PRINCIPLES OF BUSINESS CREDIT

Final Exam Study Guide

Chapters 13-22

Foreign trade collection & procedures

Letters of credit

Standby letters of credit

Factoring

Leveraged buyout

Fraud & Loss Prevention

Credit investigations

Marginal risks

Customer visits & presale credit checks

Insolvency & Distressed customers.

Settlements

Assignments

Bankruptcy

Ch 7, 11, 13

Ch 7 Liquidation & priority of claims
Sequence of reorganization of Ch 11 case

Steps involved in time line of a bankruptcy proceeding

GAAP & FASB

Balance Sheet
Income Statement
Statement of Cash Flows
Statement of Retained Earnings

Principles of Business Credit

NACM
National Association of Credit Management
An NACM® Publication

Address Inquiries to:
National Association of Credit Management
Education Department
8840 Columbia 100 Parkway
Columbia, MD 21045.

ISBN 1-888505-07-9

Principles *of Business Credit*

Principles of Business Credit Editorial Advisors

The National Association of Credit Management extends its gratitude to the following individuals, who have spent countless hours discussing and redefining the content of this book. This group has worked tirelessly to ensure that this textbook presents a comprehensive overview of business credit.

Jack R. Clark, CCE
Vice President and Corporate Credit Manager
Hughes Supply, Inc.
Orlando, FL

Dawn Wallace Cook, CCE
Treasurer
Newton Manufacturing Company
Royal Oak, MI

Stanley R. DeGroot, CCE
National Financial Services Manager
WESCO Distribution, Inc.
Phoenix, AZ

Michael J. Donnellan, CCE
Credit Manager
Honeywell-IAC
Phoenix, AZ

Marjorie L. Dyrnes, CCE
President and CEO
CrediTemps, a Division of Select Management, Inc.
Portland, OR

Pamela R. Faulk-Turnbull, CCE
Credit Manager
xpedx
Hayward, CA

Wayne Hicks, CCE
General Manager, Credit
MC Tubular, A Subsidiary of Mitsubishi International
Houston, TX

James W. Ivers, CBF
Credit Manager
Madison Electric Co.
Warren, MI

Jay E. Marcus, Esq.
Counsel
Kwiatt & Ruben, Ltd.
Northfield, IL

James A. McIntyre, CCE
President
McIntyre Enterprises, Ltd.
Edina, MN

Ronald E. Mefford, CCE
Director of Credit
Cooper Lighting
Elk Grove Village, IL

Kenneth L. Minton, CCE
Corporate Credit Manager
Southdown, Inc., Florida Mining & Materials
Tampa, FL

Ms. Dewanna L. Myers, CCE
Credit Team Leader
Aeroquip-Vickers, Inc.
Maumee, OH

Suzanne M. Pledger, CCE
Senior Manager
Digex, Inc.
Beltsville, MD

Thomas G. Sauer, CCE
Owner
Credit Crisis Management
Montgomery, TX

George A. Schnupp, CCE
Regional Credit Manager
IMC-Agrico Co.
Bannockburn, IL

James M. Sczudlo, CCE
Credit Manager
Schlumberger Oilfield Services
Houston, TX

Thomas E. Shimko, CCE
Corporate Credit Manager
Southdown, Inc.
Fairborn, OH

Joanne Simone
Credit Manager
Namasco
Atlanta, GA

Douglas B. Strobel
Assistant Credit Manager
Tarmac America, Inc.
Richmond, VA

B. Norman Taylor, CCE
Director of Credit
Avondale Mills, Inc.
Graniteville, SC

Clint B. Techmeyer, CCE
Corporate Credit Manager
Geneva Rock Products, Inc.
Salt Lake City, UT

W. Val Venable, CCE
Manager, Corporate Credit
GS Industries, Inc.
Charlotte, NC

Janice J. Welte, CCE
Controller
Fargo Tractor & Equipment
West Fargo, ND

Principles of Business Credit

Contents

Figures

1 Credit in the Business World

Overview

Credit is a privilege granted by a creditor to a customer to defer the payment of a debt, to incur debt and defer its payment, or to purchase goods or services and defer payment. This chapter provides an introduction to the topic of credit. It explores the history of credit and the primary reasons credit is offered, and presents an overview of the credit process. Additionally, the types of credit are defined and discussed. Lastly, the chapter provides an overview of the Federal Reserve System (Fed) and how the Fed controls the U.S. economy.

Learning Objectives

After reading this chapter, the reader should understand:

- The historical development of credit
- The primary reasons credit is offered
- The important elements of credit
- The credit process and where credit fits in a business cycle
- The different types of credit
- The Federal Reserve System and its impact on the economy

Chapter Outline

I. A Brief History of Credit
   A. Credit in Early America
II. Primary Reasons to Offer Credit
III. Modern Credit
   A. Five Cs of Credit
IV. The Credit Process
V. Types of Credit
   A. Public Credit
   B. Private Credit
      1. Investment Credit
      2. Consumer Credit
      3. Agricultural Credit
      4. Business Credit
      5. Bank Credit
VI. The Federal Reserve and the U.S. Payment System
   A. Federal Reserve Banks
   B. Federal Districts and Branches
   C. Demand for Reserves
   D. Changing the Reserve Requirement
   E. Supply of Reserves
VII. Federal Deposit Insurance Corporation
VIII. Federal Open Market Committee
IX. Check Processing
   A. Electronic Funds Transfer
X. Chapter Summary

A Brief History of Credit

The idea of exchanging goods or services in return for a promise of future payment developed only after centuries of trade: money and credit were unknown in the earliest stages of human history. Nevertheless, as early as 1300 B.C., loans were made among the Babylonians and Assyrians on the security of mortgages and advance deposits. By 1000 B.C., the Babylonians had already devised a crude form of the bill of exchange, so a creditor merchant could direct the debtor merchant in a distant place to pay a third party to whom the first merchant was indebted. Installment sales of real estate were being made by the Egyptians in the time of the Pharaohs.

Traders in the Mediterranean area, including Phoenicia, Greece, Rome and Carthage, also used credit. The vast boundaries of the Roman Empire, at the beginning of the Christian era, encouraged widespread trading and a broader use of credit. In the disorganized period that marked the decline and fall of the Roman Empire, credit bills of exchange or promissory notes were widely used to reduce the dangers and difficulties of transferring money through unorganized trading areas.

During the Middle Ages, a period which spanned 1000 years from about 500 to 1500 A.D., credit bills were essential to the trading activities of the prosperous Italian city-states. Lending and borrowing, as well as buying and selling on credit, became widespread practices; the debtor-creditor relationship was found in all classes of society from peasants to nobles, even including the Pope and other high dignitaries of the Church. A common form of investment and credit, especially in Italy, was the "sea loan" whereby the capitalist advanced money to the merchant and thus shared the risk. If the voyage was a success, the creditor got the investment back plus a substantial bonus of 20 to 30 percent; if the ship was lost, the creditor could lose the entire sum.

Another form of credit was the "fair letter" which was developed at the fairs held regularly in the centers of trading areas during the Middle Ages. The fair letter amounted to a promissory note to be paid before the end of the fair or at the time of the next fair. It enabled a merchant, who was short of cash, to secure goods on credit. This gave the merchant time either to sell the goods brought to the fair or to take home and sell the goods that had been purchased on credit.

Credit in Early America

The discovery of the New World provided new opportunities for the growth of capitalism and the expansion of credit. The first recorded use of open credit in early America took place with the establishment of the first permanent colony in New England. In September 1620, the Mayflower set sail from England for Virginia. Because of bad weather and navigational errors, the Pilgrims ended up off the coast of Cape Cod and eventually established the village of Plymouth in Massachusetts. While the journey itself was a tremendous achievement, so was its financing.

The Pilgrims had spent three years of arduous negotiations in England attempting to raise the funds necessary for the trip. A wealthy London merchant financed the trip and provided for "all credit advanced and to be advanced." In return, the Pilgrims contracted to work for a period of seven years. At the end of that period, payment would be made to the creditors based on the size of the individual investment.

It has been said that the growth of specialization is one of the distinguishing features of modern society. That may be so, but that specialization surely began far back in the midst of time when one of our ancestors decided that he had just had too much! He couldn't do everything himself—hunt, fish, shape axe heads, fashion spears, gather wood, salt and berries. Perhaps it was at that time that the revelation occurred. He was a good fisherman; his neighbor was not. But that neighbor certainly knew how to turn out axe heads! He could give some of the surplus of fish to the neighbor in exchange for an axe head or two. Thus, the birth of barter.

A particularly fascinating type of barter, and one that implicitly established one as a creditor, was practiced by Native Americans—a form of exchange called potlatch. The social status of the giver rose in proportion to the magnificence of the gifts offered—and the accompanying influence that was gained by having others in your debt.

Simple barter, useful as it was, had some limitations: If your neighbor didn't want any of your fish, you had to find someone who did—and fast. Commodity money, which developed out of simple barter, overcame this difficulty. Commodity money was something that had assumed some accepted value. As a portable store of value, it could be exchanged for a wide variety of items. Cowrie shells, for example, were used in China 3,500 years ago and more recently in New Guinea, Africa, many Pacific Islands and in various parts of the Middle East. Cattle were, and still are, used as money in parts of the world. Salt was also a common medium of exchange (salt bars were still being used as money as recently as the 1920s.) Early American colonists borrowed an idea from Native Americans—wampum (elaborate and beautiful strings of beads)—and declared it legal tender in Massachusetts in 1637. Other examples abound: fish hooks, feathers, amber, rice, human skulls, ivory, drums, nails, hoes and furs, to name but a few.

The original credit of £1800 could not be paid at the end of seven years, so an alternative arrangement was agreed upon: £200 to be paid annually for a term of nine years. This arrangement had to be renegotiated and finally, after 25 years, the last payment was made. This was the first example of credit in early America.

To finance the American Revolution, the Second Continental Congress made efforts to finance the Army of the United Colonies. The Congress had only three alternatives: borrow the money from sympathetic countries abroad which was an impossible task since the Colonist's credit in the world stood at zero; impose taxes which was unpopular and the very cause that had brought about the American Revolution; or issue bills of credit.

In June, 1775, the Continental Congress authorized the printing of $2,000,000 in various denominations ranging from one dollar to eight dollars. Trouble for the Continental currency began almost at once; each note had to be hand signed which was not a simple task considering 49,000 of them had to be signed. Counterfeiting of the currency was rampant. The principle behind the Continental currency was, in essence, a promise to pay the final bearer, at some point in the future, the face value in Spanish coins, the coins in widest circulation at this time.

In 1783 the Treaty of Paris was signed bringing an official end to the war and official recognition of the United States by England. Trading resumed and American importers and wholesalers extended generous terms to their customers. Generally, sales were made on terms of 12 months but even where six- or nine-month terms where offered, it was not uncommon for an account to remain unpaid for a much longer period, up to 24 months or more.

With the restoration of pre-Revolutionary trade customs and habits, credit references assumed importance, although in most instances, proper information was still lacking. Some prospective purchasers took the precaution of using the names of prominent people they knew when placing orders on credit. Credit references accompanied orders, however in most cases, merchants took their chances.

Terms of sale, as they developed during the 1800s, reflected the changes in the rapidly expanding economy. The 12-month period, which had prevailed, showed a tendency to become shorter. By the 1830s, the average term of sale was about six months.

Hard financial times hit the country in the mid 1830s. The population was rapidly growing and business was expanding. The sale of land on credit went virtually unchecked. The banking system was not centralized. By the summer of 1837, bank after bank closed its doors and thousands of businesses went into bankruptcy. The financial panic of 1837 saw the beginnings of the Mercantile Agency, established in 1841 by Lewis Tappan. It was this credit information agency which eventually became Dun & Bradstreet and helped transform credit, and with it, the course of American commerce.

The story of American credit, as we now know it, was not solely influenced by Dun & Bradstreet. Another organization important for credit managers worldwide was formed in 1896 in Toledo, Ohio. A group of credit executives, representing a hundred or so of their colleagues, organized themselves into a national association for credit managers, the National Association of Credit Men. Their exchange of credit information was initially conducted on a local and regional level. The association expanded into the **National Association of Credit Management** (NACM), which today with its network of Affiliated Associations, represents 30,000 credit executives worldwide.

The purposes and objectives of NACM are:

- To promote honest and fair dealings in credit transactions
- To assure good laws for sound credit
- To foster and facilitate the exchange of credit information
- To encourage efficient service in the collection of accounts
- To promote and expedite sound credit administration in international trade
- To encourage training for credit work through colleges, universities, home study courses and other means
- To foster and encourage research in the field of credit
- To disseminate useful and instructive articles and ideas with respect to credit management techniques
- To promote economy and efficiency in the handling of estates of insolvent, embarrassed or bankrupt debtors

- To provide facilities for investigation and prevention of fraud
- To perform other such functions as the advancement and protection of business credit may require

Primary Reasons to Offer Credit

The use of credit in the purchase of goods or services is so common that it is taken for granted. The granting of credit from one business to another for the purchase of goods or services, business or trade credit has been part of the U.S. business scene for hundreds of years. Trade credit is, and continues to be, a very important source of funds for firms. It provides more financing to businesses than does commercial borrowing or corporate bond financing. Without business credit, the economic system as we know it would not exist.

The primary reason for a company to offer credit terms to its customers is to increase its sales.

The principle reasons companies offer credit are:

- **Increase Sales:** Extending credit to buyers often involves a trade-off between holding inventory or holding accounts receivable.
- **Competition:** Matching a competitor's credit terms may be a sales necessity.
- **Promotion:** A company may offer special credit terms as part of a promotion program for a product.
- **Credit Availability:** Some buyers may not have access to any other forms of credit. In tight credit times, seller trade terms or financing may be necessary.
- **Convenience:** Trade credit provides benefits not easily obtained from other payment arrangements. One of the biggest benefits is the simple convenience of writing a single check to pay for hundreds of purchases.
- **Demand:** Credit is extended in response to customer demand for a company's products or services. This implies that the sale may or may not take place without the extension of credit.
- **Price:** The granting of trade credit is an aspect of price. The time that the buyer gets before payment is due is one of the dimensions of the product, (like quality, service, etc.) which determines the attractiveness of the product. Like other aspects of price, the firm's terms of sale and credit-granting decisions affect its sales volume.

Modern Credit

Several essential points are always included in any definition of **credit.** First, there must be an exchange of values. This sets up the transaction. Goods or services are obtained for a promise to pay, and payment is made when it comes due. This introduces the second factor: futurity and its companion, trust. The credit sale relationship between customer and supplier is based on trust and mutual need. The very derivation of the word credit from the original Latin *credere,* to believe or trust, graphically describes the entire process of credit of mutual trust and confidence. The buyer selects the supplier on the basis of its reputation as a source of a quality good at an acceptable price. The supplier accepts the order and extends the credit necessary to facilitate the sale if it believes the customer will honor the contract by paying the invoice according to the terms agreed.

Where goods or services are exchanged immediately for cash, there is no futurity, no trust and no need for the seller to have confidence in the buyer. None of these is needed since economic payment is made at the time of purchase. Credit sales represent an extension of the cash inflow time line. When credit is granted, the seller does not require cash at the time of the sale but rather permits payment to be made at a specific date in the future.

When a payment by check is offered, the seller must decide whether or not to accept it. Many times company policy will guide the seller's action, while at other times a snap judgment may be necessary. Since the check transaction involves futurity, trust and confidence, the credit concept is involved. The futurity is short; just long enough for the check to clear. Trust and confidence however, are just as significant in this example as they are on longer terms. Once the seller has transferred goods to a buyer, legal steps are necessary to repossess them.

When unsecured credit terms are offered, the seller gives up goods or provides services in exchange for the promise of the buyer to pay at a specific future date. The seller is convinced that payment will be received when it is due, that is that the buyer can be trusted. In a sale made on 30 or 60 days, for instance, the futurity aspect of credit is important; and as selling terms lengthen, the seller's analysis of the buyer's ability to pay on or by the due date becomes increasingly important.

There is no doubt that selling on credit is more costly than selling for cash. Those costs include the cost of the credit department, the investment of company funds in receivables, discounts for early payments, the cost of converting receivables to cash and collecting bad debts. All of these factors comprise the cost of credit. No matter how great these costs, however, they are more than offset by distinct sales advantages. By offering credit terms, the seller can build a greater customer base, make more efficient use of production facilities, create greater good will, expand geographical markers, accept marginal risks, earn incremental profits and ultimately realize a greater return on investment.

There are several important elements of credit:

- **Risk of Nonpayment.** The purchaser may default in making any or all of the payments due to the seller.
- **Timing.** When credit is offered, the seller must wait for payment, even if that payment is received on time. This increases the risk of losing the use of funds that are tied up in financing the credit transaction or if a payment is late, in carrying or financing the past-due customer.
- **Security.** As a means of gaining partial or full protection for the credit transaction, a seller may require the purchaser to pledge a form of collateral or provide a financial guarantee. This can be accomplished by pledging an asset, providing a personal, corporate or bank guarantee or entering into a security agreement.
- **Extra Costs.** The seller incurs the expenses associated with granting credit, such as the cost associated with the credit department, the investment of

company funds in receivables, discounts for early payments and the cost of converting receivables to cash.

- **Legal Aspects.** Federal and state laws have been enacted which affect both the credit grantor and debtor. Both businesses and consumers must be aware of both state and federal laws.
- **Economic Influences.** Changes in economic conditions such as the rate of inflation can have strong effects on credit sales. For example, in inflationary times, a seller will not want to wait too long before getting paid and will likely impose stricter credit policies.

Five Cs of Credit

Later in this book, the separate factors that enter into credit analysis are examined; but for now, they can be summarized in one statement: "Credit depends on the ability and willingness to pay." Without that, credit is meaningless.

The **five Cs of credit** summarize the important features of a credit applicant. The ability to analyze each of the five Cs provides an important foundation in the credit process.

The five Cs of credit are:

- **Character.** *Those moral qualities and actions of a credit applicant which oblige the applicant to pay as debts become due.*
- **Capacity.** *The ability to pay when a debt is due.*
- **Capital.** *The financial strength of a risk as measured by the equity or net worth of an applicant.*
- **Collateral.** *Those possessions or equities from which payment might be expected should character and capacity fail.*
- **Conditions.** *The current and expected general economic situations as they might affect the applicant.*

Companies are exposed to many changes: political and demographic changes, recession, inflation and interest rate fluctuations. Companies within a particular industry confront additional risks relating to technological change, shifting competition, rapid growth, regulation, and the availability of raw materials and labor. Management competency, litigation and the company's strategic direction are additional sources of risk. All of these factors affect a company's operating performance, net income and cash flows which affect the buyer's ability to pay. Credit in its broadest sense is based on the components of trust, risk, economic exchange and futurity. Thus, **credit** *can be appropriately described as the transfer of economic value now, on faith, in return for an expected economic value in the future.*

The Credit Process

In simple terms, the credit process begins with a **buyer** *(a company or individual consumer)* deciding to purchase a product or service from a seller which either makes or provides a product or service. The buyer offers a means of trading value, or a medium of exchange, for the goods or service. Cash is most readily accepted by the seller, but the seller may also offer a form of credit or deferred payment.

The Credit Process

- Sales makes contact and order is taken.
- Credit department reviews customer for creditworthiness.
- Order is shipped on credit.
- Payment is made on time/within terms.

Credit is part of a company's **operating cycle** *which comprises the activities a company performs to produce and sell its product or service.* Consider a typical operating cycle for a manufacturer: the operating cycle begins when the manufacturer purchases raw material from a supplier. The purchase of raw material is usually a business credit transaction. *The material is converted into goods during the* **production stage** and the manufacturer must pay its supplier for the material. The manufacturer then sells the finished goods to a customer, who ultimately pays for the goods that were purchased on credit during the **collection stage.** *A firm's* **operating cycle** *can be defined as the period of time between the acquisition of material, labor and overhead inputs for production and the collection of sales receipts.* During the operating cycle, the manufacturer is both a debtor and a creditor.

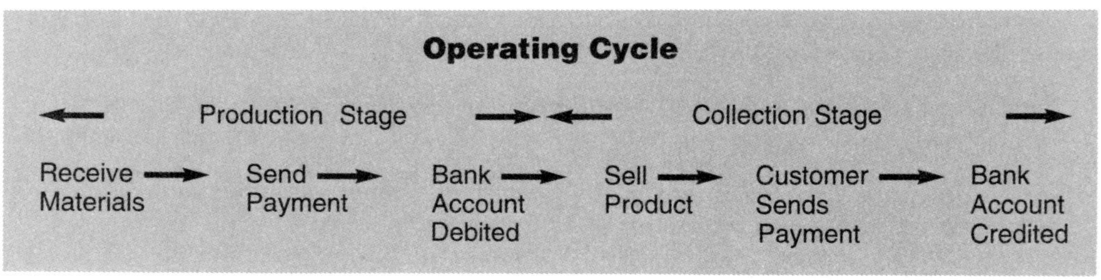

The purchaser becomes the debtor or user of credit, while the seller becomes the creditor, or grantor of credit. *The purchaser's ability to obtain a product or service based on its promise to pay at a later date is called* **creditworthiness.**

Types of Credit

Because of its different uses, credit can be classified into two broad classifications: **public or private credit. Public credit,** *which can also be called government credit, is credit extended to or used by governments or governmental divisions, agencies or instrumentalities.* **Private credit** *is extended to or used by individuals or businesses to carry on the exchange of goods and services in the private sector.*

Public Credit

Public credit *includes the extension of, or borrowing by, units of government, states and municipalities as well as the federal government.* State, local and the federal governments

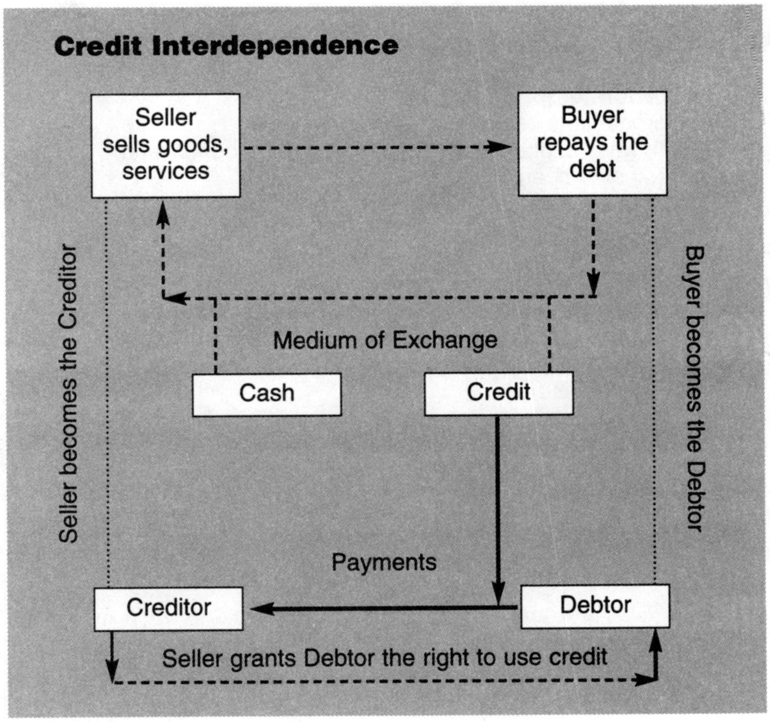

borrow money to meet the costs of public needs, including financing the cost of schools, highways, health and social welfare and military preparedness. Governments buy a wealth of products and services such as tanks, planes, food, office supplies, books, computer equipment, labor, electricity and so forth. Governments buy almost all they need from business in the private sector. In all cases where financing needs exceed revenue, governments must draw upon their borrowing capacity. This is usually done by the issuance of state, municipal or federal bonds, or in the case of the federal government, through the issuance of shorter-term Treasury bills and notes. Currency itself can be regarded in a sense as a credit obligation of the federal government, though it is usually not so classified. Analysis of public debt is usually made on the basis of government's powers of future taxation.

On the other side of the equation is federal and state lending, which often has public policy objectives. Disaster loans, loans by the Small Business Administration and many other programs serve as aids to the business community with less attention to the goodness of the credit risk and more to social aims such as employment, economic opportunity and housing.

Private Credit

Private credit *is extended to or used by individuals or businesses to carry on the exchange of goods and services in the private sector.*

Private credit can be divided into five broad categories:

- Investment credit
- Consumer credit
- Agricultural credit
- Business credit
- Bank credit

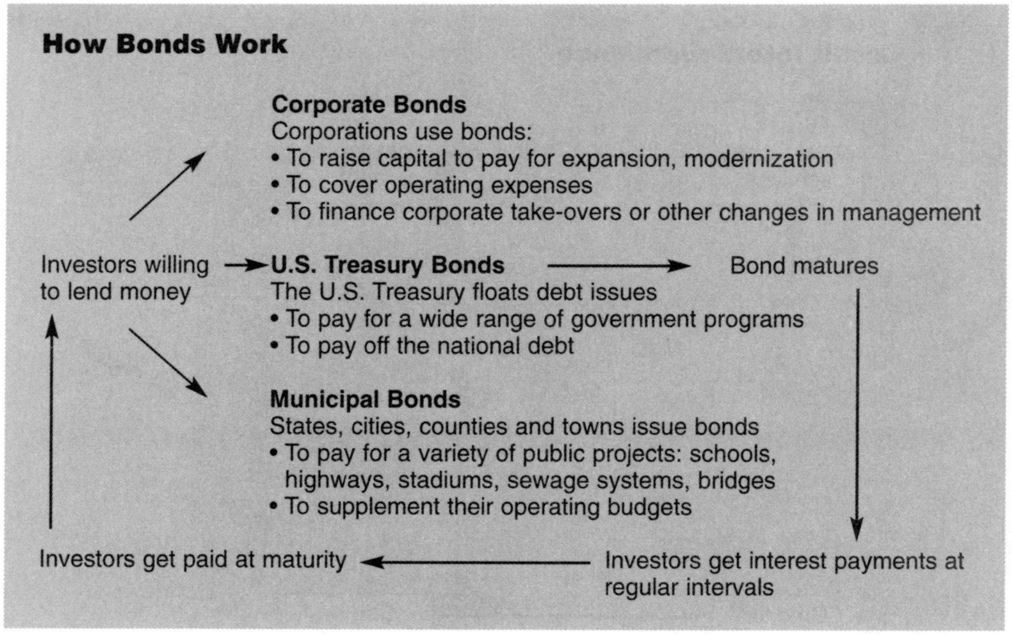

Investment Credit

This refers to the placement of funds in productive assets to earn a profit. **Investment credit** *can be defined as the long-term borrowing of large amounts of money to finance productive assets.* It consists primarily of loans made to governments or businesses to raise capital to pay for expansion, modernization or public projects such as highways or schools. An institution, a corporation, the U.S. Treasury or states, cities, towns and counties is the borrower and the investors are the lender. Investors can buy bonds issued by U.S. companies, the U.S. Treasury or by states and cities. *The loans that investors make to corporations and governments are called* **bonds.** The borrowers get the cash they need while the lenders can earn interest.

Companies often prefer to offer a bond rather than to issue stock to raise money because issuing additional stock may lessen the value of shares already owned by investors. Corporate bonds are listed on the New York Stock Exchange or the American Stock Exchange. Governments are not profit making entities and cannot issue stock to raise money. Bonds are the primary way for governments to raise money to fund capital improvements.

Bonds, or fixed-income securities, *are generally long-term (more than 10 years) securities that pay a specified sum (called the principal) either at a future date or periodically over the length of a loan, during which a fixed rate of interest may be paid on a regular basis.* Every bond has a fixed maturity date when the bond expires and the loan must be paid back in full. The interest a bond pays is also set when the bond is issued. The rate is competitive, which means the bond pays interest comparable to what investors can earn elsewhere. As a result, the rate on a new bond is usually similar to other current interest rates, including mortgage rates. Unlike stockholders who have equity in a company, bond holders are creditors.

The word bond once referred to the piece of paper which described the details of a loan transaction. Today, the term is used more generally to describe a vast and varied market in debt securities.

Asset-backed bonds, created in the mid-1980s, *are secured or backed up by specific holdings of the issuing corporation such as equipment or real estate.*

Debentures *are the most common corporate bonds. They are backed only by the financial strength or standing of the organization issuing it, rather than by any specific assets.* A debenture buyer relies on the issuer's faith and credit as the only assurance of being paid the interest and principal.

Secured bonds *have specific titles attached to them, such as mortgage bonds, equipment and trust certificates and collateral trust bonds.* **Mortgage bonds** *are secured or collateralized with specific corporate assets such as buildings.* Mortgage bonds are backed by a pool of mortgage loans. **Equipment trust certificates (ETC)** *are bonds issued to pay for new equipment, secured by a lien on the purchased equipment.* ETCs are frequently issued by airlines, railroads and shipping companies to finance the purchase of railroad freight cars, airplanes and oil tankers. **Collateral trust bonds** *are similar to mortgage bonds except they are backed by securities of any company through the pledge of stocks and bonds.*

Consumer Credit

Consumer credit *is defined as credit extended to a natural person primarily for personal, family or household purposes* and may be either closed-end or open-end credit. It excludes business and agricultural credit, and loans exceeding $25,000 that are not secured by real property or a dwelling. It also must be extended by a creditor, although it can be advertised by someone else, such as a builder, real estate broker or advertising agency. Consumer credit can be classified as **open-end, closed-end or incidental.**

Open-end credit *means credit extended under a plan which a creditor may permit an applicant to make purchases or obtain loans from time to time directly from the creditor or indirectly by the use of a credit card, check or other device.* Open-end credit generally consists of credit card accounts with small credit lines to the most creditworthy borrowers. Today, open-end credit generally includes accounts with much larger lines of credit to diverse borrowers with a variety of risk levels.

In open-end credit, the creditor:

- Reasonably expects the customer to make repeated transactions
- May impose a finance charge from time to time on the unpaid balance
- Generally makes the amount of credit available again to the consumer as the outstanding balance is paid

Examples of open-end credit are bank and retail gasoline credit cards, department stores' revolving charge accounts, and cash-advance checking accounts.

Closed-end credit *includes all consumer credit that does not fit the definition of open-end credit. It consists of both credit sales and loans.* In a typical closed-end credit transaction, credit is advanced for a specific time period, and the "amount financed," "finance charge," and "schedule of payments" are agreed upon by the lender and the customer. Single payment loans and installment loans are examples of closed-end credit.

Incidental Credit *is extended by service providers, such as a hospital, doctor, lawyer or retailer and allows the client or customer to defer the payment of a bill.* There is no credit card involved. There is no finance charge and no agreement for payment in installments. Payment must be made in four installments or less.

Agricultural Credit

In general, **agricultural credit** *relates to the farming industry and the family farmer.* This type of credit often presents more risk to the creditor and is sometimes separated into its own unique category. The farming industry is highly seasonal and is subject to natural hazards such as drought, flood, frost, wind and insect damage. Consequently, many laws and regulations which govern credit regulations treat this type of credit separately.

Business Credit

Business credit *refers to extensions of credit primarily for business or commercial purposes.*

The important characteristics of business credit are:

- Selling terms are relatively short
- Transactions are usually on open account or unsecured, but may be partially secured or secured in full
- Cash discounts may be offered for payment before the net due date
- The terms include transactions to manufacturers, wholesalers and retailers, but specifically exclude the consumer
- The timeliness in reaching a decision whether or not to extend credit is often much more critical in the business setting. Delays in the manufacturing process can increase costs and reduce the quality of perishable goods

The fact that business credit finances the intermediate and final stages of production and distribution distinguishes it from consumer credit. Business credit sales also yield a profit on goods sold rather than interest or investment income, which distinguishes it from bank and investment credit.

Unsecured, open-account credit is the most widely used form of domestic business credit. In **open-account credit,** *the creditor reasonably expects the customer to make repeated transactions and generally makes more credit available to the buyer as the outstanding balance is paid.* A typical business creditor who sells on open account terms is relying specifically on the full faith and credit of a purchaser. The seller establishes the terms of sale. Open account terms are also called ordinary terms or standard terms, which are discussed in detail in a later chapter.

A **secured credit arrangement** *is one in which collateral is provided to the creditor.* By obtaining some form of security, the creditor can reduce repayment risk. Examples where secured credit may be useful are a start-up business or an undercapitalized business or an opportunity to sell an account that cannot justify a high credit exposure. Security is obtained not only when the buyer's financial condition is weak, but in order to guarantee payment if the buyer's financial condition changes. While it cannot strengthen a buyer's financial weakness, a secured credit arrangement does reduce the likelihood of loss. Secured credit is defined in Article 9 of the Uniform Commercial Code, discussed later in this book.

It is important to note that drafts, trade acceptances and promissory notes are not forms of security. Each of these instruments is written evidence of debt. However, no security attaches to the instrument.

Sales to customers in other countries account for an important portion of U.S. business transactions. Today, there are more companies with more products entering more markets than at any other time in history. The ability to compete in the global marketplace has become a necessity and, as a result, credit has become global. The procedure for an export credit decision includes more elements than for a domestic decision. In addition to the traditional five Cs of credit analysis, other elements such as the risks associated with the economic stability of a country or country risk must be evaluated. The strength and stability of foreign currency versus the exporter's currency play a major role in the success of an international credit transaction. And, of course, the culture and customs of the buyer influence the credit transaction. These factors, country risk, currency issues and culture, add three more dimensions to the five "Cs" of credit.

Bank Credit

Depositor checking accounts constitute some three-fourths of all currency used in the United States. Backed by these resources and the strong Federal Reserve System (which will be discussed later in this chapter), the commercial banking system is the greatest generator of credit to assist the business and financial community. Bank credit is the most important kind of money in circulation. It is also the ultimate source of other forms of credit in use today.

The principle difference between bank credit and other forms of money lending is that no cash changes hand when a bank loan is made. Rather, a paper amount is set up in the borrower's account. This is called check-account credit and is backed by a specified cash reserve required by the Federal Reserve Board.

The paper transaction is in effect money, although no physical currency is printed. It acts as a multiplier to the amount of physical currency in circulation, since only a percentage of actual currency is required as reserve against checking-account currency. The ability of banks to create money is an important aspect of the economic and financial climate in the United States.

Bank credit differs from business credit in a number of ways, but primarily in terms of the type of resource which changes hands in a transaction. A bank furnishes money, while a business supplier furnishes goods or services. After the transaction is completed, however, both are creditors in the same way. The customer owes money to each.

As a general rule, business credit terms are shorter than the periods of repayment offered by banks. Payment for goods or services usually comes due in 30, 60 or 90 days, depending on the industry. Bank loans, on the other hand, are generally longer term.

The Federal Reserve and the U.S. Payment System

The **Federal Reserve System** *is the central bank of the United States.* The United States was slow to adopt a central banking system. Before Congress created the Federal Reserve system, periodic financial panics had plagued the nation. These panics contributed to many bank failures, business bankruptcies and general economic downturns. Following the financial panic of 1907, and under pressure from President Woodrow Wilson, Congress passed the Federal Reserve Act of 1913. The **Federal Reserve System,** *or the Fed, was created as an independent agency, to provide the nation with a safer, more flexible, and more stable monetary and financial system.*

The U.S. central bank, the Federal Reserve, plays a key role in supervising, regulating and providing services to the banking community. Its multiple roles have substantial impact on credit management.

The Fed plays a number of roles including:

Administrator

It provides a national clearing house for check clearance and a real-time electronic funds transfer system, called Fedwire. The Fed handles approximately 18 billion checks a year. Using high-speed sorting machines, the Federal Reserve Banks process these checks, route them to the depository institutions on which they are written, and transfer payment for the checks through accounts that depository institutions maintain with Federal Reserve Banks.

Banker

The Fed provides banking services for the U.S. Treasury and other government, quasi-government and international agencies. Each year, billions of dollars are deposited to and withdrawn by various government agencies from operating accounts in the U.S. Treasury held by Federal Reserve Banks.

The Federal Reserve Banks hold, in their vaults, collateral for government agencies to secure public funds that are on deposit with private depository institutions. In addition, Reserve Banks receive for deposit to the Treasury's accounts such items as federal unemployment taxes, individual income taxes withheld by payroll deduction, corporate income taxes and certain federal excise taxes. The Federal Reserve Banks also issue and redeem instruments of public debt, such as savings bonds and Treasury securities.

Controller

Federal Reserve banks distribute currency (paper money) and coin to depository institutions to meet the public's need for cash. During periods of heavy cash demand, such as the Christmas season, institutions obtain larger amounts of cash from the Federal Reserve Banks. When public demand for cash is light, institutions deposit excess cash with the Reserve Banks, for credit to their reserve accounts. Currency and coin received at the Federal Reserve Banks are sorted and counted. Unfit currency and coin are destroyed and replaced with new currency and coin obtained from the Treasury Department's Bureau of Engraving and Printing and Bureau of the Mint.

Guardian

The Fed handles the exchange and storage of gold bullion.

Lender

The Fed is the lender of funds to banks at the discount rate.

Regulator

The Fed buys and sells U.S. government securities to maintain controls over the U.S. monetary system. The Fed sets margin requirements, which limit the use of credit for purchasing or carrying securities. It also establishes operating rules and regulations for its member banks. Additionally, the Fed is responsible for the development and administration of regulations that implement major federal laws governing credit such as the Truth in Lending Act, the Equal Credit Opportunity Act, and the Truth in Savings Act.

The Federal Reserve is the primary conductor of U.S. monetary policy, using three major tools designed to expand or contract the money supply to control interest rates:

Figure 1-1 Boundaries of Federal Reserve Districts and Their Branch Territories

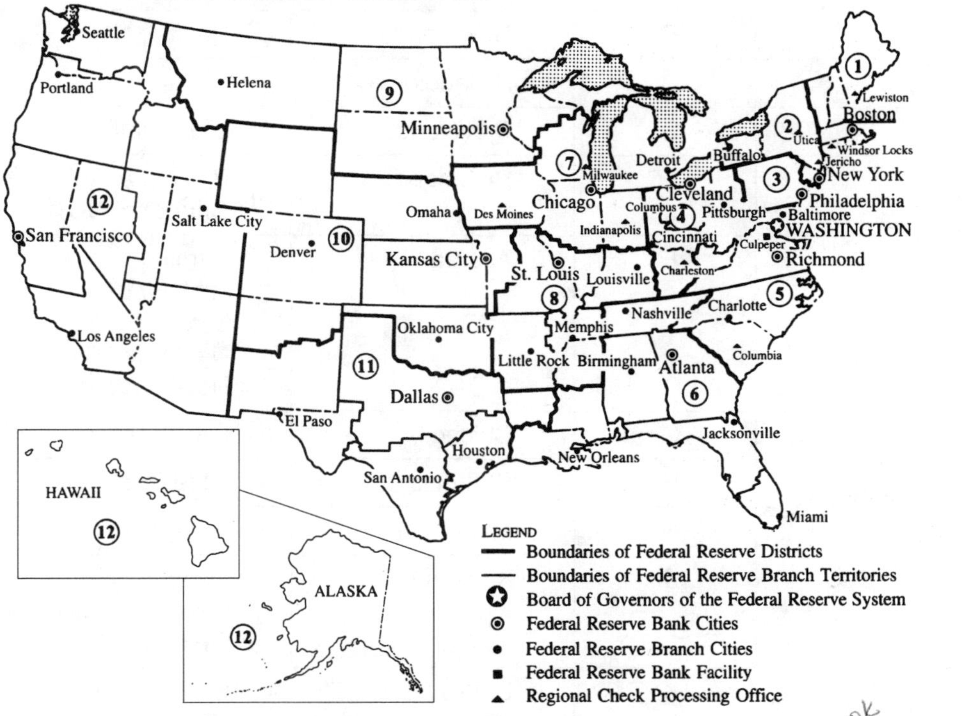

- **Reserve requirements** regarding the amount of funds that commercial banks and other depository institutions must hold in reserve against deposits.
- The **discount rate** or the interest rate charged by commercial banks and other depository institutions when they borrow reserves from a regional Federal Reserve Bank.
- **Open market operations** or the buying and selling of U.S. government (mainly Treasury) securities in the open market to influence the level of reserves in the depository system.

The Federal Reserve is run by the Board of Governors in Washington, D.C. The seven members of the Board of Governors are appointed by the President and confirmed by the Senate, to serve 14-year terms of office, which insulates them from political pressure to some extent. Members may serve only one full term. One term expires every two years. The President designates, and the Senate confirms, two members of the Board to be Chairman and Vice Chairman for four-year terms.

Federal Reserve Banks

The Federal Reserve is broken down into 12 districts. (Figure 1-1) Each district is managed by a district bank and runs somewhat autonomously from the Board in Washington, D.C. Federal Reserve Banks generate their own income, primarily from interest earned on government securities that are acquired in the course of Federal Reserve monetary policy actions. A second source of income is derived from the provision of priced services to depository institutions, as required by the *Monetary*

Number	Letter	Bank	Branch
1	A	Boston	
2	B	New York	Buffalo, NY
3	C	Philadelphia	
4	D	Cleveland	Cincinnati, OH
5	E	Richmond	Baltimore, MD Charlotte, NC
6	F	Atlanta	Birmingham, AL Jacksonville, FL Miami, FL Nashville, TN New Orleans, LA
7	G	Chicago	Detroit, MI
8	H	St. Louis	Little Rock, AR
9	I	Minneapolis	Helena, MT
10	J	Kansas City	Denver, CO Oklahoma City, OK Omaha, NE
11	K	Dallas	El Paso, TX Houston, TX San Antonio, TX
12	L	San Francisco	Los Angeles, CA Portland, OR Salt Lake City, UT Seattle, WA

Control Act of 1980. Federal Reserve Banks are not operated for profit. Each year they return to the U.S. Treasury all earnings in excess of operating and other expenses.

Federal Districts and Branches

Each of the 12 district banks, with 22 regional branches spread across the nation, has its own Chairman and nine-member Board of Directors. Each district bank is identified by a letter and corresponding number. On each U.S. currency bill, a Federal Reserve Bank number and corresponding letter symbol appear.

Approximately half of all banks, and all of the largest banks, are members of the Federal Reserve System. All national banks must be members of the Federal Reserve System. National banks must use the word national in their name or have N.A. following their name, which stands for National Affiliation. State-chartered banks can join if they meet the Fed's financial standards. All banks must maintain Federal Reserve accounts to be able to move or receive funds through the Federal Reserve System, membership not withstanding.

The initial link between monetary policy and the economy occurs in the market for reserves. The Federal Reserve's policies influence the demand for or supply of reserves at banks and other depository institutions, and through this market, the effects of monetary policy are transmitted to the rest of the economy.

Demand for Reserves

The demand for reserves has two components: **required reserves** and **excess reserves.** All depository institutions commercial banks, saving banks, savings and loan associations and credit unions must retain *a percentage of certain types of deposits to be held as reserves referred to as the* **reserve requirement.** The reserve requirements are set by the Federal Reserve under the Depository Institutions Deregulation and Monetary Control Act of 1980.

Since the early 1990s, reserve requirements have been applied only to transaction deposits or interest-bearing and non-interest bearing checking accounts. Transaction deposits are also called demand deposits. Required reserves are a fraction of these deposits; *the fraction*—the **reserve ratio**—*is set by the Board of Governors within limits established by law.* The total required reserves expand or contract with the level of transaction deposits and with the required reserve ratio set by the Board. Depository institutions hold required reserves in one of two forms: **vault cash** *which is cash on hand at the bank or* **required reserves balances** *in accounts with the Reserve Bank for their Federal Reserve District.*

Depositories use their accounts at Federal Reserve Banks not only to satisfy their reserve requirements but also to clear many financial transactions. Some depository institutions choose to hold reserves even beyond those needed to meet their reserve and clearing requirements. *These additional balances, which provide extra protection against overdrafts and deficiencies in required reserves, are called* **excess reserves.**

Excess Reserves = Actual Reserves – Required Reserves

The total amount of deposits that could be supported by any given amount of reserves can be calculated as follows:

Total deposits = Reserves / Percentage Reserve Requirements

Consider this example to understand reserve requirements: Suppose a bank is required to keep 20 percent of its deposits in reserves. The reserve ratio is 1/5. With a reserve ratio of 20 percent, reserves of \$10,000 would support \$50,000 in deposits.

$$\$50,000 = \$10,000 \times 1/5$$

The total amount of money that can be supported by a given amount of reserves can be found by multiplying the amount of reserves by what is called the **money multiplier.** *The money multiplier is the reciprocal of the reserve ratio or 1 divided by the reserve ratio.*

Using the same example, the reserve ratio is 1/5 or .2, so the money multiplier is 1/0.2 = 5. Thus, \$10,000 of reserves would support \$50,000 of deposits;

$$5 \times \$10,000 = \$50,000$$

The amount of deposits supported equals five times the amount in reserves. The five is called the money multiplier. A money multiplier of five means that a \$1 increase in reserves would lead to a \$5 increase in deposits.

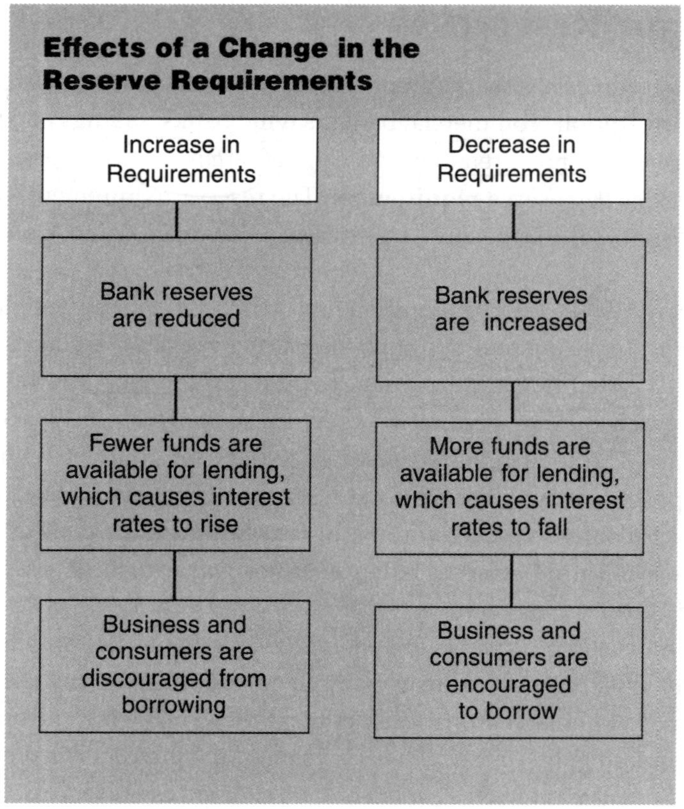

Changing the Reserve Requirement

Suppose the reserve requirement increased from 20 percent to 25 percent. The reserve ratio would be 1/4. Therefore, the multiplier would be four. With reserves of $10,000, only $40,000 of deposits could be supported. If the Fed lowered the reserve requirement, banks would have lower required reserves and could support more deposits. If the reserve requirement decreased to 10 percent, the reserve ratio would be 1/10. Therefore, the multiplier would be 10.

$$10 \times \$10{,}000 = \$100{,}000$$

By increasing the reserve requirement, it takes money out of the economy. By decreasing the requirement, it increases the money supply. In practice, the Fed rarely changes the reserve requirement more than once every few years.

Supply of Reserves

The Federal Reserve supplies reserves to the banking system in two ways: by lending through the Federal Reserve discount window and by buying government securities. *Reserves obtained through lending through the Federal Reserve discount window are called* **borrowed reserves.** Access to such credit by banks and thrift institutions is established by rules set by the Board of Governors, and loans are made at a rate of interest, called the discount rate, set by the Reserve Banks and approved by the Board.

The **discount rate** *is the interest rate banks must pay when they borrow money from*

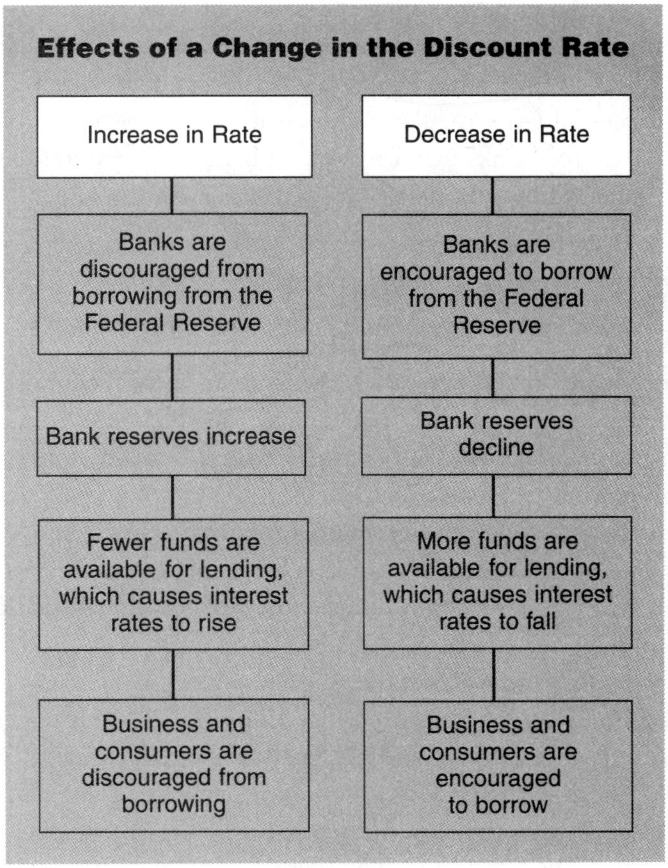

the Federal Reserves. Since banks must keep enough reserves to meet the reserve requirement, often they have to borrow from the Fed.

Although very few banks borrow at the Fed discount window at any given time, the discount rate is often viewed as an indicator of Fed policy. When the rate is lowered, the Fed is assumed to want to increase the money supply. When the rate in increased, it is assumed that the Fed wants to decrease the money supply.

The other source of reserve supply is nonborrowed reserves. When the Federal Reserve buys securities in the open market, it creates reserves to pay for them, increasing the supply of nonborrowed reserves. When the Fed sells securities, it absorbs reserves in exchange for the securities and the supply of nonborrowed reserves falls.

Federal Deposit Insurance Corporation

The Federal Deposit Insurance Corporation (FDIC) was created in 1913 by the Federal Deposit Insurance Corporation Improvement Act to provide insurance protection for depositors if their bank fails. Since 1933, the FDIC has responded to thousands of bank failures and its insurance protection has been expanded to include accounts in savings and loans associations. In the 1980s, the FDIC assisted with slightly more than 1,000 bank failures.

All insured depositors of failed banks and thrifts have been protected by the FDIC. The FDIC insures deposits up to $100,000 per personal or corporate depositor per institution in all federally chartered and most state banks. One of the most important roles of the FDIC is in determining the course of action in the event of a bank failure. The FDIC usually makes the decision that a bank is insolvent and is charged with liquidating a failed bank's remaining assets and paying insured depositors. The FDIC also is the Federal bank regulator responsible for supervising certain savings banks and state-chartered banks that are not members of the Federal Reserve System.

Federal Open Market Committee

A major component of the Federal Reserve System is the **Federal Open Market Committee (FOMC).** Five of the 12 presidents of the Federal Reserve Banks serve, along with the seven members of the Board of Governors, as members of the FOMC. The president of the Federal Reserve Bank of New York serves on a continuous basis; the other presidents serve one-year terms on a rotating basis.

The FOMC is charged under law with overseeing open market operations, which is the main tool used by the Federal Reserve to influence money market conditions and growth of money and credit. **Open market operations** *involve the buying and selling of securities by the Federal Reserve.*

When the Federal Reserve buys securities from any seller, it pays, in effect, by issuing a check on itself. When the seller deposits the check in its bank account, the bank presents the check to the Federal Reserve for payment. The Federal Reserve, in turn, honors the check by increasing the reserve account of the seller's bank at the Federal Reserve Bank. The reserves of the seller's bank rise with no offsetting decline in reserves elsewhere; the total volume of reserves increases. Just the opposite occurs when the Federal Reserve sells securities: the payment reduces the reserve account of the buyer's bank at the Federal Reserve Bank with no offsetting increase in the reserve account of any other bank, and the total reserves of the banking system decline.

A Federal Reserve securities transaction changes the volume of reserves in the depository system: A purchase adds to nonborrowed reserves, and a sale reduces them. In contrast, the same transaction between financial institutions, business firms, or individuals, simply redistributes reserves within the depository system without changing the aggregate level of reserves. The purchase of securities in the open market increases the money supply, since the Fed makes purchases by crediting the seller's account with additional reserves. The sale of securities from its portfolio reduces the money supply by taking cash out of the economy.

Check Processing

Next to cash, checks are the most frequently used method of completing transactions in the United States. The Federal Reserve system processed $15.5 billion check payments in 1997 or 35 percent of total check payments in the United States.

Since it was established, the Federal Reserve has worked with the private sector to improve the efficiency and cost-effectiveness of the check collection system. In the 1940s, the Federal Reserve and the banking industry developed routing numbers. These numbers are still printed on checks to identify the institution on which they are drawn and to which the check must be sent for payment.

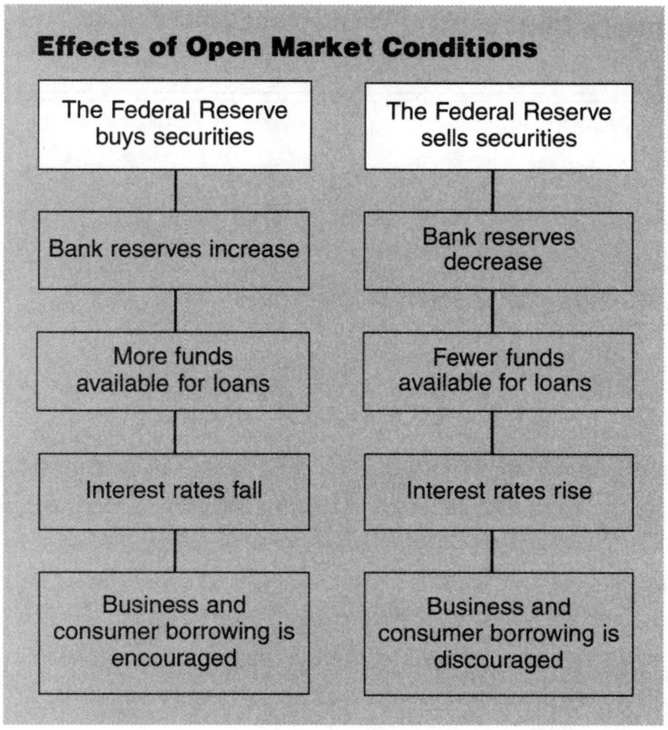

In the 1950s, the Federal Reserve developed and implemented the **magnetic ink character recognition (MICR) system** *for encoding pertinent data on checks so that the data could be read electronically. The characters are printed at the bottom of a check in what is called* **the MICR line.** This development contributed significantly to the automation of check processing.

The MICR line contains the following information:

- **The Federal Reserve District:** The first two digits identify the Federal Reserve district in which the drawee bank is located.
- **The Federal Reserve Office:** The next two digits give further information about how the check is to clear, identifying the Fed district office or branch and any special clearing arrangements.
- **Bank Identification Number:** Digits five through eight make up the the American Bankers Association four-digit identification number. Each bank has a unique number within a particular Fed District.

This first section, or the first eight digits, of the MICR line is called the **transit routing number.**

- **Payor's Account Number:** Within a depository institution, each account is assigned a unique number. This enables the bank to debit or credit the appropriate account after the check is processed.
- **Sequence Number:** This optional field enables the bank to sort checks to a particular account in numerical order. Usually, this sequence of numbers contains the check number.
- **Encoded Amount:** At the bank, the amount for which the check is drawn is read by people and then printed or encoded on the right hand side of the

Figure 1-2 Sample Check

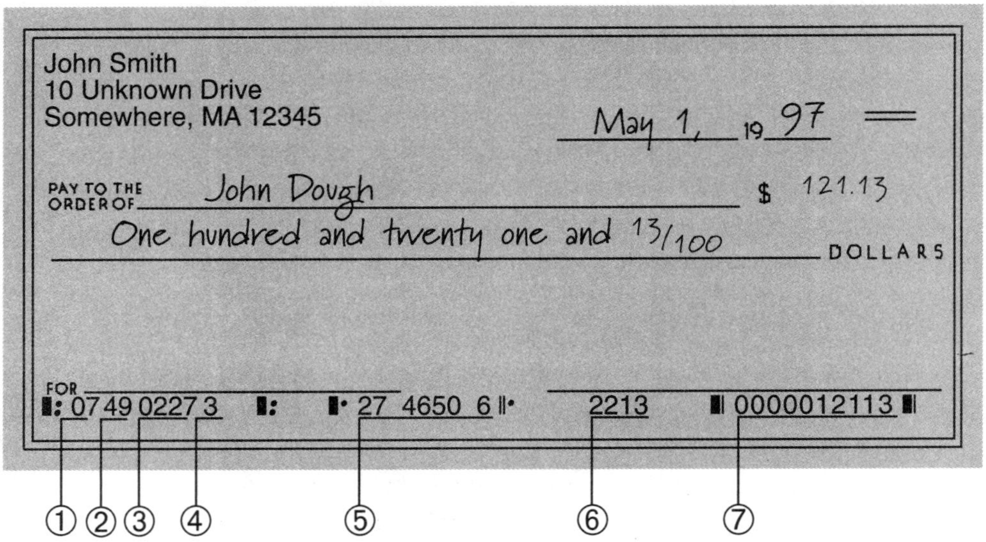

Keys to Sample Check:

1-Federal Reserve District Bank
2-Branch or city designation and clearing assignments
3-ABA bank number
4-Check digit
5-Payor account number
6-Sequence number
7-Encoded check amount (in cents)

MICR line. Unless an error has been made, this number (in cents) will agree with the amount written or typed in the body of the check. Once a check is encoded, it is completely readable from that time on. (Figure 1-2)

In the 1970s, the Federal Reserve introduced a regional check-processing program to further improve the efficiency of check clearing. The program expanded the number of check-processing facilities, which enabled the Federal Reserve to collect significantly more checks faster. As of mid-1997, there were 10 regional check processing centers (RCPCs). These centers are now located at each of the Reserve Banks, the 25 Reserve Bank Branches and 10 regional check-processing.

In the mid-1980s, the Federal Reserve began to encourage the conversion of paper checks to electronic records in order to improve the efficiency of the check collection process. The Federal Reserve has actively supported research to develop check image processing, which permits the image of a paper check to be captured, processed and stored on electronic media.

Until the late 1980s, depository institutions were allowed to hold deposited funds for an unlimited time before making them available for withdrawal. Some banks continued to use circuitous routes to clear checks to avoid presentment fees, and depositors could not be sure when their funds would be available. In 1987, Congress enacted the Expedited Funds Availability Act (EFAA), which limits the time that banks can hold funds from checks deposited into customer accounts before the funds are made available for withdrawal. The law was implemented in September 1988 through the Board of Governor's Regulation CC, Availability of Funds and Collection of Checks, also establishes rules designed to speed the return of unpaid checks.

The EFAA requires that funds be made available for deposits of cash, Treasury checks and cashier's checks no later than the business day after the banking day of deposit. Regulation CC extends this next-day availability to U.S. Postal Service money orders and to checks drawn on a Federal Reserve Bank or a Federal Home Loan Bank.

Banks and the Fed generally specify the time schedule for all other checks. The Federal Reserve has an availability schedule which details the time it takes to make funds available. A number of factors determine the availability of funds schedule, which can be from zero to five days. The average time it takes a check to clear the system is two days. If a bank uses the Fed to clear its checks, the bank's schedule will be similar to the Fed's schedule. Distance is a major factor in determining Fed and bank availability. Generally, checks drawn on distant banks or harder to reach banks are assigned longer availability than those drawn on nearby, easy to reach banks. Checks drawn and presented within the same Fed district are available faster. The time of day when the transaction is made affects the schedule. Sometimes, companies negotiate an availability schedule. Instead of using the bank's normal availability schedule, a blanket availability on all checks deposited is negotiated. *The delay between the time a check is deposited at the bank and the time the depositor's account is credited with collected funds by the bank is called* **availability float.**

Availability Float

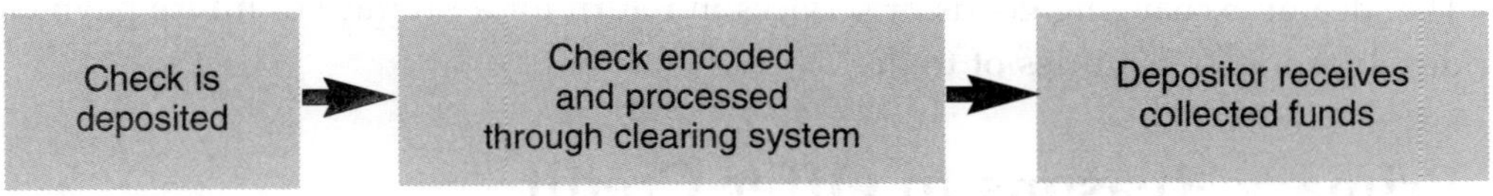

Electronic Funds Transfer

Electronic funds transfer (EFT) is a faster and more secure method of payment than either cash or check. A **funds transfer** *is a series of transactions, beginning with the originator's payment order, made for the purpose of making a payment to the beneficiary of the order.* The Federal Reserve Banks provide two types of services for electronically transferring funds: Fedwire and the Automated Clearing House (ACH). Through the Fedwire service, depository institutions typically transfer large-dollar payments. Depository institutions generally use the ACH for small-dollar payments.

Fedwire *is a real-time method of transferring cash value from one bank to another using Federal Reserve account balances.* Fedwire funds transfers are processed individually and are settled immediately. With a Fedwire transaction, the payor's account is debited and the payee's account is credited the same day. The Federal Reserve guarantees the payment to the bank receiving the transfer and assumes any risk if the bank issuing the payment has insufficient funds in its reserve account to complete the transfer.

The **Automated Clearing House (ACH)** is another electronic funds transfer system, developed jointly by the private sector and the Federal Reserve in the early 1970s as a more efficient alternative to checks. *ACH payments are pre-authorized, large-volume and are transmitted in batches to a Federal Reserve processing center by a depository institution.*

Transfers are generally processed one or two day days before the settlement date and are delivered to receiving depository institutions several times a day as they are processed. ACH credit transfers are used to make direct deposit payroll payments and corporate payments to contractors and vendors. ACH debit transfers are used by consumers to make payments on insurance premiums, mortgages, loans and other bills and by businesses to make payments to other businesses. Although the Fed is the primary operator, regional ACHs are owned by member financial institutions. The National Automated Clearing House Association (NACHA) is the member-run organization that sets policies for the ACHs and performs other functions such as research training and marketing.

The **Clearing House Interbank Payments System (CHIPS)** *is an independent message-switching system operated by the New York Clearing House Association.* It was established in 1970 to substitute electronic payments for paper checks arising from international dollar transactions such as Eurocurrency or foreign exchange between foreign and U.S. banks. It is also used for payments under letters of credit and documentary collections and for third-party transfers.

Chapter Summary

The History of Credit

The idea of exchanging goods or services in return for a promise of future payment developed after centuries of trade.

Primary Reasons to Offer Credit

The primary reasons for a company to offer credit terms to its customers are:

- Increase Sales
- Competition
- Promotion
- Credit Availability
- Convenience
- Demand
- Price

Modern Credit

Included in any definition of modern credit are an exchange of values, futurity and trust. There are several important elements of credit:

- Risk of Nonpayment
- Timing
- Security
- Extra Costs
- Legal Aspects
- Economic Influences

The five Cs of credit summarize the important features of a credit applicant. The five Cs of credit are:

- Character
- Capacity
- Capital
- Collateral
- Conditions

The Credit Process

The credit process begins with a buyer (a company or individual consumer) deciding to purchase a product or service from a seller which either makes or provides a product or service.

Credit is part of a company's operating cycle which comprises the activities a company performs to produce and sell its product or services.

The purchaser's ability to obtain a product or service based on its promise to pay at a later date is called creditworthiness.

Types of Credit

Credit can be classified into two broad classifications: public or private.

Private credit can be divided into five broad categories:

- Investment credit
- Consumer credit
- Agricultural credit
- Business credit
- Bank credit

The Federal Reserve and the U.S. Payment System

The Fed plays a number of roles including:

- Administrator
- Banker
- Controller
- Guardian
- Lender
- Regulator

The Federal Reserve is the primary conductor of U.S. monetary policy, using three major tools designed to expand or contract the money supply to control interest rates:

- Reserve requirements
- The discount rate
- Open market operations

Check Processing

Next to cash, checks are the most frequently used method of completing transactions in the United States. The Federal Reserve system processed $15.5 billion check payments in 1997 or 35 percent of total check payments in the U.S.

The Federal Reserve developed and implemented the magnetic ink character recognition (MICR) system for encoding pertinent data on checks so that the data could be read electronically. The MICR line contains information about the Federal Reserve District, the Federal Reserve Office, the bank on which the check is drawn, and the payor's Account Number.

In 1987, Congress enacted the Expedited Funds Availability Act (EFAA), which limits the time that banks can hold funds from checks deposited into customer accounts before the funds are made available for withdrawal. The law, implemented in September 1988 through the Board of Governor's Regulation CC, Availability of Funds and Collection of Checks, also establishes rules designed to speed the return of unpaid checks.

The Federal Reserve Banks provide two types of services for electronically transferring funds:

- Fedwire
- The Automated Clearing House (ACH)

Comprehension Check

1. The idea of exchanging goods or services on credit developed after centuries of trade. Explain some of the reasons why credit evolved.
2. List and explain the reasons credit terms are offered.
3. Explain why a sale may not take place, in the business setting, if credit is not offered.
4. What does the Latin term credere mean? How does it describe the credit process?
5. Explain why selling on credit is more costly than selling for cash.
6. List and explain the important elements of credit.
7. List and explain the five Cs of credit.
8. Define the term operating cycle.
9. Define and give an example of public credit.
10. Define and list the major types of private credit.
11. What is the most common type of corporate bond? List of characteristics of this type of bond.
12. What is the difference between a secured bond and a debenture?
13. Define the term consumer credit.
14. List and explain three ways consumer credit can be classified.
15. Define and explain the important characteristics of business credit.
16. Explain what open-account credit is.
17. What is the difference between unsecured and secured credit?
18. List and explain the six roles played by the Federal Reserve.

19. List the three major tools used by the Fed to expand or contract the money supply and to control interest rates.
20. Must all banks belong to the Federal Reserve System?
21. Briefly explain the concept of reserve requirement.
22. What are excess reserves?
23. What would the effect be if the Fed raised the reserve requirement? What if the requirement was lowered?
24. Define the term discount rate.
25. What role does the Federal Open Market Committee play?
26. What is the MICR system?
27. What information does the MICR line contain?
28. Define the term availability float.
29. Define the term electronic funds transfer.
30. List the two types of services for electronically transferring funds provided by the Fed.

Glossary

Agricultural credit. Relates to the farming industry and the family farmer.

Asset-backed bonds. Are secured bonds, backed by specific holdings of the issuing corporation such as equipment or real estate.

Automated Clearing House (ACH). An electronic funds transfer system, developed jointly by the private sector and the Federal Reserve in the early 1970s as a more efficient alternative to checks. ACH payments are large-volume and are transmitted in batches to a Federal Reserve processing center by a depository institution.

Availability float. The delay between the time a check is deposited at the bank and the time the depositor's account is credited with collected funds by the bank.

Bonds. Loans that investors make to corporations and governments. They are generally long-term (more than 10 years) security that pays a specified sum (called the principal) either at a future date or periodically over the length of a loan, during which a fixed rate of interest may be paid on a regular basis.

Business credit. Extensions of credit primarily for business or commercial purposes.

Capacity. One of the five Cs of credit which describes the ability to pay when a debt is due.

Capital. One of the five Cs of credit which describes the financial strength of a risk as measured by the equity or net worth of an applicant.

Character. One of the five Cs of credit which describes those moral qualities and actions of a credit applicant which oblige the applicant to pay as debts become due.

Clearing House Interbank Payments System (CHIPS). An independent message-switching system operated by the New York Clearing House Association.

Closed-end credit. Describes all types of consumer credit that does not fit the definition of open-end credit.

Collateral. One of the five Cs of credit which describes those possessions or equities from which payment might be expected should character and capacity fail.

Conditions. One of the five Cs of credit which describes the current and expected general economic situations as they might affect the applicant.

Consumer credit. Credit extended to a natural person primarily for personal, family or household purposes and may be either closed-end or open-end credit. It excludes business and agricultural credit, and loans exceeding $25,000 that are not secured by real property or a dwelling.

Credit. The transfer of economic value now, on faith, in return for an expected economic value at a specific or stated future date.

Creditworthiness. The purchaser's ability to obtain a product or service based on its promise to pay at a later date is called creditworthiness.

Debentures. A debt obligation not secured by specific property but backed by the general credit of the issuing company.

Demand deposits. Interest-bearing and non-interest bearing checking accounts.

Discount rate. The interest rate banks must pay when they borrow money from the Federal Reserves.

Equipment trust certificates (ETC). Bonds issued to pay for new equipment, secured by a lien on the purchased equipment.

Excess reserves. Additional balances on deposit with the Fed which provide extra protection against overdrafts and deficiencies in required reserves.

Expedited Funds Availability Act (EFAA). Federal legislation that establishes the time that banks can hold funds from checks deposited into customer accounts before the funds are made available for withdrawal. It also establishes rules designed to speed the return of unpaid checks.

Fair letter. A form of credit which was developed at fairs held regularly in the centers of trading areas during the Middle Ages. The fair letter amounted to a promissory note to be paid before the end of the fair or at the time of the next fair. It enabled a merchant, who was short of cash, to secure goods on credit. This gave the merchant time either to sell the goods brought to the fair or to take home and sell the goods that had been purchased on credit.

Federal Deposit Insurance Corporation (FDIC). Provides insurance protection for depositors if their bank fails. The FDIC also is the Federal bank regulator responsible for supervising certain savings banks and state-chartered banks that are not members of the Federal Reserve System.

Federal Open Market Committee (FOMC). A committee of the Federal Reserve charged under law with overseeing open market operations, which is the main tool used by the Federal Reserve to influence money market conditions and growth of money and credit. Open market operations involve the buying and selling of securities by the Federal Reserve.

Fedwire. A real-time method of transferring cash value from one bank to another using Federal Reserve account balances.

Federal Reserve System. An independent agency, established to provide the nation with a safer, more flexible, and more stable monetary and financial system.

Five Cs of Credit. Summarize the important features of a credit applicant. The five Cs of credit are character, capacity, capital, collateral and conditions.

Funds transfer. A series of transactions, beginning with the originator's payment order, made for the purpose of making a payment to the beneficiary of the order.

Incidental credit. Credit extended by service providers which defers payment of a bill. There is no credit card involved. There is no finance charge and no agreement for payment in installments. Payment must be made in four installments or less.

Investment credit. Refers to the placement of funds in productive assets to earn a profit. Investment credit can be defined as the long-term borrowing of large amounts of money to finance productive assets.

Magnetic Ink Character Recognition (MICR). A system for encoding pertinent data on checks so that the data could be read electronically.

Money multiplier. The reciprocal of the reserve ratio, that is, one divided by the reserve ratio.

Mortgage bonds. Bonds that are secured or collateralized with specific corporate assets such as buildings.

Open-account credit. Where the creditor reasonably expects the customer to make repeated transactions and generally makes more credit available to the buyer as the outstanding balance is paid.

Open-end credit. Credit extended under a plan which a creditor may permit an applicant to make purchases or obtain loans from time to time directly from the creditor or indirectly by the use of a credit card, check or other device. In open-end credit, the creditor reasonably expects the customer to make repeated transactions and may impose a finance charge from time to time on the unpaid balance; and generally makes the amount of credit available again to the consumer as the outstanding balance is paid.

Operating cycle. A firm's operating cycle is the period of time between the acquisition of material, labor and overhead inputs for production and the collection of sales receipts.

Private credit. Is extended to or used by individuals or businesses to carry on the exchange of goods and services in the private sector.

Public credit. Also called government credit, is credit extended to or used by governments or governmental divisions, agencies or instrumentalities.

Reserve requirement. All depository institutions—commercial banks, saving banks, savings and loan associations and credit unions—must retain a percentage of certain types of deposits to be held as reserves set by the Fed.

Secured bonds. Bonds with specific titles attached to them, such as mortgage bonds, equipment and trust certificates and collateral trust bonds.

Secured credit arrangement. One in which collateral is provided to the creditor.

Transaction deposits. Interest-bearing and non-interest bearing checking accounts.

References and Further Reading

Barzman, Sol. *Credit in Early America.* National Association of Credit Management, 1975.

Emery, Gary W. *Corporate Finance: Principles and Practices.* New York: Addison Wesley, 1998.

Gallinger, George W. and Jerry B. Poe. *Essentials of Finance: The Integrated Approach.* New Jersey: Prentice Hall, 1995.

Hill, Ned. C. and William L. Satoris. *Short-Term Financial Management: Text and Cases.* New Jersey: Prentice Hall, 1995.

The Federal Reserve System: Purposes and Functions. Board of Governors of the Federal Reserve System, 1994.

2 Credit in the Company

Overview

Business is basically concerned with the sale of goods or services on open account at a profit. This chapter discusses the role of the credit department within business from a strategic point of view and from an organizational point of view. The structure of a credit department is also discussed.

Learning Objectives

After reading this chapter, the reader should understand:

- Why credit is a function of business
- The strategic role of credit
- Where credit typically fits within the business organization
- The role of credit in financial management
- The role of credit in the operating cycle
- The goals and core activities of a credit department

Chapter Outline

I. Credit as a Business Function
II. The Strategic Role of Credit
  A. Collection of Information
  B. Credit Analysis
  C. Collection
  D. Cash Application
  E. Deduction Resolution
III. Credit Within the Business Organization
IV. The Role of Credit in Financial Management
  A. Managing Cash Inflows
  B. Internal Cash Flow Management
  C. Managing Cash Outflows
V. Credit and the Operating Cycle
VI. The Credit Department's Goals
VII. The Core Activities of the Credit Department
  A. Required Areas of Knowledge
VIII. The Credit Department's Multi-Functional Role
IX. The Credit/Sales Relationship
X. The Credit/Purchasing Relationship
XI. The Credit/Manufacturing Relationship
XII. The Credit/Information Systems Relationship
XIII. Credit Department Relationships with Other Departments
XIV. Organizing the Credit Department
XV. Day-To-Day Administration
  A. The Credit Approval Process
  B. Account Establishment
  C. Order Processing
  D. Accounts Receivable Administration
  E. Collections and Adjustments
XVI. Lockbox Operations
XVII. Collection Efforts
XVIII. Control and Follow-Up

Credit as a Business Function

The word, **business,** *first appeared around the 14th century and was originally defined to mean "purposeful activity."* Today, the inclusive term business designates the activities of those engaged in the purchase or sale of commodities or in related financial transactions. In other words, a **business organization** *is a combination of functions, people and materials aimed at producing goods or services, and selling them to customers at a profit.* The sale of most commodities is accomplished through the extension of credit.

Because business is basically concerned with the sale of goods or services on open account at a profit, the credit department plays an important, pivotal role within the business organization. At the same time, the role of credit and the credit department operations within the business organization have become blurred. The global business environment, coupled with leaps in technology, have changed not only the way in which and where business is conducted but who is conducting the business. The credit department is the link between customers and many other business functions such as marketing, sales, production, shipping, customer service and accounts payable.

Traditionally, the credit function was linked only to accounts receivable management. On a balance sheet, accounts receivable are reported as an asset, representing a company's claims against a customer—instead of requiring cash at the time services are provided or goods are sold, payment is accepted at a later date. Accounts receivable was the responsibility assigned to the credit department. In the management of that responsibility, the function of a credit department was to evaluate the customer's ability to pay and to manage the activities of collecting the payment. Traditionally, credit was about collecting money.

Today, that role has changed. The credit department is involved in the business process; i.e., the chain of events leading to the sale of goods or services at a profit. The credit department is involved from the time the order is solicited to the time the cash is collected. This order-to-cash responsibility reaches well beyond the financial evaluation of a customer's ability to pay and collecting that payment. The credit department represents a business decision which requires both financial and strategic decision making to assure that a proper balance of benefit is derived from sales against carrying the cost or potential loss.

Strategic decision making is part of strategic planning, which is the key ingredient that underlies credit policy and procedures. **Strategy** *can be defined as the art of devising or using plans to achieve a goal.* **Strategic planning** *entails the coordination of long-range plans with a particular focus on strategies, controls and desired results.*

External factors such as social, political and economic, legal and technological and competitive pressures impact a company's strategic plan. These external factors must be weighed in light of internal business factors such as production capacity, financial strength, human resources and marketing. Both these external and internal factors are assessed in terms of risk and reward. The role of strategic planning underlies the framework from which any policy, including credit policy, is formulated. Clearly defined goals impact upon accounts receivable to shape the resulting credit policy.

The Strategic Role of Credit

The credit department is involved with the customer cycle from the order to the collection of cash. The cycle involves the important task of information collection, credit analysis, collections and cash application, and deduction resolution. All of these elements have both financial and strategic implications in the business process.

Consider the following broad credit related areas. Each has both financial and strategic implications.

Collection of Information

The collection of information enhances the quality of financial analysis. That same information also has strategic implications; it can strengthen a company's understanding of its customer base and lead to expanding that base. The credit department is, in effect, an information warehouse within any company. The information collected by a credit department can be used by a purchasing department to screen vendors or by the marketing department to help find new customers.

Credit Analysis

Credit analysis provides financial protection—whether the customer has the ability to pay—to a business and, depending on a company's strategic goals, becomes an important factor in the sales decision.

Collection

While the credit department is responsible for the enforcement of payment terms, credit terms are a part of a company's strategic business plan. Whether credit terms are restrictive or liberal will have a direct impact on a company's strategic business plan as well as on the credit process. Cash forecasting is a natural transition for the credit department.

Cash Application

The financial impact of cash application is related to the timing of cash flow and the cost of carrying a receivable. The strategic implication of cost of carrying receivables is related to a company's financial strength and its need for cash flow.

Deduction Resolution

The financial implication of the cost of carrying unresolved deductions or customer disputes impacts a company's operating costs. Deduction resolution has very critical strategic implications because it is directly related to customer satisfaction, which in turn, impacts sales.

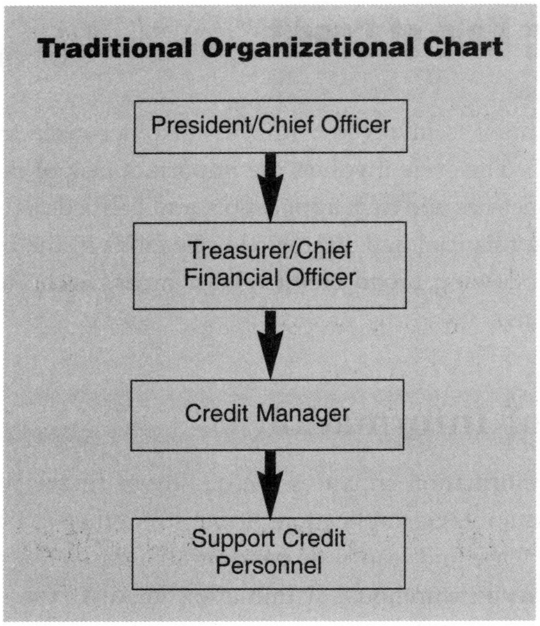

Credit Within the Business Organization

The credit department is responsible for the management of accounts receivable. To understand where credit fits within a business organization, it is important to understand the significance of accounts receivable from an accounting perspective. Accounts receivable is a current asset and a component of **net working capital,** *which is the excess of current assets of a business over its current liabilities.*

Net working capital is calculated by subtracting current liabilities from current assets:

Net Working Capital = Current Assets – Current Liabilities

In larger companies, the Finance Department or the Treasury Department is responsible for the management of working capital. In small or family owned businesses, usually the owners or top executives manage working capital.

As a result of this balance sheet logic, most credit departments report to either the treasury or finance department. In a 1995 study conducted by the Credit Research Foundation (CRF), an association dedicated to promoting a comprehensive understanding of credit and accounts receivable management, it was reported that "80 percent of the credit executives surveyed said that their credit departments report to the chief financial officer or treasurer."[1] In another study conducted by CRF in 1993, it was concluded that "the predominant reporting structure has the credit department reporting to finance related functions. This confirms the view that the formal role of credit in the corporate organization is typically defined according to the structure of a financial statement and not the strategic role of credit."[2]

A key function of every credit department is to integrate and coordinate its defined responsibilities with the treasury or finance department.

Some of the finance related functions that the credit department manages include:

- Protecting and managing the investment in the accounts receivable portfolio
- Cash forecasting
- The timely conversion of receivables into cash
- Financial analysis
- Handling of collateral which secures a customer's account
- Deposit of funds and the relationship with banks
- Handling customer deductions
- Evaluation of economic trends on sales, receivables and collections

The Role of Credit in Financial Management

Managers practice financial management when they:

- Obtain cash from investors
- Use that cash to buy productive assets
- Operate those assets to produce additional cash
- Return cash to the business and/or investors[3]

The first and fourth activities are part of the process of financing a business while the second and third are concerned with its investments and operations.[4]

A key component of a company's financial activities is managing cash flow or cash management. *The goal of* **cash management** *is the efficient management and use of cash in a manner that is consistent with the strategic objectives of the business.* Sound financial management employs a combination of managerial actions concerned with the cash flows of a business. *A major goal of cash management is to manage cash flows in order to increase the long term value of the business while balancing the inflow and outflow of cash so that the business can meet its demands for cash by creditors.*

The management of cash flow can be divided into three broad areas:

Managing Cash Inflows

These are the funds collected from customers or obtained from financial sources. Cash flows into the business from the sale of goods or services, from the return on interest earning assets in the form of interest or from the return on equity securities in the form of dividends. Cash also flows into a business when it borrows money.

Internal Cash Flow Management

This includes managing the company's cash reserves and investing cash or transferring cash among the operating units of a business or various bank accounts. Excess cash is usually invested so that it earns interest, becoming a productive asset.

Managing Cash Outflows

These are the funds disbursed from cash reserves[4] to pay for purchases of inventories, to pay for operating expenses such as salaries, rent, insurance, to pay for the purchase of long lived assets such as buildings or land, or for the repayment of debt principal or payment of dividends.

The credit department plays a crucial role in managing cash inflows from the sale of goods or services. The timely collection of cash is critical to maintain the proper balance of cash inflows and cash outflows.

Credit and the Operating Cycle

In Chapter One, credit as part of a company's operating cycle was discussed. *The* **operating cycle** *is comprised of the activities a company performs to produce and sell its product or service.* A business must first purchase the resources it needs to make its product. It then sells that product and collects the funds from the sale. *Cash flows in and out of the business during the operating cycle: cash flows out of the business, during the production stage, when it purchases the resources needed and into the business when it finally sells the product to a customer, during the collection stage.* Rarely do these events occur at the same time; the challenge of business is to maintain sufficient levels of cash throughout the operating cycle to ensure smooth and ongoing operations.[5]

The collection stage or cycle begins with the sale of a product or service. It often begins with the credit department's receipt of an order or a customer application. Depending on the size of a company, the order or application may come from the sales department or directly from the customer.

The order is received and many times is logged into a computer system for tracking purposes. Then, the customer placing the order is reviewed for creditworthiness to arrive at the credit decision. Sometimes, and depending on the credit policy, an order/customer passes all credit indicators and the order is approved. If the credit indicators point towards further credit investigation, the necessary steps are taken to make the sale while reducing the risk. Once the order is approved, it is placed into the processing mainstream as quickly as possible.

The approved order is recorded as a sale and an invoice is created. The events of recording the sale and creating an invoice are usually simultaneous. It is at this point that the receivable is created. The invoice is, in effect, a memorialization of the sale and should include an itemization of products or services purchased.

The approved order is shipped. The timing of the shipment of the order varies from company to company; sometimes the order is shipped as soon as the order is approved and the creation of the invoice follows. Sometimes, shipping and invoicing occur simultaneously. In other companies, the invoice is created after the order is shipped. The important point is that the work of the credit department continues after the order is shipped by monitoring the receivable.

In a perfect credit world, payments are received when due. The accounts receivable is reversed when the payment is received, and the cycle begins again. The reality is that not all invoices are paid as they come due. Among the reasons are errors, discount violations, duplicate payments or deductions. The disputes must be settled with

Basic Diagram of the Collection Cycle

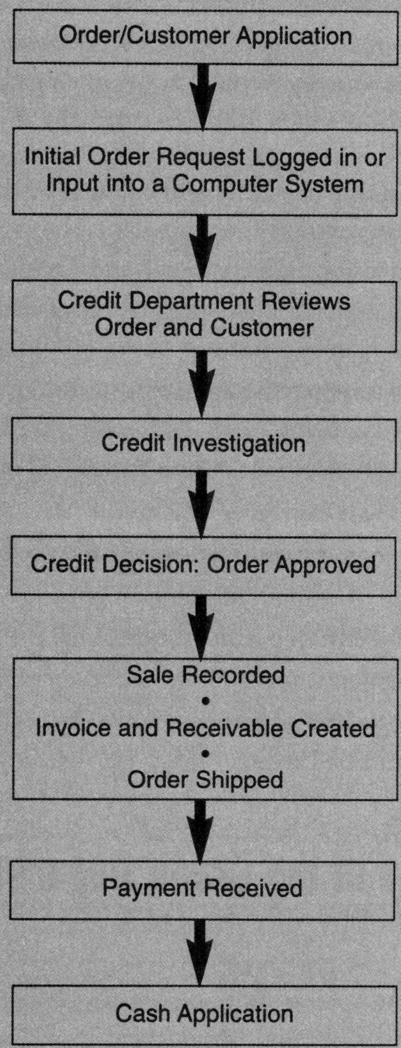

chargebacks, credit memorandum or in some cases, the order is canceled and a new invoice is issued. Invoice disputes are usually resolved by direct communication with the customer and other departments within the company key to the transaction.

In other cases, the customer is financially distressed. Customers that do not pay invoices as they are due must be followed closely with an understanding, yet aggressive collection effort. When a direct collection effort is not successful, a third party—a collection agency, a local NACM Affiliate or a collection attorney—can be used. In cases of insolvency, the business must be assessed to determine whether it can be financially rehabilitated or whether it should be liquidated. Depending on a company's policy and strategy, credit may or may not continue to be offered to a financially distressed customer. Some businesses continue to sell to customers, even during a bankruptcy proceeding. Some businesses terminate credit to customers based on the severity of the situation.

The Credit Department's Goals

It is the responsibility of the manager of the credit department to plan and direct the activities of the credit function within the guidelines of company policy.

The goals and objectives of every credit department are to:

- Increase sales and profit through a better understanding and skillful handling of all credit functions
- Match risk and reward through customer and financial analysis
- Monitor, protect and manage the company's investment in accounts receivable
- Communicate the condition, cost and trend of the company's investment in receivables to management
- Convert accounts receivable to cash in a timely manner
- Increase cooperation between sales and credit
- Maintain and increase goodwill in customer relations
- Coordinate credit activities with all departments
- Train and supervise credit department personnel
- Educate other departments about credit and the credit function
- Control operating costs and expenses
- Reduce collections and bad debt

The Core Activities of the Credit Department

The credit function is a valuable asset to a company's business. Using creative methods to structure transactions so that sales can be approved, the credit department makes a significant contribution to sales and profit maximization by knowing when and how to accomplish the sale while minimizing risk.

The core activities of the credit department are:

- Customer and credit analysis
- Developing credit policy
- Managing the collection function
- Setting credit availability thresholds
- Management reporting

Required Areas of Knowledge

To accomplish these goals and to perform these core activities, the following areas of knowledge or skill sets are required:

A Thorough Understanding of the Accounting, Financial Analysis and Finance Disciplines

All three of these disciplines come into play during the analysis of the customer. A mastery of both accounting and financial analysis is needed in the interpretation of a customer's financial reports. Basic concepts in the area of finance, such as the time value of money, assist in determining the cost of offering credit terms for the perspective of both the buyer and seller.

A Comprehensive Understanding of Business and Credit Law

Many elements of the credit function require a thorough understanding of legal concepts. For example, a credit application can be used as a contract between the seller and the buyer. A cardinal rule of any credit investigation is: Know Your Customer. Is the customer a corporation, partnership or sole proprietor? Who are the owners? Antitrust laws, the Equal Credit Opportunity Act and the Fair Credit Reporting Act all have an impact on what the credit department can and cannot do. Securing a credit transaction involves the Uniform Commercial Code. Most of the legal issues affecting the credit function are discussed in this text.

Sound Business Communication Skills (writing and presentation)

The credit department must compose and send a variety of written communications to the customer as well as create meaningful reports to management. In management meetings, credit managers must be able to clearly explain credit issues in order to have input in general business policies and practices. Excellent verbal communication skills are critical when dealing with both internal business functions and with customers.

General Management Skills Including Expert Negotiation Skills

As with most business functions, general management skills are a must. The ability to effectively manage, inspire and motivate credit department personnel is critical to the success of any credit department. As business changes, so do management techniques. There has been a shift to the team concept, which demands an understanding of how teams interface and work. Additionally, expert negotiation skills are invaluable in the collection area. General management skills also include the ability to assign responsibility, delegate authority and maintain accountability for the results.

Customer Service Skills

The credit department interacts with the customer and as discussed, also serves as the intermediary with a variety of other business units such as the sales department, the purchasing department, manufacturing or production and so on.

Analytical Skills

The ability to analyze both the customer's financial condition and general economic conditions and trends is key to a successful credit department.

Computer Skills

Many large companies have company-wide, integrated computer systems which enable the credit department to check on the status of an order at any point in time. In smaller companies, the use of stand-alone computer programs such as Lotus® or Excel® provide tools that are key to the credit function. Many companies use credit scoring programs to evaluate credit applicants. The explosive growth of the World Wide Web or the Internet have increased the need for computer skills. Information abounds on the Web; financial information on most publicly held companies is readily accessible. Additionally, participation in or the management of computer conversions are becoming common place in the every day activities of the credit department.

These skills will provide a credit manager with the tools to analyze, plan and develop credit department objectives, policies and programs to ensure its success within the business organization.

The Credit Department's Multi-Functional Role

Most credit departments confer with many departments during the credit process. The credit department is multi-functional, interacting with many business functions, departments or units. An informal organization structure exists, allowing the credit department to perform its strategic business role.

During the credit process, credit confers with the sales department, the order entry department, the production department, the shipping department, the accounting department and the customer service department. Clearly, the credit department works with more departments than ever before, creating a broader role for themselves within the business organization.

In some cases, the credit function has been merged with customer service, sales and marketing or purchasing. There has been a trend among larger companies to change the name of the Credit Department to Customer Financial Services to reflect its broader role and responsibilities. Regardless of what the credit department is called, its broader role provides it with the opportunity to provide value added services to both internal business groups and to customers.

The Credit/Sales Relationship

Establishing a viable credit-sales relationship is one of the most important tasks of the credit manager. Credit policy must be clearly defined to reduce misunderstandings between the sales department and the credit department. Participation in sales meetings is essential to clarifying the role and responsibility of credit, especially in dealings with the customer. As already discussed, *the major goal of every credit department is to help move products or sell services—make the sale—with the reasonable assurance of payment.* Additionally, there should be a clear delineation of responsibility for resolving customer disputes and unauthorized deductions.

One of the major contributions of the credit department to the sales function is to work with customers and sales representatives and to find ways to approve orders. For example, a credit manager may be able to suggest a financing method not previously considered by the customer or may be helpful in locating sources of capital for a customer.

Finally, what may be called a marketing risk should be distinguished from a credit risk. For example, to achieve adequate geographic distribution in marketing a name-brand product, it may be necessary to sell to a company that may not be creditworthy. **Marginal accounts** *or accounts with poor payment history, inadequate working capital or a deteriorating financial condition* are taken on for strategic reasons and should be identified as such when receivables investment is being analyzed. The credit department must communicate the risks to sales and management while guarding the confidentiality of the customer. This aspect of confidentiality extends to credit information that may be obtained in connection with industry credit group meetings.

The Credit/Purchasing Relationship

Purchasing departments often check the financial condition of new supply sources through the credit department to assure that the vendor or subcontractor will be able to deliver goods or services as agreed. Besides inquiring into the backgrounds of potential suppliers, the credit department can also analyze a supplier's financial condition. At times, the credit department is called upon to collect or adjust debit memorandums issued to cover claims for defective material or to settle other chargebacks. The credit department can assist in negotiating with suppliers. For example, it can arrange for other types of security, such as letters of credit, UCC-1 filings and liens. The credit department may also see to it that setoff rights are retained when its company both sells to and buys from another concern. Under most state laws, a creditor has the right to offset mutual debts it owes against the debtor's liability to it.

The Credit/Manufacturing Relationship

When overproduction leads to excess inventory, it may be necessary to dispose of the goods through sales to accounts that are not ordinarily creditworthy. Just as with marketing risk sales, these production risk sales should be followed closely by the credit department to minimize collection costs and bad debts.

Sometimes orders are put into production subject to confirmation by the credit department before shipment. **An approval subject to confirmation** *usually means that the customer is being asked to do something before goods are released, such as pay an overdue balance, reduce an outstanding balance to an acceptable level or submit an interim or annual financial statement.* This allows the goods to be manufactured for delivery on time to the buyer. While most of these conditional approvals result in the release of goods when they are ready, they do represent a production risk.

In periods of shortages, a customer may order goods well in excess of actual requirements in the hope that the amount allowed will be near to the quantity actually required. The credit department can be instrumental in spotting orders that are out of proportion to the relative size of the customer. A credit manager can usually recognize this practice and prevent the marketing and manufacturing departments from being misled into believing that growing sales has made additional production facilities necessary.

The Credit/Information Systems Relationship

If a company decides to implement a new business or technology process, computer system or package, the first goal of the credit department should be to get as involved as possible in the decision making and planning process. The credit department can present valuable data about the credit process. Applying technology to the credit process requires a detailed examination of what information is necessary and what is not. A technique called **process mapping,** *or breaking down key processes into primary activities, including actions, decision points and information/transportation flows* is critical to implementing new technology. Technology can improve the flow of information, speed decision making and standardize the credit process which will ultimately increase efficiencies and reduce costs.

Electronic Data Interchange (EDI) *is the movement of data electronically from one computer to another in a structured, processable format.* EDI has the potential to revolutionize the management of information and cash flow. The information needed in a typical business transaction might include items such as a request for a quote, a purchase order, a purchase order acknowledgment, shipping documents, an invoice, a payment advice and a freight bill. Most of these items are currently exchanged via the mail system. EDI converts these documents to electronic messages routed directly between the parties, either in a standard, widely accepted format or in a proprietary, mutually agreed upon format.

Credit Department Relationships with Other Departments

Determining the status of a customer's account often requires close cooperation with the accounting department. The credit department frequently accounts for payments received and for collateral taken in settlement of customer accounts, credit adjustments and corrections of sales.

Federal and State laws as well as the proper use of legal documents play a critical role in business and require the credit department to interact extensively with the legal department or counsel. The credit department also plays a key role in bankruptcy proceedings, including service on Creditors' Committees.

In cases when a customer has difficulty with one of the company's products, it may be necessary for the credit department to consult with engineering or manufacturing groups about corrections or replacements to be made before payment of the account can be collected. The traffic department or shipping department may wish to determine the financial responsibility of carriers and may require assistance in the collection of claims for shortages or damages.

A close relationship must also exist with the personnel department. The credit manager should take an active role in creating job descriptions for credit personnel. Recommended salary ranges must be sufficient and competitive. Training programs should be coordinated with the personnel department.

Organizing the Credit Department

Each function performed must be planned for within the organizational structure of the credit department in order to ensure a smooth flow of credit. Two essential functions briefly discussed here are **defining responsibility** and **staffing.**

The credit department's structure should be flexible and clearly delineate responsibility for each function to be performed and for each customer account. If a company classifies accounts by degree of risk, it may assign the highest-risk accounts to the more experienced and knowledgeable credit personnel and the relatively risk-free accounts to those with less experience and ability. This approach is particularly useful where a company has a large number of accounts that vary in size, quality and quantity.

The credit department must have a staff large enough for the current workload. It must have qualified individuals in each position who are systematically trained and developed for promotion to greater responsibility. Forecasting staff requirements and budgeting for growth are key functions of the credit manager, along with the need to cover each position with an accurate, up-to-date job description.

Controls and guidelines provide for a timely evaluation of key functions. This will ensure prompt and suitable decisions and enable appropriate action to be taken when required. Quantitative and qualitative data should be available for adequate reports to each control point. The goal of the department is to achieve an optimum combination of profitable sales, turnover of accounts receivable investment, bad-debt expense and credit department operating expense.

Day-to-Day Administration

The major functions performed daily by the credit department include:

- The credit approval process
- The establishment of an account
- Order processing
- Accounts receivable administration
- Collections and adjustments
- Control and follow-through

The Credit Approval Process

Certain procedures must be followed before a credit decision can be made. The relationship with the customer must be established; essential information about the account must be obtained, analyzed and stored; and the data must be evaluated so that the processing of future orders may be facilitated.

Customer relationships are usually initially established through the sales department by visits, marketing programs, and advertising and solicitation. Customer orders come through the sales department, which furnishes the necessary credit information about the prospective customer.

Few companies make shipments on open account to a new customer without some sort of credit investigation. Information about the customer's banks, other suppliers, and accountants to contact should be obtained and investigated. Credit agency reports can also be used, as can direct interviews or correspondence with the prospective customer.

The credit department is usually the only group, other than sales, to have substantial contact with the customer. This happens when the credit investigation fails to provide sufficient data to warrant approval of the amount of credit requested. When additional information is required, letters should be written, phone calls should be made or visits arranged to meet the management team of the customer and tour the customer's facilities. Although the sales force is ordinarily not involved in the financial conversations with a customer, they should be kept informed of these matters. Sales has the prime responsibility for dealing with customers, so communication should be a coordinated effort.

Special documentation may be necessary. It may require participation of the attorneys for both the company and customer. A security agreement along with filings under the Uniform Commercial Code should be made if collateral is required. A guarantee or subordination, if agreed upon, should be prepared. A letter of credit and other special documentation may be called for in international dealings.

The credit file is the place for information on a customer's account, including its history and current status. It must be readily accessible but handled in a confidential manner. Many customers require that a confidentiality agreement be signed stating that all information will be held in confidence. Credit files should be reviewed periodically to sort out obsolete material and keep files manageable. Important documents such as those used to secure a credit transaction should be carefully stored, perhaps in a fireproof cabinet.

Financial statements should be analyzed, with appropriate tools and techniques to aid the evaluation. Statements received directly from the customer should be promptly acknowledged.

All the information helps the credit manager to decide whether to approve or decline the request for credit. Determined lines or limits are an aid to processing further orders. A letter should be sent informing the customer of the credit decision and specifying the credit parameters of the relationship. This will minimize questions and future disputes.

Account Establishment

The ultimate responsibility for the status of a customer account rests with the credit department. It is essential, therefore, to set guidelines for account establishment. By having the customer complete a credit application (which is discussed in detail later in this book), much of the needed information can be obtained.

The account must be precisely identified with its correct name and address. Additional identifiers may include an alpha-numeric identifier, a D U-N-S number, bank transit number, or a social security or employer identification number (called ElNs). It is important to obtain customer billing instructions and accounts payable contacts. Also, it is important to communicate the parameters of the transaction from the start: if credit availability limits are shared with customers, they should be so communicated. Credit terms should be clearly communicated and agreed upon.

Check processors must have guidelines for handling errors, short payments or overpayments, and terms and discount violations. They should know how to communicate with customers and the sales and credit departments to resolve problems.

Collectors must be told how to minimize customer slowness and to resolve problems arising from such items as returns, traffic claims covering shortages and damage, pricing disputes or allowances for advertising and promotion.

Order Processing

Every order that falls within established credit parameters should be processed quickly for shipment to the customer. If it does not, it should be referred to the credit manager for personal handling. The reason for the referral—such as an order over the limit, a new account, or past due balances—is transmitted to the credit manager along with the account status, the credit file, or any other pertinent information. Wherever possible, orders should be released for shipment quickly. If it is necessary to hold them until a credit deficiency is remedied, the sales department and the customer should be notified.

Accounts Receivable Administration

The sum of all customer account balances must agree with the accounts receivable control account in the general ledger. This total reflects the company's investment in accounts receivable.

As a shipment is made, its invoice is posted to the customer account, either manually with a hand-posted system or as a byproduct of billing in an automated system. Credits and payments are also posted, so at any time the sum of the open items represents the balance due from the customer. From a credit perspective, accounts receivable administration reflects the credit parameters established for customers, along with a historical summary of the transactions that have taken place. Thus, it may involve customer identifiers, credit limits, credit agency ratings, daily shipping amounts, aging of open items, terms and a payment summary. Quantitative data for reports include number of invoices, checks, credits, discount or other terms violations, short payments and overpayments. The ledger should also contain a summary of order activity along with the impact on the balance due of any orders that have been approved or held but not yet shipped. This will provide an accurate view of the account as it looks when those orders are shipped and billed.

Collections and Adjustments

The collection aspect consists of cash inflows from accounts receivable. Most customers pay invoices as they are due and need no special collection effort. They may send payments to a lockbox, a third party (such as a factor) or directly to the selling company.

Lockbox Operations[6]

A **lockbox** *is a check collection system operated by a bank.* The bank picks up the mail, processes the deposit and transfers information to the company. The bank maintains post office boxes for receipt of payment at a central post office. Many banks have a unique zip code to speed delivery. The bank collects mail several times a day. Checks are removed from envelopes and either photocopied or recorded as a digital image, encoded, endorsed and entered into the clearing process. Because the bank can enter checks into the clearing system even when the bank is not open to the public, processing and availability delay can be reduced. Check and deposit information, along with other remittance data and any return documents, are sent to the company after the deposit has been processed and the checks are entered into the clearing system.

Two major types of lockboxes are offered by banks.

- **Wholesale lockboxes** are used for processing a moderate number of large-dollar remittances, usually from business payors.
- **Retail lockboxes** are characterized by a large number of relatively small-dollar remittances.

The economic benefit of using a lockbox system involves a tradeoff between the freeing of funds by faster collection and the cost of dealing with a bank or third party.

- Mail time can be reduced by selecting a lockbox close to the customer's mailing point.
- Processing time is reduced because deposits are entered even though the bank is closed.
- Availability time is reduced because checks clear faster when the deposit point is closer to the bank on which they are drawn.

Collection Efforts

A collection effort is needed when payment is not received for invoices when they are due. It may consist of only a statement but can include letters, phone calls, e-mail, visits and third-party collections. The resolution of disputes about how much is due is also a function of the collection effort. The customer may require an invoice copy or proof of delivery; clarification of prices, terms and discounts; information concerning damaged or undelivered merchandise; or explanation of some other adjustment claim. Usually the sales and other departments are consulted to resolve these items.

Control and Follow-Up

The concept of control and follow-up is to identify and remedy reasons for nonpayment. For instance, credit policy and credit guidelines should define the actions for pursuing delinquent accounts and resolving disputes. Credit policy should also establish important benchmarks such as the industry average for payment trends.

Comprehension Check

1. Discuss what the term business means.
2. What is meant by the term order-to-cash?
3. Define the term strategy.
4. What factors impact a company's strategic plan?

5. Discuss a credit-related area that has both a financial and strategic implication.
6. Define the term net working capital.
7. Using balance sheet logic, explain where the credit department falls within an organization.
8. List eight finance related functions that the credit department manages.
9. What is the goal of cash management?
10. List and describe the three broad areas of cash flow management.
11. List twelve goals and objectives of every credit department.
12. List the core activities of the credit department.
13. Discuss some of the areas of knowledge or skill sets required for credit management.
14. Why is the role of credit described as multi-functional?
15. What is an approval subject to confirmation?
16. Define the term electronic data interchange.
17. What is a lockbox?
18. List and the describe the difference between the two major types of lockboxes.
19. What benefits can be derived from using a lockbox system?

Notes

1. "Leading the Journey from Isolation to Integration: The Future of Business Credit." *The Credit Financial and Management Review*, Vol 3, No. 2, 2nd Quarter, 1997.
2. *Compensation of Credit Executive Study*. 9th Edition. The Credit Research Foundation, 1994.
3. Emery, Gary W. *Corporate Finance: Principles and Practices*. New York: Addison Wesley, 1998.
4. Ibid.
5. Gallinger, George W. and Jerry B. Poe. *Essentials of Finance: The Integrated Approach*. New Jersey: Prentice Hall, 1995.
6. Hill, Ned. C. and William L. Satoris. *Short-Term Financial Management: Text and Cases*. New Jersey: Prentice Hall, 1995.

Glossary

Approval subject to confirmation. Usually means that the customer is being asked to do something before goods are released, such as pay an overdue balance, reduce an outstanding balance to an acceptable level or submit an interim or annual financial statement.

Business organization. A combination of functions, people and materials aimed at producing goods or services, and selling them to customers at a profit.

Cash inflows. The funds collected from customers or obtained from financial sources. Cash flows into the business from the sale of goods or services.

Cash management. The efficient management and use of cash in a manner that is consistent with the strategic objectives of the business.

Cash outflows. The funds disbursed from cash reserves to pay for purchases of inventories, to pay for operating expenses such as salaries, rent, insurance, to pay for the purchase of long lived assets such as buildings or land, or for the repayment of debt principal or payment of dividends.

Electronic data interchange (EDI). The movement of data electronically from one computer to another in a structured, processable format.

Lockbox. A check collection system operated usually by a bank.

Marginal account. Accounts with poor payment history, inadequate working capital or a deteriorating financial condition.

Net working capital. Current assets less current liabilities.

Order-to-cash. The customer cycle involving all phases from the receipt of an order to the collection of cash.

Process mapping. Breaking down key processes into primary activities, including actions, decision points and information/transportation flows.

Retail lockbox. Characterized by a large number of relatively small-dollar remittances.

Strategic planning. The coordination of long-range plans with a particular focus on strategies, controls and desired results.

Strategy. The art of devising or using plans to achieve a goal.

Wholesale lockbox. Used for processing a moderate number of large-dollar remittances, usually from business payors.

References and Further Reading

Reengineering the Credit Function. The Credit Research Foundation, 1995.

3 Credit in the Department

Overview

This chapter discusses the role of the credit department within business from an organizational point of view. The structure of a credit department assures that the department functions under all conditions. To succeed at this, a measure of permanence and stability must be acheived. In large and small businesses, the components of credit functions are the same.

Learning Objectives

After reading this chapter, the reader should understand:

- How a credit department is organized
- The importance of ongoing training
- Small business organization

Chapter Outline

I. How a Credit Department is Organized

II. Centralization and Decentralization
  - A. Benefits of Centralization
  - B. Benefits of Decentralization

III. Types of Credit Organization
  - A. Centralized—Credit Controlled and Administered at a Principal Office
  - B. Credit Controlled at a Principal Office but Administered from Decentralized Locations
  - C. Credit Controlled and Administered from Decentralized Locations with a Staff Office Maintained at Headquarters

IV. General Considerations

V. Management Responsibilities
  - A. Planning
  - B. Organizing
  - C. Staffing
  - D. Leadership
  - E. Control

VI. Organization for Small Businesses
  - A. Establish a Credit Policy
  - B. Personnel Administration
  - C. Importance of the Job Specification
  - D. Appraisal of Personnel
  - E. Training
  - F. Employee Enhancement

How a Credit Department is Organized

The requirements of the business determine the size and type of credit department. Unlike most other company operations, the credit department tends to remain fairly constant in size and scope of activities during periods of changing business conditions. A credit department may face a greater number of collection problems in a depressed economy when inflation is rising and the money supply is tighter than during a period of general prosperity when inflation is low.

Consequently, the organization of the department is particularly important; a measure of permanence and stability must be achieved that will assure that the department functions under all conditions. Although the organization should not remain static, it is highly desirable to have experienced and capable employees always available within the department. Today, alternatives exist to accommodate extra heavy workloads. Today's business environment allows for the cross-training of personnel which allows for more flexibility. Perhaps accounting department personnel can be trained to perform routine tasks and called upon as necessary. Alternatively, temporary staff can be hired or work can be outsourced to companies specializing in credit-related work such as cash application and dispute resolution.

Centralization and Decentralization

The question of whether to centralize or decentralize the credit function is faced by large companies with geographically diverse operating units. It has become more important recently as many corporations are reengineering their business processes to take advantage of automation and electronic commerce. *In a* **centralized structure,** *the credit function is controlled and administered from a principal or central location. In a* **decentralized** *structure, the credit function may be report to a principal location (headquarters) with credit personnel located at remote offices.* Smaller businesses or companies operating in only one geographic area have centralized credit functions.

Benefits of Centralization

Economies of Scale

In cases where different divisions serve common customers, this can mean receiving fewer checks per customer and may reduce the number of lockboxes needed and speed up the receipt of payments. Ultimately, it means reducing staffing and operating costs. In addition, it is easier to handle vacations and other routine interruptions.

Functional Expertise and Reduction in Training

A centralized credit function permits a company to develop a staff with depth and expertise in credit management. Training is easier to administer and can be combined with on-the-job training.

Consistency and Control

Standardization of policies and procedures is easy in a centralized function. This has the advantage of providing consistent credit availability decisions across all business lines and accounts and usually prevents outside departments from having undue influence on credit decisions, which can be controlled more effectively in a centralized department.

Broader Perspective

When all information about a common customer is centralized, the credit function has more effective control over bad debt exposure and perhaps increased leverage in collection efforts.

Benefits of Decentralization

Customer Service and Improved Customer Relations

The ease with which customers can be contacted enhances a credit executive's relationship with marginal customers and develops a better rapport with customers having a sizable dollar exposure. A decentralized credit operation may be able to develop faster response times and better relationships with customers by its physical proximity.

Cooperation of Business Functions and Better Interdepartmental Relationships

Being on-site with other business functions promotes better understanding of business goals and fosters exchange of information about market and customer needs. It also enhances communications among departments and reduces the number of interdepartmental conflicts.

Involvement in Setting Strategic Priorities

Credit can integrate its objectives with those of sales and marketing into divisional goals. Also, decisions made at a local level can be implemented immediately without going through levels of review.

More Authority and Accountability

The combination of increased business knowledge, flexibility to act and accountability gives the credit function the opportunity to be more timely and efficient in responding to customer needs and market conditions.

How to Decide

Recent research suggests that centralized credit departments are better for companies that have divisions serving common customers and decentralized departments work better for corporations with products in diverse markets that have little in common. *If a company is going to focus on its core business, then it should plan a centralized credit function. If it plans to diversify into other markets, however, it should plan to decentralize.*

Types of Credit Organization

Although there may be variations among companies, the control and administration functions can be classified into three types of operations.

Figure 3-1 Credit Controlled and Administered from a Principal Office

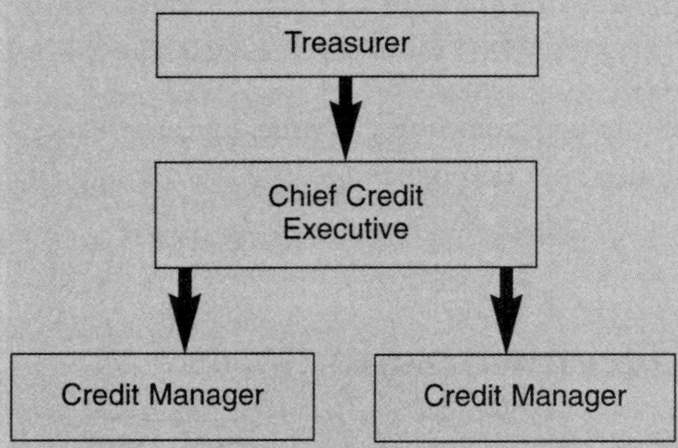

Centralized—Credit Controlled and Administered at a Principal Office

Under this type of organization, the credit department functions as a line operation. The term line is sometimes used to differentiate the organizational function of an operation or an employee. For example, in a manufacturing firm, line managers are typically in the production and sales functions, whereas executives in personnel and accounting are considered staff managers. Whether a manager's function is classified as line or staff depends on the organization's objectives.

Although the central department may service a number of different units, it is situated entirely at company headquarters where all of its business is transacted. The credit executive and staff approve credit on all orders. Contact with customers is largely by telephone or correspondence, although customer visits are made when necessary.

A centralized credit system may be modified in certain respects. In some companies, for example, most of the credit functions are carried on at headquarters, but collections offices are located in the field to assist in securing payments or making adjustments.

Figure 3-1 illustrates a credit department that is administered and controlled from a principal office. The executive level credit manager or director of credit devotes almost full time to the management of credit and reports to the treasurer or chief financial officer. This type of operation maintains a close connection with the financial function and the sales department. It is particularly suitable to small and medium-sized businesses that do not have much geographical dispersion or product diversification.

Credit Controlled at a Principal Office but Administered from Decentralized Locations

In this scenario, a mid-management level credit manager reports functionally to an executive-level credit manager at headquarters and also reports to the division head (the principle is the same for subsidiary or branch operations). *Authority in credit and collection is received from the executive level credit manager, but in all other respects, proce-*

Figure 3-2 **Decentralized Offices with Credit Controlled from a Principal Office**

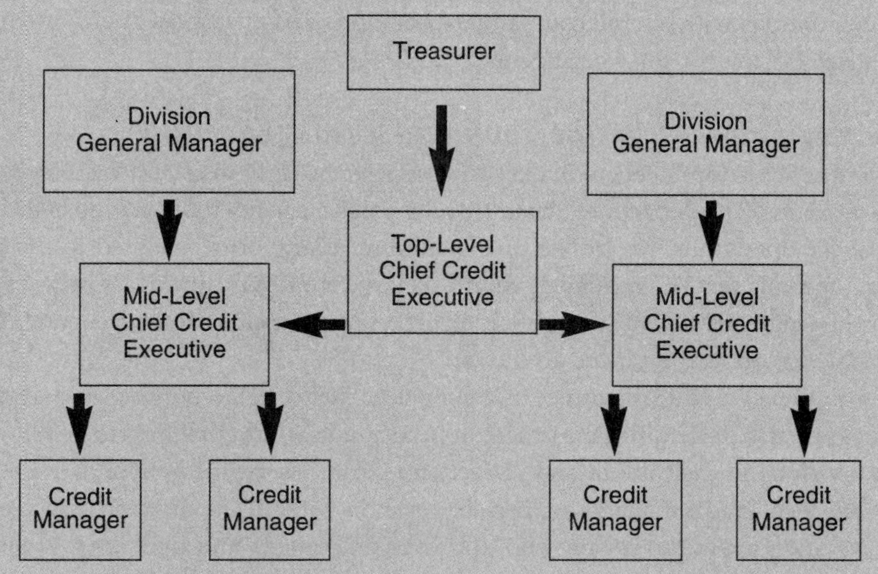

dures to which the credit executive must conform are established by middle management. Figure 3-2 illustrates a decentralized operation under which the middle-level credit manger has line authority. This type of arrangement requires close cooperation between the top-level credit executive and the division general manager regarding the dual reporting of the line credit executive.

Authority of the Mid-Level Credit Manager

The mid-level credit manager is normally authorized by the division general manager to take care of personnel problems, operating expenses and all other nonfunctional matters within the scope of local policy.

In supervising the conduct of local credit and collection activities, the top-level credit executive may follow one of several procedures. Generally, the mid-level credit manager has authority to give final credit approval on all orders not exceeding a stipulated amount; such final authority probably extends to 80 percent or more of the orders received by a division, subsidiary or branch. Orders in larger amounts are referred to headquarters for processing and approval, usually with local recommendation. In some instances, the mid-level credit manager may be authorized to give preliminary credit approval so the order may be put into production at the factory, with shipment approval to come from the top-level credit executive.

Another method is to designate certain customers as "headquarters accounts" because of special circumstances. All credit matters pertaining to these orders are accordingly processed by the headquarter's credit office. When this procedure is followed, the mid-level credit manager ordinarily has final approving authority for all other orders, and may be empowered to recommend credit limits for accounts of unquestioned financial resources whose orders normally exceed local authorization. In the area of miscellaneous adjustments or writeoffs, the mid-level credit manager is usually given a blanket authorization to process the great majority of individual cases, only those of major importance being brought to the attention of the top-level credit executive. In addition, a mid-level credit manager is often asked to recommend the amount of allowance for uncollectibles that will be required for the underlying units portfolio of accounts. The top-level credit executive can then factor in these local recommendations with overall company expectations and objectives in order to make adequate provision for this contingency.

Authority Retained by the Top-Level Credit Executive

In many firms, the top-level credit executive retains the right to establish credit policy for the divisions. The department head thereby gains a considerable degree of indirect control over operations, regardless of the amount of authority assigned to the mid-level credit manager. The top-level credit executive considers approvals in cases that exceed the limits set for an underlying top-level credit executive and is completely responsible for all headquarters accounts.

The top-level credit executive, in conjunction with the accounting and systems departments, also determines the procedures, techniques, and practices to be followed by the divisions in their credit and collection operations. In the general supervision of the mid-level credit managers, close cooperation with all the division managers is necessary and covers the review and approval of budgets and operating expenses, the status of accounts, customer contacts, and the performance of all credit functions. It is important in a decentralized operation that the activities of the various divisions be coordinated so that substantial discrepancies will not exist among them in salaries, facilities, or methods.

Training of credit personnel and the assignment of employees to the divisions—with the agreement of the division manager—are primary responsibilities of the top-level credit executive. Since mid-level credit managers frequently seek advice of the top-level credit executive in connection with unusual or special situations, the staff at headquarters must be organized in such a manner that the necessary assistance can be given promptly and expertly.

Credit Controlled and Administered from Decentralized Locations with a Staff Office Maintained at Headquarters

Under this type of organization, the top-level credit executive is responsible for collecting information and preparing reports for top management, providing advice and counsel to the line credit executives, and participating in major problem-risk analysis. Figure 3-3 illustrates a decentralized operation with a staff office maintained at headquarters. This type of arrangement requires the top-level credit executives of the underlying units to be responsible for order approvals and collections, and to control their own unit credit departments.

The top-level credit executive usually determines the overall credit policies. Divisions coordinate their activities and select the best alternative action in the light of prevailing conditions. Compliance with the overall policies is especially important, so periodic field trips and reports on division operations are the basic means for monitoring the activities of the line credit executive. In cases where control is completely decentralized, the mid-level credit manager reports only to the division general manager and has complete authority in all credit and collection matters without

Figure 3-3 **Decentralized Offices with Staff at Principal Office**

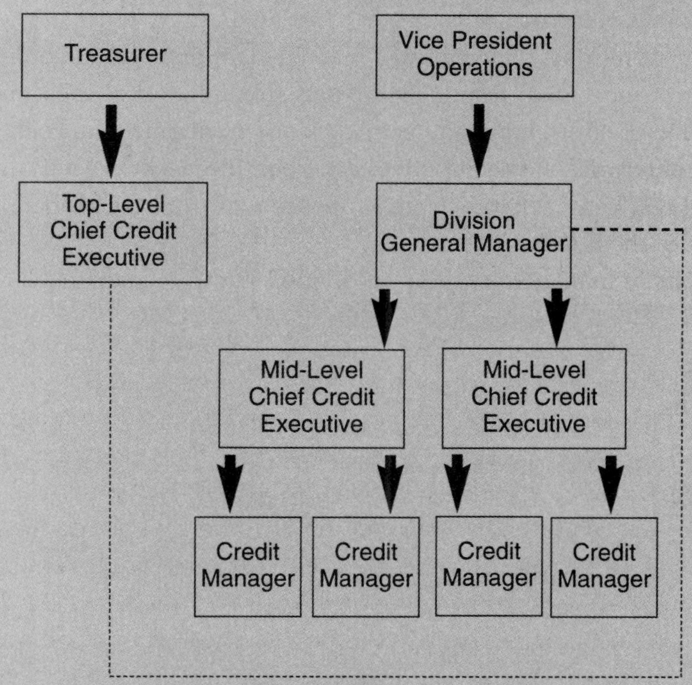

reference to headquarters. The division is required to carry out the general credit policies of the company, but the operation within those policies is the responsibility of the division. Consequently, the line credit executive is responsible to the division general manager both for the performance of the function and for the operation of the division.

General Considerations

In general, the credit department tends to be a line operation managed from a principal office, although in many cases its administration is carried on at decentralized locations. Despite the fact that their major duties are usually line, almost every credit executive performs some staff activity such as appraisal of business conditions and forecast of economic trends. This staff work becomes increasingly important as an organization grows larger, particularly in the manufacturing field, and executive management requires increasing relief from the pressures of accumulated problems. In some large corporations, particularly those whose credit departments are decentralized to the fullest extent, a credit executive will devote principal time to staff functions.

When sufficient work of a staff nature develops, the credit executive should be relieved of operating duties so that full time may be devoted to this important function. Otherwise, there is a danger that staff duties will be neglected under the pressure of line problems. Eventually, a full time staff executive will require the services of additional personnel who have a background in credit work.

Management Responsibilities

Every department needs a philosophy of management that will not only permit full development of individual responsibility and strength, but at the same time give cohesive direction of effort, maintain teamwork and harmonize the goals of the individual and the enterprise. If the objectives are clear, the credit executive and department personnel will know what they are supposed to do and the proper organization of the job enables them to do it.

The functions of management may be divided into five main areas:

- Planning
- Organizing
- Staffing
- Leadership
- Control

Planning

Many serious problems of credit management are caused by lack of adequate planning. The top-level credit executive must determine the sequence of planning steps and the scheduling of activities necessary to accomplish the desired results. Planning establishes common objectives so everyone can know the values the department hopes to achieve; it coordinates what each person must do without duplication or omission; it determines the factors necessary to perform assigned duties effectively; and it institutes control measures that can be implemented as work progresses and standards against which to check results.

Organizing

By clarifying what is to be done and maximizing the opportunity for individual accomplishment, the organizational structure gives freedom of action and reduces limitations. Therefore, it encourages high productivity and creativity. There are certain essentials in developing an improved organizational structure. It is essential to clarify in writing the overall objectives, purposes and results desired for the entire credit department. The major activities that will accomplish the objectives should be identified and grouped accordingly—that is, match the groups with the specialized abilities, interests and skills of personnel. This grouping must be simple, tailored for the credit department and accepted by those affected. It should contribute to maximum effectiveness of total department operations.

Major functions should be combined into the overall department structure. Every function and every position should be described in writing: accurately, briefly and clearly. This requires continuity of work flow, harmonious relationships, easy communications across all organizational levels, and equitable appraisal and remedial action.

Finally, the ideal organizational structure should be put into place to develop the ideal department structure. Major problems standing between the ideal structure and the present structure should be identified; viewpoints, objectives, vested interests, trends, and personnel analyzed; and the use of present staff, resources and facilities reviewed. A decision has to be reached on what improvements can and should be made immediately, and a schedule of subsequent changes prepared.

Staffing

The top-level credit executive must establish and maintain basic controls governing the selection, compensation and development of department employees.

Adequate staffing ideally means that the right person is in the right job, at the right time, at the right compensation and with satisfaction to all concerned.

To succeed, there are three steps to consider:

- First, establish the results required of each position and what criteria are used to measure them.
- Second, determine what the present occupant of each position has to do in order to secure desired results.
- Third, ascertain what knowledge, skills and personal qualifications are needed to perform the activities. Appropriate skills and abilities can be provided at points needed and instructions given clearly so they may be understood. Teamwork and cooperation then become natural and easy.

Executives are responsible for the selection, performance, training and development of their employees. Outside trainers or training specialists may help, but the final responsibility rests with the department head. Effective training requires department objectives and standards and accepted criteria for performance measurement. Manuals and instructions for uniform interpretation of established practices are essential.

Leadership

Leadership, motivation and follow-through by the head of the department are important to identify opportunities for improvement or the need for remedial action, and to point out areas where unfavorable results or trends should receive executive attention. Appraisals of employee performance, made regularly or for special reasons, are needed to identify gaps between actual performance and desired results, to ascertain specific training needs and to develop effective ways of meeting those needs. Improved performance should be recognized through nonfinancial awards, financial rewards or both.

Leadership refers to the degree of authority exerted by the top-level credit executive and the amount of freedom available to subordinates. The successful leader is one who can behave appropriately under varying conditions. The top-level credit executive must guide and oversee subordinates, delegate authority and assign duties. In all instances, company objectives must be held paramount. Instructions must be complete, clear and reasonable. Subordinates also must understand policy and procedures and the reason for actions; and be able to coordinate their actions in the department and communicate effectively.

Control

The basis of effective control is a plan based upon some realistic set of standards. Hence, a requirement of a top-level credit executive is the ability to review the operations of the department and the performance of the staff in terms of desired results and to provide conditions that encourage the staff to produce to the best of their abilities. However, the head of the department should review all operations to assure conformity with established goals and objectives and order remedial action where necessary. Because the economic climate is in a constant state of flux, every policy, control, record and report, should be reviewed and questioned periodically. Responsibility should be established for appraising the observance of credit policies, reporting lack of compliance, recommending remedial action, reviewing procedures and standards of performance, and recommending changes.

Organization for Small Businesses

Small business owners often begin to think seriously about credit management when they find they have insufficient cash flow to fuel their growth, although they are profitable on paper. In most small companies, accounts receivable becomes one of the largest assets of the company. Even if the new credit manager works only part-time, it is important to establish the credit function. Large or small, the components of the credit function are the same.

Establish a Credit Policy

A small company can rarely prevail against industry practice, even if it is not as favorable to a small company as other terms would be. In any case, policy should include the terms offered to customers (based on the level of receivables the firm can afford to carry), the guidelines for extension of credit, and prompt-payment discounts, if any.

Develop a Credit Application

The application should include enough information about the new customer to allow the credit manager to assess risk. It should be used in conjunction with commercial credit information from credit reporting agencies and the NACM Affiliated Associations. Small businesses can also learn about payment history from checking other trade references.

Keep Credit Records

It is important to maintain accurate records for easy access while preserving confidentiality. Although individual files are most common in small business, more and more information is being archived in electronic files on PCs.

Produce Accurate Invoices

Small businesses tend to lose a lot of time in the collection process due to incorrect pricing, sending an invoice to the wrong account, disagreement over the quantity shipped, and missing purchase order information. Timely payments are more likely when businesses send timely, clear and accurate statements to their customers.

Deal with Past Due and Delinquent Accounts

Small businesses tend to use collection letters and telephone calls with past due accounts. Other methods are personal visits, fax, e-mail, certified or registered mail and form letters. Regardless of collection methods, some customers will not be able to pay. If they are good potential long-term customers, it may be in a small company's best interest to try to work out new payment terms.

Measure Effectiveness and Performance

It is just as important to measure credit effectiveness and performance in a small company as it is in a large corporation.

The following list of tools, that are discussed in detail later is this book, is commonly used by small businesses:

- Bad debt as a percentage of sales
- Days sales outstanding
- Receivable days
- Delinquency days
- Percent collected by aging period
- Aging of accounts receivable in dollars and as a percentage of total A/R
- Accounts opened as a percentage of applications received
- Accounts over 90 days past due
- Accounts on credit hold as a percentage of total open accounts

Personnel Administration

Emphasis on the job to be done is the essential consideration in assigning personnel to the credit department organization. Basic tools for accomplishing this are the job description and the job specification.

Developing a Job Description

The **job description** *is a statement of the duties, responsibilities and authorities of each position.* It helps define the amount and type of training required by qualified personnel for the various credit department jobs. It is also valuable when developing measures of performance.

Components of a Job Description

The four primary elements of the successful job description are position objective; duties and responsibilities of the position; the authority of the position (should be commensurate with the duties and responsibilities); and relationships with other individuals, departments or functions that the position entails.

Position Objective

The job description should begin with a concise statement of the position's objective. In this section of the job description there should be no detail. The statement should simply describe the nature of the position in relation to the department as a whole.

Duties and Responsibilities

The longest section of the job description is usually devoted to the major responsibilities of the job, which should be stated in enough detail to guide the individual in the job. This section should also list the special activities, beyond normal business routine, that are involved in fulfilling the position objective or function.

Authority

It is extremely important to specify the authority delegated to the position with respect to the major duties and responsibilities for which the individual is to be held accountable. Responsibility and authority are usually commensurate in practice, regardless of what their relative weight may be in theory.

Relationships

The section in the job description devoted to relationships is particularly important in the case of credit positions because of the many contacts the credit department may have throughout the organization. This section should describe the types, levels and organizational location of individuals with whom the person in the job will have contact. The specific nature of the relationship (advisory, coordinating, etc.) should be stated in every instance, since these contacts can have a significant bearing upon the accomplishment of the position function.

Analyzing the Position

The method that follows is based upon factors present (though not to the same degree) in all credit department positions. The first factor to be considered is the amount of investigation, research and creative thinking that the position requires.

Organization, Planning and Administration

This relates to the formulation and execution of plans for achieving specified objectives. A further consideration is the extent to which the position is responsible for the direction, supervision and coordination of subordinates as indicated by the number of persons directly and indirectly supervised.

Planning and Execution of Operations

This factor represents the degree to which the position is involved in achieving established objectives through planning, developing and executing work programs, and maintaining controls. The complexity of the problems and the degree of participation in formulating departmental or company wide plans also are weighed.

Interpersonal Contacts

This factor represents the requirements of the position to initiate and maintain effective contacts with individuals other than subordinates. Internally it refers to consultative and non-supervisory relationships within the company. Externally it refers to contacts with customers, governmental agencies, suppliers, banks, accountants, potential employees and the community at large.

Influence on the Company Strategy

This factor represents the influence the position may exert on the general strategy and goals of the company. Among the elements to be taken into account are the scope of responsibility and authority, and exposure to opportunities and risks.

Weighting the Factors

Particularly for purposes of position grading and salary administration, the above factors may be graded by level on a ten-point scale. After assigning points to every factor, some evaluators consider the sum of the assigned points to be the rating for the job. A further refinement of such a rating system is to weight the factors, one against the other.

Importance of the Job Specification

The job specification is a statement of the qualifications that an individual should have to fill a particular job—usually including educational requirements, experience requirements, and special characteristics and abilities.

Relation to the Job Description

The job specification details "what it takes" to do the job set forth in the job description. Therefore, the job specification should clearly state the qualities, training, and experience required to accomplish the assigned task satisfactorily. The statement of specifications for a particular job should be derived from the job description, rather than being based on the qualifications of the person in the job, however competent the person may be. When the specification is kept impersonal, it becomes a yardstick by which the incumbent can be measured. At the same time, the specification itself can be tested by comparison with the individual.

Relation to Training Programs

Job specifications can be useful in establishing training goals for personnel at all levels. Initially, the job specification should be accurate and reflect the current job. It then can be modified or expanded to meet the job requirements as they may be expected to develop in the next few years. If desired, the specifications can be further revised in terms of the expanded requirements of the "job ahead"—the logical next step upward for the current occupant of the job. By comparing the modified job specification with a profile of the job incumbent, management can determine the areas in which an individual needs additional experience or training. Thus, a more meaningful training program can be developed and adapted to individual needs.

Job Qualifications

The qualifications for the position of credit executive are of two types: **technical** and **personal.** *The technical may be defined as the education and experience requirements,* while the *special characteristics and abilities of the individual would comprise the personal.*

Education

Most positions require a college degree or equivalent. A degree in business administration is most desirable. The candidate must have basic training in and knowledge of accounting, credit and collections, financial statement analysis, banking and finance, commercial law, marketing, statistics, economics, human behavior and psychology.

Experience

The length of experience required depends upon the position level. In some cases a special type of experience may be needed, such as a statistical background for the preparation of reports or familiarity with electronic data processing in order to process orders smoothly.

Special Characteristics and Abilities

The full qualifications listed below are not likely to be possessed by any one individual. However, the higher the position level the more likely it is that the executive will be able to:

- Determine appropriate methods of observing, organizing, analyzing and reporting data.
- Meet new situations and changing conditions with initiative, adaptability and ingenuity.
- Identify needs, unsatisfactory conditions and the causes of such conditions; and handle unpleasant situations with tact, diplomacy, and emotional stability.
- Analyze complex problems constructively and follow up difficult situations with resourcefulness.
- Make informed decisions and be willing to take considered risks for profitable company growth and development of the sales potential.
- Direct the work of employees effectively, exercising considerate interest and fairness in dealing with people and communicating effectively and convincingly through speaking and writing.
- Handle customer and internal relations diplomatically and firmly when required.
- Acquire and maintain the required job knowledge; have pleasing appearance, speech and personal manner; conduct affairs with uncompromising honesty; and persevere in eliciting confidential information.

Appraisal of Personnel

Appraisal is essential to determine how well individuals have been doing their jobs and to help them improve their performance. There are many useful evaluating systems and programs. An annual or more frequent personnel review should be conducted by the immediate superior of the individual being evaluated. Together, they should establish measurable goals and timetables for accomplishing them. These goals should build the strengths of the employee and correct shortcomings.

Job descriptions, coupled with annual performance evaluations, can give employees a work environment that clarifies what is expected on the job and review of how these expectations were met.

A policy of joint career development planning can be useful to the company and to selected employees. Written one-year individual career development plans appropriately related to employee interests and aspirations would ensure that such plans are implemented.

Promotions and Pay Increases

A sound promotion policy requires some form of systematic appraisal for each worker. Such a plan should cover, in addition to performance of office and routine work, relevant personal characteristics, health, emotional stability, analytical ability, initiative, ambition, ability to influence and work with others, ability to make sound decisions, and ability to assume responsibilities and carry out delegated authority.

Each of these factors should be carefully weighed so the appraisal procedure will be fair and reasonably accurate. No one, not even the top-level credit executive, should be left out of such an appraisal, though it may be necessary to modify the criteria as the position changes.

Training

Given the increasing complexity of today's business world, management personnel must continue to develop themselves so they can carry out their responsibilities. Credit and finance are increasing in importance and credit executives must keep themselves equipped to perform these expanding roles and functions.

Need for Credit Training

Credit department personnel need formalized training, not only to train new employees but also to increase the skills and talents of experienced members. Any significant change in company organization may also require an expansion of the present training program. Whenever credit employees face greater responsibilities, some provision must be made for retraining present personnel or for training new personnel.

Preparation for Credit Training

No two companies operate precisely the same. Therefore, a training program used in one company cannot be expected to satisfy all the requirements of another. Training should emphasize the advantages of working in and for the company.

After training is completed, employees should have a broad perspective of their work and its opportunities. If they like credit work, this phase of job training will reinforce their decision. Even if they decide to leave, a good training experience will make them feel well-treated. The credit executive should remember that the new employee is coming into a strange environment and that there are limits to how much new information the trainee can absorb in a given time. It is an opportunity for the department head to set the tone for effective training, to present credit functions within a broad perspective and to get to know new people as they join the staff.

Selection of Personnel

Training begins with careful selection of the personnel to be trained. The aim is to select people with ambition and capacity to become productive workers. They should have a career interest in credit and financial management.

Every good program requires clear-cut statements of the objectives of the credit department, so that both the trainee and management clearly understand why the training is being provided. Specifications for the various jobs should be clearly established and job descriptions specifically set forth. The training program must then be geared to the credit department's functions and objectives on the one hand, and to the needs of the personnel to be trained on the other. A farsighted top-level credit executive will seek to bring to the staff young associates who, with proper training and experience, will develop management abilities. One cannot be sure these abilities exist. They have their source, however, in basic qualities that may be expressed in school and social activities, and in the way the individual plans, organizes, and performs daily work, and gets along with associates.

Considerations in a Sound Training Program

The primary objective of any training program is to provide employees with the opportunity to progress to whatever level of responsibility they can achieve. This requires programs for developing one's ability to think and to analyze and formulate workable solutions to problems. Personality should be enriched, confidence inspired, and the traits and skills of leadership developed to assure the widest possible use of the available human resources for the company's benefit.

A well-designed training program should:

- Develop a higher level of performance by being more proficient on the job. This includes the ability to handle customer relations and develop more harmonious working relations with other departments.
- Provide a broad concept of the company's place in the industry and the department's relation to the whole.
- Provide basic training for another job which the trainee may eventually hold.

The basic requirements of a good training program are:

- Much of the instruction should be given and supervised by top-level personnel. This requires adequate preparation of instructional materials, maximum use of visual and other aids, a quiet environment for the instruction, and provisions for testing and follow-up to determine training effectiveness.
- Outline of job routines and procedures should be given to trainees and reviewed with them within a few days. Items include an explanation of credit forms and credit files so trainees may know the importance of the various types of credit information available in the files, and full information on collections and procedures, with emphasis on the importance of keeping these receivables current by quick conversion into cash.
- Day-to-day office operations should be described to trainees so they may better understand related responsibilities. These include describing the flow of information and work with which the trainee will be concerned, with emphasis on how important it is to keep the work flow moving so that others may not be delayed in their work; describing the successive steps in the processing of orders, from the time an order is received by the sales representative until it is ready for shipment; and developing a broad understanding of the work procedures on billing and accounts receivable, especially the payment application function.
- Explaining the importance of maintaining friendly working contacts with employees within the credit department and constantly striving for effective relationships in all their working contacts, particularly those with the sales department.

Management Support

The management team of the credit department must believe strongly in the benefits to be derived from credit training, and give unqualified endorsement and active support to it. Known antagonism by superiors frequently causes employees to underestimate the value of their training or enter into it half-heartedly. It also makes it difficult for those in charge of training to retain their enthusiasm.

Defining the Responsibilities

Good training must prepare the trainee to assume responsibility, no matter how simple or unimportant it may be. The responsibilities of subordinates should be clearly defined to help them develop their capacity for decision-making. It is often difficult for credit executives to determine the extent to which they can entrust credit analysis and credit decision responsibilities to their subordinates.

Here are a few recommended procedures to encourage delegation of authority for training purposes:

Support

The credit executive and training staff must be ready and willing to support the trainee on those decisions questioned by higher authority. Credit trainees must know that decisions based on reliable information will not result in their being reprimanded simply because someone in the front office has complained.

Mistakes

When a trainee makes a mistake, it is the duty of the credit executive or staff to correct it and also to prevent its repetition. Of course, good supervision will place a limit on the number of times a given mistake can be made. The chronic offender who cannot or will not profit by training must be replaced, and the sooner this is done the better for the morale of all other trainees.

Communications

Written communications will minimize misunderstandings. They should be used mainly for transmitting information and not for making decisions, otherwise trainees may fall into the habit of transferring all problem decisions to their superiors, thus defeating the purpose of the training program.

Making Decisions

Denying a trainee decision-making experience can be a serious deterrent to effective training. The trainee should be given assistance and guidance in solving a problem but decisions, appropriate to that function, should be made by the trainee.

Orientation

Broadly speaking, **orientation** *is the attempt to establish in the mind of new or transferred employees certain basic knowledge about an organization and its operations.* The new employee must become acquainted with company rules, regulations, and procedures in order to make an effective adjustment to the job.

The basic requirements of a good orientation program are:

Welcome

This should be a personally delivered message of welcome by the credit executive and a personally written welcome from the president of the company or some other member of top management. The purpose is to create a favorable attitude and a sense of belonging.

About the Company

The next part is an oral presentation, supplemented by a summary sheet or relevant information about the company—its size, its place in the industry, its services, and its key executive personnel.

About the Job

Then comes a carefully prepared, realistic presentation of the job to be filled, its opportunities and challenges, and how it fits into the total pattern of the credit operation.

Rules and Regulations

A review of company and departmental rules and regulations is necessary, supplemented by an explanation of the reasons for the more important ones.

Salary and Benefits

Last, employees should be given an outline of the conditions of employment, salary and wage policies, Social Security, health and life insurance, and other benefits.

On-the-Job Training

Some credit skills and functions, such as the gathering of credit information, can only be learned on the job through actual experience. In the development of a training program, it is necessary that instructional materials be related to the day-to-day operations of the credit department. Each program should be developed to meet the particular needs of the department where it will be used. Training is best if it is the direct responsibility of one supervisor, although the actual teaching assignment can be delegated to others.

After spending some time reviewing company policies, the new employee should be assigned to meaningful work duties. For example, the first few weeks could be spent studying the training manual, reading sample letters and credit files, setting up financial statements, and responding to credit inquiries. Under supervision, the trainee could gradually work into other responsibilities, such as notifying other interested departments of changes affecting the company's relations with customers. The trainee could then begin to assist in approving orders and handling new account investigations.

The extent of supervision depends on the position level, the employee's past academic background and experience, the speed of training, and the individual's overall progress. Supervision should always be available to provide direction, answer questions, discuss problems, and evaluate the individual. Any periodic progress reports should be discussed with the trainee, along with specific recommendations for improvement. Trainees on a new job must first learn the current methods of doing their work. When these techniques have been mastered, they can be encouraged to seek improved ways.

In-House Training

There is a useful supplement to the day-to-day training that is given to employees while performing their duties—namely, in-house training. It can take many forms and be given either sporadically or on a regular basis.

A well-conceived program can include weekly conferences devoted to credit problems. The program is adaptable to the training of one employee to a dozen. In some companies, credit employees are encouraged to suggest topics for discussion. This can be an effective device for raising the morale and efficiency of the department.

There must be common information regarding each employee's functions and responsibilities. There must also be a common desire to coordinate effort and eliminate conflicting work procedures. Moreover, all members of the staff must be willing to exchange ideas freely. Finally, the credit problems should be sufficiently challenging to encourage the participants to take an active part in their solution.

The requirements of such a program are:

- Advanced reading and study to assure intelligent consideration of the problem when the conference takes place
- Discussion of the nature and importance of the problem at the conference, with possible solutions to it
- After the problem has been discussed and a solution determined, a clear indication of how the employee(s) can apply the solution in practice

The credit executive will have to use ingenuity in developing problem materials and in planning the training schedule. This program makes demands on the credit executive's abilities as a writer of useful materials for staff study, as a discussion leader, and as a teacher and guide.

Instead of a conference, employees form self-instructional units comprising a cross-section of the entire department for training. Each group can consist of a specified number of credit analysts, one group leader, and a credit executive to whom they report their progress.

The group theory produces some positive developments:

- There is a greater degree of flexibility, as analysts move from one problem area to another.
- Peer pressure encourages participation by weaker members.
- Instruction is continuous and there is a greater exposure to problems and solutions.
- The group tends to cut down the flow of paperwork from subordinate to management.
- All members are included in the decision-making process, so each person feels more involvement and a greater degree of commitment to the group goals.

Observation Tours

Tours of other departments can help credit employees to understand more fully the working relations between the credit department and other divisions of the company. In addition, visits can be made to credit departments of neighboring companies. By observing how credit work is done in other companies, credit employees may learn ways of improving their own techniques.

Observation tours are a useful supplement to any training, since they give the observer an opportunity to see in operation certain processes they may have only read or heard about. This is particularly true in a company with a wide range of product lines and many different industrial classifications of customers.

Job Rotation Program or Cross Training

It is sometimes desirable to include in the training program some provision for rotating trainees from one job to another within the department, and even from one department to another. Such experience generates a broader credit perspective. The specific plan of rotation depends upon the size, complexity, and organizational setup of the department.

Popular on-the-job training methods include job rotation and understudy assignments. New employees often learn their jobs by understudying a seasoned veteran or by **vertical rotation.** *The understudy serves under an executive as an observer or assistant to become familiar with the functions and area of responsibility.* Alternatively, **job rotation or horizontal rotation** *involves lateral transfers that enable employees to work at different jobs.* To prepare for a horizontal job rotation program, each employee should list and document all the duties performed daily, weekly, and monthly, and how these tasks are performed. The credit executive should review these descriptions with each employee to be sure that all functions are fully and clearly covered. Copies are prepared so that each employee in the department will be familiar with the work of every other employee. At a departmental conference job descriptions are reviewed and discussed, and the techniques of the job interchange plan fully explained.

The following benefits are likely to be attained with little expense and with only a slight disruption of normal office routines:

- The overall flexibility of the department is greatly increased. It is better able to meet emergencies caused by illness, vacation schedules, and other work interruptions.
- Employees' enthusiasm for their work is increased. In addition, the discipline of having to think out and describe their jobs often leads credit personnel to better work habits and a better understanding of where their work fits in with that of others.
- Replacement of lower supervisory personnel is made easier since several persons in the department know several jobs.

Credit Library

Some companies have built up credit libraries containing books, articles, case histories, special reports, and other pertinent materials. Employees are encouraged to use them in their training.

In order that these reading materials may be kept in usable order and receive fair distribution, one member of the staff should serve as librarian. It should be the responsibility of the credit executive or a subordinate to keep the library up to date. Members of the staff should be encouraged to be on the alert for published materials which would be useful additions to the credit library. As new materials are received, group discussions and conferences may be arranged for the purpose of reviewing them and considering their bearing upon the work of the credit department.

From time to time, certain significant credit problems are encountered in daily operations. These can easily be written up for inclusion in the credit library. All the correspondence, special reports, and other essential information relating to a problem should be kept together in a single file. The credit executive can make these materials more useful by adding pertinent questions designed to stimulate thinking and to encourage discussion of the problem. The problem may serve as the basis for a group conference. In addition, these reports can be used for orientation of new credit employees.

Employee Enhancement

After the training phase is completed and the employee settles into a normal credit assignment, continuous efforts can be made to involve the employee in assignments of special or non-routine nature.

The credit department can hold weekly departmental meetings about subjects peculiar to the department's internal structure. Visits by customers, by debtors, and by lecturers who specialize in peripheral credit activities also can be encouraged. In addition, the credit executive can conduct periodic group meetings with the supervisory personnel to ensure a constructive team effort between line and staff people.

In order to help broaden credit understanding and as an additional aid for career planning, an accounting and financial training program can be established. It could consist of a series of seminars held over a period of about six months, where selected new employees are exposed to a detailed review of many activities within the credit department. The topics can cover such diverse fields as taxes, financial analysis, auditing, banking, corporate accounting, foreign exchange, and personnel.

Continuing Education

A continuing education program usually follows a conventional pattern with courses designed to cover a given area of instruction in an orderly manner. The purpose of this program is to offer credit employees educational opportunities not provided by their company and to enable those outside the field to train for credit work. There are continuing education programs for credit personnel at every level of experience. Continuing education is primarily based upon courses offered by local colleges, NACM affiliates, and other groups.

Local NACM affiliated associations conduct educational activities that can provide desirable supplementary training. Open forums, which provide interaction between participants or conferences and seminars focusing on core credit topics or current trends are especially beneficial.

National Institute of Credit

The National Institute of Credit, founded in 1918, is one of the many educational activities of NACM. It encourages local NACM affiliates to offer courses directly or through local colleges and universities. The courses cover the basic skills in credit and financial management and are presented in an authoritative and realistic manner. The Institute also regulates the certification awards for Credit Business Associate (CBA), Credit Business Fellow (CBF), and Certified Credit Executive (CCE).

In cooperation with NACM-National, local NACM affiliated associations offer the Credit Administration Program (CAP) and the Advanced Credit Administration Program (ACAP). The CAP program is a college-level series of courses designed to enhance a credit and financial professional's knowledge and understanding of business credit. CAP prepares credit professionals for the CBA professional designation exam. The ACAP program is a follow-up program to CAP. It is a series of college-level courses designed to enhance extra knowledge of general business, management, financial, and legal skills. ACAP prepares credit professionals for the CBF professional designation exam.

Graduate School of Credit and Financial Management

Founded in 1947, the Graduate School of Credit and Financial Management provides a program for qualified credit and financial executives who wish to prepare for greater corporate responsibilities, perform their work more effectively, develop their leadership skills, and increase their decision-making ability. The School is conducted each summer on the campuses of leading universities. The program consists of intensive sessions offered each year for two years. The curriculum covers financial analysis, treasury and credit policy, management strategy and law.

The National Credit Congress

NACM's national, annual convention, the Credit Congress, offers working sessions, educational sessions, and an exhibit area where attendees can view products and services offered by vendors to the credit management field.

Credit Training in the Small Department

The credit executive of the small centralized department may have more limited resources available for planning a training program. Management of a small company is likely to question any outlay that will throw the normal budget out of line, unless assurance can be given that the investment will produce savings and profit to the company. Even so, the need for training is probably more urgent here than in larger departments.

Time limitations may prove even more restrictive. Any large amount of time taken out for training may seriously affect the flow of work through the department. Whatever training can be managed is likely to be the credit executive's responsibility, but the problem will be to find adequate time for this important function in the midst of a busy schedule.

Training Options for a Small Credit Department

There are several things the credit executive can do to train and develop a staff, including:

- Informal training
- Training through local colleges, local NACM affiliated associations, NACM-National or other continuing education conferences or seminars
- Encouragement to undertake self-study on their own time. The department manager can set the example by offering to help them with comments or explanations

In smaller communities where outside educational facilities are limited, a number of small credit departments could pool their resources for training purposes. Group conferences, study groups, and more formal courses can be arranged at a central location, either on company time or after working hours. Often the local NACM affiliated associations can help with curriculum, material, instruction, and meeting place.

Comprehension Check

1. List and discuss the benefits of a centralized credit operation.
2. List and discuss the benefits of a decentralized credit operation.
3. Describe how the credit function would operate if credit is controlled at a principal office but administered from decentralized locations.

4. What is the goal of a well-designed training program?
5. Name and describe two popular on-the-job training methods.
6. Describe why continuing credit education is vital.

Glossary

Centralized credit operation. The credit function is controlled and administered from a principal or central location.

Horizontal rotation. A training method that involves lateral transfers that enable employees to work at different jobs.

Job description. A statement of the duties, responsibilities and authorities of each position.

Job rotation. A training method that involves lateral transfers that enable employees to work at different jobs.

Vertical rotation. A training method where an understudy serves under an executive as an observer or assistant for sufficient time to become familiar with the functions and area of responsibility.

References and Further Reading

Reengineering the Credit Function. The Credit Research Foundation, 1995.

4 The Legal Environment of Credit

Overview

There is a critical need to be aware of the specific government legislation that pertains to business credit. Government legislation not only creates and protects the rights of creditors but also imposes limitations on business activities. Moreover, credit department policies and procedures should be in place to ensure that all actions are within the boundaries of the law.

Learning Objectives

After reading this chapter, the reader should understand:

- The basic premises of the four most important antitrust acts and why they were formed at the turn of the century
- The Fair Credit Reporting Act and its applications toward consumer and commercial credit
- The rules that a creditor must adhere to under the Fair Debt Collection Practices Act when collecting from a debtor
- What information a creditor must disclose to a consumer applying for credit under the Truth in Lending Act/Regulation Z
- The applicable practices a creditor must follow under the Equal Credit Opportunity Act/Regulation B

Chapter Outline

Antitrust Regulation

The antitrust laws were first formed around the turn of the century due to the damaging repercussions that the massive companies of the mid to late nineteenth century caused. After the industrial revolution, corporate giants, among others, drove the typical American small business into the ground by creating tremendous monopolies which resulted in the emergence of many unfair trading practices such as price rigging and restraint of trade. When the monopolies got out of control, antitrust statutes started to appear in the United States to protect the common small business. Four major acts have been passed over the course of the century, each of which refine the former laws to eliminate loopholes and make new provisions. The four acts of importance are the Sherman Act, the Clayton Act, the Robinson-Patman Act, and the Federal Trade Commission Act. Although the four acts are summarized here briefly, the acts themselves are extremely complex, and counsel should be consulted when dealing with them. *The purpose of U.S. antitrust law is to encourage and protect competition.*

The Sherman Act

The Sherman Act was the first act passed in 1890 in the United States. *The Act was designed to prevent monopolies and unfair restraints of trade.* It prohibits contracts, combinations, and conspiracies in restraint of trade in interstate commerce, and declares that any person who monopolizes or attempts to monopolize, or who combines with another or others to monopolize trade or commerce, shall be guilty of a felony, punishable by a maximum $100,000 fine for corporate defendants and/or imprisonment for three years. In order for an offense to be constituted as a crime under the Sherman Act, a contract, combination, or conspiracy between two or more persons or companies which has the effect of restraining or monopolizing trade or commerce among the several states or with foreign nations must be made.

The purpose of the Sherman Act is to prohibit monopolies, contracts, and combinations which probably would unduly interfere with the free exercise of their rights by those engaged, or who wish to engage, in trade and commerce—in a word, to preserve the right of freedom of trade. A seller of goods does not violate the Act by refusing to sell to others, and may withhold goods from those who will not sell them at the prices fixed for their resale.

The Clayton Act

The second antitrust act passed was the **Clayton Act.** The Clayton Act was passed in 1914. *This act was designed to amend the Sherman Act and fix its broad language.* The Clayton Act adds offenses which were to be considered a felony when the effect is to substantially lessen competition or to tend to create a monopoly. The newly added offenses were leases and sales on conditions that the lessee or purchaser shall not use or deal in the commodities of a competitor of the lessor or seller (tie-in sales exclusive dealing arrangements, and requirements contracts); acquisitions of stock of other corporations; and interlocking directorates and senior officers of competing corporations.

The Act was amended in 1955 to add two new subdivisions. The first gives the United States a right of action for actual damages sustained by reason of any violation of any antitrust law. The second subdivision imposes a four-year statute of limitations on actions by private persons or by the United States to recover damages under the Act.

The Robinson-Patman Act

The Robinson-Patman Act was the next act passed in 1936. This act functioned partly in supplement to the Clayton Act. It declares that it shall be unlawful for any person engaged in commerce, or in the course of such commerce, either directly or indirectly, to discriminate in price between different purchasers of commodities of like grade and quality when either or any of the purchasers involved in such discrimination are engaged in interstate commerce, and where the commodities are sold for use, consumption, or resale within the United States or any other place within the jurisdiction of the United States and where the effect of such discrimination may be substantially to lessen competition or tend to create a monopoly in any line of commerce, or to injure, destroy, or prevent competition with any person who either grants or knowingly receives the benefit of such discrimination or with customers of either of them.

For credit executives, the Robinson-Patman Act is of particular importance. *This act forbids price discrimination where the effect of such price discrimination is to substantially reduce competition or to create a monopoly.* The term price discrimination includes the following types of business practices:

- A different price charged to different purchasers. A difference in price can only occur when the price difference results from differences in the cost of manufacture, sale or delivery resulting from the differing methods or quantities in which such goods are sold.
- Differences in terms and conditions of sale. For example, granting one purchaser free freight while charging freight costs to another is discriminatory.
- Preferential credit terms. Requiring one dealer to pay COD while granting another dealter credit terms can support a price discrimination claim. Likewise, granting different credit terms to similar customers can be found to be discriminatory pricing. However, any person is entitled to extend different terms to competing purchasers as long as the credit decision is made in a reasonable, nondiscriminatory manner so that the same standards of credit worthiness are applied to all customers who compete with each other.

The Federal Trade Commission Act

Lastly, the **Federal Trade Commission Act** was the last and broadest of the important antitrust acts to be past. *The Act states that all unlawful methods of competition and unfair or deceptive acts or practices in commerce to be unlawful.* Its prohibitions include false advertising of foods, drugs, devices, and cosmetics, and any other practice which is designed to deceive the public. Any practice which constitutes a violation of the Sherman Act, the Clayton Act, or the Robinson-Patman Act, or even if it falls short of a violation of such laws but is related to the type of practice which they prohibit, may constitute an unfair method of competition in violation of the Federal Trade Commission Act. The ultimate aim of the Act is the protection of the public from the evils likely to result from the destruction of competition or the restriction of it in a substantial degree. This presupposes the existence of some substantial competition to be affected, since the public is not concerned in the maintenance of competition which itself is without real substance.

Other Important Antitrust Legislation

Other acts which have come through since are the **Antitrust Procedures and Penalties Act.** Passed in 1974, the act increased the penalties for offenses under the Sherman Act, changed consent decree procedures, and revised the provisions for appellate review of antitrust cases. **The 1976 Antitrust Act** *grants the federal government new disclosure powers in antitrust litigation.* It also requires companies of a certain size to file pre-merger notices, and it permits a state Attorney General to sue for damages on behalf of the state's citizens. In addition to the above laws, almost all of the states, in one form or another, have statutes prohibiting monopolies, contracts, conspiracies, and combinations in restraint of trade.

The antitrust laws are very complicated laws and despite the simplicity that it seems to convey above, legal counsel should be consulted when dealing with these laws. For a more complete understanding of these laws, credit executives should look through all of the acts in much closer detail.

The Fair Credit Reporting Act

The Fair Credit Reporting Act (FCRA) is Title VI of the Consumer Credit Protection Act and became effective on April 25, 1971. *The purpose of the Act is to require consumer reporting agencies to adopt reasonable procedures for meeting the needs of consumer credit, personnel insurance and other information in an accurate, fair and equitable manner.* It guarantees a consumer the right to know all credit information that is maintained by credit bureaus and consumer reporting agencies and to be given a specific reason or reasons why the consumer was denied credit. The Act is intended to apply only to consumer credit transactions and not to commercial credit transactions.

New amendments to the FCRA took effect on October 1, 1997. Unfortunately, based upon the information provided by the FTC and others, there is some confusion within the commercial credit community as to the law's applicability and provisions.

The new amendments to the Fair Credit Reporting Act deal with personal or consumer credit which is defined as "credit for personal, family or household purposes". The extension of business credit, as long as it does not "cross over" into consumer credit, is not affected by the new law. Since the law does not focus on the nature of the proposed or actual credit recipient (individual, partnership or corporation) but rather focuses on the use of credit (personal, family or household purposes), it does not affect credit extended to individuals who may be sole proprietors of businesses or partners in a partnership operating a business. It is important for the credit grantor to be certain that the credit extension is for business purposes. A one or two sentence certification to that effect on a credit application or other written document can suffice to make sure that the credit grantor is protected. A credit extension is not for personal, family, or household purposes if a credit grantor receives a sales tax or other type of tax exemption from the credit recipient.

As in the past, if a report from a credit bureau providing consumer credit information is to be requested, the individual about whom the information is sought must have signed a written consent. Under prior law, it was fairly clear that a credit grantor could not request a consumer credit report without the written authority of the credit recipient. A question arose as to the use of credit reports by prospective and current employers, which raised the question as to whether written consent was necessary. The new law makes it clear that the use by a current or prospective employer or, for that matter, any use of a consumer credit report, may not be initiated or requested without the written authorization of the individual involved.

The law, as in the past, and as it is now clarified, deals only with the duties involved in connection with information provided to credit reporting agencies for consumer credit reports. As long as the information provided to a credit reporting agency or in connection with an industry group credit exchange is based upon credit for commercial purposes and not for "personal, family or household purposes", the statute's regulations do not apply. Since the law only deals with consumer credit which is limited to personal, family or household purposes, there has been no change in the long-standing practice concerning the absence of a requirement to provide information or justification for a business credit decision. (This is a complicated area which requires the advice of counsel should a particular issue arise.)

Under Section 604(f) of the Fair Credit Reporting Act, the requesting creditor must certify to a consumer reporting agency the permissible purpose for which the report is being obtained and must certify that the report will not be used for any other purpose. Should this certification be inaccurate or incomplete, the credit grantor requesting the report can be held liable.

The term "consumer report" is defined in the law to mean any written, oral or other communication of any information by a consumer reporting agency bearing on a consumer's creditworthiness, credit standing, credit capacity, character, general reputation, personal characteristics or mode of living which is used or expected to be used or collected in whole or in part for the purpose of serving as a factor in establishing the consumer's eligibility for:

- Credit or insurance to be used primarily for personal, family or household purposes
- Employment purposes or any other purpose authorized under Section 604

In general, a consumer reporting agency may furnish a consumer report relating to a consumer in connection with any credit or insurance transaction that is not initiated by the consumer only if the consumer authorizes the credit reporting agency to provide such report or the transaction consists of a firm offer of credit or insurance, and other applicable provisions are met:

- Extension of credit, or review or collection of an account of the consumer; or
- Intends to use the information for employment purposes.

The Fair Debt Collections Act

The Fair Debt Collections Act (FDCA) was passed in 1977 and became effective on March 30, 1978. Prior to its enactment, there was no federal law on debt collection. In July of 1986 the FDCA was amended to include, not only creditors, but attorneys who collect debts as well. *This Act states the ways in which a collection agency may go about pursuing payments from a debtor.* It is the most important act within the credit and collection profession. The FDCA was created to make fair laws for the benefit of debtors in a creditor's attempts to recover debts. It attempts to eliminate all unethical practices of collecting a debt that were clearly present prior to the installation of the Act. The Act prohibits creditors from attempting collection by employing tactics such as extortion, physical threats, threats of defamation among family, friends, and colleagues, and annoying inconveniences.

The FDCA states that any debt collector communicating with a third party in an attempt to locate a debtor must disclose his identity, not state that the debtor owes any debt and he must not contact the third party a second time unless requested to do so by the debtor or unless the collector believes that the earlier response from the third party was not the truth or was incomplete and that the person has since learned the correct information. Additionally, the collector may not communicate by postcard. Adhering to the correspondence by mail even further, a letter of collection must not have any symbol on an envelope which shows that the letter is from a debt collection agency or that the contents of the letter relate to the collection of a debt. A creditor must, after receiving the debtor's attorney's name, communicate solely with the debtor's attorney unless the attorney does not communicate with the debt collector within a reasonable amount of time.

This act declares certain ways that a debt collector may and may not communicate with a debtor to be legal or illegal. A debt collector may not communicate directly with a debtor with the collection of a debt if the time or place is known to be an inconvenience to the debtor. A collector will not communicate with a debtor before 8:00 a.m. and no later than 9:00 p.m. at the local time of the debtor. If the debt collector knows that the debtor is represented by an attorney, then he must contact the attorney unless the attorney does not reply within an ample amount of time. A debt collector may not communicate with the debtor at his place of employment. Also, a creditor may not without the prior direct consent of the debtor communicate with third parties. Equally so, the debt collector must cease total communication with the debtor upon his request. After this time, the collector may only notify the debtor to tell the debtor that the efforts of collecting the debt have ceased, to notify the debtor that the debt collector has the right to take specified remedies which are ordinarily invoked by such debt collector, and to notify the debtor that the debt collector intends to invoke a special remedy.

Special rules govern the harassment or abuse within the efforts to recover a debt from a debtor. This is probably one of the most important parts within the FDCA. It clearly states that a debt collector may not use threats of violence or other criminal means to harm an individual or use obscene or vulgar language. Furthermore, for the protection of the debtor, a collector may not publish a list of debtors who allegedly refuse to pay debts, except to a debtor reporting agency; advertise the sale of any debt to coerce payment of the debt; cause a telephone to ring or call a person repeatedly with the intent to annoy, abuse, or harass any person at the called number; or lastly, to place telephone calls without the meaningful disclosure of the caller's identity.

A debt collector may not make any false representation or through the use of fraudulent misrepresentations make false implications such as that the debt collector is vouched for, bonded by, or affiliated with the United States or any State, including the use of any badge, uniform, or facsimile thereof. Furthermore, a debt collector may not make false representations regarding the character, amount, or legal status of any debt or services rendered or compensation which may be lawfully received by any debt collector for the collection of a debt which can negatively stigmatize the debtor. Lastly, a creditor may not threaten the debtor of false circumstances, such as imprisonment, or take action which is not legally binding, or make false accusations or implications that the debtor has committed a crime or other act which can place a stigma on the debtor. Also, a creditor may not communicate, or threaten to communicate to any person credit information whether it be false or not. No deceptive means may be used by the debt collector to collect a debt or attempt to collect a debt or find out information regarding a debtor.

There is, within the Act, a section which describes in great detail what would make up unfair practices. The Act declares that a debt collector is in violation of the FDCA if a debt collector accepts from a debtor a check or other payment instrument postdated by more than five days unless such person is notified in writing of the debt collector's intent to deposit such check or instrument not more than ten nor less than three business days prior to such deposit. The debt collector may not solicit any postdated check or other postdated payment instrument by threatening or instituting criminal prosecution.

The FDCA says that, unless the debt has been paid, a creditor shall within five days after the initial communication with a debtor send the debtor a written notice, containing the following:

- the amount owed
- the name of the debt to whom the debt is owed
- a statement that unless the debtor disputes the validity of the debt, or any portion thereof, within 30 days after receipt of notice, the debt will be assumed to be valid by the debt collector
- a statement that says that if the debtor notifies the debt collector of the invalidity of the debt, that the debt collector shall obtain verification of the debt or a copy of a judgment will be mailed to the debtor by the debt collector
- a statement that, upon the debtor's written request within the thirty-day period, the debt collector will provide the debtor with the name and address of the original creditor, if different from the current creditor

If the debtor notifies the debt collector in writing within the 30 day period described in the above section that the debt, or any portion of the debt, is disputed, the debt collector shall cease collection of the debt until the debt collector obtains verification of the debt or a copy of a judgment from the original creditor. The failure of a debtor to dispute the validity of a debt under this section may not be construed by any court as an admission of liability by the debtor.

Penalties for violation of the FDCA vary. Any debt collector who fails to comply with any provision of the Act with respect to any person is liable to such person in an amount equal to the sum of the actual damage sustained by such as a result of such failure or any additional damages under $1,000 the court deems necessary. In the case of any successful action to enforce the foregoing liability, the costs of the action, together with a reasonable attorney's fee as determined by the court, may be enforced.

A debt collector may not be held liable in any action brought under this title if the debt collector shows by a preponderance of evidence that the violation was not intentional and resulted from a bona fide error notwithstanding the maintenance procedures reasonably adapted to avoid such error.

The Truth In Lending Act / Regulation Z

The Truth In Lending Act (TILA) was first signed in 1968 by President Johnson. Johnson passed the act with intentions of protecting and educating the consumer in the field of purchasing credit. It was thought that the information that was supplied to a consumer when purchasing credit was not thorough enough for consumers to establish whether they were receiving a good deal or not. Johnson ideally wanted the consumer to be able to buy credit the same way as a consumer might purchase any other product. This Act and its companion Regulation Z, which are the Act's rules and regulations, attempt to give the everyday consumer the opportunity and right to shop for credit in a fair and decent manner.

In an effort to protect and educate consumers, *sellers of credit are mandated to disclose certain information when offering credit*. By disclosing such information, consumers are given the opportunity to shop around and find which rates are the best for them. Not only, but quite obviously, it lets consumers know exactly what they are getting into when accepting such credit. *The consumer is now given the opportunity to know any interest rates, finance charges and fees straight from the beginning when applying for credit.*

This act, however, only applies to consumer credit. It is important to know that many exemptions do apply to the Truth In Lending Act and Regulation Z. If a credit purchase is not used primarily for personal consumer use such as business or agricultural, then it may be deemed exempt under this title.

The TILA and Regulation Z exempt transactions such as credit transactions involving extensions of credit primarily for business, commercial, or agricultural purposes, or to government or governmental agencies or instrumentalities, or to organizations. It also exempts transactions in securities or commodities accounts by a broker-dealer registered with the Securities and Exchange Commission; credit transactions, other than those in which a security interest is or will be acquired in real property; or in personal property used or expected to be used as the principal dwelling of the consumer, in which the total amount financed exceeds $25,000; and transactions under public utility tariffs, if the Board determines that a State regulatory body regulates the charges for the public utility services involved, the charges for delayed payment, and any discount allowed for early payment. Lastly, loans made, insured, or guaranteed pursuant to a program authorized by Title IV of the Higher Education Act of 1965 are exempt under the TILA and Regulation Z.

To protect consumers, the Act states that certain information must be disclosed to the applicant of credit on the credit application: Any finance charges that may or will be incurred (Regulation Z is very concise to explain what charges may be considered finance charges and what charges are not) and the APR (annual percentage rate)—probably the most important disclosure mentioned in the Act. A consumer must know how much the APR comes out to be, whether it is paid yearly, quarterly, monthly and so on. If an attempt is made by the issuer of credit to mask any information pertaining to charges to be incurred by the APR, they stand in clear violation of this Act, and whether they are applying for open-end or closed-end credit and what the differences between the two are all must be disclosed on the credit application.

Under the TILA, particular information must be disclosed for open-end consumer credit plans before a credit card is issued. The following information must be disclosed to an applicant for open-end credit before a credit card is issued:

- each annual percentage rate imposed in connection with extensions of credit under the plan, a statement that such rate does not include costs other than interest and full descriptions of any variable rate
- the maximum amount being charged, the maximum APR and a table disclosing the repayment options, and any itemization of any fees imposed by the creditor in connection with the availability or use of credit under such plan, including annual fees, application fees, transaction fees and closing costs
- the time when such fees are payable all must be disclosed to the applicant before a credit card for open-end consumer credit is issued
- a statement by the creditor showing which fees, if any, may be imposed by third parties such as governmental authorities, appraisers, and attorney(s) in connection with opening an account under the plan
- a statement that says that the extension of the credit is secured by the consumer's dwelling and if a default is taken, the consumer risks losing the dwelling
- a statement which discloses the time in which the application must be submitted to obtain the terms disclosed and if they are subject to change
- a statement which says that the creditor may under certain conditions terminate any account and demand full payment for any outstanding balance and prohibit any additional extension of credit to the account or reduce the credit limit applicable to the account
- all repayment options under the plan
- an example of an outstanding balance and the interest rate which shows how long it would take to pay the hypothetical sum back if only the minimum payment was made each month without receiving any additional extensions of credit
- if under any repayment option of the plan, the payment of not more than the minimum periodic payments required under such option over the length of the repayment period would not repay any of the principal balance or would repay less than the outstanding balance by the end of such period where a balloon payment may be imposed in full at that time
- any limitation contained in the plan on the number of extensions of credit and the amount of credit which may be obtained during any month or other defined time period

- a statement which says that consumers should consult a tax advisor regarding the deductibility of interest and charges under the plan
- any other term which the Board requires, in regulations, to be disclosed

If an amount is owed at the end of a billing cycle, a periodic statement must be sent to the consumer. This statement must contain the following:

- the credit balance
- a listing of all transactions taken place within the billing cycle
- a listing of all credit relating to credit extensions together with other types of credits
- the disclosure of any periodic rates that may be used to compute the finance charge
- the balance which the finance charge is computed
- whether any split rates were charges on the balance
- each type of separately charged finance charge
- the APR
- the closing date of the billing cycle
- the time within which a new balance shall be paid
- the address to send any notice of billing errors
- the general purpose address

When dealing with closed-end credit, the disclosure which needs to be made must be segregated from all other copy pertaining to the credit. The following information must be disclosed when applicable to closed-end credit:

- the identity of the creditor
- the amount financed, subtracting any pre-paid finance charge and adding any other amounts to the finance charge
- itemization of the amount financed
- the finance charge
- the APR
- the variable rate, if applicable
- the payment schedule
- the total of the payments
- the demand feature, if applicable
- the total sale price if it is a credit sale
- any pre-payment privileges
- any dollar or percentage charge for late payment
- the disclosure of security interest if any property is being pledged as security
- any insurance premiums
- security interest charges
- information about non-payment default, right to accelerate, or pre-payment privileges

- a statement saying whether mortgage may be assumed in regard to a residential mortgage
- the requirement of any deposit

All of the above rules (among many others) must be followed under the title of the Truth In Lending Act and Regulation Z. If any part thereof is violated, a good chance exists that the **laws of usury** have been violated as well. *The laws of usury pertain to the ceilings of interest rates.* Different kinds of credit obviously have different ceiling caps on allowable interest—a simple concept which becomes rather complicated very quickly. Although this doesn't directly deal with the Truth In Lending Act and Regulation Z, APR rates do make the two acts correlate on occasion.

The Equal Credit Opportunity Act/Regulation B

The Federal Reserve Board issued **Regulation B** to implement the Equal Credit Opportunity Act (ECOA). The act was amended and became effective April 1, 1990. *The purpose of this regulation is to promote the availability of credit to all creditworthy applicants without regard to race, color, religion, national origin, sex, marital status or age (provided the applicant has the capacity to contract); to the fact that all or part of the applicant's income derives from a public assistance program; or to the fact that the applicant has, in good faith, exercised any right under the Consumer Credit Protection Act.* The regulation also requires creditors to notify applicants of action taken on their applications and to retain records of credit applications.

The Equal Credit Opportunity Act and Regulation B apply to all credit—commercial as well as personal—without regard to the nature or type of the credit or the creditor. It applies to credit extended to any individual, partnership or corporation for any purpose. It also applies to consumer leases.

Business credit is covered by the basic nondiscrimination requirement of the Equal Credit Opportunity Act and its amendments, and Regulation B. This means that businesses may not refuse to grant business credit or discourage a business credit applicant from asking for credit because of sex, marital status or any of the reasons cited above.

The basic rules of ECOA and Regulation B state that a business credit grantor cannot:

- discriminate against an applicant regarding any aspect of a credit transaction
- make any oral or written statement, in advertising or otherwise, to applicants or prospective applicants, that would discourage a reasonable person from making or pursuing an application
- inquire whether income stated in an application is derived from alimony, child support, or separate maintenance payments unless the creditor discloses to the applicant that such income need not be revealed if the applicant does not want the creditor to consider it in determining the applicant's creditworthiness
- inquire about the sex of an applicant
- inquire about birth control practices, intentions concerning the bearing or rearing of children, or capability to bear children

- inquire about the race, color, religion or national origin of an applicant
- request any information about a spouse of an applicant unless the spouse will be permitted to use the account; the spouse will be contractually liable on the account; the applicant is relying on the spouse's income as a basis for repayment of the credit requested; the applicant resides in a community property state, or property on which the applicant is relying as a basis for repayment of the credit requested is located in such a state; or the applicant is relying on alimony, child support, or separate maintenance payments from a spouse as a basis for repayment of the credit requested
- inquire about the applicant's marital status unless the applicant resides in a community property state, or is relying on property located in such a state as a basis for repayment of the credit requested

The last two factors listed also come into play on personal guaranties. The ECOA does not permit a credit grantor to require a spouse to sign a personal guaranty if that spouse is not directly involved with the business credit applicant. Care must be taken to make sure that there are policies established for dealing with this, so that there is not an accidental dark-compliance.

The law does permit a spouse to sign a personal guaranty if certain, detailed procedures are followed to first verify that the applicant does not have the financial statement or credit wherewithal to support a guaranty. Once the fact is independently established that the applicant does not meet creditworthiness criteria, the business credit grantor would have to deny the request or ask for additional financial information to support the request. Should the applicant volunteer the additional guaranty of a spouse, even though that spouse is not directly involved in the business, it is permissible for the spouse to also sign the guaranty. The key is that the business credit grantor may not require a spouse to sign the guaranty; it must be voluntary. This is a very complicated procedure, and competent counsel should be consulted in order to establish the appropriate policies and procedures for each company.

Credit applications are not required, but if used, must conform with the requirements of Regulation B.

Notification of ECOA Compliance, Action Taken and Statement of Specific Reasons

For the purposes of noticing, the Federal Reserve Board has created a distinction for **trade credit,** to differentiate it from other types of business credit. *The Board defines trade credit as limited to a financing arrangement that involves a buyer and a seller—such as a supplier who finances the sale of equipment, supplies or inventory; it does not apply to an extension of credit by a bank or other financial institution for the financing of such items.* The Board defines **factoring** as *a purchase of accounts receivable,* and thus not subject to the Act or the Regulations. If there is a credit extension incident to the factoring arrangement, then the notification rules and the relevant provisions of the ECOA apply.

The Board created this distinction between trade and business credit in the area of noticing to curb discriminatory practices against women and small businesses seeking working or venture capital.

All business creditors must notify credit applicants that they comply with the

Equal Credit Opportunity Act. The easiest way to comply with this requirement is to add the following language to a credit application:

> Notice: The Federal Equal Opportunity Act prohibits creditors from discriminating against credit applicants on the basis of race, color, religion, national origin, sex, marital status, age (provided the applicant has the capacity to enter into a binding contract); because all or part of the applicant's income derives from any public assistance program; or because the applicant has, in good faith, exercised any right under the Consumer Credit Protection Act. The federal agency that administers compliance with the law concerning this credit is the Federal Trade Commission, Division of Credit Practices, 6th and Pennsylvania Avenue, NW, Washington, D.C. 20580.

Further, the Board has created slightly different noticing requirements, depending on the action taken by the business credit and depending on the size (measured by gross revenue) of the applicant. The Board establishes two types of business applicants: those with gross revenues of $1 million or less in their preceding fiscal year and those with more than gross revenues of $1 million in their preceding fiscal year. Small volume creditors are also given special noticing consideration.

With respect to applications from a business that had gross revenues of $1 million or less in its preceding fiscal year, a business credit (non-trade) grantor must notify the applicant either orally or in writing within 30 days of receiving a completed application concerning the approval of, counteroffer to, or adverse action taken.

If adverse action is taken, within 30 days the creditor must provide a statement about the action taken that includes either a statement of specific reasons for the action taken, or a disclosure of the applicant's right to a statement of the reasons for an adverse action within 30 days. This notice of disclosure may be given either at the time the adverse action is taken or at the time the application is submitted, provided that the disclosure is in a form the applicant may retain and contains the required ECOA notices.

An example of a statement of specific reasons for the action taken is:

> Thank you for applying to us for credit. We have given your request careful consideration and regret that we are unable to extend credit to you at this time for the following reasons:
>
> (Insert the appropriate reason, such as: value or type of collateral not sufficient, lack of established earnings record, slow or past due in trade or loan payments, etc.

An example of the disclosure of the applicant's right to request specific reasons for credit denial at the time of application is:

> If your application for business credit is denied, you have the right to a written statement of the specific reasons for the denial. To obtain this statement, please contact [name, address and telephone number of the person or office from which the statement of reasons can be obtained] within 30 days from the date of this notification. We will send you a written statement of reasons for the denial within 30 days of receiving your request for the statement.

For applications made solely by telephone, a creditor may give an oral statement of the action taken and of the applicant's right to a statement of reasons for adverse action.

With respect to applications for trade credit, or for business credit from a business with gross revenues in excess of $1 million in its previous fiscal year, the creditor must notify the applicant either orally or in writing within 30 days of the action taken. If the applicant makes a written request for the reasons of the adverse action within 60 days, the creditor has 30 days to give the applicant a written statement of the specific reasons for the action, and the ECOA notice.

There are four kinds of actions that qualify as adverse:

1. **Refusal to grant credit.** *A refusal to grant credit occurs when credit is denied in substantially the amount or terms requested by the credit applicant.* However, if the business credit grantor makes a counter offer, it is not considered as adverse action taken. For example, if the applicant has applied for $100,000 in credit availability and the business credit grantor offers to extend $10,000 rather than $100,000, and if the applicant accepts this offer, the action is not considered to be adverse.
2. **Refusal to increase credit on an existing account.** *This situation occurs when an existing customer requests additional credit and that request is denied.* This action is considered as adverse action.
3. **Reduction of credit availability on an existing account.** *This situation occurs when a business credit grantor reduces credit in any way.* For example, if a credit limit is reduced from $100,000 to $10,000, it is considered an adverse action.
4. **Termination of credit on an existing account.** *This situation occurs when credit is terminated.* For example, if a customer is placed on COD because of its credit history, credit has been effectively terminated.

Placing a customer on credit hold because of its credit history (slow paying or delinquent) is not considered as adverse action, because it is a situation that can be corrected or cured by making a payment.

Business and trade credit grantors may rely on special rules provided in Section of 202.9 of Regulation B with regard to multiple applicants, incomplete applications, notifications by small volume creditors, withdrawn applications and third-party applications.

For creditors that did not receive more than 150 applications during the preceding calendar year, the notification of action can be oral, including the statements of specific reasons.

Keeping Records

Business credit grantors must retain all information used in making a credit decision on an applicant for 12 months after the date on which the business credit grantor notifies the applicant of action taken on an application. However, for business applicants with gross revenues in excess of $1 million in its preceding fiscal year, creditors shall retain records for at least 60 days after notifying a business applicant. If, within that time period, the applicant requests in writing the reasons for adverse action or that records be retained, the creditor must retain records for 12 months.

Comprehension Check

1. What is the purpose of U.S. antitrust law?
2. What is the Sherman Act designed to prevent?
3. What does the Robinson-Patman Act specifically forbid?
4. What types of business practices does the term price discrimination include?
5. What is the purpose of the Fair Credit Reporting Act?
6. How does the Fair Debt Collection Practices Act affect the collection of a debt by a debt collector?
7. What is the purpose of the Truth in Lending Act?
8. What is the purpose of the Equal Credit Opportunity Act?
9. Under the ECOA, what is the compliance notice that all business creditors must give to credit applicants?
10. The ECOA defines the term adverse action. List the four types of action that qualify as adverse under the ECOA.

5 Credit Policy and Procedures

Overview

A policy is a general course of action developed for recurring situations, designed to achieve established objectives. In business concerns, complementary policies exist at several levels: some apply to the activities of the company as a whole, others to the activities of a major division, and still others to a single department. With regard to the credit function, credit policies apply to the credit department's activities for the company as a whole. They establish a framework or guide for consistent credit decisions directed toward attaining the goal established by the company for the credit function.

Learning Objectives

After reading this chapter, the reader should understand:

- The components of a credit policy
- The steps used in establishing a credit policy
- How a credit policy is implemented
- The types of credit policies
- The components of a credit manual
- How to create a credit application

Chapter Outline

I. Defining Credit Policy
   A. Importance of Credit Policy
   B. Objectives of a Credit Department
   C. Policy and Procedures
   D. Policy and Practice
II. Establishing Credit Policy
   A. General Considerations
   B. Credit Policy Focal Points
   C. Other Influences on Credit Policy
   D. Formulating the Policy
   E. Reasons for a Written Policy
   F. Checklist for a Well-Defined Credit Policy
   G. Example of a Credit Policy
III. Implementing Credit Policy
   A. General Considerations
   B. Communication of Policy
   C. Assignment of Responsibility
   D. Establishing Procedures
   E. Applying Policy Under Varying Conditions
   F. Factors Influencing Short-Term Policy Application
   G. Conditions that Can Cause Credit Policy To Change
   H. Review of Credit Policy
IV. Types of Credit Policy
   A. Analysis of Risk
   B. Degree of Collection Effort
V. Credit Procedures Manual
   A. Importance
   B. Format
   C. Recommended Contents
VI. Credit Applications
   A. Important Features of a Credit Application
   B. Preparation of a Credit Application

Defining Credit Policy

Importance of Credit Policy

It is important to distinguish among a credit policy, procedure, and rule. A **policy** *is a general course of action developed for recurring situations and designed to achieve established objectives.* It is a general statement that serves as a guide for the credit manager's decision making.

A **credit procedure** *describes the actual working steps that should be followed in the appropriate order to accomplish the desired credit result or decision.*

A **credit rule** *is a statement that defines and/or restricts the actions that a credit manager can take (or not take) in a specific situation or decision.*

All companies, whether they sell on credit or for cash, have a **credit policy.** Cash only is a form of credit policy. *The policy provides a framework for making effective credit decisions.* When a company sells on credit, individual credit decisions follow a pattern consistent with the company's overall aims and policies. A company that makes all its sales for cash has adopted a credit policy to the effect that no credit will be extended. This is just as much a credit policy as any other.

Companies vary widely in the extent to which they express a stated policy. In this sense, credit policy is not fully developed in many companies. It is often formulated in very broad terms, such as "to effect maximum sales with minimum losses," and fails to differentiate one customer from another or to provide a useful basis for individual credit decisions.

Further difficulties arise from confusion of policy with objectives, procedures, or practices. All of these are interrelated in the process which leads from the statement of goals to the daily operation of a credit department. It is helpful, however, to distinguish among them. The scope of credit policy is shown in Figure 5-1. The wide range of terms suggests that credit policy in many companies is far-reaching.

Objectives of a Credit Department

Typically, a company has written and defined objectives over stated periods of time. These may involve sales volume, return on capital employed, profit levels, and general recognition of prestige for the company, its products, and its management. The objective of a company's credit policy might be expressed as "serving the customer and maintaining the company's profitability."

Credit policy should address the authority to do the job, establish consistent credit guidelines, and assure credit and sales cooperation.

To help the company achieve these overall objectives, each functional department, including the credit department, must reach certain specific goals. For the credit department, these might be stated in terms of sales volume to customers in various risk classifications, relationship to the sales department, training and development of credit personnel, amount of capital committed to accounts receivable, and measurement of the status of the accounts receivable investment. These objectives set forth in the credit policy define desired accomplishment for each department. The policy is established to meet the objectives of the company, which are determined before any other actions can be taken.

Figure 5-1 Scope of Credit Policy

P — **Purpose**, Plan, Performance, Performance Measure, Preparation, Profitability, Protection, Printed Instructions, Procedures, Process, Productivity, Positive Results

O — **Organizational** Expectations (Goals/Objectives) and Behavior

L — **Level** of Understanding, Limit of Authority, Liberality, Language of the Industry

I — **Investment**, Impact, Individual Responsibility, Individual Department Needs

C — **Corporate** Goals and Desires, Credibility, Consistency, Cooperativeness, Critique of Current Methods, Chain of Command

I — **Intentions**, Important Points, Instructions, Implementation, Innovation

E — **Established** Ground Rules, Employee Training Manual, Effectiveness, Energy, Employee Input, Sales, Service

S — **Stability**, Sensitivity, Support, Security, Strategic Planning, Standardization

Policy and Procedures

Credit policy serves as a guide in determining how to handle given kinds of problems, but it does not offer a definitive solution—it presents a range of solutions within which the credit executive is free to exercise judgment.

In the process of decision-making, credit policy is constantly interpreted and applied to actual situations with the help of specific guidelines or procedures. These procedures are generally devised by the chief credit executives to standardize the actions of their subordinates in specific situations. They are usually published in procedure manuals as ready references for employees. They allow little discretion since they formalize reactions to particular situations.

Policy and Practice

In practice, the range of possible decisions provided under a firm's credit policy is narrowed for particular personnel, kinds of situations, or time periods. Considerable scope for individual judgment may still be provided, although in some instances company practice imposes stricter constraints on the decision maker.

Changes in practice within a given policy provide flexibility in meeting changing conditions. A change in the effective range of decisions that will be made serves to change emphasis within the same policy. In this way, for example, the extension of credit can be made more conservative without any change in the basic policy under which the department operates.

Handling Exceptions

A company's credit policy is intended to be applicable to the majority of credit situations over a long period of time. Even within such a broad context, however, exceptions do arise. The fact that credit policy is explicitly stated does not preclude decisions contrary to the policy. The authority to make such decisions is usually reserved to the head of the department.

In addition, not all of the decisions required of a credit executive will fall within the areas covered by existing credit policy. In most companies, non-policy decisions are also reserved for the head of the department. Like the credit policy itself, they must be consistent with overall company policy and objectives.

Establishing Credit Policy

General Considerations

Because credit policy concerns the company as a whole, it is usually established officially by top management. Sometimes responsibility for its formulation lies altogether with top management, but more commonly the chief credit executive and associates play an active role in its development. The heads of other interested departments may also be consulted.

Credit policy is probably most effectively implemented when all who are directly affected have some voice in its development. A credit policy assures that there will be consistency across departmental functions. It requires the endorsement of top management, preferably the board of directors.

While credit policy is the cornerstone of credit administration, there is no exclusive acceptable format. If a credit policy is to have practical value, it must be related to a specific company, reflecting the goals that the company has set for receivables management. Every credit executive is entitled to a written policy statement from the officers of the company—one that is fully understood and accepted by sales as well as credit people. *An effective credit policy permits and encourages the fullest development of the opportunities in administering credit.* It can be a blueprint for action as well as a training aid for the development of credit personnel. It provides the latitude to plan departmental operations within the scope of the company policy, to create effective procedures and techniques to implement that policy, and to establish adequate controls. It can assure that there is consistency in the company's dealings and interactions with its customers, and it provides a means of recognizing the importance of the credit function to the company.

In general, there are several key questions that should be answered when developing a credit policy.

- What is the credit department's mission? This also can be called a vision or purpose. It states the overall objective for the credit function.
- What are the goals? Goals can be specifically stated, such as a quantifiable measure, or more generally as an expressed desire to achieve improvement in a specific area.
- What are the roles and specific authorities of the credit department management and staff? This defines the boundaries of the credit function, often in terms of interactions with other departments.
- What are the primary criteria for evaluating customer credit? This describes credit procedures in more detail, listing key aspects of the credit review and analysis processes.

- What are the normal collection procedures? This describes the steps to be taken in customer collection activities.
- What are the company's terms of sale? Terms should be spelled out by major product line, with any qualifications or restrictions included.

Credit Policy Focal Points

When a company is developing a new credit policy or is reviewing an existing one, a number of factors should be considered. Some of these are internal in nature while others are external. Depending on the company, they vary in relative importance. All of them together establish the context within which credit policy must operate. There are four major focal points.

- Credit policies and procedures that focus upon development of an optimal level of sales:
  - a. New customer policy and procedures:
    1. a credit application with each request (sample in manual)
    2. procedures that outline expected turnaround time for making a credit decision on new accounts
    3. procedures that outline the specific mode for communicating the request for credit and the credit decision
    4. responsibility for establishing and keeping current credit department files (includes nature of contents to be included in file)
    5. a policy for authorizing and communicating credit limits
  - b. Policies and procedures that relate to terms of sale:
    1. terms established by industry; clear communication internally and to customers
    2. a discount chargeback policy; procedures for follow-up consistently applied and monitored
    3. a late payment service charge policy; procedures for follow-up consistently applied and monitored
    4. a policy for requests for extended term arrangements; necessary approvals clearly specified
    5. a blanket approval policy (Small orders below a specified amount are either cash or automatically approved)
    6. a policy and procedure for consignment sales
    7. a policy for export sales and letters of credit
    8. a policy for terms for sales to a debtor in possession in Chapter 11 bankruptcies
  - c. Policy and procedures that govern credit investigations:
    1. a sign-off policy for responsibility of the control of the account developed by the size of the account
    2. use of credit-reporting agencies clarified by the requirements for types of reports to be utilized
    3. a policy and procedure that outlines obtaining bank references detailing the type of information needed

4. a policy and procedure that outlines obtaining trade references with details of information needed
5. financial statement requests from customers and procedures for the analysis of statements with key focal points
6. policies and procedures that govern the use of collateral (include sample documentation, specify authorized signatures and clarify the safeguarding of documents held in storage)
7. perfecting liens under Article 9 of the Uniform Commercial Code
8. guarantees (personal and corporate)
9. warehouse receipts
10. letters of credit (details by types of L/C)
11. subordination agreements
12. lien searches
13. pledge of stocks, bonds or certificates of deposit

- Credit policies and procedures that focus upon minimizing the carrying costs of receivables:

a. follow-up system for past-due accounts:
  1. responsibility and time interval for initial follow up
  2. a systematic program for additional follow up
  3. use of the computer for monthly statements or automated dunning letters
  4. a policy and procedure for holding orders
  5. a policy for deductions and open credits
  6. a policy for personal visits (written summary report required)
  7. a policy for the exchange of credit information related to customer payment experience
  8. a policy for unauthorized shipments
  9. a policy and procedure for cash application

b. internal credit department reports (assign responsibility, clarify timing and include a distribution list for each report):
  1. aging of receivables (Do all items age out?)
  2. an over credit limits report
  3. a response on open items by category and age (deductions, credits, unearned discounts, service charges)
  4. a highly leveraged transaction report
  5. a report for accounts with collection agencies or in litigation
  6. a bad debt write-off report
  7. travel and expense reports

- Credit policies and procedures that focus upon minimizing bad debt losses:

a. a policy for conversion of an open account to a note (interest bearing? collateralized?)

b. policies and procedures governing customer counseling

c. a policy for use of collection agencies

d. a policy related to the use of outside attorneys and lawsuits

e. policies and procedures related to customer bankruptcy, bulk sales and assignments for the benefit of creditors
f. a policy for credit manager participation on creditors' committees
g. authorization for accounts written off to bad debts

- Credit policies and procedures that focus upon credit department organization and cost containment:
  a. a formal organization chart that clarifies the positions of each member of the credit department (authority and responsibility should be clear)
  b. policies and procedures that govern human resources within the credit department:
     1. recruiting and hiring guidelines
     2. educational requirements by position
     3. experience requirements by position
     4. training and development guidelines
  c. performance review criteria with procedures for a regular periodic performance review
  d. membership in professional organizations
  e. workshop and tuition reimbursement guidelines
  f. promotion and termination guidelines
  g. credit department budget guidelines:
     1. responsibility for preparation and content
     2. specific items for which policies and procedures need to be developed, including salaries/incentives, space and equipment, supplies, training and education, travel and entertainment, and collection and investigation expenses

Other Influences on Credit Policy

Credit practices within the industry also bear upon the credit policy of an individual company. Depending upon the industry, competitive conditions place a high degree of importance on credit availability.

Where credit is a fundamental factor in competition within the industry, the credit policy of a company is important for maintaining or improving its competitive position. Even where credit is not generally a competitive tool, an individual company can use it in this way if it is willing to do so. In considering credit policy in relation to competitive conditions within the industry, the credit executive must also evaluate the company's long-range ability to compete. This would include analysis of the company's present position in the industry and its financial strength, as well as a general awareness of such factors as the strength of its marketing organization and its position in product development.

Within every industry some companies are leaders and others are followers. The relative standing of a company in its industry will, in many cases, influence the course of action it sets to meet credit problems. If its position is undisputed, a company may demand more from its customers. A company that is just getting started, on the other hand, may find it advantageous to be more lenient in its credit policy. This factor ties in with the marketing aspects of the company. The role of credit is influenced by a number of general factors, including tradition, the stability of demand for the industry's products, and the rate of technological change.

The type of customer has a direct limiting influence on the credit policies of all companies in an industry. Where the buyers' line of business is characteristically short of capital, it is unrealistic for credit policy to be unduly restrictive. A company that operates on that basis will not maintain its market. If an industry has many well capitalized customers, the company that takes additional risk must expect additional return for this added risk. With enough good credit risks available to provide adequate profits, there must be an added incentive to make sales to fair or marginal risks.

The number of different classes of customers will also have a direct bearing on the variations in credit terms offered. Credit terms affect the company's credit policy in a number of ways. The market share a company has may affect the types of terms. For example, if the buyers are in control of the industry, the seller will probably have to offer longer terms. Also, if a seller is not a major market leader, it will have to match the best terms, instead of being in firmer control over what terms it offers.

The length of terms offered will also be a function of the product's shelf life (for example, those that can spoil will require shorter terms, so terms are usually net 10 in the food industry), variations in demand (for example, seasonal products may have differing terms depending on the time of year), and cost/price of the product (for example, more expensive items such as jewelry may have longer terms while cheaper products may have shorter terms).

The type of merchandise affects the credit policy of the seller in a number of ways. There is a tendency to sell on a more liberal basis if the merchandise has a relatively high profit margin or there is intense competition for the sale among a large number of suppliers. Also, terms may be somewhat more liberal if the merchandise can be repossessed in the same condition as it was sold (rather than if the appearance of the merchandise were changed by the buyer). Yard goods in the bolt, for example, can be taken back if they have not been cut by the clothing manufacturer. Once they have been on the pattern table, however, they lose much of their repossession value. Similarly, steel fabricated to specification has less reclamation value than that prepared in an ordinary run.

The merchandising policy of a company often influences credit policy. For example, a company may be required to place machinery in the hands of a limited number of franchised dealers on some basis to enable them to sell a maximum volume during a relatively short retail buying season. This might involve long terms of sale to coordinate it with the problems of manufacturing and shipment.

Large extensions of credit may be required in relation to the financial responsibility of many dealers. Reliance is placed on the character and capacity of the dealer to a far greater extent than on capital. The essential factors are experience and proven ability in selling competitively, collecting effectively, and operating profitably.

Markup of the merchandise is important. When profit margins are slim, the credit department may be more careful in the selection of its accounts. High-markup goods entice credit executives to approve sales to fair and marginal accounts. On a percentage basis, they may find it more profitable to check orders and rely on overall profits to cover relatively large bad-debt losses.

Price range of merchandise similarly influences credit policy. It is generally easier to establish a uniform liberal policy that applies to all customers when the unit price of merchandise is relatively low. Even on a wrong decision, the dollar amount of risk is not great. On a big ticket item, however, credit exposure is greater. A more detailed analysis is usually conducted before a customer order is approved.

When merchandise can be obtained readily by the supplier, there is no need to restrict sales to customers unless warranted by financial or credit risks. When a particular item is scarce, however, credit policy may be influenced to the extent that stricter requirements are set for customers needing that item. This situation might occur during shortages of material because of production shutdowns, other restrictions, or in instances where supplies of materials may be scarce.

When goods have been stored in inventory for some time and an opportunity arises to dispose of them, credit policy should be sufficiently flexible to approve the transaction. An extreme example of this is the case of the shoe wholesaler that has stored some out-of-style shoes for a number of years, then receives an offer for the entire lot. Even if the customer wanted extra terms or was not a good credit risk, it is doubtful that the offer would be refused.

The geographical distribution of customers determines credit policy to some degree. Widely separated markets require particular modifications in credit analysis and in collection efforts. A highly concentrated selling and buying area, on the other hand, involves a special type of price competition and service requirements.

In the case of particular commodities, such as spirits and liquors, government regulations specify credit policies or procedures which must be followed by the seller. There, the overall policy must take the regulations into consideration. In a very general way, expected long-range trends in the economy also influence credit policy.

Economic or business conditions are of much greater significance, however, in determining how policy is to be applied over a shorter period of time. When times are prosperous, ability of debtors to pay their bills is somewhat improved; however, there is a danger that they may tend to overbuy. During slack business periods, debtors tend to delay payment of their bills and credit requirements may tend to be stricter. Concurrently, as sales drop, the company is faced with the problem of maintaining volume in the face of decreasing sales and more demanding selection of credit customers.

Formulating the Policy

The actual formulation of credit policy begins with the establishment of objectives. What does the company want to accomplish during the period of time for which policy is to be established? If these objectives are to be attained, what should be the role of the credit department? The next step is a thorough analysis of the context within which the credit policy must operate over this period of time. This includes those factors which, according to a realistic appraisal, will act in some way to define what the credit department will be able to do:

- the established company policies
- the objectives and policies of the other departments
- the primary industry characteristics, such as current credit practices, the role of the credit in competition, the company's position in the industry, and the company's financial resources.

After these steps have been completed, the credit policy can be formulated. Within the given context, it sets a course of action that is expected to lead to the accomplishment of the objectives.

Credit Policy Can Be Disseminated as an Implied Policy

This means that it exists but is not officially stated (or written). It has little or no official expression of approval and may be difficult to perceive and, therefore, be left to interpretation. It is protected from public view and dissemination is very informal.

The effects of an implied policy may be favorable or unfavorable. Implied policy is often used when the true policy is unlikely to obtain approval from one or more company groups.

Credit Policy Can Be a Stated Policy

This means that it is set forth in writing. It usually has the backing and authentication of senior management. There are usually fewer misunderstandings as the policy is available to everyone in the same form. A stated policy indicates a basic honesty and integrity in intentions. It generates confidence and stability and serves as a good training tool.

There are four essential components of credit policy:

- Establishing the credit standard. This describes the profile for an acceptable credit customer, including appropriate details and examples.
- Determining credit availability. This describes how the maximum amount of available credit is computed and managed, including decision criteria for reducing or increasing a customer's availability of credit.
- Setting credit terms. This stipulates the exact terms of sale for each class of customer.
- Defining collection policy. This provides criteria for regular collections and exception collection procedures for past due amounts.

Reasons for a Written Policy

Careful consideration should be given to writing the credit policy. By definition, the understanding of unwritten policy depends on oral communication or on inference from the decisions made by senior credit personnel. Once established, a credit policy that is written has many advantages. It is thought through carefully, with the result that any vagueness in the unwritten policy becomes apparent and can be modified. Consideration of a written policy by the executives concerned also helps to reveal differences in their understanding of what the policy is and areas in which it is inadequate. *A written policy is more useful because it can be a source of stability and continuity in the operation, not only of the credit department but of the company as a whole.*

Individual credit executives and other administrators tend to vary unconsciously in their credit thinking as they interpret and react to the conditions and problems with which they work. Unwritten policy is thus subject to gradual, unnoticed changes while a written policy lessens the possibility of this kind of variability; it requires that changes in policy be conscious and intentional. In this way, policy becomes a more effective vehicle for review of the credit department's total situation.

Removing credit policy from dependence on the knowledge and experience of one or a few individuals tends to ensure consistency regardless of changes in department personnel. There is a greater probability of consistent decisions under a written policy, especially in large and complex credit organizations, where many people are dealing with the same types of problems and where they may be separated organizationally or geographically. Customers can be shown a copy of the policy statement, so they can see that they are not being given unusual or discriminatory treatment.

A clearly stated credit policy is a valuable aid in training credit and sales personnel. The trainee in the credit department can enhance his or her learning by reviewing the written statement of policy, which provides orientation to the company's point of view on credit and a frame of reference within which the trainee can proceed. Sales trainees can learn the credit framework that applies to sales.

Checklist for a Well-Defined Credit Policy

A well-defined and complete credit policy includes:

1. formal organization of department
2. job description, titles, and review process
3. credit department budget guidelines
4. credit documentation required for credit file
5. methods of gathering credit information
6. time limits for credit decisions
7. established credit lines and procedure for establishing new lines
8. procedure for communicating the decision to the customer
9. procedure for communicating the decision to management
10. procedure for communicating the decision to the sales department
11. procedure for communicating the decision to operations
12. guidelines for dealing with and assisting marginal accounts
13. a collection policy that reduces borrowing cost
14. a collection policy that deals with slow-paying accounts
15. a collection policy that minimizes bad debts
16. a policy for unearned discounts/unauthorized deductions
17. a policy for the handling of disputes
18. a policy for the handling of returned and damaged merchandise
19. establishment of terms of sale
20. policies for using secured transaction for protection
21. a policy for the use of guarantees
22. guidelines for reporting to upper management

Example of a Credit Policy

An example of a credit policy is shown in Figure 5-2. It is not presented as a complete or perfect policy statement, but it provides a concrete illustration of some of the concepts discussed. Like many policy statements, this one interweaves the department's objectives, such as "to help build a broad and durable customer relationship"

Figure 5-2 Example of a Credit Policy

The credit department shall function under the supervision of the treasurer, and its activities shall be coordinated with overall corporation policy and the activities of the sales department.

It shall be the responsibility of the credit department to help build a broad and durable customer relationship for [company name] Corporation. In the performance of this duty, the credit department shall maintain a positive and constructive attitude toward [company name] Corporation's customers. Discrimination in customer relationships is to be avoided. Likewise, the credit and sales departments shall maintain a cooperative attitude, with an aim toward promoting sales.

Within the bounds of sound credit practices, the credit department shall endeavor to find a suitable credit basis on which to deal with every customer that the sales department desires to have purchase our products. The decision as to what constitutes a suitable credit basis shall rest with the credit department. From the standpoint of credit, no customer shall be denied the right to purchase our products until every means of selling to that customer has been exhausted.

Standards by which credit risks are accepted or rejected shall be flexible enough to permit the maximum of profitable sales by [company name] Corporation. Marginal credit risks are to be dealt with when they are needed to complete operating schedules, and as long as they constitute a source of added net profit to [company name] Corporation.

Customer contacts are to be kept on a dignified and friendly basis, conducted so as to promote a wholesome respect for [company name] Corporation and its business practices.

Credit department practices shall be designed to permit the maximum number of orders to flow without interruption through the sales department, but to provide for interception when necessary as a means of safeguarding credit extensions.

The credit department shall keep the sales department fully informed regarding the status of a customer's account when the free flow of orders from that customer is in jeopardy.

The credit department has the collection responsibility. Sales department advice or direct help may be sought in exceptional cases.

All credit decisions shall be independently made and shall conform to requirements of law.

and "with an aim toward promoting sales." These lead directly into policy statements: "The credit department shall endeavor to find a suitable credit basis on which to deal with every customer"; "Marginal credit risks are to be dealt with when they are needed to complete operating schedules, and as long as they constitute a source of added net profit to [company name] Corporation."

Specific practices are implied in the policy statement but are detailed in other documents. The procedures designed to find a credit basis for sales to every customer, for example, cover such matters as obtaining financial information, establishing terms of sale, and setting credit lines.

Implementing Credit Policy

General Considerations

To be effective, policy must be directly and explicitly related to action. Credit management should take the steps necessary to translate broad, flexible policy statements into guides that can be used by credit personnel in the daily operation of the department. This usually begins with establishing short-term objectives and determining for the short run what the emphasis is to be within the range of decisions provided by policy.

Probably the most significant single step in the implementation of credit policy is the creation of an atmosphere that encourages subordinates to think in terms of policy and to be aware of the effect of their individual credit decisions upon the company's commitment to the accounts receivable investment and to the total department and company operations.

Communication of Policy

In creating this atmosphere, as in all phases of administration of credit policy, a basic requirement is **effective communication of policy,** both inside and outside the credit department. Whether policy is disseminated orally or in writing, there must be clear mutual understanding as to what it is and how it is to be applied. The company may also wish to make its credit policy known to organizations and individuals outside the company, such as its banks, its customers, and its competitors, and depending on the situation, the purpose such publication is expected to serve, the nature and duration of the relationship, and the competitive role of credit.

Top management should endorse the credit policy, with that endorsement made known to others. Undoubtedly, the financial officers will be familiar with it, but it is just as important for the heads of purchasing, sales, and production to know it. Credit executives and department personnel should be fully aware of the implications of the company's credit policy. The policy should be explained to all personnel in the department and be made a part of the initial training of all new credit employees. In most cases, a statement of policy to the sales department should be followed up with information concerning the specific application of the policy as it affects sales personnel. For example, sales representatives should know what information they are expected to furnish with new orders, have some knowledge of the standards by which the credit department decides whether to accept an order on regular credit terms, etc.

Understanding how credit decisions are made improves the sales representatives' knowledge of the business. The customers themselves are better prepared to deal with a supplier if they understand its credit policy, the need for current facts, the importance of financial information, and the significance of a good payment record.

The ideal time to describe credit policy to a customer is when the first order is placed. As the business relationship continues, it is wise to remind the customer occasionally of the credit policy of the organization. In that way, the customer's mind can be refreshed on a routine basis rather than at a time when an account is in dispute. This makes it easier to refer to terms and policy when a misunderstanding does arise.

Assignment of Responsibility

While the organization of a credit department is not determined by credit policy, it plays an important part in putting policy into action through specific assignment of responsibility and delegation of authority. *Credit policy establishes the broad limits for decisions over a long period of time.* To make these limits a workable guide to decision making, it is necessary to specify who has the authority to make specified types of decisions and within what range personnel may exercise their judgment.

Guides of this sort take several forms. For example, the authority to make exceptions to basic policy is usually limited to the chief credit executive. Authority for various levels of personnel is often stated in terms of the amount of credit involved. The definition of authority should make clear the channels through which an order must move until it is finally approved.

Establishing Procedures

Closely allied to assignment of responsibility is the development of detailed procedures for day-to-day operations. These translate the general policy instructions into clear cut rules for specific situations, including such matters as order flow, maintenance of credit files, and preparation of periodic reports.

One of the principles for delegating authority and establishing procedures is to include as many situations as possible in the routines administered by lower level personnel. This frees credit executives who are more highly qualified by training and experience to deal with more complicated situations.

Typical credit activities that can require written procedures are shown in Figure 5-3.

Applying Policy Under Varying Conditions

Because credit policy is intended to apply to the great majority of the company's credit activities over a long period of time, it is often necessary to provide for varying interpretations within the one policy. For example, a company producing two products marketed under widely different competitive circumstances might well develop different interpretations of credit policy for the two products.

These varying ways of applying the same policy work toward the same objectives but take into account the difference in application. Similarly, for a given product it may be necessary to shift the emphasis in applying credit policy in different geographic areas, considering the nature of business or the general conditions in each area. This would be true, for example, for companies selling to farmers in various sections of the United States.

Factors Influencing Short-Term Policy Application

The short-run application of policy should be flexible, consistent, fair, and allow for the credit manager's judgment.

Figure 5-3 Credit Activities Appropriate for Written Procedures

- Processing new customer accounts
- Processing foreign (export) accounts
- Handling updates to current credit files and systems
- Processing requests for extended credit terms
- Assigning risk categories to customers
- Planning for and completing customer on-site visits
- Dealing with collateral
- Selecting, using, and evaluating outside collection agencies
- Processing requests for credit references
- Obtaining customer credit references from bank and trade sources
- Charging off bad debts
- Managing and using credit and receivables computer systems
- Preparing regular management and department activity reports
- Evaluating department personnel

Flexibility is the result of the way in which a credit manager applies the credit policy. Some policy statements describe the degree of tolerance by using such phrases as whenever possible or under usual conditions. Building in flexibility allows the policy to be used intelligently and in different approaches without the need for a formal change in policy.

Consistency assures that the policy will be applied in a similar manner for the same situations. **Fairness** assures that all relevant facts and issues will be considered for each customer credit decision. Allowing for judgment encourages personal insight, develops better perspective, and helps assure a correct analysis of relevant matters.

The factors that underlie the credit policy also influence the way it is applied. A company's **current financial position** may be decisive in the short-term application of policy. For example, severely limited operating capital may require emphasis on prompt collections and rapid turnover of accounts receivable. New companies often have cash flow problems. As they age and cash flow improves, policy can be changed.

Business conditions affecting the areas or industries in which the company operates are also of major importance in policy application, such as those in a particular region, in the United States as a whole, or in areas of foreign trade.

Cyclical movements in the economy and **changes in the general level of prosperity** affect the credit department along with the whole company. During prosperity and expansion, the credit department may help develop new markets or new products. In a recession, the emphasis may be on greater care in selling to marginal accounts. The same credit policy would be in effect during all phases of the cycle, but its application would be changed.

Similarly, business conditions within a given industry affect the interpretation of credit policy. Not all segments of the economy change at the same rate or in the same direction. Occasionally, the company may change emphasis, redefine responsibilities, and adjust procedures in order to meet changing conditions.

Conditions that Can Cause Credit Policy To Change

Increases or decreases in **critical factors,** *such as profit margins, regular monthly cash flows, aged accounts receivable, bad debts (as a percent of sales), competition, and market share* can cause credit policy to change.

For example, the personal computer and fax machine business had low profit margins when first beginning. Accordingly, credit policy was probably very tight. As profit margins increased, credit policy was probably loosened. Changes in economic and political conditions and increased litigation in the collection of accounts can also cause changes in policy.

Review of Credit Policy

Both the credit policy and its application should be reviewed at definite stated intervals. Additional reviews may also be planned or made necessary by unexpected developments of major importance. The frequency of planned reviews depends upon such factors as the difficulty of reaching goals and the probability of change in the competitive situation.

One means of reviewing credit policy is by conducting a credit department audit. The audit should review all department activities in light of the overall policy. The product of the audit should be an objective evaluation of the department's effectiveness as well as the identification of any areas that need improvement.

Policy and application are evaluated in terms of their effectiveness in reaching the established goals. At the time of review, information must be gathered indicating the present position and progress of the department in relation to its objectives. Short-term goals provide convenient intermediate benchmarks toward long-term objectives. If performance is satisfactory, the existing policies are reaffirmed or new objectives set. If credit performance is less than expected, there should be a critical examination of both the policy and the way it has been applied.

The steps for changing policy are much the same as those used for its initial development. Proposed changes should be discussed with the same people who participated in the formulation of the policy. When the changes become definite, they should be carefully communicated to all the individuals and departments concerned with it.

Types of Credit Policy

Analysis of Risk

One type of policy deals with the **analysis of risk.** *How much risk is the firm willing to take in granting credit to its customers?* This question seeks to determine whether the credit analysis of the customer will be strict or liberal. It should also set the basis for analysis, whether it be purely on the financial showing of the customer or include other factors such as the principal's background.

Risk classifications should be assigned for each customer. **Risk criteria** *include the likelihood that the customer will pay on terms (i.e., it has sufficient funds available); the*

Figure 5-4 Different Types of Credit and Collection Policies

Strict analysis of risk and liberal collections
The assumption is that if precautions are taken up front by concentrating on good credit risks, then these good credit risks will pay on time. Any additional time is less expensive to carry than the cost of following up accounts that are only a few days past-due.

Liberal analysis of risk and heightened collection effort
Credit is granted to nearly everyone, but payment activity is monitored closely. This policy may apply to low unit priced goods with a high markup. Collection costs are usually quite high.

Liberal analysis of risk and liberal collections
Few businesses would find it profitable to function under this policy. Although credit costs are low, the cost of carrying bad debts and of carrying receivables for extended periods of time would offset the savings. A company might use this policy to avoid offending customers.

Strict analysis of risk and strict collections
Only high credit-rated accounts are accepted, and very little variation from terms is allowed. The risk analysis risk is thorough, collections require more effort, and sales would be restricted.

success of the customer in staying within the maximum amount of credit made available; the customer's overall creditworthiness and general financial stability; and the likelihood that the customer will not have sufficient liquid reserves, over the medium term, to be able to pay on terms.

Degree of Collection Effort

Another type of policy deals with the degree of collection effort a company will consider. This means answering several questions. The answers to these questions will determine the strictness of collection effort.

- How much money and effort is the company willing to spend in collecting amounts owed to it?
- How will it treat past-due accounts?
- Will unearned discounts be permitted?

A number of different credit and collection policies can be set when these questions are answered. Four such policies are shown in Figure 5-4. Within these four broad categories there are innumerable shadings of policies, depending upon the particular degree of strictness in credit analysis and in collections.

Credit Procedures Manual

Importance

A **credit manual** is important as a ready reference. Large companies need it as a standard guide for their many department personnel, and even small companies find it useful. *The manual should cover rules, regulations, and procedures necessary for consistent department operations.*

In larger organizations, it should aid in the delegation of authority and in workload control, and give other departments a ready reference to company credit practices. It is also a useful tool in job training programs.

The chief credit executive should have nominal charge of the manual. Actual writing may be done by someone in the credit department or by a special outside group. Whether the final writing is done within the credit department or outside, all other departments should be given the opportunity to approve those sections of the manual pertaining to procedures in which they are directly involved.

Format

The credit manual may be issued as a separate book or as part of the manual of general company instructions. If included in the general manual, it should be a separate section. Because credit procedures are characteristically subject to change, it is advisable to issue materials in loose-leaf form. Wherever possible, illustrations, diagrams, flow charts, and sample forms should be included to make content graphic and readily comprehensible.

In companies with highly specialized departments, it is advisable to issue two manuals. A detailed manual for credit department use and a shorter version in the company instruction manual. Some credit departments that issue instruction letters or memoranda to their staffs compile them into a brochure of credit department policy and procedure. This is not a true manual (and is not recommended). The individually addressed memorandum may achieve results with the person to whom it is addressed but will not necessarily influence a successor. With changes in personnel, changes in procedure often take place. Moreover, there is nothing in a memorandum to indicate that an action is definite policy or procedure.

The credit manual must be kept current. Those responsible for its maintenance must be alert to changes in the credit situation, both inside and outside the company, that would necessitate revision of the manual. Information obtained from banks, customers, credit associations, company attorneys, and the sales department should be carefully reviewed for such possible changes.

The method of indexing should be flexible and logical. The index will direct the choice of material, so it is important to begin with an efficient working index. It should be capable of meeting future needs as the manual expands in size and scope. Once an indexing system is established, it is difficult to change. A poor index can hinder the usefulness of the manual.

Headings and subheadings should be used freely within the text to permit cross-referencing. It is desirable to identify each heading and subheading with a letter or number. When a decimal indexing system is used, the whole number indicates the general subject area and the decimals identify specific subjects within the general area.

Recommended Contents

Table of Contents

The table of contents is a ready reference of the topics in the manual. The original date of issue of the manual can be shown in the foreword. This eliminates the need

Figure 5-5 Checklist for Content of Credit Policy and Procedures

Credit Department Structure

Credit Department Organization

Titles of key department personnel are shown

Credit Policy Statement

Operation

Describes how the credit department functions, whether it is centralized or decentralized, and the chief credit executive's responsibility to senior management for the overall credit function. The procedures should also provide the mechanics for the chief credit executive to monitor credit, comments on the handling of account referrals and how they are resolved, and the procedure for handling developments in an account's business activity or financial condition.

to date each page of the manual; only those pages containing revised material would need to show the date that material was revised. The foreword should point out that the manual is the official reference source on credit department policies and procedures. It should emphasize that the manual only outlines the framework that credit department personnel should follow and does not attempt to provide a specific blueprint for handling each and every credit decision.

Figure 5-5 offers a sample checklist for topics ordinarily covered in a department manual. The information is not a comprehensive treatment, and a company writing this type of manual should consult its own attorneys on items that may have legal consequences to the company or its employees.

Investigation

Direct Inquiry. A normal inquiry should be in the form of a written request. Also included in this subsection could be such exhibits as a copy of a letter to a new customer, a balance sheet, an operating statement, a statement of changes in financial position, a spreadsheet for displaying successive financial statements, significant financial ratios, and a brief description of how they are calculated and how they are used.

- Outside Agency Reports—Exhibits could include sample reports from Dun & Bradstreet, National Credit Office, NACM's Business Credit Report, Equifax, and Moody's Industrial.
- Bank References—These range from a single statement of a customer's average deposit balance to a comprehensive report. A standard request for bank credit information could be included as an exhibit.
- Inquiries to Other Suppliers—A trade inquiry normally will incorporate a request for high credit, amount owing, amount past due, terms of sale, and payment performance. A copy of the company's trade inquiry form should be included in this subsection.
- Customer Visitation Guidelines—List of items to be covered, questions to be answered, and normal items to review on-site.

Security Devices

- **Guarantee**—*An instrument containing a promise by a person, persons, or company to pay or perform an obligation owed in the event the debtor does not pay or perform.* It can take the form of a personal or corporate guarantee, both of which should be included as exhibits.
- **Irrevocable Letter of Credit**—*This substitutes a bank's credit for that of the customer.* It allows the supplier to initiate a draft against the letter of credit upon delivery of goods. Copies of all types of letters of credit should be in this subsection.
- **Subordination Agreement**—*This agreement can improve a supplier's priority position by establishing a higher priority claim to the customer's assets, especially if a significant portion of a customer's debt is owed to officers or stockholders.* A copy should be shown as an exhibit.
- **Security Agreements and Financing Statements**—Article 9 of the Uniform Commercial Code, entitled Secured Transactions, deals with the creation of security interests in personal property. *The most common forms are inventory, accounts receivable, and equipment.* A copy of a financing statement should be in this subsection.
- **Mechanics Lien**—*A statutory lien on a building (and usually the land it occupies) in favor of suppliers of material and contractors to secure their interest on a particular construction project.*
- **Payment and Performance Bonds**—Before relying on a payment bond, the supplier should send a letter to the bonding company to confirm the existence of the bond and learn its coverage with respect to the material. Since the type of project and the notification rules vary substantially, questions should be referred to the legal department through the chief credit executive. A sample letter to the bonding company should be included in this subsection.
- **Joint Check Agreements**—*A joint check agreement is a device whereby the ultimate user or beneficiary of material supplied by an original seller agrees with the original seller and its supplier to make all payments to the supplier by checks payable to both the seller and the supplier.* A copy of the agreement should be shown as an exhibit.
- **Real Estate Mortgages (Deeds of Trust)**—Sometimes a customer will offer a first or second real estate mortgage (deed of trust) as security for open-account arrangements. This can be an effective method of securing an account but a number of factors must be considered, such as determining the value of the property, the marketability of the property, liens and encumbrances on the property, the payoff on the first mortgage, and whether the first mortgage permits a second mortgage. Guidelines and sample documentation should be included in this subsection.

Credit Approval and Administration

- Terms of Sale—A complete list of the terms offered by the company and a brief explanation of how they are used should be shown in this subsection.
- Terms Codes—Terms of sale may be coded to facilitate the processing of

information into the computer, and the code should be shown on all sales orders and invoices. The procedure for administering the codes should be described, including the treatment of multiple codes and exceptions. This subsection should include a complete list of terms codes.

- Credit Instructions—Daily routines used to process all orders in accordance with prescribed credit lines and terms. Forms should be shown wherever used.
- Credit Recommendations—Organizations using referral limits that recommend credit for approval to a higher level can use this section to show the recommendation form, properly filled out.
- Credit Files—List of information that must be kept up to date, such as a current agency report, a current credit recommendation, and current financial figures.

Collections

- Normal Procedures—Each account is a separate collection problem. Placing it into a category by size or type assists in determining the intensity of collection effort required. Several means for collection follow-up are letter, phone, personal visit, and joint credit and sales action. Copies of the series of form collection letters should be part of this subsection.
- Collection Schedule—Collections should use a definite schedule that will provide for systematic review. Details should be described in this subsection.
- Lockbox System—Descriptions, such as bank procedures and company guidelines for returned check processing, and other tasks, should be included in this subsection.
- Advance Payments—Procedures for handling these items should be described in this subsection.
- Customer Deductions—Copies of typical correspondence and departmental guidelines should be included in this subsection.
- Note Arrangements—Copies of the notes used by the company should be included in this subsection. In addition, important points in preparing notes should be included, such as correct maturity date, correct interest rate, and correct signature.
- Account Referral—If normal collection procedures fail to net the necessary results, the account should be placed with an attorney or collection agency. Typical documentation should be included as exhibits.
- Creditors' Extension Agreements—As a major creditor, a company may initiate or join in a creditors' extension agreement to permit a debtor to set aside existing debt under an established plan. Standard documentation should be included in this subsection.
- Bankruptcy Proceedings—Standard documentation and procedural guidelines should be included in this subsection.
- Allowance for Uncollectibles and Write-offs—Guidelines for reporting and handling these items should be discussed in this subsection.

Reports

This section includes procedures and examples for writing reports on past-due accounts, control and inspection reports, forecasts, annual reports to management, and the like as called for by company policy. It is important to include in this section a timetable for all credit reports, along with details of approval and distribution.

Credit Applications

Important Features of a Credit Application

Credit applications serve several purposes for the credit professional. A well-planned credit application can assist the seller during the four stages of the creditor-debtor relationship: prior to extending credit (pre-credit), during the credit relationship with a debtor (during the credit cycle), during problems in a credit relationship (problem credit) and during litigation (after credit).

It is very important for a seller/creditor to know its applicant/debtor. The credit application begins the relationship-building process and is an initial source of information to begin a fact-finding, fact-verification mission to help investigate the applicant.

In addition to using the credit application as an investigative tool, the credit application should create a contract between the seller/creditor and the customer, the applicant/debtor. The application should include all of the seller's essential terms of sale. Having the seller's terms agreed upon by the applicant in advance of sales will better enable the seller to prevail in a lawsuit against the applicant when it argues that its terms of sale (as may be contained in the applicant's purchase order) govern the sales transaction(s) between seller and applicant. After a judgment has been obtained by the seller/creditor, the credit application will become a useful tool to locate and retrieve the applicant's assets for collection purposes.

Preparation of a Credit Application

Most credit investigations start with the information supplied by the applicant on the credit application. Since businesses vary in product, needs, size, volume, it is almost impossible to create a one-size-fits-all credit application. Therefore on an annual basis, each seller should carefully review its needs, and the potential credit problems it faces based on experience, and restructure a sound credit application accordingly. It is wise to seek the advice of legal counsel, well versed in commercial transactions, prior to finalizing your corporate credit application.

Keep in mind that the key goal of a credit application is to assist the seller in learning as much as possible about the applicant/debtor before making a decision to extend credit. The credit application is often considered to be the cornerstone of the customer's file. It should provide basic information about the customer and be updated at least every two years.

Appropriate information must be gained with respect to the business operations of the applicant/debtor. Too often, extensions of credit are given based upon too little information. The credit application must contain sufficient factual information to permit an intelligent decision to be made with respect to the extension of credit.

The key points to consider in a credit application are listed and discussed in the remaining pages of this chapter. Sample language has been included for guidance purposes only.

Key Points in a Credit Application

■ Date of application

By dating the application, it is easy to identify it in a file and determine the start date of the agreement. If financial information is supplied, the date will provide a frame of reference for the information supplied.

■ Applicant's full firm name, including any trade names or DBAs

The key is to be able to determine the legal name of the applicant. This will also assure that the contract is legally binding. By using the legal name, a judgment and lien search can be made. In addition, federal tax lien and state lien searches can be conducted. Credit reports and assumed name filings can be obtained. With all of this related information, the seller can check facts and information presented on the application. New DBAs should be gathered and added to the credit file.

■ Address information including mailing address, physical address, P.O. box

Address information can be verified through directory assistance or an address verification program. Get the sales department involved with this investigative process by asking it to verify physical address information. A physical address indicates a physical location of an applicant. The applicant's assets will probably be located at the physical address location. Be careful about an applicant/debtor who lists a mail drop. Most credit frauds occur through the use of a mail drop.

■ Telephone number, fax number or e-mail

Verify telephone numbers with directory assistance. This simple verification can uncover many irregularities or inconsistencies.

■ Legal status of company: corporation, LLC, partnership, sole proprietorship

It is important to understand the legal structure of the applicant. A sole proprietor is liable for the debts of his/her entity. When dealing with a partnership, the partners and the individual partners may be held liable for debts of the partnership. A corporation is a separate legal entity that exists under the authority of the state in which it is incorporated. A corporation can sue and be sued in its name. Annual reports can be obtained for corporations from the Secretary of State. If the applicant is a public corporation, 10K (annual reports), 10Q (quarterly reports), and 8K (other reports upon particular circumstances, such as a change in auditor, bankruptcy or other important corporate events) information can be obtained from the Securities and Exchange Commission (SEC).

Check the legal status of a company with the Secretary of State's office or corporation commission which is usually located in a state's capital. Each state office (except Hawaii) has a corporation information center. The corporate information center can verify whether a company is, in fact, a corporation, that corporation's status (active, inactive or suspended), the full legal name of the corporation, the date of incorporation, the name of the resident agent and, in some states, the names and addresses of the corporate officers and directors.

If a company changes its legal status, a new credit application should be signed. For example, if a sole proprietorship should incorporate, the credit application for the sole proprietorship will not necessarily be valid for the new corporation. Following mergers and acquisitions, new credit applications should also be obtained. Consider placing language in the credit application stating that the applicant is required and agrees to inform the seller of any change in legal status.

- **Information about the owners and/or officers, including name, title and address**

For a sole proprietor, gather the name of the sole proprietor, social security number, home address and telephone number. Remember, a sole proprietor and an individual are considered to be one and the same with respect to liability.

For a partnership, gather the partners' names, social security numbers, home addresses and telephone numbers. Usually, a partnership agreement will dictate the parameters of liability. Generally, each partner in a general partnership is personally liable to the full extent of the partnership debts. General partners in a limited partnership are jointly and severally liable for the partnership debts and obligations. Limited partners are not liable beyond the capital contributed to the partnership.

Under provision of state laws, a corporation or a limited liability company (LLC) is considered to be a legal person. Each (a corporation and LLC) can sue and be sued. For a corporation or an LLC, gather the state and date of incorporation/organization (formation), shareholders'/members' names, social security numbers, home addresses, telephone numbers, and names of all officers and directors (managers).

- **Federal Tax Identification Number (FEIN)**

If a company is engaged in business, it needs a federal tax ID number in order to file a tax return. Inability to supply a FEIN may be a sign that there is a problem.

- **Accounts payable contact name, address, phone and fax number**

This information saves time should the creditor need to contact the accounts payable department. A billing address (if different from other addresses) will ensure that no delays in payment occur due to non-receipt of invoices.

- **Type of business (wholesale, retail, distributor, manufacturer)**

A general description of the business will help the seller/creditor understand the applicant's/debtor's business. An applicant/debtor may have more than one business.

- **Years in business**

The longer a firm has been in business, the more stable it would appear to be. If the application indicates whether it owns or leases its premises, this information can also be useful. If the premises (office, warehouse, retail space, etc.) is leased, information can be obtained from a landlord. Should a seller/creditor ever be in a position of searching for assets, knowledge about ownership of real estate or an office building is useful.

- **Sales tax exempt**

In some businesses, sales tax status is important to learn before invoicing. The seller/creditor would want to obtain a copy of a sales exemption certificate up front, rather than waiting until a credit situation arises.

Sample language can be:

Sales Tax Permit #:

I certify that [name of applicant/debtor] located at [address, city, state of applicant] is engaged as a registered

❑ Retailer ❑ Manufacturer ❑ Lessor ❑ Other, and is registered with the state and cities listed on the attached use tax exemption certificate, within which seller/debtor would deliver purchases and that any such purchases are for wholesale, resale, ingredients, or components of new products to be resold, leased, or rented in the normal course of applicant's business. Applicant is in the business of retailing, manufacturing, leasing (renting) the following:

Description of Business:

I further certify that if any property so purchased tax free is used or consumed by the firm as to make it subject to a Sales or Use Tax, that applicant will pay the tax due directly to the taxing authority when state law so provides, or inform the seller/creditor for added tax billing. This exemption certificate shall be part of each order which applicant may hereafter give to seller, unless otherwise specified, and shall be valid until canceled by applicant in writing or revoked by the city or state.

Under penalties of perjury, I swear or affirm that the information on this form is true and correct as to every material matter.

____

Authorized Signature Date Title

■ **Related previous business ventures**

It is helpful to obtain as much information about previous business ventures as possible.

■ **Bank references, including bank name, address, account numbers (checking, savings), bank contact name and phone number**

The seller/creditor must be able to contact the applicant's/debtor's bank directly. Obtain a contact name or a loan officer's name. Account numbers (checking/savings) are important should any post judgment garnishment action ever need to be taken. Regarding loans, useful information includes the type of loan, the original amount of any loan, the total amount due, loan payment trends and whether a personal guaranty was provided, or whether any collateral secures the loan.

■ **Authorization for bank references to release information requested**

Obtain proper authorization to contact the applicant's/debtor's bank. Do not assume that because the applicant furnished information about its banking relationships that the seller/creditor has an automatic right to obtain information.

Sample language can be:

The applicant hereby authorizes the bank references listed herein to release all information requested. It is understood that all information will be kept confidential.

■ **Information about bank, insurance or other creditor security interests**

Are the applicant's accounts receivable, inventory and/or equipment encumbered by a present lien or security interest? If yes, be sure to obtain names, addresses and telephone numbers of secured parties.

> **Sample language can be:**
>
> The following is a list of all creditors of the undersigned who hold liens or security interests in assets of the undersigned. (Please list names of creditor, a brief description of secured assets and amount of debt.)

■ **Financial Information**

For customers that are small companies, financial statements can be difficult to obtain. Many small companies do not have audited annual financial statements. If this class of customer represents the largest sector of your customer base, include an easy-to-complete balance sheet and income statement form as part of your application. If your customer base is made up of larger companies, financial statements should be available. In either case, it is very important for the seller/creditor to obtain financial information, signed by an authorized official, and to attach such financial information by reference into the credit application.

A section should be included in the credit application asking that the applicant agree to provide updated financial information upon request. Changes in legal status can be detected by financial statements.

> **Sample language can be:**
>
> Attached to (or included within) this credit application is the most recent financial statement of the applicant/undersigned. The undersigned agrees to provide to creditor updated financial information on request, and to timely provide an annual financial statement to creditor as a condition of the continuation of this credit.
>
> If the applicant is a corporation, a balance sheet can be copied from an 1120 tax return. Not all applicants can provide an audited financial statement, but it is recommended that the seller/creditor obtain financial information to evaluate creditworthiness.
>
> The application can include a question about whether the applicant/debtor has ever filed for bankruptcy, been involved in an involuntary bankruptcy proceeding, an assignment for the benefit of creditors or a composition agreement, which are all insolvency proceedings.
>
> Because the Equal Credit Opportunity Act (ECOA) has rules based upon an applicant's gross revenues, at a very minimum, it is prudent to determine whether the applicant is a business with more or less than $1 million in gross revenues.

■ **Trade Reference Information: Reference name, address, contact, phone and fax numbers, account number and average or high monthly purchases amount**

Be sure to obtain complete information about a trade reference, including a contact name. Before contacting trade or business references to verify or seek information, the seller/creditor may want to seek authorization to do so. It may be best not to assume that because references are listed, the applicant has granted permission for a seller/creditor to contact any of them. Contacting references without permission can be interpreted as an infringement of a business relationship.

> **Sample language can be:**
>
> Applicant authorizes seller/creditor to contact the financial and trade references (including those listed herein) and any credit reporting agencies to obtain, verify and reverify credit information.

■ Equal Credit Opportunity Act (ECOA) Notice

The ECOA prohibits a business credit grantor from discriminating with respect to the extension or renewal of credit based upon race, color, religion, national origin, sex, marital status or age. It is important that a credit application does not contain questions which could be interpreted as discriminatory. And, both credit and sales personnel should take care to not verbally ask questions which could lead to a claim of discrimination.

The seller/creditor must provide notice of the action taken on a credit application within 30 days of its receipt. Further, the seller/creditor must provide a notice of the applicant's right to a statement of reasons why the application was not accepted.

> **Sample language for the notice of an applicant's right to a statement of reasons is:**
>
> The Federal Equal Credit Opportunity Act prohibits creditors from discriminating against credit applicants on the basis of race, color, religion, national origin, sex, marital status, age (provided the applicant has the capacity to enter into a binding contract); because all or part of the applicant's income devices from any public assistance program; or because the applicant has in good faith exercised any right under the Consumer Credit Protection Act. The federal agency that administers compliance with this law concerning this creditor is the Federal Trade Commission.

■ Fair Credit Reporting Act

Changes to the Fair Credit Reporting Act require that the seller/creditor is required to obtain written permission from the principal officers of a corporation to allow the release of consumer reports on the officers prior to obtaining a credit report.

> **The following language can be used in a separate paragraph and require a separate signature or signatures in order to permit a seller's/creditor's use of a consumer credit report of a principal of a company as part of the credit extension or renewal of the business and trade credit process:**
>
> The undersigned hereby consent(s) to [your company name]'s use of a non-business, consumer credit report on the undersigned in order to further evaluate the creditworthiness of the undersigned as principal(s), proprietor(s) and/or guarantor(s) in connection with the extension of business credit as contemplated by this credit application. The undersigned hereby authorize(s) [name of seller/creditor] to utilize a consumer credit report on the undersigned from time to time in connection with the extension or

> continuation of the business credit represented by this credit application. The undersigned as [an] individual(s) hereby knowingly consent to the use of such credit report consistent with the Federal Fair Credit Reporting Act as contained in 15 U.S.C. @ 1681 et seq.

■ Application Provisions

Many different provisions can be included in a "provisions" section of a credit application. Not all provisions may fit the seller's/creditor's needs, but the following key provisions should be considered:

Agreement of Sale—The credit application should state that is an agreement for the sale of goods or services as well as serving as a credit application. This brings it into the purview of the UCC to create the language necessary for an enforceable written agreement. Under the UCC, a sale of goods for $500 or more must be made through a written contract for it to be enforceable.

> **Sample language can be:**
>
> The terms and conditions of this application shall, upon extension of credit by the company, constitute an agreement of sale.

If the contract or agreement of sale is clear and unambiguous, oral testimony cannot be used to change its terms. In other words, a clear and unambiguous agreement created by a credit application cannot be changed by conversation.

Credit Availability/Credit Limit—Do not use the term "credit line" in an application. Credit grantors give credit limits, credit availability—banks extend credit lines. The terminology "credit line" implies that the credit is available to the applicant for a certain amount of time and the law construes it to be a reasonable amount of time. Credit grantors must have the right to change the terms of credit granted anytime circumstances dictate a change. It is helpful to include wording in the provision stating that, should a credit availability be granted, all decisions for extending or continuing that credit availability will be at the sole discretion of seller. Be sure to state that seller/creditor may terminate credit availability at its discretion.

> **Sample language can be:**
>
> Should a credit availability be granted by seller/creditor, all credit shall be extended at the sole discretion of seller/creditor. Seller/creditor may increase, decrease or terminate any credit availability at any time within its sole discretion.

Application Updates—Remember, it is good credit practice to update a credit application at least every two years.

> **Sample language can be:**
>
> The applicant/undersigned agrees to provide seller/creditor with an updated credit application each year/every two years as a condition for the continued extension of credit.

Payment Terms and Delinquency—All applications should provide that the applicant agrees that all invoices will be paid according to their terms when due. The provisions should also provide that any payment made which is not in accordance with the terms on the invoice is a delinquent account. Absent an agreement, invoices are not contractual agreements, but merely memorializations of the terms of the transaction. An invoice does not constitute an agreement in writing which is enforceable between the parties. If the credit application incorporates, by reference, the provisions of an invoice (such as payment terms), the terms of an invoice may become part of the written agreement. Terms must be agreed to before the sale. Terms on an invoice that is not incorporated into the credit application by reference may be useless, since they are delivered after the sale. Also, the application can state that payments received from the application/customer may be applied against whichever invoice the seller chooses.

> **Sample language can be:**
>
> The undersigned hereby makes this application for credit and agrees that all amounts payable on or before the net due date, as shown on each invoice, will be paid, and, if not paid on or before said date are then delinquent.
>
> The payment for all sales of goods or services will be according to the terms stated on the company's invoice for the sale of goods or services. The failure to pay on the net due date on each invoice shall deem the debt to be delinquent.

Waiver of the Right to a Jury Trial—It is important to seek the agreement of the customer to waive the right to a jury trial. Virtually every state will permit the waiver of a jury trial by a business debtor, provided that it is created in a commercial setting.

> **Sample language can be:**
>
> The parties hereto knowingly and intentionally waive the right to a jury trial on any issue or dispute that may arise between them.

Prejudgment Remedy Waiver

> **Sample language can be:**
>
> Applicant does hereby expressly and irrevocably waive any notice and/or hearing which may be required for prejudgment remedies under the statute of the state of [state].

ADR-Alternative Dispute Resolution—Following the provision dealing with the waiver of a jury trial, can be language which activates the alternative dispute resolution procedure established by the American Arbitration Association or other such arbitration forums or companies. The binding arbitration clause should be clearly set forth. With this type of provision, both parties are agreeing that all disputes will be handled through arbitration. Both parties can agree to waive the arbitration clause.

Sample language can be:

The seller/creditor and applicant/debtor agree that any claim or dispute between or among them, their agents, employees, successors or assigns, related to this application, the credit extended thereafter or otherwise (other than the exercise of rights under security interests created by purchases or otherwise), including disputes related to the applicability of the agreement, regardless against whom made, shall be resolved by binding arbitration by and under either (a) the Code of Procedure of the National Arbitration Forum or (b) the Rules of the American Arbitration Association. Any award may be entered and enforced as a judgment in any court of competent jurisdiction. Claims may be filed at any office of the (a) National Arbitration Forum or (b) the American Arbitration Association. This Agreement shall be subject to and interpreted under the Federal Arbitration Act.

Service, Finance, and Interest Charges—A provision dealing with the imposition of service or finance charges should be included in the credit application. While Regulation Z and other federal regulations and statutes do not currently apply to the imposition of interest, finance charges and service charges in a commercial transaction, it is important to have a particular agreement memorialized in the credit application.

Care should be taken when imposing late fees and service charges in addition to interest charges. Many courts will uphold separate default interest if the amount of the interest are somehow related to losses suffered. For example, administratively, a firm can incur extra costs.

Service charges can be legally charged to some, but not all invoices if the following language is used:

a finance charge of _____ may be imposed. The word "may" does not bind the seller and allows the seller to be able to retroactively (for up to four years) charge interest because of the UCC.

Always state that the interest rate will be the lower of whatever your rate is or the highest rate allowed by law. States have default rates of interest. Some states do not allow service fees to be charged in addition to the highest interest rate allowed by law. Usury is a state specific area. Be sure to check your state's allowable interest rate.

Attorneys' Fees and Collection Costs—The credit application should provide for the imposition of, not only attorneys' fees, but also costs and expenses involved with collection should there be a breach or default by applicant/debtor under the credit application. This permits the creditor to seek to recover these in the event of litigation. Most states will permit the imposition of attorneys fees as well as costs and expenses of the creditor if they are written in an agreement.

Under the UCC, the seller can recover incidental damages as a seller, provided that there is a provision in your contract that says it can. Collection costs can mean your time, or your staff's time, preparing for litigation.

The credit application should provide that the terms and conditions of purchase orders and other similar documents submitted by the customer will not become part of any agreement with the seller unless accepted in writing. Under the UCC, if a creditor sells goods in response to a purchase order, the creditor is agreeing to the terms and conditions stated in the purchase order.

Because of the complexity of today's business activities, many creditors neither take the time nor have the personnel to adequately review each purchase order. By placing a provision in the credit application that no terms or conditions of a purchase order or similar document shall become part of the contract unless approved by the creditor in writing, the creditor eliminates the problem that may be encountered if there are unusual or unique provisions included in a purchase order. This provision will guard against any "battle of the forms".

Governing Law and Venue—The credit application should indicate which state laws will apply. There should be a relationship between the transaction and the state selected. If the contract is formed in your state, the laws of your state will reasonably apply.

> **Sample language can be:**
>
> Venue shall be in x county, x state.
>
> Any sales that result from an extension of credit by seller shall be construed under the laws of [seller's state] and any lawsuits resulting from this extension of credit may be commenced in the state of [seller's state].

Warranties—Provisions dealing with any warranties which are or are not to exist should be included in the credit application. Because this will become the contract between the parties, it is important that all warranty provisions be carefully spelled out in order to be enforceable by each party.

Shipment Terms—The transfer of goods from seller to buyer presents an element of risk. The goods can be lost, damaged, or destroyed while in the care of a transportation carrier. Therefore, the issue of who is responsible for the risk of loss must be defined. The Uniform Commercial Code has specific rules governing risk of loss, which is an issue separate and apart from title (ownership). Risk of loss depends upon the terms of the agreement, the moment the loss occurs, and whether one of the parties was in breach of contract when the risk of loss occurred. Risk of loss can be contractually addressed by using commonly accepted shipping terms. The following are commonly used shipping terms that create **shipment contracts**, *whereby the seller turns the goods over to a carrier for delivery to the buyer*. In a shipment contract, both title and risk of loss pass to the buyer when the goods are given to the carrier. The seller has no responsibility for seeing that the goods reach their destination.

FOB (Free on Board) the Place of Shipment—requires the seller to deliver the goods free of expense and at the seller's risk to the place of shipment.

FAS (Free Alongside)—at a named port requires the seller to deliver the goods, at his/her own risk, alongside the vessel or at a dock designated by the buyer.

CIF (Cost, Insurance, and Freight)—means that the price of the goods includes the cost of shipping and insurance. The seller bears this expense, and the risk of loading the goods.

C&F (Cost and Freight)—means that the price of the goods includes the cost of shipping. The seller bears the risk of loading the goods.

If the contract requires the seller to guarantee delivery of the goods to a specific destination, the seller bears the risk and expense of delivery to that destination. Commonly used shipping terms that create **destination contracts** are:

FOB Destination or an *FOB Term with the Place of Destination*—of the goods puts the expense and risk of delivering the goods to that destination on the seller.

Ex-Ship—places the expense and risk on the seller until the goods are unloaded from whatever ship is used.

No Arrival, No Sale—places the expense and risk during shipment on the seller. If the goods fail to arrive through no fault of the seller, the seller has no further liability to the buyer.

If no agreement has been made for either a shipment contract or a destination contract, then the risk passes to the buyer on receipt of the goods if the seller is a merchant. If the seller is not a merchant, the risk passes to the buyer when the seller tenders (offers) delivery of the goods.

Authorization—Language should be included, seeking permission to contact financial and trade references furnished in the application by the applicant.

> **Sample language can be:**
>
> Applicant authorizes creditor to contact the financial and trade references (including those listed herein) and any credit reporting agencies to obtain, verify and reverify credit information.

Certification—Language should be included stating that the information supplied is true and correct.

> **Sample language can be:**
>
> The applicant certifies under the penalty of perjury that the statements contained in the application are true and correct. Applicant understands that the seller intends to rely on all of the information presented in this application in determining its creditworthiness.

■ Signatures

The credit application must be signed by a person authorized on behalf of the applicant to do so. The person signing an application does not necessarily have to be an officer of the corporation. The signer's title or capacity should be included with the signature.

■ Personal or Corporate Guaranty

A personal guaranty should not be included within the body of the credit application. It must be provided for separately and apart from the application, and it must include a separate signature by the individual guarantor. The guarantee can appear after the application signature line, as a separate section, provided that it is conspicuously labeled as a guarantee and provided there is a separate signature line. Keep in mind the separation of the application, which is signed by a firm, and a personal guaranty, which is signed by an individual.

The ECOA will not permit a credit grantor to require a spouse to sign a personal guaranty if that spouse is not directly involved with the business credit applicant. Care must be taken to make sure that there are policies established for dealing with this that there is not an accidental dark-compliance. The law does permit the requirement for a spouse to sign a personal guaranty if detailed procedures are followed to first verify that the participant spouse does not have the financial credibility or credit wherewithal to support a guaranty. Once that has been independently established, and if the credit were to then be turned down because of the lack of sufficient creditworthiness of the guarantor, the guaranty of the spouse may then be required.

This is a very complicated procedure and competent counsel should be consulted in order to establish the appropriate policies and procedures for each company.

If a guarantee of another corporation, an affiliated corporation, a parent or a subsidiary is obtained, always get a copy of the corporate resolution authorizing it. A parent corporation can guarantee the debt of its subsidiary. The official corporate seal should be placed on the documents.

Checklist for the Personal Guaranty—

- Absolute and Unconditional Guaranty
- Guarantor(s) agree to seller's/creditor's specified interest rates
- Guarantor(s) agree(s) to pay all costs of collection (attorneys fees and court cost(s)
- Guarantor(s) agree(s) to the specified governing laws
- Guarantor(s) agree(s) to be joint and severally liable with the debtor to the seller/creditor
- Guarantor's consent to jurisdiction (optional)
- Guarantor's waiver of a jury trial (optional)
- Guarantor's signature

Sample language can be:

The undersigned individual(s) in consideration of the company's extension of credit to the applicant hereby agrees to personally guarantee any and all obligations of the applicant and the company. This guaranty shall be continuing and unlimited and may be terminated only on 30 days' written notice to the company. The company may exercise its rights under this guaranty without first taking any action against the applicant. The undersigned waives notice of default and non-payment, and consents to the extension or modification of credit terms to the applicant without notice.

Dated Witness Guarantor

Sample language can be:

This guaranty is given by the undersigned to seller, in order to induce and extend credit to, sell goods to, or otherwise become the creditor of, the above-named sole proprietorship or corporation.

I hereby guaranty to seller, the prompt payment, in accordance with the terms of credit, of every claim of seller, including claims relating to goods sold, open accounts and accounts stated, against the above-named sole proprietorship, partnership or corporation. This is a continuing guaranty and shall remain in force until revoked by the written consent of seller. This obligation shall cover the renewal of any claims guaranteed by those affected by any surrender or release by the seller of any security held by it for any claim hereby guaranteed.

The undersigned additionally guarantees the payment of interest at the maximum lawful rate on all monies outstanding to seller, by the above-named sole proprietorship, partnership or corporation, together with costs and reasonable attorney fees whether suit be brought or not and any attorneys' fees on appeal, which the seller may incur in the collection of any claims. Further, the undersigned hereby submits himself (or herself) to the jurisdiction of the course of [STATE] in the event suit is brought in connection with any claims by seller regarding the guaranty of payment, and agrees that venue shall be in the county where seller has its principle place of business. It is understood and agreed by the undersigned that this personal guaranty shall remain in full force and effect regardless of whether the above-named corporation, partnership or sole proprietorship files bankruptcy, becomes insolvent or is otherwise dissolved.

The guarantor signature(s) below must be dated and witnessed.

In witness whereof, I/We have signed, sealed and delivered this guaranty for the purposes set forth above on the ____ day of ____, ______.

____

Witness to Guarantor   Guarantor (husband), with personal liability

____

Witness to Guarantor   Guarantor (wife), with personal liability

Or, sample language can be:

Please sell and deliver to [applicant name/purchaser], or representatives, pursuant to the terms and conditions of sale contained in this credit application incorporated herein by reference and made a part hereof, such merchandise as they or their management may order or select, and in consideration thereof, the undersigned (Guarantor(s), which shall include guarantor, of only one, and Guarantors if more than one) hereby fully guarantee and agree that the Guarantor(s) shall be personally responsible, jointly and severally for the payment at maturity of the purchase price of all such merchandise so sold or delivered whether by open account acceptance, note or otherwise. The Guarantor(s) hereby waive notice of acceptance hereof, amounts of sale, dates of shipments or deliveries, notice of default in payment and legal proceedings against Purchaser.

Guarantor(s) acknowledge that the Guaranty is a condition for the extending credit to Purchaser.

This is intended to be, and shall be construed to be, a Continuing Personal Guaranty ("Guaranty") applying to all sales made by Seller to Purchaser and shall not be revoked by

1. the death of the Guarantor(s) 2. the sale or transfer of Purchaser subsequent to the execution of this Guaranty; or 3. the departure, resignation and/or disassociation for any reason, of Guarantor(s) from the Purchaser.

This Guaranty shall remain in full force and effect until the Guarantor(s) shall have given notice in writing to Seller to make no further advances on the security of this Guaranty, and until such notice shall have been received by an authorized agent of Seller. Unless Seller agrees in writing otherwise, this Guaranty shall extend to the transactions between Seller and Purchaser, as well as any successor or related business entities or to any other business entity in which the undersigned owns or holds an interest. Guarantor(s) agree to notify Seller in writing of any changes in the form of the Purchaser's business or ownership of Purchaser's business within five days of such change, otherwise this Guaranty shall extend to Purchaser, and any successor companies, individuals or assignees, or related entities, as a condition of maintaining an open account with Seller. The obligation of the Guarantor(s), where more than one, shall be joint and several, and the death, discontinuance or discharge for any reason as to one or more of the undersigned shall not operate as a discontinuance or discharge as to the other or others.

It is understood and agreed that the Guarantor(s) liability under this Guaranty shall be unlimited.

The undersigned consents to an investigation into the creditworthiness of the Guarantor(s) and further agrees to dissemination of credit information about Guarantor(s) to inquiring sources.

In witness whereof, the undersigned hereby executes the Guaranty this _____ day of _____, _______.

Do not use corporate or business titles, as they are inapplicable.

____

Signature Name

Comprehension Check

1. What is a policy?
2. What is a procedure?
3. What is a rule?
4. Why is it important for a company to have a written credit policy?
5. List the key questions that should be answered when developing a credit policy.
6. What are the four major focal points that should be considered when developing a credit policy?
7. List four factors that influence a company's credit policy.
8. What are the four essential components of a credit policy?
9. List ten credit activities that should be addressed by a credit policy.
10. List four different types of credit and collection policies.
11. A well-defined credit policy can assist the seller during the four stages of the creditor-debtor relationship. What are the four stages?
12. Why is it important to have the correct legal name of a credit applicant?
13. Where can the legal status of a public corporation be checked?
14. Why do terms of sale have to be set forth in writing in a credit application?
15. What is the difference between the terms, credit line and credit availability?

16. If there is no agreement, are credit terms printed on an invoice enforceable?
17. Why should terms of an invoice be incorporated by reference in a credit application?
18. In a shipment contract, when does title and risk of loss pass to the buyer?
19. What is the difference between the terms FOB the Place of Shipment and FOB Destination?
20. What are the essential elements of a personal guaranty?

6 Terms of Sale

Overview

Arrangements between seller and buyer that specify the conditions of payment for goods or services are known as **terms of sale.** They indicate if credit is to be part of the sales transaction, the length of time for which credit is to be granted, and other features such as discounts. Because most business transactions involve a title transfer prior to the requirements of payment from the purchaser, terms of sale play an important role in financing the growth of a business enterprise. Terms of sale are made up of many factors. Some are similar from industry to industry and some are different. They represent a commitment of operating funds by the seller and should therefore be carefully understood.

Learning Objectives

After reading this chapter, the reader should understand:

- The role played by terms of sale
- The major factors that influence terms of sale
- The key elements of terms of sale
- The types of terms and how they differ

Chapter Outline

I. Role of Terms of Sale
   - A. Purpose
   - B. Important Considerations

II. Influencing Factors
   - A. General Considerations
   - B. Competition
   - C. Market and Product Characteristics
   - D. Type of Customer
   - E. Profitability

III. Categories of Payment Terms
   - A. Prepayment Terms or Cash Terms
   - B. Ordinary or Standard Terms
   - C. Discount Terms
   - D. Late Charges

IV. Other Terms
   - A. Consignment
   - B. Floorplan Financing
   - C. Sight Draft/Bill of Lading
   - D. Contra Accounts
   - E. Extra Dating Terms
   - F. Seasonal Dating Terms
   - G. Guaranties
   - H. Pledge
   - I. Advances
   - J. Progress Payments
   - K. Commitments

V. Export Terms
   - A. Role of Terms of Sale
   - B. Letters of Credit
   - C. Pro Forma Invoice
   - D. Barter Arrangements

Role of Terms of Sale

Purpose

There are many different terms of sales, ranging from prepayment of cash to permitting the customer considerable time within which to pay for the goods after received. From a practical standpoint, there is a direct relation between the terms of sale and the seller's perception of the buyer's ability to pay. If the seller has little or no confidence in the buyer's paying ability, the immediate payment of cash may be required. On the other hand, the payment period may be extended if the seller believes that the customer is a good credit risk. Careful thought and understanding of all of the elements of terms of sale is critical to selecting the appropriate terms for a customer.

The expression **terms of sale** has an exact meaning. *A term in a contract is any contractual condition.* Thus, terms, when set forth in a contract, include the kind of goods, the time of delivery, the carrier to transport goods, and the time for payment. In other words, *terms of sale are actually the terms of payment.* To be enforceable, it is important that terms of sale be **contractual;** *agreed to by both the seller and buyer.* Terms of sale can be clearly set forth in a credit application, if the application is also a contract.

Terms of sale, also referred to as credit terms, selling terms, or payment terms, must be set independently by each seller, without collusion or conspiracy with other sellers, to avoid violation of the antitrust laws. They are different from other provisions of sales contracts, such as warranties, guarantees, and cancellations privileges, which are more usually considered as conditions of sale, are not within the scope of business credit.

Important Considerations

Terms of sale are an integral part of each sales contract and, like the price, require agreement by both buyer and seller. The seller sets terms for its products. The sellers' terms of sale can be set in its credit application, provided that the application is also a contractual agreement.

The law governing this concept can be found in Section 207 of Article 2 of the UCC and is commonly referred to as the **battle of the forms.** As with all contracts, there must be an offer and acceptance. If the seller's offer of sale limits acceptance to the terms set forth in the contract, they cannot be altered. For example, if the seller's credit application contains a provision that states that no terms or conditions, different from those stated in the application will become part of the agreement of sale, the terms may not be altered. *Where there is no contract stating that terms cannot be altered, the last document sent will be considered as the prevailing document, hence the term "battle of the forms."* If there is no contract and if a seller receives a purchase order from a buyer which contains different terms, which the seller does not acknowledge or object to, the seller agrees to the different terms. With paperwork flowing from seller to buyer and buyer to seller, it is of critical importance that the seller establish contractual terms of sale that may not be altered.

The Robinson-Patman Act

Because the courts have ruled that credit terms are part of price, the seller should be fully aware of the provisions of the Robinson-Patman Act regarding discrimination in terms of sale if any departure from regular terms is contemplated. The Robinson-Patman Act makes it "unlawful for any person engaged in commerce to discriminate in price between different purchasers of commodities of like grade and quality . . . where the effect of such discrimination may be substantially to lessen competition or tend to create a monopoly in any line of commerce." The Robinson-Patman Act applies to interstate commerce when commodities, or goods, of like grade and quality are involved.

In a successful antitrust case (*Rose Confections, Inc. v. Ambrosia Chocolate Company*), the courts said that granting one purchaser free freight while charging freight costs to another purchaser is discriminatory. In another case, (*Conoco, Inc. v. Inman Oil Co.*) the courts said that charging one price for goods delivered to a customer and charging the price for goods delivered f.o.b. terminal was found to be discriminatory. And, the courts said that requiring one dealer to pay COD while granting another dealer credit terms can support a price discrimination claim (*Cemar, Inc. v. Nissan Motor Corp.*).

However, companies are entitled to extend different terms to competing purchasers provided that the same standards of credit worthiness are applied to all customers who compete with each. The key is to apply the same standards to determine credit-worthiness for all customers. For example, if a buyer has a history of late payments and financial difficulties, that is sufficient to make the business decision to deny credit and to use prepayment terms. It is legal to alter a credit term to a particular customer provided that the decision to make that change is based on factors such as credit records, a review of the customer's financial information and your company's own position in the market. It is also legal to adjust a price in order to meet a price being offered by a competitor. Documentation to support the use of adjusting terms to meet competition should be carefully documented. Price differences may be permitted if reasonably justified by other factors such as cost, volume or delivery schedule.

The facts of unusual situations should be carefully studied and the advice of counsel obtained. In any event, the supplier should insist that the customer meet regular terms as soon as possible. To avoid misunderstanding, companies should include their credit terms on important documents relating to the transaction, such as credit applications, price lists, purchase orders, sales contracts, statements, quotes and the invoice itself.

Influencing Factors

General Considerations

Once terms of sale are established, they may be difficult to change. Since they have both marketing and financial aspects, it is important that decisions related to establishing or changing terms be made jointly by the company's sales and financial management. Terms vary widely according to products and marketing situations within the same industry. These dissimilarities are in the broadest sense a reflection of **competition** and **market and product characteristics,** which are two important factors that influence terms of sale.

Competition

Credit is extended in response to either direct or indirect customer demand for the firm's products or services. This implies that sales might not occur without the extension of credit. The decision to extend credit and the decision about the terms offered can be viewed as similar to a change in the price of the product or service. Price is the result of a great number of market forces, some of which are controllable, some of which are not. Although the firms products or services may be similar to those offered by competitors, sufficient diversity of product or service can be created by the firm through customer relations, pre and post sale services and pricing policies or credit terms.

A company that contemplates offering terms to all of its customers that differ significantly from standard terms for its product line or from terms of competitors must weigh the competitive aspects and the ultimate influence on profits. Unless the product holds a large share of the market or is priced much lower than competing items, terms that are shorter than standard can divert business to competitors that offer less stringent arrangements. Conversely, while unusually long terms may help build sales, they produce higher costs, greater capital investment and cost of carrying accounts receivable, higher collection expenses, heavier losses from bad debts, and reduced margins of profit.

Any competitive advantage may be only temporary, since it can lead competitors to offer other inducements to the same customers. Shorter terms reduce the seller's burden of financing the transaction, but buyers seek longer terms or larger cash discounts. Payment arrangements balance these opposing interests. Basically, terms are an element much like prices in the overall competitive scene. Uniformity of terms within an industry minimizes their competitive aspects, but even under these circumstances, a change in competitive conditions is likely to produce changes in terms. For instance, in a buyer's market there is a tendency to offer longer terms as an inducement to buy. When demand for products or services exceeds their availability, terms may be expected to shorten.

Market and Product Characteristics

Market and product characteristics range widely in impact and complexity, from production time to physical characteristics of raw materials. There is a direct relationship between the time it takes to convert goods or materials into cash and the time allowed to repay the debt created by the purchase of the materials. The operating cycle is the period of time between the acquisition of material, labor and overhead inputs for production and the collection of sales receipts.

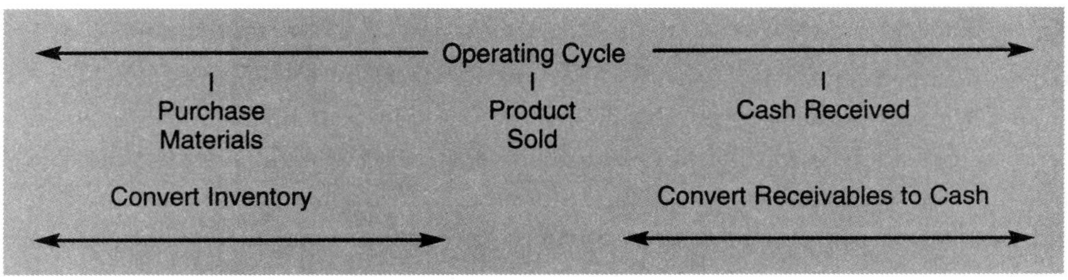

In practice, however, a portion of the customer's operating cycle is usually funded by its own capital, especially if there is further production involved, or if the goods are not ready for resale when purchased. During the inventory conversion period, raw materials are purchased, machinery and labor transform it into a product before it is sold. If selling terms are shorter than the customer's operating cycle, the supplier is said to have a favorable spread. If longer, then the buyer is said to have the advantage. In the latter case, for instance, suppliers could be furnishing a disproportionate share of the funding for a customer that buys on long terms and sells on short terms.

Basic materials are sold to manufacturers on shorter terms than intermediate or finished goods, primarily because of the short period of time raw materials retain their original form in the hands of the manufacturer. Terms of sale rarely exceed the normal manufacturing cycle and storage time. Chemical products such as agricultural oils and minerals, are normally sold on longer terms than their raw components. In the textile industry, cotton goods frequently call for shorter terms than the finished fabrics and garments.

Perishable items, such as meats, fresh vegetables, and dairy products, have a short shelf life, rapid turnover rate, and short selling terms. It is fairly common to find 10-day terms in the food industry. Less perishable foods, such as canned goods and manufactured or processed foods products, have a longer turnover period, since they can be stocked in larger quantities by the retailer. They are sold on longer terms.

Merchandise having a seasonal demand often carries longer terms during the off season than during the active period. For instance, accounts receivable generated from the sale of toys build up during the year in contemplation of the Christmas season. The supplier finances a great portion of the buyer's needs, but maintains steadier production levels during the year and reduces storage problems that would have been created by large pre-season stocks.

Goods protected by trademarks or those in very high demand enjoy widespread consumer acceptance and frequently turn over more rapidly than unknown brands, which translates into shorter terms for the more popular products. Inexpensive items tend to be sold on shorter terms than more costly products. For example, terms for drug items are shorter than terms for floor coverings and many furniture items. Diamonds and expensive jewelry, which generally have a longer operating cycle than any of the above products, are purchased by retailers on terms that range from four to six months.

Type of Customer

Companies often employ different terms for different types or classes of customers. Customers can be classified in many ways, for example by size of order or by type of buyer. Retailers may receive one set of terms, wholesalers another, and institutional buyers still another. For example, a paint manufacturer may grant longer terms to retailers than to industrial accounts purchasing for use rather than resale.

Profitability

Products with higher profit margins may allow longer terms than those with lower margins, and selling terms should take this factor into consideration. In practice, however, competition may nullify this by forcing a seller to offer longer terms in lines where depressed prices yield little or no profit.

Categories of Payment Terms

Terms of sale can be separated into different categories: **prepayment, cash, standard or ordinary, and special.** Regardless of the kind of terms used by a seller, they should be clearly communicated in writing and agreed to by the buyer.

Prepayment Terms or Cash Terms

Cash terms, *also referred to as prepayment or closed terms, include payment before the transaction, at the time of the transaction, or in a short period after the transaction, usually no longer than 10-14 days.* Cash terms do not ordinarily offer any discount. The short credit period allows the buyer sufficient time to examine and accept the merchandise. When cash terms requiring payment before the merchandise is delivered are offered, this is an indication that the seller does not wish to extend credit to the buyer. Net cash terms often are used for the sale of raw materials. The seller takes some risk with cash terms in cases such as seasonal items, where the time elapsed in shipping goods to the purchaser, then having them rejected and returned, makes the vendor less able to sell the goods to someone else.

The following terms are prepayment terms, requiring payment before delivery:

- **Cash in Advance (CIA)**—*These terms require the buyer to make payment via one of the cash methods (wire, bank check, etc.) before an order will be shipped.* This is used for very weak credit. It is the most stringent form of cash terms.
- **Cash before Delivery (CBD)**—*No delivery is required until the buyer has made payment.*
- **Cash on Delivery (COD)**—*These terms require payment to the transportation company for the full invoice amount at the time of the delivery.* There is the risk that the buyer will not accept the shipment, which means that the seller will have to bear the costs of freight charges to and from the buyer's location, preparation and packaging costs, and possible deterioration of the product. This risk may encourage the seller to consider other forms of credit terms. COD terms are used extensively where credit has not been established and where the merchandise is standard.
- **Cash with Order (CWO)**—*These terms are offered when the seller requires payment before shipment can occur.* The seller requires that a check be included with the order or that some form of cash payment be received at the time the order is placed. These are the most severe from the buyer's standpoint since the seller assumes little or no risk. Their use is largely on customers with no credit standing. Goods can be prepared for shipment and held until payment is received.
- **Bill-to-Bill terms**—*These are also called drop delivery or load-to-load terms and require payment for the previous shipment when a new delivery is made.* These terms are often found in lines involving weekly deliveries. Perishable foods sold to retail stores and gasoline sold to retail service stations are representative of this type of credit term.

Except in the few cases where these types of terms are an industry standard, these terms indicate the seller's unwillingness to accept a credit risk. The advantage of prepayment terms is that they do offer the seller an alternative way to make a sale when extending credit is not an option. When prepayment terms are used, there is little risk of nonpayment. Some risk exists with a cash on delivery, if for example, the delivery agent forgets to pick up payment. There is a chance that the buyer will refuse delivery, which creates risk.

There are several kinds of **cash;** *cash can mean a buyer's check, a certified check, or a cashier's check.* **A cashier's check** *is drawn by a bank on the bank's own funds.* The seller/creditor looks to the bank for the risk of payment. Therefore, the risk to the creditor is the credit risk of the bank itself when a cashier's check is accepted. Courts have held that payment cannot be stopped on a cashier's check because the bank, by issuing it, accepts the check in advance. A **certified check** *is where a bank guarantees that funds are on deposit when the check is certified.* At the request of either the depositor or the holder, the bank acknowledges and guarantees that sufficient funds will be withheld from the drawer's account to pay the amount stated on the check. Certified checks are virtually guaranteed, but there is some risk of bank offset in several states, so the guarantee is not perfect. This is rare, but it does create some risk to the credit grantor. In addition, more banks are encouraging the use of bank checks for these purposes and discouraging the use of certified checks.

Cash payment methods can include wire transfer and electronic transfer via **automated clearing house (ACH).** *In a* **wire transfer,** *the buyer arranges to move funds electronically from its bank account to the seller's bank account electronically.* The most common method to do this is via the Federal Reserve's Fedwire system, which all banks have access to. Funds move in a real-time mode via Fedwire, and all Fedwire transfers are final once they have been made. Banks handling the transfer can provide a Fedwire identification number to verify that the transfer has been made. In an ACH, customers can also arrange to transfer funds electronically by instructing their banks to use the ACH for the transfer or by allowing their supplier to automatically debit their bank account by using an ACH debit transfer. ACH transfers are not real-time, however, and require at least one business day to be completed. They are also not final and can be returned, much like a check that does not have enough funds on deposit to cover the clearing. ACH transfers are substantially cheaper than Fedwire transfers. Many electronic commerce/electronic data interchange transactions also use the ACH to finalize the payment. The credit manager should alert the bank as to the incoming transfer and have the bank call as soon as the wired funds are received so the order can be released.

In more and more industries, there have been concerted efforts to shift from payment by check to an electronic form of payment, usually through the ACH network. Float loss by the paying firm usually has to be negotiated. ACH transfers are usually much more economical than checks. Receipts are more predictable when made electronically because the uncertainty of mail time is eliminated. Electronic payments are the typical form for international, cross-border payments. Selling companies may be able to recognize a different cost for buyers that pay electronically, thus making such buyers qualify as a separate class of customer entitled to its own set of credit terms.

Ordinary or Standard Terms

Most businesses grant credit according to an industry-wide set of terms. **Open account terms,** *also called ordinary terms, or standard terms include three elements: the net credit period, the cash discount and the cash discount period.*

Net Credit Period + the Cash Discount = Credit Term

The **net credit period** *is the length of time allowed for payment of the face amount of the invoice.* It is usually computed from the date of the invoice, although in a few industries it is computed from the date the goods are received by the customer. When the net credit period is expressed as a net term or net 30, payment must be made in full within 30 days from the date of the invoice.

Next month terms *specify payment in the month following shipment.* Under this type of terms, invoices are usually sent at the time of shipment rather than once monthly. An example of a next month terms is: Net 10th prox. This terms means that payment of the full amount of the invoice is due on the tenth day of the following month. These terms are also referred to as proximo terms.

End-of-Month (EOM) terms are usually offered for a consolidated bill that represents purchases and shipments of goods during the monthly period. *Payment is due for the credit period shown or by the end of the month billed, especially if the invoice is dated on the first of the month.* For example, if the terms are 10 EOM, payment for all purchases made in one month is due on the tenth of the following month.

Middle-of-Month (MOM) terms *are a variation of EOM terms, with payments due by the middle of the month, instead of the end of the month.*

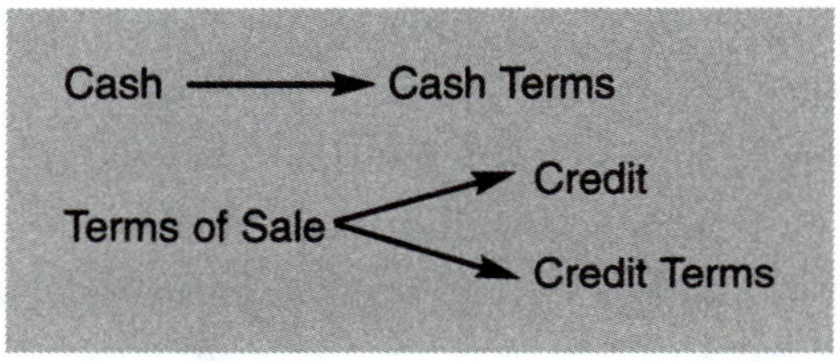

Discount Terms

Net terms with a cash discount offer an inducement for the purchaser to pay ahead of maturity. A cash discount is offered off the invoice amount if the customer pays within a specified period of time called the discount period. It is usually expressed as a percentage but can also be stated as a dollar amount. For example, terms of 1%, 10/net 30 allow the buyer to deduct 1% from the face amount if the invoice is paid within 10 days. If the buyer does not take the discount, the full amount of the invoice in due within 30 days. The discount rate is 1% and the discount period is 10 days.

The following are examples of discount terms:

1% 10 Prox—a 1% discount is earned if paid in 10 days, the net period is the 10th of the following month.

1% 10 MOM—a 1% discount is earned if paid in 10 days, the net amount is due the middle of the month

2% 15 EOM—a 2% discount is earned if paid in 15 days, the net amount is due at the end of the month

The necessity and value of cash discounts is widely disputed by credit executives. Cash discounts offer substantial financial advantages to buyers. Assuming that a majority of customers pay within the discount period, the seller may expect a quicker turnover or receipt of funds, with reduced net working capital requirement, reduced credit and collection expenses, and reduced delinquencies and credit losses. These advantages are sometimes disputed, with the argument that prompt payments are at least partly a matter of habit or fulfillment of agreement on terms. This presumes that collections would be as prompt on terms of net 10 days as on 1% net 30 days. This assumption may be valid if the seller's customers are all strong financially and if competitors sell on similar terms. If cash discounts shorten the average collection period, they could be a very real advantage to a business that has exhausted most of its possible sources of financing and has a strong need for faster turnover of its accounts.

Trade discounts *are allowances made to purchasers because of the line of business and for quantity purchases.* They should not be confused with the cash discount, since trade discounts bear no relationship to time of payment and may be deducted regardless of when the bill is paid. Two separate trade discounts are sometimes offered, one for being in the trade and another for quantity purchases. In other words, manufacturers may offer trade discounts to wholesalers or retailers, wholesalers to retailers, etc. Chain discounts, or successive discounts from the original price, are a form of trade discount. The amount of discount is calculated by successively applying the discounts to the quoted price. For example, terms of 10% and 5% on a $100 invoice would allow a 10% reduction of $100, then a 5% reduction on the remaining $90, for a net due of $85.50.

Once discount terms are established, customers may try to take unearned discounts by deducting them from payments made beyond the prescribed discount period. Administration of discount terms can become a major problem in customer relationships. If cash discounts are to serve their purpose, the seller must not allow unearned discounts because they can be an important influence on seller's costs, and therefore on profits. Strict administration of discount terms may cause customers to claim they are being penalized if there is no allowance for mail time, transportation time, and other delays. Correspondence between seller and buyer over these matters is costly and often impairs good sales relationships. Enforcement of discount terms varies widely, but most firms allow only a few days grace beyond the discount period and do not allow unearned discounts. Most companies charge back unearned discounts, although some actually return the customer's uncashed check as not acceptable.

Offering a Cash Discount

A seller offers customers a cash discount for several reasons. The primary reason is that the seller believes it can increase sales by encouraging customers to buy its products at reduced purchase prices. Another reason often expressed for the use of cash discounts is that a seller believes that it has no other alternative since its major competitors offer them. In either case, the seller finances customers' purchases for some period of time. Presumably, the seller is sharing its financial capacity with buyers and can afford to do so. However, the issue that is generally overlooked by the seller is whether the cash discount adds economic value to the firm. That is to say, is the reduced invoice amount received at the discount date more profitable than the non-discounted amount that would be received at a later date? To answer this question, the selling firm's credit manager should perform a detailed analysis to understand the economic value of offering cash discounts for early payment.

If a seller offers a discount, the credit manager may be able to help customers enhance value in their firms by showing them how costly trade credit can be if cash discounts are forgone. The next two sections address these issues.

Cost of Cash Discounts to the Seller

The credit manager must analyze two opposing costs associated with offering customers cash discounts. On the one hand, there is the cost associated with the loss of funds received as a result of the discount reducing the invoice amount. Opposing this cost is the gain of having funds received earlier as a result of the buyer accelerating payment from its normal non-discount payment period. The credit manager must measure these opposing costs in a time value of money framework that employs an opportunity cost of funds. The opportunity cost represents the interest rate that the seller could obtain by investing funds elsewhere at comparable risk.

To illustrate, assume that a seller offers credit terms of 1%, 10/net 30 on a $2,000 sale that has a cost of $1,600. For simplicity, assume that costs are paid 15 days after the sale. The seller's opportunity cost of funds is 6%. What is the present value of profits from this sale when the buyer takes the discount? You calculate it using the following equation.

$$\text{Profit} = \frac{\text{Sale} - \text{discount}}{(1+\text{rate})^{\text{days}/365\ \text{cost}}} - \frac{\text{cost}}{(1+\text{rate})^{\text{days}/365}}$$

$$\text{Profit} = \frac{\$2000 - \$20}{(1+.06)^{10/365}} - \frac{\$1600}{(1+.06)^{15/365}}$$

$$\text{Profit} = \$1976.84 - \$1596.17 = \$380.67$$

The $2,000 sale has an accounting profit, net of discount, of $380:

$2,000	face value of the invoice
– 20	the discount of 1%
$1,980	discounted face value of the invoice
–1,600	cost of items
$ 380	accounting profit

Think of the events along a time line:

Day 1	Invoice Sent by Seller
Day 10	Payment for discounted invoice amount received from buyer
Day 15	Goods Paid for by Seller

Because the payment of $1,980 (the discounted value of the invoice amount) will be received 10 days after the sale, the present value of that amount must be calculated. In other words, how much is a payment received ten days from now worth today? Assuming the interest rate of 6%, the present value of $1,980 is $1,976.84. Receiving $1,980 in 10 days is the same as having $1,976.84 on day one.

Since the seller's payment, or cash outflow, for cost of the goods ($1,600) occurs

15 days after the sale, its present value can also be calculated. The present value of $1,600 is $1,596.17.

The result is an economic profit of $380.67:

Present value of payment received	$1,976.84
less the present value of the cost of the goods	–$1,596.17
Economic Profit	$ 380.67

The higher economic profit relative to the accounting profit, of $.67, results from delaying payment to suppliers beyond the receipt of funds from the customer. The firm retained the funds in other aspects of the business and earned income at an annual rate of 6%.

As an exercise, assume that costs are paid 10 days after the sale; that is, the seller pays for the cost of the goods when the account pays on day 10. Substituting 10 days for 15 days in the above equation results in an economic profit of $379.39. See if you can derive this answer. The economic profit of the selling firm declines relative to paying for costs in 15 days because cash outflows are accelerated 5 days.

Now it is necessary to calculate the profit if the customer does not take the discount and pays on day 30. Continue to assume that the seller pays all costs 15 days after the sale.

$$\text{Profit} = \frac{\text{Sale} - \text{discount}}{(1+\text{rate})^{\text{days}/365}} - \frac{\text{cost}}{(1+\text{rate})^{\text{days}/365}}$$

$$\text{Profit} = \frac{\$2000 - \$0}{(1+.06)^{30/365}} - \frac{\$1600}{(1+.06)^{15/365}}$$

$$\text{Profit} = \$1990.44 - \$1596.17 = \$394.27$$

The interpretation is straightforward when you compare this answer with the above result of $380.67. The seller is better off if the customer does not take the discount. Economic profits increase $13.60 (= $394.27 – $380.67) if the customer foregoes the discount and pays at the end of the credit period.

What is the economic profit to the seller if the buyer stretches payment 20 days beyond the credit period to day 50? Substitute 50 in place of 30 in the equation and solve. The answer is $1,984.10 – $1,596.17 = $387.93. The seller is still better off by not having the buyer exercise the discount—now by $7.26. Obviously, the credit manager should enforce payment at the end of the credit period if the discount is not taken. However, this example illustrates that even if the customer is delinquent in payment, but does pay in 50 days, the selling firm is still better off than if the customer took the discount. The credit manager could expend up to $7.26 (on a present value basis) to collect the overdue account and be as well off as if the discount was taken.

Let us look at the initial example but now assume that the seller's opportunity cost is 12%.

$$\text{Profit} = \frac{\text{Sales} - \text{discount}}{(1+\text{rate})^{\text{days}/365}} - \frac{\text{costs}}{(1+\text{rate})^{\text{days}/365}}$$

$$\text{Profit} = \frac{\$2000 - \$20}{(1+.12)^{10/365}} - \frac{\$1600}{(1+.12)^{15/365}}$$

Profit = $1973.86 – $1592.57 = $381.29

The economic profit, when the customer takes the discount and pays in 10 days and the seller pays suppliers 15 days after the sale, is $381.29. If the customer does not take the discount and pays 30 days after the sale, the economic profit is $388.89.

$$\text{Profit} = \frac{\text{Sales} - \text{discount}}{(1+\text{rate})^{\text{days}/365}} - \frac{\text{costs}}{(1+\text{rate})^{\text{days}/365}}$$

$$\text{Profit} = \frac{\$2000 - \$0}{(1+.12)^{30/365}} - \frac{\$1600}{(1+.12)^{15/365}}$$

Profit = $1981.46 – $1592.57 = $388.89

Again, the seller is more profitable—this time by $7.60—if the buyer does not take the discount and pays at the end of the credit period.

If the customer pays 50 days after the sale date, and the seller continues to pay suppliers 15 days after the sale, the economic profit is $376.62. Now the economic profit of the seller is $4.67 less than if the customer had taken the discount and made payment at the end of the discount period.

Consider the preceding analysis from a different perspective. Assume that a seller has a customer who normally pays 50 days after the sale date on terms net 30. Is the economic value added to the selling firm improved by offering a cash discount? The answer is, it depends. Review the profit results for the above examples, as summarized in the following table.

Terms: 1%, 10/net 30	Cost of funds: 6%	Cost of funds: 12%
Discount Taken	$380.67	$381.29
No Discount Taken: Payment on Day 30	$394.27	$388.89
No Discount Taken: Payment on Day 50	$387.93	$376.62

Under the assumed condition that the seller pays suppliers 15 days after the sale date, the exercising of a 1% discount by the customer erodes economic value to the selling firm when the seller's cost of funds are relatively low (e.g., 6%). When the cost of funds increases to a significant interest rate (e.g., 12%), the seller can increase economic value of the firm by offering, and having customers take, a discount when customers stretch payment significantly beyond the credit period. For instance, economic profit increases $4.67 (= $381.29 – $376.62) by enticing the customer to pay on day 10 by offering a 1% discount. However, when customers normally pay at the end of the credit period, it is not advantageous for the selling firm to offer a 1% discount even when its opportunity cost of funds is 12%. The selling firm loses $7.60 (= $388.89 – $381.29) in value by doing so.

Missing from this analysis is what happens to sales volume if the seller fails to offer customers a discount. Assume that credit terms are net 30 and customers pay on day 30. Further assume that sales would decline 10% without a discount, whereas costs would only fall 5%. Sales will be $1,800 and costs will be $1,520.

$$\text{Profit} = \frac{\text{Sales} - \text{discount}}{(1+\text{rate})^{\text{days}/365}} - \frac{\text{costs}}{(1+\text{rate})^{\text{days}/365}}$$

$$\text{Profit} = \frac{\$1800 - \$0}{(1+.06)^{30/365}} - \frac{\$1520}{(1+.06)^{15/365}}$$

$$\text{Profit} = \$1791.40 - \$1516.36 = \$275.04$$

In this example, if the seller fails to offer a cash discount the economic profit of the transaction is $275.04. Compare this result against the initial illustration where profitability realized by offering a cash discount was $380.67. It is obvious that the discount should be offered. The selling firm's value increases $105.63 (= $380.67 – $275.04).

The lesson for the credit manager from this analysis is that he or she needs to be engaged in decisions with other people in the organization who are responsible for setting credit policy. It is impossible to make a blanket statement about whether it is profitable to offer cash discounts without doing analysis of the expected cash inflows and cash outflows associated with the credit policy. However, without any sales improvement, it is questionable how much value a cash discount contributes to the economic value of the firm. The credit manager must engage the managers of sales and marketing in a forecasting exercise to estimate the effect on sales of a cash discount. A cash discount without any sales stimulus will probably result in decreased firm value—a value eroding decision instead of a value adding decision. By taking time to understand the present value concepts discussed here, the credit manager can make a real contribution to the company.

Cost to the Buyer

The credit manager may also be able to add value to the company by showing buyers the cost they incur by not taking cash discounts. Of course, it is only worthwhile for the credit manager to reveal this cost to the buyer when it is advantageous to the selling firm to offer a discount to stimulate sales.

The credit manager can explain the cost of a missed discount by the buyer using the following equation:

$$\text{Cost} = \left(\frac{1}{1\text{-discount}}\right)^{365/\text{acceleration}} - 1$$

Discount represents the discount offered by the seller, stated in decimal form. Acceleration is the number of days payment is advanced by the buyer to the seller in order to take advantage of the discount.

Let's continue to use the example discussed in the preceding section where terms are 1%, 10/net 30. Further assume that the customer is not currently taking the discount and is paying on day 30.

$$\text{Cost} = \left(\frac{1}{1\text{-discount}}\right)^{365/acceleration} -1$$

$$\text{Cost} = \left(\frac{1}{1\text{-}.01}\right)^{365/20} -1 = .201$$

If the customer took the 1% discount, payment would be accelerated 20 days (= 30–10). By not taking the discount, the buyer incurs an annualized cost of 20.1%. Hopefully, the buyer can borrow money cheaper than at this rate. If so, then the buyer can add value to her or his firm by borrowing from, say, a bank and paying the seller within the discount period.

If the discount is 2%, the annualized cost to the buyer in the above example is 44.6%. This cost is significant. Again, if the buyer can borrow at a rate less than the annualized cost, the buyer's firm will realize economic profit improvement.

Now look at the "cost to buyer" equation from a different perspective. Assume that the buyer is constantly strapped for cash and stretches paying invoices well beyond the credit terms of 1%, 10/net 30. If the buyer normally pays 90 days after invoice, it has stretched payment 80 days beyond the discount period. What is the annualized cost to the buyer of not taking the discount? Substituting 80 in place of 20 in the equation results in an annualized cost of 4.7%. This cost is probably less than the rate a bank would lend to the buyer. Thus, the buyer uses the seller as a source of relatively cheap financing. And needless to say, the credit manager should be actively pursuing payment well before 90 days after invoice date.

The credit manager should play an important role in determining credit terms. By using a time value of money approach to capture relevant cash inflows and cash outflows associated with selling the firm's products or services, the credit manager can show whether offering credit enhances firm value. For slow paying customers that the firm has extended a cash discount to, the credit manager can use the "cost to the buyer" technique to help convince the buyer that a bank loan may be cheaper than trade credit. In this way, the credit manager helps the buyer add value to the buyer's firm. The result may be a more loyal and timely paying customer.

Late Charges

When goods are purchased on credit, the supplier finances the purchase during the credit term period. This financing is regarded as a necessary cost of business and is included in the selling price. However, unless the bill is promptly collected at maturity, the cost for carrying the account thereafter is greater than anticipated and is an additional cost of business. **Late charges** *for payment services on overdue accounts receivable represent a way in which the seller can recover capital advanced to the customer.* Late charges should be clearly distinguished from **interest payments,** *which are changes made by financial institutions for loans.*

Many suppliers do not impose late charges for a number of reasons, such as the fear of losing good will; doubts about their ability to collect these charges cost effectively; the fear that sales will be lost if such charges are applied, especially if their competitors do not use them; and the belief that the costs of carrying overdue accounts are comparatively small, so it is easier to absorb them. Others favor service charges for such reasons as payment made beyond invoice terms uses the supplier's capital without consent. Not charging for the use of this capital provides the customer with an unfair advantage over competitors that pay promptly. This may also be construed as a price concession on the purchase of merchandise, determined solely by the slow payer. Also, many sellers do not consider the costs of carrying overdue accounts receivable to be confined to the cost of money but are increased by added collection expenses and more likely bad-debt losses.

Corporate attorneys emphasize that late charge programs should be applied uniformly to all like customers or to like groups of customers, or they may be interpreted as a form of price discrimination. Each corporation must seek legal counsel before instituting a service charge program to make sure it is applied properly under the law. The main concern centers around treating all like customers fairly, with a clear definition of like customers. In other words, the issue is not the validity of using late charges but how to implement them under the law. Further, under some state laws, late charges can constitute a violation of the usury laws if the amount is in excess of the maximum permitted by state law.

Other Terms

Receipt of Goods (ROG) terms *permit the buyer to compute the cash discount period from the date on which the merchandise is received rather than from the invoice date.* A distant buyer wanting the cash discount is not pressed to remit before examining the shipment, as may happen when the discount period commences from the invoice date. The net credit period, however, is always calculated from the invoice date and not from the date of arrival. ROG terms are common in the importing of raw sugar and are used by firms in other lines for water shipments between the coasts of the United States. This method of terms enforcement places a burden on the seller to determine when the merchandise arrived at the buyer's facility.

Consignment

Consignment terms offer an alternative to an open-account sale. Consignment is not a true sale until the buyer, called the consignee, actually sells the goods; until then, title remains with the owner, usually the manufacturer, called the consignor. By definition, a **consignment sale** *is one in which a consignee has taken possession of merchandise from the goods' owner. The consignee has the obligation to pay the consignor from the proceeds of the sale of the merchandise. The consignee receives a commission or some other compensation for making the sale. If the consignee does not sell the goods, they may been returned without obligation. Title to the goods remains with the consignor until the sale takes place.*

Consignment terms are not strictly selling terms because title to the goods need never pass to the receiver of the goods. Consignment arrangements may be used in cases where a customer does not have a sufficiently high credit rating but may be considered capable of selling the product. Consignment is often used when the goods are high priced and have a high margin, such as precious gems, jewelry, and antiques. While there is no binding obligation on the receiver to buy or pay for the goods, there is an obligation to account for the proceeds when the goods are sold or to return the goods if they are not sold. The seller may also require the receiver to maintain adequate insurance on all consigned goods with the seller as beneficiary.

Creditors who ship consigned goods should receive regular inventory reports, require insurance coverage designating the creditor as a loss payee and consider perfecting a security interest under the UCC. Compliance with the perfection requirements of the UCC protects ownership of inventory, and in the event of a dispute over goods, the consignor will prevail over a competing creditor. Consignment terms are most often used for other than credit reasons (for example, agricultural products).

Floorplan Financing

Floorplan financing *involves an inventory financing company called the floorplan creditor, that has contractual arrangements with both the supplier/seller and the buyer.* In some cases, the seller can serve as the financing company. The supplier ships the product to the buyer, but sends the invoice to a third party. The third party pays the supplier and the buyer pays the third party over a longer period of time, with interest. A floorplan agreement, which states all of the terms (such as repayment terms, repurchase agreements, and recourse), must be developed and signed by all of the parties involved. Floorplan financing is used when individual goods or items are very expensive. Motor vehicle or boat dealer frequently use floorplan financing. Large retailers, distributors and wholesalers also commonly use floorplan financing because of the need for large inventories and volume.

Trust receipts are commonly used in floor planning high-priced durable goods such as automobiles and household equipment. As with any other inventory loan, the manufacturer and the customer can execute a single security agreement. The manufacturer, as the secured party, can protect its interest by filing a financing statement covering the goods and proceeds without having to execute new agreements as more items are sold.

Sight Draft/Bill of Lading

The seller usually issues an order bill of lading, to his own order, indorses and forwards it attached to a sight draft to a bank in the buyer's city. The buyer pays the draft and obtains the bill of lading. With the bill of lading, the buyer obtains the goods and the bank transmits the funds to the seller. Under these very secure terms, a negotiable bill of lading together with the invoice and a sight draft drawn on the buyer is forwarded by the seller to the customer's banking connection and the merchandise cannot be obtained from the carrier without the bill of lading. The bill of lading will not be released by the bank until the customer honors, or agrees to pay, the draft. As with COD shipments, the seller faces the risk in paying for transportation and packaging costs if the buyer does not pay the draft. These arrangements are employed fairly frequently in sales of carload quantities of meats, grains, and flour.

Contra Accounts

Some companies find that they are reciprocal suppliers with their customers, so *only the net amount needs to be paid regularly.* Certain industries, such as the energy companies, have set up netting arrangements of this sort to facilitate payments without the need of moving large amounts of duplicate funds. The technique of contra-account settlement may be perfectly natural between two strong companies, but it can also be useful in cases where a strong supplier wants to protect itself against a customer that is financially weak. The supplier may insist on a contra-account arrangement. When the right of offset is to be exercised, the selling terms should be specific in stating that a contra-account arrangement has been made. It is important for a creditor to know if a customer has made such arrangements with other suppliers, since the supplier with the contra-account arrangement has a potentially stronger call on the customer's assets.

Extra Dating Terms

Extra dating arrangements, *found primarily in the farming and textile industry, extend the discount period.* For example, terms of 2% 10, 60 extra extend both the discount period and the net credit period to 70 days from the date of the invoice. Since extra terms have identical discount and net credit periods, there is no inducement for the buyer to pay prior to maturity. To overcome this, extra terms are sometimes expressed as 3% 10, 2% 10, 60 extra. This indicates that 3% may be deducted if payment is made within 10 days, but only 2% is deductible if payment is made by the end of 70 days. The extra 1% is in effect an anticipation discount.

Seasonal Dating Terms

Seasonal dating terms *are used when there is a high seasonal demand for a product and sellers wish to encourage off-season purchases by granting terms that postpone payments to coincide with the buyers' selling seasons, such as in the agricultural industry.* The customer benefits from having the goods on hand without any immediate investment of funds. The seller benefits by having more consistent and predictable sales, production cycles with lower storage requirements. The seller usually dates the invoices as of the beginning of the production season with regular terms are computed from that date. Additional incentives may be offered to the buyer in the form of anticipation for early payment. Seasonal datings create the problem of a build up for accounts receivable. The increase in dollar exposure due to one payment date per year can create substantial credit risk.

Guaranties

In situations where the buyer's financial position is not strong enough to warrant open-account credit, the seller may ask that the obligation be guaranteed by someone else, such as a parent corporation or individual. **Guaranties** *are a promise by a third party to satisfy a debt and may be in various forms and by individuals or entities.* Governed by state law, a guaranty can be an effective method to insure repayment of an obligation. To the extent that guaranties protect creditors in the event of a default, they are a useful tool to reduce credit risk.

Guaranties may be arranged as either a guarantee of payment or a guaranty of collection. A guarantee of payment allows the creditor to present an obligation to the guarantor immediately upon default by the debtor. A guaranty of collection requires the creditor to first attempt to collect from a debtor, and if unsuccessful, then seek payment from the guarantor.

A personal guaranty should be signed by the obligor as an individual, not as someone acting in the capacity of an officer of a company. Although governed by state law, a guaranty can be an effective method to insure repayment of an obligation. Principals of a corporation are good candidates to sign a personal guaranty because they have a direct financial interest in the corporation's success. By using a personal guaranty, a creditor can gain a personal financial commitment from the principals operating a corporation.

The Equal Credit Opportunity Act (ECOA) does not permit a credit grantor to require a spouse of a principal to sign a personal guaranty if that spouse is not directly involved with the debtor's business. Care must be taken to make sure that there are policies established for dealing with this so that there is not an accidental dark-compliance. The law does permit the requirement for a spouse to sign a personal guaranty if detailed procedures are followed to first verify that the participant spouse does not have the financial statement or credit wherewithal to support a guaranty. Once that has been independently established, and if the credit were to then be turned down because of the lack of sufficient creditworthiness of the guarantor, the guaranty of the spouse may then be required. This is a very complicated procedure and competent counsel should be consulted in order to establish the appropriate policies and procedures for each company.

Corporate guaranties can be difficult to enforce. When a guaranty is obtained from a corporate entity, creditors should obtain a Board of Directors' resolution that authorizes the corporation to guarantee an obligation.

Pledge

Some sales may be secured by a pledge of an asset to allow the seller to salvage a default situation. *When a debtor places personal property in the possession of a creditor, a* **pledge** *occurs.* Stocks and bonds can be pledged as collateral. Other assets that are sometimes pledged include the cash surrender value of insurance, a certificate of deposit or a savings account. Pledges are useful when a sale is made to a high-risk account, the terms of sale are long, a large dollar amount is involved, or if material is going to be at the customer's location for an extended period of time.

The creditor should obtain a separate pledge agreement. This agreement authorizes a creditor to sell items pledged in the event of nonpayment. The creditor should take physical possession of the item pledged. Finally, creditors should consider notifying an insurance company or bank to block any potential withdrawal of funds by the debtor until the credit commitment is fulfilled.

Advances

When work is done to the customer's specification, it is customary to ask for a partial payment with the order to provide the seller with some working funds for the job and to offer some protection in case the customer cancels the order. Where advances are not usual, they may nevertheless be used for partial protection when a customer is not in a strong financial condition.

Progress Payments

Partial payments are sometimes made on a contract as it progresses, especially when manufacturing or construction time is long and the creditor cannot afford to finance production, such as in the construction industry.

Commitments

These are agreements to deliver or accept merchandise of definite specifications at a fixed price sometime in the future. Commitments are mostly used in buying and selling commodities and raw materials, typically by using the futures markets.

Export Terms

Role of Terms of Sale

The *terms of sale in an* **export transaction** *are a matter of prior arrangement between the buyer and the seller.* Usually the actual collection of payment for goods sold abroad is accomplished through the international facilities of a commercial bank. The choice of payment method or financial instrument will depend on such factors as the credit standing of the foreign buyer, possible foreign exchange restrictions, geographic location of the buyer, and competition locally and internationally.

An exporter may choose to request payment in cash, in part or in whole, before shipping merchandise. This payment arrangement could arise when any of the following conditions exist:

1. The customer's credit standing is not satisfactory.
2. Currency exchange conditions within the customer's country are such that the return of funds from abroad may be delayed for an unreasonable period.
3. A letter of credit cannot be obtained.
4. The goods are manufactured to special order and would have little resale value elsewhere.

In some countries, because of local exchange restrictions, importers are not permitted to make payment in advance of shipment. In addition, foreign buyers may be unwilling to tie up capital for the length of time involved in a foreign transaction, and may hesitate to bear the risk of the shipper's possible default or bankruptcy. As a result, the volume of business handled on cash terms is negligible.

Exporters often use open-account credit terms to break into a new market or to meet competition. Open-account terms are used because they are convenient for both the buyer and the seller. The advantages of these transactions are simplicity and avoidance of additional charges connected with other payment arrangements. The economic and legal atmosphere of the buyer's country should be stable for an exporter to sell on open account. This type of credit is confined to customers of good credit standing in established markets. In other cases, the exporter may market directly through its own sales department. Direct exporting gives a manufacturer full control of sales promotion and distribution, and permits close cooperation with foreign outlets. It allows for a greater degree of coordination with domestic operations and gives first-hand experience with the requirements of the market.

Foreign credit administration poses no new problems for the company that markets its product abroad indirectly through export marketing agencies, such as export commission houses, manufacturers' export agents, export merchants, buyers for export, export and import brokers, and combination export managers that handle a number of noncompetitive products for different manufacturers. The export agency not only assumes many of the sales expenses but sometimes assumes all credit and exchange risks. The U.S. manufacturer is thus permitted to engage in export business on almost a riskless basis. The export agent charges a service fee or commission.

Merchandise may also be shipped on consignment to a foreign branch or subsidiary of the exporter, to a resident agent or representative abroad, to an import house, or to a foreign bank, but consignment shipments to other than branches or subsidiaries are infrequent in export trade.

As a means of some security in countries with free ports or free trade zones, consigned merchandise may be placed under bonded warehouse control in the name of a foreign bank. Arrangements can then be made to release partial lots of the consigned merchandise against payments on specified terms. Merchandise would be cleared through customs after the sale has been completed. This type of consignment arrangement should not be made until regulations and conditions are verified, and storage facilities are assured. Many foreign banks will not accept merchandise consigned directly to them, so goods should not be consigned until prior arrangements have been made. It is also advisable to verify that goods not sold may be readily returned to the country of origin.

Letters of Credit

Letters of Credit are used heavily in international trade and provide substantial protection when a company sells a product overseas. The **letter of credit** *substitutes the financial institution's credit for the buyer's credit and specifies the terms and conditions under which payment will be made.* Letters of credit can also be used domestically, in a similar manner to overseas. In addition, a standby letter of credit can be used to provide a financial guarantee underlying a trade transaction.

Pro Forma Invoice

Widely used in the export trade, **a pro forma invoice** *is an abbreviated invoice sent in advance of a shipment, usually to enable the buyer to obtain an import permit, an exchange permit, or both.* The invoice closely approximates the weights and values of the shipment, but it is not binding on the seller until the order is confirmed. This device enables the buyer to receive goods without unusual delays and the exporter to receive payment without lengthy exchange restriction delays. It can be used domestically when sent in advance of shipment and treated as a memo item. It does not appear on the books until the customer requests shipment, when a regular invoice is sent to the customer.

Barter Arrangements

This form of payment allows a buyer to pay with merchandise instead of currency, often using a third party clearing house as in intermediary. The intermediary facilitates the transaction and collects a fee for its services. The intermediary can also function as a broker, working with buyers and sellers that wish to take part in barter arrangements. Barter is often used when a country does not have a fully convertible currency or is an early stage of development and the country risk is significant.

Comprehension Check

1. The term, terms of sale, has an exact meaning. Provide an explanation.
2. Explain what is meant by battle of the forms.
3. How does the Robinson-Patman Act apply to terms of sale?
4. Explain how a company could extend different terms to competing purchasers.
5. What four factors influence credit terms? Provide an explanation of each factor.
6. What are prepayment terms?
7. What other expressions are used to describe prepayment terms?
8. List five types of prepayment terms.
9. What other expressions are used to describe standard terms?
10. List the three elements of standard terms.
11. What are net terms?
12. What are discount terms?
13. Give three examples of discount terms.
14. What are trade discounts?
15. Why are discounted credit terms offered?
16. What are receipt of goods terms?
17. What is a consignment term?
18. What is floorplan financing?
19. What are extra dating arrangements?
20. What are seasonal dating terms?
21. What is a guarantee of payment?
22. What is a guarantee of collection?
23. What is a pledge?
24. Briefly describe what a letter credit is and how it works.
25. What is a pro forma invoice?

7 Negotiable Instruments

Overview

As commerce and trade developed, people moved beyond the reliance on barter to the use of money. Gradually, there was a need to use substitutes for money or commercial paper. **Commercial paper** *is a contract for the payment of money.* It can serve as a substitute for money payable immediately, such as a check, or it can be used as a means of extending credit. Commercial paper, consisting of notes and drafts, has played an important role in business and commerce since the 12th century. Today, it reflects the needs of merchants, traders, and importers. These groups were responsible for the development of the negotiable instrument and the eventual establishment of a set of rules for the settlement of their disputes in courts they established for that purpose. A **negotiable instrument** *can be transferred from party to party and accepted as a substitute for money.* Their "Instruments Rules" became known as the law of negotiable instruments.

Gradually, the rules were codified and a uniform negotiable instruments act was passed by every legislature. When the **Uniform Commercial Code** was adopted, its Article 3 contained the statutory law that governs commercial paper. This Article (as enacted in the different states) was in part superseded in 1987 when Congress passed the Expedited Funds Availability Act, implemented by Availability Act Regulation CC of the Federal Reserve Board, which effectively superseded prior state laws. Article 3 of the UCC was then rewritten to comply with these Federal Laws and Regulations and is now the principal source of law governing negotiable instruments. The new UCC provision has now been adopted in most states.

Learning Objectives

After reading this chapter, the reader should understand:

- The concept of negotiability
- The difference between the various kinds of negotiable instruments
- The difference between the various special types of checks
- What Certificates of Deposit are
- What negotiation of commercial paper means
- What checks marked "In Full Account" mean

Chapter Outline

I. The Concept of Negotiability
  A. Written Document
  B. Signed by the Maker or Drawer
  C. Unconditional Promise To Pay
  D. A Sum Certain in Money
  E. On Demand
  F. Payable to Order Certain in Money
II. Kinds of Negotiable Instruments
  A. Drafts
  B. Checks
  C. Special Types of Checks
III. Certificates of Deposit
IV. Negotiation of Commercial Paper
  A. Assignment
  B. Negotiation
  C. Indorsements
  D. Four Common Types of Indorsements
V. Checks Marked "In Full Account"

The Concept of Negotiability

The concept of negotiability is one of the most important features of commercial paper. Because of this feature, negotiable instruments are highly trusted and are used daily by millions of people. A **negotiable instrument** *is a written document, signed by the maker or drawer, and containing an unconditional promise to pay (or order to pay) a certain sum of money on delivery or at a definite time to the bearer (or to the order).* (Figure 7-1)

Written Document

The requirement that the instrument be a **written document** is very flexible. *The writing may be done in pen, printing, typewriting, or pencil (although this invites alteration) as long as it is legible. The surface on which the writing is executed must be capable of being circulated.* The fact that an instrument is in writing means that the parole evidence rule governs the admissibility of oral evidence to contradict the terms of the instrument. Therefore, evidence of fraud, incompleteness, inconsistency, etc. is required before testimony on the terms of the instrument are allowed in court. Also there are rules for interpreting problems that tend to recur frequently in the making out of such an instrument. Where there is a conflict of terms, the written terms take precedence over the typewritten terms, or over any printed form term. In other words, if there is a conflict between the written amount and the amount expressed in numbers, the written amount wins out, due to the deliberation required to state it.

Signed by the Maker or Drawer

This second requirement is relatively straightforward. *The actual or authorized signature of the issuer is required for the instrument to be negotiable.* The **maker** *is the person (or company) who makes or executes a note.* The **drawer** *is the person (or company) who makes or executes a draft.* Oral evidence is admissible to identify the signer of an instrument. For example, there are typically several people bearing a common name—such as John Smith. The appropriate person is allowed to testify as to which John Smith actually was the maker of the note.

Figure 7-1 Negotiable Instrument

$ 1,500.00 Anytown, USA, March 10, 19--

Sixty Days after date I promise to pay to

The order of June Goldberg

One thousand five hundred and 00/100 Dollars

Payable at Third National Trust

Value received with interest at 7.0%

No. 746 Due June 18, 19-- Arn McMichaels

If another person signs for the issuer (for example, all corporations must employ this method to utilize commercial paper), the person signing must be authorized to do so or be bound personally to pay the instrument. A failure to indicate that a person is signing in such a capacity, even if so authorized, obligates the signer personally.

Any form of signature is permissible as long as it indicates an intent to issue the instrument. Therefore, an instrument signed with an "X" is sufficient; witnesses to such a signing are a good idea, but not required technically. Also, the signature may appear anywhere on the face of the instrument.

Unconditional Promise To Pay

The requirement that maintains the promise or order to pay contained in the commercial paper must not be conditional on any outside event. To enhance the transferability of such instruments as checks and notes, avoid a situation in which every potential purchaser of an instrument must somehow take time to determine whether a condition has been fulfilled. Requiring that something be done, or that a specific event occur before an instrument can be collected on, reduces the instrument to the status of a simple contract whose rights, at best, can merely be assigned.

A Sum Certain in Money

The requirement of a sum certain means that the amount must be clearly ascertainable from the face of the instrument. To qualify the instrument as negotiable, the sum certain must be calculable at two distinct times at purchase and at maturity. When the holder considers buying the instrument, the exact minimum amount payable on it must be calculable from the information on its face. At maturity, the holder must be able to calculate from the face the exact amount due.

A second requirement is that of a "sum certain," or that the instrument be payable in money. **Money** *is defined as the medium of exchange that any government has officially adopted as part of the currency.*

On Demand

To satisfy this requirement, the time the instrument is payable must be determined in one of two ways. **On demand** *is synonymous with "at presentment" or "at sight". These terms mean that the holder has the option of choosing the time to receive payment.* Equally acceptable is specifying the time when the instrument matures. Such expressions as "due and payable 60 days from March 3, 19XX," "due and payable 60 days from sight," or "due and payable on or before March 3, 19XX," are all acceptable. The holder must be able to determine from the face of the instrument the latest possible time it can be paid without default.

Even if the instrument is subject to an acceleration clause, as long as a specific date is otherwise named, the instrument is still negotiable. An acceleration clause allows the obligee to declare the full amount due and payable upon the occurrence of a particular event, such as the failure to make a payment. An acceleration clause hastens the maturity date. An example is, "In case of default in payments of interest (or of an installment of the principal), the entire note shall become due and payable."

Payable to Order Certain in Money

The last requirement is the most straightforward. An order or to Bearer instrument must be "payable to the order of the named payee(s)," "payable to the named payee's order", or some equivalent wording. A bearer instrument must be written "pay to bearer," "pay to cash," "pay to the order of the bearer," "pay to the order of the named payee(s) or bearer," or the like. Finally, if an instrument is made out to an obviously fictitious person, such as Superman, it is treated as a bearer instrument.

Kinds of Negotiable Instruments

There are two basic kinds of negotiable instruments: promises to pay money and orders to pay money.

- drafts (including checks)
- notes, including certificates of deposit

Drafts

A **draft** *(also known as a bill of exchange) is an instrument that orders someone else to pay.* The order is given by the drawer, who issues the draft usually by signing it in the lower right hand corner. The one who is ordered to pay the money is called the drawee. The one who is to receive the money is known as the payee.

Drafts may be presented to the drawee for payment or for acceptance. When a draft is presented for acceptance, the drawee is asked to become liable on the instrument. To accept a draft, the drawee writes "accepted" across the face of the instrument, and dates and signs it. By doing this, the drawee agrees to pay the instrument at a later date when it becomes due.

Checks

A **check** *is a draft on which the drawee is a bank that is ordered to pay on demand.* It is the most common form of a draft. It is drawn on a bank by a drawer, who has an account with the bank, to the order of a specified person or business named on the check, or to the bearer. Ownership of a check may be transferred to another person by indorsement by the payee. In this manner, a check may circulate among several parties, taking the place of money. Banks provide regular and special printed check forms. These check forms display a series of numbers printed in magnetic ink, which makes it possible to process checks accurately by computers. The first set of figures is the bank's Federal Reserve number. This number is followed by the bank's own number. The second set of numbers is the depositor's account number. The use of printed forms is not required. Any writing, no matter how crude, may be used as a check if it is a draft drawn on a bank and payable on demand.

Special Types of Checks

Bank Drafts

A bank draft, *sometimes called a teller's check, or a treasurer's check, is a check drawn by one bank on another bank in which it has funds on deposit in favor of a third person, the payee.*

Cashier's Checks

A cashier's check *is a check drawn by a bank upon itself.* The financial institution is both the drawer and the drawee. The bank, in effect, lends its credit to the purchaser of the check. Courts have held that payment cannot be stopped on a cashier's check because the bank, by issuing it, accepts the check in advance.

Traveler's Checks

A traveler's check *is similar to a cashier's check in that the issuing financial institution is both the drawer and the drawee.* The purchaser signs the checks in the presence of the issuer when they are purchased.

Certified Checks

A certified check *is a check that is guaranteed by the bank.* At the request of either the depositor or the holder, the bank acknowledges that sufficient funds will be withheld from the drawer's account to pay the amount stated on the check. The UCC provides that "certification of a check is acceptance." This means that a drawee bank that certifies a check becomes primarily liable on the instrument just the same as the acceptor of a draft. The bank has absolute liability to pay.

Whether anyone is secondarily liable depends upon who had the check certified. If the drawer had the check certified, the drawer and all indorsers remain secondarily liable on the instrument. If, on the other hand, the holder had the check certified, the drawer and all prior indorsers are discharged. The UCC places no obligation on a bank to certify a check if it does not want to do so.

Postdated Checks

A check may be **postdated** *when the drawer has insufficient funds in the bank but expects to have sufficient funds to cover the amount of the check at a future date.* A postdated check is not usually covered in the bad check laws of the states. Third-party collectors subject to the Fair Debt Collection Practices Act are restricted on their reliance on postdated checks.

Sight and Time Drafts

A **sight draft** *is payable as soon as it is presented to the drawee for payment.* A **time draft** *is not payable until the lapse of a particular time period stated on the draft.* A **trade acceptance** *is a draft used by a seller of goods to receive payment and also to extend credit.* It is often used in combination with a bill of lading, which is a receipt given by a freight company to someone who ships goods. For example, a seller ships goods to a buyer and sends a bill of lading, with a trade acceptance attached, to a bank in the buyer's city. The trade acceptance is drawn by the seller ordering the buyer to pay the money either to the seller or to someone else. If it is a sight draft, the buyer must pay the draft immediately to receive the bill of lading from the bank. If it is a time draft, the buyer must accept the draft to receive the bill of lading from the bank. The freight company will not release the goods to the buyer unless the buyer has the bill of lading. (Figures 7-2 and 7-3)

Domestic Bill of Exchange

A **domestic bill of exchange** *is a draft that is drawn and payable in the United States. A draft that is drawn in one country, but is payable in another is called an* **international bill of exchange, or foreign draft.**

Figure 7-2 Sight Draft

$ 576.00 Anytown, USA, May 3, 19--

At sight Pay to

the order of First Bank of Jonesdale

Five hundred seventy-six and 00/100 Dollars

Bill of lading attached

Value received and charge the same to account of

To Vernau Shipping

No. 361 Anytown, USA

Corlene Brothers

Joseph Corlene

Notes

A note *(often called a promissory note) is a written promise by one party, called the maker, to pay money to the order of another party, called the payee.* In contrast with drafts, notes are promise instruments rather than order instruments, and they involve only two parties instead of three. They are used by people who loan money or extend credit as evidence of debt. *When two or more parties sign a note, they are called* **comakers.**

Demand Notes

A **demand note,** *as its name implies, is payable whenever the payee demands payment.* A **time note** *is payable at some future time, on a definite date named in the instrument.* Unless a note is payable in installments, the principal (face value) of the note plus interest must be paid on the date that it is due. In an **installment note,** *the principal, together with interest on the unpaid balance, is payable in installments at specified times.* (Figure 7-4)

Promissory Notes

Promissory notes come in the following forms:

- A **single-name paper,** *a note signed by only one maker.* No one else is liable on it.

Figure 7-3 Time Draft

$ 250.00 Anytown, USA, July 8, 19

In or within 30 days Pay to

the order of James Burton

Two hundred fifty and 00/100 Dollars

Accepted
Jim Wilkes
July 12, 19--

Value received and charge the same to account of

To Jim Wilkes

No. 831 Anytown, USA

Brian Gates

Figure 7-4 Demand Note

Anytown, USA, July 7 ,19 --

On demand, the undersigned, for value received, promise(s) to pay to the order of

ANYTOWN TRUST COMPANY

Five thousand two hundred and 00/100 Dollars,

at its offices in Anytown, USA, together with interest thereon from the date thereof until paid at the rate of 10 percent per annum.

500 Anyroad Street
Anytown, USA

Anthony Andolini

- **Double-name paper** *is a promissory note signed by two or more makers or signed by the maker and endorsed by others.* With additional people standing behind the note, the likelihood of payment is increased.
- A **straight note** *is the more common instrument, used merely as evidence of indebtedness.* In order to make certain that the note is negotiable, the word "order" in one form or other must be used.
- In a **serial note,** *the amount to be paid is covered by a series of notes usually of equal amounts and with maturity dates equally spaced.* Usually, a provision is added, stating that in the event of a default in payment, all subsequent notes become due and payable. Thus, notes with stated maturities are converted into demand instruments under this provision.

Promissory notes are commonly used for bank loans. They are not frequently used for merchandise transactions. However, some credit executives will ask their customers to sign a note for past-due accounts, believing that it will stimulate payment and make collection of the account easier. This practice provides written acknowledgment of the past-due debt, but also postpones the due date of the account until the date stated on the note.

Collateral Notes

A **collateral note** *is a note that is secured by certain collateral, such as stocks, bonds, personal property, or mortgages.* Its outstanding feature is that the collateral is held by the creditor while the note is outstanding. Such a note may be negotiated in the same manner as any negotiable note, whether the collateral be assigned or not.

Judgment Notes

Judgment notes *are controlled by state law and have many technical requirements associated with them.* These promissory notes are generally given in connection with a separate agreement by the maker who consents to have a judgment entered should payment not be made on the note when due. *The separate agreement consenting to the judgment is known as a* **confession of judgment.** Clauses that sanction confession of judgment prior to maturity are not authorized by the UCC, because they do not contain an unconditional promise to pay at one definite time.

The note may be endorsed and negotiated by the payee in the same manner as any other negotiable instrument. The confession of judgment is not negotiable but may be assigned by the payee to an endorsee along with the note. *In essence, the confession of judgment enables a creditor to enter a judgment without going to trial.* Because it can be usually entered without advising the debtor, it has been criticized as violating the constitutional rights of due process.

Certificates of Deposit

A **certificate of deposit (CD)** *is an acknowledgment by a bank of the receipt of money and its promise to pay the money back on the due date, usually with interest.* Certificates of deposit generally pay more interest than regular savings accounts because the depositor cannot withdraw the money before the due date without penalty.

Negotiation of Commercial Paper

Assignment

Commercial paper that does not meet all of the requirements of negotiability cannot be negotiated. It can only be transferred by assignment, which is governed by the ordinary principles of contract law. An **assignment** *is the transfer of a contract right from one person to another.* Commercial paper is assigned either when a person whose indorsement is required on an instrument transfers it without indorsing it or when it is transferred to another person and does not meet the requirements of negotiability. In all such transfers, the transferee has only the rights of an assignee and is subject to all defenses existing against the assignor.

An assignment of commercial paper also occurs by operation of law when the holder of an instrument dies or becomes bankrupt. In such cases, title to the instrument vests in the personal representative of the estate or the trustee in bankruptcy.

Negotiation

Negotiation *is the transfer of an instrument in such a form that the transferee becomes a holder.* A **holder** *is a person who is in possession of an instrument issued or indorsed to that person, to that person's order, to bearer, or in blank.*

If an instrument is payable to order, such as "pay to the order of," it is known as **order paper.** To be negotiated, order paper must be indorsed by the payee and delivered to the party to whom it is transferred. *If an instrument is payable to bearer or cash, it is called* **bearer paper** *and may be negotiated by delivery alone, without an indorsement.* When order paper is endorsed with a blank indorsement, it is turned into bearer paper and may be further negotiated by delivery alone.

Indorsements

An instrument is **indorsed** *when the holder signs it, thereby indicating the intent to transfer ownership to another.* Indorsements may be written in ink, typewritten, or stamped

Figure 7-5 **Blank Indorsement**

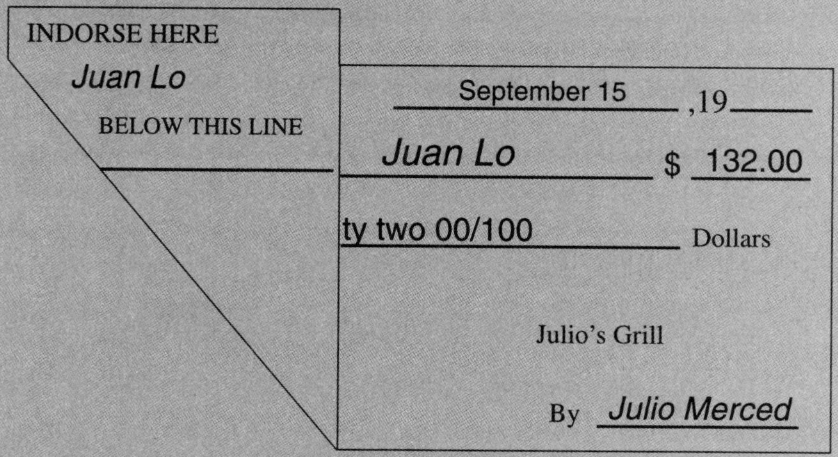

with a rubber stamp. They may be written on a separate piece of paper that becomes part of it. Although the UCC does not require indorsements to be on the back of the instrument, for convenience purposes they are usually placed on the back of the instrument. Each indorsement of a negotiable instrument is a separate contract, standing apart from that of the maker or any other indorser.

Six Common Types of Indorsements

Blank Indorsement

A **blank indorsement** *consists of the signature alone written on the instrument.* No particular indorsee (person to whom an instrument is indorsed) is named. When an instrument is indorsed in blank, it becomes payable to bearer and may be transferred by delivery alone. If the instrument is lost or stolen and gets into the hands of another holder, the new holder can recover its face value by delivery alone. (Figure 7-5)

When an instrument is made payable to a person under a misspelled name or a name other than that person's own, the payee may indorse in the incorrect name, in the correct name, or in both. Signatures in both names may be required by a person paying or giving value to the instrument.

Special Indorsement

A **special indorsement** *(also called an indorsement in full) is made by writing the words pay to the order of or pay to followed by the name of the person to whom it is to be transferred (the indorsee) and the signature of the indorser.* A special indorsement is one that specifies to whose order an instrument is payable. (Figure 7-6)

Restrictive Indorsement

A **restrictive indorsement** *limits the rights of the indorsee in some manner in order to protect the rights of the indorser.* An indorsement is restrictive if it is conditional, attempts to prohibit further transfer of the instrument, includes the words for collection, for deposit, pay any bank, or like terms signifying a purpose of deposit or collection, or otherwise states that it is for the benefit or use of the indorser or of another person. (Figure 7-7)

Figure 7-6 Special Indorsement

Figure 7-7 Restrictive Indorsement

Conditional Indorsement

A **conditional indorsement,** *a type of restrictive indorsement, makes the rights of the indorsee subject to the happening of a certain event or condition.* (Figure 7-8)

Indorsements for Deposit or Collection

Indorsements for deposit or collection are designed to get an instrument into the banking system for the purpose of deposit or collection. *When a check is indorsed "for deposit only" the amount of the instrument is credited to the indorser's account before it is negotiated further.* Retail stores often stamp each check "for deposit only" when it is received. This wording provides protection in the event the check is stolen. Checks mailed to a bank for deposit should always be indorsed in this way.

Qualified Indorsement

A **qualified indorsement** *is one in which words have been added to the signature that limit the liability of the indorser.* By adding the words without recourse to the indorsement, the indorser disclaims liability on the instrument and cuts off his/her obligation to future indorsers and holders to pay on the instrument. The mere use of the words "without recourse" do not wholly relieve the indorser from liability. Under UCC 3-417, it is provided that every person who signs his name as a qualified indorser of a negotiable instrument warrants, by his signature, that:

Figure 7-8 Conditional Indorsement

INDORSE HERE

Pay to the order of Fred Wright
when he turns twenty-one years old.
Sam Wilson

DO NOT WRITE, STAMP OR SIGN BELOW THIS LINE
RESERVED FOR FINANCIAL INSTITUTION USE*

Figure 7-9 Qualified Indorsement

INDORSE HERE

Pay to the order of Pete Lorenzo
without recourse
Rita Will

DO NOT WRITE, STAMP OR SIGN BELOW THIS LINE
RESERVED FOR FINANCIAL INSTITUTION USE*

1. He has good title to the instrument or is authorized to obtain payment or acceptance on behalf of one who has good title and the transfer is otherwise rightful;
2. All signatures are genuine or authorized;
3. The instrument has not been materially altered;
4. He has no knowledge of any defense of any party that is good against him; and
5. He has no knowledge of any insolvency proceeding instituted with respect to the maker or acceptor or the drawer of an unaccepted instrument. (Figure 7-9)

Checks Marked "In Full Account"

Does a check given in payment of an account, marked "In full account," which does not as a matter of fact pay the entire account, constitute payment in full, and is the payee who holds the check estopped from moving for the uncovered balance?

The general rule is as follows: If the claim is liquidated and there is no dispute as to the amount due, a check for a lesser amount than the claim, even though marked "In full account" does not settle the account. The creditor may keep the check and sue for the balance. If however there is a bona fide dispute as to the amount of the claim, and the same claim is not liquidated, a check sent and marked "In full payment of account" is payment in full and the creditor must either return the check and sue for the amount claimed or accept the check in complete payment. Whether a bona fide dispute exists can be a matter of dispute in itself and obviously a debtor wishing to pay a lessor sum can very easily make such a claim.

The retention and use of the check by the creditor will constitute an accord and satisfaction even though the creditor notifies the debtor that it is received only as a partial payment on account. The creditor is therefore placed in a difficult position: either he must reject such a check and demand payment of the full amount or accept the check and possibly be deemed to have made an accord and satisfaction. One possible solution to this problem is to stamp all collection checks with a legend that states:

> "The check is accepted without prejudice and with full preservation of all rights pursuant to Section 1-207 of the UCC."

Under this section of the Code, a party who explicitly so reserves his rights does not prejudice the rights reserved. Some courts have held that this section of the Code applies only to Code-covered transactions such as the sale of goods, and does not apply to service contracts; other courts have entirely rejected the application of the Code to checks marked "In full payment." In some instances, however, the courts have held that where a creditor gave a release under seal, the acceptance of a smaller amount than the amount due, even in a liquidated claim, releases the debt.

Comprehension Check

1. Define the term negotiable instrument.
2. Give a brief explanation of the elements of a negotiable instrument.
3. List the two basic types of negotiable instruments.
4. What is a check?
5. Define the following terms:
   a. Bank draft
   b. Cashier's check
   c. Traveler's check
   d. Certified check
   e. Postdated check
   f. Sight and time draft
   g. Domestic bill of exchange
   h. Note
   i. Demand note
   j. Single-name paper promissory note
   k. Double-name paper promissory note

l. Straight promissory note
m. Serial note
n. Collateral note
o. Judgment note

6. Define the concept negotiation.
7. List and describe the six most common types of indorsements.
8. What is a special indorsement?
9. What is a restrictive indorsement?
10. What is a conditional indorsement?
11. What are indorsements for deposit or collection?
12. What is a qualified indorsement?
13. What is the general rule for handling a check marked "paid in full?"

8 The Legal Forms of Business

Overview

Part of the risk creditors undertake has to do with the legal form of the debtor's business. Consequently, it is important that the credit executive understands the different forms of business, particularly as they affect the rights of creditors and debtors. For the most part, state laws govern the legal forms of business, and for particulars of how the topics in this chapter relate to the states, it is best to consult special sources, such as the *Credit Manual of Commercial Laws*, which is published by the National Association of Credit Management.

This chapter focuses on the legal form of an organization as a factor in credit analysis. It is not so much concerned with the advantages and disadvantages of the various legal forms to the business itself, but rather how those vendors and bankers dealing with the business are affected.

Learning Objectives

After reading this chapter, the reader should understand:

- The importance of the customer's form of organization in credit decisions
- The major features of sole proprietorships
- The major features of partnerships
- The major features of corporate organizations
- The major features of S corporations
- The major features of estates, limited liability companies, common law trusts, joint ventures, and cooperative societies
- Other features of organizations that are relevant to credit managers

Chapter Outline

I. Creditor's Interest in Legal Composition
   A. The Importance of Legal Form
   B. Principal Forms
II. Proprietorships
   A. General Considerations
   B. Management
   C. Continuity
   D. Capital
   E. Liability
III. Partnerships
   A. General Considerations
   B. Continuity
   C. Capital
   D. Liability
IV. Corporations
   A. General Considerations
   B. Certificate of Incorporation
   C. Stock
   D. Continuity
   E. Capital
   F. Liability
V. S Corporations
   A. General Considerations
   B. Continuity
   C. Capital
   D. Liability
VI. Estates
   A. Proprietorships—Continuity
   B. Capital
   C. Liability

The Creditor's Interest in Legal Composition

The Importance of Legal Form

The credit executive must consider the form of business organization used by the debtor. It is important to know if the business will remain viable in the event of the sickness or death of one or more of the principals. Certain forms of organizations—namely, corporations—can raise additional funds more easily than others. Many business undertakings are so costly, they require a large investor pool from which to solicit funds. The ability of the debtor to raise these funds is an important factor in the analysis of a firm.

Principal Forms

On the form of the business, the personal assets of the principals may or may not be available to support its debts. In smaller businesses controlled by an individual or a family, assets such as real estate used by the company can be easily manipulated so that they are outside the reach of the firm's creditors. The three principal forms of business are the proprietorship, partnership, and corporation.

Proprietorships

General Considerations

This form of enterprise is the easiest to organize and requires a minimum of legal knowledge and financial resources. It is simple to set up. Of course, the business must engage in a legal activity, and comply with local health, safety, and zoning regulations. There may also be registration or qualification fees required by the community, and an advertisement of a fictitious firm name if one is used. The owner may then begin operations.

Management

The most obvious concern about a proprietorship, from the creditor's viewpoint, is that the owner has total control over the business. The owner may direct the entire business: marketing, production, and financial management. If he or she gets sick—or worse—the business may simply stop, and along with it the cash flow that was destined to pay creditors.

Another factor is that the owner may not possess all the skills required to successfully operate the company. A sole proprietor may hire one or more managers. The structure of a sole proprietorship makes it difficult to "take in a partner" if the business is successful.

Continuity

The business of a proprietorship ceases when the owner dies. In some cases, it might be continued by the family or estate, provided someone suitable to run the business can be found. If the proprietor has a living trust will, the will could create an ongoing business.

In the event of a proprietor's death and liquidation of the business, the creditors may not receive payment until the will is probated and the estate is settled. This doesn't necessarily mean a loss of the money due, but payment may not be forthcoming for some period of time.

The creditor is also interested in the proprietor's health and the amount of life insurance carried. As the driving force in the business, the owner must be in good physical and mental condition. Generally, the strain of running a business is great, particularly when it rests on the shoulders of one person. Banks have long made it a custom to require sufficient insurance on the life of a proprietor–borrower to pay off the loan. That may be a good policy for a business creditor as well, depending upon how much money is at stake, with the proceeds of the insurance paid directly to the estate.

Capital

The proprietorship generally seeks credit based only on the assets of the business and those of the owner. If they are inadequate, the owner may be forced to moderate expansion plans, or to allow outside interests to invest in the business. As soon as someone else invests money in the firm, the proprietorship may have to be changed to another form. Consequently, the total amount of assets available to a proprietorship is usually limited.

The limited capital of the proprietorship may be a significant factor in a credit analysis. In some cases, it is a controlling influence; but in many others the capital invested is adequate for the scope of operations. By and large, the credit executive is interested in seeing that the capitalization is sufficient for the current needs of the business, and not in determining the capital requirements of some theoretical program of expansion.

The sole owner also receives the full benefit of a successful operation; he or she may retain as much of the profits in the business as they please. In some cases, the credit decision will be influenced by what the owner does with the profits. Does the owner leave them in the business to strengthen its financial position, or does the owner use them and continue to rely on creditor financing for operating funds? In accounting parlance, the money a proprietor takes out of the business for personal use is called the owner's "draw". Its counterpart in a corporation would be the salaries and dividends paid to the principals.

While the draw in a sole proprietorship is meant to reflect the work done by the owner in the business—or the salary that would have to be paid if the owner hired someone to do his or her work—other factors seem to have a greater bearing on the amount withdrawn. The first of these is the owner's personal needs. If there is a costly illness in the family, or the owner has an expensive hobby, the business may be the only recourse for money available. Another factor is the needs of the business. There are many, perhaps a majority, of small companies that don't earn enough to fairly compensate the owner for the time and energy put into the business. Either of these factors is a negative element in the credit decision.

Liability

The owner has a personal, unlimited liability for the debts of the business, which makes the proprietor very vulnerable to creditors. With certain exceptions, the personal assets may be claimed for the payment of business debts. This may not include, however, assets held jointly with the owner's spouse.

The owner's personal liability for the debts of the business often can strengthen its credit position. It is equivalent to having the principal's personal guarantee for the debts of a corporation. The credit executive should be satisfied, however, that the personal liability means something in terms of assets. Frequently, the owner's personal wealth is all tied up in the business, and the benefit to creditors of the personal liability is largely theoretical. Any personal wealth must be shared with all general creditorsbusiness, as well as personal.

In cases where the company offers only marginal support for the credit requested, the credit executive should verify any outside assets the owner claims to have. If they are owned jointly with the spouse, the creditor will have difficulty in acting against them. A husband and wife can be a proprietorship in every state in the United States. Homestead laws passed in most states exempt the real estate from attachment or forced sale to meet general debts, including a proprietor's business debts.

Partnerships

General Considerations

A **partnership** *is defined as "an association of two or more persons to carry on as co–owners of a business for profit."* While no particular form of contract is necessary to create a partnership, a partnership contract usually provides what the partners' rights and duties are, and the extent of liability.

A partnership may be formed by the method of doing business, such as sharing profits, even though no formal contract exists. *When a third party is led to believe a partnership exists even though no partnership has been created, it is called* **partnership by estoppel.** This has no benefit for the purported partners. It is used legally to correct or prevent injustice.

The contract, or articles of partnership, formalizes the conditions of the business partnership and is the basis for solving any questions that may come up during the life of the partnership. The following points are usually covered:

- the type of business to be conducted
- the amount of money or other valuable consideration to be invested by each partner
- the division of profit and losses
- the power and duties of each partner
- the compensation to be paid to each in the form of salaries or drawings
- the duration of the partnership and how it is to be dissolved
- the division of assets in case of dissolution
- provisions for withdrawal or admission of partners
- how differences of opinion are to be settled
- provision for continuation in the event of one partner's death or incompetence
- anything else of importance

The Uniform Partnership Act (UPA) *covers the rights and duties of partners.* The provisions of the UPA can be changed by partners as they create their own contract. In addition, the partners should know each other fairly well and be compatible, that is, willing to cooperate in their common interest. It is important that they can get along, and can resolve differences in ways that won't hurt the business. Partnerships are of three types: general, limited, and silent.

General Partnership

In a **general partnership**, *all partners are entitled to take an active part in the affairs of management, unless this is amended by the partnership agreement. Despite their various roles, each partner is considered an agent for the firm; as such, each can commit the firm for business obligations and each has unlimited liability for the business.* In comparison to a proprietorship, two or more partners will normally have more cumulative business experience, but by the same token, there will be less flexibility in decision making. With more than one principal in the business, it is logical to assume there will be a greater pool of the production, marketing, and financial management skills required to operate successfully.

Limited Partnership

The **limited partnership** *differs from the general partnership in that it is composed of one or more general partners and one or more limited partners. The rights and obligations of the general partners are the same as those in a general partnership, except where they may be modified by the partnership agreement.* They control the management, have unlimited liability, and participate actively in the day-to-day operation of the firm. *Limited partners, however, risk only the amount of their investment.* In exchange for this limited liability, they relinquish their voice in the management of the firm.

This type of partnership attracts people who are primarily interested in investment. They are not partners in the usual sense, in that they depend upon return on investment much like those who invest their money in the stock market. The attraction is often a higher rate of return; it is also a convenient way of helping a relative or friend start a business without the backer getting too involved.

Silent Partnership

Silent partners *are those whose actions are such that the law will deem them general partners with liability for the firm's obligations even though their relationship with the firm may not be known in public.*

Continuity

The partnership normally dissolves automatically upon the death of a general partner if there are only two partners, although it may continue long enough to enable the surviving partners to wind up the affairs of the business. This may be modified if the partners agree beforehand that the interest of the deceased partner will be purchased by the remaining partners and a new partnership formed simultaneously. Alternatively, the partnership agreement could provide that the interest of the deceased partner will pass to another partner. Failure to make some such provision would be a glaring mistake for the partners and a hazard for the firm's creditors. Moreover, the skills and experience lost upon the death of a partner may be difficult to replace; candidates of sufficient ability may hold out for a partnership for themselves. The death of a limited partner does not usually terminate the partnership. It may be necessary, however, for the remaining partners to purchase the interest held by the estate of the deceased partner.

The impact of ill health is not so great as it is in a proprietorship. One partner may become sick, yet the business may continue to operate in a satisfactory manner. Disagreements among the partners, though, may have a detrimental effect on the business. If they do not have the personal funds to buy each other's interest, they may be forced to remain together despite personal disagreements.

Capital

Compared to a proprietorship, the partnership can obviously command more invested capital. Very often partnerships are formed because one party can contribute business leadership and another party has the money to invest. Nevertheless, partnerships are usually confined to fairly small businesses lured by the ease of formation; in fact, many have been formed over coffee at a local café. The limited partnership has the potential to attract large numbers of investors, because shares can be sold on a pro rata basis in much the same way as a corporation sells shares of ownership. Essentially, the limited partners are investors who do not take an active part in running the business. Certain industries such as oil and gas producers and pipelines, leasing, and real estate, have huge limited partnerships run by a general partner that is itself a large corporation, formed primarily for certain tax advantages not available in most other business activities.

With regard to benefits, profits are shared equally by the general partners, unless another agreement has been specifically reached and set down in writing by the partners. There is, however, no restriction as to what agreement may be reached.

One of the attractions to the partnership form is that it does not pay federal income taxes as a business entity; the partners pay individual income taxes on their proportionate shares of partnership income. Therefore, there is no double taxation on business profits, as there is when a corporation pays a tax on its profits and the shareholders pay a tax on their dividends. Thus if the tax savings are retained in the business, the firm may be able to grow more rapidly than a corporation of comparable size.

Liability

All general partners are jointly and severally liable for the debts of the business. This means that every partner has unlimited liability for the debts of the business. Each may also be required to pay the debts even though they were incurred by the general partners. Under the laws of most states, creditors may sue any one partner, as well as the partnership, for the amount owed to them. Because creditors are always looking for the easiest way to collect their money, the partners with the "deep pockets" are the ones most likely to be sued. If made to pay, those partners, in turn, may be legally entitled to recover proportionate shares of this amount from the other partners.

Corporations

General Considerations

The **classic definition of a corporation** was made by U.S. Supreme Court Chief Justice John Marshall (1755–1835). He termed it "*. . . an artificial being, invisible, intangible, and existing only in contemplation of the law.*" A **corporation** *may also be defined as a voluntary association of persons, natural or legal (i.e., other corporations); organized under state or federal law and recognized by the law as being a person, fictitious in character, having a corporate name, and being entirely separate and distinct from the people who own it; having continuous life; and set up for some specified purpose or purposes.*

As a legal institution, the corporation has its roots in the medieval fiefdoms of England. One reason for its establishment was that it could get big things done, undertakings beyond the capacity of individuals or families. The corporation could lure money from the warm folds of a thousand mattresses. In fact, one English corporation, the South Sea (Bubble) Company, attracted and accepted money way beyond the firm's ability to earn a reasonable return with it. Its crash in 1720 so discredited the corporate institution that it was outlawed for nearly a hundred years afterward.

A corporation, being a creature of the state, has no "natural" rights and powers; it has only those granted by law. Thus, the corporation must be organized in accordance with the laws of the state of its domicile. While it is afforded protection as a "person" by our federal Constitution, including its right to engage in interstate commerce, it cannot do business in another state without first getting permission from that state. *A corporation is known as a* **domestic corporation** *in the state in which it is organized; in other states it is considered a* **foreign corporation**. Its powers and purposes are fixed by charter and cannot be changed at will as in the case of an individual or partnership. Such a change as entering into a new type of business or increasing its capitalization—in fact any variation from the rights or powers conferred by its charter—can be effected only by amending that charter in accordance with the laws of its home state. However, most corporate charters are drawn broadly enough so that the need for amendments rarely arises.

For purposes of credit analysis, the financial responsibility is that of the corporation. Nevertheless, the business backgrounds of the principals are an important deciding factor, for they are the conscience of the corporation.

Certificate of Incorporation

The **articles or certificate of incorporation** *includes a description of the powers which the corporation expects to exercise. These are called the* **express powers of the corporation.** In addition, there are certain **implied powers**. *Examples of implied powers include the right to buy and sell real estate when used as a plant location, the right to borrow, the right to have a bank account, and the right to have a corporate seal as part of the corporate signature.*

The corporation is required to comply with the conditions of its charter. Ultra vires acts—those outside the powers of the corporation—are forbidden, and the officers and directors of the corporation may be held personally responsible for such acts. For example, in some states if corporate dividends are paid out of invested capital and not from earnings, the directors and officers may be required to replenish the capital from their personal assets.

Stock

Capital Stock

Stock certificates *issued by a company are evidence of corporate ownership in a proportion of the number of shares held to the total number of shares outstanding.* Some capital stock is issued with a **par value,** *a specific dollar amount that is shown on the face of the stock certificate.* This purports to represent the minimum original investment in cash, property, and services behind each share at the time of the original issue. As a company grows and matures, the par value becomes meaningless except as a historical curiosity.

For that reason, in most cases, the capital stock is authorized with no par value. A stated value is assigned when the stock is sold, which establishes the amount that is entered in a corporation's books as capital. Any funds received in excess of the par or stated value are shown on the books as capital surplus. The presence or lack of par value has no credit significance, nor has the classification of equity investments as capital stock or capital surplus. The most significant number is the total equity.

Common Stock

On the balance sheet, **common stock** *represents all or a portion of the money that was received when the company issued its shares.* The figure has virtually nothing to do with the market price of the shares. These latter prices are fixed by investors buying and selling shares from one another. Common stock represents the basic, and sometimes only, form of ownership in a corporation. By virtue of this ownership, common stockholders have certain rights:

- to vote and thus participate in the selection of directors
- to share in the profits of the business by receiving dividends if and when declared by the directors
- to share in the distribution of assets should a company be dissolved

In addition, state laws, the charter, or both can give another right (called the **preemptive right**), *which prevents dilution of stockholders' equity without their consent*—that is, the right to purchase new stock in proportion to the stockholder's holdings at the time of a new issue. This ownership is in effect a semi-permanent investment, as common stockholders are not entitled to any distribution of earnings or assets until the respective prior claims of preferred stockholders, if any, have been satisfied. If there is no preferred or other special class of stock, common stock and capital stock are synonymous. Because this class of stock frequently has all the voting power, if it is concentrated in just a few hands, the credit executive should be interested in determining who actually controls the common stock. Closely held corporations have the potential to be drained of value by the payment of excessive salaries, rent, interest, and dividends to those who control them. Creditors can often protect themselves by obtaining the personal guarantees of the principals. Occasionally, an organization may have established more than one class of common stock, maintaining voting rights in only one class, but permitting equal participation by both classes in dividends and giving each class equal rights in liquidation. There is a large variety of capital stock, much of it arising out of complex negotiations in mergers and acquisitions.

A common measure of the financial operation of a business is its earnings per share of common stock. Regular high earnings enhance the market value of the stock, for dividends are paid out of accumulated earnings. Dividend yield is expressed as a percentage of the dividend to the market price of the stock. Thus, a $5 annual dividend payment on a share that has a market value of $100 would constitute a yield of 5 percent. *The percentage of earnings distributed to common stockholders in the form of dividends is known as the* **payout ratio**. Accordingly, a company is deemed to have a 50 percent payout ratio if it earns $10 per share and pays a dividend of $5 per share. The lower the payout ratio, the greater the amount of earnings a company retains in the business to improve its financial condition and finance its growth.

Preferred Stock

As implied in the title, holders of preferred shares enjoy certain preferences over common shareholders. These normally include:

- the payment of dividends and assets in liquidation
- sometimes voting, convertibility, and redemption preferences

Dividends

Preferred stock *almost always provides for a fixed dividend, which must be paid before a distribution is made to common stockholders.* This is not an automatic dividend, because it is paid out of profits. Dividend preference may be cumulative or noncumulative, and participating or nonparticipating. The offset to the investor for the preferred treatment afforded this stock is the fixed dividend. Most investors in the stock market bank heavily on future growth. There is no growth attached to the preferred stock dividend because no matter how prosperous the business, that dividend will not increase. With **cumulative preferred stock**, *dividends not paid when due accumulate and must be paid in full before any common stock dividend is paid.* Under **noncumulative preferred**, *the preferred dividend is lost if not paid.* This is less desirable from the viewpoint of the preferred stockholder. A special form of preferred stock is the **participating preferred stock** *which is entitled to dividends in excess of those stipulated in the charter.* The most popular form is to permit the preferred to share further dividend distributions with the common after both have received their stipulated rate. *Where the stock is* **nonparticipating, or straight preferred**, *no additional dividend over the contract rate is received by the holders.*

Assets in Liquidation

After claims of all creditors have been paid in full, preferred stockholders are entitled to receive the full par value of their shares before distribution is made to common stockholders.

The priority granted to preferred shareholders in dividend payments and liquidations is more apparent than real. If a company is experiencing trouble and profits are not sufficient to pay common stock dividends, it is seldom adequate to pay preferred dividends either. Likewise in liquidation, any payment to stockholders is likely to be moot, for it's a rare dissolution that generates enough cash to pay administrative costs and all the creditors, never mind anyone else.

Voting

Unless the charter provides otherwise, preferred stockholders have the same voting rights as common stockholders. In actual practice, the charter usually denies the preferred stockholders such voting power or limits it so long as the affairs of the company are conducted in a satisfactory manner.

Convertibility

Preferred stock sometimes has the right to convert (usually into common stock) at the option of the holder, and at a conversion ratio fixed at the time the stock was issued. This is of little consequence to credit executives, for debt claims precede both types of stock.

Redemption

Preferred stock may be redeemable after a certain period at the option of the corporation. Since the late 1970s the **"sinking fund preferred" stock** has become somewhat popular. *The issuing company promises to buy back or redeem the preferred stock at some fixed time in the future.* This provision creates a paradox for creditors. Outstanding preferred stock, because it is part of equity, provides a cushion for creditors. But if the issue has a buy–back or sinking fund provision, that cushion will be systematically reduced in the future.

Continuity

Nearly every corporation is granted a charter in perpetuity. The corporation survives the death of any principal. New talents and new financing may be necessary, but the surviving management generally has time to find them. The credit executive must keep an eye on the situation, but it is not like having the problems that arise during a forced liquidation of a proprietorship or partnership.

Notwithstanding a liberal charter, all corporations, like the people who create them, are mortal; they are born, they have their season, and they pass from the scene. There are some notable exceptions, but it's a rare firm that lasts a century. Responsibility for the overall performance of a corporation is vested in the board of directors; the stockholders elect the board at the annual meeting.

The board selects the officers who manage the corporation, set their salaries, decide policy, and have an oversight responsibility for the conduct of the business. This arrangement creates a sharp division between those who own the corporation and those who run it. The significance to creditors is twofold: The business is able to hire expert help in marketing, production, and financial management, in short be run by professionals. There is less likelihood of the corporate wealth being siphoned off for the personal benefit of the owners. Moreover, even though shares of ownership may change hands, the creditor has an amount owing from the same debtor—the corporation. The relationship of the parties is not changed by the buying and selling of the common stock.

Capital

Because a corporation can issue stock, it usually has a larger potential source of capital for operations and expansion than the other forms of organization. In addition, shares of stock in a corporation can be bought and sold by shareholders without any effect on its capital structure. This permits a continuity of operation and financial strength. That stability, so important to creditors of the corporation, can be jeopardized if one individual or family owns a majority of the shares. Such a situation is more akin to a proprietorship or partnership in that there is a potential for enriching the controlling shareholder at the expense of the company.

The corporation, being a legal entity, is required to pay taxes on its earnings in addition to those paid by its stockholders on the corporate dividend payments.

Liability

The stockholders have limited liability for the debts of the corporation. This liability is restricted to the amount each stockholder has invested. When the amount invested is equal to the par value of the stock, it is designated as fully paid and nonassessable. Most states prohibit a corporation from issuing shares for less than par value (not fully paid for). Any amount owing for common stock is treated much like an account receivable. The stockholder is liable for the unpaid balance if the corporation becomes insolvent and the money is needed to pay creditors.

Despite the fact that stockholders may limit the amount of money they invest in a business, a creditor may ask the principals to guarantee or endorse the business obligations. Thus, the capital funds available for creditor protection may be larger than they would appear to be to the casual observer. Before a principal is asked for a guarantee or endorsement, however, the creditor should ascertain whether there are tangible assets to support the personal guarantee. If not, there may still be some psychological value to the guarantee; a businessperson facing the decline of his or her company will likely have an incentive to first pay off those debts subject to guarantees. Should a bankruptcy ensue, such a pay-off might be judged a preference. Any creditor can request a guarantee, and once a principal gives it to one creditor it may make little difference to him or her to do the same for any or all of the others.

The legal procedure for forming a corporation is more detailed and complicated than that required for a partnership or proprietorship. In addition, the corporation is subject to more control by state and federal governments, especially if it intends to offer its stock to the investing public. Much information, not normally obtainable from the partnership and the proprietorship, is filed with regulatory bodies. Such information is available to the public and can be readily obtained from data services companies. This gives the credit executive an additional source of facts about customer accounts.

Much has been done by the credit profession and others to promote the adoption of the Uniform Commercial Code among the several states. Nevertheless, the rights of a creditor are not the same in every state. For a full description of those rights, see such references as the *Manual of Credit and Commercial Laws*.

S Corporations

General Considerations

S Corporations were formerly known as **Subchapter S corporations**. *In 1958 some of the tax advantages enjoyed by proprietorships and partnerships were granted to small, newly formed corporations.* This came about with the passage of the Technical Amendments Act, which modified the federal income tax laws to permit such corporations to be taxed as the individuals who owned or controlled them. The Tax Reform Act of 1976 gave shareholders of these pseudo corporations a variety of new benefits. In legislation passed in 1985, the allowable number of shareholders was increased to 35.

Continuity

The life span of an S Corporation is the same as that for other corporations provided it meets certain requirements. It must have been organized in the United States and not be a member of an affiliated group of corporations responsible to a common parent. It must also meet these additional requirements:

- the corporation has no more than 35 stockholders
- stockholders must be individuals, estates, or one of the following types of trusts:
- a **revocable trust**, *which is one that is set up and owned by the grantor*
- a **voting trust**, *in which each beneficiary is counted a separate shareholder in computing the maximum number allowed*
- a **testamentary trust** *that holds the pseudo corporation stock for not more than 60 days*
- the individuals must be U.S. citizens or resident aliens

Every co–owner, tenant by the entirety, tenant in common, and joint tenant is considered a shareholder when counting the total number. If husband and wife are treated as one stockholder because of the form of ownership, the death of either husband or wife or both will not change the number of stockholders, providing the stock continues to be held by their estates in the same proportion as before death.

The S Corporation must earn 75 percent or more of its gross income from its normal business function. If a company's passive earnings, such as rent, interest, royalties, dividends, or capital gains, exceed 25 percent for three consecutive years, the S Corporation status will be terminated. In the meantime, such earnings exceeding 25 percent are subject to the corporate income tax. When an S Corporation is created, every stockholder must agree to have the corporation taxed as individuals. When a new shareholder is added, however, this consent is not needed.

Capital

The net income of an S Corporation is divided into two general classes: that distributed to stockholders; that retained in the business. The distributed yearly income from the corporation is taxed to the stockholders based on the amount each receives. Undistributed income is taxed to the stockholders based on the percentage of ownership. Undistributed income from prior years' earnings, for which the owners have previously paid personal income tax, can be distributed in later years to the stockholders without any tax liability. The credit executive can determine the amount of the available undistributed income by reviewing the capital section of the balance sheet. Where a corporation previously operated as a taxable corporation and had retained earnings not previously taxed to the stockholders, the balance sheet will distinguish between retained earnings and undistributed income.

Because S Corporations usually pay out profits each year, the net worth tends to remain the same, but cash funds may eventually be depleted. These funds are often used by the stockholders to pay their personal income taxes on distributed and undistributed earnings. In some cases, however, the stockholders will pay their personal income taxes and return any remaining cash to the business as a loan. With such a practice, stockholder loans will grow and *the relationship of debt to equity* (which is referred to as **leverage**) will deteriorate.

Liability

An **S Corporation** *is a corporation in all respects, except that the federal income taxes are paid by the stockholders rather than the corporation.* Likewise, any losses sustained by an S Corporation pass to the shareholders and can be used as deductions from other business income the stockholder may have on their personal tax returns. These losses are based on the percentage of stockholders' ownership and are limited to the total sum of the stockholders' investments in and loans made to the corporation.

From the creditor's point of view, shareholders of an S Corporation have the same immunity from business debts as any other shareholder. If their loans to the corporation become inordinately high, creditors should consider obtaining a subordination agreement or an assignment of the stockholders' loans receivable. Personal guarantees from the stockholders would also lend credit support. Of course, an alternative would be for shareholders to reinvest the profits.

Estates

Proprietorships—Continuity

The operation of a business by an estate is normally of short duration. *It is the* **duty of the executor** *to take possession of the assets of the decedent, pay the expenses of administra-*

tion and the claim of creditors, and dispose of the balance of the estate in accordance with the decedent's will. If there is no will, the administrator will do the same in accordance with the laws of the state governing the distribution of the decedent's estate. In such a case, it is also possible for a creditor, or a group of creditors, to apply for and receive letters of administration. Of course, a creditor that becomes the representative of the estate must administer, not only for his or her own benefit, but for the benefit of all interested parties. A creditor so proceeding is entitled to receive, in addition to its claim, the ordinary commissions and fees which the law allows.

Capital

If a significant amount of money is owed by an estate–run business, a creditor should verify that the assets are properly classified as business or personal and that they are not dispersed prematurely. The creditor should also be satisfied that the executor or administrator is qualified to manage the disposition of the estate. Unless the decedent's will provides otherwise, the executor must be bonded in the amount the court may direct; in the case of an administrator, a bond is always required.

Liability

Under the laws of most states, the representative, who may be either the executor or administrator, is required either to advertise for claims or to notify creditors to present their claims on or before a specified date. In some states, no such notice is required although creditors must file their claims within a time prescribed by law after the appointment of the representative.

Once a creditor determines that a customer has died, steps should be taken promptly to file a claim with the representative, without waiting for some official notice. Except for possible procedural difficulties and delay, the death of a debtor generally does not affect the validity of a debt. Where a debt has been reduced to judgment prior to death and has become a lien on real or personal property, the lien of the judgment generally continues as if death had not intervened.

Death usually does not shorten the applicable statute of limitations with respect to unsecured claims; in most cases, the time allowed to enforce collection is extended for a short period of time to enable creditors to assert their claims against the estate. Mere written notice by the creditor to the representative of the estate generally suffices to stop the running of the statute of limitations without the necessity of instituting legal proceedings. Where written notice is given to the representative and the claim is acknowledged, the creditor need do nothing further, since the claim will generally be paid after the account has been audited or confirmed by the court.

If, after the passage of a **statutory period of time** (*from six months to one year in most states*), the representative has not paid the creditor nor filed an account for audit or confirmation by the court, a creditor may institute proceedings to compel the payment of the account.

If a creditor has given written notice of its claim and it is denied or disputed by the representative, the creditor must submit the claim directly to the court. Unless the creditor is prepared to prove the claim at the time of audit or institute legal proceedings against the representative, the claim will be barred.

Limited Liability Companies (LLCs)

General Considerations

Limited liability companies, or LLCs, are a rather recent development in the United States, having first come into existence in this country in 1977 in Wyoming. *The basic concept of the* **LLC** *is that an unincorporated business association which desires to do business under the corporate structure may do so by combining the benefits of a traditional C corporation and a partnership.* The designation C corporation is that given for tax purposes only to the "ordinary" corporation as one is familiar with and used to dealing with. Like an "ordinary" or C corporation, the members of LLCs (similar to stockholders) enjoy limited liability. At the same time, a properly structured LLC avoids the double taxation of C corporations, and, therefore, enjoys the pass-through tax advantages of a partnership. LLCs are different from S Corporations in several ways:

- LLCs are not limited to a specific number of shareholders.
- They are not restrictive in the type of individuals who can hold an interest in the association or the amount of interest the association can hold in another corporation.
- The Internal Revenue Service has imposed strict limitations upon S Corporations as to when the election to become an S Corporation can be made, and when and how it can, or must be eliminated.

Throughout all of the discussion of LLCs, the credit executive should be constantly aware of the fact that LLCs are creatures created for tax advantages only and, by and large, do not differ in the overall corporate structure for those extending credit. They receive a distinct advantage when dealing with an LLC in that because it avoids the double taxation of corporate profits it could use more of its revenues to satisfy debts of creditors.

States Authorizing LLCs

Prior to 1988, LLCs had been authorized in just two states: Wyoming and Florida. The reluctance of states to enact LLC legislation and of businesses to enter into LLCs, even if available, stems from the question of whether or not the companies would retain the tax advantages of a partnership. This reluctance was more on the part of those already enjoying tax advantages of the partnership which would convert to an LLC, rather than traditional C corporations considering conversion. Every state, except Vermont, has adopted limited liability company legislation.

In 1988, the Internal Revenue Service issued Revenue Ruling 88–76, which held that an LLC organized under the Wyoming law would be seen as a partnership for federal taxation purposes, though an LLC must still meet certain federal standards to retain this tax status. With the basis for the tax benefits of an LLC thus being solidified by the Internal Revenue Service, states moved quickly to enact appropriate legislation.

How an LLC Is Formed

The advantage of the LLC is that it possesses both the limited liability of a corporation for the benefit of its members, and the tax advantages of a partnership. If one were to lose the tax advantages present in a properly structured LLC, there would be virtually no use of an LLC as opposed to a traditional C corporation. In order to retain the tax status of a partnership, an LLC must conform to certain requirements set out in the federal law. Credit executives should be familiar with these requirements, as the failure of a customer that is an LLC to comply with these standards could create a substantial adverse tax impact which could seriously impair the entity's ability to pay its debts to its trade creditors. It is for that reason that the requirements are listed here: In 25 CFR 301.7701-2(a)(1), the federal government has outlined the six characteristics found in "pure corporations". They are:

- associates
- an objective to carry on business and to divide the gains therefrom
- continuity of life "of the entity"
- centralized management
- limited liability
- free transferability of assets

To be considered a partnership for federal taxation purposes, the Internal Revenue Service requires a business association, like an LLC, to possess more non-corporate than corporate characteristics. Since the government has acknowledged that the first two characteristics above are found in both partnerships and corporations, one uses the remaining four characteristics to determine tax status. In other words, an LLC must not possess more than two of the characteristics of continuity of life, centralized management, limited liability and free transferability of assets.

Because one of the primary purposes of forming an LLC is to retain limited liability, one can usually assume this characteristic will be present in an LLC, although it is not necessary. This leaves the LLC with the ability to utilize only one of the remaining three characteristics. In order to gain the full benefit of an LLC, it must be carefully structured to avoid having two of these remaining three characteristics.

Retention of Partnership Status

There are three specific ways one can avoid possessing the three characteristics that can tip the balance toward being more of a corporation and less of a partnership:

- *Continuity of Life.* If the LLC is structured so that other members of the association must agree to continue the LLC or it will be dissolved upon the withdrawal or removal of any member, it will be considered not to possess continuity of life.
- *Free Transferability of Assets.* If the LLC is structured so that a member may not transfer any non-economic rights without the consent of all of the other members, it will be considered not to possess free transferability of assets. This means that there must be a clear restriction on the transfer of membership interests, which can be a positive or a negative for the credit grantor.

- *Centralized Management.* It is known that more than than 20 percent of equity must be represented in the management in order for an LLC not to possess centralized management. Due to the relatively new nature of LLCs in this country, it is not clear at this time how much equity must be involved to avoid this characteristic. This further creates problems with subsidiary entities that wish to be part of a consolidated tax return where an 80 percent stock ownership is required.

A properly structured LLC will avoid at least two of these three characteristics. If it does so, it will probably retain the past or retained tax benefits of a partnership, while permitting its members to enjoy the limited liability of a traditional corporation.

Considerations for Creditors

At first blush, an unsecured creditor dealing with an LLC would seem to think that dealing with an LLC would be no different than dealing with an ordinary corporation. In most instances this is true, as absent a personal guaranty from one of the principals, the creditor could only look to the assets of the corporation to satisfy its obligations. In general, an LLC has the authority to conduct business, enter into contracts, and transact any type of business in accordance with its bylaws just as if it were a C corporation. There are, however, some considerations which should be reviewed when dealing with an LLC:

- Usually, LLCs are startup operations and are not part of an established group of entities.
- While there are tax advantages for both profits and losses, the pass-through of losses to the members is a very distinct advantage.
- Many times, when it is assumed that the entity will be losing money in its early stages, the LLC structure (or an S Corporation) is chosen to maximize the tax benefits of the losses for those involved on an individual basis.

Thus, when dealing with an LLC, creditors should recognize that there may be an anticipation of losses by those who have formed the entity. Even though the corporation itself will escape tax liability as it will be "imposed" upon the members, a creditor must assume that provisions for these taxes will be somehow made by way of distributions to the members. Careful review of the annual financial statement of an LLC entity should be undertaken to make sure that cash is not removed at such a rate which, while satisfying the tax obligations of the members, depletes the entity of cash needed in order to carry out its functions and pay its creditors in the ordinary course of business. If the principals of an LLC will not provide a credit grantor with personal guaranties, consideration should be given to securing a subordination agreement from the members that provides that the LLC may not distribute income to them unless and until the debts due to the credit grantor are current.

In many instances, this can have an even greater impact upon the individuals involved than would a personal guaranty. By selective monitoring of the financial statements of the entity, the credit grantor can keep in touch with the situation, and make sure that the provisions are being honored. If a substantial amount of credit is being extended, it may be wise to receive an opinion from the legal or accounting professional for the LLC that it has been properly structured in order to receive the tax advantages. Were the LLC to anticipate the tax benefits but not receive them because of improper structuring, this could create a serious tax burden on the entity, which could interfere with the cash flow needed to pay debts in the ordinary course of business.

There is no reason or prohibition why a creditor cannot seek such an opinion from the legal or tax professional of a substantial customer. Indeed, the reluctance to provide one could signal the possibility of a problem.

Special Tax Exceptions

While most states will view an LLC as a partnership for state taxes when properly structured, at least two states (Florida and Texas) view LLCs as corporations for state taxes. In this minority of states, LLCs may lose some of their appeal as a pass-through tax entity, since they may be at a federal level, and not at the state level. The law on LLCs is new and quickly evolving. In this area, one should consult state law, if appropriate, to determine if there will be any impact.

Common Law Trusts

General Considerations

This form of organization, also referred to as a Massachusetts trust or business trust, has been used in England for centuries. Here it was first used extensively in Massachusetts and has since been recognized and used throughout the United States. In some states, notably Texas, it has been regarded more as a partnership than a common law trust. Unlike the corporation, the powers of the common law trust are not generally derived from statutory law. They come rather from the trust agreement, subject to the rules that govern trusts generally. *It is formed by agreement between owners of property (or a business) and a trustee or group of trustees.*

The beneficiaries are issued trust certificates proportionate to their interests. The trustees hold legal title to all of the property of the business, and manage its affairs. Some of their powers may at times be delegated to one of their number, though the trustees normally function as a unit. The certificate holders, or shareholders of beneficial interest as they are sometimes called, participate proportionately in the income from the trust. They also share proportionately in the proceeds when the trust is dissolved, much the same as the partners in a partnership do.

Continuity

Depending upon the agreement creating it, a trust may continue for a specified duration, or may intend a perpetual existence. The death of a certificate holder does not cause a dissolution of the common law trust. The share passes through the estate of the deceased in much the same way as a share of corporate stock.

Capital

The capital of the common law trust is equal to the value of the property transferred to the trustees. Profits are generally distributed at the end of the fiscal period. For purposes of credit appraisal, the credit executive should obtain a balance sheet, income statement, and statement of cash flows, as with any other type of business. Initially, the common law trust was not required to pay income taxes; instead the beneficiaries paid personal income taxes on their proportionate earnings distributions. This advantage has been reduced over the years, and the common law trust has increasingly been taxed as a corporation.

Liability

Primarily, the credit executive will be interested in determining the liability of the beneficiaries for the debts of the business. In most cases where a trust has been organized, the certificate holders are protected from claims over and above the extent of their investments. The principal exception occurs when the beneficiary is shown to have a voice in the affairs of management. In those states where the common law trust is treated like a partnership, the certificate holders are not exempt from personal liability for debts. The creditor can then act as it normally would against a partnership.

Trustees are held accountable for the fiduciary affairs of the common law trust. They are accountable to the certificate holders for the property entrusted to them and for any loss due to misconduct or mismanagement. In acting with third parties, the trustees are liable personally for their commitments unless they have been absolved from this responsibility by agreement with the party with which they have made a contract.

In dealing with common law trusts, it is important for the creditor to know how that entity is viewed by the courts in the states where merchandise is to be shipped, as well as the state where the headquarters of the trust is located.

Joint Ventures

General Considerations

A **joint venture** *(also called syndicate) is a combination of two or more persons (including corporations) formed to undertake a specific, and usually large, contract or project.* Often the transaction is too large in scope to be handled by any one of the venturers alone. For example, a large construction job or a public offering of securities or a large real estate transaction might be undertaken by a joint venture.

Participants often bring unique resources to the group, such as technical knowledge, capital, ability to negotiate for the business with the proper persons, competent personnel to handle the work, and sources of materials which are needed to meet the contract specifications. Occasionally a firm will form a joint venture to develop a new product that is only partially within the range of their own expertise.

For credit analysis purposes, a joint venture is similar to a partnership. It is defined in case law as "an association of two or more persons (corporations) to carry out a single business enterprise for profit, for which purpose they combine their property, money, effects, skill, and knowledge." In general, a creditor dealing with a joint venture can presume that the venturers can bind each other to contracts that are "reasonably necessary to carry on the business" they have undertaken. If the credit extended is for products or services that are not normally associated with the joint venture project, or if the amounts of credit involved are very large, the credit executive would do well to get legal assistance in analyzing the liability of the parties.

Continuity

The continuity of the joint venture is fairly well established by the length of time it will take to complete the transaction as specified in the contract. A contract drawn properly will bind the co-venturers to meet the obligations of the joint venture, either together or individually, if one or the other fails to perform. Naturally, when the project is completed the presumption is that co-venturers can no longer bind each other to an extension of credit.

Capital

The capital available to the joint venture includes all resources of the co-venturers, in a technical sense. It is usual for the venture to keep a separate set of books. In that way, the assets committed to the contract are segregated. Similarly, the creditor should set up a separate account for sales to the joint venture.

Liability

As mentioned above, co-venturers are usually held jointly and severally liable for the debts of the joint venture. However, there are some states where a different interpretation is given. In these states, the creditor may encounter difficulty in establishing that the co-venturers are individually liable for all debts of the joint venture. In such cases the credit executive might ask the joint venture to state in writing who is liable for what.

Where the liability of the co-venturers is established, it is important to know the financial strength of the parties. A co-venturer that is not a good credit risk in other business transactions is not likely to be a better risk just because it entered into a joint venture. In such an instance, the credit position of the other co-venturers would weigh heavily in the overall analysis of the combination.

Other Forms of Organizations

Cooperative Societies

This form of organization is not usually encountered by the credit department, except in such industries as lumber, groceries, and dairy products. **Cooperative societies** *are organizations of mutual help and betterment, formed when individuals or corporate businesses combine their financial, capital, and other resources to advance their particular trade or industry.* By this combination, they seek to obtain marketing and/or purchasing advantages. Savings are distributed to the membership periodically in the form of a patronage dividend, dependent upon each member's participation during the dividend period.

Methods by which cooperative societies obtain funds for their operation may vary from one state to another, or may be specified in the charter or bylaws of the society if not restricted by state law. Similarly, the liabilities of the officers, directors, and membership of the society may vary, as may the circumstances which affect its legal life. In general, cooperative societies are not heavily financed. Members may be small producers, such as dairy farmers, or even consumers who join a supermarket cooperative.

The extension of credit should be based on balance sheet numbers and member support as indicated by the "profits" earned.

Not-For-Profit or Nonprofit Organizations

The designation, not–for–profit, is recognized for certain organizations by the Internal Revenue Service. **Not-for-profit organizations** *may be either corporations or associations.* They are often formed to carry out work or business as a service to the community rather than for profit.

Capital for the operation may come from governments, charitable endowments, social service agencies, as well as fees for goods and services furnished to their constituents. Like for–profit businesses they prepare financial statements which can guide creditors in their dealings with them. They are not normally seekers of large credit; many, in fact, do not spend money until they have it.

Other Features of Organizations

General Considerations

In addition to knowing the legal form of customers, the credit executive is often asked to appraise the credit significance of organizational changes. Some of the more frequent situations are:

- principals of one business are also principals of another, and there may be many transactions between them
- changes being made in legal composition, as when a proprietorship becomes a corporation
- one company having its operations split into one or more divisions using separate names
- two or more businesses merging or consolidating, or one corporation acquiring another

In each instance, these actions could affect the creditworthiness of the customer. It may be advisable to determine the effect of these changes on the financial strength and credit position of the accounts. Generally, if no additional borrowing is required for these changes, the financial condition will not suffer. Should outside borrowing be necessary, however, another look at the credit position is in order.

In any case the credit executive should determine if the change is brought about by favorable circumstances, such as a growth in business, or something unfavorable, such as a decline in market strength and profitability.

Affiliated Interests

A person is said to have **affiliated interests** *when he or she is a principal in more than one company.* If each of these businesses is incorporated, they are all separate entities even though they may provide similar goods and services to their customers. Thus, a person may control a number of stores selling the same type of goods, yet each is a separate corporation. Legally, the assets of one store are not available for payment of the others' debts. Further, the individual's personal assets are also insulated from the debts of each corporation.

The credit executive should examine the financial statements of each corporation dealt with. Any weaknesses found may be cured by getting one or more of the affiliated corporations to guarantee the debts of the weaker one. Affiliated interests are also important because they provide a more complete picture of the principal's character and capability. An unfavorable business record can often be uncovered by investigating the affiliates of a new concern.

Changes in Legal Composition

One of the more complex problems faced in credit analysis is a change in the legal composition of an account. A business often progresses from proprietorship to partnership to the corporate form. As the benefits of the various legal forms become better known, changes are made to take advantage of them. In a business succession, the exact details of the change should be determined. The following examples are three situations that may appear similar on the surface, but have differing ramifications to creditors. They demonstrate why further questioning is necessary when a partnership is succeeded by a corporation:

- The corporation is formed. It then purchases the assets of the partnership and assumes its liabilities. In exchange for their proportionate holdings in the old partnership, the partners receive shares of stock in the new corporation.
- The corporation is formed. The partnership is then liquidated and the partners receive a pro rata distribution of the proceeds of liquidation. They then invest their funds in the new corporation for shares of stock.
- The corporation is formed. After the partnership is dissolved, the partners invest only a portion of the proceeds of liquidation in exchange for shares of stock in the new corporation.

From the viewpoint of credit analysis, three different situations are described above. In the first, there is no change in the net worth of the business. The change from the creditor's point of view is that a new corporate customer has come into being. However, the former partners have now insulated their personal assets from the claims of business creditors.

In the second situation, the new business is formed independently of the old partnership's liquidation. There, the partnership would pay all outstanding obligations before it could dissolve. Although there is now limited liability on the part of the principals, there has been no change in net worth or financial strength of the business, provided the principals do indeed take the cash they will have in hand and invest it in the corporation as planned.

The third situation reflects a complete change in the form of organization, in the liability of the principals, and in the financial strength of the business. By deciding to invest only a portion of the assets in the new corporation, the principals have kept out some of their interest in the old partnership.

It is not unusual for a business to be incorporated under the circumstances of the third illustration. The details are often left to the accountant and attorney. Consequently, the creditors may not be readily aware of the specific change nor of its effect on the financial condition of the concern. When a succession takes place, a typical incident that often confronts a credit executive is the following: In answer to a question on the ownership change, the principal may reply, "Yes, we have incorporated, but there is no other change in the business." This information can be misleading and may cause the credit executive to make an unjustified favorable appraisal of the account. It is always good practice to obtain the financial statements of the newly formed corporation. Any changes in equity or debt or the cash position should then be apparent.

Parent–Subsidiary Relationships

A corporation which owns more than 50 percent of the stock of another corporation is said to be the **parent of its subsidiary**. Thus, subsidiaries may be partly owned or wholly owned. In the eyes of the law, the parent and its subsidiary are generally considered as separate entities, with no intercompany liability for debts. It is therefore important to find out if any debts of the subsidiary have been guaranteed by its parent. Should that be the case, they represent a contingent liability claim on the parent's assets which may not be reflected on the parent's financial statement.

Under special circumstances, the parent and its subsidiary have been ruled by the courts to be one organization. These cases have been decided on their individual merits, however, and do not fit in with the usual parent–subsidiary relationships. They have to be proved in court with the burden of proof on the creditor to show that, in effect, the subsidiary was an instrumentality of the parent and that the separate corporate indentures were ignored. This is normally very difficult to do. The safer approach is to regard the subsidiary as a separate entity and to rely upon analysis of its financial condition for appraisal of credit risk. Naturally, if the parent will guarantee the obligations of the subsidiary, the credit task is diminished (assuming of course, that the financial condition of the parent makes its guarantee meaningful).

One of the touchiest situations for a credit manager is where a giant corporation sets up an operating subsidiary with virtually no equity, and that subsidiary seeks credit. To ask the parent for a guarantee, which may involve getting approval from the giant company's board of directors, may appear ludicrous. In the majority of cases the parent corporation will stand behind the debts of the subsidiary, but every now and then we are reminded that if serious money is at stake, a giant corporation may cut loose the subsidiary and wrap itself in the corporate veil.

Operating Divisions

A credit executive who approves sales to a division of a customer need not analyze the division as a separate entity. A **division** *is an internal arrangement of a corporation made for the convenience of its management.* It does not affect the legal status of the corporation. Thus, there is no separation of credit liability.

Mergers or Consolidations

Mergers and consolidations *are statutory procedures regulated by state law. They involve the complete integration of corporate entities, not just their assets and liabilities.* In a merger of two corporations, the shares of stock in one company are exchanged by their holders for shares in the other, which will be the survivor corporation. The absorbed corporation files a certificate of succession and its files are assimilated by the survivor. The liabilities of the absorbed corporation are in effect taken over by the survivor corporation.

A consolidation is a somewhat different procedure. A new corporation is formed. The shares of the corporations that are to be consolidated are exchanged for shares in the newly formed corporation. Certificates of succession are filed by the corporations that will discontinue. Their files are absorbed by the brand new corporation. Here, the liabilities of the old corporations are assumed by the new one.

The credit executive must determine what factors have been brought into the credit situation by the consolidation or merger of the two or more companies. New capital resources may be available; new or different principals may be in control; there is a new legal responsibility. In the consolidation, the creditor must look to the reorganized corporation for payment of debts existing before the change took place. The combination of facilities in the new organization may broaden the potential for expanded operations.

Purchase of Assets

This type of transaction between two corporations does not affect their positions as separate and unrelated concerns. Any assets may be purchased, though usually it will be inventory, fixed assets, or intangibles such as methods, processes, or patents. The purchase of assets is a private contract, and a variety of terms may be specified by the buyer and the seller. If assets are sold subject to liabilities, the purchaser assumes the secured debts on the assets bought. Such assumption, however, does not relieve the seller of his or her obligation to the creditor. Assets may also be sold net, in which case the seller pays any obligations from the proceeds of the sale. From the creditors' viewpoint, there is no change in the legal form of either corporation. The sale or purchase may affect their financial condition, but the two companies remain separate and unrelated.

Creditors of the selling companies have these further protections: If securities of the purchasing corporation are taken instead of cash, a creditor of the selling company can proceed against such securities if any judgment is unpaid. If the selling company goes bankrupt, its assets may be sold by the trustee with the approval of the court. If the assets purchased are subject to any outstanding obligations on them, the new owner is also responsible to the creditors of the original owner. Any purchaser of all or a substantial part of a firm's inventory assets is subject to Article 6 of the Uniform Commercial Code—Bulk Transfers—and must notify creditors that the purchase is being made. This refers to the transfer of a major part of inventory outside the ordinary course of business. A transfer of a substantial part of equipment is also a bulk transfer if it is made in conjunction with a bulk transfer of inventory, but not otherwise.

Comprehension Check

1. Why does a credit manager need to be concerned with what form of business a debtor is?
2. What factors does a credit manager need to consider when dealing with a proprietorship?
3. Define the term partnership.
4. Describe the differences between a general partnership, limited partnership and silent partnership.
5. Define the term corporation.
6. What is common stock?
7. What is preferred stock?
8. To what extent do stockholders have liability for the debts of a corporation?
9. List the requirements of an S corporation.
10. How does an LLC differ from an S corporation?
11. List the six characteristics of a "pure corporation."
12. Define the term joint venture.
13. Briefly discuss the relationship between a parent corporation and its subsidiary.
14. What is an operating division?

9 The Uniform Commercial Code

Overview

Laws governing sales began in England when merchants developed the law of merchants or a system of rules, customs and usages which regulated their transactions. Eventually, the law of merchants was combined with British common law. By 1882, the English Bills of Exchange Act was adopted by the British Parliament, followed by the Sale of Goods Act in 1893.

Using these two English laws as an example, two sets of laws were created by the National Conference of Commissioners on Uniform State Laws in the United States: the Uniform Negotiable Instruments Act (1896) and the Uniform Sales Act (1906). Other laws relating to commercial transactions were also created in the early 1900s such as the Uniform Warehouse Receipts Act (1906), the Uniform Stock Transfer Act (1909), the Uniform Bills of Lading Act (1909), the Uniform Conditional Sales Act (1918) and the Uniform Trust Receipts Act (1933). By the mid-1900s, it became clear that these various laws needed revision to keep current with business and to be integrated into one set of laws.

In 1942, the Uniform Commercial Code was designed as a joint project between the American Law Institute and the National Conference of Commissioners. It took ten years for the appointed editorial board and drafting committees to produce an official text, which underwent several revisions. Today, the Permanent Editorial Board (PEB) for the UCC is the body responsible for the uniformity of enactment and construction of the UCC and for evaluating and preparing proposals for amendment of the UCC.

The UCC is not federal law; each state adopts the Code. Pennsylvania was the first state to adopt the Uniform Commercial Code in 1954, and Louisiana is the only state that has not adopted the Code in its entirety. The Code applies to sales made in the District of Columbia and in the Virgin Islands, but it is not valid for sales made in Puerto Rico.

The basic premise on which the **Uniform Commercial Code** *is based is that commercial transactions is a single subject of the law, involving the sale of and payment for goods.* A single transaction may involve a contract for the sale of goods followed by a sale, which is the subject of Article 2 of the UCC. Article 2: Sales replaced the former Uniform Sales Act. The transaction may involve the giving of a check or draft, which will ultimately pass through one or more banks for collection, for all or part of the purchase price. This is the subject of Article 3: Commercial Paper and Article 4: Bank Deposits and Collections. Transactions made using letters of credit are covered in Article 5: Letters of Credit. If the goods are shipped or stored, the sale may be covered by a bill of lading or warehouse receipt or both. These transactions are covered by Article 7: Documents of Title. Because the transaction can involve not only a contract for the sale of goods followed by a sale, the giving of a check or draft for part of the purchase price but also the acceptance of some type of security for the balance, Article 9—Secured Transactions was created. *The concept of the* **UCC** *is to cover every phase of commerce involved in the sale and payment of goods.*

Learning Objectives

After reading this chapter, the reader should understand:

- The history of the UCC
- Article 2: Sales
- Article 2A: Leases
- Article 6: Bulk Sales
- Article 9: Secured Transactions

Chapter Outline

I. A Brief Guide to the UCC
II. Article 2: Sales
    A. Title
    B. Risk of Loss
    C. Reclamation Clause
    D. Warranties
III. Article 2A: Leases
    A. General Default

IV. Article 6: Bulk Sales
   A. Creditors' Actions
V. Article 9: Secured Transactions
   A. Security Interest
   B. Attachment
   C. Records Search
   D. Perfection
   E. Priority of Security Interests
   F. Credit Analysis of Secured Debtors

A Brief Guide to the UCC

The UCC is divided into nine articles and extends over the laws of sales, negotiable instruments, bank deposits and collections, letters of credit, bulk sales, documents of title, investment securities, and secured transactions. The following lists each Article and the basic subjects covered:

Article 1	General	Presents purposes and policies, definitions
Article 2	Sales	Contracts for Purchase/Sale of goods
Article 2A	Leases	Transfer of the right to possession and use of of goods for a term in return for consideration
Article 3	Commercial Paper	Negotiable Instruments, Promissory notes, checks Certificate of Deposit, Money Orders, Drafts
Article 4	Bank Deposits and Collections	Deposit/Collection of checks
Article 4A	Wire Transfers	Electronic transfers of funds (CHIPS, Fedwire)
Article 5	Letters of Credit	Domestic and Foreign commercial letters of credit
Article 6	Bulk Transfers	Special protection for creditors of seller in bulk inventory sales
Article 7	Warehouse Receipts Documents of Title	Special rules for documents that evidence ownership or right to possession of goods
Article 8	Investment Securities	Stock Certificates
Article 9	Secured Transactions	Security interests, collateral, priority among secured creditors

Article 2: Sales

Article 2 of the UCC *applies to transactions in goods, which includes leases, rentals, gifts of goods as well as sales.* **Goods** *are defined as all things (other than money, stocks and bonds) that are movable.* Goods also includes the unborn of young animals and growing crops. *Goods that are not yet in existence or not yet under the control of people are called* **future goods.** Examples of future goods are fish in the sea, minerals in the ground, goods not yet manufactured and commodities futures. Article 2 does not cover contracts to provide services or to sell real property; these are covered by general contract common law and real property law.

Article 2 of the UCC is generally a part of the law of contracts. Therefore, general contract common law applies to sales laws unless displaced by a particular provision of the Code. And, the **elements of contract common law**—*offer and acceptance, mutual assent, capacity to contract, legality of subject matter and consideration*—all apply. Article 2 states that a contract for the sale of goods for the price of $500 or more is not enforceable unless there is some writing sufficient to indicate that a contract for sale has been made between the parties.

The sales article of the Code distinguishes between merchants and casual or inexperienced sellers. The Code defines a **merchant** *as "a person who deals in goods of the kind . . . involved in the transaction or a person who regularly deals in the kind of goods being sold."* The Code recognizes that more reliance can be placed on professional sellers, holding them in effect to a higher standard.

A significant aspect of Article 2 is that it states the law without reference to the location of title. Historically, many controversies between buyer and seller were answered by early common law decisions, and then by the Uniform Sales Act, by determining the location of title to the goods. However, the drafters of Article 2 took the position that this "lump concept thinking" or merely determining the location of title to goods created many uncertain and unfair results since it is frequently difficult to predict when title passes or is even established. Furthermore, passing of title may have no logical relationship to the rights in question. There is however a general title provision in Article 2.

Article 2 addresses the terms of the contract for sale and the various steps of its performance. In other words, Article 2 says that title passes when the seller completes his performance by delivery of the goods, or if there is to be no delivery of goods, when the documents of title are shipped, or if there is to be no shipment of goods at the time and place of shipment; otherwise, title passes at the time and place of contracting. In no event will title pass until it is clear that the goods are those to which the contract refers (identified to the contract) or in the case of future goods, when they are designated by the seller as goods. Under Article 2, the rights, obligations and remedies of the seller and the buyer are determined without regard to title, except where the provisions refer to such title. The Code resolves issues in terms of contract for sale and the various steps of performance.

Within the UCC, every contract has an obligation of good faith, or honesty in fact in the transaction concerned, in its performance. This is an important concept because if a contract contains an unfair or unconscionable clause, or the contract as a whole is unconscionable, the courts have the right to refuse to enforce the unconscionable clause or contract.

In general, the performance obligation of the seller is to tender delivery of goods that conform to the contract with the buyer. Tender delivery means that the seller must make the goods available to the buyer. The basic obligation of the buyer is to accept the goods and to pay in accordance with the contract. Additionally, the buyer has the right, before payment or acceptance, to inspect the goods, to reject the goods if they fail to conform to the contract or to accept the goods in spite of non-conformity and the seller has the right to correct or cure improper delivery. Acceptance of goods occurs when a buyer, having had a reasonable opportunity to inspect the goods, either indicates that he will take them or fails to reject them.

If the goods delivered by the seller do not conform to the contract, the buyer has several options. The buyer can (1) reject all of the goods, (2) accept all of them or (3) accept any commercial units and reject the rest. A **commercial unit** *is any unit of goods that is treated by commercial usage as a single whole (such as a machine, or a dozen, bale, carload of something).*

The buyer must state the grounds for rejection where a defect in the tender could have been ascertained by reasonable inspection and could have been cured by the seller. The Code introduces the concept of cover which applies where the seller fails to perform; it gives the buyer an alternative right to purchase substitute goods and to recover from the seller the difference between the contract price and the cost of cover as an absolute measure of damages, provided the buyer purchases in a reasonable manner.

If the buyer refuses to accept goods that conform to the contract or repudiates the contract, the seller does not have to resell the goods. The seller has two ways of determining the damages that the buyer is liable for because of the buyer's breach of contract: (1) the difference between the contract price and the market price at which the goods are currently selling and (2) the profit the seller lost when the buyer did not go through with the contract.

If the buyer rejects a shipment, rightly or wrongly, the seller must first resell the goods at the best price obtainable; then sue for the difference between the proceeds and that which was due, plus any incidental damages. The only exception is where the merchandise is of a special nature and not readily salable at a reasonable price; in that case, the old rule still applies and the seller can sue for the full purchase price. Of course, if the buyer retains the shipment and then tries to return it much later, the seller is not obligated to accept the return and can sue for the full amount.

There are many variations of this kind of problem, and the UCC provides all sorts of rules to deal with them. The above rule covers the simplest and most common situation. Consequently, a seller can no longer hold rejected merchandise for a buyer and then sue for the purchase price, but has to sell the goods first and then sue only for any loss. If the seller has no loss on the resale, then only the profit on the original sale can be recovered.

The Code acknowledges the fact that terms are frequently omitted from agreements or contracts by defining common trade practices. The UCC recognizes that a contract for the sale of goods may be performed even though the price is not settled. An open-price term may occur when the parties intend to be bound by a contract but to not mention a price or agree to set a price at a later time.

Title

The Code does contain a general title section. It provides that title passes to the buyer when the seller has completely performed his/her duties concerning physical delivery of the goods. Therefore, if the contract only requires the seller to ship the goods, title passes to the buyer when the seller delivers the goods to the carrier. If the contract requires delivery of the goods by the seller, title passes to the buyer when the goods are delivered and tendered to the buyer. If delivery is made without moving the goods, the title passes at the time and place of contracting, if the goods have been identified in the contract.

Risk of Loss

The Code also has specific rules governing risk of loss, which is an issue separate and apart from title. Risk of loss depends on the terms of the agreement, the moment the loss occurs and whether one of the parties was in breach of contract when the risk of loss occurred. Risk of loss can be contractually addressed by using commonly accepted shipping terms.

The following are commonly used shipping terms that create shipment contracts, whereby the seller turns the goods over to a carrier for delivery to the buyer. In a shipment contract, both title and risk of loss pass to the buyer when the goods are given to the carrier. The seller has no responsibility for seeing that the goods reach their destination.

FOB (Free on Board) *the place of shipment requires the seller to deliver the goods free of expense and at the seller's risk to the place of shipment.*

FAS (Free Alongside) *at a named port requires the seller to deliver the goods, at his/her own risk along side the vessel or at a dock designated by the buyer.*

CIF (Cost, Insurance, and Freight) *means that the price of the goods includes the cost of shipping and insurance. The seller bears this expense and the risk of loading the goods.*

C&F (Cost and Freight) *means that the price of the goods includes the cost of shipping. The seller bears the risk of loading the goods.*

If the contract requires the seller to guarantee delivery of the goods to a specific destination, the seller bears the risk and expense of delivery to that destination. Commonly used shipping terms that create destination contracts are:

FOB Destination or an FOB term with the place of destination of the goods *puts the expense and risk of delivering the goods to that destination on the seller.*

Ex-Ship *places the expense and risk on the seller until the goods are unloaded from whatever ship is used.*

No Arrival, No Sale *places the expense and risk during shipment on the seller.* If the goods fail to arrive through no fault of the seller, the seller has no further liability to the buyer.

If no agreement has been made for either a shipment contract or a destination contract, then the risk passes to the buyer on receipt of the goods if the seller is a merchant. If the seller is not a merchant, the risk passes to the buyer when the seller tenders (offers) delivery of the goods.

Reclamation Clause

Unless the seller has agreed to extend credit to the buyer, the buyer must pay for the goods at the time they are delivered. When the seller is ready to make delivery of the goods, the seller may withhold delivery until the payment is made. If the seller discovers that the buyer is insolvent before making delivery, the seller has the right to withhold delivery until the buyer pays cash for the goods and for any goods previously delivered for which payment has not been made. The seller has the right to require the buyer to return any goods the insolvent buyer obtained from the seller within the previous 10 days.

If a seller demands the return of merchandise from an insolvent buyer within 10 days of the receipt of the shipment and the buyer fails to comply, the seller may recover the goods without proving any misrepresentation of solvency or fraud. **Insolvency** *under the UCC is defined to include the so-called equity rule (inability to pay debts as they mature) as well as the bankruptcy definition (liabilities exceeding assets.)* If the buyer misrepresented solvency in writing within three months, then the 10-day limitation does not apply and the demand can be made at any time. If a seller discovers that a buyer is insolvent, the seller has the right to stop delivery of any goods in transit. Except in these two situations, the seller may not recover merchandise on the basis of any misrepresentation of solvency. For example, if the seller fails to demand the return of merchandise within 10 days of its receipt, it cannot be reclaimed from any insolvent buyer even though the buyer had made all kinds of misrepresentations of solvency, unless they were in writing and made within three months of delivery.

In addition to the provisions of Article 2, reclamation can also be negotiated between a debtor in Chapter 11 of the Bankruptcy Code and the creditors' committee. Section 546 of the Bankruptcy Code recognizes the rights of a reclaiming seller.

Warranties

Article 2 addresses several warranty issues. A **warranty** *is a contractual promise by the seller regarding the quality, character or suitability of the goods sold.*

An **express warranty** *is an oral or written statement, promise or other representation about the quality of a product.* Express warranties are created in three ways: by a statement of fact or promise made by the seller to the buyer which relates to the goods, by a description of the goods which is made part of the basis of the agreement that the goods will conform to the description and by a sample or model of the goods. Whenever a seller of goods makes a statement of fact about the goods to a buyer as part of the transaction, an express warranty is created.

An **implied warranty** *is a warranty that is imposed by law rather than by statements, descriptions or samples given by the seller.* Implied warranties are designed to promote high standards in business and to discourage harsh dealings. There are three types of implied warranties: an implied warranty of merchantability, an implied warranty of fitness for a particular purpose and an implied warranty that is derived from a course of dealing or usage of trade.

The Code provides three alternatives to the extension of an express or implied warranty. Each state must select only one of these three alternatives:

1. A seller's warranty, whether express or implied, extends to any natural person who is in the family or household of his buyer or who is a guest in his home if it is reasonable to expect that such person may use, consume or be affected by the goods and who is injured in person by breach of warranty.
2. A seller's warranty, whether express or implied, extends to any natural person who may reasonably be expected to use, consume or be affected by the goods and who is injured in person by breach of the warranty.
3. A seller's warranty, whether express or implied, extends to any person who

may reasonably be expected to use, consume or be affected by the goods and who is injured by breach of the warranty.

Disclaimer of warranties is permitted as a matter of freedom of contract, but with the condition that if in a written contract, the disclaimer must be conspicuous; to disclaim the implied warranty of merchantability the writing must mention the word "merchantability." Aside from the provisions mentioned here, the Code is silent on the question of privity between the seller and buyer as a prerequisite for a breach of warrant claim.

Article 2A: Leases

In recent years, the leasing of goods has become very popular. Consumers and businesses lease cars, television sets, furniture, and a variety of tools and equipment. Leasing allows the lessee to use valuable assets without making an initial large capital investment. Leases allow firms with limited capital budgets an alternative way to obtain resources. Additionally, leases are frequently tailored to meet the cash budget requirements of the lessee.

Leasing of goods is a type of **bailment** *which is the transfer of possession and control of personal property for the benefit of both parties.* Traditionally, bailment was governed by bailment law which turned out to be inadequate to address today's modern lease agreements. Therefore, the National Conference of Commissions on Uniform State Law added Article 2A Leases, to the UCC in 1987. It was revised in 1990.

Included within the scope of the Article 2A are transactions as diverse as the lease of a hand tool for a few hours and the leverage lease of a complex line of industrial equipment. The Article generally preserves the concept of freedom of contract except that there are special rules for consumer leases. A **finance lease,** *which is a lease in which the lessor does not manufacture or produce the goods and only acquires the goods in connection with the lease,* is also governed by the Article.

A lease contract is enforceable if the total payments to be made, excluding payment for options to renew or buy, are more than $1,000 or if there is a written agreement. A lease contract can be made in any manner which shows agreement between the parties. As with sales contracts, if a court finds as a matter of law that a lease or clause is unconscionable at the time it was made, it can refuse to enforce the lease or clause. A lease imposes an obligation on each party that the other's expectation of receiving the performance will not be impaired.

A lease is also enforceable if the goods are to be specifically manufactured or maintained for the lessee and are not suitable for lease or sale to others in the ordinary course of business, or if a party admits that the lease was made or if the goods have been received and accepted by the lessee.

Promises made by a lessor to a lessee create a warranty that the goods will conform to the promises. Any description of the goods creates an express warranty that the goods will conform to the description, and any sample or model used creates a warranty that the goods will conform to the sample or model. In a finance lease, there is an implied warranty of merchantability in a lease contract if the lessor is a merchant with respect to goods of that kind.

General Default

If either party is in default under the lease, the party seeking enforcement may obtain a judgment or otherwise enforce the lease by self help or any available judicial or non-judicial procedure. Remedies are cumulative. An action for default under a lease, including a breach of warranty or indemnity, must be commenced within four years after the cause of action accrued. The parties, however, may reduce the period of limitation to not less than one year.

If a lessor discovers the lessee to be insolvent, the lessor may refuse to deliver the goods; and if the lessee is in default, the lessor may take possession of the goods without judicial process. After default by the lessee under a lease contract, lessor may recover from the lessee damages for goods accepted by the lessee and for conforming goods lost or damaged within a commercially reasonable time, accrued and unpaid rent, the value of the lease and incidental damages.

Article 6: Bulk Sales

Bulk transfers have created special problems for business people. Merchants, owing debts, would sometimes sell out their entire stock of inventory for less than what it was worth. This left creditors with no way of reaching and selling the goods to obtain the money owed to them. Article 6: Bulk Sales, protects creditors from this practice, called bulk transfer. A **bulk transfer** *is any transfer of a major part of the materials, supplies, merchandise or other inventory of an enterprise that is not made in the ordinary course of business.*

The general concept of Article 6 is to protect creditors of a merchant by voiding a bulk transfer of his merchandise out of the ordinary course of trade, unless the merchant (who is the transferee) gives notice of the contemplated transfer to all known creditors at least 10 days before he takes possession. The creation of a security for the performance of an obligation is not a bulk transfer under Article 6 but a legitimate financing transaction. However, any transfer of a major part of inventory not in the ordinary course of business is subject to Article 6. A transfer of a substantial part of equipment is also a bulk transfer if it is made in conjunction with a bulk transfer of inventory, but not otherwise. Creditor protection under this Article is designed to prevent two types of fraud:

1. To stop the conveyance type of sale where both parties, the debtor and the buyer/transferee, may have conspired to defraud creditors by transferring goods at less than their true value so the debtor may then reestablish the business.
2. To prevent a debtor from selling the bulk of stock in trade, even for full value, to a buyer/transferee that may not be in collusion with the debtor, and then either dissipating the proceeds or disappearing with them, leaving creditors unpaid.

The Code lists four requirements that must be followed whenever a bulk transfer is made. If the four requirements are not met, the transferee of the goods can lose all ownership rights to them. Further, creditors who suffer damages can demand the return of all goods bought, with no obligation to reimburse the buyer. The four requirements are:

1. The buyer/transferee must require the transferor/seller to furnish a list of any existing creditors with their addresses and amounts owing;
2. The parties must prepare a schedule of the property being transferred so that it can be identified;
3. The buyer/transferee must maintain or preserve the list and schedule for six months following the transfer and make it available for inspection, and
4. The buyer/transferee must give notice of the transfer to all creditors at least 10 days before taking possession of the goods or paying for them, whichever happens first.

After following these four requirements, the transferee may pay for and take possession of the inventory.

Creditors' Actions

A creditor receiving notice that a customer is selling under a bulk sale must immediately contact both the debtor and buyer to ascertain how much time will elapse before the sale; obtain a description of the property to be sold, its value, and the names of other creditors and the amounts due them; determine whether the debtor's debts are to be paid in full or in part from the proceeds; and find out where claims should be sent.

A creditor that did not receive any such notice but learns that a sale of the debtor's goods has been made which may be subject to Article 6 should find out whether the debtor, the sale, or both are subject to the UCC; whether a claim can be filed; or, if a claim cannot be filed, what rights creditors have against the buyer/transferee if either the debtor or buyer has failed to comply with the UCC. The creditor must move quickly in order not to be barred from relief under the law. Creditors who have not taken any action to interrupt the transfer lose their right to do so.

Article 9: Secured Transactions

Article 9 is probably the most important Article of the Code for credit executives since its scope reaches transactions whose intended effect is to create security interests in personal property.

Using Article 9, an unsecured creditor can become a secured creditor. A creditor's right, or security interest, is in specifically identified personal property, tangible or intangible, or in fixtures. Article 9 is the set of rules governing how those rights are created, extinguished, and reconciled with the rights of the debtor, the rights of the debtor's other creditors and the rights of third parties who may also acquire or claim rights in the property subject to the security interest.

Article 9 is divided into 5 parts:

Part 1 is the general part covering definitions, exclusions, general provisions, multi-state transactions and special rules.

Part 2 addresses security agreements and the requisites for validity, attachment, after-acquired property and future advances.

Part 3 addresses perfection and its effect, requirements, the rights of third parties and priorities among conflicting secured creditors.

Part 4 addresses filings, formal filing requirements, the place to file, the effectiveness, lapse and termination of a filing and the release of a filing.

Part 5 addresses collection and repossession of collateral and disposition of collateral.

According to Article 9 of the UCC, a **secured transaction** *includes any transaction that is intended to create an interest or right in personal property, to secure either the payment of a debt or the performance of some other kind of obligation.* Property is divided into two types: real property and personal property. **Personal property** *refers to movable assets whereas* **real property** *includes land, buildings and anything that is firmly attached to land or embedded under land.* It is crucial to determine the type of personal property, that is, whether it is tangible personal property or intangible personal property. **Tangible property** *has a physical existence or substance and includes equipment, inventory, farm products and goods.* **Intangible property** *is property that is not perceptible to the senses and cannot be touched.* Examples of intangible property are accounts receivable, instruments, documents, and **chattel paper**, *which is a writing which evidences both a monetary obligation and a security interest in specific goods.*

While Article 9 applies to all personal property, some important sections state special rules with reference to particular types of collateral. In the Code, collateral is divided into different types.

Tangible Collateral:

1. Equipment—goods are equipment if they are used or bought for use primarily in business (including farming or professional) or by a debtor who is a non-profit organization or a governmental subdivision or agency, or if the goods are not included in the definitions of inventory, farm products or consumer goods.
2. Inventory—goods are inventory if they are held by a person for sale or lease or to be furnished under contracts of service or if they are raw materials, work in progress or materials used or consumed in business.
3. Farm products—goods are farm products if they are crops or livestock or supplies used or produced in farming operations or if they are products of crops or livestock (such as milk and eggs) and if they are in the possession of a debtor engaged in farming.
4. Consumer goods—goods are consumer goods if the are used or bought for use primarily for personal, family or household purposes.

Intangible Collateral:

1. Accounts refer to any right to payment for goods sold or leased or for services rendered which is not evidenced by an instrument or chattel paper, whether or not it has been earned by performance.
2. Instruments are writings, expressly excluding leases and security agreements, that evidence the right to receive payment of money and that are

transferred in the ordinary course of business by the act of delivery, including, for example, check, money orders, certificates of deposit, commercial paper, bearer or registered bonds and debentures and stock certificates in publicly traded corporations.

3. Documents are writings such as bills of lading, dock receipts, and warehouse receipts, that are generally recognized in the ordinary course of business as evidence that the bearer has the right to receive, hold and dispose of the documents and the goods that it covers.
4. General Intangibles are rights to payment not otherwise described in the UCC, including the goodwill or customer list of a business, the right to an income tax refund, the rights to receive payment under a license agreement and the right to receive a partial rebate of a purchase price because of a bulk discount.

While certain types of collateral, such as accounts, do not change classification depending upon their use, some do. For example, a computer in the hands of a wholesaler or retailer is inventory, but may become a consumer good when sold to an individual for home use or equipment if sold to a doctor for office use. Distinction in use is critical.

Security Interest

The goal of a creditor is to obtain a security interest in certain personal property that will be good against the debtor, other creditors of the debtor and any person who might purchase the property from the debtor. By definition, a **security interest** *is an interest in personal property or fixtures that a creditor obtains to secure payment or performance of an obligation.*

Attachment

Obtaining an enforceable security interest is a two-step process consisting of attachment and perfection. *To be effective, a security interest must be legally enforceable against the debtor. This is known as* **attachment.** The attachment of the security interest takes place in a legal sense rather than in a physical sense. *A security interest is said to attach when the secured party (the creditor) has a legally enforceable right to take that property and sell it to satisfy the debt.* There are two basic requirements for a security interest to be attached to the goods of a debtor. First, there must be an agreement by the debtor granting the creditor a security interest in particular property in which the debtor has an interest. In other words, the security agreement is an agreement that creates a security interest. Second, the creditor must give something of value to the debtor by advancing goods on credit. Unless a debtor owes a debt to the creditor, there can be no security interest.

The agreement in which a debtor grants a creditor a security interest in the debtor's property is called a **security agreement,** *which establishes the obligations and contractual rights between the debtor and creditor.* The security agreement must be in writing and signed by the debtor. A written agreement is required in all cases except where the creditor has possession of the collateral.

A security agreement must clearly describe the collateral so that it can readily be identified. Model numbers and serial numbers of equipment or other complete descriptions collateral should be used. The agreement lists the terms of the arrangement between the creditor and the debtor, containing a promise by the debtor to pay certain amounts of money in a certain way and what constitutes a default by the debtor.

A security agreement can be written to grant a creditor a security interest in **after-acquired property of the debtor,** *which is property that the debtor does not currently own or have rights in but that may be acquired in the future.* However, the security interest in the after-acquired property cannot attach to that property until the debtor obtains some property rights in the new property. The after-acquired property clause does not apply in a bankruptcy setting. Under the Bankruptcy Code, property acquired by the debtor after the commencement of a bankruptcy proceeding is not subject to any interest resulting from a security agreement entered into by the debtor before the commencement of the case.

A security agreement can provide that the security interest will not only cover the collateral described in the agreement but will also attach to the proceeds if the collateral is disposed by the debtor. **Proceeds** *can be defined as that which is received upon the sale, exchange or other disposition of collateral.* To create a security interest in proceeds, the word proceeds must be added to the description of the collateral in the security agreement.

In review, at a minimum, any security agreement should contain:

1. Identification of the parties. Generally there are two groups of parties to any security agreement: the seller/lender/creditor who is the secured party and the debtor or debtors who are jointly called the debtor. While mailing addresses are not required, it is advised to include them.
2. The law requires a granting clause or words granting a present security interest in all the collateral described in the security agreement to secure all present and future indebtedness of the debtor to the creditor.
3. The description of the collateral covered by the security interest created in the security agreement is the essence of the agreement. The agreement should have a space to insert a written description of the collateral and should contain language stating that the security interest attaches to all similar types of collateral now owned or subsequently acquired by the debtor as well as any proceeds generated by the sale of the collateral.
4. A typical security agreement contains provisions setting out various warranties, such as that the debtor owns the collateral, and gives a comprehensive list of events of default. Additional provisions for insurance of inventory or governing accounts receivable general by the sale of the collateral are also common.

Records Search

Initially, the creditor should search the records of the Secretary of the State in the state where the customer is located to learn the names of creditors that have perfected security agreements. The search can be done by completing a **UCC-11 form or Information and Copy Request form.** *This form directs the Secetary of State's office to list any effective financing statements on file against the named debtor.* There is a fee to file a UCC-

11 and an additional fee if copies of the statements are to be furnished. These filings determine the order of priority as against third parties, regardless of when the secured transactions take place. In light of the order-of-priority filing rule, filing before the attachment of the security interest is preferable. In addition, filing before giving value allows an adequate search for prior filings and also prevents intervening filings.

This search enables the creditor to decide whether the security agreement should take the form of a security interest or a purchase money security interest. Enforcing the security interest literally depends on the adequacy of the search for conflicting security interests. In transactions involving inventory, accounts, and chattel paper, the financing statement eliminates the necessity to refile on each of a series of transactions where the collateral changes from day to day. Once filed, it serves to establish the priority of the creditor's position as to future extensions of credit and as to after-acquired property. Except for a purchase money security interest, a new creditor perfecting on the same type of property covered by an earlier filing will generally be subordinate to the priority extended to the earlier filing.

Perfection

When a security interest attaches, it is effective only between the debtor and the creditor. A creditor wants to make sure that no one else can claim the collateral if the debtor defaults in any way. To protect a security interest in collateral against other creditors of the debtor, it must be perfected. **Perfection** *is the process of taking the legal steps necessary to insure that a secured creditor's interest in collateral will withstand attack by competing creditors attaching judgment holders and a bankruptcy trustee.* Under the Code, there are three ways to perfect a security interest:

- by filing a public notice, or security agreement or a financing statement
- by possession of the collateral where the creditor takes possession of the collateral
- by attachment alone (automatic perfection)

Perfection by Filing a Security Agreement or Financing Statement

The most common way of perfecting a security interest is by filing either a security agreement or a financing statement, generally referred to as a UCC-1, in the appropriate public office. Such filing serves as public notice that the creditor claims an interest in collateral that belongs to a named debtor. The financing statement usually consists of a multicopy form that is available from the Secretary of State's office.

The security financing statement should contain at a minimum:

- the exact legal name of the debtor. This can be confirmed by calling the Corporations Division of the Secretary of State in the debtor's state. Usually, any trade names that the debtor uses are also listed
- the debtor's address must also be included
- the name and address of the secured party from which additional information about the security interest can be obtained
- a description of the collateral which must reasonably describe the goods or the real estate if the collateral is growing crops or timber to be cut, and
- the signature of the debtor

The financing statement can contain additional optional information such as a provision granting a security interest in the collateral described, an after-acquired property clause, a provision covering the proceeds and products and a blank for the secured creditor's signature.

There is a national standard financing form which is accepted in Alaska, Arizona, California, Colorado, Connecticut, Delaware, the District of Columbia, Florida, Hawaii, Idaho, Kansas, Kentucky, Maryland, Massachusetts, Michigan, Mississippi, Missouri, Montana, Nebraska, Nevada, New Jersey, New Mexico, New York, North Dakota, Oklahoma, Pennsylvania, Tennessee, Texas, Utah, Virginia, Washington and Wyoming.

The following Secretary of State offices will accept the national standard financing form with a penalty fee: Alabama, Illinois, Indiana, Iowa, Louisiana, Minnesota, Ohio, South Carolina, South Dakota, Vermont, West Virginia and Wisconsin. The Secretary of State offices in Georgia, Maine, New Hampshire, North Carolina, Oregon and Rhode Island will not accept the national standard financing form.

Where To File a Security Agreement or Financing Statement

Once the security agreement financing statement is properly completed and signed, it should be filed. Each state specifies by statute where the security agreement or financing statement has to be filed. State law varies as to whether financing statements that concern commercial collateral are to be filed locally and/or in a central state file, usually in the Secretary of State's office. Most states require local filing where the transaction is local in nature. As a general rule, when the debtor is an individual, the filing should be made in the state and location where the debtor normally maintains his/her residence. If a debtor has multiple residences, multiple filings are advisable. If the debtor is a corporation or partnership, the location controlling the filling will be that of the physical location of the office or the main office from which the business is managed.

Filing is complete upon presentation of a properly executed security agreement or financing statement and the necessary filing fee. If the security agreement or financing statement is filed through the mail, it is important to check to insure actual receipt.

Samples of financing statements are shown for illustrative purposes. The security agreement or financing statement should be typewritten because many filing jurisdictions microfilm these documents. Some states require a Federal ID number or a social security number for both the debtor and the secured party. NACM's *Manual of Credit and Commercial Laws* details the filing requirements by state. Additionally, private firms can perform nationwide filing and search services.

When To File a Security Agreement or Financing Statement

A security agreement or financing statement may be filed prior to a transaction or within a reasonable time, which is generally 10 days after the transaction.

How Often To File

Generally, a filing is effective for a period of five years from the date of filing. Amendments adding collateral do not extend the effective period. Further, additional filings covering additional types of collateral may result in different effective dates and different lapse dates. **Continuation statements,** *referred to as a UCC-3, must be filed within six months of the termination date to continue the priority of perfection.* A continuation statement is also valid for five years. The continuation statement must contain the secured party's signature, the filing number identifying the original financing statement to be continued and a statement that the original financing statement is still effective. An "amended" security agreement or financing statement may need to be refiled sooner if there is a name change of the business or if there is a change in the location of the debtor or collateral. When all of the debts that are secured by a security agreement are satisfied, the debtor is entitled to a termination statement signed by the secured party.

Perfection by Possession

Security interest in most types of tangible collateral may be perfected by the secured party taking physical possession of the collateral. In a limited number of cases, such as when the collateral is money or stock, possession may be the only method of properly perfecting a security interest. Where perfection is created through possession, a determination of what constitutes possession must be made. Most courts have said that if a creditor has exclusive control of, access to or the use of the collateral, it has possession of it. For example, if a negotiable instrument such as a stock certificate is in your safe, it is in your possesion. If inventory or equipment is stored in a warehouse in your name, it is in your possession.

Perfection by Attachment (Automatic Attachment)

In a few, limited situations, automatic perfection pertains to certain types of instruments, negotiable documents and certain types of collateral proceeds. A security interest in these types of collateral is perfected automatically (without filing or possession) for a period of 21 days from the time a security interest attaches, if and only if the security interest arises from new value given to the debtor and if there is a written security agreement. At the end of the 21-day period, any interest becomes unperfected unless the lender perfects by filing or possesion within that time.

Priority of Security Interests

To review, a **security interest** *is an interest in personal property created by the debtor to insure repayment of a debt.* A security interest is consensual and requires that the debtor sign a written security agreement which describes the goods to be covered, or collateral. *A security agreement* **attaches** *when the security agreement is executed and the debtor acquires the rights in the goods.* A *security interest is* **perfected** *when the secured creditor either takes possession of the collateral or files a properly executed security agreement or financing statement with the appropriate state authority.* Unperfected security interests have priority account to the date of attachment. Perfected security interests have priority over all unperfected security interests. Competing or conflicting security interests have priority in the order in which they are perfected, or if all competing interests are unperfected, the order in which they are attached.

The Floating Lien

Article 9 permits a single creditor to create a security interest in the debtor's inventory, equipment, and accounts receivable; and to provide for future advances on after-acquired property. **Future advances** *means that the lender agrees to make additional loans from time to time, with those future loans secured by the same collateral as the original* *advance.* An **after-acquired property clause** *states that all property subsequently acquired by the debtor shall constitute additional collateral for the lender.*

The floating lien is an integral part of this approach. A **floating lien** *attaches to all of the debtor's property of a particular kind, property described in the security agreement and financing statement, even though the property of that kind is acquired long after the execution of the loan documents.* Since inventory is always changing, a floating lien related to an after-acquired clause can be used on inventory replacement goods as they are acquired by the debtor. Thus, merchandise sold by an unsecured creditor may serve as collateral for the secured creditor.

Used to extreme, a floating lien could tie up a debtor's entire inventory. For example, one creditor may have a security interest in every item of merchandise coming into the debtor's shop, from the moment it crosses the threshold, from the moment it arrives at the train station, or from the moment the seller puts the goods on the train. Even before the goods have arrived at the buyer's place of business, that creditor, possibly a financing company or bank, may have a lien on the goods. This weakens the position of other creditors.

Purchase Money Security Interest

The usual rule is that a properly perfected security agreement which contains an after-acquired property clause permits a priority interest in property purchased thereafter. However, the "first-to-perfect rule" is subject to an important qualification: property purchased under a purchase money security interest is not subject to the after-acquired clause. A creditor who holds a purchase money security interest to secure the purchase of newly acquired property has a priority claim over another creditor who claims the purchased property under an after-acquired clause, provided such supplier complies with the UCC requirements.

A **purchase money security interest** *may be created by either a seller of collateral who secures all or part of the price for the collateral (i.e., a seller who sells its product on credit and secures the credit by the product it sells) or a person who, by making advances or incurring an obligation, gives values to enable the debtor to acquire rights in or the use of collateral if such value is, in fact, so used (i.e., a lender who lends money directly for the purchase of a specific product and who secures its loan by the product purchased.)*

A purchase money security interest in inventory is established by giving written notice of the purchase money security interest (usually by certified letter) to the competing/conflicting secured party. This includes filing a financing statement before the debtor receives the inventory. Written notification by certified letter is then given to the holder of the filed security interest that a purchase money security interest in inventory is expected to be acquired. For example, Bank ABC takes and perfects a security interest in all present and after-acquired inventory of a debtor. That debtor acquires additional inventory from XYZ Wholesalers. XYZ Wholesalers checks the public records and finds that Bank ABC holds a now owned and after-acquired security interest in all inventory. XYZ Wholesaler perfects a security interest in its inventory to be shipped to the debtor and sends notice of its purchase money security interest before the inventory is shipped. The key elements are to perfect the security interest before the debtor takes possession of the collateral and that notice of the purchase money security interest was given to the competing security interest holder.

A purchase money security interest can also be established in non-inventory collateral. This can be accomplished without notice to the holder of the conflicting security interest, by making certain the security agreement is entered into and the financing statement is filed, at or before the time the debtor gains possession of the collateral, or within 10 to 20 days thereafter.

Default Under a Security Agreement

The UCC does not define the term default but gives the parties latitude in defining it. Therefore, a creditor should define default in such a fashion as to cover most of the probable bases for the need to foreclose. Depending on the nature of the collateral involved, a creditor has a range of options upon default by a debtor in a commerical situation. The options range from simply writing off the debt to foreclosing on the collateral and pursuing any deficiency.

In many cases, a debtor in default may not be willing to abide by provisions outlined in the security agreement, despite the fact that the holder of the security interest has a right, according to the UCC, to peacefully take possession of the collateral. Therefore, a creditor should take preparatory steps at the time the security agreement is negotiated to strengthen its right of domain.

Where the collateral is accounts receivable, the creditor should obtain the right to inspect the debtor's books; obtain periodically a list of the customers along with outstanding balances; and obtain a presigned, undated letter, that requests the debtor's customers to pay the creditor directly in the event of default.

The procedure is different in the case of inventory. The creditor should obtain the debtor's permission in advance to employ a bonded warehouse to protect the inventory in the event of default. The value of the security interest in inventory must be carefully assessed: is repossession practical, what is its expected value upon repossession, and will it still be in possession of the customer.

Credit Analysis of Secured Debtors

Because the UCC has made the use of secured credit more uniform, there is a greater tendency to use this type of transaction in sales to marginal accounts. The decision to sell to a buyer that is involved with a secured creditor will depend upon the merits of each case. The credit executive cannot readily ascertain the amount of debt being secured where there is a security interest in inventory and its proceeds. Every asset of the business, except machinery and equipment not specifically identified, may be subject to the lien of the secured creditor. This type of problem did not exist prior to the UCC. In most states, the earlier law did not give a secured creditor such broad protection. Extreme caution should now be exercised in extending credit to any business that has a financing statement covering inventory and proceeds filed against it.

On the other side of this question, the UCC includes a specific provision requiring the exercise of good faith in all transactions. A secured lender that has obtained a complete package—namely, a security interest in equipment, inventory, and accounts receivable, including provisions for future advances and after-acquired property—is still required to exercise good faith with regard to the debtor's business. It is the task of the unsecured creditors to aggressively preserve their rights in situations where undue emphasis may be placed upon security agreements rather than upon straightforward credit analysis.

When a debtor is in default under a security agreement, secured creditors may reduce their claims to judgment, foreclose, or otherwise enforce the security interest by an available judicial procedure. Unless otherwise agreed, secured creditors have the right to take possession of their collateral. This may be done without judicial process, providing it can be conducted without breach of peace.

A secured creditor may sell, lease, or otherwise dispose of the collateral through public or private sale. Any sale of goods is subject to Article 2 of the UCC. The secured creditor must give the debtor reasonable notice of the time and place of a public sale or a private sale, unless the debtor has signed after default a statement renouncing or modifying the right to notification of sale. In cases other than consumer goods, the secured creditor must also give notice of the sale to any other creditor that has filed a security interest or is known by the secured party to have a security interest in the same collateral.

It is important that a creditor that forecloses on property subject to a security interest conduct the sale in a commercially reasonable manner. Otherwise the creditor may be subject to damages and may not be able to obtain a deficiency judgment, depending on state law.

If the proceeds from the sale exceed the amount owed to the secured creditor, plus allowable expenses, the excess monies must be given to subordinate creditors, providing they ask for the excess sum in writing. If there are no subordinate creditors, then any excess proceeds are returnable to the debtor. When the proceeds fall short of the debt, the debtor is liable for the deficiency.

At any time before the secured creditor has disposed of the repossessed collateral or contracted for its disposition, the debtor may redeem the collateral by making payment in full satisfaction of the debt, plus reasonable and allowable expenses.

Comprehension Check

1. Article 2 applies to which kind of transactions?
2. Under Article 2, what rule applies to sales worth more than $500?
3. Why does Article 2 distinguish between a merchant and casual or inexperienced sellers?
4. Within UCC Article 2, every contract has an obligation of good faith or honesty in the transaction concerned. Why is this an important concept?
5. What does tender delivery mean?
6. What options does a buyer have if goods delivered by the seller do not conform to the contract?
7. If a buyer refuses to accept goods that conform to the contract, how can the seller determine the damages for which the buyer is liable because of the breach of contract?
8. What does the general title section of the code state?
9. List three conditions that relate to risk of loss.
10. What is a shipment contract?
11. What is a destination contract?
12. What does reclamation mean under Article 2?
13. How is bankruptcy defined under Article 2?
14. Define the term warranty.
15. What is an express warranty?
16. What is an implied warranty?

17. Article 2 provides three alternatives to the extension of an express or implied warranty. What are they?
18. Leasing is a type of bailment. Explain this statement.
19. When is a lease contract enforceable?
20. What is the general concept behind Article 6?
21. UCC 6 lists four requirements that must be followed whenever a bulk transfer is made. What are they?
22. Under UCC 9, what does a secured transaction include?
23. In UCC 9, into what two broad categories can collateral be divided?
24. List four types of tangible collateral.
25. List four types of intangible collateral.
26. What is a security interest?
27. Obtaining an enforceable security interest involves a two step process. What are the two steps?
28. What is a security agreement?
29. What does a security establish?
30. At a minimum, a security agreement should contain four essential elements. What are they?
31. Explain how a creditor can conduct a records search.
32. What is perfection?
33. List three ways to perfect a security interest.
34. List five elements that should be included in a security financing statement.
35. When is filing of a security agreement or financing statement complete?
36. As a general rule, how long is a filing valid?
37. Explain what is meant by the term perfection by possession.
38. Explain what is meant by the term perfection by attachment.
39. What is a floating lien?
40. How is a purchase money security interest established?

10 Credit Investigations

Overview

Sound credit decisions can only be made on the basis of adequate information about the customer's business, its financial condition, the character of the principals, and other matters. This chapter opens with a discussion of the legal and ethical aspects of credit investigation. The remainder of the chapter is devoted to various methods of credit investigation in the United States and internationally and to the management and storage of information collected about customers.

Learning Objectives

After reading this chapter, the reader should know:

- The difference between direct and indirect credit investigations
- How to conform to the ethical and legal requirements of credit investigation
- How to open a new credit account
- How to gather information in a direct credit investigation
- How to gather information in an indirect credit investigation
- How to gather foreign credit information
- How to conduct credit investigations on existing accounts
- Why the Internet is a good tool for credit investigations

Chapter Outline

I. Direct and Indirect Credit Investigations
   - A. Traditional Definitions
   - B. Current Practice

II. Ethical and Legal Aspects of Credit Investigation
   - A. Confidential Nature of Credit Information
   - B. Ethical Considerations
   - C. Company Policy
   - D. Legal Aspects of the Exchange of Credit Information
   - E. References
   - F. Resources

III. Opening a New Credit Account
   - A. Standard Procedure
   - B. Customer-Supplied Information

IV. Direct Investigation
   - A. Types of Direct Investigation
   - B. Bank Information
   - C. Ways to Make a Bank Investigation
   - D. Information Sought in a Bank Inquiry
   - E. Trade Information
   - F. Other Sources for Direct Investigation

V. Indirect Investigation
   - A. The Impact of Automation
   - B. Credit Reporting Agencies
   - C. Specialized Agencies
   - D. Voluntary Trade Groups

VI. Getting International Credit Information
   - A. Customer-Supplied Information
   - B. Bank Information
   - C. Exporter's Foreign Sales Representative
   - D. Reporting Agencies

VII. Investigating Existing Accounts
   - A. When to Investigate an Existing Account
   - B. Methods of Contact
   - C. Sources of Information

VIII. Using the Internet for Credit Investigation
   - A. Credit Reports
   - B. Specialized Information
   - C. Government Information
   - D. Industry-Specific Sites
   - E. Association Sites
   - F. General Information

Direct and Indirect Credit Investigations

Traditional Definitions

Credit investigations have been traditionally divided into two types: direct and indirect.

Direct Investigations. **Direct investigations** *are those where credit information is collected by the creditor either through direct contact with the customer or through direct contact with noncommercial sources of information such as individuals, banks, or other trade references that may have useful credit information.* Customer supplied financial statements or information gathered through a telephone interview are examples of information gathered through direct investigation.

Indirect Investigations. **Indirect credit investigations** *usually refer to acquiring information from sources that are in the business of preparing information on companies.* A credit report purchased from a commercial credit reporting agency is an example of information obtained by indirect credit investigation.

While these terms are still used, wide sweeping changes in technology and the speed at which information can be gathered has created only a subtle difference between them.

Current Practice

Most companies today rely on third-party credit reports for the bulk of their credit investigations. There are several reasons for this. Computerized data base technology allows large collections of credit data to be assembled and accessed quickly. For companies that do business nationally, using a credit report is much easier than contacting references all across the country. This is particularly true of large companies that have thousands of credit relationships. Because of access to instant information through either a fax machine or e-mail, a credit manager can obtain a credit report on a credit applicant in one day or less. Direct investigation cannot produce information this quickly. Also, the numbers of credit staff needed for adequate direct investigation is rarely available in most credit departments. The cost of credit reports is nominal compared to the cost of additional personnel.

Ethical and Legal Aspects of Credit Investigation

Confidential Nature of Credit Information

Businesses are subject to a variety of laws that affect the work of the credit manager. In addition, there are ethical standards of behavior in conducting a credit investigation that credit managers should comply with as business professionals.

In the United States, almost unlimited sources of credit information are normally available. Over the years, these sources have steadily expanded on the basis of mutual confidence and respect among credit executives themselves and among credit executives and customers.

The concept of the confidential and privileged nature of credit information has been vital in the development of these relationships. What exactly does this mean? Using the literal meaning of "secret" or "private" a confidential relationship would prevent a company from giving any credit information about its customer to anyone. Under these conditions, the free interchange of credit information could not survive.

The average commercial credit user today is well aware of the interchange of credit information. Therefore, it may be more accurate to say that customer information is held in "trust", rather than on a confidential basis, by the credit department. The customer knows that credit departments will only release factual credit information to other creditors that have a legitimate interest. The customer trusts the good judgment of the credit department personnel in knowing to whom they may release information and how much information may be properly divulged. Most customers realize this relationship makes credit easier to obtain, and available in larger amounts and with less delay. They also appreciate that the record of their creditworthiness will follow them wherever they go.

Ethical Considerations

The purpose of a **credit investigation** *is to obtain information to make a specific decision about granting credit to a company.* The goal of the investigation is to obtain factual accurate information that will lead to an appropriate decision.

Personal Behavior. The credit manager has an obligation to his or her firm and the credit profession, as well as a personal obligation, to behave professionally and to guard against violating—even unintentionally—any laws against restraint of trade.

Honesty. The credit manager should always present himself or herself honestly to any source of information. Misrepresenting oneself or one's firm can have serious legal consequences and may later embarrass the credit manager or the company.

Objectivity. Information requested must be factual. It is important to phrase questions and requests objectively to avoid charges of slander or libel. However, the credit manager can ask questions such as: Does the respondent handle the account personally? Does the respondent know the applicant personally? Are there a lot of requests for credit information for this account? Have there been recurring problems with the accounts?

Topics To Avoid. Credit managers should avoid discussing the following topics with anyone outside the credit department: future prices, future terms, or future discounts. Furthermore, credit managers should avoid any conversations touching on discriminatory trade practices or anything that might be construed as restraint of trade or in violation of antitrust legislation.

Company Policy

Credit information must be kept confidential within the organization itself, and should be released with great care to companies, agencies, and others. A strict policy should be established as to who may have access to the credit files. This policy must be appropriate to the size of the organization, the extent and nature of information contained in the files, and the use to be made of it. An untrained person could seriously jeopardize the relationship between the customer and the company, and even subject the company to a lawsuit, by unwarranted or unguarded revelations of information which the customer might consider detrimental to its situation, reputation, or character. It is most important, therefore, that all persons dealing with credit inquiries be properly indoctrinated in credit ethics and principles.

Legal Aspects of the Exchange of Credit Information

The exchange of factual credit experience information is legal and proper, but the information exchanged must be restricted to factual information. The courts of the United States have recognized in numerous decisions the legitimate business interest in the exchange of factual credit information among businesses with legitimate interests. As early as 1925, the U.S. Supreme Court held that:

> "...The gathering and dissemination of information which will enable sellers to prevent a perpetration of fraud upon them, which information they are free to act upon or not as they choose, cannot be held to be an unlawful restraint upon commerce, even though, in the ordinary course of business, most sellers would act upon the information..." (*Cement Manufacturers Protective Association vs. United States*, 268 US 588, 603–604)

In a 1976 case, the U.S. Court of Appeals for New York commented on the exchange of credit information as follows:

> "...Unlike exchanges regarding prices which usually serve no purpose other than to suppress competition, and hence fall within the ban of the Sherman Act ... the dissemination of information concerning the creditworthiness of customers aids sellers in gaining information necessary to protect themselves against fraudulent or insolvent customers. . .Given the legitimate function of such data, it is not a violation of the Sherman Act to exchange such information, provided that any action taken in reliance upon it is the result of each firm's independent judgment, and not of agreement." (*Michelman vs. Clark Schwebel Fibre Glass Corp.*, 534 F 2nd 1036)

Conspiracy

While the courts, in these cases and others, have held the exchange of factual credit information to be legal and proper, any agreement, express or implied, between competitors on any action concerning a common customer or class of customers is clearly illegal. Such an illegal agreement or conspiracy could be an agreement not to do business with a certain customer or class of customers or it could be an agreement on terms to be offered to a customer or class of customers. Thus, while exchange of factual information about the credit experience with customers is perfectly proper, care should be taken that no agreements are made for any common action, nor should there be any effort made to influence the credit decision of another credit executive.

Libel and Slander

When exchanging information, credit executives must also be careful to avoid defamation, which is legally actionable. **Defamation** *is a false statement made to others that injures the name or reputation of a third party.* The broad two types of defamation are

Figure 10-1 Libelous Per Se

It has been ruled that the following are **libelous per se**:

1. to charge by letter that a person is a swindler, or knowingly made false representation with intent to deceive, or lacks veracity
2. to publish a false statement imputing insolvency to a merchant or trader
3. to charge falsely that a person has failed in business or has made an assignment for the benefit of creditors
4. to publish that a merchant has not succeeded in obtaining the implicit confidence of local people, and is looked on locally as an itinerant trader of small financial responsibility and uncertain prospects
5. to charge in writing that a business individual is embarrassed, inferring insolvency or lack of creditworthiness

libel and slander. **Libel** *is defamation in some permanent form, such as printed media, writing, film, CD-ROM, or laser disc.* **Slander** *is defamation in a temporary form, such as speech.*

The law has always been very protective of the reputation of businesses and business individuals, and the law of defamation includes the protection of the reputation of business firms. Legislatures and the courts have recognized that a person or business firm may suffer real damages by being lowered in the esteem of any substantial and respectable group, especially when that group may represent suppliers.

Examples of Libel and Slander

While it is proper to pass on information that is of public record to another supplier, such as the filing of liens, legal actions, or criminal convictions, such information should not be reported with any malicious intent. Continuous reference to a person's unfavorable past history, for instance, could hinder a person with such a record from being reestablished in society. This is especially pertinent where many years of good conduct have ensued, or where nothing either good or bad is definitely known about the intervening years.

It is not defamatory to say that a subject is dead, is overly cautious with money, has led an eventful life, or owes money. These statements lack the element of personal disgrace necessary for defamation in the eyes of the law. However, saying that a business "refuses to pay its bills" or that a firm is "insolvent" (unless it is an established fact) obviously damages that business firm in the business community and may be subject to a charge of defamation.

Matter Libelous Per Se. Generally, **matter libelous per se** *is any communication that falsely suggests a criminal act or immorality, or which tends to deprive a person in business of public confidence and esteem.* Examples would be to accuse someone of fraud or of being dishonest. The charge need not be made in a direct, positive, and open manner. If the words used, taken in their ordinarily accepted sense, convey a degrading imputation—no matter how indirectly—they are libelous. A letter that states a particular debtor has not paid debts which are owing and past due is not libelous, if true. But if the letter imputes insolvency, bankruptcy, or lack of credit on the basis of this fact, it becomes libelous. Figure 10-1 gives examples of statements that are libelous per se.

Figure 10-2 Privileged Communications

The courts have considered the following as **privileged communications**:

1. statements made by a former employer whose name has been given as a reference to a prospective employer of an employee
2. communications between creditors of the same debtor in reference to their respective claims
3. communications by banks, such as a statement as to the financial standing of a person offered as a surety

Publication. The second element essential to an action in libel is **publication,** *which means communication of the libel to some third person.* Communication to the defamed person alone is not actionable because no third person has learned of the defamatory matter; consequently, there is no possible injury to the defamed party's reputation. If the defamed person, moreover, exhibits the defamatory matter to a third person, there is no publication for which the writer is liable, since the defamed person's own act is the cause of the injury. If the writer reads the defamatory matter to a third party, however, before sending it to the defamed person, there is a publication—that is, a slander.

Defenses to Charges of Libel

Truth is a complete defense to an action in libel and must be so pleaded. Where several statements are published, however, only some of which are true, the defamer does not escape liability. Some defamatory statements are not actionable as libel because they are **privileged communications**: *statements made by one person in pursuance of a duty to another person having a corresponding duty or interest.* Such privilege is conditional, however, in that a community of interest must exist and must be exercised in good faith; malicious intent or a wanton and reckless disregard of the defamed person's rights will destroy the privilege. A person bringing suit must prove the existence of malice in order to sustain the action. Figure 10-2 gives examples of privileged communications.

References

Legislation. Credit managers should be familiar with the following federal laws dealing with antitrust and restraint of trade.

The Sherman Act of 1890 (15 USC §§ 1-7). This act prohibits contracts, combinations in form of trust or otherwise, and conspiracies in restraint of trade in interstate commerce or with foreign nations. It declares that any individual, partnership, corporation, association or other legal entity that combines, contracts, or conspires with one or more other parties to restrain trade or commerce shall be guilty of a felony. Further, any person or other entity that monopolizes or attempts to monopolize, or that combines, contracts, or conspires with one or more other parties to monopolize trade or commerce among the United States or with foreign nations, shall be guilty of a felony.

The Clayton Act of 1914 (15 USC §§ 12-27 and 29 USC §§ 52 & 53). This followed the Sherman Act and was created to "correct" the defects in the Sherman Act. This statute prohibits acts that will reduce competition or create a monopoly. Congress passed the Clayton Act in order to promote competition through protection of viable, small, locally owned businesses. Under the Clayton Act it is unlawful to enter into a) leases or sales on condition that lessee or purchaser shall not use or deal in the commodities of a competitor of the lessor or seller, b) exclusive dealing arrangements, c) tying leases and agreements.

The Robinson-Patman Act of 1936. The Act was partially an amendment to the Clayton Act. It makes it unlawful for any person engaged in commerce to:

> "discriminate in price between different purchasers of commodities of like grade and quality . . . where the effect of such discrimination many be substantially to lessen competition or tend to create a monopoly in any line or commerce . . ." [15 USC § 13(a)]

The Robinson-Patman Act is designed to prevent discriminatory practices adversely affecting free competitive enterprise, to preserve competition generally, and to protect small businesses that usually are unable to buy in quantity against large competitors. It is equally unlawful for any person engaged in commerce "knowingly to induce or receive a discrimination in price which is prohibited by this section." [15 USC § 13(f)]

Violations of 15 USC § 139(a) are subject to civil liability. However, Section 3 of the Robinson-Patman Act (15 USC § 13(a)) provides criminal liability for any person who discriminates through the use of discounts, rebates, allowances, or advertising service charges; or by selling at unreasonably low prices to destroy competition or a competitor. This section, technically, is not an "antitrust" law.

The Federal Trade Commission Act of 1914. This act prohibits all "unfair methods of competition in or affecting commerce, and unfair or deceptive acts or practices in or affecting commerce." [15 USC § 45] The Federal Trade Commission Act is the broadest of all antitrust statutes. Its coverage includes acquisitions, mergers, monopolies, unfair trade practices, unfair trade arrangements between suppliers and dealers, deceptive sales approaches, and discrimination in prices, services, or facilities. Its prohibitions cover false advertising of foods, drugs, devices, and cosmetics, and any other practice which is designed to deceive the public. Any practice which violates The Sherman Antitrust Act, The Clayton Act, or the Robinson-Patman Act, or even falls short of an actual violation of those laws but is related to the types of practice which those laws prohibit, may constitute an unfair method of competition under the Federal Trade Commission Act.

The Antitrust Procedure and Penalties Act of 1976. This lesser known antitrust statute increases penalties for violation of The Sherman Antitrust Act. The 1976 Antitrust Act gave the federal government new disclosure powers in antitrust litigation. This statute also permits a state attorney general to sue for damages on behalf of a particular state's citizens and requires companies of a certain size to file premerger notices.

In addition, almost every state has State Antitrust Statutes. These are independent laws prohibiting monopolies, contracts, conspiracies, and combinations in restraint of trade.

The Equal Credit Opportunity Act of 1977, Regulation B. This law applies to consumer transactions and to credit extended to any individual, partnership, or corporation for any purpose.

- It prohibits creditors from discriminating against an individual because of sex, marital status, race, color, religion, national origin, age, welfare assistance, or the exercise of a debtor's rights assured by the Consumer Credit Protection Act.
- If an applicant is denied credit and requests in writing the reasons for the denial within 60 days of being notified, the credit grantor must issue a written response within the next 30 days. This response can be brief, such as "insufficient credit references."
- A written notice of the rights of the applicant can be given in three ways: by providing a written notice of a right to a statement; by providing the specific reasons for denial of credit; and by providing a notice to all business applicants on any document sent to them that they can keep.
- If an application for business credit is made only by telephone, then the creditor is allowed to provide an oral notice of rights to a written statement.
- Credit decisions may be given in writing or orally, but must be given within 30 days after the creditor receives a completed application. A completed application is one where the creditor has all the information it requires to make a decision.
- Creditors may not ask about the marital status of a business credit applicant for unsecured credit. They may ask about marital status if the application lives in a community property state and plans to use property in that state to repay a debt or as collateral for a secured loan. They may also ask about ownership rights or the names of any co-owners of property a credit applicant plans to use to satisfy a debt in case of default.
- Creditors must maintain all records for a minimum of 60 days. If an applicant requests a written statement of the specific reasons for credit denial, the creditor must retain those records for at least 12 months.

Resources

In addition to copies of the actual legislation, there are some published materials that should be in every credit manager's office.

- The *Manual of Credit and Commercial Laws*—published annually by the NACM and contains summaries and explanations of relevant state and federal statutes
- *Statement of Principles for the Exchange of Credit Information*—published jointly by the NACM and Robert Morris Associates. (Figure 10-5)
- *Yes You Can Exchange Commercial Credit Information*—This brochure is also published by Robert Morris Associates

Opening a New Credit Account

Standard Procedure

Some pieces of information are standard for every credit relationship. Therefore, it makes sense to have a standard procedure for collecting credit information.

The Credit File

The credit department should have a credit file for every customer and every credit applicant. It will contain all the relevant pieces of information pertaining to its credit investigation—documents, reports, correspondence, notes, and summaries of telephone conversations. Each piece of information should be dated. The savvy manager will have a check list for each credit file to make sure all the information needed to make a credit decision is available.

Credit Application

The credit application is the cornerstone of the customer's credit file. It should provide the basic credit information about the customer.

Working with the Sales Department

If possible, sales representatives should be trained to submit credit applications with all prospective accounts, new accounts, or both. They may inform the credit department of the approximate amount of credit required and give an estimate of annual purchases, or initial purchases for a new or prospective customer. The forms used by the sales representatives should have a section for bank and trade references, and one for the credit department reply, with a suggested credit line. Some sales personnel are provided with balance sheet forms they give to the customer to complete and mail directly to the credit department.

Financial Statements

Financial statements aid in understanding the company's financial condition. A sales representative can collect financials easily from a new customer as a standard procedure. It can also be a matter of credit policy or included as a provision of the credit application. If it is not received when the account is opened, the credit manager should continue to request it through friendly but firm letters. If a customer cannot provide a financial statement, the credit manager may request the customer to complete a financial statement form. (Figure 10-3)

Other Forms

One of the first steps in a credit investigation is to check the references given in the credit application. A sample form for bank references is shown in Figure 10-4.

Customer-Supplied Information

The most accurate source of information about a business, its operation, and its financial condition is often the business itself. Direct contact with the principals provides the credit executive with financial details, bank and trade references, and other information. Through direct contact the credit executive also has the opportunity to establish a close and friendly working relationship with the applicant and build mutual confidence and respect.

Direct contact with the customer depends on the customer's degree of cooperation, proximity to the seller, the time available to conduct the investigation, and the amount of credit requested.

Figure 10-3 Sample Financial Statement Form

Please supply the following balance sheet information or attach a current copy of your company's balance sheet.

Balance Sheet at (date): ____________________

CURRENT ASSETS		
Cash	$______	______
Marketable Securities	______	______
Accounts Receivable	______	______
(less allowance for doubtful accounts)	______	______
Inventory	______	______
Prepaid Expenses	______	______
Total Current Assets	______	______
Plant Assets	______	______
Land	______	______
Buildings (less accumulated depreciation)	______	______
Equipment (less accumulated depreciation)	______	______
Total Plant Assets	______	______
Total Assets	$______	______
CURRENT LIABILITIES		
Accounts Payable	______	______
Notes Payable	______	______
Salaries Payable	______	______
Total current liabilities	______	______
Long-Term Liabilities	______	______
Notes payable	______	______
Total Liabilities	$______	______
STOCKHOLDERS' EQUITY		
Paid in Capital	______	______
Excess of Issue Price Over Par	______	______
Total paid-in capital	______	______
Retained Earnings	______	______
Total retained earnings		$______
Total stockholders' equity		$______
Total Liabilities and Stockholders' Equity		$______

Direct Investigation

Types of Direct Investigation

Direct investigation for credit applications is undertaken by the credit manager or other credit personnel to assess the creditworthiness of the applicant and to form a conclusion about the level of credit to offer. Direct correspondence by mail, personal

Figure 10-4 Sample Bank Reference Form

Request For Bank Credit Information

INQUIRER TO COMPLETE THIS SECTION

Date: ____________________

To: ____________________

RE: ____________________
Company
____
Street Address
____
City/State/Zip
____
Bank Account Number

The above referenced account has applied to us for an open credit line of $__________ and has given your bank as a reference. Please fill in the information requested below. We would appreciate any additional information which would prove helpful.

We will be pleased to reciprocate at any time.

Sincerely,

____
Signature

Please return a copy of this completed form to my attention at the following address:

Name ____________________ Title
Company ____________________
Street Address ____________________
City/State/Zip ____________________
Phone Number ____________________ Fax Number

BANK TO COMPLETE THIS SECTION

CHECKING ACCOUNT:

Opened: __________ Average Balance: __________

Returned Items: ☐ Yes ☐ No
Satisfactory: ☐ Yes ☐ No

LOANS:

Opened: __________ High Credit: __________ Balance: __________
Secured by: ____________________ Unsecured: __________
Payment History: ____________________

Opened: __________ High Credit: __________ Balance: __________
Secured by: ____________________ Unsecured: __________
Payment History: ____________________

COMMENTS: ____________________

Signature ____________________ Title ____________________ Date

rma

NACM®

This form and the "Statement of Principles" (see reverse side have been approved by the Robert Morris Association and the National Association of Credit Management.

Additional copies of this form may be purchased from NACM Publications Dept., 8815 Centre Park Dr, #200 Columbia, MD 21045-2158

Form 19

interview, telephone contact, and research are all ways of directly investigating a credit applicant.

Direct Correspondence

This is the most common basis for contact with all customers. Opening accounts presents an excellent opportunity to set a tone that will keep the customer providing credit information. Today, correspondence can be conducted by telephone, facsimile (fax), and by e-mail, as well as through the U.S. Postal Service. However, the credit executive must use discretion and match the medium with the nature of the communication.

Order Acknowledgment

The most economical and convenient means of establishing contact with a new customer may well be a friendly letter requesting information, in addition to acknowledging and approving an initial order. A letter of this type, giving honest recognition to the credit standing that the customer has already established in other places, can build mutual respect and good will in the very process of obtaining information. Even when the seller is not ready to approve the order, it may be desirable to acknowledge it, and to list the seller's terms and other conditions. If the customer's credit is questionable, the acknowledgment should be confined to a simple statement that the order has been received; no commitment to accept the order or ship the material on a credit basis should be implied.

Request for Financial Statements

The best place to put a request for financial statements is in the credit application. The application should have a requirement for the customer to provide regularly audited financial statements, or to provide them on request. Enclosing a blank financial statement form with the application serves several purposes. It reveals to the customer that supplying financial information is indeed a common practice; it makes it easier to comply with the request; and it helps ensure that all information desired by the credit department will be submitted. The use of a standardized form also makes analysis of information easier. It is particularly advisable to send a standard check list of questions rather than an individual request when a follow up is necessary to amplify items on a statement already submitted. By showing that this type of investigation is routine enough to merit a printed form, the follow up avoids the impression that any particular buyer has been singled for extra investigation.

Terms of Sale

Terms of sale and expected payment performance should be clearly explained to the customer early in the establishment of a new account and before a sale takes place. However, unless terms of sale are part of a contract, they are not binding.

Additional Information

Most companies subscribe to credit agency services that provide detailed reports on potential customers and records of their paying habits. When additional information is required, the customer may be asked directly. The letter should be carefully worded so the customer will want to give this information freely. If an order is to be held up until the credit investigation has been completed, the customer must be convinced that the delay is worthwhile.

Refusal of Credit

Even the letter refusing open-account credit to a new customer can serve a useful purpose. The customer must be encouraged to do business on special terms at present so that open account terms may be offered later. Credit executives should be ever mindful of the provisions of Regulation B of the Equal Credit Opportunity Act and transact their business accordingly. The Act requires a creditor to notify an applicant orally or in writing of the action taken on an application. If credit is denied and the applicant makes a written request for the reason within 60 days, a creditor must advise the applicant in writing of the reason(s) and provide the notice requested by statute. Negative phrasing should be held to a minimum. The positive aspects should include the favorable factors in the customer situation, and an expression of confidence that the customer will soon improve the factors which prevent open account credit at this time.

Acknowledgment Letters

Although sometimes routine, these letters play an important part in reaffirming terms of sale, expressing appreciation of an order, or completing a contract by asking for counter signatures.

Personal Interview

One of the best occasions for the credit department to gather information, promote good will, and build sales is the personal interview with the customer. While the time and expense involved usually restricts this method of contact, a personal interview may uncover enough information to permit the granting of credit even though the customer has not submitted financial statements. Moreover, a personal call may be the only means to persuade the customer to submit or discuss financial statements, or to accept cutbacks on terms or order quantities. Face-to-face dialogue can go beyond a discussion of financial condition. Credit contact can be both a sales tool and a chance to establish mutual confidence, respect, and good will.

While it may be highly desirable to conduct personal interviews at the customer's office, they may also be held in the credit executive's office if the customer prefers this arrangement. After any interview, a complete memorandum for the credit file should note the date, the occasion, all pertinent points of information, and the credit executive's own impressions.

Telephone Contacts

The telephone can be used to supplement financial information on statements submitted to the company or to a credit agency, to obtain references, to bring financial information up to date, and to verify reported contracts. Often the next best thing to a personal visit, the telephone has the added advantage of being less costly and time consuming.

Before making telephone contact, it is wise to prepare a form noting the points to be covered and the information needed. This will be very helpful, particularly for the inexperienced, or when a large number of points are to be discussed.

As in the case of the personal interview, a memorandum of the telephone conversation should be written promptly and placed in the credit file.

Sales Representatives

Sales representatives can obtain a great deal of information just by keeping their eyes and ears open. They can judge the location and appearance of the place of business

Figure 10-5 Statement of Principles for the Exchange of Credit Information

1. Confidentiality is the cardinal principle in the exchange of credit information. The identity of inquirers and sources should not be disclosed without their permission.
2. All parties involved in the exchange of credit information must base inquiries and replies on fact.
3. The purpose of the inquiry and the amount involved should be clearly stated.
4. If the purpose of an inquiry involves actual or contemplated litigation, the inquirer should clearly disclose this fact.
5. The inquirer should make every effort to determine the subject's bank(s) of account before placing an inquiry, and indicate the extent of information already in the file.
6. Proper identification should be provided in all credit communications.
7. Replies should be prompt, containing sufficient facts which are commensurate with the purpose and amount of the inquiry. If specific questions cannot be answered, the reasons should be clearly stated.

and the presence or absence of competition. They can observe the names of other brands and products carried, and the personalities of employees and of management. To obtain the full benefit of the sales representatives' observations, a spirit of mutual confidence and cooperation must be developed between the sales and credit departments.

Bank Information

Because of all the services they can provide to their customers, banks are valuable sources of credit information. Trade creditors can make direct inquiries of the customer's bank, or may ask their own banks to inquire of the customer's bank. In either case, the information is helpful in obtaining a rounded picture of the customer's financial ability.

Statement of Principles for the Exchange of Credit Information

Recognizing the need to foster and maintain a high level of ethical standards in the exchange of business credit information between banks and business credit grantors, the National Association of Credit Management (NACM) and the Robert Morris Associates (RMA) formed a joint committee in 1955, which developed a *Statement of Principles for the Exchange of Credit Information Between Banks and Business Credit Grantors*. The *Statement of Principles* was revised in 1978 to reflect current usage. Figure 10-5 lists the seven principles with explanatory comments.

The *Statement of Principles* is designed for commercial transactions and is subject to applicable federal and state laws. Such laws include securities statutes regulating disclosure of inside information and could under particular circumstances include the antitrust laws, credit reporting regulations, and limitations on the use of confidential records and customer information or computerized data. Both RMA and NACM encourage their members and others with whom credit information is exchanged to become familiar with and respect the *Statement of Principles.* In addition, each party must understand its obligation to its customers and the need for fair, considerate, accurate, and prompt replies in relation to the extension of business credit.

Ways To Make a Bank Investigation

The name of the customer's bank is generally obtained through direct inquiry or by noting the bank on which a customer's checks are drawn. It is desirable to establish some relationship and rapport with the customer's banker as part of the relationship that exists between the seller and the customer.

Telephone

This has the advantage of speed. Many bankers do not mind telephone inquiries if they know the individuals initiating the inquiry. However, bankers are reluctant to talk freely about an account to someone they do not know well.

Mail Inquiry

This is often necessary because of distance. Form 19, *Request for Bank Credit Information,* published by NACM, is recommended for this use. (Figure 10-4) A postpaid return envelope should be enclosed.

Telephone Facsimile

Depending on the relationship with the credit executive, some banks may be willing to supply information by fax.

Personal Visit

This is the best means of obtaining complete information from a bank. The credit executive should make a special point of becoming well-acquainted with local lending officers, as that builds confidence and respect between the credit executive and the bank officer.

Bank-to-Bank

It is possible for the credit executive's bank to check with the customer's bank when the credit department's efforts are unsuccessful or when special information is needed. Often this is a successful technique, as banks might disclose more information to other banks than they do to trade creditors that are not their depositors. There is usually a fee charged for this service.

Information Sought in a Bank Inquiry

The credit executive should explain the scope, nature, and reason for the inquiry. The depth of response rests on several basic factors: the amount of money involved; being certain that the proper person is contacted at the bank; being well prepared with precise questions before calling or writing; and being careful not to violate the following caveats. Banks will not usually volunteer unsolicited information. They will, however, answer specific legitimate questions that do not violate confidentiality. An inquiry that involves large dollar amounts and includes specific data, such as terms

Figure 10-6 Robert Morris Associates' General Figure Ranges

Low 4 figures	$1,000 to 1,999
Moderate 4 figures	$2,000 to 3,999
Medium 4 figures	$4,000 to 6,999
High 4 figures	$7,000 to 9,999

The ranges are adjustable to accommodate all amounts in the following manners:

Nominal	under $100
3 figures	from $101 to $999
4 figures	from $1,000 to $9,999
5 figures	from $10,000 to $99,999
6 figures	from $100,000 to $999,999, and so on

of sale and a request for financial details, may well receive a more detailed reply than one that refers to a small dollar amount with vague reference to the terms of sale and other factors. Banks will generally decline comment about a company's ability to pay a specified amount.

Questions To Ask

While all questions might not be answered, key questions to ask include:

- How long has the bank had the account? If the account was opened recently, who introduced the account?
- What are the average balances? The banker's reply usually will express the customer's average bank balance in such terms as "medium four figures" or "low six figures." To ensure accuracy and consistency in interpretation, Robert Morris Associates' General Figure Ranges should be used. (Figure 10-6)
- Have any loans been granted? If yes, how high have they been during the past year, and what is owing now? How are cleanups—that is, are loans repaid on time with a regular period during which no money is owed?
- When, why, and how often does the account borrow? "Why" is most important.
- Are loans made on straight paper? Are they endorsed or guaranteed? If so, by whom? If endorsements are given by someone not officially connected with the business, this person may be the principal behind the business and a full investigation should be made to determine personal reputation and financial responsibility.
- If borrowings are on a secured basis, what is the collateral: accounts receivable, inventory, real estate, marketable securities, or cash surrender value of life insurance?
- If loans are secured, has the bank perfected a financing statement under the Uniform Commercial Code? This is normal procedure. If filing notices of a security interest are important to a credit decision, verification of the filing should be obtained through the office of the Secretary of State of the state in which the financing statement was filed.
- What was the date of the latest financial figures filed with the bank?

- Ask for highlights on current assets, current liabilities, net working capital, total assets, and net worth.
- Ask for a summary of the customer's latest operating figures, and an indication of profitability.
- Ask for a summary of the latest trade clearance conducted by the bank.

Reason for an Inquiry

The credit executive should explain the reason for the inquiry, describing the size and basis of the order, experience with the account, and other available facts. The banker may also ask some pertinent questions:

- Is the customer a new account, is the file being revised, or is this a delinquent account about which the seller is concerned?
- On what line of merchandise is credit being extended, and on what terms?
- What has been the experience of the inquirer, and how much is now owing?
- How much does the seller know about the account already?

Caveats on Requesting Credit Information from Banks

When a request discloses the nature and scope of the inquiry, the bank normally furnishes whatever data it is free to give. Sometimes, however, it may not answer an inquiry because of previous poor experience with the particular inquirer. Certain practices should be avoided by the credit executive:

- disregarding the confidential nature, accuracy, identity, and source of the inquiry and data.
- requesting credit information from banks without citing the precise amount of credit involved—When this is not given on the inquiry, banks sometimes ask for it so they may answer properly. The credit executive can avoid delay by providing the information in the first place.
- not specifying the spread of the sale—Banks should be informed whether the amount of credit involved (especially when it runs high) is a one-time request or whether the amount is requested for one year.
- disguising or hesitating to disclose the reason for an inquiry—Credit executives should be aware that there are situations in which the bank cannot or should not give detailed information to an inquirer. If, for example, the inquirer has a lawsuit pending against a customer and calls the bank for the purpose of locating the customer's assets, this is not a customary credit inquiry. The bank would understandably object to this type of deception.
- making competitive inquiries—Banks also will not handle competitive inquiries, in which the information sought may be used competitively against the subject of inquiry. This is not considered a legitimate trade inquiry. Merger and acquisition inquiries would be considered of a similar nature.
- making repeated rush requests—Banks realize that businesses sometimes need rush information, but will naturally object when a rush becomes the routine rather than the exception.
- making several requests for information on the same company during the same day—This underscores the need to be well-prepared before calling a bank.

- using unsigned or rubber-stamped form inquiries that give the impression that the inquirer is not concerned about receiving credit information—These inquiries draw limited response.

Trade Information

Trade information, like bank information, is an important part of the credit file. If not complete, it should at least be representative of the customer's pay record. A customer opening a new account is asked for the names of suppliers. The experienced credit executive will also check with other likely suppliers, since references given by the customer almost always will report a good paying record. The payment pattern with all suppliers is needed, including those which the customer may be paying slow.

Trade References

Trade information consists of facts obtained from merchandise suppliers of the customer. It includes recent high credit, amount owing, amount past due; whether customer payments are discounted, prompt or slow and, if slow, how many days; whether a supplier has referred the account to a collection agency; and other facts about the buying and paying record of the customer. This is vital information. It describes how the customer actually pays bills, regardless of other financial facts.

The payment record should be examined for specifics as well as for the trend of payments, and be reconciled with the condition indicated by the customer's financial statements. Though slow trade payments is often a sign of trouble, it may also characterize a business that is having growing pains but is substantially healthy; its slowness may be seasonal or due to expansion.

Sources

Depending upon the customer, the industry, location, size of order, and other factors, the credit executive has several places to get this information. Those most commonly used include credit reporting agencies that report on all industries, industry credit groups, direct interchange with other suppliers, and agency trade checks.

Direct exchange of information with other suppliers is costly and time consuming but can be very useful when there is substantial credit exposure, when agency and bureau reports are inadequate, or when industry group interchange is not practicable. Personal acquaintance, proper identification, and mutual trust and confidence play a key part in these direct exchanges. Also, credit executives should bear in mind the legal limitations to such an exchange, as noted earlier in this chapter.

Standard Practices

Some companies will exchange trade information only when contacted in writing. It is useful to have a standard form to record credit or trade experience where the credit manager can note the reason for the inquiry, the size of the order, and the inquirer's own credit experience. Other rules to follow on direct interchange are:

- Always volunteer available pertinent information.
- Provide other suppliers a standardized reply form to be completed, as well as a return postage-paid envelope.

Figure 10-7 A Typical Trade Summary Report

High Credit	Now Owing	Past Due	Selling Terms	Payments	Sold Since	Remarks
$10,000	$7,500-	$-0-	2/10, n/30	Discount	Yrs	Good acct.
8,000	8,000-	0-	2/10, n/30	Discount	1960	Good
9,500	3,000-	0-	Net 30	Prompt	—	
7,350	4,000	750	2/10, n/30	Usually ppt	1 yr	Dispute

- Stress the importance of a confidential relationship between the two companies.
- Have the letter signed by a responsible person in the credit department.

Summarizing Trade Information

After trade experience is gathered, it can be compiled, arranged by high credit and method of payment, and then tabulated into a summary. A typical trade summary report is shown in Figure 10-7.

Other Sources of Direct Investigation

Sources of information are plentiful and limited only by a credit executive's creativity. The following sources are by no means exhaustive of the information available for credit investigations.

State Government

Perhaps the office contacted most frequently is that of the Secretary of State. This is the site of information about a customer's incorporation: the date, the officers, the type of corporation, any changes to the articles of incorporation, and whether assumed names must be registered with the state. Depending on the customer, it may be prudent to obtain a copy of the articles of incorporation. Other things to check at the state level are professional licenses and permits, driver's licenses, and UCC filings. See Appendix B for contact information for the Secretary of State for each of the 50 states.

Federal Government and Federal Agencies

The U.S. Postmaster will respond to a written request with an enclosed fee of $1.00 for the name, business and residence addresses and telephone number of people renting post office boxes. This is very useful when a customer's business address is a box number and the shipping address is geographically removed. Depending on the seller's industry, different branches of government, such as the Department of Agriculture or Health and Human Services, have regulations or program data that may influence a credit decision.

Local Government

The County Clerk's office can supply information about unsatisfied judgments or liens filed against property as well as who has title to the property. City offices are helpful for verifying addresses and getting information to check on ownership, taxes, zoning, and licenses and permits. Of course, this varies by city and state. Also, if other methods fail, the police can be useful in locating or verifying a distant address.

Chamber of Commerce

Applications for chamber membership require information similar to that on credit applications. An initial query could be made to see if the information matches. Chambers usually can supply additional background about a town, the business climate, the applicant, the location of the business, etc. They also should be able to provide the telephone numbers of local government offices. When selling to retail stores, it also may be helpful to check with the Better Business Bureau regarding consumer inquiries about complaints.

Newspapers

The *Wall Street Journal* and local newspapers are important, essential reading for a credit manager. First, it is important to understand the current economic climate. Second, there is a lot of company specific news that can affect credit decisions, or at least suggest further investigation.

Directories and Other Reference Materials

There are a host of printed materials useful in a credit investigation. First of all, there are the standard sources: *Thomas Register, Wards Business Directory, Directory of Corporate Affiliations, MacMillan Directory of Leading Private Companies, Moody's Industry Review, Million Dollar Directory, Experían Trade Payment Guide, Value Line Investment Survey,* and several different publications from Standard and Poor's and Dun & Bradstreet. Specific industry references can be helpful, as can directories of state businesses and chambers of commerce.

Bankruptcy Court Information

To research a bankruptcy filing or possible filing, the credit manager needs to know the name of the owner, as well as the name of the company and in what county of the state the company was doing business. The procedure is to contact the U. S. Bankruptcy Court Clerk with jurisdiction for the particular county.

Indirect Investigation

Every experienced credit manager can recount instances when direct investigation or a personal visit turned up pertinent information about a credit applicant that was otherwise unavailable. However, the truth is that many credit executives today have neither the staff nor the time needed to conduct thorough direct credit investigations. Instead, they turn to a third party. There are several agencies that provide credit reports. Three of the largest private agencies will be discussed later in this section, as well as the credit reporting services provided by NACM Affiliates.

The Impact of Automation

All information today is automated and is usually obtained via CD-ROM or downloaded directly from a mainframe computer. Automation and technology have made credit reports more attractive to credit executives for several reasons.

Large Quantities of Data

Combined with vast data bases, computers can provide information about companies nationwide. Large companies today deal with tens of thousands of customers that are more and more often not geographically local to them. The level of effort required for direct investigations on large numbers of customers is beyond the means of most companies and would take far too much time.

Speed

Reports can be generated instantly and sent electronically or faxed for same day responses. Decisions about credit applications are time sensitive. There is usually an urgency for a fast decision in order to make a sale. The ability to obtain a credit report on a same day or one-day basis can affect a company's revenues.

Relatively Low Cost

The cost benefit of using credit reports is high. The salary of a credit investigator can pay for more credit reports in one year than the investigator could produce in one year. There are also additional savings in telephone, postage, supplies, storage, and overhead costs.

Additional Uses for Data

Credit reports can provide additional marketing data for the company. Examples are checking a customer's trade lines for growth and, therefore, the possibility of additional sales or reviewing trade terms for customers according to their credit risk. Some credit reporting companies also provide relational information reports.

Credit Reporting Agencies

Agency reports not only cover trade payment information, but usually attempt to cover all of the major factors involved in the credit decision. Credit reporting agencies accumulate credit, financial, and allied information from various sources; consolidate and prepare such information in readable form; and disseminate it to clients or subscribers for a fee. They may be classified into three broad categories: general agency, specialized agency, or voluntary trade groups.

Dun & Bradstreet

The largest general reporting agency is Dun & Bradstreet (D&B). It has information on more than 11 million firms, although not all of it is complete. While firms have to voluntarily give trade data, D&B is the only agency that uses reporters to gather information about companies.

Business Information Report

This is the basic credit report, which is developed by D&B reporters. (Figure 10-8) Information is obtained from direct interview with the business owner, partner, or corporate officer. It is then confirmed and expanded through investigations with the business accountant, banks, and supply sources (for payment experiences); by checking public records at federal, state, and county levels; and from a review of D&B's own internal files. After all the information is analyzed to determine the strength and desirability of the account as a credit risk, a D&B rating is assigned, and the data are compiled into the written *Business Information Report*.

Figure 10-8 A Dun & Bradstreet Business Information Report

Dun & Bradstreet

Business Information Report

SUBSCRIBER: 123-4567L
PREPARED FOR:

ANSWERING INQUIRY

DUNS: 80-473-5132	DATE PRINTED	SUMMARY
GORMAN MANUFACTURING CO. Inc.	APR 11 199-	RATING 3A3

COMMERCIAL PRINTING STARTED 1965

492 KOLLER STREET	SIC NO.	SALES	F	$13,007,229
AND BRANCH(ES) OR DIVISION(S)	27 52	WORTH	F	$2,125,499
SAN FRANCISCO CA 94110		EMPLOYS		105(100 HERE)
TEL: 415 555-0000		HISTORY		CLEAR
		FINANCING		SECURED
		FINANCIAL CONDITION		FAIR

CHIEF EXECUTIVE: LESLIE SMITH, PRES

SPECIAL EVENTS
10/22/9

On Oct 1 199-, the subject experienced a fire due to an earthquake. According to Leslie Smith, President, damages amounted $35,000 which were fully covered by their insurance company. The business was closed for two days while employees settled personal matters.

* * * CUSTOMER SERVICE * * *

If you need any additional information, would like a credit recommendation, or have any questions, please call our Customer Service Center at (800) 234-3867 from anywhere within the U.S. From outside the U.S., please call your local D&B office.

* * * SUMMARY ANALYSIS * * *

The Summary Analysis section reflects information in D&B's file as of April 7, 199-.

RATING SUMMARY . . . .

The "3A" portion of the Rating (the Rating Classification) indicates that the company has a worth from $1 million to $10 million. The "3" on the right (Composite Credit Appraisal) indicates an overall "fair"credit appraisal. This credit appraisal was assigned because of D&B's assessment of the company's financial ratios and its cash flow.

Below is an overview of the company's D&B Rating(s) since 06/10/9-:

RATING	DATE APPLIED
3A3	06/10/9-

* * * PAYMENT SUMMARY * * *

The Payment Summary section reflects payment information in D&B's file as of the date of this report.

The PAYDEX for this company is 74.

This PAYDEX score indicates that payments to suppliers average 9 days beyond terms, weighted by dollar amounts. When dollar amounts are not considered, approximately 53% of the company's payments are within terms.

Figure 10-8 A Dun & Bradstreet Business Information Report

Dun & Bradstreet

Business Information Report

Page 2

Below is an overview of the company's dollar-weighted payments, segmented by its suppliers' primary industries:

TOTAL	LARGEST TOTAL RCV'D	% DOLLAR AMOUNTS	HIGH CREDIT	DAYS W/IN TERMS	SLOW <31	31-60	61-90	91+
	#	$	$	%	%	%	%	%
Total in D&B's file	10	1,181,000	1,000,000					
Payment By Industry:								
1 Management consulting	2	50,000	40,000	80	20	-	-	-
2 Nonclassified	1	1,000,000	1,000,000	50	50	-	-	-
3 Business consulting	1	5,000	75,000	-	100	-	-	-
4 Engineering services	1	20,000	20,000	50	-	50	-	-
5 Natural gas transmssn	1	15,000	15,000	100	-	-	-	-
6 Ret fuel oil dealer	1	10,000	10,000	100	-	-	-	-
7 Refuse system	1	7,500	7,500	50	-	-	50	-
8 Natural gas distrib	1	2,500	2,500	-	-	-	100	-
9 Surety insurance	1	1,000	1,000	-	-	100	-	-
Other Payment Categories:								
Cash experiences	0	0	0					
Payment record unknown	0	0	0					
Unfavorable comments	0	0	0					
Placed for collection								
with D&B	0	0						
other	0	N/A						

The highest "Now Owes" on file is $25,000
The highest "Past Due" on file is $15,000

The aggregate dollar amount of the 10 payment experiences in D&B's file equals 109.0% of this company's average monthly sales. In Dun & Bradstreet's opinion, payment experiences exceeding 10% of a company's average monthly sales can be considered representative of payment performance.

PAYMENTS (Amounts may be rounded to nearest figure in prescribed ranges)

Antic — Anticipated (Payments received prior to date of invoice)
Disc — Discounted (Payments received within trade discount period)
Ppt — Prompt (Payments received within terms granted)

REPORTED	PAYING RECORD	HIGH CREDIT	NOW OWES	PAST DUE	SELLING TERMS	LAST SALE WITHIN
01/9-	Ppt	40000	10000			
	Lease agreement					
	Ppt	15000	10000			
	Ppt	10000				
	Ppt-Slow 60	20000	15000	5000		
	Ppt-Slow 90	7500	5000	2500		
	Slow 15	75000	25000	15000		
	Slow 30	10000	7500	1000	N30	
	Slow 60	1000				
	Slow 90	2500				
05/9-	Ppt-Slow 15	1000000	-0-	-0-	N30	2-3 Mos

* Payment experiences reflect how bills are met in relation to the terms granted. In some instances payment beyond terms can be the result of disputes over merchandise, skipped invoices etc.

* Each experience shown represents a separate account reported by a supplier. Updated trade experiences replace those previously reported.

Figure 10-8 A Dun & Bradstreet Business Information Report

Dun & Bradstreet | **Business Information Report**

Page 3

FINANCE
10/22/9-

	Fiscal DEC 31 199-	Fiscal DEC 31 199-	Fiscal DEC 31 199-
Curr Assets	4,643,821	4,825,611	5,425,125
Curr Liabs	3,595,821	3,625,000	4,125,718
Current Ratio	1.29	1.33	1.32
Working Capital	1,048,000	1,200,611	1,299,407
Other Assets	1,468,291	1,485,440	2,191,690
Worth	1,879,451	1,912,112	2,125,499
Sales	9,321,118	10,325,582	13,007,229
Net Profit (Loss)	32,661	213,387	26,014

Fiscal statement dated DEC 31 199-:

Cash	$ 925,000	Accts Pay	$ 2,125,114
Accts Rec	1,725,814	Bank Loans	1,100,000
Inventory	1,643,311	Notes Pay	450,000
Other Curr Assets	1,131,000	Other Curr Liabs	450,604
	--------------		--------------
Curr Assets	5,425,125	Curr Liabs	4,125,718
Fixt & Equip	1,667,918	L.T. Liab-Other	1,365,598
Other Assets	523,772	CAPITAL STOCK	50,000
		RETAINED EARNINGS	2,075,499
	--------------		--------------
Total Assets	7,616,815	Total	7,616,815

From JAN 01 199- to DEC 31 199- sales $13,007,229; cost of goods sold $9,229,554. Gross profit $3,777,675; operating expenses $3,751,661. Operating income $26,014. Net income $26,014.

Submitted MAY 11 1996 by Leslie Smith, President. Accountant: Ashurst & Ashurst, P.C.

ACCOUNTANTS OPINION: A review of the accountant's opinion indicates the financial statements meet generally accepted accounting principles and that the audit contains no qualifications.

--0--

Accounts receivable shown net less $12,586 allowance.

------------------ Statement Item Explanations ------------------

OTHER CURRENT ASSETS: Consist of prepaid expenses $64,471 and $1,066,529 of a loan from an affiliated concern.

OTHER ASSETS: Consist of deposits.

BANK LOANS: Due to bank at prime interest rate, are secured by accounts receivable and inventory, and mature in 3 years.

NOTES PAYABLE: Are due on printing equipment in monthly installments of $37,500.

OTHER CURRENT LIABILITIES: Are accrued expenses and taxes.

LONG TERM DEBT: Consists of the long term portion of the equipment note.

On OCT 22 1996 Leslie Smith, president, referred to the above figures as still representative.

He submitted the following interim figures dated SEP 30 199-:

Cash	$ 1,011,812	Accts Pay	$ 1,801,559
Accts Rec	1,936,118	Owe Bank	986,557
Inventory	1,456,384	Notes Pay	500,000

Sales for the 9 months ended Sep 30 1996 were $15,486,435.

Profits for the 9 months ended Sep 30 1996 were $345,016.

------------------ INVESTIGATIVE PROCESS ------------------

On Oct 22 199-, an on-site interview was conducted with Leslie Smith, President, at 492 KOLLER STREET, SAN FRANCISCO, CA.

Figure 10-8 A Dun & Bradstreet Business Information Report

Dun & Bradstreet

Business Information Report

Page 4

PUBLIC FILINGS

The following data is for information purposes only and is not the official record. Certified copies can only be obtained from the official source.

* * * JUDGMENT(S) * * *

DOCKET NO.:	94CV321		
JDGMT AWARD:	$5,003	STATUS:	Unsatisfied
JDGMT TYPE:	Default judgment	DATE STATUS ATTAINED:	08/13/199-
AGAINST:	GORMAN MANUFACTURING COMPANY, INC	DATE ENTERED:	08/13/199-
		LATEST INFO COLLECTED:	10/02/199-
IN FAVOR OF:	JOHN SMITH		
WHERE FILED:	CONTRA COSTA COUNTY SUPERIOR COURT/MARTINEZ, MARTINEZ, CA		

* * * SUIT(S) * * *

DOCKET NO.:	96CV123		
SUIT AMOUNT:	$1,000	STATUS:	Pending
PLAINTIFF:	JOHN SMITH	DATE STATUS ATTAINED:	08/13/199-
DEFENDANT:	GORMAN MANUFACTURING COMPANY, INC	DATE FILED:	08/13/199-
		LATEST INFO COLLECTED:	10/02/199-
CAUSE:	Civil Rights		
WHERE FILED:	CONTRA COSTA COUNTY SUPERIOR COURT/MARTINEZ, MARTINEZ, CA		

DOCKET NO.:	SC19951218		
SUIT AMOUNT:	$20,000	STATUS:	Pending
PLAINTIFF:	DUN & BRADSTREET, BETHLEHEM, PA	DATE STATUS ATTAINED:	12/18/199-
DEFENDANT:	GORMAN MANUFACTURING COMPANY, INC	DATE FILED:	12/18/199-
		LATEST INFO COLLECTED:	12/19/199-
CAUSE:	Breach of contract		
WHERE FILED:	KERN COUNTY MUNICIPAL COURT / WEST DISTRICT, BAKERSFIELD, CA		

* * * LIEN(S) * * *

A lienholder can file the same lien in more than one filing location. The appearance of multiple liens filed by the same lienholder against a debtor may be indicative of such an occurrence.

BOOK/PAGE:	23/506		
AMOUNT:	$230 Sales and use	STATUS:	Open
TYPE:	State Tax	DATE STATUS ATTAINED:	08/13/199-
FILED BY:	STATE OF CALIFORNIA	DATE FILED:	08/13/199-
AGAINST:	GORMAN MANUFACTURING COMPANY, INC	LATEST INFO COLLECTED:	10/02/199-
WHERE FILED:	CONTRA COSTA COUNTY RECORDERS OFFICE, MARTINEZ, CA		

BOOK/PAGE:	32/506		
AMOUNT:	$50,000 Corporate income tax	STATUS:	Open
TYPE:	Federal Tax	DATE STATUS ATTAINED:	08/13/199-
FILED BY:	INTERNAL REVENUE SERVICE	DATE FILED:	08/13/199-
AGAINST:	GORMAN MANUFACTURING COMPANY, INC	LATEST INFO COLLECTED:	10/02/199-
WHERE FILED:	CONTRA COSTA COUNTY RECORDERS OFFICE, MARTINEZ, CA		

Figure 10-8 A Dun & Bradstreet Business Information Report

Dun & Bradstreet

Business Information Report

Page 5

* * * UCC FILING(S) * * *

COLLATERAL: Leased Inventory including proceeds and products - Leased Accounts receivable including proceeds and products

FILING NO:	UCC951218	DATE FILED:	12/18/199-
TYPE:	Assignment	LATEST INFO COLLECTED:	12/19/199-
ASSIGNEE:	DUN & BRADSTREET, BETHLEHEM, PA	FILED WITH:	SECRETARY OF STATE/UCC DIVISION, CA
DEBTOR:	GORMAN MANUFACTURING COMPANY, INC		

The public record items contained in this report may have been paid, terminated, vacated or released prior to the date this report was printed.

BANKING

(8-95) Balances average in a low 7 figure amount. At Jun 30 199-, a low 7 figure was outstanding under short-term lines of credit which are secured by accounts receivable and inventory.

HISTORY
01/23/9-

LESLIE SMITH, PRES KEVIN J HUNT, SEC-TREAS
DIRECTOR(S): THE OFFICER(S)

Incorporated California May 21 1965. Authorized capital consists of 200 shares common stock, no par value.

Business started May 21 1965 by Leslie Smith and Kevin J Hunt. 100% of capital stock is owned by officers.

SMITH born 1926. Graduated from the University of California, Los Angeles, in June 1947 with a BS degree in Business Management. 1947-65 general manager for Raymor Printing Co, San Francisco, CA. 1965 formed subject with Kevin J Hunt.

HUNT born 1925. Graduated from Northwestern University, Evanston, IL in June 1946. 1946-1965 was general manager for Raymor Printing Co, San Francisco, CA. 1965 formed subject with Leslie Smith.

Affiliates: The following are related through common principals, management and/or ownership. Gorman Manufacturing Company, San Francisco, CA, started 1965. DUNS #80-480-0217. Operates as commercial printer. Intercompany relations: None reported by management.

OPERATION
01/23/9-

Commercial printing specializing in advertising posters, catalogs, circulars and coupons.

ADDITIONAL TELEPHONE NUMBER(S): Facsimile (Fax) 415 555-1000; Toll-Free (800) 555-5555.

Has 175 account(s). Net 30 days. Sells to commercial concerns. Territory : United States. Nonseasonal.

EMPLOYEES: 105 which includes officer(s). 100 employed here.

FACILITIES: Rents 55,000 sq. ft. on first floor of 1 story cinder block building in good condition.

LOCATION: Central business section on well traveled street.

BRANCHES: Subject maintains a branch at 1073 Boyden Road, Los Angeles, CA.

04-11(554 /554) 00000000 052052052 H

While reports are normally scheduled for updating every six months, revisions are made whenever circumstances warrant. Other information, when uncovered, is issued in a report form called the *Special Notice*. These flyers contain data on such items as fires, floods, deaths, tax liens, suits, judgements, new products, and branch openings. When the information is of such nature as to affect the credit rating, either upward or downward, the entire report is revised and a new rating is assigned.

D&B Rating

Each full rating involves two factors: first, a double-letter or number-and-letter combination identifying financial strength; second, a single-digit number on a scale of one to four, indicating the composite credit appraisal as high, good, fair, or limited. (Figure 10-8) Ratings are a convenient method of measuring accounts in addition to serving as a broad basis for credit insurance classifications. For example, an account rated DD2 by Dun & Bradstreet means the concern's estimated financial strength is between $50,000 and $74,999, and the composite credit appraisal is good. A business rated DD3 is less desirable although it has the same financial strength. The fair composite credit appraisal would normally reflect a weaker financial or operating position, perhaps some slowness in payments, or both.

D&B Reference Book

Key information extracted from the *Business Information Report* forms the basis for listing in the *D&B Reference Book*. A "P" at the end of the listing indicates that a *Payment Analysis Report* is available on the particular business. Some listings are prefixed by the letters "A" or "C." The "A" identifies a business listed for the first time. A "C" prefix signals a change in rating since the prior edition. (Figure 10-9) *The Reference Book* contains nearly three million listings of commercial enterprises in the United States, Puerto Rico, and the Virgin Islands, arranged alphabetically by cities within states. *The Reference Book* is updated and republished every 60 days.

Payment Analysis Report

This features the PAYDEX (a numerical scoring system) score in the upper right-hand corner of the report for an instant overview of the firm's payment habits. Seasonal variations, payment performance trend, and the historical payment pattern are graphically illustrated. The bottom portion of the first page provides a "Detailed Summary of Firm's Payment Habits." The second page shows the "Payment Habits by Industry." (Figure 10-10)

Experian

Experian is the credit reporting business that was formerly TRW. It differs from the other reporting services by including very small businesses and sole proprietorships in its data base as well as larger companies. Experian has an easy-to-follow menu on its website that allows a credit manager to obtain either of the two reports below via the Internet using a credit card to pay the fee.

Experian Intelliscore

Experian uses statistical methodology to give each business in its data base a composite credit risk ranking between 1 and 100 (best). It is designed for credit managers processing large volumes of credit applications or transactions. Companies using this

Figure 10-9 A Dun & Bradstreet Reference Book Listing

Page from Reference Book Listings

	2512	Jones AF & Co.	464-5051	DC3
	7392	K & B Resources, Inc.	464-0204	ER6
A	52x11	Keeton Lumber Corp.	464-0859	——
	2952	Lakeside Roofing Company, Inc.	464-3366	INV
C	5399	Lane Bros., Inc.	464-4402	DD2 P
	7231	Laura's Beauty Place	464-2121	ER5 F
	3469	Mark Boring Parts, Inc.	464-9163	EE3
	5621	Paris Fashions of Crestview, Inc. Sub of Paris Fasions, Inc. Longview, VA	464-3004	3A1 P
	54x11	Russell AF	464-2512	1A1 PF
	5541	Thomas Bros. Industrial Corp. Br. of Johnstown, PA	464-0023	2A1
	1211	Wells Coal Co.* Br. of Pittsburgh, PA	464-5550	1A2
	2321	Wilson John Jacob & Co., Inc.	464-6222	EE3
	5042	Zindler & Dahl	464-5664	FB
	5912	Zoby John*	464-1073	8 2R2 P

Figure 10-10 A Dun & Bradstreet Payment Analysis Report Page 1

Who is my customer?
Business Summary – Check on basic company data, including name, parent company, location, type of business, years in business, size and CEO.

When will I get paid?
PAYDEX Score based on all trade in D&B's file – This unique, dollar-weighted indicator helps you determine how quickly a firm is likely to pay you. It is calculated based on up to 875 payment experiences reported to D&B by various vendors.

How will I spot changes in payment patterns?
90-day PAYDEX Score – Provides an instant overview of a firm's payment patterns as reported to D&B, over the most recent 90 days.

How often does this company pay within terms?
Percentage of Payments within Terms – Determine the frequency of payments within terms using this convenient feature.

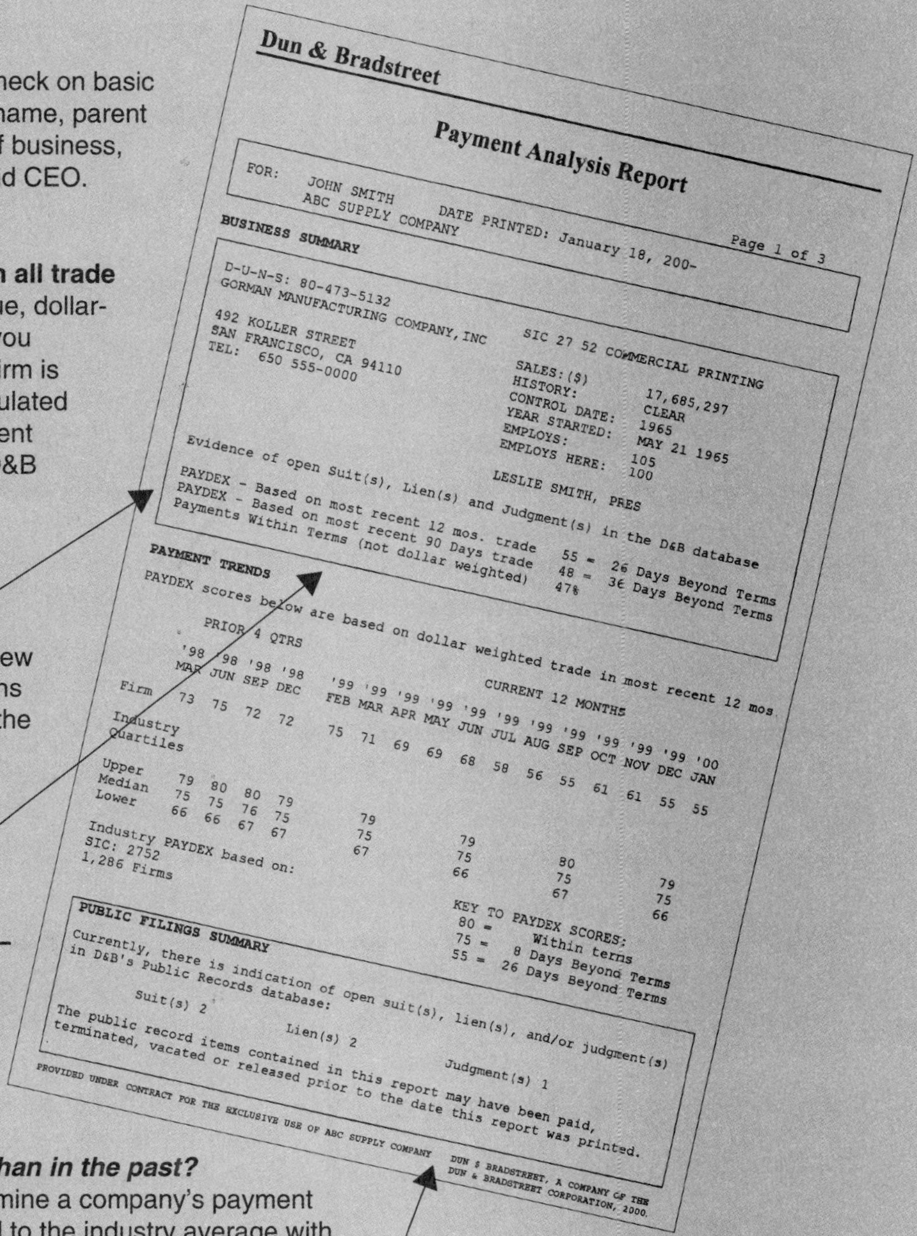

Dun & Bradstreet

Payment Analysis Report

FOR: JOHN SMITH
ABC SUPPLY COMPANY
DATE PRINTED: January 18, 200-
Page 1 of 3

BUSINESS SUMMARY

D-U-N-S: 80-473-5132
GORMAN MANUFACTURING COMPANY, INC
492 KOLLER STREET
SAN FRANCISCO, CA 94110
TEL: 650 555-0000

SIC 27 52 COMMERCIAL PRINTING
SALES:($) 17,685,297
HISTORY: CLEAR
CONTROL DATE: 1965
YEAR STARTED: MAY 21 1965
EMPLOYS: 105
EMPLOYS HERE: 100
LESLIE SMITH, PRES

Evidence of open Suit(s), Lien(s) and Judgment(s) in the D&B database
PAYDEX - Based on most recent 12 mos. trade 55 = 26 Days Beyond Terms
PAYDEX - Based on most recent 90 Days trade 48 = 36 Days Beyond Terms
Payments Within Terms (not dollar weighted) 47%

PAYMENT TRENDS

PAYDEX scores below are based on dollar weighted trade in most recent 12 mos.

PRIOR 4 QTRS | CURRENT 12 MONTHS

	'98 MAR	'98 JUN	'98 SEP	'98 DEC	'99 FEB	'99 MAR	'99 APR	'99 MAY	'99 JUN	'99 JUL	'99 AUG	'99 SEP	'99 OCT	'99 NOV	'99 DEC	'00 JAN
Firm	73	75	72	72	75	71	69	69	68	58	56	55	61	61	55	55
Industry Quartiles																
Upper	79	80	80	79		79			79			80			79	
Median	75	75	76	75		75			75			75			75	
Lower	66	66	67	67		67			66			67			66	

Industry PAYDEX based on:
SIC: 2752
1,286 Firms

KEY TO PAYDEX SCORES:
80 = Within terms
75 = 8 Days Beyond Terms
55 = 26 Days Beyond Terms

PUBLIC FILINGS SUMMARY

Currently, there is indication of open suit(s), lien(s), and/or judgment(s) in D&B's Public Records database:

Suit(s) 2 Lien(s) 2 Judgment(s) 1

The public record items contained in this report may have been paid, terminated, vacated or released prior to the date this report was printed.

PROVIDED UNDER CONTRACT FOR THE EXCLUSIVE USE OF ABC SUPPLY COMPANY

DUN & BRADSTREET, A COMPANY OF THE DUN & BRADSTREET CORPORATION, 2000.

Is this company paying better or worse than in the past?
Payment Trends – Determine a company's payment performance as compared to the industry average with this helpful report. It indicates a firm's payment habits over the past 24 months, as reported to D&B.

How can I check on legal activities?
Public Filings Summary – Find out immediately about important legal activities in D&B's files, such as bankruptcy filings and number of suits, liens and judgments that may impact a firm's ability to pay.

Figure 10-10 A Dun & Bradstreet Payment Analysis Report Page 2

Use the Payment Analysis Report to help you spot potential slow-payers.

How much does a slow-paying customer cost you?

- Let's assume you have a $5,000 credit decision on your desk with a 20% profit margin.

  This means that you would get $1,000 in profit, if collected immediately.

- A general rule of thumb is that the carry cost interest rate on outstanding accounts receivable is 12% annually.

  This means the monthly carry cost interest rate is 1% or $50 on a $5,000 receivable. Assuming 30-day terms, you lose $50 in profit, even on prompt-paying accounts. For every month the amount remains outstanding, you lose another $50 in profits.

- You can see how quickly this adds up. It only takes ten, $5,000 receivables—paid one month slowly—to cost you $500 in profits.

  The Payment Analysis Report can help you determine which of your accounts may become delinquent, so you can better manage your profit margins.

- The chart below illustrates the impact on profits for the receivable from Company A vs. Company B when the same $5,000 with 30 day terms gets paid on time vs. 60 days beyond terms.

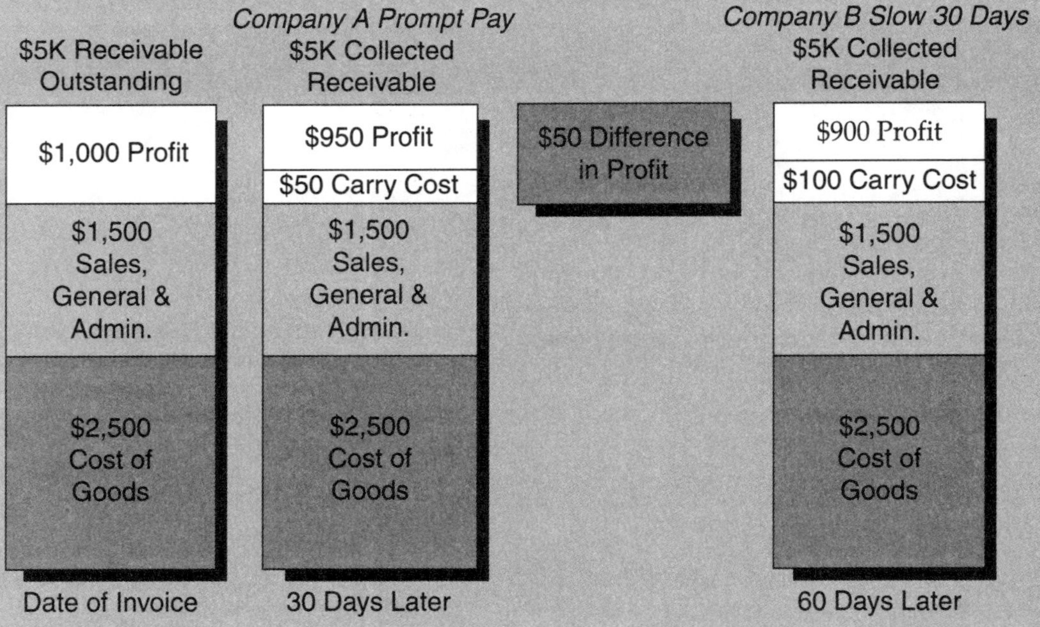

service can establish multiple scoring ranges with assigned actions, so accounts that need further investigating are clearly indicated. A sample is shown in Figure 10-11.

Relational Information

Experian also offers companies relational credit information that they can use with electronic filters to enhance their credit decisions, set benchmarks, and fine tune sales tactics.

Business Profile

Companies can obtain a business profile of a customer that includes financial information from Standard & Poor's, the average number of days late (DBT) a company pays its bills past the invoice due date and a predicted DBT 60 days in the future, payment trends for the company and its industry, and UCC filing data.

Creditors' Information Network, LLC (CIN)

CIN began as a regional cooperative among four NACM affiliates to deliver business credit information. In 1996 CIN was formed as a separate legal entity. The databases of the 13 affiliates that now comprise CIN will be linked by the end of 1998.

CIN Business Credit Report

The *CIN Business Credit Report* has eight major elements: payment history, trade line totals, monthly payment trend, quarterly payment trend, inquiry record, historical information, bank and branch reference information, and legal information. (Figure 10-12)

The Data

The system has three million subjects (credit reports) and seven million items of information. The databases include public record information, such as ownership, bankruptcy proceedings, and legal suits. Information from the affiliates is an important component, and there are plans to include information from industry trade groups. All the information is objective. It includes trade experiences of members, accounts placed for collection, judgements, liens, etc. CIN uses state-of-the-art technology to create its reports.

Differences from Other Data Bases

The CIN database is believed to be different from other credit reporting databases because more than half of the members who contribute data do not contribute to any other organization. Members receive a discount on the cost of credit reports if they provide their trade tapes, and between one-third and one-half of members choose this option.

Pricing

As a member-owned organization, CIN has cooperative pricing, which means it costs less than competitive credit report agencies. Companies can join as members of a local affiliate or by arranging for a contract directly with CIN. Like its competitors, CIN offers different levels of service on an annual basis.

The National Association of Credit Management (NACM)

NACM provides business credit reports and industry credit group meetings through its affiliate network.

Figure 10-11 An Experian Intelliscore Sample

PAGE	RPT DATE	TIME	PORT	TYPE	(1) FR-I901100455
1	05-01-97	10:27:11	C218	PROFILE	340

(2) **Sample Company**
223 S Main St
Hollywood CA 92222
Phone: 213.222.9999
Experian File No: C12345678
Experian File Established: Jan 1988

(3) **Jon Consumer**
10655 Birch Street
Burbank CA 91502

Small Business II Intelliscore

(4) **Credit Information For Sample Company**	**VALUE**
Days Beyond Terms (DBT)	11
Worst Ever DBT	32
Trade Account Balance From 14 Trade Lines (All) $	113,300
Recent High Credit $	50,000
Median Credit $	12,000
Number Of Good Trade Lines	9
Number Of Late Paying Trade Lines	3
Number Of Bankruptcies	0
Number Of Judgments, Liens And Collection Accounts	0
Number Of Original UCC Filings	8
Legal Balance $	500
SIC Code......................8721 (Accounting, Bookpng Svce)	

(5) **Credit Information For Jon Consumer**	**VALUE**
Trade Account Balance From 18 Trade Lines $	86,541
Total Monthly Obligation $	1,250
Number Of Open Revolving Trades	8
Open Revolving Trade Balance $	950
Revolving Credit Available	21.00%
Number Of Installment Loans	4
Installment Loan Balance $	0
Number Of Bankcard Trades	9
Total Number Of Bank Trades	2
Worst Ever Status On Any Trade	PD WAS 90
Number Of Trades Over 30 Days Or More Past Due	5
Date Opened For Oldest Trade Line	20 YRS 2 MOS
Legal And Collection Balance $	0
Number Of Bankruptcies	0

(6) **Score :** **50.61** (7) **Action: As specified by customer**

(8) 29% Of Businesses Score Lower (Indicating Higher Risk) Than This Business.

(9) **The Key Determining Score Factors Are:**
High consumer risk indicated by consumer risk model
Risk associated with the company's industry is higher than avg
Low risk based on long commercial credit history

1. **FR Number -** Use the FR number to order an Experian Business Profile and/or an Experian Business Owner Profile within three days at a reduced rate.

2. **Sample Company -** The business for which you have requested information is shown here along with the address, phone number, Experian File Number, and the date when the company information was established in the business information database.

3. **Jon Consumer -** The proprietor(s) for which you requested information are listed here along with the address.

4. **Credit Information For Sample Company -** Lists pertinent summary business data relating to the company's business credit performance.

5. **Credit Information For Jon Consumer -** Lists pertinent summary consumer data relating to the owner's personal credit performance.

6. **Score -** Is a statistically-based credit risk score which integrates business and owner information. The score ranges from 0 to 100, where lower scores indicate high risk and higher scores indicate low risk.

7. **Action -** Shows the decision alternatives you set based on a given set of score ranges and your credit policy/process.

8. **Percentile -** Shows the percentage of small businesses which would have scores below that of the business on the report.

9. **Score Factors -** Indicate which variables contribute most significantly to the score.

Figure 10-12 A CIN Business Credit Report

THE CREDITORS' INFORMATION NETWORK, LLC

REPORT ON 051490 DATE 5/05/98 FOR MEMBER 38-00038 PAGE 1

SAMPLE REPORT	NACM OHIO
41 WHITE ALLEN AVE	E. Pat O'Brien, CAE, CCE
BOX 1377	PO Box 1377
DAYTON OH 45401	Dayton OH 45401-1377

ON FILE SINCE 9/87 PH. 513-228-6113

BUSINESS CATEGORY	DATE REPD	DATE OPEN	LAST SALE	HIGH CREDIT	TOTAL DUE	CURRENT DUE	* * DAYS BEYOND TERMS * * 1-30	31-60	61-90	OVER90
AUTO ACCES N30DAYS PROMPT	7/97	YRS	7/97	50000	30000	30000				
BEVERAGES COD	7/97		0/00							
CHEMICALS NET 15 PROMPT	7/97	YRS	7/97 DISC	50000	2800	2800				
FOOD DISTR N30DAYS	7/97		7/97	779						
GENERAL X10FOL 60 DYS SLO	7/97	1982	7/97	30081	900			900		
GENERAL D10N30 PROMPT	7/97	YRS	7/97	22000	18000	18000				
RUBBER N10&25 PROMPT	7/97	YRS	7/97	2000	2000	2000				
SUPPLIER N20DYS 14 DYS LTE PWD	7/97	YRS	7/97	2500	500	500				

		TOTAL DUE	CURRENT DUE	1-30	31-60	61-90	OVER90
TRADE LINE TOTAL	8 ACCOUNTS	54200	53300		900		
			98.3 %	%	1.7 %	%	%
TRADE CURR TOTAL	ACCOUNTS						
			%	%	%	%	%
QUARTERLY 7/97	7 ACCOUNTS	54200	53300		900		
			98.3 %	%	1.7 %	%	%
QUARTERLY 10/97	7 ACCOUNTS	54200	53300		900		
			98.3 %	%	1.7 %	%	%

*** BANK INFORMATION ***

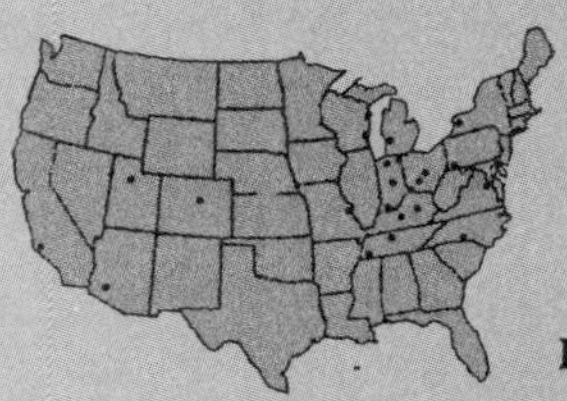

PO Box 1062, Louisville, Kentucky, 40201 Phone 502-583-4471/Fax 502 585-5453

Figure 10-12 A CIN Business Credit Report

THE CREDITORS' INFORMATION NETWORK, LLC

REPORT ON 051490 DATE 5/05/98 FOR MEMBER 38-00038 PAGE 2

SAMPLE REPORT
41 WHITE ALLEN AVE
BOX 1377
DAYTON OH 45401

NACM OHIO
E. Pat O'Brien, CAE, CCE
PO Box 1377
Dayton OH 45401-1377

ON FILE SINCE 9/87 PH. 513-228-6113

BANK 1195 BANK ONE DAYTON NA, BOX 1103, DAYTON OH
(937)449-7440
BANK 1195 BANK ONE DAYTON NA, BOX 1103, DAYTON OH
(937)449-7440
BANK 1195 BANK ONE DAYTON NA, BOX 1103, DAYTON OH
(937)449-7440

*** ACCOUNTS PLACED FOR COLLECTION ***
DATE 3/96 AMT 230.70 REF # 6640M UNCOLLECTIBLE
DATE 3/96 AMT 657.96 REF # 6640M UNCOLLECTIBLE
DATE 3/96 AMT 303.49 REF # 6640M UNCOLLECTIBLE

*** PUBLIC RECORD INFORMATION ***
ST TAX LIENS 05/10/96 BOONE
ST TAX LIENS 06/20/97 $175 BUTLER
SUITS-MUNCIPAL 06/24/97 $2,532 BOONE
PLAINTIFF KNOCHELMANN, DAVID PLUMBING

7/97 *****
7/97 GENERAL INFORMATION:
7/97 OUR INVESTIGATION REVEALS THAT THIS FIRM WAS ESTABLISHED IN
7/97 1915 AND IS A PARTNERSHIP BETWEEN JOHN BROWN, DON SMITH &
7/97 IRVING GREEN.
7/97 # OF EMPLOYEES: 16 (SIXTEEN)
7/97 TYPE OF BUSINESS: GENERAL CONTRACTOR
7/97 INFORMATION VERIFIED PER JOHN BROWN

*** INQUIRIES ***
SERVICES 5/05/98 INQUIRY

THE ACCURACY OF THIS REPORT IS NOT GUARANTEED. ITS CONTENTS ARE GATHERED IN GOOD FAITH AND SENT TO YOU BY THIS BUREAU WITHOUT LIABILITY FOR NEGLIGENCE IN PROCURING, COLLECTING, COMMUNICATING OR FAILING TO COMMUNICATE THE INFORMATION SO GATHERED. THE PURPOSE OF THIS REPORT IS INTENDED FOR USE IN THE EXTENSION OF COMMERCIAL OR BUSINESS CREDIT ONLY AND CANNOT BE REPRODUCED.
* * END OF REPORT * *

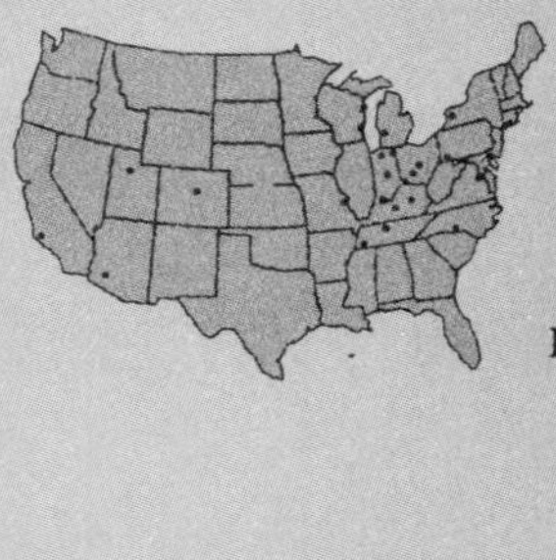

PO Box 1062, Louisville, Kentucky, 40201 ■ Phone 502-583-4471/Fax 502 585-5453

Industry Credit Groups

These groups, which operate in virtually every industry, provide credit executives with a mutual interest in the same class of customers, an opportunity to participate regularly in informative round table discussions of accounts and to evaluate credit management procedures and techniques. More than 1,500 industry credit groups are sponsored and operated by NACM affiliated associations, with association personnel acting as secretaries and meeting monitors. The industry credit groups are organized and function on a local, regional, national, or international basis. The industry credit groups are secretaried by an NACM association employee to provide services and to ensure compliance with antitrust provisions. The groups exchange information in a written or oral manner.

Written Credit Reports

Written reports are prepared using payment information furnished by group members. These reports are compiled by the local NACM offices and distributed at group meetings.

Oral Account Discussion

This frequently replaces or supplements written reports. Where groups do not require written reports, round table discussions only are held. A member desiring information about a particular account notifies the local office, which compiles a list of these accounts and mails it to members for their reported experience. The results are used by members to discuss their accounts.

Delinquent Account Reports

Members regularly submit lists of their delinquent accounts. The local NACM association collates these lists and prints a *Delinquent Account Report* that is provided to group members for discussion at the next group meeting.

Local NACM Affiliates

NACM affiliates offer business credit reports through CIN, D&B, and Experian. There is some variation by individual affiliate organization. If there are no records for a specific company, some affiliates will undertake direct investigations for members. This data is then added to the main database.

Specialized Agencies

Specialized reporting agencies usually restrict either their scope of operation or their function. They generally issue reports to only their subscribers and may or may not publish reference books. This type of agency can be helpful for accounts in a particular industry. Analysts can maintain a more personal contact with companies and more of the contact work may be done on the phone.

Examples of this type of agency are the Jewelers' Board of Trade, for the jewelry trade; the Lyon Furniture Mercantile Agency, for the furniture industry; and Proudfoot Reports, for investment houses and financial institutions.

Trade Reporting Agencies

Trade reporting agencies restrict their operations to a single line or allied lines of trade. Their coverage may be local or national in scope. They may prepare reports and issue reference books.

Credit Agencies with a Narrow Focus

A number of agencies offer credit services in several industries but the scope of their operations is usually smaller than that of the general agencies. They may provide special features that are useful to their subscribers. Examples of this type of agency are National Credit Office (NCO), which provides credit reports on apparel, textile, mass merchandisers, department stores, toy and drug wholesalers, supermarkets, aerospace, electronics, automotive and mobile home, and chemicals and coating. The Credit Exchange provides credit reports in the apparel, giftware, golf, and tennis fields. It also provides collection services for all industries.

Voluntary Trade Groups

These groups may be formed within a local credit association or be national in scope to cover a specific trade. As in the case of industry credit groups, a NACM-affiliated association services the group by accumulating and compiling pertinent factual trade information for the group. Members generally pay a subscription fee, and the information developed by the group is essentially restricted to its membership.

Getting International Credit Information

Credit information is available on international customers and their countries, but financial statements are not as easy to obtain. Furthermore, they are difficult to evaluate because accounting practices and tax regulations differ widely from country to country. The time required to gather information is greater than in domestic operations, so many export credit executives build a comprehensive file of information on prospective foreign customers so they may make quick decisions when necessary. Credit information sources range from the customer to the comprehensive economic and business data compiled by U.S. governmental agencies, by the international departments of banks, by private trade promotion organizations, and by publishers and organizations that foster foreign commerce.

Customer-Supplied Information

The best starting point for credit information is the customer. A tactful way of soliciting this information is for the U.S. manufacturer to initiate an exchange of antecedent and financial information between the seller and the buyer. At best, the buyer may volunteer valuable data, including financial reports, a detailed biography of the principals, and a history of the business going back over several generations. At worst, the buyer will provide no information at all, feeling that such a request reflects upon the integrity of the principals. Due to differences in accounting methods, financial statements cannot generally be analyzed in the same way as domestic statements.

Bank Information

An excellent source of credit information is the exporter's bank. An inquiry directed through this source stands a better chance of obtaining useful information than one directed to the foreign customer's bank. Bank information generally includes a history of the foreign firm, antecedents of the principals, and some financial data. A fairly complete picture of a firm's credit standing often may be obtained, but, depending on the seller's risk, bank reports should be supplemented by information from other sources.

Domestic Banks

Domestic banks usually have extensive credit information on many foreign firms. Credit executives should address a letter to their bank's credit department, giving the full name and address of the foreign customer, its local bank if known, and the nature of the sale including terms and amount. Credit information on a buyer may already be in the bank's file or may be obtainable from other domestic sources, and a reply will be received very quickly. In other cases, it will be necessary for the bank to get the information from its foreign offices or correspondents abroad.

Foreign Banks

Foreign banks vary widely in their cooperation with requests for information and, like information received from the customer, the credit information secured directly from the foreign bank varies in value. It may include business history, business background of the principals, financial data, or consist merely of a comment that the foreign buyer is a respected member of the community.

Exporter's Foreign Sales Representative

The exporter's sales representative abroad can also be a valuable source of information. In all probability, the sales agent has had the opportunity to study the customer's business practices firsthand. The agent is known in the customer's trade circle and has access to credit information from local banks and commercial sources. The representative can therefore offer a fair picture of a customer's financial condition, as well as confidential data which would be difficult to obtain from any other source.

Reporting Agencies

A number of agencies provide business information reports on companies located outside the United States. Some of these also provide domestic credit reports, while others focus primarily on non-U.S. companies. Dun & Bradstreet, Experian, Equifax, Graydon America, Creditel and Veritas Business Information are some of the groups that report on non-U.S. companies. In general, reports on foreign companies are similar in content and format to domestic reports. They may be purchased individually or contracted for in advance.

Companies Which Sell International Credit Reports

FCIB-NACM

FCIB-NACM, an association of executives in Finance, Credit and International Business, is a wholly owned subsidiary of NACM which serves professionals involved in worldwide export financing, credit, treasury and international subsidiary management. The purpose of the association is to raise the level of expertise and professionalism of members and to provide enhanced job enrichment through relevant discussion and exchanges of experiences. Among the services FCIB provides are:

- Conferences. FCIB holds regional US meetings, three international conferences and an annual Global Conference, all of which focus on current worldwide credit, collection and exchange problems as well as in-depth country discussions.
- Industry Export Credit Groups. FCIB operates eight export credit groups in the US and Europe. The groups meet to discuss past experiences of individual mutual accounts as well as general country problems specific to the industry.
- International Bulletins and Newsletters. Current changes affecting credit, collection and exchange conditions throughout the world are reported in the FCIB international bulletin which is distributed to all members. The bulletin presents a "reader's digest" for members and is an invaluable aid to keep them abreast of ever-changing conditions in world markets normally not discussed at meetings.
- Country Reports. These reports summarize current experience of international finance and credit managers, capturing timely, in-depth information on the credit risks of export sales in 16 countries. FCIB's country reports assist international credit professionals to forecast foreign exchange availability, transfer risks and prospective currency changes.
- International Credit Reports. FCIB, because of its large volume, is about to offer its members access to the major international credit reporting agencies at attractive prices.

Organization for Economic Cooperation and Development (OECD)

The OECD is a Paris-based intergovernmental organization, established under a 1960 convention, whose purpose is to provide its 29 member countries with a forum in which governments can compare their experiences, discuss problems they share and seek solutions which can be applied within their own national contexts. The fundamental task of the OECD is to enable its members to consult and cooperate with each other in order to achieve the highest sustainable economic growth in their countries and to improve the economic and social well-being of their populations.

The original members of the OECD were the countries of Europe and North America. Next came Japan, Australia, New Zealand and Finland. Just recently, Mexico, the Czech Republic, Hungary, Poland and Korea have joined.

The OECD publishes various booklets which assess economic trends and prospects. Many statistics are available through its on-line bookstore.

Investigating Existing Accounts

Every credit policy should include procedures for updating customer credit applications on a systematic, periodic basis. Of course, sometimes specific events will trigger an immediate reevaluation.

When To Investigate an Existing Account

Periodic Updating

Credit experts recommend that credit applications be updated routinely every six months or so. In the process of verifying information, the credit manager should take the opportunity to review the contents of the file and discard all out-dated or irrelevant materials. This will prevent errors and make it easier to find items when they are needed.

Event-triggered Updating

The credit manager should begin an update whenever any of the following events occur:

- an account that usually purchases small amounts suddenly starts to place large orders
- a prompt payer suddenly begins to pay slowly
- a lot of inquiries suddenly come in about an account
- there is a change in ownership or legal business structure of an account

Methods of Contact

Written Communications

All too frequently a good account is not commended for the manner in which it has conducted its affairs. Credit correspondence should not be limited to the collection letter but should also include all facets that will build a solid customer relationship.

Periodic Requests for Financial Statements

Business finances can change greatly from one period to the next, so financial statements covering the year, or even a shorter period, are very important. A request can point out that it is routine for all customers and that the current statements are used to continue or expand the customer's credit line.

Offer of Advice

Often the credit executive's knowledge can be made available for counseling customers, but only if the legal implications of such counseling are carefully considered. Some firms minimize the risk by requiring the customer to ask for counseling or assistance in writing, and to sign a form which could be referred to as a letter of release. This establishes a proper relationship between those offering counseling services and those seeking assistance.

Revision of Credit Availability

If the seller firm makes it a practice to notify customers of their credit lines, the revision of a line offers an opportunity to express the seller's position to the customer. With a marginal account, particularly, notification may be worthwhile. It is always a pleasing task to advise a customer that its line has been increased. To be most effective, it should emphasize that the increased credit line is a direct result of the customer's payment performance and financial growth. Less easy, is the letter to a customer advising of a downward revision. Here, it is best to state the facts in a logical, friendly manner, with sufficient explanation so the customer will understand the reasons for the downward revision. If possible, the letter should close on a hopeful note that the circumstances causing the downward revision will soon be remedied.

Sales Reps

Through frequent calls on customers, salespeople may receive early news of changes in sales trends, collections, or movement of inventory. When changes are promptly reported, the credit executive can be alerted to investigate further.

Sources of Information

The sources of information for updating a credit file are the same ones used for opening a new account. In addition, it may be useful to use the Internet to check a company's Web site and see what they are saying about their business. The Internet also is a good, fast way to access newspaper and periodicals for articles or news items about a company.

Using the Internet for Credit Investigation

Computers, telecommunications, and the Internet are radically changing the practice of credit investigation. They bring more information to the credit executive faster and at a cost far less than it would be to collect the same information manually. (See Figure 10-13 for the Uniform Resource Locators (URLs) of the sites mentioned below.)

Credit Reports

Many of the services providing credit and business information reports already make them available on-line for subscribers and for non-subscribers, although the latter must pay by credit card when requesting a report. This will soon be possible with all the services.

Specialized Information

There is a wealth of information already posted on the Internet. Databases: Lexis-Nexis is the prime example of a fee-for-service research data base. CompuServe has two kinds of research capabilities; some are free, some have time charges.

Government Information

The federal government has a lot of information available on the Internet. One of the most useful for credit executives is EDGAR, the Electronic Data Gathering, Analysis, and Retrieval system of the Securities and Exchange Commission (SEC). EDGAR contains the 10K and other reports filed with the SEC.

Figure 10-13 Useful Internet Sites for the Credit Executive

American Bankruptcy Institute (ABI)	http://www.abiworld.org/
Bloomberg.com	http://www.bloomberg.com/
businessfinancemag.com	http://www.businessfinancemag.com
CNNfn, The Financial Network	http://www.cnnfn.com/
Commercial Law League of America (CLLA)	http://www.clla.org
CompaniesOnLine	http://www.companiesonline.com/
Coopers & Lybrand L.L.P.	http://www.colybrand.com/industry/finserv/
Cornell Law School	http://www.law.cornell.edu/
CreditRiskMonitor.com	http://www.creditriskmonitor.com/
Dun & Bradstreet	http://www.dnb.com/
Equifax Business Information Services	http://www.infocheck.co.uk/
Experian	http://www.experian.com/
F & D Reports	http://www.fdreports.com/
Federal Filings Online	http://www.fedfil.com/
Fortune.com	http://www.pathfinder.com/fortune/
Graydon UK	http://www.freesearch.graydon.co.uk/
NACHA, The Electronic Payments Association	http://nacha.org/
National Association of Credit Management (NACM)	http://www.nacm.org/
Organisation for Economic Co-operation and Development (OECD)	http://www.oecd.org/
PR Newswire (PRN)	http://www.prnewswire.com/
Quote.com	http://www.quote.lycos.com/quote.com
The Economist	http://www.economist.com/
The New York Times on the Web	http://www.nytimes.com/
Thomson Financial	http://www.tfn.com/
Treasury Management Association (TMA)	http://www.afponline.org/
U.S. Census Bureau	http://www.census.gov/
U.S. Department of Commerce, STAT-USA	http://www.stat-usa.gov/
U.S. Department of Commerce, The Commercial Service	http://www.ita.doc.gov/fcs/uscs/
U.S. House of Representatives	http://www.house.gov/
U.S. Library of Congress	http://www.loc.gov/
U.S. Security and Exchange Commission, EDGAR Database	http://www.sec.gov/
U.S. Senate	http://www.senate.gov/
Uniform Commercial Code (UCC) Constitutions & Codes	http://www.law.cornell.edu/
Uniform Commercial Code (UCC) Index	http://www.law.cornell.edu/ucc/
Wall Street Journal	http://www.wsj.com/

Industry-Specific Sites

A little exploring on the Web quickly leads to new sites, which will be of varying usefulness. For instance, Thomson BankWatch follows commercial banks. Coopers and Lybrand has an on-line library of accounting and financial papers as well as a focus on risk management, and the Uniform Commercial Code is available at the Cornell University site.

Association Sites

Associations generally have helpful sites that are linked to other related sites. In addition to the sites of the NACM and the NACM affiliates, credit executives might be interested in those of the American Bankruptcy Institute (ABI), the National Automated Clearing House Association (NACHA), and the Treasury Management Association (TMA).

General Information

The amount of general information on the Internet is truly overwhelming: publications, periodicals and news services. Internet access does make it easy for the credit executive to check out many more publications than one would normally purchase to read. All the major newspapers are available on the Web. Right now, the *Wall Street Journal* is one of several charging an access fee. Publications such as *Fortune* and the *Economist* are on-line, as is *Business Credit* (on the NACM site). Also useful are the financial networks, such as CNN Financial News and Bloomberg.

Company Information

In addition to investigating a company in the press or through regulatory filings with the SEC, for example, the Internet allows the credit executive to investigate a company by going to its Web site and seeing what's there.

Electronic Mail (E-Mail)

Finally, the Internet offers a fast, efficient, and effective way to communicate with customers. E-mail seems to work faster, and has an inherent friendliness that is a bonus in credit management situations. Somehow, people find it easier to compose e-mail messages rather than to use regular mail.

Of course, the credit executive must ensure that e-mail messages adhere to the same standards as regular letters. A relaxation of style does not mean relaxing credit policy or normal business practices.

Much credit information is confidential in nature. Credit executives should take every precaution to maintain standard levels of confidentiality. This may mean using encryption or otherwise securing messages and transmissions. Security also means controlling access to the computer where e-mail messages are stored.

Comprehension Check

1. Credit investigations have been traditionally divided into two types. Name the types and provide and explanation of each.

2. Explain the terms libel and slander, providing an example of each as it pertains to credit management.
3. Provide three examples of communications that courts have deemed as privileged.
4. List the seven principles for the exchange of credit information as developed by Robert Morris Associates and NACM. Provide a brief explanation of each principle.
5. When contacting a bank for information about a potential account, what questions should be asked?
6. Provide the numeric figure ranges for the following dollar ranges:
    a. Nominal
    b. 3 figures
    c. 4 figures
    d. 5 figures
    e. 6 figures
7. If a bank reports that an account balance is in the medium 4 figure range, what is the numeric balance range for this account?
8. If a bank reports that an account balance is in the high 4 figure range, what is the numeric balance range for this account?
9. Provide an explanation of the term trade references and provide some common examples.
10. Provide an explanation of the kind of information that can be obtained on a customer by reviewing a commercial credit report.

11 Nonfinancial Analysis

Overview

Character and experience were recognized as important factors in evaluating creditworthiness as far back as colonial times. These are certainly contributing factors in determining a potential debtor's creditworthiness. It is important that a full picture of the credit applicant be obtained. This means that, in addition to extensive financial analysis, there must be analysis that is nonfinancial. Much of this nonfinancial analysis focuses on the applicant's management, namely their experience, background, knowledge, aggressiveness, honesty, and ingenuity.

This chapter focuses on the nonfinancial aspects of credit decisions, especially detailing the five "Cs" of credit, which are the mainstays of nonfinancial credit analysis.

Learning Objectives

After reading this chapter, the reader should:

- Understand the importance of nonfinancial analysis
- Know how to apply each of the five "Cs" of credit
- Understand the importance of the background of the principals and the business
- Know how the debtor's method of operation and industry characteristics affect creditworthiness
- Know the major nonfinancial aspects of bank investigations
- Know the major nonfinancial aspects of trade investigations

Chapter Outline

The Importance of Nonfinancial Analysis

General Considerations

Credit investigation procedures should be standardized and comprehensive. By standardizing the steps taken to investigate a risk and determine its desirability, the credit department minimizes the possibility of oversight in the investigation. By assuring that all aspects of a credit applicant are reviewed, the credit executive can make a better decision.

Credit investigations are not complete if they only consider the financial information about a credit applicant; there are other areas not appearing in financial statements that are relevant to the credit decision.

The factors examined in a credit analysis are generally known as the five "Cs" of credit—character, capacity, capital, conditions, and collateral. These factors provide the credit manager with a framework for evaluating credit applications.

Understandably, each factor may be more important in one case than in another. In every case the credit executive must measure the account against all the factors before giving a final opinion.

Facts and Opinions

Credit executives must attempt to gather facts as much as possible, in order to make the best credit decision. This is difficult sometimes, because it may be impossible to differentiate between a fact and an opinion. Thus, all questions should be worded to obtain as factual an answer as possible. This is especially true for nonquantitative information.

Behavior

Much of nonfinancial analysis deals with the **behavior** *of the credit applicant, ranging from payment behavior to other related business behavior.* The credit executive must decide whether past behavior has been satisfactory and whether it is likely to be indicative of future behavior.

The Five "Cs" of Credit

Character

Character *is often believed to be the most important of the five "Cs" of credit. It refers to the willingness of the debtor to pay obligations, and imputes a level of morality, integrity, trustworthiness, and quality of management to the credit applicant.* To properly examine the business character of an individual, the credit executive must know as much as possible about the individual's previous business background. Individuals who have been in business on their own or who have been officers of corporations should be judged on the record of their success, past payment records, and information from current suppliers. For example, a long-standing record of operation without litigation or financial embarrassment is a prima facie indicator of a favorable business record. On the other hand, an individual who has a record of bankruptcies, litigation, or both is a questionable risk insofar as this factor is concerned.

Where information is detrimental to an individual, full details should be sought. Accurate, comprehensive information is essential for practical credit analysis. If an individual has been involved in failures, it should be determined how much on the dollar was paid in settlement to unsecured creditors. Intangibles, such as family background, employment record, and personal credit history, can be judiciously used to form a tentative opinion. People who have set up a business for the first time are judged on their ability, conscientiousness, integrity, and aggressiveness as employees. It is essential to secure the names of their previous employers and to check antecedents with responsible persons in these concerns.

Capacity

This aspect deals with the ability of the business to operate successfully and the ability to pay when a debt is due. Capacity can be measured by the applicant's ability to generate cash flows. Previous business experience is a valid indicator of the capacity of a firm. Particularly when large volume orders, exacting specifications, or tight delivery schedules are involved, the credit executive is interested in knowing whether the concern has actual prior experience in that type of operation. In the building contracting industry, for example, a job may be let on the basis of previous performance and capacity, as well as on the basis of low bid.

Capital

Capital, *the credit applicant's equity or net worth, signifies the financial strength of the applicant as a credit risk.* In evaluating capital, the credit executive seeks to determine whether the account will be able to pay its obligations. This approach is different from the first "C", which seeks to judge if the account will be willing to pay. This factor highlights the financial condition and trend of operations. Each case is judged on its own merits, since many factors affect the financial condition of a business. Some lines need a large investment in fixed assets. Others require only a minimum investment in machinery and fixtures. This affects the financial picture of the concern. Similarly, some lines of business must have large amounts of ready cash and liquid assets to meet seasonal operating expenses, while others can rely on regular cash inflow to meet maturing debts.

The trend of business is significant and weighs heavily in the overall judgment of the account. The credit executive looks more favorably on a business that shows increasing sales, profits, and net worth.

Conditions

By examining conditions, the credit executive analyzes how the current and expected general economic situations may affect the applicant's business. Credit executives should analyze the business cycle of credit applicants and customers as well as their own. The likelihood of a satisfactory credit experience is greater when the subject is in an industry that is in a period of dynamic growth.

In addition, it is important to know about creditors' industry cycles and consolidations and if the industry is subject to booms and busts. Community conditions also affect the likelihood that merchants will pay their bills on time, as they must rely upon receipts from their own customers.

Collateral

This factor considers *whether the account has additional resources, in the form of equities or other assets, that can be used for payment should the creditor's capacity or character fail.* Specific assets, such as receivables or inventories, can be pledged via liens against these assets. Other forms of collateral may include standby letters of credit from the applicant's bank, guaranties by the firm or its parent, personal guarantees from the principals, and pledges of investment holdings such as stocks or bonds, or other investments. It is important to determine whether potential collateral is free and clear and has not already been pledged to other creditors.

Background of the Principals and the Business

Essential Demographics of the Principals

It is true that no business situation is completely stable. The possibility always exists that a debtor company may encounter financial difficulty. But when a company has a good business record and is operated by capable people who are good moral risks, the likelihood of this kind of trouble is decreased. Business reputation takes a long time to build. It includes the ability, integrity, and experience of the principals, and is a valuable indicator of a firm's future actions.

To develop the information needed for understanding the personal and business background of an account, the credit executive follows a prescribed method of investigation, inquiring into a number of key points.

Names of the Principals

This is the normal starting point of this phase of the investigation. The people who have invested money in the business should be identified and their backgrounds checked. This may not be practical when companies are widely or publicly held. In these instances, background investigations of the chief stockholders, officers, and members of the board of directors are usually enough. More usually, however, companies are closely held, with a handful of people owning control. Then, the background of each person should be investigated. It is especially important to uncover hidden ownership in case the business may be controlled by people who have unfavorable backgrounds.

Credit judgments based on the integrity and ability of the principals cannot be realistic when facts regarding the true ownership are kept from creditors. For example, it is important to know the business record of the husband when the wife is listed as an officer or principal. It is entirely possible that she has active control over the firm, in which case her record would govern. But if she is a "front" for her husband, whose business record may not be able to stand scrutiny, then his business record becomes an important part of the total picture.

A similar situation is sometimes encountered when a person starts a business with an abnormal initial investment from supposed "savings." The credit executive should be able to gauge the amount of money a person would have normally saved, and ask for a detailed explanation about the source of larger amounts. Aliases are sometimes uncovered during a credit investigation. The simplest way to proceed in that case is to turn the information over to a credit agency, and ask for a detailed record search.

If aggression and ambition are not tempered with experience and judicious action, the firm may find itself in difficult situations. On the other hand, a conservative attitude may lead to less willingness to take a chance. It is important to be sure that the combination of traits is made in the right way.

Business Experience

To say that principals have business experience is not enough. It must be ascertained that the experience is in the same line of business or that the skills required are transferrable from previous business experience. The size of previous ventures is also an important point in the experience of principals.

Financial Worth of the Principals

By law, the personal assets of partners and proprietors are available for the payment of business debts; this may also be true for corporations. Though a corporation protects its principals' personal assets from the debts of the business, the individuals may be asked by creditors to endorse or guarantee business debts. Thus, principals who are wealthy in their own right are able to reinforce the credit position of their companies.

Relatives

This feature of a business background is not important in many cases, but it arises often enough to make some mention of it worthwhile. It may be discovered that a relative has lent financial support to the company, either as a loan or as an investment. Significant family relationships may suggest additional methods of approving an account on a secured basis, or with endorsement or guarantee.

Integrity

The ultimate decision in any credit analysis is based on the creditor's confidence that the debtor will pay its obligation. The ability to pay is important in this determination, but more important perhaps is the debtor's willingness to pay. This makes the debtor's integrity a key point in the analysis of credit risk.

Record Information

Generally, it is assumed that a person has good moral character unless there are specific facts to the contrary. To uncover unfavorable information, it is usually necessary to check agency reports and local records. Any facts concerning fire, failure, or fraud should be examined carefully. The circumstances surrounding the particular situation should be ascertained by direct investigation or through an agency, and clearly understood before a decision is made.

When a fire has occurred, it is important to know if the account carried insurance coverage. Where this is so, it should be determined if payment was made without question or if the fire was criticized. The number of fires may also be significant, though they are more common in industries working with flammable materials. Failures may have been caused by actions of the principals or may have resulted from the incompetent actions of others. If the individual was a dominant principal, this information becomes more important in the overall analysis of the person's capabilities. The credit executive must also be aware of the circumstances under which the difficulty occurred.

A bankruptcy filing during a time of serious business recession would not be viewed in the same perspective as a petition filed during a prosperous period. Similarly, as events recede into the years, they may become relatively less important than current events. The number and frequency of failures are likewise significant, because they indicate inability to operate successfully.

Fraud is a difficult thing to prove and requires court proceedings. This aspect of one's business history can be uncovered by a check of court records in the locales where the principal has conducted business. In this connection, it is important to obtain a complete listing of the individual's prior business interests, because those which did not meet with success might be omitted by the principal. An effective way to do this is to go over a chronological listing of prior affiliations and obtain explanations for any years not covered. It goes without saying that when this procedure is followed, it is necessary to check the listing against agency and public records.

Other Important Personal Factors

Ability of the Principals

The ability of principals is largely determined by their past records. In starting a new business, one who has had a successful business for many years would normally be considered a better risk than one who is beginning a first venture. That comment holds true on a general basis, but needs refinement in terms of the specific management skills required to operate a business—namely, production, marketing, and finance. Some of these skills may be furnished by employees or consultants, but the management of a company must still be responsible for them. Thus, when a company is analyzed, the credit executive must be satisfied that the necessary skills are provided in adequate proportions to ensure successful operation.

Distribution of Functions

Individual control of a complicated business venture is usually inadequate, because the demands are too great for any one person to meet. Preferably, the managerial functions should be divided among the principals. This not only allows each to specialize in a particular phase of operations, but it also spreads the danger of serious business loss if one principal becomes ill or incapacitated. In addition, it is wise for a company to provide management in-depth, with subordinates trained to take over a more senior job, should one become available.

Outside Interests

Principals having several interests must be expected to divide their time among them. As a result, they do not give full attention to the affairs of any one business. This may not be unfavorable in many cases where a company has made adequate provision for the day-to-day operations, but it becomes a serious matter when one individual takes on too many responsibilities. The extent of intercompany relations between commonly owned companies must also be examined. Where a principal operates and controls a number of separate entities, there may be a tendency to consider them as one group. Consequently, their affairs may be directed to the mutual benefit of all, but particularly for personal gain. While this is not undesirable in itself, it may create some problems for creditors of any one company. They must understand these intercompany relations and how they affect their own positions as creditors.

Personal Habits

The personal habits of the principals are of natural concern to creditors. Undesirable traits, when carried to excess, can influence business operation and take the principal's time and attention away from business. This jeopardizes the creditors' position.

Primary Characteristics of the Business

Business Name

A proprietor or a partnership using a trade style should register that name and keep a bank account under it. Orders should be placed and payments made in the legal name of the business. If that is not done, it may confuse creditors when they invoice the company. A check with the firm's bank will disclose the name under which its account is maintained. When it is convenient, court records may also be searched for details of trade style registration. Charter details of a corporation may be obtained from the Secretary of State where the company is organized. These list the date of incorporation, the state of incorporation, the number and type of shares authorized, and their par value. During the personal investigation, it can be determined how many shares are outstanding, and who holds them. This identifies the control of the business.

Age and Reputation of the Business

Businesses have their own personalities in much the same way as the principals who operate them. Thus, it is important to determine how long a concern has been in existence, the extent of its success, and its public image. It is generally acknowledged that the first five years of business operation are the most trying. During that time, the concern must become established in its industry or community, must develop a following of customers, and must demonstrate its ability to compete effectively for a share of the market. During the same period, the business is slowly establishing its reputation in the trade. Some are known as price cutters, others stress quality and service, while still others develop a reputation for effective performance on schedule. Credit executives are interested in these aspects of their accounts, since they reflect their stability of operations.

Legal Form of Organization

The legal form of organization influences the capital, continuity, and liability of the business and of its principals. In reviewing a case up for credit decision, the credit executive should be satisfied that the seller's position will be protected if it becomes necessary to press for collection.

Method of Operation and Individual Characteristics

Function

It is important for the understanding of an account to know whether it retails, wholesales, or manufactures merchandise. This may seem relatively simple to do, but the lines are not clearly drawn in practice.

For instance, one company may purchase raw materials for manufacture and sell the finished products directly to customers; another may purchase some products ranging from semi-finished to ready made for manufacture and sale. To determine the function of a company, a percentage breakdown is needed in terms of retailing, wholesaling, and manufacturing done by the account. It is likely that the different functions will have different buying and selling terms, which in turn will influence the financial requirements of the company. In addition, the function breakdown may indicate the amount of dependence the company places on local business, as well as the stability of its share of the total market.

Industry

The industry in which a company operates is extremely important for evaluating a given company. Every line of business has characteristics that apply to it alone and distinguish it from other industries. These should be known by the credit executive, as they vitally affect its financial operation. For example, a company selling to a growth industry plays an active part in a dynamic sector of the economy that is growing more rapidly than the economy as a whole. Continued growth is characterized by companies whose sales and profits rise rapidly and are usually not subject to business downturns. However, companies in this group are vulnerable to technological changes and to the transition from rapid growth to slower growth. This could then lead to a period of stabilization which may ultimately develop into a decline. Because cash needs are relatively high and capital turns rapidly in growth industries, creditors occasionally may be required to carry their customers. By the same token, suppliers selling to companies in growth industries can expect a more satisfactory profit.

A firm's customers also exert an influence on liquidity. If a company sells to customers in a strong industry, the likelihood is greater that it will have little trouble with collections. By the same reasoning, if a company sells in an industry that is cyclical, collection problems are more likely. Also, since a cyclical industry moves up and down more rapidly than business in general, purchase of its product can be readily postponed in times of adverse economic conditions.

Many companies in cyclical industries are prone to **leverage** their operations. *This means that a prime source of their funds is long-term debt, used to finance plant expansion when the prospects for business are good.* Companies in this type of industry are vulnerable to business downturns, however. With high fixed costs, a sharp reduction in sales volume paves the way for losses. These drains cause a sharp reduction in their liquid assets and their ability to meet trade obligations when they become due.

On the other hand, a company selling in a relatively stable industry would normally expect its customers to show a more consistent financial condition with sales and profits holding or rising. Those customers sell goods that are consumed or used immediately and their replenishment cannot be postponed.

While there are basically three patterns of industrial progress—growth, cyclical, stable—not all companies within a given industry will always follow the industry pattern. Moreover, the categories are not mutually exclusive. For example, the sales and profits for an industry may fluctuate during a business cycle but have better than average growth from one business cycle to the next. Such an industry would have both cyclical and growth characteristics.

Credit executives can obtain a fair picture of their customers' business outlooks by knowing industry trends. While there is a spread between good, marginal, and poor accounts within every industry, the general industry characteristics will influence all companies. It is conceivable that marginal companies in slow growth industries would be less desirable risks than marginal companies in fast growth industries. When prospects are good, it is naturally easier to look favorably upon a credit risk; when the trend is downward, more careful examination of the facts is required.

Some industries are characterized by concerns that forego customer service and rely upon price competition as a chief attraction. If that is the case, their operating costs should be lower and their profit margins carefully shaved. At the same time, the companies should have vigorous collection procedures. Operations are so delicately balanced that the slightest slowdown of collections will have a major influence on the liquidity position of the seller. This type of operation relies upon smooth functioning of the entire buying-selling-collection-payment cycle.

Other companies that enjoy higher profit margins have a built-in buffer in their accounts receivables. Consequently, the companies may be able to carry accounts for longer periods of time. The creditor helps to finance the customer but charges for the service in the form of higher profit margins.

Products and Terms

Products

The actual products sold by a company do, in the final analysis, reflect company success. Pricing, quality, and service are related to each other. Usually when quality and service are good, prices tend to rise. By the same token, prices are sometimes less important to buyers when a supplier can deliver good quality merchandise and provide adequate service. In every instance, the acid test of this combination is reflected in the profit and loss statement.

The number and type of accounts sold also bear directly on the vulnerability of a company. For instance, a company selling to a few large accounts can expect a good volume of business and fair success in projecting its cash needs. Profit margins can be predicted with close accuracy. Should the same account lose a single customer, however, the impact of this loss would be much greater than the loss of an account by a company having many customers placing relatively small orders. A company that sells to many accounts could normally expect larger selling and administrative expenses.

Selling and Buying Terms

A supplier helps to finance customers by providing goods or services on credit. To obtain a clearer picture of the importance of this feature, the buying and selling terms of customer accounts can be compared. For instance, a company that buys material on 30-day terms and sells its products on 30-day terms is in effect obtaining one month's financing from its suppliers and furnishing one month's financing to its customers. Meanwhile, a second company buying on 60-day terms and selling on 30-day terms has an advantage over the first company. Its suppliers are furnishing material on terms that are long enough to allow the company to fabricate it, sell the finished merchandise, and make its collections before the original invoices for raw materials are due. On the other hand, a third company buying on 30-day terms and selling on 60-day terms is in the worst position of the three. It is expected to pay for raw materials purchases before its own receivables have been collected. This third position is critical and will eventually lead to financial distress, unless additional funds are constantly pumped into the business.

The spread between buying terms and selling terms is naturally of concern, since it is a potent indicator of the long-range cash demands on a customer's business. Seasonal datings also fall into this category and must be compared in terms of buying and selling datings. Ideally, a company wishes to purchase on longer terms than it requires to manufacture, sell its products, and collect the resulting receivables. This is hardly ever permitted by a company's suppliers, since they realize the dangers of totally financing the customer's operations.

Factors Affecting Delivery and Timing

Distribution

Geographical separation of market areas has become less distinct with the improvement of rail, air, water, and truck transportation. Consequently, a company may have customers in all parts of the United States and in many parts of the world. This broadened market is generally favorable, as it spreads the base of company operations. Firms having a purely local distribution are more vulnerable to community economic fluctuations, since they have no way to spread their credit risk geographically.

The influence of local economic conditions on collections from any particular area pursues a distinct pattern. Usually a slowdown begins at the retail level, when consumers are laid off from their jobs and cannot pay charge accounts and installment purchases. As the retailers' collections slow down, they look to their suppliers for cooperation in carrying these slow receivables; they pay their own obligations slowly. By that time, wholesalers have felt the deteriorating local economic conditions and may seek to pay their own accounts slowly to manufacturers. As a result, the local influence has extended to areas many miles away.

If the economic conditions are very serious, their effects may be felt throughout the country. In most instances, however, large manufacturers and suppliers spread their markets to more than one geographical location. Consequently, drastic curtailment of collections from any one area has been offset by good collections in other areas serviced by the company.

Seasons

Many industries operate on a seasonal basis. During some part of the year, sales activity is high; during other months it is low. For purposes of credit analysis, this means that an account would normally require high trade and bank credit at particular times during the year. Once its season had passed, merchandise would normally have been manufactured and sold. Immediately following a heavy selling season, an account would be expected to have large accounts receivable, relatively low cash, and low inventories. At that same time, chances are high that payables had not yet been paid, so its balance sheet would show heavy accounts payable and bank debt. After the normal selling term period had passed, the company should have collected its receivables. This would change the balance sheet: cash would be high, accounts receivables would be relatively low, and inventory would still be small. When debts are paid, cash decreases and payables decline. Following this period, the account would start to buy for the next season. Inventories would rise, accounts payable would start to get heavy, and bank loans would start to appear on the balance sheet. As manufacturing progresses, cash balances would tend to decline because of the daily cash needs of the business. Receivables should be relatively low, but bank loans would increase. As sales are made in the next active season, receivables rise and inventory declines, but payables and bank loans are still at seasonally high peak. This cycle is repeated for each season.

The credit executive takes the seasonal aspects of business into account when analyzing a risk. Not only are the balance sheet and profit and loss figures important, but the frequency of seasonal activity also influences a firm's earning power and ability to recover from a poor season. Thus, a company that relies principally on Christmas trade is affected more seriously by a poor Christmas season than one that can count on Christmas, Easter, June graduation, and September back-to-school flurries of activity. In the first case, nine or more months must pass before strong prospects for earnings again become evident. The second firm has another chance at earnings in a much shorter period of time.

Time Lags

This feature of manufacturing and wholesale operations affects inventory positions, collection of receivables, and predictions of cash needs. It determines in large part the established buying and selling terms in an industry. Two examples illustrate this feature:

> Example 1. The infant's wear industry specializes in hand-embroidered baby garments. Much of this hand detail is done in foreign countries. The manufacturer must purchase the raw materials, ship them abroad by boat, have the hand work done and the dresses shipped back to the United States. This may take up to six months. In the meanwhile, the merchandise has been purchased but is not in condition to be sold. The time lag involved in manufacturing plays an important role in the capital requirements of this line of business.
>
> Example 2. Automobile designs for the next models have already been developed and tooling up has started, while current models are being sold. Planning for cash and materials requirements in this industry is detailed and exacting. Cash resources are projected up to five and ten years in advance. Time lag is a critical factor in the planning and placement of orders for component parts.

Other Industries Do Not Need Long Periods of Manufacture

When high style is an important consideration, time lags are cut as short as possible. Industry terms usually follow this trend and are likewise shortened. The reason for this is obvious: styles are volatile and vulnerable; consequently, long selling terms restrict the supplier's ability to press for collection and threaten the value of merchandise sold.

Changes in Operation

A business that has been established for a long time may occasionally find it necessary to adapt its method of operation to meet changing conditions. Technology, market locations, labor markets, and economic conditions may change and influence the market position of a concern. Consequently, the credit executive is interested in finding out what changes have taken place in the operations of customer accounts, and what has caused these changes. As an added step, an investigation should be pursued to determine the success of these changes.

Location Factors

The location of a business affects the cost of operation and nearness to buying and selling markets. Physical facilities should be large enough for efficient operations, yet not so large that space is wasted.

Rent or Own

Many well-established concerns own the buildings in which they operate. There are, however, just as many that prefer to rent physical facilities, claiming it gives them more financial flexibility. On the balance sheet, a company that rents its plant and equipment may show a relatively small investment in fixed assets. This increased liquidity improves the apparent financial condition of the company. On the other hand, a company that owns its own property shows investment in fixed assets much larger in relation to current assets; hence, lower liquidity. When the idea of leasing equipment gained acceptance, there was a simple interpretation of the balance sheet. Liquidity improved when assets were sold and then leased back. As analysts gained experience with this type of situation, however, they became more sophisticated. They now recognize that a lease to pay specified rentals is a constant drain on the earnings of the company. Obligations must be met, whether facilities are used or not. In addition, charges for rental are calculated to provide a yield to the owners.

The credit executive must be concerned with the gross charges for a plant and equipment. This is true whether the physical facilities are owned or rented. When buildings and machinery are owned, the charges are in the form of depreciation which do not require cash to be paid out. Leased equipment charges show up as a rental lease expense and require cash outlay.

Size of Premises

Several illustrations will point out that the size of the premises must be related to the type of activity performed and their geographical location. A company that does its own manufacturing would naturally be expected to have larger premises than one that uses outside contractors. Similarly, a company that uses public warehouses to store merchandise will need smaller premises than one that maintains its own warehouses. Companies requiring small machinery for manufacturing may be able to operate on smaller premises than those needing large capital equipment. By the same token, a company located in a metropolitan area can be expected to build up, while one situated in an urban area can take advantage of low land values and build long structures one or two stories high.

Size of Building

When a company's physical facilities are located in a metropolitan area, the firm often occupies a portion of a multi-storied loft building. In addition to knowing the number of square feet occupied, the credit executive should have an idea of the size of the building and the number of floors it has. This influences some of the production and materials handling methods and consequently affects the costs of operation.

Type of Construction

Floor loads and type of equipment which can be placed in the building are determined by the type of construction. This also protects the company's materials from damage. A fireproof building, arranged so the spread of fire can be effectively prevented, provides maximum assurance to creditors that the danger of fire loss is minimized. Conversely, a frame building without adequate fire protection equipment increases the possibility of a fire that will interrupt operations or destroy the business.

Surrounding Area

This also affects the fire hazard of a particular location. Located in an area where inflammable materials are stored or processed, a company is more vulnerable to fire loss. The type of construction used in the adjoining buildings also affects the fire hazard. A retail company must pay particular attention to its location, which must be accessible to its customers. There is more flexibility in the operation of a wholesale or manufacturing concern, since its products can be shipped directly to customers.

Transportation Facilities

The ability of a manufacturing company to receive raw materials economically and to ship out finished products affects its overall costs of operation. Locations near main roads or on railroad spurs are ideal. Retail stores should provide adequate parking facilities for their customers. Suburban shopping centers apportion a large amount of their total space for parking cars. In downtown areas, retailers may make arrangements with nearby garages and parking lots for customer parking. Also, locations near bus stops make it easy for customers to reach the store.

Bank Investigations

Significance of a Bank Relationship

A significant factor in the background of a business is its relationship with its bank. The bank check helps provide the credit executive with a more complete understanding of an account.

What Bank Loans Mean

There are basically two ways a bank lends money: unsecured loans and secured loans. An **unsecured loan** *relies only upon the customer's promise to pay.* Consequently, this form of loan is made only to customers having a good credit standing and the financial ability to repay the loan. *A loan granted on a* **secured basis** *is generally backed by a personal guarantee or by collateral such as marketable securities or other pledged assets.* When a personal guarantee is given, the financial strength of the names backing the notes determines the ability to pay the loan. When collateral is given, the lender usually looks in whole or in part to liquidation of the pledged property in the event that the loan is not regularly paid. A credit executive may, on occasion, come across an account that is considered a prime credit risk, eligible for an unsecured loan, but borrowing on a secured basis. To properly evaluate the credit risk, the executive should discuss the account with the bank to determine the quality of the loan and collateral. It may be that the customer requested such an arrangement in order to obtain a lower interest rate, and thus reduce the cost of carrying the loan.

Trade Investigations

Importance

Part of the background of a business also consists of the way in which it has conducted its affairs with trade creditors. If the integrity of management and its business acumen are examined, the credit executive should, and generally does, learn how the company pays its bills. Thus, a company with a record of honest dealings and principals that have demonstrated their skill and experience generally want to discount or pay its obligations promptly. It is able to do so because it knows how to buy, how to sell, and how to manage its finances.

Interpretation of Trade Clearances

The payment record of an account is actual evidence of how it pays its bills. It is therefore natural for a credit executive to examine paying records when evaluating company's credit risk. The information contained in a trade clearance presents a clear and current picture of the firm's paying habits, and covers:

- how long sold
- date of last sale
- highest recent trade
- now owing
- past due
- payment terms
- paying record
- comments

Trend of Payments

A comparison of one trade report with an earlier one establishes the trend of company payments. A trend toward slower payments should be investigated. An account may be expanding sales and relying upon trade creditors to finance this expansion. On the other hand, an account may be experiencing difficulty in the collection of its own receivables. Knowing these two alternatives, the credit executive can proceed with the investigation to determine the actual cause of the slowing trend. An improving payment trend is favorably regarded as the account may be improving its own collections or may have obtained additional financing (either equity or borrowings) in order to pay its bills more promptly.

Age of the Business

If all respondents report the account as new or if a large number of first orders appear on the clearance, it is reasonable to assume that the firm has recently begun operations. There is, of course, the possibility that the company has recently changed all of its suppliers, but that is not likely.

Size of the Business

By examining the dollar amounts of individual and total high credits, it is possible to estimate the scope of business conducted by the buyer. Large orders from many suppliers indicate a large operation. Smaller orders characterize a smaller business.

Confidence of Suppliers

A report on the actual dealings with suppliers reveals their degree of confidence in the account. This is shown by the actual terms of credit which they extend.

Selling Terms

These should be noted for every reply from suppliers and can be compared to find out if special terms are being received by the account. Seasonal datings or extra time or discount allowances put the credit executive on notice that further investigation is required.

Seasonal Clearance

When a trade clearance shows amounts owing very close to the high credits approved, it is likely that the clearance has been taken at the height of the season. This type of clearance is useful in that it gives an idea of how heavy a payable position the debtor is willing to accept. Cleanup position shows relatively small amounts owing when contrasted to recent high credits. Past-due amounts after cleanup time point to the possibility of a poor season.

Concentration of Purchases

A thorough trade clearance that shows three or four major suppliers and a number of smaller ones indicates that the company concentrates its purchases. A supplier asked to become a new source should determine the risk position it will occupy in the overall debt picture of the account.

Changes Indicated

In a comprehensive trade investigation, the respondents are asked to furnish any additional information they may have concerning recent personnel or operational changes in an account. These serve as leads to further investigation. For example, a retailer of drugs that had discounted all invoices consistently for four years might begin to allow the discount period to pass by. An investigation could disclose that the retailer was not successfully meeting the competition of a new supermarket. The trade report spotted a change brought about by the competitive situation.

Personal Quirks

Trade investigations reveal what might be called personal quirks that affect payments. For example, a manufacturer might receive a poor trade report on a potential customer that showed that some of the suppliers were being paid promptly while other suppliers were forced to collect their money through attorneys. After checking with a substantial number of the suppliers, the manufacturer might learn that the concern was paying sales personnel of suppliers promptly when they made calls for their money but was delinquent in mailing out checks. Having learned the peculiarity of this customer, the manufacturer would be able to open an account and handle profitable business while others were shutting down on the account.

Special Financial Arrangements

Unpublicized arrangements, guarantees, requests for special terms, and extensions can be discovered during a trade check. They are of considerable importance in analyzing a business.

Analysis of Sample Trade Clearances

In Figure 11-1, six sample trade clearances are shown to illustrate the kinds of information that can be obtained by a careful interpretation of these results. The first trade checking shows a relatively new business with no payment experience reported. Initial orders have been approved by at least six suppliers in moderate amounts. The owner has some previous business experience, according to one supplier, and that has apparently been satisfactory. The clearance is made at the peak of the buying season, ready for manufacturing or selling, since high credits equal amounts now owing. Terms are regular for the line of business.

The second account is better established than the first. Purchases are fairly concentrated and in larger amounts. Payments are good on terms characteristic of the garment industry. This is a seasonal clearance, with amounts owing equal to recent high credits. There is one new supplier reporting; this may be a company that is trying to get this account as a customer, because it has offered terms of "60 plus 60," or it may carry merchandise needed by the account for a new line.

The third account has spread its purchases more than the first two. It has been buying from at least eight large suppliers, with two smaller ones starting to show some activity. The clearance is taken past the peak season, with most of the amounts already past due. Apparently the account has had some trouble with its own collections or is expanding sales without sufficient equity financing. The first supplier seems to have foreseen this difficulty and restricted its credit exposure. The supplier reporting "first deal" may be replacing the one that is withdrawing.

The fourth trade clearance was evidently conducted on a company which is working itself out of difficulty. The trend of payments is consistently better. Regular suppliers have cooperated with the account and now note some improvement. The clearance seems to have been made just after season, since high credits and amounts owing are fairly close.

The fifth clearance shows a very satisfactory experience with a well-regarded account. It is taken at cleanup time, with outstanding debts low in relation to high credits. With nothing past due, except the obviously disputed $1,500, the company

Figure 11-1 Sample Trade Clearances

High Credit	Now Owing	Past Due	Terms	Payments and Comments
(1)				
1,000	50,000+	0	30.00	new account
800	35,000+	0	2/10 n/30	first transaction
600	25,000+	0	10 EOM	ppt on samples
450	20,000+	0	30.00	just opened
400	5,000	0	10 EOM	new—knew owner from previous
250	250	0	net cash	OK
(2)				
50,000+	50,000+	0	70.00	ppt
35,000+	35,000+	0	60.00	as agreed
25,000+	25,000+	0	60.00	ppt—occasionally antic
20,000+	20,000+	0	2/10/60x	ppt
5,000	5,000	0	60 plus 60	new account
(3)				
28,000	1,000	0	30 plus 30	ran slow—sold for years
25,000	25,000	15,000	2/10 n/30	30 slow—ran for years
20,000	20,000	18,000	2/10 n/30	45 slow
20,000	16,000	16,000	2/10 n/30	30 - 45 slow
18,000	18,000	18,000	net 30	first deal
15,000	13,000	8,000	net 30	55 slow—good account
13,000	12,000	3,000	net 30	30 - 50 slow
12,500	12,500	12,500	regular	10 days past due
5,000	1,500	0	2/10 EOM	ppt
1,000	—	0	net 30	ppt—new account
(4)				
25,000	15,000	5,000	60.00	fmly 60 slow—now avgs 30 slow
20,000	20,000	5,000	60.00	fmly 45 slow—now 20 days slow
18,000	15,000	1,000	60.00	about cleaned up; pay improved
15,000	13,000	5,000	60.00	improving; now 15 days p d
8,000	6,000	5,300	60.00	working along; friendly account
6,000	3,000	1,500	30.00	recently 60+ p d; now 45 p d
(5)				
22,000	5,000	0	2/10 EOM	sold for years—antic & disc
25,000	3,000	0	2/10 n/30	discount for years
18,000	6,000	0	n/30	sold years—pays prompt
15,000	6,000	0	2/10 EOM	mostly ppt—some discount
13,000	3,500	0	n/30	good discount
12,000	—	0	regular	ppt
30,000	1,500	1,500	2/10 EOM	ppt except one bill 45 days p d
(6)				
12,000	12,000	12,000	n/30	placed for collection
10,000	10,000	1,000	n/30	in hands of attorney
8,000	8,000	8,000	2/10 EOM	wants to return first shipment

shows an excellent record. Purchases are spread quite evenly among the seven suppliers that reported.

The sixth clearance speaks for itself. It has all the earmarks of a distressed debtor.

Comprehension Check

1. When conducting a credit investigation, the 5 "Cs" of credit provide a framework to analyze an applicant. List the 5 "Cs" and explain the implications of each on the credit decision making process.
2. Provide an explanation of the following trade clearance lines of information:

High Credit	Now Owing	Past due	Terms	Payment and Comments
50,000	50,000+	0	2/10 n/30	new account
35,000	35,000+	0	net 30	30 slow - sold for years
20,000	25,000+	18,000	2/10 EOM	ppt
12,000	24,000+	24,000	regular	placed for collection

12 International Trade

Overview—Banks and International Trade

Companies that trade internationally usually rely on their banks for special trade services. In a world where all customers paid cash in advance this would not be necessary. However, because most companies will not pay for goods they have not yet received, and because foreign governments do not always permit advance payment, international trade, like domestic trade, relies on extending credit to trading partners.

The simplest way of extending credit is with an open account (O/A). Selling on open account means that no draft is drawn. The transaction is payable when specified. If no term is specified, O/A usually implies payment by return mail. Selling on open account is risky to the seller unless the customer is a subsidiary or a very well-known customer. A company doing business abroad will often use letters of credit or documentary collections. Both methods, which are extensively used in international trade, are discussed in this chapter.

Learning Objectives

After reading this chapter, the reader should understand:

- Banks and international trade
- Common problems for the exporter
- Commercial letters of credit
- Standby letters of credit
- Bankers' acceptances
- Foreign exchange
- Sources of government and private sector support
- Finance support
- Overseas Private Investment Corporation (OPIC)
- Other agencies and programs

Chapter Outline

I. Banks and International Trade
   A. Collections
   B. Types of Collection and Drafts
   C. The Role of the Banking System
II. Common Problems for the Exporter
   A. Collection Advantages and Disadvantages
   B. Rules Governing Collections
III. Commercial Letters of Credit
   A. Participants Under a Letter of Credit
   B. Types of Letters of Credit and Types of Drafts
   C. Special L/C Arrangements
   D. Discrepancies
   E. Advantages and Disadvantages of L/Cs
IV. Standby Letters of Credit
V. Bankers' Acceptances
   A. Regulations Governing Bankers' Acceptances
   B. Discount Eligibility
VI. Foreign Exchange
   A. Delivery Conventions and Credit Risk
   B. Hedging
VII. Government and Private Sector Export Finance Support
   A. Insurance Programs
VIII. Overseas Private Investment Corporation (OPIC)
IX. Other Agencies and Programs

Banks and International Trade

Collections

The collection procedure in foreign trade usually involves four parties:

1. **Drawer** *(exporter) is the customer who entrusts the collection of its draft and documents to a bank in its country.*
2. **Remitting bank** *is the bank chosen by the exporter to forward the documents to the importer's country for collection through a collecting bank.*
3. **Collecting bank** *is any bank, other than the remitting bank, involved in processing a collection.*
4. **Drawee** *(importer) is the party to whom the documents are presented, in accordance with an instruction letter (sometimes referred to as the transmittal letter).*

A fundamental wish of any exporter is to maintain title to the goods until the importer either pays for the merchandise or provides satisfactory assurance of payment at a future date. Thus, an international transaction includes much more documentation and formal assurances than domestic transactions.

The **collection procedure** *is the process by which the remitting bank, acting upon the instructions of an exporter, presents document(s) associated with a sales transaction to the importer.* Documents may include:

- a sight or time draft.
- a bill of lading or other transport document.
- commercial invoices.
- a certificate of origin.
- insurance policies or certificates.

Acceptance is when the importer undertakes an obligation to make payment upon the maturity of a time draft drawn on and accepted by the importer.

Types of Collection and Drafts

There are two types of collection. **Clean collection** *is a collection involving only "financial" documents.* When the bill of lading or transport document is consigned directly to the importer, the importer has title to the goods. Such transport documents are said to be "straight consigned." **Documentary collection** *is one that transmits "commercial" (or shipping) documents.*

A **draft** *is a written order by the drawer directing the drawee to make payment at sight (sight drafts) or at a determinable future date (time drafts).* When the draft is drawn at sight, the documents are released to the buyer (drawee) upon payment of the draft. If the draft is a time draft (payable 30, 60, 90, etc., days after sight, or date), the documents are released to the buyer upon its acceptance of the draft. A time draft is also called a usance draft.

The Role of the Banking System

Under a documentary collection, a bank acts only as a collecting agent to assist the exporter in obtaining payment or acceptance of his draft before the release of documents to the importer. Collecting banks are responsible only for verifying that certain conditions are met before the release of these documents. They are not responsible for either verifying the quantity or quality of the merchandise being shipped against the documents or for guaranteeing payment in the event of nonpayment or non-acceptance of the draft.

Common Problems for the Exporter

There are a number of common problems with which exporters contend. First, if not taken by the importer, the goods may incur demurrage, warehousing, insurance, and other related charges billable to the exporter until such time as the importer wishes to pay for the collection or the exporter makes other arrangements to sell the goods. A related problem is that the insurance coverage by the seller or buyer may be inadequate. If the merchandise is either damaged or lost, the importer would probably refuse to honor the collection. There is always the possibility that the exporter might have to wait an indeterminate length of time to receive payment/acceptance.

Finally, the importer may not have a valid import license, which could result in the refusal to accept the goods or in a delay in payment or in acceptance of the draft.

Collection Advantages and Disadvantages

As a method of obtaining payment, the risks involved in a collection fall between open account, which favors the importer, and cash in advance, which favors the exporter. For the exporter, the advantages and disadvantages are:

Advantages	Disadvantages
Less risk of premature release of goods	Delays or slowness in payment
Enhanced competitive position	Additional costs due to non-payment or non-acceptance by the importer
Convenience	
Availability of financing	

For the importer, the advantages and disadvantages are:

Advantages	Disadvantages
Convenience	Damage to reputation if nonpayment or non-acceptance claimed
Reduced costs	
Deferred payment	

Rules Governing Collections

International collections are usually governed in their treatment by the International Chamber of Commerce (ICC) Uniform Rules for Collections. The general provisions and definitions of this ICC publication are binding on all parties to a collection unless otherwise expressly agreed or unless contrary to the provisions of a national, state, or local law and/or regulation from which no departure may be made.

Commercial Letters of Credit

A letter of credit (L/C) *is a written undertaking by a bank (issuing bank), acting at the request and on the instructions of its customer (applicant for the credit) to:*

- *make payment to, or to the order of, a third party (the beneficiary)*
- *accept and pay bills of exchange (drafts) drawn by the beneficiary*
- *authorize another bank to effect such payment or to pay, accept, or negotiate such bills of exchange (drafts)*

The terms and conditions of the credit must be complied with before payment, negotiation, or acceptance can be made.

A variety of documents may be included in a letter of credit, such as a draft, a bill of lading or other transport document, which may be a document of title in negotiable form, commercial invoices, certificate of origin, and insurance policies or certificates. International L/Cs are generally governed by the current ICC Publication, the Uniform Customs and Practice for Documentary Credits, commonly referred to as the UCP.

Participants Under a Letter of Credit

The buyer or importer is referred to as the **applicant or account party**. *The beneficiary is the* **seller/exporter**. Upon the instructions of the applicant (importer), the issuing bank opens or "issues" the letter of credit. The advising bank, usually a branch or correspondent of the issuing bank located in the beneficiary's locale, "advises," or checks the apparent authenticity of the letter of credit it transmits to the beneficiary.

Other banks may become involved in a letter of credit transaction. The **paying/accepting bank** *is the bank on which the draft is drawn.* The **negotiating bank** *is the bank that gives value for drafts and/or documents under the credit.* The **confirming bank** *is the bank that may, at the request of the issuing bank, "confirm" or obligate itself to the beneficiary to insure payment/acceptance of a draft under the letter of credit.*

Types of Letters of Credit and Types of Drafts

There are several kinds of letters of credit. They tend to be named in pairs, with the name indicating if they do or do not contain a special condition. They include:

Revocable: This L/C allows the issuing bank the right to cancel (revoke) or modify the terms of credit without the consent of the beneficiary.

Irrevocable: This L/C constitutes a definite undertaking by the issuing bank to pay or accept drafts drawn under the letter of credit, provided that the stipulated documents are presented and that the terms and conditions of the credit are met.

Confirmed: The L/C is "confirmed" when the second bank, usually in the locale of the exporter, has added its confirmation (obligation of assurance of payment) to that of the issuing bank.

Unconfirmed: The L/C is one for which the advising bank only advises the beneficiary, without adding its own confirmation.

Straight: This L/C is one in which the obligation of the issuing bank to pay/accept drafts or to incur a deferred payment obligation extends only to the beneficiary of the credit.

Negotiation: This L/C is one in which the obligation of the issuing bank to pay/accept drafts or incur a deferred payment obligation extends not only to the beneficiary, but also to the nominated bank in the credit.

There are two types of drafts associated with L/Cs: sight drafts and time drafts. A **sight draft** *is when a letter of credit requires the beneficiary to draw the draft "at sight."* It is expected that the beneficiary will receive payment at soon as the documents are presented and the negotiating/paying bank has had a reasonable time to examine the documents to determine if they are in compliance with the credit terms.

A **time draft** *may also be called an acceptance draft or a usance draft. If a letter of credit requires the beneficiary to draw a time draft for acceptance with payment at some determinable future date,* it is expected that the bank on which the draft is drawn (drawee) will accept the draft as soon as the documents complying with the credit terms are at the nominated bank and the nominated bank has had a reasonable time to examine those documents.

Special L/C Arrangements

Letters of credit may include special arrangements. Some common additional arrangements are:

Transferability

A transferrable credit allows the beneficiary of a letter of credit (the exporter) to transfer all or part of the rights under the credit to a third party (the transferee). For a credit to be transferable, the exporter must arrange for the importer to have a credit opened expressly stipulating that it is transferable.

Assignment of Proceeds

The beneficiary of a letter of credit assigns all or part of the proceeds under a credit to a third party (the assignee). Unlike a transferred credit, the beneficiary maintains sole rights to the credit and is solely responsible for complying with its terms and conditions.

Back-to-Back

When one letter of credit is used as security to obtain the issuance of a second letter of credit to cover the same transaction, that arrangement is known as a "back-to-back" letter of credit. Most banks are reluctant to enter into back-to-back credit arrangements because of the associated risks.

Red Clause

A red clause in a letter of credit is used when a beneficiary needs financing in order to complete the manufacturing of merchandise or to purchase items to fill a particular order. A red clause permits the exporter to obtain an advance of part or all of the amount of the credit, as specified in the credit.

Installment Credit

The applicant for an L/C may need to be assured of receiving the merchandise over a period of time in specific installments. *When a bank issues an installment credit or a credit stipulating shipments by installment within given periods, that credit should clearly state, "Shipment must be effected in the following installments."*

Revolving

A revolving letter of credit contains instructions that allow the beneficiary to draw up to a specific limit for a specified period. Revolving credit uses the same letter of credit to cover numerous scheduled shipments over a long period without the necessity of issuing new credits or amending the existing credit. However, it restricts the amount available for each shipment and controls the frequency of shipments and amounts available. Revolving credits are either cumulative or noncumulative. A cumulative revolving credit allows an unused portion of a credit to be added to a subsequent period. In a noncumulative credit any portion not used in one period cannot be added to the next.

Deferred Payment

Under a deferred payment L/C, after shipment the exporter presents complying documents to the negotiating/paying bank.

Discrepancies

All documents under a letter of credit must comply with its terms and conditions before payment/acceptance can be made. Yet, surveys of banks in major money centers reveal that approximately half of all drawings presented contain one or more discrepancies.

When the documents presented do not conform to the terms of the L/C, the exporter has the following options:

- to ask the negotiating/paying bank to return the documents for corrections and then resubmit the documents
- to request that the negotiating/paying bank contact the issuing bank, preferably by telecommunication, for permission to negotiate/pay or accept despite discrepancies
- to instruct the negotiating/paying bank to forward the documents to the issuing bank on approval, that is, for honor under the L/C
- to request that the negotiating/paying bank honor the drawing under reserve or against a guarantee

It is important to examine all the documents for compliance with terms and conditions of the credit. Common discrepancies are:

- unclean bills of lading (i.e., indication of merchandise damage, etc.)
- date of bill of lading later than called for in the credit

- consignment shown on bill of lading not as required in the credit
- bill of lading does not indicate goods have been shipped "on board"
- unauthorized "on deck" shipment
- no evidence on bill of lading of payment of freight
- unauthorized charter party bill of lading
- ports of loading and destination not as specified in the credit
- unauthorized transshipment
- draft and documents presented after expiration date
- description of goods on invoice differs from that in the credit
- marks and numbers on packages not identical on all documents
- weights not identical on all documents
- amount on invoice differs from that on draft
- draft, shipping documents, or insurance documents not properly signed or endorsed
- insurance document not as specified in the credit
- insurance coverage in currency other than that of credit
- effective date of insurance not as specified in the credit or shown on shipping documents
- cargo underinsured

There are also other key items to consider in international trade. The more important ones are:

- A **green clause** *is very similar to a red clause in that it also allows the drawing of a clean draft, but it requires the merchandise to be stored by the paying bank until all documents are received.*
- A **telegraphic transfer clause** *speeds payments when the receiver of funds is not located in a financial center.*
- An **evergreen clause** *provides a periodic expiry date with an automatic extension and usually states one final date.*
- A **bill of lading** *(transport document) is a title document issued by a carrier and serves as a receipt for the goods and as a contract to deliver the goods to a designated party or to its order.*
- *The person shipping the goods is the* **shipper** *or* **consigner**. *The company or agent transporting the goods is the* **carrier**, *and the party to whom the goods are destined is the* **consignee**.

Advantages and Disadvantages of L/Cs

The lists of advantages and disadvantages of L/Cs are for an irrevocable letter of credit, the most common form of letter of credit. For the exporter, the advantages and disadvantages are:

Advantages	Disadvantages
Minimal risk of non-payment	Reduced competitive position
Prompt and convenient payment	
Access to financing	

For the importer, the advantages and disadvantages are:

Advantages	Disadvantages
Availability of credit and financing	Increased cost and less convenience
Security	No guarantee of receiving proper merchandise

Standby Letters of Credit

A bank will issue a standby letter of credit on behalf of a customer (the applicant) who is required to provide assurances of his or her ability to perform under the terms of a contract between the applicant and the counterparty in the contract (the beneficiary). A **standby letter of credit** *is any letter of credit or similar arrangement, however named or described, that represents an obligation to the beneficiary on the part of the issuer to:*

- *repay money borrowed by the applicant, or advanced to or for the account of the applicant*
- *make payment on account of any default by the applicant in the performance of an obligation*
- *make payment on account of any indebtedness undertaken by the applicant*

Standbys are similar to commercial letters of credit in that they represent the irrevocable obligation of the issuing bank to make payment to the beneficiary upon presentation of the required documents. Standbys differ from commercial letters of credit in that the parties involved do not expect that the standbys will ever be drawn upon.

Commonly, standbys are issued by banks in the United States for the following reasons:

- to assure the refund of advanced payments
- to support **"bid" and "performance" obligations** *(the obligation of a successful bidder to accept a contract and the obligation of the applicant to perform under the terms of the contract)*
- to back up bonds issued by insurance companies
- to stand behind a monetary obligation under a promissory note or a like commitment

Bankers' Acceptances

A **bankers' acceptance** *is a time draft drawn on and accepted by a bank and payable at a fixed or determinable future date.* It can be created either from letter of credit transactions or from time drafts drawn independently of a letter of credit.

The following is a simplified example of how a bankers' acceptance is used in the United States:

A time draft is drawn on a U.S. bank by an exporter or an importer.

The drawer endorses the draft and presents it to the bank for acceptance.

The bank accepts the draft, discounts it, and pays the net proceeds to the drawer.

The bank has the option to hold the draft in its own portfolio as a loan or to rediscount it in the open market.

At maturity of the draft, the bank pays the face amount to the holder/presenter (if it has been rediscounted) and looks to its customer for reimbursement.

Regulations Governing Bankers' Acceptances

The Board of Governors of the Federal Reserve system regulates the bankers' acceptance market in the United States. It does this by modifying the definition of eligibility, by placing restrictions on the types of transactions from which eligible acceptances may arise, and by setting restrictions on amounts banks may create for individual customers and in the aggregate.

Discount Eligibility

Acceptances are generally classified as eligible for discount at the Federal Reserve or ineligible for discount at the Federal Reserve. Currently, the basic criteria for eligibility are as follows:

- the term of the draft cannot exceed six months (for example, 180 days)
- the shipment must be "current," that is, the acceptance must be created within a reasonable time (usually 30 days) after the shipping date of the goods

The underlying transaction must fall into one of the following categories:

- the import or export of goods, either to or from the United States or between foreign countries
- the domestic shipment of goods within the United States crossing state borders or traveling a minimum of 25 miles from point of origin
- the storage of readily marketable staples in the United States or a foreign country, provided the bank possesses a warehouse receipt or other such documents conveying the security title to the goods at time of acceptance until maturity

Acceptances that are not eligible for discount by the Federal Reserve are defined as "ineligible" acceptances. The Federal Reserve requires that, unlike eligible acceptances, ineligible acceptances are not exempted from the definition of deposit and as such an ineligible acceptance is subject to reserve requirements.

Foreign Exchange

Foreign exchange *is the conversion of freely usable or freely convertible currencies of one country into the currency of another.* Foreign exchange transactions differ depending upon when they are scheduled to occur. A **spot transaction** *is for the immediate sale and delivery of a foreign currency, normally two business days from the transaction date for Europe and Asia and one day for Canada and Mexico.* A **forward transaction** *is a contract between two parties that have agreed to exchange currencies at a fixed rate on an agreed-upon future date.* Forwards can be done for any traded currency for any date and for any amount although there are standards for each of these variables. For instance, regular trades are in 30-day increments, with maturities that fall on weekends or holidays (for either currency's country) rescheduled to the nearest business day.

Delivery Conventions and Credit Risk

There are well-established procedures for settling foreign exchange trades. In the United States, for example, the U.S. dollar portion of the trade is settled through the **Clearing House Interbank Payment Systems (CHIPS)**, *which consists of the major clearing banks in New York City.* CHIPS settles more than one trillion dollars daily. A customer's bank has access to CHIPS directly (through an account with a New York City bank) or indirectly through its bank's account with a New York City bank. There are similar systems in other major money centers worldwide.

The foreign currency portion of a U.S. dollar transaction is usually handled with a bank transfer through the SWIFT (Society for Worldwide Interbank Financial Telecommunications) system or through one of the internal systems offered by the largest banks. All transfer or delivery instructions are confirmed verbally at the time of the transaction and usually in writing afterward.

In trading foreign currencies with a bank (counterparty), there is a financial risk. The risk is that one of the trading parties may not be able to meet its obligation on the settlement date. Banks try to limit this exposure by establishing internal limits on the amount that a customer can trade—either on a cumulative basis or on a daily basis. Corporate customers try to minimize their risk by dealing with the largest banks (worldwide), assuming that there is safety in size.

Hedging

A **foreign exchange (FX) hedge** *is a financial transaction that reduces risk by fixing the rate for a foreign currency.* A foreign exchange hedge reduces the degree to which fluctuation in the FX rate affects financial results.

There are three basic hedging approaches—forward contracts (as described above), foreign currency futures and options, and natural hedges. **Foreign currency futures and options** *are contracts between two parties, the holder of the option (the buyer of the option) and the writer of the option (the seller-bank or option exchange corporation).* Most futures and options are traded through an exchange. **Natural hedging** *occurs when a company has both future payment obligations and receivables in the same foreign currencies and can use the cash flows to offset each other, either fully or partially.*

Note that forwards, futures, and options are all kinds of **derivative securities**. *That is, their value is "derived" from an underlying security.* They are the most common form of derivatives and are used by companies of all sizes to manage their FX exposures.

Government and Private Sector Export Finance Support

In order to encourage domestic exports, most industrialized nations have government programs designed to improve an exporter's ability to provide attractive financing terms to its foreign buyer and to protect the exporter and banks involved in export financing against certain commercial and political risk losses. In the United States, the EXIMbank is a U.S. government agency that provides flexible short- and medium-term insurance programs to U.S. exporters and banks, medium- to long-term guarantee programs to U.S. banks, exporters, or other parties extending a loan to a foreign buyer.

Insurance Programs

Eximbank issues several distinct policies divided between those for exporters and those for banks. Coverage designed for banks is principally provided by:

- The Bank Letter of Credit Policy: protects banks against commercial and political risk losses on irrevocable letters of credit issued by foreign banks in support of U.S. exports
- The Financial Institution Buyer Credit Policy: protects financial institutions against commercial and specified political risk losses on short-term direct credit loans or reimbursement loans to foreign entities importing U.S. goods and services

Coverage designed for exporters is principally provided by:

- The Multibuyer Export Credit Insurance Policy: a one-year blanket policy that provides coverage for an exporter's short-term credit sales to different buyers.
- The Single Buyer Export Credit Insurance Policy: insures an exporter's short-term credit sales to a single buyer.
- The Medium-Term Export Credit Insurance Policy: insures an exporter's credit sales for varying periods up to five years, depending on the value of the goods exported.
- The New to Export Credit Insurance Policy: a one-year blanket policy that insures export sales to several buyers with payment terms ranging from sight up to 180 days, or for certain capital or bulk agricultural goods, up to 360 days.

EXIMbank's loans and guarantees to exporters, foreign importers, or banks offer assistance for U.S. exports of capital goods and services eligible for medium- and long-term financing. EXIMbank offers four basic types of direct loans and guarantees:

- direct loans to foreign buyers
- intermediary loans to lenders financing importers
- working capital guarantees to U.S. companies involved in exporting
- guarantees to lenders providing financing to a foreign buyer

These medium- and long-term programs are designed to support sales of U.S. manufactured capital goods. Under the Direct Loan Program, Eximbank provides a fixed rate loan to the buyer of U.S. exports that face officially subsidized foreign competition. Under the Intermediary Loan Program, EXIMbank provides the lender with a standby commitment to fund the export loan at a rate that is .5% less than EXIMbank's Lending Rate. Under the Guarantee Program, EXIMbank guarantees the repayment to a U.S. bank or foreign bank in the U.S., the exporter or other party extending a loan to a creditworthy foreign buyer of U.S. capital goods or services. Under the Working Capital Guarantee Program, EXIMbank will guarantee 100% of the principal and interest on working capital loans extended by lenders to companies for the production of exported goods and services.

Overseas Private Investment Corporation (OPIC)

The Overseas Private Investment Corporation (OPIC) is an independent U.S. government agency that sells investment services to assist U.S. companies investing in some 140 emerging economies around the world. A self-sustaining government corporation with current reserves of more than $3.7 billion, OPIC assists U.S. private investment overseas because it is in America's economic and strategic interest.

OPIC's mission is to mobilize and facilitate the participation of U.S. private capital and skills in the economic and social development of less developed countries and areas, and countries in transition from nonmarket to market economies, thereby complementing the development assistance objectives of the United States. OPIC accomplishes this mission by assisting U.S. investors through four principal activities designed to promote overseas investment and reduce the associated risks: insuring investments overseas against a broad range of political risks; financing of businesses overseas through loans and loan guaranties; financing private investment funds that provide equity to businesses overseas; and advocating the interests of the American business community overseas.

Other Agencies and Programs

The Commodity Credit Corporation (CCC), a U.S. government agency, was established to encourage U.S. exports of agricultural goods by providing guaranteed medium- to long-term financing through a U.S. bank to foreign importers.

The Private Exporting Funding Corporation (PEFCO) is a privately held corporation established in 1970 with the support of the U.S. Treasury and EXIMbank. PEFCO is a supplemental lender, through its Direct Loan Program, and provides fixed-rate dollar loans to foreign buyers of U.S. goods and services.

Exporters Insurance Company Limited (EIC) is a user-owned underwriter of trade credit and political risk insurance. EIC offers trade credit insurance covering terms from sight letters of credit to 10-year financings with no produce sourcing requirement.

Just as the U.S. government has programs to aid exporters so, too, do the governments of most developed countries. Support for export credits is available through government-sponsored agencies such as EDC (Canada), COFACE (United Kingdom), Hermes (Germany) and JEXIM (Japan).

Comprehension Check

1. The collection procedures in foreign trade usually involved four parties. List the four parties and provide a brief explanation of each.
2. Provide a list of the typical documents involved in collecting an international payment.
3. List the advantages to the seller and the disadvantage to the buyer of an international open account transaction.
4. List the advantages to the seller and the disadvantages to the buyer of an international secured account transaction.
5. What is a letter of credit?
6. Provide a list of the parties under a letter of credit.
7. Provide a brief explanation of the following types of letters of credit:
    a. Revocable
    b. Irrevocable
    c. Confirmed
    d. Unconfirmed
    e. Straight
    f. Negotiation
8. List and provide and explanation of the two types of drafts associated with a letter of credit.
9. Provide an explanation of the following special L/C arrangements:
    a. Transferability
    b. Assignment of proceeds
    c. Back-to-back
    d. Red Clause
    e. Installment credit
    f. Revolving
    g. Deferred payment
10. When the documents presented under a letter of credit do not conform to its terms, what options does the exporter have?
11. Provide a list of 20 common discrepancies of an L/C.
12. Define the term green clause as it pertains to an L/C.
13. Define the term evergreen as it pertains to an L/C.
14. What is a standby letter of credit?
15. What is a bankers' acceptance?

13 Financing and Insurance

Overview

Customers often require additional forms of financing to help meet their operating or expansion needs. These requirements are beyond the scope of trade credit but usually have a direct effect on the customer's creditworthiness and represent competition to the creditor for repayment. In addition to commercial banks, other financial entities provide financing. Business insurance, in all its forms, also serves as a financial resource for many customers. Both of these topics are discussed in this chapter.

Learning Objectives

After reading this chapter, the reader should know:

- The basic reasons for borrowing
- How factoring works and what it means to the creditor
- How finance companies work and what a creditor should know about them
- Features of the various kinds of term loans
- Different forms of leasing and leasing arrangements
- Aspects of leveraged buyouts and what a creditor should know about them
- Key points about federal government finance programs
- Types and features of business insurance

Chapter Outline

- I. Financing Needs
  - A. Reasons for Borrowing
- II. Factors
  - A. Background
  - B. Factoring Procedure
  - C. Features of Factoring
  - D. Cost of Factoring
  - E. Evidence of a Factoring Agreement
- III. Finance Companies
  - A. Functions
  - B. Financing Procedure
  - C. Types of Loans
  - D. Cost of Financing
  - E. Evidence of a Financing Arrangement
  - F. Impact of Liens Under UCC
- IV. Term Loans
  - A. General Considerations
  - B. Restrictive Covenants
  - C. Public and Private Placements
- V. Leasing
  - A. Background
  - B. Operating Leases
  - C. Finance Leases
  - D. Sale-Leaseback Arrangement
- VI. Leveraged Buyouts
  - A. General Considerations
  - B. Structure
  - C. Characteristics of Good Buyout Candidates
  - D. Credit Analysis of the Leveraged Buyout
- VII. Government Programs
  - A. Background
  - B. Small Business Administration
  - C. Small Business Investment Corporations
- VIII. Business Insurance
  - A. Role
  - B. Insurance and the Creditor
  - C. Credit Executive's Interest in Insurance Coverage
  - D. Prerequisites of Insurance
  - E. Insurance Agreements
- IX. Other Forms of Insurance
  - A. Property Insurance
  - B. General Liability Insurance
  - C. Life Insurance
  - D. Credit Insurance

Financing Needs

Reasons for Borrowing

A successful business often needs outside financial support, and obtains it from its principals or shareholders, trade creditors, and a variety of non-trade sources. Most business loans are short-term in nature, either in time or demand. A maturity date is specified in the time loan, usually in 30-day periods, for up to six months or longer. A demand loan may be repaid by the borrower or called by the bank/lender at any time.

The lender may also ask for collateral or may simply make an unsecured signature loan. One reason for a cash shortage could be that the borrower had a poor year and is unprepared financially to meet some major expenses in the near future. Another is that extra funds are needed for the seasonal requirements of the business.

In all short-term loans, the borrower is expected to repay, once the need for the loan ceases, usually within a year. This means a sound company will be expected to clean up its borrowings at least once a year. However, this isn't always the case as some industries and major companies function with a "constant" amount of short-term debt (but at varying levels). To relieve this dependence on short-term funds on an ongoing basis, most creditworthy companies seek relief in the medium- and long-term debt markets, either through public issue or private placements.

Because many companies use external, non-bank sources of financing, such as factors and finance companies, as regular sources of outside financing, a knowledge of these techniques is a necessity for the credit executive and is essential for proper analysis of a customer's financial situation. The receivables in both factoring and financing are open-account, not installment-account sales. A business firm may make use of outside financing for a large number of reasons:

- to avoid dilution of ownership equity and control that would result from raising funds through issuing more common stock or taking in partners; issuance of debt is also likely to be less expensive than issuing equity because the interest on debt is tax deductible
- to obtain large amounts of operating cash expeditiously and simply; the ability to draw on these sources is one of the primary liquidity reserves of most creditworthy and successfully operating businesses
- to secure operating cash on a flexible basis, thereby avoiding the tying up of other company assets in the form of ready cash
- to improve the net working capital position
- to take advantage of cash discounts and other profit opportunities that will provide greater financial returns than the borrowing costs
- to benefit from the technical assistance provided by the specialized financing institutions

Factors

Background

Factoring grew out of the specific need for working funds in some industries, such as the textile and fur trades. *It provides the means for business executives to convert* *receivables to cash before they are due without retaining liability for their payment.* It began in early America, when factors acted as commission merchants, handling goods on consignment. During the latter years of the 19th and the early years of the 20th centuries, factors ceased acting as sales agents for their clients and gradually evolved into modern factoring operations. The great growth of factoring, the entrance of a variety of financing institutions into this field, and the widespread use of such financing in many different lines of business are all quite recent phenomena.

Among the principal reasons that modern day companies use factors are:

- to limit credit and collection expense, including credit losses, to a definite percentage of credit sales
- to reduce the credit and collection expense ratio (including credit losses), or obtain a more efficient performance of credit and collection
- to increase sales through the credit granting and collection services provided by the factor
- to increase profits by concentrating on product development, production, and sales

Factoring Procedure

Accounts receivable of the client are purchased by the factoring concern, which assumes the credit risk without recourse to the seller. The seller's customers are usually notified to make payment directly to the factor, but this may not always be the case. The business firm entering into a factoring agreement not only contracts to sell its receivables to the factor, but also relieves itself of the credit and collection function, including personnel and the cost and risk of decision making. This role is assumed by the factor for a fee. Under no other method of short-term financing do business firms shift the credit and collection job to the financing institution. When a business firm is being factored in this manner, a notice that payment for the goods is to be made to its factor usually shows on the firm's invoices.

The factor approves credits for its client. As the client makes shipments, it sends copies of the invoices and the shipping documents to the factor. The client may obtain immediate cash for the full net face value of the invoices (i.e., the gross amount of the invoices, less any discounts and allowances granted to the firm's customers), minus only the commission and a reserve to offset returned goods, merchandise claims, and the like. The remainder is made available at the average due date of the invoices. Any credit losses (net of the reserve) are borne by the factor.

Features of Factoring

Credit Checking

When a factor checks credit, it takes over the credit and collection functions of its client. The client no longer needs to conduct credit investigations and analysis, make credit decisions, keep records of accounts receivable, collect accounts receivable, and sustain bad-debt losses. When an order is received from a customer, the client calls the factor for a recommendation. The factor usually has a credit file on the account or will set one up when the request is received. The file contains agency reports, memoranda of the factor's interviews with the principals and the accountant, financial statements, trade reports, bank investigations, and other information normally contained in a credit folder.

In addition, there is a record of inquiries on the account, the factor's current exposure, and the recommendation. If the recommendation is favorable, the factor approves the client's order.

Purchasing Accounts Receivable

When the factor approves a client's order, there is a concurrent agreement that the receivables resulting from the order will be purchased by the factor. This distinguishes factoring from pledged borrowing. In factoring, title to the claim passes from the client to the factor, while in pledged borrowing, title remains with the client. In this way, the client is assured of a stated amount of money each time the factor approves an order. There is no need for accounts receivable follow up or for collection procedures. The likelihood of bad-debt losses for the client is completely eliminated on approved accounts. The only exception to this procedure occurs when a client ships an order which has not been approved. In that case, the factor is not obligated to participate in the transaction, and the order is shipped at the client's risk. There, the factor reserves the right to turn down the receivable arising from that particular transaction or may advance money against it with recourse, which makes the client contingently liable on the account.

Cashing Receivables

At any time after the receivable is created, the client may turn it over to the factor. This function of the factor is called **cashing receivables**, *or cashing sales, on an advance basis (prior to maturity) or at maturity.*

Advancing Funds to the Client

Upon the request of the client, the factor advances funds against the receivables that have been checked or approved. The client forwards the invoices and usually receives 85 to 90 per cent of the face amount purchased before maturity; the factor holds back the balance for such contingencies as returns and discounts, disputed receivables, and client's risk receivables. This provides funds to the client before the due date of the invoice.

A company that is trading actively on its invested capital and does not want to tie up its assets in receivables will find this feature useful. Much of the need for borrowing is eliminated, ownership of the business can remain undiluted, the liquidity of the firm is strengthened, and net working capital is turned actively. However, this does come at a price. The factor's fee is not negligible, and it should be measured against alternative forms of financing.

Receiving Funds at Maturity

In this type of arrangement, *the factor does not advance any funds, but remits monthly on the average due date of the invoices purchased in any given month.* Banks will often make unsecured loans with greater confidence to a client factored under a maturity agreement.

Notification

This means the factor's clients notify their customers that their invoices are being sold to the factor, stamping each invoice to show this. The client's customers pay directly to the factor which now owns the receivable. Thus, the factor acts as a middleman in the regular creditor-debtor relationship. In industries such as textiles and furs, where factoring is common, factors keep extensive files on companies. Their clients are constantly asking for recommendations on their customers. By the same token, the customers recognize the role of the factor and are willing to submit complete credit information so their account can be analyzed.

Purchase Without Recourse

Under an "old-line" factoring agreement, *the factor purchases accounts receivable without recourse and bears the entire burden of collection and risk of bad-debt losses.* This means that the client selling the receivable is immediately relieved of any responsibility concerning its payment. This feature is especially attractive to a company that must plan cash requirements very carefully and cannot afford extraordinary bad-debt losses. However, the factor's fees are likely to be substantially higher for such an arrangement.

Loans on Inventory

In addition to purchasing clients' accounts receivable without recourse, factors offer a number of other services, including loans against inventory. This method of secured borrowing is often used by clients to finance temporary needs for working funds. *When the client sells inventory, it turns over the resulting receivable to the factor and liquidates the loan.*

Other Types of Loans

The factor will sometimes make loans or advances for other purposes in the same way as any other financial institution to finance fixed asset purchases, finance expansion, or reorganize the client's financial structure.

Cost of Factoring

The factor charges a commission or fee for performing the credit and collection function and for purchasing the firm's receivables without recourse for credit losses. In addition, the factor charges a substantial rate of interest on funds provided when it cashes receivables.

The factor's commission for service is a percentage of sales. It is negotiated beforehand by the client and the factor and depends upon a number of conditions, including:

- the nature of the client's industry, including style considerations, seasonal aspects, stability of items; and whether customers are manufacturers, wholesalers, or retailers
- annual sales volume of the client; as volume mounts, the percentage charged will usually tend to decline
- average size of the orders processed: Large orders are no more time-consuming to process than small orders and produce more revenue for the factor. Therefore, the factor's commission rate may be expected to decline as the size of the individual orders rise.
- average annual sales volume per customer: As this figure rises, there is less work and follow up for the factor, since the client's business is becoming

concentrated in few accounts. The commission rate will therefore tend to decline.

- credit position of the client's customers: Where the client sells only to high quality accounts and the risk is relatively small, the factor's commission may be lower. On the other hand, a company that concentrates its sales on accounts of questionable credit desirability should expect to pay a higher commission if the factor is willing to go along with those accounts.
- client's selling terms; if they are long, the factor must wait to collect its receivable, necessitating a higher fee
- other services such as billing, may be provided by the factor; these will increase costs and therefore raise the charge to the client

Evidence of a Factoring Agreement

Credit executives should develop an understanding of why companies need additional cash, what methods they may choose to obtain it, and what to look for on the financial statement of their customers that would indicate the presence of such outside financing. The balance sheet of a company that uses a factor on an advance basis may list a small amount of money Due from Factor, because most of the proceeds from the sold receivables have already been realized. The balance sheet will not list accounts receivable, because they will have been sold to the factor.

When analyzing the balance sheet of a company on an advance arrangement, the credit executive should be alert to the fact that the customer is not only obtaining a credit service but an increase in the availability of cash. This calls for a further analysis of how that cash has been applied. Where the arrangement is on a maturity basis, the amount Due from Factor will usually reflect the total amount of current sales sold to the factor but not yet cashed. The balance sheet will show little or no accounts receivable.

Due to the confidential, contractual relationship between the customer and its factor, it may be difficult to obtain frank answers to all of the questions posed in Figure 13-1. It may be necessary to have the customer authorize the factor to disclose whatever information may be sought.

General

Under either an advance or maturity basis, it is important to determine if the item Due from Factor has been diluted by such contingencies as returns and advances, disputed receivables, or receivables taken at the client's risk; or through advances on overdrafts where additional collateral may be taken.

Upon inquiry, a factor will usually state, in either an advance or maturity arrangement, the customer's range of credit balances, or the gross difference between the accounts receivable purchased and the advances that the factor has already made. It should also be determined whether the factor will apply a reserve against that amount for returns and discounts, disputed receivables, or accounts receivable not guaranteed by the factor and therefore at client's risk.

If the customer has credit balances under either an advance or maturity arrangement, it should be ascertained to what extent these credit balances can be diluted as outlined above. Moreover, even when the customer has a credit balance, the factor may have additional collateral to cover contingencies. If overdrafts are granted, the factor may have taken additional collateral.

Figure 13-1 Questions To Ask about a Factoring Arrangement on an Advance Basis

Initially, it is important to determine whether the factoring arrangement is on an advance basis. If so, the balance sheet of the customer may hide more meaningful data than it reveals, and any figure shown as Due from Factor should not be taken at face value. If the arrangement calls for advances on accounts receivable, the factor should be asked the following:

1. What is the contractual advance percentage? Is it fully used?
2. Are there any arrangements for unsecured overdrafts? If so, what are they? An overdraft is a verbal agreement by the factor to provide funds in excess of the contractual advance percentage on receivables, usually to a stated limit for a specific period of time.
3. Are there any overdrafts outstanding? If so, how much?
4. When an arrangement calls for overdrafts in addition to advances, the reason should be determined. It could indicate that the customer is financially strained, because inordinately high sales would necessitate increased purchases of merchandise. Therefore, it is essential to obtain profit and loss figures to ascertain whether this increased activity yields commensurate profits and does not weaken the firm. In addition, interim trial balance figures are an aid in determining the current profitability of operations.
5. Are the overdrafts stated as an amount over 100 percent of the purchased receivables or over the contractual advance percentage?
6. Have overdrafts been requested but refused or restricted?
7. If the maturity arrangement calls for payment on the average due date, it is essential to determine the following:
   - Is the item Due from Factor pledged to a third party, such as a bank, to secure a loan?
   - Is there any intercompany offset situation?
   - Does the factor have other affiliates or subsidiaries that are suppliers of credit to the customer?

The client's profit and loss statement should also be examined carefully to note the added costs of using a factor. They may offset the decreased credit and collection costs of using the factor.

Finance Companies

Functions

Finance companies make loans against pledged or assigned collateral, such as accounts receivable, inventory, or fixed assets. Their services differ from those of factors in that the finance companies do not actually purchase receivables or other assets, they make loans based on the value of the asset and expect repayment of the loans by their clients.

Finance companies are different from commercial banks in that they do not create bank deposits with the proceeds of the loan as banks do. When a commercial bank makes a loan, it usually creates a credit in the borrower's demand deposit (checking) account. The borrower can draw on these funds by writing checks or transferring funds electronically to make payments. A finance company lends funds directly to the borrower. However, if the borrower deposits the funds in its bank account, it will create the same effect as a bank loan.

Accounts receivable financing, as a method to advance operating cash to business, was pioneered in the early 20th century, but did not become a significant source of funds until 1941. Now practically all of the major banks in America have financing operations and many finance companies are subsidiaries of bank holding companies. Also, many commercial finance companies specialize in accounts receivable financing, and many factors have accounts receivable financing departments. Moreover, some finance companies are owned by manufacturers, while some of the larger finance companies own their own commercial banks.

One important result of the development is that accounts receivable financing has become increasingly important in the world of finance. The necessity for the use of receivables as collateral arises because the borrower is trading actively on invested capital and needs funds to finance current operations. With the variety of institutional sources available, small businesses as well as mid-sized and large companies are able to obtain funds through receivables financing when they might not be able to obtain unsecured financing.

Financing Procedure

In financing, a loan is secured by accounts receivable assigned to the finance company, or purchased by it with full recourse to the borrower in the event of a default by the debtor. A company entering into an accounts receivable financing agreement continues to operate its own credit department as before. It makes credit decisions; maintains customary detailed accounts receivable records; and handles its own collections, dealing directly with debtors. Meanwhile, the company signs a formal covering agreement with the finance company. *This is known as an* **underlying agreement** *or working plan and is a continuing arrangement for funds to be advanced by the finance company.*

Banks frequently use a collateral loan form of agreement, as they do not have statutory authority to purchase open accounts receivable outright. Commercial finance companies use the purchase form of agreement; accounts are purchased for 100 percent of their value, but a reserve is retained to secure the collection of the accounts. The effect of both procedures is the same. The agreement specifies what percentage of the value of the assigned accounts will be available to the borrower. The percentage varies depending upon such factors as industry, current economic conditions, and the financial condition of the borrower.

The agreement also outlines the overall conditions, such as maximum limit, interest rate, service fee, if any, and the rights and liabilities of each party. The procedure for obtaining funds varies according to the agreement. In some instances, the borrower signs a note and submits it with a schedule of specific accounts to be assigned, duplicate invoices, and evidence of shipment or delivery. In other cases, invoices and shipping documents are not required, and the borrower continuously assigns its total accounts receivable, which are certified by an outside accountant. The method used to collect pledged accounts depends upon whether the arrangement is on a notification or non-notification basis. For the most part, banks and finance companies use the non-notification method, and the borrower's customer is not aware that the account has been pledged. Consequently, payment is made by the customer to the borrower in the normal manner, and in turn by the borrower to the lender. If the notification plan is used, the original invoice sent to the customer carries a notice that the invoice has been assigned and that payment is to be made directly to the financing agency. If an account is not paid at maturity, it is carried 30 to 60 days, after which the amount advanced is charged back to the borrower. In the event that the account was purchased outright, other accounts are substituted as collateral or the borrowed amount is repaid.

Types of Loans

Loans against Accounts Receivable

In accounts receivable financing the borrowing firm makes its own sales, conducts its own credit investigations, makes its own credit decisions, passes on its own orders, makes its own collections, and absorbs its own bad-debt losses.

As it makes deliveries, the borrowing firm notifies the financing company how much money it wants to borrow against receivables. The amount that can be borrowed is a predetermined percentage of the face amount of the invoices presented. Usually the finance company will require some evidence that the borrower has shipped or delivered the goods covered in the arrangement.

The finance company and the client agree upon the percentage to be advanced based upon the borrower's number and quality (credit ratings) of customers, volume of business, selling terms, line of business, type of merchandise, collection efficiency, bad-debt experience, average size of orders, number of returns, and other specific details of the business.

The advance is paid back from the proceeds of the pledged receivables. The borrower generally endorses and delivers the customers' checks directly to the finance company.

After waiting a stated number of days (three to five normally) for checks to be collected, the finance company credits the client's account for sums collected on the individual pledged accounts. It then deducts the amounts already loaned and sends the balance to the client or makes the funds available to the client upon request.

Loans against Inventory

A finance company will make inventory loans in much the same way as a factor. These loans are generally made to meet short-term capital requirements of the client, but occasionally a client will borrow this way on a fairly steady basis. The method is quite satisfactory from the viewpoint of the finance company. As inventory is used in manufacturing or is sold, chances are it will be or has been replaced through additional purchasing. When the periodic reports show a reduction, then a loan reduction may be in order.

Unsecured Loans

In this instance, the finance company's analysis of the borrower is based on the five "Cs," in much the same way that a commercial bank would consider a request for an unsecured loan. Usually these loans cover temporary capital needs of the client.

Mortgage Loans

These are usually made on the client's plant and equipment. They are long-term in nature and are repaid on a regular schedule.

Loans Secured by Miscellaneous Assets

These are negotiated to meet the particular needs of the client. They may be secured by life insurance policies, bank books, stocks and bonds, or any other valuable assets owned by the borrower company, its endorsers, or its guarantors.

Equipment Financing and Leasing

Equipment financing enables a company to acquire fixed assets, such as industrial equipment and machinery, and pay for them on an installment basis. The plans are arranged by finance companies and instituted through dealers that are their clients. Terms are arranged at the convenience of the borrower and include such considerations as the financial strength and cash requirements of the borrower, useful life of the equipment to be purchased, and the seasonal characteristics of the borrower's line of business. The borrower makes a down payment at the time the equipment is purchased, then pays the balance, including installation, delivery, and carrying charges, in a series of installments. These may be paid monthly or arranged to correspond to the seasonal periods when the borrower has large amounts of cash on hand. Sometimes payment schedules and amounts are geared to the depreciation charges to be taken on the purchased equipment. The length of the contract does not exceed the useful life of the equipment. If the borrower prefers, however, it may accelerate payments to reduce the carrying charges on the installment loan. This method permits the borrower to have use of the asset while it is being paid for. At the same time, it releases funds that would otherwise have gone to retire the debt created when the equipment was purchased.

If the user of the equipment prefers to lease rather than own it outright, finance companies can offer complete programs to meet those needs. Title is held by the finance company, and a monthly leasing charge is paid by the client for the use of the equipment. This arrangement has been extended to include all types of fixed assets used in industry, such as plant and equipment, automobiles and trucks, and conveyors and other materials handling facilities.

Cost of Financing

There is only one charge incurred by a business firm in making use of accounts receivable financing at any major finance company. Throughout the period of the financing agreement, the borrower firm is billed at the end of each month in accordance with the extent of its borrowing activity during that month. Every business firm does not pay the same rate. In fact, the rate usually runs substantially above bank rates. Differences in rates tend to reflect the differences in the size of accounts accepted, in the degree of risk assumed, and in other services rendered by the financing institutions.

Evidence of a Financing Arrangement

The balance sheet of a company borrowing against receivables should show evidence of this fact, either on the statement or in the accompanying footnotes. Often, receivables and corresponding short-term loans are linked together by an explanatory note. If that is not done, the credit executive should look for signs that a financing arrangement does exist. Questions to ask are shown in Figure 13-2.

Impact of Liens Under UCC

Both factoring and financing require a security agreement between the parties and a filing of a financing statement under the Uniform Commercial Code. The credit executive should also be aware that there may be additional hidden liens against the collateral held by the factor or finance company. Factors that finance companies sometimes take inventory as collateral and do not record this lien under the UCC. This can be done through the use of a field warehouse, a third-party public warehouse, or through direct possession of the physical asset. In all of these instances, a valid lien can exist under the Uniform Commercial Code.

In addition, with floating liens and after-acquired clauses, the pledge may extend to a lien on every tangible asset on the customer's balance sheet. Furthermore, while guarantees or letters of credit issued by the factor or finance company are only a contingent liability, they can become real, thereby increasing the customer's indebtedness to the factor or finance company and possibly diminishing the availability of funds.

Term Loans

General Considerations

During a period of expanding business growth, many firms cannot fill their financial needs solely through additional investment and retained profits. Consequently, they are forced to look for long-term outside funds, which may be further broken down as intermediate or long term. For purposes of this discussion, no distinction between these two will be made.

Although long-term borrowing cannot be considered part of the owner's investment in a business, the company does have the opportunity to use those funds over a relatively long period of time. Generally, they are used to purchase machinery, fixtures, equipment, real estate, and other assets of a durable nature. This procedure frees the invested capital to carry accounts receivable, pay for inventories, and meet the daily cash needs of the business.

This type of financing has a usual maturity date of between three and five years. When interest rates are low and banks have funds available for lending, the terms can be longer. Terms tend to shorten when interest rates rise and the supply of money declines.

Each loan is a separate agreement between borrower and lender, so the terms of the transaction may be specified in the contractual agreement. Installment payments are common and may be made quarterly, semiannually, or annually. Payments may also be made at irregular intervals, depending on the capital needs of the business. Prepayment of the loan is usually allowed, although a prepayment penalty may be part of the agreement. Administrative costs are higher and there may be a provision in the loan agreement for the interest rate to change over the period of the loan.

Figure 13-2 Questions To Ask about Arrangements with a Finance Company

An understanding of a customer's arrangement with its finance company may be properly reached by obtaining answers to the following questions:

1. Is the arrangement normal? With a normal financing arrangement there is no notification to the client's customer that receivables are being pledged to secure a loan. If the agreement differs from the normal arrangement in that it provides for notification, this should act as a warning that the finance company considers the client a higher than ordinary risk.
2. What is the contract percentage advanced by the finance company against pledged receivables?
3. What is the customer's overall line with the finance company? A finance company will advance a contract percentage against pledged assets, although there is an overall dollar limit to the loan.
4. Does the customer draw the full amount available? Are there any arrangements for advances above the contractual percentage? If the customer does not draw the full loan amount available, this is probably a favorable sign. If it is doing so, it either signals full dependency on the finance company or possibly indicates that finances are in a strained position. On the other hand, overadvances may indicate a great deal of confidence by the finance company. A conclusion as to which way the scale is balanced can only be drawn after all the facts and circumstances are weighed.
5. What is the customer's gross receivables amount and its current loan balance with the finance company? The difference between these two items is the customer's equity. Equity can be diluted by discounts and reserves, contras and concentrations, or delinquent accounts receivable. Discounts and reserves are direct reductions of the face amount. Contras are potential reductions, in that the client's customer may offset an amount owed by the client to the customer. Concentration of receivables from a few large companies poses a danger to those receivables and the market position of the seller. Finally, delinquent accounts are potential bad debts.
6. What is the usual delinquency percentage? The quality of the account's receivables gains in importance because the company is contingently liable on them.
7. What is the accounts receivable turnover experience?
8. Is there any pledge of the accounts receivable equity to the finance company, the finance company's affiliates or subsidiaries, or to any other third party?

Restrictive Covenants

The lender may make an unsecured term loan, require a pledge of collateral, or obtain a lien against the property as an additional margin of safety. Most kinds of personal property may be pledged or serve as collateral for a UCC lien, while a lien on tangible property is created by a mortgage. The arrangements are quite similar to those made in short-term financing. In addition to a promissory note, however, the borrower

Figure 13-3 Typical Covenants in a Long-Term Borrowing Agreement

The borrower may not pay excessive dividends, borrow from other sources, sell business assets, guarantee the debts of other companies, merge or consolidate with other companies, or buy back any outstanding shares of stock.

The borrower generally is required to maintain an acceptable relationship between current assets and current liabilities (often as a minimum financial ratio, such as the current ratio), maintain the physical and real assets of the company in good condition, employ the proceeds of the loan in the way prescribed, provide adequate insurance coverage on the business, maintain accounting records and have them available for review, and submit periodic financial statements to the lender.

Property acquired by the borrower after the agreement is signed may become subject to the terms of the loan agreement by the **after acquired clause.** *This means that the property is automatically pledged, although the borrower did not own it at the time the loan was made.*

The interest rate may change during the life of the agreement through the use of an escalator clause.

The entire loan may become due immediately if the borrower fails to live up to the agreement. This is called an **acceleration clause.** Where the borrower cannot meet the terms of the note, the lender may institute foreclosure proceedings. The court renders a judgment and orders the property sold to satisfy the claim. If the proceeds of the sale satisfy the amount owed to the creditor, any excess is returned to the debtor. Should the proceeds be insufficient to pay the claim, the creditor may seek a deficiency judgment against the personal assets of the debtor for the difference.

There will also be a **cross-default clause**, *which states that if the borrower defaults on any long-term borrowing agreement, all such agreements will be in default (including the one being negotiated).*

signs a term loan agreement that specifies how the business may be conducted while the loan is outstanding. Some of the points usually covered in the agreement are shown in Figure 13-3.

Public and Private Placements

Many of the institutions making long-term loans are not required to keep a major portion of their resources in liquid assets and can therefore provide money for buildings, machinery, and equipment. Their loans are usually evidenced by collateral bonds, mortgages, or debentures of high-quality credit risks. This enables a borrower to obtain funds without having to repay the loan in one year. It enlarges the financial resources available to a business and releases other funds for day-to-day operation.

When a public offering is to be made, the borrower decides what terms will attract the investor at minimum cost to the borrower. The distribution and administrative details of the bond issue are usually handled by an investment banker specializing in this field. The investment banker usually guarantees a minimum price for the bonds.

When a private placement is to be made, the buyer can exert somewhat more influence on the terms of the issue. The indenture, deed of trust, or contract will specify the terms of the loan and repayment. Some features may be included that are particularly desirable to the borrower or to the lender. Because the contract is only between two parties, these points can be readily determined.

Leasing

Background

Leasing is a long established practice. In the period following World War II, rapid industrial expansion and inadequate depreciation allowances enabled leasing to become widely accepted as a method of acquiring the use of assets other than real estate. **Lease contracts** *allow use of equipment by lessees in return for periodic rental payments to lessors over a specified time period.* They stipulate the number, size, and time sequence of lease payments, and include clauses covering cancellation rights, conditions for renewal or a purchase option, the treatment of tax benefits and obligations, and the servicing responsibilities of lessor and lessee. Where no purchase option is provided in a lease contract, residual value reverts to the lessor, which may recoup costs by selling or releasing the asset. The Financial Accounting Standards Board (FASB) sets forth comprehensive guidelines for classifying leases into two broad categories: operating leases and capital leases.

Because leases are designed to transfer substantially all of the benefits and risks associated with ownership of property from one contracting party (the lessor) to another (the lessee), these leases are tantamount to completed exchanges, and the accounting for them should mirror that reality. Further, if a lessor can effect such a full transfer of benefits and risks through a lease, the lessee has assumed those very same benefits and risks through the lease. Thus a form of proportion should exist in the accounting by lessees and lessors. The lessor, by transfer through the lease, has converted its ownership of property into an investment in a lease contract (a receivable in accounting terms). The lessee has acquired an asset (an intangible) and incurred an obligation (a liability in accounting terms). *Leases of this full transfer variety are called* **capital leases** *by accountants* and **finance leases** *by other finance people. All other leases are called* **operating leases**.

With either form of lease, additional charges may be added for services that the lessor is providing, but which the lessee could provide either itself or through an outside contract. These might include administration, insurance, maintenance, and property taxes. In both types of contracts, legal title is retained by the lessor. Entering into a finance lease has many of the characteristics of an investment decision in that once the contract is signed the stream of payments to be made cannot be changed by management's subsequent decisions.

Operating Leases

These leases are typically short-term or spot rentals of equipment and property and are cancelable on short notice. Such nonfinancial services as insurance, delivery, maintenance, and repair are provided by the lessor. The most important feature is that the sum of the rental payments bears no direct relationship to the total cost of the assets being leased. Therefore, a user can acquire use of an asset for a fraction of its useful life, and count its cost as a straight operating expense.

Lessors include manufacturing companies, independent leasing companies, lease brokers, commercial finance companies, and most of the nation's largest commercial banks. Many equipment manufacturers use leasing as a marketing tool, offering equipment either for sale or on operating leases.

Finance Leases

These leases are completely net leases and are noncancelable over the basic lease term. The lessee is required to make a series of rental payments, which sum is equal to the initial cost of the asset being leased plus interest. Thus, the lessee has a definite fixed commitment as in any other form of term financing. Conversely, lessors with excess earnings obtain ownership benefits, which include depreciation allowances, interest tax deductions, and investment tax credits. These benefits can be shared with the lessees in the form of lower rental rates.

There are basic requirements inherent in any lease before it is considered a true lease. As owner, the lessor must bear the risk of ownership, which includes the possible decline in the economic value of the equipment. In addition, the lessee cannot build equity interest in the leased equipment with lease payments nor can the lessee assume title after making a specified number of lease payments. The lease terms must be less than the economic life of the equipment so that it has a residual value. A common practice in the past was to disclose the pertinent details of a lease agreement in the footnotes to a balance sheet. Recently, however, the balance sheet of the lessor under a finance lease shows the receivable from the lease as an asset, classified into current and noncurrent portions.

As for the lessee, the lease rights are shown as an asset and the lease obligations as a liability, classified into current and noncurrent portions. Consequently, the balance sheets of business enterprises transacting finance leases now show significantly larger investment in property and larger liabilities. These larger liabilities mean a larger debt-to-equity ratio. The number of times interest charges are covered by earnings also is affected. Since the lessee's obligation is declining over the term of the lease, interest charges in the early years are higher than in the later years. For a company with growing commitment to finance leasing, the effect would be to decrease net income.

An interesting feature of a finance lease is that it may be leveraged. Such leases are called leveraged leases, leveraged tax leases, and tax shelter leases. They have been popular with financial institutions and with individuals in high tax brackets who act as the lessors. The **leveraged lease** *is a segmented financing arrangement whereby up to 80 percent of the purchase price of equipment is supplied by long-term lenders, with the lessor of the equipment, typically a financial institution, providing the remainder amount as equity.* The debt in these arrangements is secured by a security interest in the equipment, a pledge of the lease payments, and an assignment of the rights of the owner under the lease document. It is serviced from lease payments during the life of the lease. The leveraged lease is also tax-oriented, in that the equity investor receives tax benefits based upon the total costs of the equipment. These benefits consist of investment tax credits and tax deferrals arising because the accelerated depreciation and interest expense exceeds rental income in the early years of the lease.

The lessor also receives nontax-oriented benefits to the extent of lease payments in excess of debt service requirements and whatever residual value of the equipment is realized following the end of the lease. A portion of the lessor's tax benefits is transferred to the lessee in the form of reduced rental payments, thus making the structure attractive to lessees, especially those users that are not in a tax situation whereby they could efficiently utilize the tax benefits through direct ownership of the equipment.

Sale-Leaseback Arrangement

In a **sale-leaseback arrangement**, *a company sells property or equipment to an insurance company or other institutional investor, and arranges for a long-term lease.* The rental consists of a predetermined rate of return plus amortization of the purchase price over the life of the lease, which generally runs from 25 to 30 years. The company, as lessee, continues to assume all of the risks, taxes, insurance, maintenance, and other costs of ownership. Moreover, the company sometimes can obtain an option to make an offer to buy the property for the remaining unamortized balance of the investment plus a penalty payment. If the offer is rejected, the company has the right to either continue in possession or vacate.

The institutional buyer's decision to enter into the sale-leaseback arrangement depends heavily on the lessee's credit standing, earnings record, and management ability. The location and quality of the property or equipment in question is also an important factor. In addition, commercial buildings such as apartment houses and office buildings have greater appeal than industrial property to institutional investors. The sale-leaseback device is used by many cash-poor companies to raise cash. While raising cash under this method alleviates the debtor's short-term cash inflow crunch, credit executives must be alert to the distortion it makes in their debtor's financial position despite the relief of knowing that current bills can now be paid. The balance sheet appears more liquid because cash has been built up, but short- and long-term obligations have been increased, the profit and loss statement will show increased rental payments, and the overall capital strength has been weakened. This does not mean that sale-leaseback arrangements should not be used as well as all types of leasing arrangements. But rather that their use must be taken into account when reviewing the credit decision.

Leveraged Buyouts

General Considerations

A **leveraged buyout** *is a special acquisition process that uses debt (leverage) to acquire or control (buy out) a company.* Specifically, a management group borrows substantial capital by pledging the company to be acquired and its assets as collateral. Then, simultaneously, the group uses that capital to purchase the equity necessary to acquire or control the company. This is accomplished with only a token amount of capital coming from the buyers. The technique can be used to take a public company private, to purchase a division or subsidiary spun off by the parent company, or to fulfill the financial goals of a company owner who may be seeking to retire.

To ensure the completion of the buyout, the company's other stockholders are usually offered premium prices for their equity. The buyers must then rely on company profits or strong cash flow to pay down the heavy debt load incurred and on the continued growth of the company to increase the value of their equity. At an appropriate later time, buyout companies may arrange for public underwritings. Equity sold to the public at handsome prices can provide large profits for the management group and investors.

Structure

Leveraged buyouts arrange financing in tiers for successful completion. The first tier consists of the corporate management. They usually make token capital contributions of about one percent. This is hardly enough capital to qualify for the large loans necessary to launch the buyout, so they seek additional financing from other investors.

The second tier is made up of investment bankers, venture capital pools, pension funds, and wealthy investors. They contribute about 25 per cent of the capital needed and frequently receive between 20 per cent and 70 percent of the total equity. Their goal is to sell their equity to the public at capital gain rates sometime in the future.

The last tier consists of financial institutions that lend funds to pay for the leveraged buyout. As inducements for the loans, the lending institutions may be offered an equity position in the company, interest rate premiums of up to 3 percentage points, and other benefits such as upfront charges, points, and prepayment penalties. Best of all, the company's assets are pledged as collateral. These are tangible properties that creditors appreciate.

Characteristics of Good Buyout Candidates

There are two types of lenders for the leveraged buyout: commercial lenders and asset-based lenders. Although both examine the company's track record and prospects in the same way, commercial lenders emphasize cash flow, while asset-based lenders look to inventories, receivables, and the fixed assets of the company to secure their creditor position. The main factors that these lenders use for evaluating buyout candidates are shown in Figure 13-4.

Credit Analysis of the Leveraged Buyout

All of the general rules for credit analysis apply, except that some need added attention. From the personnel viewpoint, the added incentive for skilled entrepreneurs who not only manage but also own their companies is a positive intangible factor. The greater stake in the company by management tends to spur productivity. Often, because of the risk involved with these customers, it is advisable to segregate them as a separate portfolio of accounts and have corporate management share the decision making with the credit executive. Properly structured buyouts can be good customers.

Ownership via a leveraged buyout appears to contradict sensible financial practices. The new owners and their backers incur large debts to buy the company's stock or assets. The company's assets are pledged against loans, causing an extraordinarily high debt-to-equity ratio. If successful, leverage can bring tremendous rewards, but it can create major problems if the investment's value declines or if the debt burden

Figure 13-4 Factors for Evaluating Leveraged Buyouts

- The company must have proven products and markets. Unlike venture capital financing, leveraged buyouts aim for reliability and staying power.
- Key management personnel must have a proven track record. They must be experienced in production, sales, finance, and operating the company or one like it.
- Management should have its own cash invested in risk equity, enough to ensure their total commitment.
- The company must have a steady and reliable cash flow to support the purchase price, carrying charges, and related debt.
- The physical plant should be reasonably modern so that heavy capital expenditures can be avoided during the payback period.
- The company's industry should not be vulnerable to sudden technological shifts that can cause obsolescence.
- Preexisting debt should be minor because the leveraged buyout will add a major layer of new debt.
- The company should be willing to supply sufficient detailed financial information to creditors, to convince them that the company can handle the heavy debt load.
- Suppliers should be consulted so that previous trade terms will continue after the buyout. Harsher terms can cause liquidity problems.

becomes unsupportable. Debt heavy companies can fall into bankruptcy if cash flow falters.

A bankrupt leveraged buyout that benefited shareholders at the expense of creditors could be considered fraudulent under the Bankruptcy Code. This is particularly true where the buyout was financed almost entirely by debt, leaving the company with almost no equity. Under the Code, fraud occurs when the leveraged company is left insolvent, with unreasonably small capital or more debts than it can repay. However, the tests to determine actual or unintentional fraud are not applied until the leveraged company files for protection under Chapter 11. With few unencumbered assets, the chances for a successful reorganization are minimal.

Key to understanding the leveraged buyout is the awareness that the new owners rely almost completely on continuing strong earning power to provide the profits and cash inflows that will reduce the heavy debt load. In addition, there are tradeoffs to take into consideration. A write-up of the assets as part of the purchase increases depreciation, reduces tax liabilities, and improves cash flow. What can look like an impossibly high debt load may end up being manageable. Conversely, the new owners should not be committed to expand or modernize plant facilities, because such expenditures will take sizeable cash flow from operations and will not be available for the general creditor.

Balance sheets and operating statements should be compared with pre-buyout ones so as to evaluate cash flow and debt. Current ratio should be especially analyzed and compared to industry standards. When the credit risk seems too high, the creditor firm may try to bolster its position by using a standby letter of credit. It is best to

Figure 13-5 Analyzing Financial Statements for a Leveraged Buyout

- Examine cash to uncover any seasonal peaks and valleys.
- Check trade receivables for the average age of past-due receivables and their rate of change. Significant customers that provide 10 per cent of sales should be listed. The probability of collecting long overdue accounts needs to be evaluated.
- Check notes receivable from customers as to nature of loan, terms, and history of collection.
- Examine inventories to determine the current market value, pricing sensitivity, and obsolescence factor.
- Evaluate plant and equipment to assess their remaining useful life by comparing the appraised value with the remaining book value.
- Check short-term borrowing requirements for peaks and valleys beyond the debt service associated with the buyout.
- Analyze accounts payable to determine whether there are any payment problems arising from a reduced inventory turnover or slowdown in accounts receivable turnover.
- Review operating income by product lines, industry segments, geographic locations, trend of major customers, pricing strategies, sales agreements, and customer base.
- Review operating expenses to establish the stability of cost structure by looking into each major element of expense. Lease rates, labor and fringe costs should be checked. Leases need to be examined to see if they are assignable and if they are economically advantageous to the buyer.

review three years of pre-buyout balance sheets and operating statements and do the analysis shown in Figure 13-5.

Government Programs

Background

The U.S. Government has set up various agencies to assist small business in meeting their capital needs. The principal agency for accomplishing this goal is the Small Business Administration, which was given the authority under the Small Business Act of 1953 to make direct loans and to guarantee portions of loans made by commercial banks and other lenders.

Small Business Administration

Designed to assist small businesses to finance capital needs for growth and expansion, the Small Business Administration (SBA) participates in loans made by private lenders or may lend directly when the private institutions do not consider the prospect a satisfactory credit risk. For business loan purposes, the SBA defines a small business as one that is independently owned and operated, not dominant in its field, and meets sales standards developed by the agency. Its clients are businesses that may be undercapitalized, lack sufficient collateral, and have not established an operating history. Consequently, the SBA establishes loan ceilings and provides its clients with free management assistance.

By law, the SBA cannot make a loan if a business can obtain funds from a bank or other private source on reasonable terms. The prospective borrower must first seek financing from at least one bank (or two within a city of a population greater than 200,000) before applying for an SBA loan. The prospective borrower is also not eligible for an SBA loan if funds can be secured through the sale of assets that the business does not need in order to grow.

Types of Loans

Of the loans participated in by the SBA, the guaranteed loan is the more common. Under the guaranteed program, all funds come from the commercial lender. The SBA guarantees up to 90 percent of the loan up to $500,000 (in special situations). If the borrower defaults on the loan, the SBA reimburses the bank for its share of the defaulted loan. Where the SBA participates with a bank, the SBA advances a maximum of $150,000 and the bank provides the remainder. If the bank will not participate in an SBA guaranteed loan, then the agency will consider making a direct loan up to a maximum of $150,000. However, funds may not be available for the agency to lend because of federal fiscal restraints.

Small firms that cannot get a line of credit from a bank may apply to the SBA for regular and seasonal lines of credit. However, the firms must supply proof of their ability to perform on contracts and show repayment capabilities. Regular business loans are also available for those firms that have a reasonable amount of capital invested. Where the firms have principals of minority origin, the application procedure is simplified and the loan processing is expedited. However, the term, interest rate, and loan limit are the same. A large variety of special loans are also available for low-income disadvantaged persons to start a small business; to small firms that must make changes in their equipment, facilities, or operations because of new federal, state, or local laws and regulations; to firms that have deviations from the normal safety code standards and must make additions to or alterations in their plant, facilities, or methods of operation; and to small businesses that have suffered economic injury because of a large number of economic circumstances.

Restrictions

In addition to the usual commercial loan restrictions and covenants, government lenders may require an assignment of insurance concerning net proceeds, cash surrender value, loans, distributions, and other benefits. The loan agreement also restricts the use of the proceeds and places limits on fixed asset acquisitions, distributions, and compensation.

Small Business Investment Corporations

Given its power through the Small Business Investment Company Act of 1958, the SBA makes private capital and long-term credit more readily available to small businesses. It grants licenses to small business investment corporations (SBICs) and provides them with financial assistance. In turn, these SBICs provide funds and managerial assistance to businesses in their area. This type of investment company has grown considerably since its inception and now plays a significant role in the small enterprise sector of the economy.

The Act provides tax breaks not only for the investor but also to the SBIC itself. The earnings of the SBIC are not subject to the holding company surtax or penalty on accumulation of retained earnings, assuming the accumulation is properly invested. Most of the funds invested in SBIC represent the private capital of individuals, commercial banks, and investing public; the balance comprises money borrowed from the federal government.

An SBIC may be eligible for a government loan up to twice its paid-in capital and retained earnings, thus providing significant leverage. There is no limit to the private capital that may be used to establish an SBIC.

Business Insurance

Role

The position of the going concern may change radically if something unforeseen happens to its earning power and financial strength. Fire, death of a principal, embezzlement, robbery, business interruption, or extraordinary bad-debt losses can change the financial condition of a business overnight. Concurrently, these circumstances can change its creditors' position. It is important therefore for creditors to know the types and amounts of insurance carried by their customers.

There is no way to foretell many of the misfortunes that can hit a business. The competent manager, however, can provide adequate insurance coverage against these contingencies and thereby protect company assets and earning power, and creditors' interest. The creditor should be satisfied that major risks are covered.

Numerous descriptions of insurance have been made. Though they differ in detail, they all have these points in common: people join together to protect the value of their lives and property, and each participant contributes a relatively small amount in exchange for protection against a disastrous personal loss. The ultimate purpose of insurance is self-protection, but each participant cooperates with all others to carry common risk. Payments for this protection can be budgeted and paid in an orderly manner.

Insurance and the Creditor

Creditors must be primarily concerned with their customers' ability to withstand disastrous loss. Insurance offers several advantages to a business. Adequate insurance coverage offers security to the business and to its creditors. It enables the manager to plan for the future, knowing that the financial strength of the business is protected from disaster. Insurance reduces the need for financial reserves. A company that does not carry insurance would not necessarily have to set some of its assets to provide for unforeseen emergency cash needs. By carrying insurance against these contingencies, the firm releases additional assets for business operation. This strengthens its credit position. The manager can devote more time to efficient operations. This means that the firm can plan more effectively for the coming year with greater certainty that it is protected against unforeseen loss. Costing procedures can be based on more realistic appraisals of expenses.

Creditors are likewise protected. Credit analysis is based largely upon business assets and assumes they will maintain their values. Since these assets are liable to dissipation or destruction, the creditor assumes an additional risk when customers do not protect business assets with insurance. It therefore follows that the insured account is a better credit risk. The greatest advantage to a creditor lies in having a good knowledge of the customer's line of business. That makes it easier to determine the adequacy of the insurance coverage. In this respect, however, the cost of overprotection can be as harmful as losses due to underprotection.

Credit Executive's Interest in Insurance Coverage

Creditors are interested in the ability of a company to recover from financial loss and to stay in business. The types and amounts of insurance carried affect this ability and should be known in every detailed credit analysis. Emphasis up to this point has been on the protection of tangible and intangible assets of the debtor, but there are other related points that a credit executive should know. First, a company's insurance program should be kept under continuous review by knowledgeable persons, either directly employed or retained on contract. A growing company adds new products, expands its territory, purchases new equipment, adds new employees, enters into new contracts, and so on. Each of these represents a consideration that needs attention.

Second, business insurance is seldom a fixed cost item. The larger the cost the more likely this will be true. Business insurance contracts usually involve an estimated premium charge at inception, to be followed by an adjustment at the end of the period based on a physical audit conducted by the insurer that determines the actual premium. A business that has grown or changed substantially during the period could owe a sizable additional amount to its insurer. Many times this has not been anticipated and provided for, and may result in a financial strain.

Third, a financial statement issued by a customer may not reflect the contingency or added obligations to its insurer. The best safeguard is to inquire whether the financial statements have been audited and through what date. In this respect, insurance is similar to federal income taxes and should be approached on the same basis. An insurer's audit privilege may extend beyond one year. This contingency can be missed in audited reports.

Finally, there is one more area of business insurance that usually relates to the larger firms. It is referred to as **retrospective**. In this case, *the insured buys a contract with a built-in fee to compensate the insurer for servicing the firm's claims.* This can become an important consideration due to the amount of money and time involved. Many claims involve litigation that can extend as much as 10 to 15 years. Until the claims have been settled, the costs between the insured and the insurer cannot be fully determined.

Prerequisites of Insurance

Because the purpose of insurance is to protect owners and creditors, it should not be considered a means by which property owners can realize a profit. This makes it necessary to examine the requirements and circumstances surrounding the use of insurance.

Real Risk

An insurance contract should be based upon an actual possibility that the insured party may sustain a financial loss from a hazard to which it is exposed, and which cannot be eliminated. The threat may be to life, physical property, or intangible interests. Insurance against real risk must be clearly distinguished from risk that can be eliminated completely. For instance, the possibility of a fire loss is always presentthat is a real risk. It is different from the risk of financial loss by gambling. There, the risk is self-created and should not rightfully be considered insurable.

Necessity of Insurance

Normally a business is not expected to carry insurance on values which are negligible. Premiums are a cost of doing business. If premium payments exceed the value of the insured property over a short period of time, they would represent a foolish expenditure. The business should have saved those premiums. From the viewpoint of the insurance company, too, the costs of writing and servicing contacts on negligible values are greater than the value of the protection furnished. It therefore is customary to fix a minimum premium on insurance contracts. In fact, most business insurance programs are designed with layers of protection, wherein the insured and insurer share the responsibility. The insured may pay numerous small claims up to an agreed-upon maximum with the insurer paying claims beyond that figure.

Reasonable Costs

Insurance is based upon the banding together of many people against financial loss from real risk. In order to attract the necessary numbers of people, the cost of insurance must be relatively low for the protection offered. The insured must initially be convinced that the premium is reasonable. In addition, the business must be able to afford the payment or it will take a chance without adequate coverage.

Large Number of Individual Risks

It is necessary from the insurer's point of view to have a large number of individual risks for safe operation. Generally, as the number of insured parties increases, individual losses can be absorbed more readily by the insurer company.

Extent of Hazard Calculable

The insurer should be able to estimate the risk to which each insured party is exposed. This estimate should be close enough to permit adequate and equitable premium rates to be established. In this way, the insurance company is able to operate effectively and can meet its obligations when an insured sustains a loss. At the same time, an equitable premium structure pro rates contributions according to the extent of risk in each case.

Principles of Insurance

Over the years, a body of knowledge has been built up that clarifies the use of insurance. Many claims are settled quickly and without disagreement between the insured and the insurer. Others are brought to court and decisions obtained. These decisions help in subsequent interpretations of insurance cases and thus refine the principles that guide insurance practice.

Indemnity

Ideally, insurance should restore to each member of the group the exact amount of financial loss sustained from disaster. This prospect is the chief attraction to the insured, and the need to join with others for protection is only incidental. *The essence of* **indemnity** *is compensation in event of loss.* It is not intended that the insured realizes they have a profit from a disaster. Occasionally insurance coverage exceeds the value of the property insured. Usually this overinsurance provides no additional protection to the owner, because indemnity can be no more than the actual financial loss suffered. Exceptions are found in some states—under a **valued policy law**—*additional compensation is allowed when a total loss is suffered.*

Insurable Interest

A number of different interests may be represented by the same assets. This can be illustrated by a shipment of merchandise from a supplier to a wholesaler. Before the merchandise has been sold, the supplier has an insurable interest in it. As soon as title changes hands, the new owner has an insurable interest in the merchandise. While the merchandise is being shipped to the wholesaler, the carrier transporting the merchandise has an insurable interest in it. Furthermore, if the inventory is pledged as collateral for a loan, the lender also has an insurable interest in it. Thus, the same merchandise may represent an insurable interest to one or more parties. Title to the goods is not the chief consideration. Rather, it is the risk of loss that determines insurable interest.

In addition, a person cannot obtain an insurance policy on property, but only on an interest in property. It is the risk of financial loss that prompts an insured to purchase a policy, not the opportunity to guarantee that a property will not be destroyed. For example, to assure that business premises do not burn down, the owner makes them as fireproof as possible, using fireproof construction and adequate protection measures. To protect against financial loss resulting from a fire, however, it would be necessary to carry a fire insurance policy.

Mutuality

This principle has developed from the original joining together of people to protect themselves against a common risk. *It expresses the method in which funds are obtained to pay losses of insured individuals.* The members (subscribers or policyholders) furnish these funds as premiums. This pool of money is used to pay insured losses and operating expenses of the insurance company and to set up certain reserves.

Theory of Probability and Law of Large Numbers

Certain statistical principles form the bases for insurance operation. The first of these is known as **the theory of probability**. *This states that if certain events have taken place repeatedly in the past, there is equal likelihood the event or result will be repeated in the future, so long as the conditions do not change. The second is called* **the law of large numbers** or **the law of averages**. It complements the theory of probability, stating that *as the number of past occurrences becomes greater, the likelihood increases that the event will happen again.* Consequently, the averages or forecasts drawn from the past experience become more reliable. *The law further states that forecasts based on past events* *are more reliable when they are drawn from many experiences than when they are drawn from few experiences.*

In applying these principles, insurance companies collect accurate records of losses and examine them carefully for statistical significance. The information developed from these studies aid the companies to make forecasts of future events. Naturally no forecast can be considered completely accurate. But those based on statistical treatment of comprehensive information give good working results for the insurers. On this basis they can set rates and establish insurance limits.

Uniformity and Distribution of Lines

To make the laws of probability and large numbers effective in practice, insurance companies reduce the chance of extraordinary losses to a single insurer from one or several related disasters. They do this in two ways:

1. The unit amounts at risk are kept fairly uniform. Otherwise, a disproportionately large loss would upset the averages. *The insurer will often limit the amount of coverage for any single risk and transfer any amount which exceeds that limit to another company. This is called* **reinsurance**.
2. The various units of risk are separated geographically or physically as much as practically possible. This is done to reduce the likelihood that any one disaster will affect a large number of units.

Equity Among Policyholders

While technically not a principle of insurance, this has a great effect on insurance operations. Part of the responsibility carried by the management of insurance companies is to distribute the costs of insurance equitably among policyholders. The establishment of fair and uniform rates for similar and equal risks, together with the elimination of the usual forms of discrimination, can be accomplished by the insurance companies quite easily. The problem facing them is that all policies do not bear the same proportion of insurance to value.

Further, all disasters do not result in total loss; in many instances the loss is only partial. Consequently, it becomes difficult to establish equitable rates in terms of percentage coverage and degree of risk. The practical rule used by many companies is that they reimburse for partial loss in the same ratio as the insurance coverage bears to the value of the property covered (the coinsurance clause).

Insurance Agreements

The agreement between insured and insurer is known as an **insurance contract**. It falls under the law of contracts, and court actions arising from insurance agreements are normally tried under this category. For the contract to be valid and enforceable, it must meet the following conditions:

- the parties to the contract must agree to its conditions
- both parties must be competent to enter into a contract
- there must be a legal object
- there must be some consideration

Agreement (Offer and Acceptance)

The legal interpretation of an offer and acceptance in an insurance contract is somewhat different from the ordinary contract. The person who requests protection from the insurer is, according to law, making the offer. The acceptance is made when the insurance company agrees to the offer and puts the insurance in force. The courts have declared that the activity of insurance representatives soliciting business does not constitute an offer. The offer must be more specific and detail the terms of the agreement. Technically, these specific terms cannot be known until the prospect makes the offer.

Competent Parties

While both parties must be legally competent to enter into an insurance contract, contracts signed by minors are enforceable in behalf of the minor and cannot be dissolved by the insurer. In some states, automobile and life insurance have been declared exceptions to this rule. Similarly, a person who is officially declared insane does not lose the protection of any policy already purchased.

Legal Object

Insurance contracts that do not have a legal objective in the public interest are not enforceable. Goods or merchandise illegally held, such as illegal drugs or contraband, cannot be made the subject of an enforceable contract.

Consideration

In an insurance contract, **consideration on the part of the insurer's company** *consists of its promise to make payment if certain events occur.* **The insured party's consideration** *is payment of, or promise to pay, the stipulated premium.* By its nature, an insurance contract differs from other contracts in that the values exchanged are not equal. The premium is small when compared to the potential reimbursement in case of loss. There is no reimbursement unless a loss is suffered.

The terms of other contracts may be changed to suit the needs of either party. In insurance, the forms of contracts are prepared by the companies and by state regulatory bodies. When a change is desired by the insured, it is made by using a standard rider or endorsement.

Other Forms of Insurance

Property Insurance

Most business firms begin fulfilling their insurance needs by purchasing protection for the assets of the business; both tangible and intangible assets can be and often are insured. Tangible assets include buildings, merchandise, accounts receivable, and production equipment. Intangible assets relate to business interruption, such as earnings insurance, extra expense insurance, rental value protection, tuition fees coverage, and consequential damage. While it is possible for a customer to insure against almost every possible risk, a sound program will not necessarily include all available types.

Some customers may prefer the most costly **"all risk" form of coverage** *with* *certain specified situations of loss unprotected.* Others may be completely satisfied by a **"named peril" policy** *with protection for only those perils named, such as fire or windstorm.* There is also the extent of the risk that the insured is willing to assume. For lesser cost, one may elect not to cover minor exposure, or may select a larger-than-normal deductible. There are generally two parties to the property insurance contract: the owner of the property to be insured (or some entity charged with responsibility for the property to be insured); the insurance company. There may be a mortgagee or a loss payee also named whose interest in the property must be settled by the insurance company prior to any settlement with the owner.

Fire and Extended Coverage Insurance

Insurance on a building or its contents against fire, lightning, and removal is **direct fire loss coverage**. The insurance normally applies only to the location described, and the property covered is stationary and not on the move. There must be a form of unfriendly conflagration in order for a fire loss claim to be payable. To these perils most often are added the extended coverage perils of windstorm, hail, explosion, riot and civil commotion, aircraft damage, vehicle damage, and smoke damage.

Often vandalism and malicious mischief coverage is made a part of the fire insurance policy. Dealing with buildings only, a special extended coverage endorsement may make the fire insurance policy an all risk protection to the building. However, this type of policy does not insure accounts, bills, deeds, money, or securities. There are other forms of insurance designed to protect those items.

War risk is never covered nor are losses that take place under any ordinance or law regulating the use of property. Power failures that take place away from the insured's premises are not covered. Earthquake, flood, and water backup are not insured. Many items are excluded from the protection of windstorm and hail insurance. Some may be insured for extra premiums, while others may not be insured at all. Among the extra premium items are windmills and their towers, crop silos, metal smokestacks, awnings or canopies, signs, radio or television antennas, sprinkler leakage, and sonic shock waves. Even the addition of the special extended coverage endorsement fails to remove many of the limitations on coverage involving buildings. The insured should be aware of the policy limitations on freezing and what must be done to have coverage for the explosion of a steam boiler or electrical short circuit, to name a few. Fire insurance forms dealing with business property involve coinsurance requirements. The normal requirement is 80 percent of the true value of the property covered. The insured becomes a coinsurer or a contributor to a partial loss if coverage falls below 80 percent.

There are also two bases of insurance: the actual cash value basis and the replacement cost basis. The difference is that the **replacement cost basis** *envisions no depreciation in the adjustment of losses.* Obviously the replacement cost provides better coverage, but it also costs more. Creditors of businesses with some type of "package" insurance should be sure the package includes direct fire and allied peril coverages.

Business Interruption Insurance

Business interruption coverage may be essential to maintain the financial position of a business, protect profits, and pay key employees during an insurable shutdown. The amount of the coverage depends on the length of time that it takes to get the damaged property operating again. The profits can be regarded as intangible, since they are not necessarily guaranteed. Business interruption insurance is available under package policies at discounts. It is nearly always advisable to package insurance where possible because of lower costs to the customer.

Burglary and Theft Insurance

There are three types of insurance available for this type of risk: two offer limited protection while the third offers a package of protection.

Mercantile Open Stock Insurance

This is available for almost any type of business that manufactures products or has merchandise for sale or storage. *It insures against loss of merchandise, furniture, fixtures, and equipment, and pays for damage to the premises described in the policy if the insured is the owner or is liable for the damage.* The coverage is effective while the premises are not open for business. Generally there are discounts for deductibles and for first-class alarm systems.

In one form the insurance does not cover theft; the other form covers both theft and burglary. Burglary means abstraction from within the premises by someone making an entry by force or violence with visible marks left as evidence. Theft is a broader protection term than burglary.

Mercantile Robbery and Safe Burglary

This is another form of limited coverage in a crime area. *The* **robbery** *portion is nothing more than holdup insurance and may be the least expensive form of crime insurance that deals with money.* It provides protection for both money and merchandise taken through force or threat of force from a business premises or from a messenger of a business. *The* **burglary** *portion protects both money and merchandise locked up in a safe on the business premises.* Both of these forms exclude mysterious disappearance and infidelity of employees, and should not be purchased unless one of the broader crime coverage policies is too expensive.

Storekeepers' Burglary and Robbery Insurance

This is a package protection that covers the loss of money and merchandise through safe burglary on the premises, holdup of night watchman or messenger, or imposition of duress upon an insured or an employee to open the premises or the safe within the premises. The latter is called kidnapping. All of these burglary coverages are available in package policies.

Inland Marine Insurance

This type of insurance deals with a number of situations requiring broad insurance coverage. The objects covered may not be stationary or they may be excluded directly from fire and allied peril insurance. Coverage generally includes accounts receivable, camera and musical instrument dealers, cargo insurance, equipment dealers, contractors' equipment, garment contractors, jewelers, physicians' and surgeons' equipment, agricultural equipment and livestock, signs, and valuable papers. Appropriate inland marine coverage may be purchased on either all risk or named peril basis. Because the coverage often involves expensive materials or equipment, it is more often written on an all-risk basis. There is generally a deductible amount. Most of this coverage is available for incorporation in a package policy. While some companies discount the coverage when packaging them, others refuse to do so because of the breadth of the protection.

Ocean Marine Cargo Insurance

All exported goods (whether they are initially transported by railroads, trucks, or air) that are waterborne during any time of their shipment can be insured by this policy. The open cargo type covers all shipments. The shipper (the insured) reports the shipments made and protection is automatic once the report of a shipment is filed. The protection can be tailored to meet special requirements. For example, it may provide all risk or named peril protection. The policy contains a valuation clause that states the amount of insurance per shipment is equal to the amount of the invoice and all contingency charges. Many special clauses can be added to make this into exactly the type of protection a shipping business desires.

Data Processing Policy

This covers electronic data processing equipment, plus component parts and data processing media owned or leased by a business. Insurance is on an all-risk basis subject to certain exclusions. The policy may be extended to include extra expense incurred as a result of damage to equipment or media. Business interruption loss attributable to total or partial suspension of operations can be purchased. The policy can be extended to cover valuable papers and records of accounts receivable.

Difference in Conditions Policy

This form of property insurance provides all-risk insurance for perils not normally available through fire and extended coverage. It covers catastrophic perils such as flood and water damage, earthquake, collapse, burglary, and transit exposure, and is subject to a sizable deductible amount. This can be purchased as a supplement to fire, extended coverage, vandalism, and sprinkler leakage insurance. It is simply supposed to repay the purchaser for the difference in condition of the property insured after a loss has occurred. It is about the only source of coverage that provides flood insurance outside the federal program. No standard policy is available and many insurance companies offer varying clauses dealing with protection and exclusions. Therefore, protection of this type should be examined thoroughly.

Flood Insurance

This is made available and partially subsidized by the federal government through acts of Congress. It protects against both flood and mud slide (mud flow) for all types of buildings and their contents, subject to a deductible. The condition causing the flooding or inundation must be of a general nature; coverage is not provided when damage results solely from causes on the insured property or from causes within control of the insured.

Plate Glass Insurance

This is generally a replacement insurance. It provides protection on scheduled glass and (if separately described) lettering and ornamentation. In addition, the insuring company will also pay for repair or replacement of frames, installation of temporary plates, and boarding up of openings necessitated by glass breakage from almost any cause except fire. There may be a limitation on damage to frames, temporary plates, and boarding-up requirements.

General Liability Insurance

Every business may sustain a financial loss caused by injury to the person or property of an individual or another business entity. The **general liability policy** *transfers the legal liability for such injury from the insured to the insurance company.* The major sources of potential injury may include premises, operations, contractual agreements, products liability, completed operations, or work done by independent contractors. Historically, coverage was provided by narrow contracts that addressed the insured's primary exposurethat is, an Owner's, Landlord's, and Tenant's policy for a premises exposure or a Manufacturer's and Contractor's policy for operations coverage.

While many of these policies are still written and provide the necessary coverage for the particular circumstances, protection now is usually provided by a **Comprehensive General Liability policy**, *which addresses itself to all of the policyholder's liability exposures.* The Comprehensive General Liability policy is broad and can protect the policyholder for most liability exposure. Often it is broadened further by the addition of special endorsements to provide coverage excluded in the basic contract. Very briefly, the following hazards are covered:

- the ownership, maintenance or use of premises, and all operations
- the ownership, maintenance, or use of any elevator designated in the declarations
- operations performed by independent contractors for the insured, if the accident occurs during operations (with certain exceptions)
- goods or products manufactured or sold—and title has passed—that cause an accident away from the premises
- completed or abandoned operations, if the accident occurs away from the premises
- other coverages that may have been separately endorsed into the policy, such as when an insured has entered into a written contract assuming certain liabilities of others
- property damage, known as coverage B (this coverage can be excluded by the insured)
- medical payments, known as coverage C (this coverage is usually endorsed into the policy)

The commercial insurance industry has followed the personal lines insurance industry in including property insurance and liability insurance in one policy. These multi-peril or package policies have become widely accepted, but the liability coverage is the same as that provided by a separate liability policy.

Life Insurance

Creditors must be concerned with the effect that the death of a principal or a key employee will have on the earning power and financial condition of a customer. For instance, the death of a proprietor dissolves the business. It may continue to be operated by an estate, but the valuable contribution of the owner is no longer available. The earning power of the business will be radically affected; it should be protected for the good of the estate and of the creditors.

In another case, a partnership may suffer when a principal dies. Again, the deceased partner's talents are no longer available to the business. Just as important, however, the heirs of the deceased may wish to withdraw their interest from the business. This can cause a serious drain on the finances of the company. Similarly, a corporation may suffer a loss of earning power when an officer or key employee dies. In addition, it may be forced to buy back a deceased officer's interest and thus decrease its own capitalization.

Insurance on the lives of the principals and key employees relieves some of the financial loss caused by their deaths. A number of different policies are written to cover this contingency. Usually premiums are paid by the business and the firm is named beneficiary. This protects the earning power of the business and enables the company to buy back the interest of a deceased principal without decreasing its usual financial resources.

Credit Insurance

Credit insurance *provides protection against disastrous bad-debt losses while retaining the risk of ordinary losses.* It is not a substitute for competent credit analysis but does relieve some of the pressure on the credit department. It is different from a factoring agreement in that receivables are not sold by the client to the insurer. It also differs from a financing arrangement because receivables are not pledged as collateral for secured loans. It serves chiefly to protect the company investment in receivables.

Major Benefits of Credit Insurance. A credit insurance policy protects against excessive bad-debt losses, promotes safe sales expansion, provides effective collection assistance, strengthens borrowing and purchasing power, improves planning and budgeting accuracy, and provides loss prevention guidance on key risks.

Elements on the Contract. For a contract of credit insurance to apply, there must be a sale, shipment, and delivery; or a service must be provided for which there is a legally sustainable claim against the debtor or the debtor's estate. Generally, coverage is limited to sales on regular terms of not more than one year.

Policy Coverage

Credit insurance is available only to firms engaged in manufacturing, wholesaling, and certain service businesses. It is written with a deductible provision, primary loss provision, and may provide for coinsurance. In every policy, the insured and the insurer agree on a maximum amount of coverage, which is the policy amount. It is the maximum amount the insured can recover for all covered losses sustained during the one-year term of the policy.

Coinsurance. The insured company participates in 10 or 20 percent of the bad-debt loss sustained on a debtor. This **coinsurance feature** *causes the insured to participate in each loss.* A higher premium is charged if the insured wants a policy without coinsurance.

Primary Loss. Because credit insurance is not intended to eliminate all credit risk, the policy covers losses over and above an agreed-upon annual deductible. This deductible is based on the normal expected loss for the business and the overall risk to be insured. *This initial deductible loss is termed the* **primary loss** *and is not reimbursed to the insured.* It is set as a percentage of sales, but in no case less than a stated dollar amount.

Policy Endorsements. A number of endorsements can be made to the credit insurance policy to cover particular situations, including the following:

- *Bank Endorsement.* This endorsement is used when an account uses its receivables as collateral for bank borrowing. It gives the lending bank the right to file accounts in the same way as the insured does.
- *Construed Coverage.* In case a customer's credit agency rating is changed downward between the time an order is accepted and the merchandise is shipped, this endorsement provides coverage at the higher rating for up to 120 days after the order is accepted.
- *Interim Claim Settlement.* This endorsement allows the insured to request three interim settlements within 60 days after filing a claim rather than waiting until the end of the policy term.

Claim Settlement

Within one month after the expiration of the insolvency period of the policy, the insured submits a Final Statement of Claims listing all claims to be included in the loss settlement. A settlement date is made with the insured within two months after receipt by the insurer of the Final Statement of Claims, at which time the amount ascertained to be due the insured will be paid.

Comprehension Check

1. Briefly describe what a factor is.
2. List nine important questions to ask about a factoring arrangement.
3. How do finance companies differ from factors?
4. List some typical covenants found in a long-term borrowing agreement.
5. What is an operating lease?
6. What is a finance or capital lease?
7. Define the term leveraged buyout.
8. List nine factors to consider when evaluating an LBO.
9. List nine important items to analyze when reviewing the financial statement of an LBO.

14 Business Credit Fraud

Overview

The National Association of Credit Management operates a Loss Prevention Department at its national headquarters to assist creditors in the ongoing battle against credit swindlers. The following information is the culmination of years of analysis of frauds that have been referred to NACM's Loss Prevention Department. The facts of these real-life cases have been distilled into the "fraud warning signs".

While these serve as primary clues that a fraud against a company may be in the making, it is important to note that there can be some extenuating circumstance explaining possible signs of fraudulent behavior. The greater the number of signs, the greater the odds that a fraud may be occurring.

Learning Objectives

After reading this chapter, the reader should understand:

- Why unsolicited orders are suspect
- Why a large number of reference requests should be checked out
- How the credit manager can be used as a reference in a fraud
- Why unverifiable references, unusual product mixes, and unverifiable backgrounds are suspect
- The hallmarks of the "same name scam"
- How to spot misrepresentations
- How to spot the warning signs of hidden ownership, the principal being unavailable, and NSF and counterfeit checks
- How to spot financial irregularities
- How to spot a skip
- Which assets may be removed from a business

Chapter Outline

I. Unsolicited Orders
II. Large Number of Reference Requests
III. Being Used as a Credit Reference in a Possible Fraud
IV. Unverifiable References
V. Increased Orders and Unusual Product Mixes
  A. Unusual Product Mixes
VI. Fraud Warning Sign: Same Name Scam
VII. Fraud Warning Sign: Misrepresentations (Lying)
VIII. Changes in Ownership
IX. Unverifiable Backgrounds
  A. Dealing with an Unverifiable Background
X. Fraud Warning Sign: Hidden Ownership
  A. Sources of Information
XI. Fraud Warning Sign: Principal Unavailable
XII. Fraud Warning Sign: NSF Checks Received
XIII. Counterfeit Checks Received
XIV. Financial Statement Irregularities
XV. Skip
XVI. Assets Removed
  A. Any Assets Can Be Removed

Unsolicited Orders

One sign that something may be amiss is an unsolicited order. Generally speaking, no matter how good your product is, your sales force needs to work hard to come up with business. When a customer comes to you unsolicited, it is often a warning sign of fraud.

Unsolicited orders can come to your company any number of ways, but they generally arrive via phone, mail or at a trade show.

Trade show orders often lead to disaster. One of the biggest sources of losses, due to business credit fraud over the years, has been trade show orders.

The definition of an "unsolicited order" can be tricky. Is an order at a trade show really unsolicited? After all, everything about a trade show is designed to sell, sell, sell! Aren't all vendors at a trade show putting their best foot forward in an effort to sell as much as possible? Of course! So how can a trade show order be "unsolicited"? The answer often lies with the number of orders placed.

Often there are reports of a company going to every booth at a trade show and ordering large amounts of goods at random. This is clearly a tip that something is amiss. However, an isolated, carefully planned order, placed after consultation with your sales staff would likely not be a warning sign.

In addition, it should be noted that many companies receive the vast majority of their business via unsolicited orders. For example, catalog businesses receive calls soliciting their wares routinely. As a credit professional, the questions to ask yourself are: (1) how common is an unsolicited order? and (2) is there a rational explanation for the order? Does it make sense?

Another tip is the relationship between sales and the customer placing the order. If the customer seems to be "trying just a little too hard" to give you what you're normally looking for, perhaps it is time to back off and be careful. Many experienced credit managers feel that the harder someone presses, the more they back off. Perhaps the key statement to remember is the often quoted, "If it seems too good to be true, then it probably is."

Large Number of Reference Requests

Typically, clever bustout artists establish a good credit history on a relatively smaller scale with several companies. They plan to use those companies as references when their "big ordering" begins. Often there is very little a credit manager can do to detect that this is a problem—until the inquiries begin flooding in.

What constitutes a "large" number of inquiries? It's all relative. Most who manage a credit function receive credit reference requests as a part of their daily routine. What is "normal" for you, might not be "normal" for another credit professional. Generally speaking, you have a sense of how many inquiries are "routine." So, when something deviates from what you perceive as routine, consider it a red flag—a reason to dig deeper.

Often, there may be an explanation for the ordering. Perhaps the inquiries are coming in on a major customer that is expanding. The best action for a credit professional to take is to simply call the customer and ask why they are giving your company as a reference so often. A legitimate company will be quite open and have a plausible explanation.

However, it must be noted that clever bustout artists are thoroughly prepared for questions about their ordering. Over the years, numerous companies that have established credit over a period of time used the excuse of "expansion" to justify huge increases in ordering from suppliers. A two-store chain is suddenly opening six more; or a wholesaler is suddenly "going national." You may hear a similar story, but if the company is one you really don't know much about, it often pays to dig deeper.

If the customer claims to be opening new stores, have your sales representative visit the locations. What do the locations look like? Are they well-stocked? Do they even have locations? Don't laugh. Many companies that have claimed they were expanding were able to give only a vague explanation. It's your job to pin them down and to ask for specifics. Why can't they give you exact locations for their stores, when they've just told you that their "new stores" are the reason they have increased orders?

Being Used as a Credit Reference in a Possible Fraud

The problem of high inquiry rates also brings up the question of what credit managers should do when their company is set up as a reference. Suppose you receive many calls and your credit experience has been quite good. What if you've sold for a fairly long period of time, had substantially high credit and prompt payments? What if the phone is ringing off the hook and you are being flooded with written inquiries? You could suspect a fraud is in the making, but you worry about liability.

What do you tell the people inquiring? Under all circumstances, tell the truth. However, you can (and should) advise the caller that you have received many inquiries. You are not offering any value judgement about whether the customer is "good." You are simply offering factual information about your credit experience with the customer in question. Interpretation of this information is up to the user.

When companies begin to receive numerous inquiries about a particular customer, and then conclude that something is wrong, they stop offering references altogether. The Loss Prevention Department disagrees with this practice, as it reduces the valuable flow of information at a time when it is needed most. What about liability? If you stick to the facts, and leave the interpretation up to others, there is no reason not to offer credit references when you suspect a fraud.

Unverifiable References

One of the foundations of the credit checking process is the credit reference. The theory behind reference checking is that past performance can be an indicator of future performance. Often, with modest-sized accounts, a credit manager has little other than references from which to base a credit decision.

The problem, of course, is that any business applying for credit knows this, and is unlikely to submit references that don't reflect favorably on it. Worse still, in the case of fraudulent operators, a potential creditor can simply make up their own references. In fact, Loss Prevention archives document that perhaps 50 percent of all business credit frauds have fake references.

So, what is a credit manager to do? How can a credit manager recognize when someone is fabricating their own credit references? First, as with all the fraud warning signs that we will examine, it is important to recognize that most references that cross your desk are completely legitimate. Don't become paranoid!

However, there are certain questions you can ask yourself about the references you are checking:

- Are the references unknown to you?
- Do some or all of the references sound vaguely familiar to known businesses?
- Do the references have an ostentatious sounding name, like "World-Wide," "International," or "National"?
- Are most of the references in the same general geographic area as your prospective customer?

If the answer to any of the questions is yes, you should dig deeper. The first and easiest step you can take is simply to check with directory assistance in the reference's locale. Believe it or not, this small step will uncover many, many frauds.

If you do find that the reference is listed with directory assistance, but still have a "funny feeling" about the references you are checking, what's next? A second very simple step you can take to help verify the legitimacy of your references is to look them up in your credit rating guide book (often available in CD form). By checking your credit rating book, you can find out a wealth of information. First, is the reference listed at all? Second, if it is listed, is it in a line of business that makes sense? If not, and they are offering a glowing reference, it is a warning sign.

Even when a company is listed with directory assistance and the credit agencies, it is not a guarantee that the reference is legitimate.

Another tip-off that you might be dealing with a questionable reference is the use of a mail drop or answering service. While a business that sells some product or service might operate from a mail drop, most businesses generally need some physical location.

Ask to call the reference back. If you find that you are leaving messages at answering services, and your suspicions are aroused, here is a technique which will help you get to the bottom of the situation. When you receive a return call, simply say you are momentarily tied up, and need to call them back in a couple of minutes. If they give you their answering service number again, ask for the number at their current location, as you will be calling in just a minute. Fraud operators hate to give their number, as they don't want you to know their location.

Often, fraud operators will stall indefinitely with a myriad of excuses as to why they will not be in their office, and simply ask you to leave your number with their answering service. The excuses generally will sound plausible, so good common-sense judgement is required. As with all situations, there are a number of legitimate reasons why a business person might want to give an answering service number. However, when you see a pattern of this activity, and the references in question are overly "glowing," you should treat the reports with more than a small amount of skepticism.

A post-mortem of many credit frauds shows that many achieved "success" by relying on references that called back with glowing reports.

Following the above steps, a credit manager should still look for obvious discrepancies in the reference's "story." If you have done your homework, and found that a reference does exist, does it's story make sense in light of other information that you might have about your potential new customer? For example, is the reference reporting sales for longer than your new account appears to have been in business? Or, is the figure given for high credit too high, in light of the size of the reference? If so, then you should discount the information received from the reference, and perhaps ask more questions.

Quantify your "gut feeling." As always, one of the best indicators is a credit manager's instinct. When you have a "gut feeling" that something is wrong, the chances are that some of the steps outlined here will help you quantify that feeling. When you feel something might be wrong, a little extra digging will usually help you feel much more comfortable with your ultimate decision!

Increased Orders and Unusual Product Mixes

Certainly, the primary goal in any business endeavor is to get your customers to increase their orders. But, this can also be a warning sign and another technique for spotting business credit fraud. An increase in orders could very well indicate fraud.

In most credit fraud situations, the operator ultimately wants to order as much as possible. The "window of opportunity" for the heavy ordering is often just a few months. Thus, there comes a time in almost every credit fraud when ordering increases drastically. It is simple greed. If they're going to "take the business down," they can't resist doing it on a big scale. The results are orders that are out of proportion in relation to the size of the business.

Again, like all fraud indicators, a credit analyst can only make use of this indicator in the context of other factors. Without knowing something about the business' history, its previous order history or its ability to move products, the credit analyst can't really make a judgement about whether a significant rise in orders is a warning sign.

Here are some things you should make yourself aware of:

- If your order is from a retail store, what is the square footage?
- How many locations does the business have?
- Has your sales representative visited any of the stores or the headquarters? What did he or she find?
- If your customer is a wholesaler, do you know the reason for the increase? Under normal circumstances, a wholesaler knows his or her sales reps. If this is a mystery, try to find out who needs the product.
- Does the business have the usual signs of permanence or does everything look like they're ready to pick up and leave on a moment's notice?
- Do you know the background of the principals?

When in doubt, call your sales representative—a good sales rep can be one of your best fraud-fighting allies. If you experience a significant increase in ordering, coupled with any of the other fraud warning signs, the odds are something is wrong.

When questioned after the fact, many fraud operators have told NACM and law enforcement agencies that an increase in ordering should be viewed by credit managers as a "red flag." Convicted bustout operator Alan Levy, who made a 20-year career of bustouts, said, "Normal businesses do not routinely increase each order, but for bustouts, this is par for the course. When a bustout is gearing up, the orders generally increase each time."

Like all fraud warning signs, this is merely a circumstantial "red flag"—something that should cause you to look carefully at the customer in question. Dig until you know the reason and feel comfortable, prior to authorizing increased credit.

Unusual Product Mixes

A classic indicator that a fraud may be in progress is the receipt of an order for an unusual product mix. This indicator comes in two forms. First, it can be a customer placing an order for a product that it wouldn't normally place (for example, a single restaurant ordering 12 copiers). Or, it can be a routine customer who places an order for a mix of your product that does not seem to make sense (for example, six of every item you sell).

Examine the first situation. Regardless of the product or service you sell, you begin to develop a sense for the type of customer from whom you normally receive orders. When an order comes through that deviates from this norm, it generally stimulates that "sixth sense."

When this happens, your game plan should always be the same—throw out your "normal" credit checking routine, and become a detective. You should not stop until you are satisfied that you understand the reason for the "odd" order. As with all fraud warning signs, it is important to keep in mind that many situations which look suspicious on the surface are easily explainable after further examination. Maybe there's an explanation. Until you call the customer and ask, it's difficult to know. Often, a conversation with your customer will alleviate your fears of questionable activity. But more often than not, it will confirm your original suspicions.

The second way in which this indicator can manifest itself is when the customer seems routine, but the order seems unusual. Most credit managers don't take the time to look at what is ordered. Most of the time, the dollar value is what counts. But, the composition of the order is often a clue that the people ordering are up to something. At trade shows, bustout artists often place orders for each and every item in a company's catalog. Just as strangely, they might place an order for only one of your products, when normally an order would be a variety of items.

Through experience, you can develop this sense of which orders are unusual. Bustouts have been detected by alert credit managers who noticed that an order came in at a higher price (retail, instead of wholesale, for example) than normal. This indicates that price is not a big concern. Either you've got a confused customer, or a customer who intends for his or her price to be zero! Be alert to the composition of orders. When in doubt, keep digging until you are satisfied that you understand the reason for the order.

Fraud Warning Sign: Same Name Scam

Since the beginning of credit ratings, enterprising crooks have taken advantage of systems designed to rate business's credit worthiness. To illustrate how the same name scam works, we will look at a hypothetical case. (Any similarity to real businesses is strictly coincidental.) Let's say that there is a reputable business with an excellent credit rating in Detroit named Detroit Distributing. The enterprising crook knows that credit professionals don't always order credit reports for businesses with excellent credit ratings, particularly when the dollar amounts are relatively small.

He thus sets up an office and/or warehouse under a name very similar, if not identical to "Detroit Distributing." In this case, he calls his new business, "Detroit Distribution," and locates it in Detroit. The variation on the name is a very subtle difference, and will probably not be noticed by the majority of suppliers who receive orders. Most credit departments have a credit scoring system that allows orders under a given level to be shipped, depending upon the credit rating.

The crook proceeds to place a number of small to modest-sized orders using the name of his "Detroit Distribution." Unwary suppliers, finding the excellent rating of Detroit Distributing, ship without a thought. By the time the bills come due a month later, the operator is long gone. All suppliers find is a disconnected phone number and an empty office or warehouse.

Upon further in-depth observation, most thoughtful credit managers will point out that there is an obvious flaw to this scheme. Suppose the supplier already sells to the real "Detroit Distributing," and sends the invoice to the real company. Immediately upon receipt of the invoice, the real company's purchasing or payables department will likely call the supplier and point out that they never ordered the product in question. And, should the supplier review the ship-to address, which is also likely at that point, they will note that the shipping address is not connected with the real Detroit Distributing. This often happens, but for some reason, it hasn't stopped credit crooks from trying it—and succeeding—often.

The notorious Harold Goldstein, for example, has set up an operation as the West Coast branch of the well established Comb Company. He was caught because a supplier sent an invoice to the real Comb Company. Goldstein obviously didn't learn his lesson, because following a stint in prison, he began operating as "Citicorp."

While the same name scam isn't the most common form of business credit fraud, it does pay to keep this possibility in the back of your mind. The best way to trip up a potential same name scam is to pay attention to detail. It simply won't work if you verify addresses.

Fraud Warning Sign: Misrepresentations (Lying)

The question of whether something is a "fraud" ultimately rests on whether there is "intent," and a misrepresentation of some sort generally proves intent. Therefore, anytime you spot a misrepresentation, a warning flag should go up.

What are some examples of misrepresentations? Anything can be misrepresented, including financial information, business or educational background, or reasons for a late payment.

Often, a credit manager may stumble onto a misrepresentation accidentally. And often, everything else about the potential account might look positive, causing the credit professional (often with sales or marketing pressure), to ignore the one "minor" infraction. However, any misrepresentation, however small, is ignored only at the peril of the creditor. While there may be occasional reasons to use an assumed name, it certainly is a warning sign that more questions are in order.

How do you find a misrepresentation? As with most fraud spotting techniques, knowledge of the industry you are in and diligence are the two elements needed to spot misrepresentations. The first is critical, because it helps you know when something doesn't fit the norm for your industry, and gives a clue that further digging is in order. But even when there is no obvious sign of something wrong, diligence is really the key. Ask for information from the prospective customer, and check it. Call an accountant and ask a few questions. Call directory assistance to check on a phone listing. Call a former employer to find out if the person really worked there during a particular period. The more stones you turn over, the more likely you are to find something significant. The key is that the "C" for Character is the most important of all. And evidence of a misrepresentation is critical in your analysis of a person's character.

Changes in Ownership

Changes in ownership occur every day, and the vast majority are completely legitimate. However, there are many individuals who specialize in buying businesses with the sole intention of driving them into insolvency, keeping the assets for themselves and leaving creditors in the lurch. This form of business credit fraud causes greater losses than all other forms of credit fraud put together.

How can you tell the difference between legitimate ownership changes and questionable ones? There are several key warning signs. One warning sign is a new owner with a track record of bankrupting businesses. Unfortunately, most are not so obvious.

A second warning sign is an ownership change with little or no notice given to creditors. In most instances, suppliers (trade creditors) and others associated with the business are notified of an ownership change. But credit fraud operators often like to capitalize on the good name of the business, and downplay the new ownership.

Another indication that something might be wrong is a new owner with little or no background information available. Often, fraud operators (also called "take-down" artists) take over businesses through "fronts." The real owner (or take-down operator) has such a bad track record, that his or her name cannot appear on a business without raising suspicions. The object is to find a "clean" front man. In this case, you might see a new owner of a business whose prior business experience seems insufficient to have provided either the capital or the experience to purchase and operate the business in question.

Another warning sign is when a company is owned by a series of corporations, and a trace "up the corporate ladder," only seems to reach more parent companies—no actual people. After all, people run any business and a business is only as good as the people running it. If trying to find out who is in charge is difficult, it may be an indication that something is being hidden on purpose.

Work your way "upstream" in an attempt to determine the owners of the ultimate "top parent." If you've been specifically advised that the names of the owners are not going to be released, this is clearly a warning sign.

Can you imagine extending a million dollar line of credit to a company with multiple parent companies, and "secret" owners at the top? This seems absurd, but it happens often.

In cases such as this, knowing that others are involved may make you feel better, but it isn't the right way to determine creditworthiness. Find out everything you can about the owners until you are comfortable with their background, abilities and most importantly, their integrity.

Unverifiable Backgrounds

Perhaps the most important criteria in the evaluation of the creditworthiness of a business is the background of the principal(s) of the particular business. Of course, if someone has a long and verifiable track record, a credit analyst can feel comfortable that a successful past will likely be prologue to a good future.

Therefore, when studying a business for the extension of credit, you should pay particular attention to the antecedents of the principals. Experience and criminology studies have shown that white-collar criminals will continue their schemes until caught. Thus, after the first bustout, a bustout operator has several choices: (1) he can tell credit agencies and creditors the truth (in which case, credit likely will be withheld); (2) he can make up his background; or (3) he can simply defer it.

The first scenario isn't likely, but it does occur. Some debtors are upfront about their past problems and attempt to convince creditors that they have "turned over a new leaf." This works occasionally. However, the second or third possibilities are more likely scenarios.

Bustout operators will sometimes supply credit agencies with personal background information which, for whatever reason, cannot be verified. They do this by saying they worked for firms which are now bankrupt, or which never existed. Saying that he or she worked at "AA Distributors in New York City," from 1980 until 1986 is a very difficult statement to verify. It is just as difficult to verify if someone really worked for W.T. Grant, the notorious retail bankruptcy in the early '70s.

Dealing with an Unverifiable Background

When you have a large order, it pays to keep asking questions until you are comfortable with the principal's background. The key is to ask for specific addresses of previous employers. Once you have this information, you are in a better position to verify the background.

Another method is to ask for the principal's supervisor at a particular company. If the person is reluctant to supply this information, it should be a clear red flag for the prospective creditor.

Fraud Warning Sign: Hidden Ownership

As we have often stressed, the most important "C" of the 5 "Cs" of Credit is Character, so knowing all you can about the owners of your companies is critical to good credit analysis. While there may be some legitimate reasons why someone would want to conceal their ownership of a business (such as being a publicity shy celebrity), in most instances, it should be a warning sign to the credit analyst. However, at this point, the astute credit professional will probably ask two questions: First, how can a business operate with a "hidden owner." Secondly, assuming they are "hidden," how will I know?

The first question is more common than you might think. The second question is tougher, and will be the subject of this section. It should be noted, hidden ownership most often occurs after an ownership change, so control changes should be monitored very carefully. Whether you have new owners or not, here are a few signs that should alert you:

1. Reluctance of the listed principals, or managers, to make decisions without consulting someone else. Clues that you are dealing with a "front" for the real owners by the way in which the purported "owners" answered questions. Generally speaking, if you are dealing with an owner of a business, they are able to answer routine questions. However, if someone is merely a front for a hidden owner, they will be unable to answer your questions without first checking with the "real" owner.
2. A control change where the owners are not immediately disclosed. Most ownership changes are not kept secret. If they occur with little or no fanfare, you might want to take a look at the individuals who are represented as "principals," to see if, in fact, they have background commensurate with their new positions.
3. A confusing chain of command at a company. NACM Loss Prevention Department staff sometimes ask company representatives at suspect businesses for the names and titles of the principals of the company. In a very recent case, we were given the name of the president, the general manager, and another person who had no title. When pressed for this person's title, the individual being interviewed advised that he was simply "the boss." This seemed to us to be a rather curious situation in which the "boss" was more important than the "president," and was the clue which caused us to keep digging deeper. Eventually, we learned that an individual with a decade-long record of involvement with bustouts was "the boss" at this company.
4. A confusing corporate structure. Did a corporation take over your long time customer? If so, it is important to find out who the people are who own the corporation. Sometimes, individuals with checkered backgrounds hide behind a series of corporations. This tactic also makes it harder for the eventual law suits to reach them personally! In cases where you find a series of corporations going up the ladder, each with unknown principals, you should not consider your credit analysis done until you reach actual people with whom you feel comfortable. This sometimes happens legitimately, of course, but it is also a method used by this country's various "mafias" to remain hidden from the scrutiny of creditors and regulators.

   The case of the now defunct P-I-E Trucklines is a perfect example of a confusing maze of companies. As with most leveraged buyouts, a well established firm was taken over by a holding company. The only trouble in the P-I-E case was that the corporate structure was extremely confusing, and determining the owners of the various companies involved was very difficult. It was eventually determined that Leonard Pelullo, a reported associate of Philadelphia organized crime figures, was in control of P-I-E. Authorities charged Pelullo with numerous fraud counts in connection with his financial dealings, and P-I-E filed for bankruptcy.

5. Signers on checking account. An old adage in white collar crime investigations is "follow the money." If you suspect that you are dealing with a questionable situation, and may not know who the real owners are, try to determine who the signer(s) are, on the checking account. When you find that the signers are different than the purported "owners," it clearly raises the question as to why someone other than the owner has control of the funds!

Sources of Information

While it is possible to find out about hidden ownership on your own, it is often very difficult, and simply happens by accident on many occasions. You certainly don't want to be alone when trying to learn information as important as this! What are the best sources of information to help the you keep on top of potentially hidden ownership? There are at least three key areas to look for help:

1. Your sales force. Some of the best leads may come from credit managers who paid attention to what their sales reps told them. Keeping open lines of communication with your sales reps is one of the best ways to gather useful information about your customer base. There is no better set of "eyes and ears" for your customer base than your own sales reps!
2. Your industry group. No one, no matter how efficient, can find out everything on their own. The industry groups in which you participate are a valuable source of information about ownership changes and irregularities. In this case, you have not only your own set of "eyes and ears" helping you (your sales force), but also that of many of your peers!
3. If you have a case of suspected "hidden ownership," call the Loss Prevention Department and we will be glad to discuss your concerns.

Fraud Warning Sign: Principal Unavailable

You've been calling your customer for weeks on end. Each time, you receive a plausible explanation for the unavailability of the person in charge. But now that your invoice is more than 90 days past due, you begin to get really worried. You realize that you haven't been able to speak to the "decision maker" for the last 60 days! "Something must be wrong," you say. And indeed, you are probably right! This fraud warning sign is something you usually find out about after its too late, but sometimes just the knowledge of what is happening will enable you to make better credit and collection decisions.

Often, the unavailability of the principal will signal that an operation is winding down. The end is often near, unfortunately, when this occurs. Generally speaking, when a fraudulent debtor wants to order from you, he will be readily available. In fact, he may be so aggressively courting you, that you wish he would go away!

Believe it or not, there are also numerous instances where fraudulent debtors are unavailable even at the time of ordering. This occurs with operations that place orders for delivery to mail receiving agencies or mini-storage warehouses. Unfortunately, because we are all taught that "the customer is always right," we usually bend over backwards to attempt to fill orderseven from blatantly questionable operations. However, consider that if you are having a hard time reaching a person before you've extended creditwhat are the odds of reaching that person after you have shipped, and are trying to collect!

Some of the classic excuses by fraudulent debtors include:

- "He's in the field, collecting from our customers." (It's hard to fault someone who's out trying to shore up cash flow. And, most credit professionals can relate to this excuse.)
- "She's overseas, on a buying trip." (While this may be what creditors' hear, there is often no basis in reality for such statementsunless you consider buying margaritas at a Caribbean beach to be an "overseas buying trip.")
- "He's had a heart attack." (You wouldn't believe the number of white collar criminals who have "heart attacks" when creditors are breathing down their necks!)
- "She's in a meeting." (The next time you call, a half hour later, she's gone home!)
- Front: A principal may be unavailable because the person listed "on paper" as the principal may, in fact, be a front for another. In such a case, it will be unlikely that you will deal with the listed principal on matters of substance.

Any of these scenarios should raise a red flag for the credit professional. Most importantly, the "unavailable principal" is a clue which can help you understand the nature of your debtor. If you can identify a problem up front, you will be much more effective in steering clear of possible frauds.

Fraud Warning Sign: NSF Checks Received

"NSF check received." A fraud warning sign? "You've got to be kidding!" you say. "Everyone miscalculates and bounces a check at some point! If I thought that every business that issued an NSF check was a fraud, we wouldn't be able to sell to anyone!" True. Our purpose is not to cry wolf, or make you paranoid, but to shed light on how NSF checks can sometimes be used as tools in a fraud by a credit crook. Like virtually all potential signs of fraud, this warning sign should only be taken in the overall context of the business at which you are looking at.

The NSF check is simply one more indication that something may be amiss. The key in determining fraud is always "state of mind," or "intent." Most of the time, an NSF check reflects simply poor management or a miscalculation, and would thus not reflect a fraud. However, when you are dealing with a fraud, the bounced check you receive is probably intentional.

So, how does an NSF check serve as a warning sign of a possible fraud? Some factors to consider are:

- Patterns of activity. While not generally admissible in court, patterns can nonetheless serve as strong circumstantial evidence that something is amiss.

If you receive a large number of NSF checks, or if other suppliers receive many such checks, perhaps it is an indication that something more than poor management is involved.

- Checking accounts supported by other bogus checks from related parties. Fraud audits conducted after the fact often uncover other NSF checks going into a crook's checking account. The checks are often submitted from related parties just prior to the issuance of a flurry NSF checks. The perpetrator can then claim that he thought he had money in the account, and show deposit slips to prove that his intentions were good. "How could I have known the checks I got from my customers were going to be bad?" he will say.
- Obvious misrepresentations. If you hear from a business owner that money is in the account, but the bank tells you that it has been overdrawn for two weeks, you are more likely to be dealing with a fraud than a case of poor management!
- An increase in ordering at the time an NSF check is submitted. Is the NSF check you have the largest check you have ever received from the account? Does it correspond to an increase in ordering? If so, it could serve as a tip-off that a fraud may be in the making! However, if the check is the same size as numerous previous transactions, it is relatively unlikely that you are dealing with a fraud.

An NSF check is not by itself an indication of a fraud, generally. But looked at in connection with other information you have at your finger tips, it can be one more clue that you are dealing with a potential fraud, rather than a routine business transaction.

Counterfeit Checks Received

Passing counterfeit checks is a growth industry of the 1990's. With the advent of inexpensive desktop publishing systems, laser printers, and color copiers, an individual con man can manufacture checks quite easily. And statistics bear that out! According to *Ernst & Young*, more than 500 million checks are forged annually, with losses totalling more than $10 billion.

The following tips work to help spot forgeries. They can save you a costly error in trusting too much in appearances and take almost no time to use. Remember, no one is ever obligated to accept a check from anyone. Part of the trick in catching check forgeries is to focus special attention on those accounts that appear suspect.

The warning signs to look for when you suspect a bad check are:

- check numbers do not change
- checks do not have perforated sides
- checks drawn on new accounts
- checks which smudge when rubbed with a moist fingertip
- inverted watermark on paper
- slightly raised rather than flat numbers
- printed on low quality paper

- misspelled words
- poor printing quality
- checks presented near the end of the business day by customers who seem unwilling to wait until the next business day for their order
- checks received from customers whose accounts are themselves suspect
- normal checks presented to honor a previously submitted bad check
- irregular signatures, such as those with an interruption or gap where the pen has lifted off the paper completely. Ask the signer to write his signature again if possible. Beware of those who seem to be unusually careful and slow as they sign.
- first two digits of routing code are not in the proper Federal Reserve District with the location of the bank or S&L
- first four digits of routing code are not valid
- district in routing code does not match District in transit number
- bank identification number in routing code does not match bank identification number in transit code
- check identification in optical scan numbers at bottom of check does not match check number on face of the check

Financial Statement Irregularities

One of the best ways to uncover potential frauds is through the careful analysis of a business' financial statements. You need not be a CPA. But you do need to have more than a working knowledge of the basics, along with an eye for detail.

Financial statement analysis gets to the core of the five "Cs" of credit. Statements are used to determine whether the "capital" and "collateral" of a business are sufficient to extend credit. But unless the "character" of the maker of the financial statements is totally sound, your analysis will be based on faulty information. We have seen many a careful analysis of completely phony information.

How does a credit professional determine that a financial statement has been fabricated or doctored? A full discussion of all of the methods of financial statement manipulation is beyond the scope of this chapter, so we will introduce some concepts to help you get started in your journey toward a higher understanding of statements. Context is critical. First, it should be noted that statements should always be looked at in the context of other information that you know about a business. By itself, a financial statement is almost meaningless. In essence, a financial statement is designed to "paint a picture" of a business both at a given point in time (through the balance sheet), and its progress over time (the income statement). Both should clearly make sense, in light of other information that you have about the business. What should one look for "in the context" of other information? The simple answer is "anything that is misrepresented or does not make sense." Dig in to the statement as if it were a puzzle. This is where your knowledge of the conditions (the fifth "C") in your industry and the economy will help you find a financial statement that may not be fully reflective of a business' true picture.

Cash flow versus Net Income: Often, credit managers and investment professionals are taken completely by surprise by the bankruptcy of a company that appeared, based on years of audited statements, to be making money. However, the infamous bankruptcy of W.T. Grant in the early '70s is a great example of a "surprise" bankruptcy, which, in retrospect, offered clues in its financial statements that "trouble was ahead." Unfortunately, most everyone was taken by surprise, and suffered their greatest losses in many a year in the case.

W.T. Grant, one of the largest retailers in the country, had shown good income numbers over the years leading up to its sudden bankruptcy. While it did pay slowly, creditors felt comfortable that the risks were reasonable, given the fact that W.T. Grant was an old-line, profitable account. What was the big clue in the financial statement? Severely negative cash flow.

It is important to keep in mind that Generally Accepted Accounting Principals (GAAP) allow a business a very wide latitude in its accounting policies. Those with very aggressive policies may often overstate the soundness of their financial status. But one report which shows problems which can be "papered over" with aggressive accounting policies is the Statement of Cash Flows. W.T. Grant's negative cash flows gave significant advance warning, but its income statement did not. It "made money" only based on highly aggressive policies (which were nonetheless within GAAP) until it declared bankruptcy.

Skip

"The account skipped." Nothing adds more finality to the collection process than a determination that your customer has skipped. While there might be explanation in certain circumstances, we believe that the term "fraud" can often be substituted for "skip."

This fraud warning sign is about as obvious as it can get in the "fraud warning signs department." While it may seem to be too late to do anything, either internally, or through a general warning to your fellow creditors following a skip, that is not always the case. Until now, most of the warning signs that we have addressed have been designed to help you spot a fraud as early as possible in the credit extension process. This warning sign may leave you with more of a feeling of helplessness than usual.

NACM is diligent in its efforts to keep track of suspicious businesses, and "skips" fall into the category. Numerous leads relating to questionable businesses are put into NACM's SEARCH database on a daily basis. These leads often end up being important clues in future cases, which may save you and other creditors millions of dollars, or which may assist law enforcement in a case with little other evidence. The leads come from NACM members, and often involve what may seem to be an insignificant nuisance we call "the skip."

Assets Removed

Last, but not least, of our specific fraud warning signs is a catch-all: "assets removed." This is essentially the essence of any business credit fraud. While bustouts are often thought of in terms of the removal of inventory, a business compromises far more assets than inventory, and any asset of a business is subject to looting.

Generally, the removal of assets is not noticed until it is too late, but in some instances, an alert credit or finance professional can spot this early, before the damage is too severe.

But, shouldn't the owner of a business be entitled to remove cash or other assets from his or her business? After all, they are the owners, and can do what they want! Of course, this is true. But the issue, as with all fraud issues, revolves around the question of intent.

One question to ask, in an effort to show intent is, Does the removal of assets occur to such a degree that keeping the business afloat is impossible? In many instances, the rapid speed and huge quantity of assets removed make it obvious to any creditor that a business was being pillaged solely for the purposes of enriching its owner, and there was no intent to keep it a going enterprise, and pay creditors.

But, what may seem obvious to professionals, may not be obvious in a court of law. There are difficulties one must keep in mind when studying the removal of assets from this angle. Even if "too much" of a business' assets are removed, showing intent can be tough. After all, legitimate businesses go under every day, and the owners draw salaries, often exorbitant, right up to the end. What constitutes too much? The business world is full of individuals who draw huge salaries at companies good and bad. So who's to say that a salary or draw for a given business is too much? This is a tough question, and a reason why many high level criminals like to take over businesses.

One way to show intent, in the case of removal of assets, is a misrepresentation. One example is the case of Coats Distributors, a business purchased by convicted bustout operator, Jon Miller. Miller claimed to be infusing money into the business. He actually transferred several hundred thousand dollars into Coats. However, investigators found that it was only a partial return of an even greater amount that he had already removed from Coats' operating accounts. On a net basis, Miller had removed more than $400,000 almost immediately after gaining control of the business, while at the same time purporting to be infusing cash into the business. After the fact, this appears obvious, but at the time, credit, financial, legal, and law enforcement investigators didn't have the benefit of seeing the whole picture. They had little but the word of Jon Miller to believe.

Any Assets Can Be Removed

What kind of assets can be removed from a business? As noted above, asset removal is not limited only to inventory or operating cash. Corporate pirates will take anything of value. Just look at the balance sheet of any one of your customers. There are all kinds of items of value. One of the biggest is, of course, accounts receivable. They simply can be collected and pocketed, or they can be sold (factored) to a third party. (Many crooks, when factoring their accounts receivable, supplement the real receivables with phony receivables.)

Even harder assets, such as equipment or real estate, can be converted to the owner's use, through sales, or sale-leaseback arrangements.

Despite the difficulty of proving intent, credit and finance professionals should nonetheless always keep a lookout for a business removing assets at a fast pace. It can be more than mismanagement. The removal of assets can be at once the most obvious or the most subtle of all the fraud warning signs.

Comprehension Check

1. Explain how an unusually large number of credit reference requests may indicate a possible business credit fraud?
2. List four basic questions that can be asked about a credit reference to protect from business credit fraud.
3. Why can a sudden increase in orders or an unusual product mix be an indicator of a business credit fraud?
4. List 18 warning signs of a bad check.

15 Credit Availability Decisions

Overview

The basic objective in making decisions about granting credit is to find ways to approve an order with reasonable expectation that the customer will pay in accordance with credit terms. A decision to grant credit affects income, sales, profits, production, and procurement. If the customer is a good credit risk, the order may be approved as is. Otherwise, an alternative must be developed that is acceptable to the credit departments, the sales department, and the customer.

It is desirable to establish routine procedures for making most credit decisions. Credit approval, through the use of order limits or overall credit limits, reduces the work load in the credit department. This means minimum delay, improved service to customers, and reduced administrative costs. Equally important, it frees the credit executive to give more attention to borderline cases and exceptions. This chapter discusses the approach and decision factors associated with credit limits.

Learning Objectives

After reading this chapter, the reader should know:

- The factors and approaches to handling credit requests from new customers
- Reasons for establishing credit limits
- How to establish and implement limits for regular customers
- Factors to consider in making decisions on marginal credit accounts
- How to handle credit decisions using limited customer information
- When and how to conduct reviews of credit limits

Chapter Outline

I. Dealing with New Customers
   A. Overview
   B. Blanket Approval of Small Orders
   C. Approval Based on Agency Ratings
   D. Non-Routine First Orders
   E. Terms Other Than Open Account

II. Credit Availability and Limits for Regular Customers
   A. Purpose
   B. Difference Between Credit Line and Credit Limit or Availability
   C. Underlying Factors
   D. Methods for Establishing Credit Limits
   E. Implementing Credit Limit Decisions
   F. Communicating Credit Limit Decisions
   G. Informing Customers of Credit Limits

III. Handling Marginal Business
   A. General Considerations
   B. Profit Issues
   C. Other Decision Factors

IV. Decisions Based on Limited Information
   A. Reasons for Limited Information
   B. Other Factors

V. Review of Credit Limits
   A. Regular Reviews
   B. Improved Credit Situations
   C. Changes in Business Conditions
   D. Exceeded Credit Limit
   E. Extraordinary Credit Needs
   F. Extended Terms
   G. Overdue Accounts
   H. Other Reasons for Reviews

Dealing with New Customers

Overview

All orders should be processed quickly, particularly first orders from new customers. Prompt handling of initial orders often means continuing sales. It is difficult to replace past experience with a customer, so many credit granters take a conservative approach with initial orders, unless the customer's credit rating and size is such that credit risk is not a major concern. Under certain circumstances, the Equal Credit Opportunity Act requires the business credit grantor to notify the applicant of adverse action in connection with an applicant for credit. Procedures for prompt handling of initial orders from new customers can also be used for old customers that have not bought for some time. In processing first orders, there are several key concerns:

- How much credit is required?
- Does the customer have the current resources to pay (i.e., is credit really only a convenience in this instance)?
- If the customer does not have apparent resources currently, is it likely that the customer will have them by the time payment is due?
- How much credit do other suppliers/vendors offer this customer, and is this request in line with these figures?

Blanket Approval of Small Orders

If initial orders are so small that the time and expense of a credit investigation is unwarranted, blanket approval may be given for all orders lower than a specified amount. The maximum amount for blanket approval should be influenced by the nature of the company's operations and by overall company and credit policy. It could be changed from time to time according to market conditions, credit terms, loss experience, and other circumstances. Experience shows that more initial orders are paid than not. While individual losses will occur, the impact of extra collection expenses on overall results can be reduced by accelerating the collection procedure, writing off slow accounts, or placing them earlier for collection by outside agencies. Follow-up work is an important requirement of a blanket approval system. Because the first small order may be a trial shipment that could lead to larger ones, the system should require the sales department to supply an estimate of each customer's credit requirements. This enables the credit department to conduct an investigation so future larger orders can be handled expeditiously.

Approval Based on Agency Ratings

Another method of handling initial and future orders without extensive investigation is to use agency ratings as the basis for the amount to be approved. This method of approving orders provides the following advantages:

- general understanding as to why certain actions are being taken
- little need for exhaustive investigation for each account when it falls within the criteria set for routine handling

- approval of larger orders than would usually be covered by a blanket approval system, providing the sales personnel have been trained and understand how to use agency ratings reports
- time saved for other, more exacting duties when routine cases are handled quickly and efficiently
- exceptions and marginal cases are more easily identified and can be examined carefully by the credit staff

Many concerns have developed a credit limit and an initial order limit key based on reports from Dun & Bradstreet or other agencies. This type of system is efficient because it uses agency ratings for first-order approval. (They may also be used to set credit limits, as discussed in a later section of this chapter). Since the agency rating is assumed to be up to date, the credit department can be fairly sure of the degree of credit risk. The rating keys of other reporting agencies may similarly be adapted. Figure 15-1 shows an example of how a company might use the D&B Rating from a Dun & Bradstreet *Business Information Report* to establish credit limits, both for regular credit limit decisions as well as for new customers. There are four decision categories shown, with decisions indicated for various rating classifications. Credit limits decrease for weaker credit categories. The form also provides suggested activities for various ratings.

Non-Routine First Orders

If a first order fails to meet the requisites for automated approval, the decision to investigate may rest on the answers to the following questions:

- Is the order large enough to warrant the cost of investigation?
- Is the potential for future sales large enough that the account should be cultivated?
- How will the prospect react to a request to do business on other than regular terms?
- Is it company policy to establish credit terms for all customers for the public relations benefit which might result?

Terms Other Than Open Account

If the circumstances do not warrant open-account credit, the sale may be made on some other basis, such as cash in advance, cash on delivery, sight draft, certified check, cashier's or bank check, or standby letter of credit. Of these methods of payment, only a cashier's or bank check and standby letter of credit can guarantee payment, since in these instances the bank's credit is substituted for the customer's. A payment on a certified check technically can be stopped for just cause by the customer, and many banks are encouraging their depositors to use bank checks instead of certified checks. Sight drafts are not a common tool in domestic transactions because they require special consignment instructions that can be cumbersome. Cash on delivery can be troublesome if the cash is not available when delivery is attempted. If materials are produced especially for the buyer and are not salable through other outlets, the buyer's refusal to accept delivery could cause loss to the seller. In such cases, if the credit risk is not acceptable, the seller might want to ask for full cash in advance.

Even on goods that are standard, the terms described above (except for cashier's or bank checks and standby letters of credit) expose the seller to the risk of paying for such expenses as round-trip transportation, repacking, and losses in transit if the buyer refuses to accept delivery. This risk should be considered in evaluating the prospect.

Credit Availability and Limits for Regular Customers

Purpose

As soon as possible after first-order approval, controls should be established to ensure prompt and appropriate disposition of further orders. The basic means of control is the credit limit, or maximum amount of risk to be taken on any customer.

Difference between Credit Line and Credit Limit or Availability

Credit line is sometimes used when credit limit is meant. The two terms are not the same because a **credit line** *implies that credit will be or has been granted up to a specific amount usually for a given period of time, as in the case of a bank line of credit.* On the other hand, a **credit limit** *does not have this same implication, and, by using this term or credit availability, a creditor retains discretion over credit granting.*

Underlying Factors

A **customer's credit limit** *is usually based on the requirements for the supplier's products and the ability of the customer to pay its debts. Other factors include the seller's policy, demand for the product, the size and financial condition of the buyer and seller, and the extent of competition.* In all cases, the ability to pay debts must be evaluated by a thorough analysis of financial information, agency ratings and reports, bank checks, trade clearances, and similar data. A new customer's requirements can often be estimated by the sales staff at the time the initial order is placed, or the credit executive may be able to determine requirements through direct contact with the customer. A customer that furnishes financial information is usually treated more liberally than one unwilling to do so. Where the seller is the main supplier, the credit limit may be more liberal. If the profit margin on the particular product is high, the seller can afford to accept greater credit risks and make more credit available. If the company's credit policy is conservative and profit margins are slim, credit limits are more restrictive. If demand for a company's product is greater than its production capacity or there is an industry-wide supply shortage, sales can be made primarily to the most select class of customers, with credit limits to marginal customers minimized. Consideration must always be given to the long-term supply outlook for the product. Greater credit risks may be taken when a company exhibits one of the following characteristics:

- high overhead, which necessitates a high capacity utilization to show a profit
- competing in a highly competitive market
- introducing a new product

- opening a new manufacturing plant
- attempting to enter a new market

The size and financial condition of the selling company influences its credit decisions

The seller needs to decide if it can afford to take the risk of nonpayment or slow payment. The credit limit for a weak customer would have to be lower than that of a well-financed concern. All classes of trade will produce some bad-debt losses. While it is not possible to foretell which particular customers in the class will be responsible for the losses, certain variables are related with failure (e.g., length of time in business, financial ratios, payment patterns, line of business). Outside factors (e.g., external credit pressure, overall health of the company's industry) also determine whether a business will fail. A company has to decide what opportunities it wants to pursue and what risks it is willing and able to accept. Competition influences credit limits. If, for example, a competitor is extending $25,000 to a customer, the seller may have to meet competition to avoid losing the account.

Terms of sale affect limits

Financial exposure is greater when terms are longer. A credit limit of $10,000 might be adequate for a company purchasing $5,000 per week on terms of net 10 days. But if the terms were net 60 days, a much larger limit would be required. The credit limit is also influenced by the collection effort that may be required. The seller must determine if sufficient personnel, time, and information are available to follow a large number of high-risk accounts. If such factors are inadequate, lower limits would have to be set. In the final analysis, profits on the good sales should exceed losses on the bad sales. A high bad-debt record is not necessarily the mark of poor credit judgment because it may be an indication that excellent credit judgment is being used to maximize net profit. On the other hand, low bad-debt losses with a high record of order refusals could hurt the company's selling efforts and restrict net profit. A certain amount of bad-debt loss has to be anticipated and should be acceptable to management.

Methods for Establishing Credit Limits

Companies use different methods in establishing credit limits and are not restricted to using one of the following for all customers. **Credit limit** *is determined by payment record*. This "method" may not really be a method as the amount of the credit limit can fluctuate, depending on the customer's ability to pay on terms. This does have the advantage of making credit decisions more routine, unless the customer does not pay on time, when a more detailed credit review process would be triggered. This type of limit encourages additional sales and is popular with sales personnel. **Credit limit** *is determined by the amount competitors grant the customer*. In this method, the amount of the limit is determined by matching the amount (or average) amount granted by appropriate competitors. The accuracy of the competitors' limits is critical to assure that proper limits are used. External reports and market information are usually used to determine competitive limits. If the creditor is not the same size as the competitors or plays a distinctly different supply role (much larger or smaller), it will be difficult to establish reasonable credit limits using this method.

Credit limit is low to begin with and increases as the customer displays acceptable payment performance

This popular method adopts a conservative risk management approach and rewards new customers as they continue to do business with the company. This is often used when little payment history is available. While limiting the company's exposure, it does limit the speed at which sales can grow. Credit limit is set for a defined period of time. Purchases made over the time period, such as a week or month, cannot exceed the credit limit. This is useful in cases where many shipments may be made to a customer from various company locations. Orders can be approved in a more routine manner using this method, as long as the overall credit limit has not been exceeded.

Credit limit is set by credit agency rating

This method is similar to that used for new customers and shown in Figure 15-1. Again, it can be set up to operate routinely. It is fairly simple to communicate credit limits to other departments.

Credit limit is set by formula

In this method, several calculations are made and averaged to determine the credit limit to be assigned to the customer. Key financial data, such as net worth, inventory, current assets, and/or net working capital are used. These data items are divided by the number of creditors to determine the amount per creditor. These amounts are averaged to set the credit limit. It may be difficult to obtain an accurate estimate of the number of creditors. This method is often used to develop a preliminary estimate and is then augmented by one of the other methods. Credit limit is determined by how much the customer is expected to use in a period of time (usually one year). Sometimes referred to as the requirements method, this method sets a credit limit based on the expected dollar volume of business for the year. This figure is divided by the number of orders expected throughout the year to estimate the credit limit. This method, like the formula method, is usually used to obtain a preliminary estimate, which can be defined further by one of the other methods.

Implementing Credit Limit Decisions

Credit limits serve as guides for order approval, minimize upward referral of orders, and call immediate attention to any change in a customer's purchasing or paying habits. Any order that does not exceed the limit can be approved without further investigation or analysis. An order exceeding the limit signals the need for examination of the account and halts all shipments of products to the customer until the exceptional situation has been resolved.

Some companies would rather not establish a firm credit limit, opting instead for a flexible limit, based on previous experience with the account. Flexible limits have the advantage of being easy to implement with little upset to the customer and the sales department, unless payments are not made on time. Those who favor a more formal system of establishing credit limits point out that the account may become overvalued quickly, that prompt payments may be a buildup for later, larger, and unpaid orders, or that a formal analysis might have set a credit limit high enough to eliminate the need for a review every time a new order was received. Often, the tendency is to let the credit limit become simply a matter of course, which means

Figure 15-1 Using Credit Agency Ratings for Credit Limit Decisions

The following example has been provided by Dun and Bradstreet Information Services and is for illustrative purposes only. D&B is not recommending adoption of this chart for use in credit decisions. Individual credit approval processes may vary, depending on internal credit policies and costs.

Rating Classification	1	2	3	4
5A 4A 3A	Up to: $5 million 1 million 100,000	Up to: $2.5 million 500,000 50,000	Up to $5,000	Approval for routine decisions: • Small orders COD • Larger orders 50% deposit with secured financing
2A 1A	Up to: $1 million 50,000	Up to: $500,000 25,000	Up to $2,500	Higher credit limits may require review of: • Historical payment information, including • Management background • Number of years in business • Financial trend and profitability
BA BB CB CC	Up to: $50,000 30,000 20,000 12,500	Up to: $25,000 15,000 10,000 6,250	Up to $2,500	
DC DD EE	Up to: $7,500 5,000 3,500	Up to: $3,750 2,500 1,750	Up to: $2,000 with 50% COD Larger orders COD and/or carefully review all information in BIR	
FF GG HH	Up to: $2,000 1,000 500	Up to: $1,000 500 250	Up to $1,000 with 50% COD Larger orders COD and/or carefully review all information in BIR	
1R 2R	N/A N/A	Up to: $50,000 Up to: $5,000	Up to: $5,000 Up to $1,000 with 50% COD Larger orders COD and/or carefully review all information in BIR	
— (no rating)	Approve credit limits after careful review of: • Payment information, including analysis by supplier's industry • Public filing information • Management background • Number of years in business • Financial trend, profitability, and other factors			

that any order the customer places is approved. Only very substantial and financially sound customers can be sold on this basis. *An* **order limit** *specifies the dollar amount that may be released without delay on any single order.* It differs from a credit limit, which is established without regard to the size of any particular order and is generally set at an amount that can be justified by the available credit information. Some companies place an order limit on every account. This usually serves as a secondary credit check, so the customer's file is reviewed when either the credit limit or order limit is exceeded. This kind of order limit may be particularly useful in a decentralized credit organization where it is impractical for order processing points to keep complete records of receivables. One variation of the credit limit is based upon the amount that the creditor is willing to have outstanding at any time. This method requires complete records of unpaid invoices and of orders approved but not yet shipped. When the total outstanding balance exceeds the limit, any further orders are referred for approval.

There is a growing tendency to use formulas for assigning credit limits, with companies using the factors they consider most meaningful and adapting them to computer systems. This may be more attractive to larger companies who can afford more sophisticated, automated systems. Computers have made it possible to use statistical and probability analysis for assigning credit limits, using credit scoring techniques. These techniques can help predict the outcome of certain credit decisions regarding various classes of customers. The knowledge can be useful in minimizing high-risk exposure where the potential reward is not commensurate with the risk or in situations where a large number of credit decisions must be made regularly. There are specialized firms that develop more sophisticated and expensive credit scoring models. A well-designed model can help establish consistent evaluation of customer risk and save time and expense in appraising marginal accounts. By the use of statistical devices, qualitative information can be assigned numerical values that are compared to an established rating scale for a particular industry.

Communicating Credit Limit Decisions

Many companies advise their sales department of the credit limits assigned to customers, often expressing the limits in terms of units (300 tons, 20 carloads) or dollars allowed during a given period of time. If, for example, a customer has a credit limit of $5,000 on terms of 1/10, net/30 and consistently discounts, this customer could be sold from $10,000 to $15,000 per month. Because of discount payments, the highest credit would still be expected to remain within the credit limit of $5,000.

Informing Customers of Credit Limits

Credit executives disagree as to the advisability of telling customers their credit limits. Some credit executives say customers may interpret the credit limit as a reflection of their financial responsibility. This may damage good will, and it may also lead the customers to confine their purchases to the original limit, even when a larger limit has become reasonable. Those who hold this view claim that a credit limit should be for internal use only. Those who favor it say the practice gives them an opportunity to discuss the credit limit and to offer suggestions which may help the customer. Furthermore, it informs the customer that there is a credit limit and reduces embarrassment and misunderstanding that may result when an order over the limit is held.

Handling Marginal Business

General Considerations

Marginal customers *fall short of the mark in one or more ways, so a sale to one presents an abnormal risk even when full information is available.* Many companies define marginal risks as having one or more typical characteristics:

- Management is weak. It is either inexperienced or lacks depth.
- Finances are inadequate. Companies are not adequately capitalized for their transaction volume or are not generating sufficient profits.
- Payments are slow. Terms of sale are not observed, so extra collection efforts are required.
- Merchandise is bought in too small quantities and provides low profitability.
- Orders often exceed predetermined credit limits.
- The customer has a low Dun & Bradstreet composite credit appraisal.

There is a growing trend to consider marginal customers an important source of business. Those with good growth prospects offer an excellent opportunity for a supplier to make profitable sales, despite the fact that credit requests are high in relation to net worth. A well-balanced receivables portfolio should include a percentage of marginal accounts because they satisfy the need for additional business in a specific market. A supplier that has excess production capacity or needs a wider market base should be willing to take a greater credit risk. This is especially true when the better customers have absorbed the fixed costs, and marginal accounts are required only to cover the incremental or out-of-pocket costs.

Profit Issues

Profit on incremental sales to marginal customers may materially improve the earnings of the business, even allowing for increased credit losses. This can be shown as follows: Assume a company is operating at less than capacity. If all of its fixed costs and an acceptable profit are covered at present levels of production, any increase in output would require expenditure only for the direct, out-of-pocket costs of the additional sales. If these make up 40 percent of the selling price, the remaining 60 percent would be profit. Hence, any incremental sales that sustained less than 60 percent bad-debt losses would increase the company's profit. A number of factors related to profit margins may influence the decision to sell to marginal accounts. As a rule, a seller with a wider profit margin can afford to take greater credit risks. The higher the prospective customer's profit, the fewer units it must sell to pay its supplier. Disposition of the customer's profit should also be considered. Reinvestment of earnings during good times will not only improve a marginal risk but tend to assure its continued existence during bad times.

Other Decision Factors

Product distribution affects the credit decision on marginal business. When new products are being promoted or when new distribution channels are being developed, marginal risks offer the seller an opportunity to maximize effectiveness. Alternative outlets must also be considered. Selling to one of a few marginal jobbers may be considerably more economical than handling hundreds of direct retailer or manufacturer accounts, for example. On the other hand, it may be constructive to refuse credit to a marginal risk and explore the possibility of selling to alternative outlets that present a more attractive financial picture. Finally, obsolete or slow-moving inventory may be better sold to a marginal risk than junked. As might be expected, marginal accounts are better risks during prosperous times than they are during recessions, and their industry often affects their ability to survive. Despite this tendency, there are a number of ways to reduce the risk on marginal accounts. Protective measures such as guarantees or security agreements perfected under the Uniform Commercial Code may serve this purpose. Terms shorter than standard terms, C.O.D., part cash in advance, and cash before delivery may also be considered. The adequacy of fire insurance on property, life insurance on the principals, public liability insurance on hazardous operations, and other types of insurance carried by the buyer may also affect the credit decision. The credit executive should carefully consider the insurable risks and their coverage in evaluating a marginal account.

Decisions Based on Limited Information

Reasons for Limited Information

Credit information is readily available from many sources, and normal investigation usually produces adequate data for sound credit appraisals. Despite this, a credit department is sometimes obliged to act upon limited information. A customer refuses to supply customary banking and trade references or financial details. Bank and trade reports can be gathered independently but with delays and greater cost. When customers refuse to supply information, the reasons for such refusal should be ascertained. It is often possible to work out a basis on which they will furnish adequate information. For example, financial data are sometimes refused because "We don't want our competition to know what we're doing." Assurances of confidential handling may satisfy this objection. Time is of the essence and the urgency for credit action does not permit normal investigation. If the credit executive can find no way to obtain adequate information within the time available, the decision must be made on whatever information can be gathered. Unless the business is new, a payment record is almost always available. Full information is not available due to recent formation of the business or inadequate records kept by the customer. Here, the principals' past business records may be more important than financial details. Without exception, if historic information is lacking, credit grantors should proceed with extreme caution. Sales may ask credit not to press for information because of possible adverse effects on future sales. This is an internal problem that should be resolved by discussion between the sales and the credit departments. What action to take and how to go about it should be decided after a factual, realistic review of the situation.

Other Factors

Decisions based on limited information involve factors that relate not only to the prospective customer but also to the supplier company. The general condition of the economy is very important. If times are prosperous, the risk of financial loss is reduced and the credit executive would be more prone to approve orders. Under depressed conditions, the risk of loss is higher and the credit executive would be more prudent in extending credit to customers.

Competition is also a factor. If it is extremely heavy, it may be necessary to approve orders on limited information. When there is an overabundance of products or a buyer's market exists, it is common to extend credit on a more liberal basis to maintain a reasonable share of the market. Conversely, when products are in short supply and a seller's market exists, credit analysis can be stricter. Compiling information costs time and money, and a point is eventually reached at which more information is not worth the added cost. Properly interpreted and evaluated, limited information may be adequate for a yes-or-no decision, while delay in reaching a decision may cause the seller to lose the order, the customer, or both. The factors that apply to setting credit limits enter into decisions based on limited information. It is helpful to review the situation with immediate superiors and top sales management. Such discussion creates common understanding of the problem, broadens the perspective of the credit executive, and makes salespeople more aware of why it is desirable for them to obtain information from customers.

Review of Credit Limits

Regular Reviews

Credit limits *are based on information, assumptions, experiences, estimates, forecasts, and economic conditions.* Since all of these factors are subject to change, it is important for a well-organized credit system to provide for review of credit limits, and to identify the criteria that trigger such reviews. A well-organized credit procedure should provide for a periodic review of all active files. For normally active customers, the review should be made annually, timed if possible to coincide with receipt of the fiscal financial statements or before the customer's active season. For marginal risks, the review should occur at more frequent intervals; semiannually, quarterly, or in extreme cases, monthly. The periodic review can help keep credit limits flexible to provide satisfactory customers, and to accommodate the development of business obtained from aggressive and expanding concerns. The frequency and scope of review will vary with the type of customer, quality of risk, and the amount of credit exposure involved. For top-quality or prime accounts, it will tend to be very nominal. As the quality of the accounts declines and the risk increases, the scope and intensity of the review will increase. A thorough and complete review should include the following steps, with particular attention to trends:

- Secure from the sales department an estimate of the customer's current and near-term needs.
- Request from the sales department an estimate of the customer's potential growth.
- Review the customer's recent payment record with the company.
- Review the latest agency reports to check for changes in ownership, operation, payment record, rating, and financial information.

- Review and analyze latest financial statements, whether received directly or contained in an agency report. Obtain current figures if necessary.
- Review the most recent interchange report and compare it with previous reports.
- Review the latest direct interchange with other suppliers and obtain new information if necessary.
- Review the latest information from the customer's bank and obtain new information if necessary.
- Review notes and memoranda resulting from direct contact with the customer.
- Make a personal call, if considered advisable, on the customer.
- Appraise historical information on the new principals when important changes in management take place.
- Decide whether the credit limit and payment terms are reasonable for the customer's financial strength and credit standing, in line with company credit policy, and adequate to supply the customer's needs.

Improved Credit Situations

The most desirable reason for an off-schedule review of a customer's credit limit is a marked improvement in its credit position. Alertness to this type of improvement offers great sales possibilities. When a customer's financial condition and payment performance improve substantially, it may be possible to extend larger amounts of credit, with fewer orders referred for review. These steps can result in increased sales and profits and in better service to the customer. A compliment to the customer on such improvement can reinforce good will, and some companies regularly send Thank You letters to customers whose payment habits remain good or improve.

Changes in Business Conditions

Changing conditions in business, in a particular industry, or in a geographic area generally may warrant review of accounts. Improving conditions in the country, market area, or industry of the customer should trigger a review for the purpose of raising its credit limit. Conversely, a nationwide depression, poor crops in a given section, a prolonged strike, and many less dramatic changes can each have serious consequences for individual concerns. If prolonged or severe enough, they can affect not only the marginal business but the well-financed, well-managed concern as well. Reassessment of credit availability in terms of new situations can be advantageous to both supplier and customer.

Exceeded Credit Limit

Orders that exceed the customer's credit limit require a review to determine whether the customer will pay and when it will do so. The credit executive will need financial and background material that justifies additional credit. Answers must be obtained to such questions as:

- Are customer debts in line with trading assets?
- Are trade payments prompt?
- What is the experience of other suppliers on the risk?
- Are other suppliers placing undisputed claims for collection?
- Is there any evidence of careless or unreliable performance by the customer?
- Are there any special marketing conditions?

If satisfactory answers to these questions cannot be obtained, it may be possible to work out a collateral security or other special arrangement reducing or eliminating the credit risk. Concurrently, if the available information indicates ability to pay but not within terms, the question is whether additional cost of the expected delinquency will make the receivable unprofitable.

Extraordinary Credit Needs

Requests for credit not warranted by the customer's financial condition may lead to sales and profits which otherwise would not materialize or, on the other hand, to increased credit losses or expanded slow receivables. Thorough investigation and current information should support a decision to extend unusually high credit.

Reasons for Unusual Needs

The common reasons for extraordinary credit needs are:

- Expanding sales. This is perhaps the most frequent reason.
- Initial or seasonal buildup of inventory.
- Special contracts.
- New or recently established business. In a highly competitive economy, buyers frequently count heavily upon credit from suppliers as the principal source of operating capital.
- Continuing credit for normal needs when there is a moratorium on previously incurred debts.

Probability of Collection

Once the reasons for unusual needs have been established, the seller must evaluate the probability of collection. Since the amount of credit is excessive by accepted financial standards, the decision must usually be based on nonfinancial factors, such as the personal background and integrity of the principals, business ability, experience with other suppliers, relations with their bank, and willingness to supply financial information. Legal advice should be sought on special contracts to avoid difficulty in connection with performance, payment specifications, or quality of goods. Payment specifications merit particular attention. Long-term payments carry greater hazard than short-term payments. A general guide is to negotiate for payment schedules that match the customer's cash receipts.

Seller Considerations

It is also important to determine whether the seller's accounts receivable will be adversely affected. If unusually high credit concentrates the credit risk in one customer, it may be advisable to refuse the request. Accounts should be classed into risk categories and incremental sales should be compared to incremental profits for each category. Overall company policies should also be considered on requests for unusually large amounts of credit. Such factors as profit margins, desirability of the business, distribution needs, competitive situations, marketing of a new product, opening a new sales territory, and efficient utilization of production facilities must be weighed.

Extended Terms

While the element of risk is common to all credit transactions, the degree of the risk varies with the credit period: the longer the credit period, the greater the risk. When circumstances appear to justify credit terms that extend longer than the usual period, the advice of company legal counsel must be sought before any decision is made. Terms of sale may be considered a part of the price. Credit executives should be aware that extended payment terms may be regarded as a change in price favoring a particular customer. If extended terms are granted to one customer, they should be available to others under comparable circumstances. In addition, it should be recognized that terms concessions to some customers may be unfair to those that pay on standard terms. Accordingly, the seller should make some provision for penalty or recovery of the added cost of carrying the extended receivables.

Establishing the Necessity for Extended Terms

In any individual case, the need for additional time must first be established. The conditions that bring about this need are similar to those that underlie requests for unusually high credit, such as expanding sales, seasonal financing of accounts receivable and inventory, and special contracts. Occasionally a customer with limited resources requests longer terms until additional capital becomes available. Current financial information is essential. In a new business, the financial data alone may justify the decision. Where the customer seems to lack operating capital to finance expanding sales, the credit executive should try to determine whether the sales forecasts are realistic. Here, the views of the sales representative handling the account can be valuable. If the need stems from a special contract, it should be examined with particular regard to the payment schedule. When additional time is needed until other capital becomes available, it might be well to seek verification from the source of expected funds.

Terms Offered by Competitors

Another reason for considering extended terms, and an important one in many industries, is often simply a matter of meeting competition, and is not related to actual customer need. This is more of a sales-management problem than one of credit. The credit executive can and should counsel as to the risks involved, but the decision belongs to top management, to be reached in the light of overall company policy. It is appropriate, however, to emphasize the need to verify alleged competitive practices before a decision is reached, for extensive terms competition can have severely demoralizing effects. Requests for lengthened terms to meet competition frequently stem from customers' reports of special arrangements offered by competing suppliers, which may be misleading. Inquiries directed to the sales department can usually determine their accuracy. If the reports are verified, a decision mutually acceptable to sales and credit management can be worked out. Extended terms can have far-reaching effects. For example, rather than reduce prices, companies may offer extended terms as non-price reductions. Sales management may justify this practice as a business decision. However, competitors or competing customers are affected by this action, and it could have serious legal implications to the seller. The effect of extended terms is much more difficult to evaluate than the effect of price changes.

Determining Whether Extended Terms Are Realistic

If the customer's need is established, the credit executive must decide whether the proposed extended payment arrangements are a realistic means of meeting this need. This means answering such questions as:

- Will temporary assistance from the supplier give adequate financing?
- Does available information, including sales forecasts and cash inflow forecasts, indicate that funds will be available to meet obligations as they mature?
- Will there be adequate funds to resume normal payments as agreed?
- Does close analysis indicate that such aid would serve no long-term purpose and that the actual need is for equity capital or long-term debt?

A manufacturer can help a customer by supplying products on extended terms, but this is not realistic if the supplier-customer relationship is relatively new and not profitable to the seller. On the other hand, if a long-time customer fails, the profit earned by the supplier over the years may more than offset any one-time loss. In deciding whether to offer extended terms, the determining factor is often the larger picture of the entire relationship between buyer and seller. If a customer's need is established and extended terms are considered, the credit executive should give close attention to the amount of credit to be granted under these terms, keeping in mind the increased risk and the legal implications.

Overdue Accounts

Slow payment is probably the factor that most frequently leads to account review. If slow-paying customers are approached with a frame of mind that seeks knowledge or answers, it may be possible to convert them to prompt and profitable accounts. As a starting point, credit information should be reviewed and brought up to date. The sales department's appraisal of the risk and potential may also help decide how a past-due account should be handled. If the review indicates that additional credit is too risky, friendly but firm efforts should be initiated to collect the past-due amount. Internal controls can be set up to prevent shipment of new orders until the past-due amount has been paid. If a new order is received, the credit department may tell the customer that additional credit will be extended after past-due bills are paid. Some problems of past-due accounts may be solved by amortizing payment of all or a portion of matured balances over a period of time, with a provision for prompt payment of any new credit. Amortization plans may also provide for conversion of extended open-account balances to interest-bearing notes. The objective is to return the accounts to a current basis by liquidating the frozen balances. However, unless such plans are based realistically on ability to meet the schedule of payments out of profits or otherwise, they may serve only to complicate the situation. The assessment of late-payment service charges can provide inducement to pay promptly and is used for that purpose in a number of industries.

Other Reasons for Reviews

A credit file should also be reviewed upon receipt of information that is deemed unusual or significant, such as receiving a new financial statement, a change in the accounting method for reporting sales and income, new auditors, the death of one of the principals, the admission of a new partner or other change in management, a change of banks, the business being incorporated, a merger, or an acquisition. Information from other sources may also cause a review. Local newspapers often publicize changes in ownership and management, the start of legal actions, and information on customers. Industry and trade publications are useful sources of information both on individual customers and on conditions in the industry. General business conditions are discussed in financial newspapers and financial sections of leading newspapers, and periodic analyses are issued by prominent banks and a number of government publications. Credit executives should be alert for any indications of a customer's financial difficulty, including reduced agency ratings, increasingly irregular or delayed trade payments, reports of contentiousness, protested checks, filing of tax claims, perfected security agreements, or failure to maintain scheduled payments on debentures, mortgages, or other fixed obligations. There is a great danger in presumptions based on incomplete surface indications. These should always be explored. Thorough investigation is often required to assess their significance. Any decision to curtail credit or to question a customer's creditworthiness should be delayed until complete information can be obtained. A selling firm's own experience with bad debts, slow collections, financial requirements, or marketing strategy can cause credit policy changes that would call for review of all customer credit files.

Comprehension Check

1. Some companies establish a way to automatically approve small orders. Supply a justification of this policy.
2. What is the difference between credit line and credit limit or availability?
3. Explain how the statement, the size and the financial condition of the selling company influence its credit decisions.
4. Discuss three common methods used to establish a credit limit.
5. List and discuss the characteristics of a marginal account.
6. Why can selling to a marginal account be important to a business?
7. Explain the statement: The longer the credit period, the greater the risk.

16 Customer Visits

Overview

It is arguably the main function of the credit department to know the customer. As the customer is usually the best source of information about itself, the importance of customer visits is obvious. Second perhaps only to the sales force, the credit department has the highest need to visit customer sites and meet the key individuals involved in the operation. Unfortunately, this is often not clearly understood by others in the organization. Thus, credit executives often face the task of clearing up misunderstandings and responding to the following kinds of objections:

- high travel expenses
- too much lost time from the office
- too confrontational
- leads to too much familiarity with the customer
- belief that there is a hidden agenda (the personal benefit of the credit executive)
- belief that credit and sales work at cross purposes, and should not make a joint visit

For example, upper management might suspect that the underlying purpose of a visitation program is to accumulate personal benefits, such as frequent flier miles, or to engage in favored leisure activities. Internal management education on this subject therefore becomes a responsibility of the credit professional and is the starting point for any visitation strategy. Sincerity is foremost here. The program cannot succeed unless the credit manager firmly believes its purpose is professional education and organizational accomplishment.

Learning Objectives

After reading this chapter, the reader should understand:

- The credit manager's main objectives of visiting a customer
- What a credit manager should look for and question during a customer visit
- How to use a customer visit to build a stronger relationship with your customer clientele
- How to prepare for a customer visit

Chapter Outline

I. Objectives of Customer Visits
   A. Developing Relationships
   B. Observe the Facilities
   C. Discuss and Review Financial Information
   D. Observe the Customer's Competition
   E. Develop Linkages, Resolve Disputes

II. Addressing Liquidity Issues with Lenders

III. Advice on Receivables and Other Matters

IV. Collections
   A. Preparation

Objectives of Customer Visits

This section addresses the objections listed above by discussing what can be accomplished through credit visits:

- develop a relationship with the customer
- develop a relationship with the sales department
- observe the facilities (the inventory, the condition of the equipment, the plant, the location and attractiveness of retail operations, etc.)
- discuss financial information in more depth than is permissible on the phone
- review financial information that might otherwise be unavailable
- observe the impact of your competitors, and how their products are being used
- develop linkages between various internal company functions and the customer's counterparts (i.e., traffic departments, advertising departments, etc.)
- resolve disputes
- join with the customer to visit lending institution(s) to help resolve liquidity issues
- provide advice to the customer with regard to his own receivables, and other matters
- collect money

Collecting money appears at the end of this list by design. Making collections the focus of the visit means ignoring all of the other factors that will make the collection effort more successful. Figure 16-1 is a checklist of questions to ask during a customer visit.

Developing Relationships

Except in the most extreme cases where all hope of preserving the account is lost, this is the principal goal of a visit. An understanding of the customer's organization (the structure, the mission, his competition) and of the individuals involved (employees, management, their roles, their personal viewpoints) are all part of building the relationship. Most customers simply cannot pay every bill when it falls due. If they could, there would probably be little need for a credit department. This reality underscores the importance of understanding factors that influence customer pay patterns. These include seasonality, competition, unforeseen disasters, and outside personal factors or family issues such as divorce, which may impact either management attention or cash flow.

Most customers are embarrassed about an inability to pay on time and are often reluctant to disclose the true reason. Consequently, it is often extraordinarily difficult to identify problem sources when telephone lines are the only connections between companies and their customers. Visitation provides a proven method of stripping communication barriers, especially when accompanied by a demonstrated knowledge of (or a willingness to learn) the customer and his organization. Valuable insights into the ability and character of management are also acquired.

Figure 16-1 Questions To Ask on Customer Visits

1. Please describe your corporate structure:

   Is it a corporation, partnership, LLC, LLP or proprietorship?

   To what entity are you really extending credit?

2. Are there affiliated companies?

   If so, what is their relationship to the company you are visiting (vertical : supplier or end-user; horizontal: differentiated by product type or geography, etc.)?

3. Describe the product cycle, from ordering to shipment of raw material to finished product to receipt of cash.

   Explain the impact of seasonality.

4. Describe inventory policies.

   Are there markdown procedures in place, or other plans to relieve slow-moving stock?

   What is the size of order backlogs?

5. Who are your principal customers?

   Describe their creditworthiness, and the impact of seasonality on their business.

6. What terms of sale do you offer to your customers?

   Describe customer payment performance.

7. What is your market share?

   Describe your product niche.

   Describe your competition, their advantages or disadvantages (price/quality/delivery), and their relative market shares.

8. Are there plans for expansion, new product developments, or curtailments of unsuccessful lines?

   In the former case, how will this be financed?

   In the latter case, how will overhead be eliminated or absorbed?

   What are the lease expense implications where facilities to be closed?

   Are the plans realistic?

9. Who are your major suppliers?

   What terms do they offer?

   Do any of them hold letters of credit, guarantees, or security instruments such as liens?

10. What are projections for sales and income?

    What factors would influence possible variances?

11. Describe borrowing arrangements (availability, advance rates, factoring arrangements, security held, mandatory cleanup periods).
    - What is the impact of seasonality?
    - Is refinancing under consideration?
    - Are personal assets or assets of affiliated companies pledged?

Figure 16-2 Plant Tours

This is a checklist to use when visiting a customer's plant.

1. Prioritize. Visit the most important sites first, but not necessarily the site the customer seems most inclined to have you visit.
2. Observe the impact of competition in terms of product use, amount on hand, etc. Try to insure that you are not misled by what you observe. If there is a large backlog, what factors are involved (heavy buying in advance of season, poor acceptance of the suppliers' product, spot buying due to advantageous pricing, purchase of supplier's product due to credit problem with us, etc.)?
3. Observe the efficiency of customer logistics. Is the facility located advantageously to customer locations and supply routes?
4. Observe the traffic flow of both employees and receiving and shipping facilities.
5. Observe manufacturing efficiency and productivity. Look for signs of excess capacity.
6. Does employee morale seem high or low? If possible, ask employees to describe their functions in the organization.
7. What is the condition of equipment and other fixed assets?
8. Are there plans to relocate any facilities?
9. Have your salesperson accompany you to help explain the facility and add his interpretation. Ask your salesperson to compare this operation to competitors' facilities.

Visitation also permits building relationships with the sales team. Credit executives are able to gain the respect of the sales department by willingness to live in the world of the industry and to learn to speak a common industry language.

Observe the Facilities

Customers come in a wide variety of configurations. For example, a value-priced retailer might be an off-price store that buys marked down seasonal close-outs and resells at a full markup. Or the business might be a discount store that buys basic products at a normal wholesale cost and sells at a reduced markup. While trade publications, such as *Discount Store News,* have developed definitions to deal with much of this differentiation, there are still many unnamed subcategories in just this one segment of the business world. (Note that SIC codes do not differentiate a high margin department store from a discount store.) This kind of diversity can be found in all industries.

Visitation breaks down barriers to understanding the customer. Credit executives can observe an operation and compare the subject company's performance to other similar businesses that were visited. What is the condition of inventory? Are markdowns being taken at an accelerated rate for this industry? Is the equipment rundown? Is retail traffic light or heavy? Are stores well located? Are the office facilities too extravagant (too expensive)? For some further thought on this, see Figure 16-2.

Discuss and Review Financial Information

Many private companies will only permit on-site examination of financial information. In such instances, if there were no visit, financial information would be unavailable to the credit department. It is important in these cases to capture as much information as possible. If the customer will permit it, take some written notes.

Even when copies have previously been given to the credit manager, a face-to-face discussion with customers about their financial statements provides a clearer understanding of the numbers. There are two reasons for this. First, the assets are now visual, or potentially visual, to the credit professional. Second, there is usually more unrestricted time allotted for the review, than for a telephone conversation. This permits more time for clear, concise questions, and the ability to see how the customer responds to certain questions.

A visit is a good time for the credit manager to learn in detail about the components of the customer's cash flow, especially if balance sheet analysis indicates weakness (heavy debt to worth, low working capital). For example, can the customer demonstrate an ability to turn receivables and/or inventory faster than normal through EFT (Electronic Funds Transfer) or EDI (Electronic Data Interchange) replenishment programs? Can this be observed and confirmed on-site?

The credit manager should be alert to signs of fraud or misrepresentation. The customer's body language in response to certain inquiries, or conflicting answers from different employees to the same question, may be a tip-off. Here also, industry knowledge is a cornerstone to detection.

The interaction of sales, the customer, and credit is sensitive. Many customers, even if they do not mention it beforehand, are reluctant to discuss financial information in the presence of the local sales representative. This issue should be addressed before the visit through individual conversations with the participants. Usually, it is best to prearrange a separation point when the salesperson can join the buying staff. Then the credit executive and the business principals or their designates can discuss finances.

Observe the Customer's Competition

Are a competitor's products in use and, if so, in what quantities? Does this enhance or conflict with previous interpretations of the situation based on reference information alone?

The credit executive who knows his customer best may utilize this information in many healthy ways. Product differentiation, favorable to the subject company, may be used to induce better payments in exchange for the advantages. Or, the industry-educated credit executive may be able to point out better uses of his company's product or favorable contract terms.

Develop Linkages, Resolve Disputes

The credit department is in a very unique position to develop linkages. Perhaps no other department has more boundary spanning contact between the customer, other departments, and other suppliers. This may be used in a wide variety of favorable ways, especially where dispute resolution is involved. It also provides opportunities for reengineering the credit department to absorb functions related to these resolutions.

Freight and Traffic

Without visitation, differences in interpreting or accepting routing guides is often reduced to a paper war between the logistics departments of two companies. The credit department, by virtue of its role in resolving customer deductions, is able to coordinate joint visits to attack these problems. Quite often a basic understanding can be reached that eliminates the problem entirely and also offers the subject company potential competitive advantages.

Pricing and Terms

Often, due to vague coding of customer purchase orders and other documents, visits become the only way to fully understand the impact of document language affecting pricing and terms. Many customers use a terms master, which means that the order itself does not reflect all the terms. That information can be passed back to the subject company's customer service department so that conflicting passages may be screened and addressed prior to shipment of product.

Advertising

Interpretation can differ widely between supplier and customer on so-called cooperative advertising programs (which can become anything but cooperative). These are often not properly understood at time of sale and become apparent only when deductions surface. Credit's role in arranging on-site meetings of the advertising functions of both companies can become instrumental in resolution of the dispute.

EDI (Electronic Data Interchange) Programs

All the issues here, and more, can be addressed by the implementation of EDI programs between supplier-customer. Here again, credit can take the lead role in the formation of an EDI team to coordinate with the customer in effecting a permanent solution. Constant frustrations from payment deduction problems can mask the fact that the customer also has problems tackling all the paper, and has incentive to achieve a permanent partnership solution.

End-Users

Perhaps a dispute exists involving an end-user (the customer's customer). For example, perhaps a delivery dispute exists on a drop-shipment made directly to the end-user, or there is a quality or product application misunderstanding. Visitation provides an opportunity to assemble the parties to arrive at a resolution or settlement.

It may be advantageous to network with other credit executives who have visited the account recently to learn about successful resolution methods that they employed. (Caveat: Do not be overly discouraged by competitor's failures or overly encouraged by their successes. They may suffer from a competitive disadvantage, or conversely enjoy an advantage.)

In summary, these and other areas provide chances to define process improvements between the companies. Distinct opportunities are provided for credit executives to redefine their function from primarily collection-oriented activities to broad problem-solving activities. Also, credit's unique contact with competing companies permits sharing of information, within legal boundaries. For example, it is not unusual for a credit executive to coordinate a visit between competitors in which systems information is shared that is common to resolving a problem with a specific customer.

Addressing Liquidity Issues with Lenders

If the relationship with the customer has become adversarial, this step is often difficult. However, with stronger relationship building, the credit executive can be instrumental in this process. Assistance may be given to the customer in the presentation of his loan application and in identifying (to the lender) the customer's strengths relative to the marketplace. Also, the credit executive may help the lender understand the impact on the customer of lost discounts due to slow payments caused by insufficient lender credit lines.

In some instances, lenders may be convinced to subordinate their notes receivable for the benefit of trade creditors, also benefiting the customer by allowing him to obtain or increase trade lines. The industry-informed credit executive may also be able to make his customer aware of new S. B. A. programs or similar advantageous borrowing opportunities.

Advice on Receivables and Other Matters

Smaller businesses may be unaware of several benefits available to them in the event of bankruptcy among their customer base, specifically:

- reclamation rights
- preference defenses
- ability to sell their claims to generate cash

The informed credit executive may be able to consult or refer consultants to address other specific problem areas. For example, in severe distress situations, the credit executive may be able to suggest work-out specialists and NACM-based assignees and trustees.

Collections

Many areas of potential benefit have been identified so far that are independent of collecting money. In fact, "accidental information" gathered during a customer visit is often the most valuable of all. Now we turn to the problem area of collections.

First of all, it is important to assess the severity of the situation. Extreme cases require immediate action and firmness, as well as continued professionalism. Teamwork with sales is often crucial. It is often possible to have the sales department arrange a face-to-face meeting with an evasive customer, even in these circumstances. The opportunity for a personal meeting often proves invaluable to recovery.

When presented with a check of questionable value, the prudent credit executive immediately visits the customer's bank to attempt to exchange the company check for a certified or cashier's check. In less extreme situations, regular collection visits are instrumental in providing the visitor with competitive advantages—the opportunity to keep marginal accounts reasonably current, to maintain shipment levels, and to save the account.

In taking a credit position with regard to resuming shipments to a still-overdue account or to raising a credit line, it is often best to give advance notice that a decision will be deferred until a later date. This has two positive affects. It reduces the potential for confrontation, and also provides for a less stressful meeting. The credit executive usually has the opportunity to set the tone for the meeting beforehand.

Preparation

There is no substitute for preparation. The credit executive must take care to bring all the information needed for the visit. Once on-site, there is rarely the opportunity to recover missed information that is still at the office.

The following preparation checklist will help to insure a successful visit:

- Review all relevant receivables information (statements of account, date of last payment, etc.).
- Review all relevant financial information, mercantile reports, etc.
- Obtain as much information as reasonably possible from other departments. What is the sales department's opinion of the account? Are distribution and other policies being properly observed by the customer? What is the unshipped order position? Review customer purchase orders for terms, prices or other issues. Are invoices being billed to the correct address?
- Assemble all needed participants, either internal or external (i.e., internal employees, customer employees, outside agencies).
- Contact other credit managers who may have visited the account recently.
- Prepare a prioritized list of things to be accomplished or learned.
- Structure the meeting to your advantage.
- Educate the staff to deal with issues in your absence.

The last three points warrant further discussion. Prioritization permits maximum meeting productivity in the event of an unexpectedly short visit. If the meeting time is cut short, you will at least have been able to cover the most important thing(s) on your agenda.

Structuring provides an opportunity to minimize conflict by using various techniques. First, it allows for get-acquainted time at the beginning of the meeting. Second, by prearranging different group discussions, the credit executive is able to separate potentially combative participants.

Employee education is a long-term project that addresses the "too much time lost from office" objection. Proper staff development through educational programs sponsored by NACM and others benefits the entire credit department and the company as a whole, and permits a visitation program that is not disastrous to overall office productivity.

Comprehension Check

1. Explain the benefits of visiting a customer.
2. What questions can a credit manager ask a customer during a visit?
3. What key factors should be observed during a visit of a manufacturing plant?

17 The Credit and Sales Partnership

Overview

Credit and sales are two distinct functions in any business. Even though both departments deal with new customers and with repeat customers, they usually operate independently. Over the past few years, as corporations have begun to integrate their business functions, the sales and credit areas have been one focus of attention. Not only do they both use some of the same data, but at times each department can provide information that helps the other department do its work better. This chapter looks at some of the ways credit and sales can work together and points out some critical areas.

Learning Objectives

After reading this chapter, the reader should understand:

- Why credit is an important sales tool
- The usefulness of the pre-sale credit check
- When to offer special credit terms
- How the credit staff can help customers
- How the credit department contributes to the sales effort

Chapter Outline

I. The Basis for the Sales-Credit Partnership
   A. Credit as a Sales Tool
   B. The Three "Cs" of the Credit-Sales Partnership
II. Promoting the New or Potential Buyer
   A. Pre-Sale Credit Check
   B. Special Credit Terms
   C. Cash Sales
III. The Established Customer
   A. The Sales Person's Role with Established Credit Customers
   B. Credit's Role with Established Credit Customers
IV. The Credit Department's Contribution to Sales

The Basis for the Sales-Credit Partnership

Credit as a Sales Tool

Today, credit is a fact of life—in our personal lives as well as in business. The few businesses that do not accept credit cards for purchases usually accept checks in lieu of cash, which is a form of short-term credit. The availability of credit is a potent selling tool, and suppliers of goods and services use credit for several reasons:

- to create sales (via installment plans)
- to improve profit margins (by adding an additional charge for items sold on credit)
- to enlarge the potential market to include customers who cannot pay cash, such as governmental organizations, big businesses, or cash-poor prospects
- to differentiate their deals and to strengthen customer loyalty
- to position the company as financially successful and be able to afford to extend credit
- to meet customer demand

Because customers and potential customers want to make purchases on credit, salespeople want to give them credit. This is where the caution and checking required by the credit staff can be perceived as an obstacle by the sales staff.

Although their functions cause them to look at credit granting differently, sales and credit staffs can cooperate. It takes some effort, but salespeople and credit managers can find ways to increase sales while minimizing risk. Instead of the traditional "yes/no" credit decision, they can find ways to say "yes, if. . . ."

The Three "Cs" of the Credit-Sales Partnership

Every financial executive knows the three "Cs" of credit: character, capacity, and capital. In order for the credit and sales staffs to develop a real working partnership, they need three additional "Cs":

Cooperation

Credit and sales are interdependent. Without sales, there is no need for a credit department. Without a credit making it possible for customers to buy, there is no need for salespeople.

Communication

Credit and sales each has account information the other needs. Communication works only if it goes both ways.

Courtesy

Cross-functional cooperation requires courtesy in order to succeed.

There are times when the sales staff knows that obtaining the business of a particular customer is important to a company's distribution plans, to developing a new market, or for maximizing shipping efficiency, for example. If the sales staff can explain this importance to the credit staff, a more informed credit decision will result that combines both credit information and sales strategy. The three "Cs" help the two staffs to reconcile their differing missions for the good of the company. By cooperating, they work together to make the prospect a customer. By communicating, they discuss the reasons why the prospect is worth the credit risk. Courtesy enables them to fulfill their own functional responsibilities and continue to work on a creative solution to finding a way to grant credit.

Promoting the New or Potential Buyer

A company's customer base is always changing. Customers go out of business, merge or are acquired, become holding companies, or file for Chapter 7 or Chapter 11 proceedings. Some companies grow too big or change their lines of business.

The antidote for account attrition—as well as for increasing sales—is to get new customers. The two types of sales prospects are the new-to-you customers and the new-to-view customers. Because they are new to your company, both will require substantial work by the credit department.

New-to-you customers are companies that have established credit histories with other firms. Although they have not been your customer, they have been a customer to other firms you may know. The seasoned credit executive knows that regardless of its reputation, all new customers should be have a credit check. New-to-view prospects have no credit history and may have no business history. These can be totally new businesses or spinoffs of established businesses.

Pre-Sale Credit Check

By requesting a pre-sale credit check by the credit department on every prospect before making an initial contact, the sales staff can make sure it is spending its time, money and effort in pursuing the legitimate prospects. In addition, you don't waste the potential customer's time, and you don't put the prospect in the embarrassing situation of being turned down for credit. The benefit to the credit department is that it is not under time or sales pressure.

The credit staff have the right to expect complete and accurate prospect information from the sales department whenever they request a pre-sale credit check. Three pieces of information are needed: the company's legal name, the complete company address, and the names of the corporate owners, officers and/or registered agents. This preliminary check, especially of the individuals involved, is the first line of defense against fraud.

If the pre-sale credit check indicates that the prospect is not credit worthy, having information on the organization's owners/officers/agents will enable the credit department to investigate the possibility of personal guarantees. As a result, what would otherwise have been a corporate credit check/refusal can lead to a personal credit check and an array of credit alternatives.

The sales department should include a realistic estimate of the prospect's current and future credit requirements as part of the request for any pre-sales credit check. The more the credit department knows about a prospect's credit needs, the better it can determine if your company can meet them. Also, knowing the amount of credit that a prospect will need allows the credit department to estimate the level of effort required for its investigation.

The sales staff can be a valuable source of information for the credit department. They observe or learn of things that may substantiate or negate other credit information, such as credit reports, credit references and financial statements. For instance, sales staff can be alert to signs of financial trouble. They may notice that the purchasing agent continuously seems to be dealing with crises and problems that indicate a cash flow problem.

This kind of information is particularly important with marginal prospects, those that have incomplete or questionable credit histories. In most cases, they make up the majority of your customers. Here, too, the sales staff can assist in obtaining prospect-supplied credit references, financial statements, and personal financial guarantees.

It may be more difficult for sales people to collect financial information (balance sheets, profit and loss statements, cash flow projections, lists of current guarantees/liens/pledges/ leases, etc.). Most firms are cautious about releasing financial information in general, and particularly wish to keep it out of the hands of their competitors. Some techniques that may help the sales staff get the information are:

- Ask for the necessary information at the proper time. Sales people shouldn't ask for confidential credit information before the prospect is convinced about the product.
- Project the proper attitude. The sales staff must convey the fact that the company is happy to give credit where credit is due. Creditworthy customers are not expected to subsidize non-payers.
- Stress that your credit request is standard operating procedure, both in your company and in your industry.
- Demonstrate that your request for credit information is, in fact, beneficial to your prospect. Sales people may be able to convince the prospect to provide additional data.
- Prove your ability and willingness to handle confidential information in an appropriate manner. If a sales person can gain a prospect's trust, the sales person can gain access to its sensitive files.
- Calmly walk the prospect through your firm's personal guarantee form. If the guarantee is treated like a standard part of the transaction, it will be more easily accepted by the prospect.
- Stress that the personal guarantee is for a limited time only. Once the prospect proves its creditworthiness, the personal guarantee can and will be canceled.
- Indicate that a personal guarantee shouldn't cost the prospect (or its guarantor) any money. Only in the event of a payment problem does the personal guarantee come into play.

During the pre-sale credit check, the sales person should estimate for the credit manager the profit margin your company would receive from a prospect's business. The greater the profit margin a company can make, the greater the risk it will assume. The seller is likely to give more leeway to a high credit risk buyer for a high profit margin product than for a low profit margin product. Here is where sales and credit

Figure 17-1 Criteria for Special Credit Terms

- Special credit terms must not be a Standard Operating Procedure.
- Special credit terms are offered for just cause.
- Special credit terms are only offered when a company has something to gain from a cash-poor prospect.
- Special credit terms are always offered for a limited time only.
- Special credit terms always require the approval of both the sales manager and the credit and collections department.

can work creatively to develop credit and/or payment terms that turn the prospect into a customer while protecting their company's ability to collect.

In addition to gathering information, the sales person is well placed to educate prospects about the company's terms of sale. It makes sense to define and explain them up front, before there is a credit line or a sale. This may prevent collection problems later on. There are a number of steps the sales people can take with marginal prospects to ensure that a credit relationship starts off on the right footing:

- Before the first sale is completed, meet with the potential customer and discuss or define all payment terms, what they mean, and how they work.
- Ask the potential customer to initial every related section of the credit application form or sales contract after the terminology has been reviewed.
- Make sure the prospect understands that in signing the credit application contract, the prospect legally commits to paying all invoices in accordance with the company's credit terms and that compliance with the terms is a requirement of doing business.
- Point out that when conditions of the credit contract (payment terms) are violated, your company may, on the advice of legal counsel, forward that fact to certain credit bureaus.
- Communicate the benefits of prompt payments.
- Show the consequences of payment procrastination.

Special Credit Terms

One of the reasons special credit terms are "special" is that they are infrequently given—and then only when the sales to a prospective customer will have a big impact on company profits. It is important for the sales and credit departments to understand and agree about this. **Special credit terms** *mean that the supplier is giving an advantage to the buyer.* If a company is not careful, the advantage can have a negative impact on revenues. This is why special credit terms must not be overused and why they must be given only to prospects whose purchases will have a high profit margin. Figure 17-1 lists criteria for special credit terms.

It often happens that the time and effort spent negotiating special credit terms are never recaptured. Some special terms customers are constant comparison shoppers. Their loyalty is as good as the most recent "good deal." They often take an offer of special credit terms and shop around with competitors, playing one against the other to lengthen the payment terms, for example.

Sales staff should never offer special credit terms before the prospect requests them. In fact, special terms should be formally and specifically requested by the prospective customer. A prospect that really needs special credit terms should be able to ask for them and to document the need. Finally, special credit terms are really for those companies that otherwise would not be able to buy your company's products.

It is important for the sales staff to accept the fact that, no matter what, there are some prospective customers that will never be approved for credit by the credit department, even though they may receive credit from company competitors. This is one of the times when a good relationship between credit and sales is important.

Cash Sales

Prospects that are willing to pay cash for their purchases can still become customers. Chances are, if you aren't giving them credit other suppliers aren't either. Thus cash-only sales terms will not likely be met with surprise. There is even a chance that your willingness to establish a business relationship will earn good will and keep the customer's business as they stabilize their finances.

With **cash sales customers,** *the sales person must learn to ask for cash payments in advance.* This should be done matter-of-factly. After all, the customer is probably doing this with other suppliers. One way to let a customer save face with the first order is for the salesman to say that the timing of the order does not allow for a thorough credit check, and a check is required in advance to cover the initial order. On a subsequent order, the sales person should ask for a check to be cut, "as it was last time." This enables the sale to go through and does not embarrass the customer by making its lack of creditworthiness an issue.

The Established Customer

Companies are continuously gaining new customers and losing established ones. Sometimes this is due to mergers, relocation, changes in business functions, technological changes, and other non-financial reasons. Other customers are lost because the relationship has frayed and broken. At some point, one of the parties terminates what has become an unsatisfactory relationship.

It is important for both the sales and the credit staffs to realize that the financial status of individual customers change—for better or for worse—and this means that established customers require periodic credit checks, too. Taking an account for granted could mean financial loss for the supplier. Possible signs of trouble include major changes in purchasing or payment behavior and changes in management or purchasing personnel, for example. In brief, the same kinds of guidelines should be used with established customers as with prospective customers.

The Sales Person's Role Vis-à-Vis Established Credit Customers

Companies should have a policy about the salesman's role when payment problems arise. No company will expect sales people to handle credit situations by themselves.

Figure 17-2 Customer Benefits for Prompt Payment

Salespeople should keep this list handy to remind themselves and customers that customers that pay their bills promptly:

- save money via fast-pay discounts
- avoid paying interest or finance charges, legal or collection fees, court costs, etc.
- receive their suppliers' best credit terms and highest possible lines of credit
- keep their good credit record
- develop a list of good credit references
- avoid the embarrassment and long-term repercussions of having a collection agency action on their credit record.
- can continue to remain customers

However, all companies will expect that their sales staff will forward to the credit department any debtor-damaging information they may find. Figure 17-2 lists arguments sales people can use in their communications with customers about collections.

In the case of an overdue invoice, companies usually take one of the following approaches:

- Salespeople are expected to personally collect past due payments. The rationale for this policy is that the sale is not complete until the bill is paid. Collecting cash is part of the sales cycle and, therefore, the salesperson's responsibility.
- Salespeople make the first attempt at collection. If that works, nothing further is needed. If that attempt is unsuccessful, the credit department assumes responsibility for collecting.
- Salespeople have no collection responsibilities at all so as not to negatively affect their sales effectiveness. In these companies all collection efforts are handled by the credit and collection department.

The salesperson's first act should be to contact the customer when there is a problem, such as a past due payment or a credit purchase that can't be processed. When a customer's payment is late due to legitimate extenuating circumstances, the sales person should let the credit department know about it as soon as possible. There are times when a late payment isn't really a collection problem but the sign of a problem that occurred somewhere in the sales and delivery cycle. Among the reasons customers don't pay on time are:

- They have an allowance claim pending.
- They haven't received the shipment yet.
- The merchandise was received after the specified acceptable arrival date.
- The merchandise was misrouted.
- The customer received the wrong merchandise.

Figure 17-3 Customer-Friendly Credit Services

Professional credit assistance to the customer ignorant of credit terms and practices involves the following.

Financial Analysis
The credit department can compare a customer's sinking, current, or quick ratios to those of others in the industry, highlighting problem areas, and perhaps even identifying the problem(s).

Cash Flow Control
The credit department can analyze a customer's credit terms and help it identify ways to increase cash flow, such as using net due dates, fast-pay discounts, interest or finance charges to encourage prompt payments. It can also suggest how customers can manage outflows more effectively through the use of leases instead of outright purchases, accessing fast-pay discounts, eliminating inventory overages, etc.

Credit References
The credit department can show a company how to develop a good credit reputation with suppliers and how to leverage that reputation in future business relationships.

Loan Referrals
The credit department may know of other companies or lending institutions that would be willing to extend credit or lend money to the buyer.

- The customer received only a partial shipment.
- The order was accidentally duplicated.
- The order was overshipped and the customer had no place to put it.
- Some or all of the merchandise was damaged in transit or defectively manufactured.
- The merchandise was refused without being reviewed and then returned.
- The shipment was billed to the wrong company/department or the invoice contained the wrong prices, quantities, credit terms, etc.

When dealing with overdue payments, the sales department and the credit department must work together to ensure that customers do not abuse the terms of sale: net payment dates, fast-pay discounts, interest charges, and special credit terms. This is another time where good communication between the departments is important. By close monitoring of payments, both departments can work together and resolve overdue payment situations quickly before they become complicated by time.

Credit's Role with Established Credit Customers

Another positive, pro-sales technique is to stress the service that the credit department can offer the customer. The customer may not really be aware of the "helpful" side of the credit function. Some of the services the credit department can offer are listed in Figure 17-3.

The Credit Department's Contribution to Sales

So far, this chapter has discussed the ways sales people can work together with the credit staff to enhance the credit function. Most of the material has dealt with what the sales staff can do to help the credit staff; however, a true partnership benefits both parties. Thus, the chapter will conclude by discussing the obligations of the credit staff to the sales staff.

Here is what a salesperson has the right to expect from the credit staff:

- neutral, open minded investigation of all prospective and current customers
- monitoring of established customers for changes in financial stability
- diagnosing potential problems in individual prospects and customers
- recommending when potential credit problems can be prevented or avoided with cautious credit terms and conditions
- working with sales to develop a collection approach that collects cash, reduces risk and enhances customer relations

- Immediate action on overdue invoices, such as:
  - prompt identification of overdue invoices
  - quick action to collect all past due accounts
  - using tact and diplomacy in dealing with overdue account, giving the customer a chance to save face and/or avoid long-term credit record repercussions.
  - providing counseling or education services to customers that will profit from them.

- Assistance with customers in financial difficulty:
  - helping to determine why a customer is in trouble
  - helping a customer work out a solution to its financial woes without filing for bankruptcy.
  - keeping open communications among sales staff, top management, and problem accounts.

- Up-to-date information about accounts:
  - keeping sales people posted on the credit status of prospects and customers so that sales people know where to concentrate their efforts.
  - informing customers about their accounts and changes in their credit terms.
  - letting top management know about any aggregate changes in the company's credit position.

- A pro-sales attitude:
  - being focused on increasing overall company sales and profits rather than credit department operations.

- being objective and fair.
- willing to take a credit loss, although it will only extend credit to those companies it thinks can and will pay.
- identifying flexible credit approaches that allow extending credit to even the most marginal customers.
- maintaining a credit program that is consistent with your industry, your region, and with customer economic conditions.

Developing a strong and mutually supportive relationship between credit and sales is much easier if the staffs of both departments can remember that they are members of the same corporate team. The common goal is profits; the game plan is cooperation, courtesy and communication. Every position on the team is important. Working together, each unit helps create a whole team greater than the sum of its departmental parts. There are no second string players when team players are the ties that bind a successful business.

Comprehension Check

1. What are the additional three "Cs" of credit in the credit-sales relationship?
2. List five general rules that should guide the establishment of special terms.
3. How can the sales department assist in the collection of past due accounts?
4. Discuss what the sales department can reasonably expect from the credit department.
5. Discuss what the credit department can reasonably expect from the sales department.

18 Out-of-Court Settlements

Overview

There are two ways of handling the affairs of insolvent or financially distressed business debtors. One is to keep the debtor in business and restore the business to profitability. The second is to put the debtor out of business, realize the assets, and distribute the proceeds among creditors.

Creditors usually prefer to rehabilitate a distressed debtor by voluntary out-of-court settlement. When rehabilitation is not possible, however, they may liquidate assets outside of bankruptcy proceedings through a general assignment for the benefit of creditors. The credit executive who is familiar with both of these methods, and their advantages and disadvantages, will be able to participate effectively in whatever action is taken when a customer becomes insolvent.

Learning Objectives

After reading this chapter, the reader should know:

- How to identify a financially distressed debtor
- What is involved in a voluntary settlement of claims
- The different kinds of settlement plans
- The two types of assignments for the benefit of creditors
- How to evaluate settlement offers

Chapter Outline

I. Identifying the Distressed Debtor
   A. Warning Signs
   B. Public Information
   C. Insolvency and Illiquidity

II. Voluntary Settlements
   A. Advantages and Complications
   B. Initiating the Voluntary Settlement
   C. Creditors' Committee
   D. Alternative Dispute Resolution

III. Settlement Plan
   A. Importance of Unity in Voluntary Settlements
   B. Extension Agreement
   C. Composition Agreement
   D. Combination Settlement
   E. Administration Costs
   F. Execution of the Settlement

IV. Assignment for the Benefit of Creditors
   A. Common Law Assignment
   B. Statutory Assignment

V. Evaluating Settlement Offers
   A. One-Time Partial Payment
   B. Present Value of Serial Payments
   C. Methodology
   D. Summary

Identifying the Distressed Debtor

Prompt action must be taken if a distressed debtor is to be restored to solvency and maintained as a customer. The astute credit executive learns to recognize symptoms of approaching business difficulties.

Warning Signs

The credit executive must learn to be alert to changes in a customer's business behavior that may signal financial distress.

There are several warning signs:

- The debtor has stopped discounting bills.
- The debtor's credit payments are lagging.
- Lawsuits are being instituted against the debtor.
- Tax liens are being filed against the debtor.
- The debtor constantly is shifting from one source of supply to another.
- The debtor is in default with its lending institutions.
- The financial condition of the company is deteriorating.

Public Information

In most metropolitan centers, daily legal newspapers list new actions brought and liens filed. Credit executives may subscribe to such newspapers or instruct their counsel to check these listings daily, to ascertain whether lawsuits are being instituted or tax liens are being filed against the debtor. Reports of credit agencies and trade associations should also be consulted regularly.

Insolvency and Illiquidity

In business, a debtor may be insolvent or may be solvent but not liquid. *A debtor with liabilities exceeding assets is deemed* **insolvent**. *A debtor that cannot pay debts as they mature is* **not liquid**.

Credit executives should learn to distinguish between a business that can be salvaged and rehabilitated financially and one that should be liquidated for the benefit of creditors, in or out of bankruptcy. Credit executives should also learn to recognize the dishonest debtor that could be rehabilitated but should instead be liquidated and prosecuted.

Voluntary Settlements

A **voluntary settlement** *is a contract between the debtor and its creditors that settles their claims for the most the debtor can pay and the most the creditors can get.* It keeps the debtor in business and avoids court costs. The creditors may take a temporary loss but expect the debtor to emerge stable and solvent, a prospective future customer. Voluntary settlements between debtors and creditors are the preferred answer to a financial problem.

Advantages and Complications

The principal advantage of a voluntary settlement is its simplicity. There are no cumbersome court proceedings. They are essentially informal, round-the-table transactions that are legally binding on the debtor with specific penalties for nonperformance.

Because they are uncomplicated, voluntary settlements are economical. There are no court costs, and the general costs of administration are lower than for court proceedings. This means there is likely to be more assets left to satisfy creditor demands.

The use of non-bankruptcy alternatives is not available in every situation. They are difficult to arrange when there are secured or priority claims on the debtor. Because partners in partnerships require a discharge as part of any workout, compositions and out of court workouts are only practically available to corporations and limited liability companies.

Secured Claims

Secured claims *may consist of mortgages on the debtor's real property, personal guarantees or perfected security interests in property subject to the Uniform Commercial Code.*

Priority Claims

Priority claims *may consist of taxes, wages, unpaid rent, and the like, entitled under federal or state law to priority of payment over unsecured claims.*

General creditors should not accept voluntary settlements or extensions unless they are given absolute assurance that secured and priority claims have been adequately disposed of by the debtor. The validity of such claims should be reviewed by counsel for the creditors.

Initiating the Voluntary Settlement

Voluntary settlements may be initiated by either the debtor or the creditors. Most frequently, a debtor in financial difficulty goes to an attorney for advice. The attorney may consult with a few of the largest creditors and arrange a meeting attended by the debtor, a limited number of the largest creditors, and representatives of both sides. A meeting may also be called by a few of the most interested or largest creditors that have reason to be suspicious of the debtor's financial condition. In this case, the creditors usually work closely together through a local NACM affiliate or adjustment bureau.

Creditors' Committee

At the first meeting, a creditors' committee should be selected. This committee generally consists of five or seven of the largest unsecured creditors and perhaps one or two representatives of the larger body of smaller creditors. Even though the proceedings are out of court, the committee should be limited in number, with other creditors serving as alternates or ex-officio members. Sometimes only the larger companies will go to the expense of sending a representative to the creditors' meetings. Some company names can lend prestige to the proceedings.

The people serving on the committee must be knowledgeable in this type of work and have the time to serve and work in the best interest of all creditors. There must be complete disclosure by all members of the committee.

The committee should select a chairman, secretary, and counsel. The chairman is often from the largest creditor, but it is more important to have a chairman who is knowledgeable and willing to serve and work. The secretary is usually a representative of a local adjustment bureau and has facilities for communicating with all creditors. Counsel is usually a lawyer experienced in this work and may be recommended by the local adjustment bureau, represent one or more of the larger creditors, or be independent of all creditors. The counsel sometimes acts as the secretary.

The creditors should also ask that an auditor be retained to make an independent audit of the debtor's books and records at the expense of the debtor or its estate. It is most helpful to the creditors if the debtor will come to the first meeting well-prepared, accompanied by both counsel and accountant. The debtor should have current financial statements, be prepared to give the entire financial history of the business as well as the reasons for its distressed condition, and be able to answer most questions.

It is possible, but unlikely, that a satisfactory plan of settlement will be agreed upon at the initial creditors' meeting. In order to assess any settlement plan the debtor proposes, the creditors need their own evaluation of the debtor's business and financial situation.

Objects of the Investigation

The creditors should obtain an up-to-date inventory count and valuation. One or more members of the creditors' committee who are experts in the type of business may evaluate the inventory, or an appraiser may be retained, again at the expense of the debtor or its estate. It is important to ascertain what the assets would realize at forced sale; this is an indication of what the dividend might be in bankruptcy proceedings and sets the floor for a voluntary settlement. Creditors should also seek information about income tax payments over a period of years.

Causes of Financial Distress

Creditors should try to ascertain the reasons for the current financial distress: excessive rent and overhead, high general and administrative expenses which include salaries, exorbitant withdrawals from the business, declining sales volume, or inadequate markup on goods. Questioning the debtor about all these matters can help determine the size of the settlement, and help creditors determine whether the offer is the best possible. During its investigation, the creditors' committee may uncover indications of dishonesty.

Questionable Actions by Debtor

These include sudden increases in purchases without corresponding increases in sales, materially false financial statements, an unaccountable or unexplained reduction in inventory or cash, recent repayment of loans, hypothecation of assets, missing books and records, evasiveness by the debtor in answering questions or supplying information, and exorbitant salaries or expense accounts.

Reaction of Creditors' Committee

In such instances, the reaction of the creditors' committee to the debtor may be unfavorable. The committee may decide that court proceedings are preferable, with opportunities for investigating fully, for denying the debtor a discharge from its obligations, and even for imposing criminal sanctions. The committee may decide to retain a fraud prevention bureau to investigate the debtor or turn the case over to the Federal Bureau of Investigation.

Positive Findings by the Creditors' Committee

If the committee finds that the debtor has been honest and a worthwhile customer in the past and that the business can be salvaged, it should ask the debtor to present a plan.

Alternative Dispute Resolution

Because of the increasing complex nature of commercial agreements, as well as the very substantial delays and expense associated with litigation, efforts have been ongoing to find a way to accommodate the needs of creditors when disputes arise. There are two types of alternative dispute resolution, or methods of resolving conflicts between parties without litigation. There is mediation and arbitration. While not totally inconsistent with one another, arbitration and mediation are different and have their own uses.

Normally, both parties must agree to use ADR, which makes it appropriate for voluntary settlements. Mediators and arbitrators are neutral, they represent neither side. Each of the parties in a voluntary settlement should have its own legal counsel for the ADR process.

Mediation

Mediation *is the non-binding attempt by parties to solve a dispute using an independent mediator or facilitator in order to allow the parties to reach a common ground.* Unlike arbitration, mediation can be chosen after the dispute has arisen. The parties usually select one mediator, who has completed appropriate training for the task.

The mediator's role is to separately review each party's contentions as to their respective claim or defense, and then bring the parties together on sufficient common grounds so that a settlement can be effected. The mediator does not make a decision as to who is right or who is wrong, nor is there any final order or award entered as a result of mediation, unless the parties reach a voluntary settlement. The mediator manages the process, helps the two sides prioritize their demands, and keeps negotiations on a realistic basis. The mediator may suggest compromises or terms but cannot impose them. Mediators are usually lawyers but can be business people or mental health professionals. They all have special training in mediation and can be located through state and national associations.

Arbitration

Arbitration *is where the parties use an independent arbitrator to act in lieu of a judge and/or jury in resolving a dispute.* Arbitration is usually provided for in a contract. In arbitration, both parties present their case to an impartial arbitrator. As with mediation, it is critically important that the arbitrator not only have the training necessary, but also be well schooled in the law and industry practices.

Figure 18-1 Advantages of Arbitration

- may be faster and less expensive than litigation
- may continue the business relationship while arbitration is occurring
- may select an arbiter with special knowledge of the industry
- subject matter may remain confidential

In most arbitrations, the normal courtroom evidence rules do not apply. (Figure 18-1) This permits the parties to present their case and the arbitrator to hear the entire case. After the presentation of all of the evidence, the arbitrator announces a ruling and an award, which is binding on the parties. Arbitrators are often lawyers or retired judges who have additional training in dispute resolution. They can be located through national and state professional associations.

Settlement Plan

Working out a settlement plan is largely a matter of bargaining. Armed with the information it has acquired, the creditors' committee is in a position to bargain for a settlement that will ensure maximum return to creditors but will still enable the debtor to emerge solvent.

Voluntary settlements usually take one of three forms: extension, pro rata cash settlements, or combination settlements. Which plan evolves depends in large part upon the negotiating ability of the creditors' committee. Occasionally the committee may arrive at a plan in which an extension is accepted by some of the creditors, while a pro rata cash payment is made to other creditors preferring that kind of settlement.

Importance of Unity in Voluntary Settlements

The success of a voluntary settlement depends upon the full cooperation of all creditors as well as the debtor. For example, a secret or previously undisclosed preferential arrangement between the debtor and even one creditor, giving this creditor a larger settlement than others will receive, is a valid basis for any creditor to rescind the settlement for fraud.

During the negotiation period, objecting creditors are free to institute suit or to levy against or attach the debtor's assets in satisfaction of their claims, or taxing authorities are free to levy. Thus, one creditor or taxing authority may prevent the settlement from being consummated.

The debtor can prevent this only by executing a statutory assignment for the benefit of creditors or by filing a petition under Chapter 11 or 7 of the Bankruptcy Reform Act.

Extension Agreement

Under an **extension plan**, *the debtor proposes to pay creditors in full over a period of time.* An extension is, in effect, a moratorium on any workout arrangement. The debtor remains in possession and continues to operate the business and buys on a cash basis temporarily. The creditors' committee acts in an advisory capacity only and does not assume active control of the business. Obviously, an extension requires an optimistic prospect of future operations.

Establishing Controls

Creditors should make sure that adequate controls are instituted for the operation of the business and, in the event rehabilitation is not possible, over the liquidation of assets and disposition of the proceeds. This is done to provide reasonable assurance that assets are protected from improper use and to produce records from which reliable reports can be prepared. Ways for exercising this control are described below.

Assignment for the Benefit of Creditors

One technique assumes that the business in effect belongs to the creditors. The creditors' committee may request or insist that the debtor execute an assignment for the benefit of creditors to be held in escrow by the committee. If the debtor defaults in performance of extension payments, the assignment becomes effective. The assignee may then liquidate the assets for the benefit of all creditors.

Transfer of Stock

This is effective when the debtor is a corporation. In addition to the assignment, or as a substitute, the creditors' committee may have the stockholders transfer their stock certificates to the committee or to an adjustment bureau, to be held in escrow. If the extension plan is fully performed, the shares are returned. If not, the transfer becomes effective and the entire corporation becomes the property of the committee, to be liquidated for the benefit of creditors.

The committee may also receive and hold in escrow the written resignation of all officers and directors of the debtor corporation. The committee will thus be in a position to assume complete ownership and control if the debtor defaults under the plan.

Financial Controls

During the extension period, the committee may designate its accountant to supervise operations or have a representative countersign all checks and control expenditures.

Security

Under the extension plan, the debtor presumably will execute extension notes to the creditors, payable in installments. In addition, the committee may request or demand some form of security for payment.

Types of Security

The form of security may be:

- a mortgage on the debtor's real estate, which is frequently owned by the debtor and spouse
- a mortgage on the inventory and fixtures, to give existing creditors priority over new ones created during the period of extension
- an assignment of accounts receivable

- a guarantee of the extension notes by a responsible third party acceptable to the committee.

Mortgages on inventory and fixtures and the assignment of accounts receivable must be perfected under the Uniform Commercial Code.

New Trade Creditors

In order to obtain the cooperation of new trade creditors, a security interest under the Uniform Commercial Code (UCC) could be given to creditors with the old debt, and they in turn could subordinate that debt to the new trade creditors to give them a priority and thus encourage shipments to the debtor.

This type of arrangement has to be fully documented, and comply with the UCC with respect to the lien and the subordination. It is widely used in rehabilitation cases and does give a good measure of flexibility in working out problems.

Composition Agreement

This is a pro rata settlement in which the debtor proposes to settle with creditors for less than the full amount owed. A composition agreement is the quickest of all voluntary settlements.

How it works:

1. The debtor pays a uniform percentage of its obligations in cash to all its creditors, who accept the partial payment in full settlement of their claims.
2. The percentage depends upon what the debtor's assets are, what the debtor is able to pay, and what the creditors are able to procure in the bargaining proceedings.
3. The debtor may obtain third-party loans or equity capital to make a settlement with creditors.

The Settlement Percentage

The most important criterion in determining the rate of settlement is what the dividend would be in bankruptcy proceedings. A pro rata voluntary settlement should be at least as high as the proceeds would be from bankruptcy proceedings. The costs of administration are low, and the debtor avoids the stigma of bankruptcy. Bargaining for a pro rata cash settlement is sometimes difficult. Some creditors will, as a matter of policy, accept extensions of time but not pro rata cash settlements.

If all creditors cannot agree to accept the pro rata cash settlement, it may be necessary to proceed to liquidate under Chapter 7 or 11 of the Bankruptcy Reform Act, and creditors may realize a smaller percentage of their claims.

Creditors With Small Claims

Creditors with small claims frequently hold out for payment in full. It is often advisable to provide that those creditors with claims of $100 or less, or some other specified small amount, shall be paid in full to reduce the number of creditors and eliminate the nuisance of those claims.

It may be wise to provide that creditors agreeing to reduce their claims to the specified amount will receive 100 per cent of their claims. Thus, if a plan provided for payment in full to creditors with claims of $100 or less and payment of 25 percent to larger creditors, a creditor with a claim of $104 would receive only $26; but if the claim were reduced to $100, it would be paid in full.

Combination Settlement

Most voluntary settlements combine both a pro rata cash payment and an extension of time. For example, the settlement may provide a cash payment of 20 percent and three future installments of 5 percent each, or a total of 35 percent in full settlement. The installment payments, usually evidenced by notes, may be payable at 3-, 6-, 9-, or 12-month intervals. The disbursements are usually made by an adjustment bureau rather than by the debtor company. Since this method involves a time settlement, careful control over the debtor's business and security for creditors during the extension period should be carefully provided.

Administration Costs

Over and above the settlement amount to creditors, the plan must provide for payment of all administration costs. Administration costs include any expenses incurred by the committee, such as cost of counsel and auditor, court costs, and out-of-pocket expenses of committee members. The costs of administration for voluntary settlements are usually lower than for formal proceedings.

Execution of the Settlement

When the committee has approved a plan, it should, with the aid of counsel, prepare a letter to all creditors explaining what has happened and recommending that creditors accept the settlement plan. A form of acceptance should accompany the letter for signature by creditors and for return to the committee. If the transaction is complicated, the letter should include a form of agreement drafted by the committee's counsel. Funds necessary for immediate payment to creditors are usually deposited by the debtor with the secretary of the creditors' committee. The secretary may also hold the outstanding notes on behalf of creditors.

Assignment for the Benefit of Creditors

While creditors' efforts are ordinarily directed toward rehabilitating the distressed debtor, some debtors are so hopelessly insolvent and lacking in prospects that they cannot be rehabilitated. In those cases, the debtor may be asked to execute a general assignment for the benefit of creditors, a liquidation technique by which the debtor goes out of business. There are two types of assignments: common law assignment and statutory assignment.

Common Law Assignment

The **common law assignment** *is a device whereby a debtor transfers title to all assets to a third party, designated as assignee or trustee, with instructions to liquidate the assets and distribute the proceeds among creditors on a pro rata basis.* The assignment may be made by a debtor without prior consultation with creditors, or it may be executed after meetings with creditors or a creditors' committee, when it becomes obvious that a voluntary settlement cannot be made. In the latter instance, an adjustment bureau is frequently appointed assignee.

Sale of Assets

The assignee proceeds to liquidate the assets, most frequently by public sale through a recognized auctioneer with adequate advertising to ensure competitive bidding. In rare instances, the assignee may sell at a private sale when a better price can be gotten that way. The assignee also takes steps to collect or sell accounts receivable.

Distribution

After deducting administration costs, the assignee distributes the proceeds from the sale of assets pro rata among all unsecured creditors. Because a common law assignment is not under the supervision or control of a court, administration costs are low and dividends to creditors may be correspondingly higher.

Acceptance

No creditor is obliged to accept a pro rata settlement. The creditor may refuse it and claim in full. As a practical matter, however, creditors usually accept, since the dividends are apt to be larger than those obtainable in bankruptcy, and their old claim may have little or no value unless the debtor subsequently acquires new assets.

Discharge from Obligations

In a common law assignment, the debtor does not receive a discharge from obligations. The debtor merely has its assets sold and the proceeds distributed among creditors. If, for example, the pro rata distribution is 35 percent, creditors retain their claims against the debtor for the balance of 65 percent. The principal users of this device are corporations that are going out of business; a claim for the balance is immaterial since the corporation will be dissolved. Individual debtors seeking discharge from their obligations will couple the assignment with a proposal for settlement in full.

The credit executive should bear in mind that if dividend checks issued under a common law assignment are not accompanied by an agreement for discharge, no discharge is granted. The creditors may therefore cash the checks and receive their dividends without agreeing to discharge the debtor. Claims for the balance are retained.

The creditor must read the wording on the check to determine whether it can be cashed only by creditors accepting it in full settlement.

Statutory Assignment

Most states regulate assignment for the benefit of creditors. Some statutes are simple; others provide machinery for administration as complicated as that found in the Bankruptcy Reform Act. In some, a common law assignment may be completely invalid. In others, a debtor may execute either a common law or a statutory assignment.

Distinguishing Between Assignment and Bankruptcy

If the state statute on assignments provides for involuntary petitions against the debtor and for compulsory discharge from obligations, it is considered by the courts as a bankruptcy law and is superseded by provisions of the Bankruptcy Reform Act. If the state statute provides merely that the debtor upon executing an assignment may offer the dividends in settlement with an option to the creditors to accept or reject (thereby retaining their claims in full), the statute remains in force.

A statutory assignment accomplishes much the same results as a common law assignment but requires more formalities. The debtor executes an instrument of assignment, which is recorded, thus giving notice to all third parties. The court may appoint an assignee or the statute may permit the debtor to designate an assignee to supervise the proceedings, including sale of the assets and distribution of the proceeds. The debtor does not receive a discharge from remaining obligations. If a dividend check is not accompanied by a statement or endorsement indicating that payment is made in full settlement, creditors retain their claims for the balance. In order for a debtor to get a discharge under an assignment for the benefit of creditors, it must be a voluntary discharge agreed to by the creditors so as not to conflict with the federal supremacy of bankruptcy. For example, in New York, under its assignment for the benefit of creditors statute, a discharge can be granted if two-thirds of the creditors agree to grant the debtor a discharge.

Involvement of the Court

By placing the assignment under control of a court, the state statute often provides a means to examine the debtor's affairs. Creditors can uncover facts to guide them in determining whether to accept or reject the debtor's proposal. Statutory assignment involves extensive court proceedings. Thus, it is apt to be as expensive as bankruptcy but without clear-cut discharge provisions or the same opportunity to uncover voidable transactions of the debtor.

Evaluating Settlement Offers

Traditionally, these offers are made and considered with little attention given to the time value of funds involved. Thus, 100 percent settlement over two years, or even over five years, is usually deemed full recovery of a claim. Furthermore, in tax accounting, write-offs and recoveries are always depicted at face value, regardless of when they are made. In order to choose effectively, the credit executive should be familiar with the cost of capital and time value of funds concepts.

To establish the analysis, it is assumed that a creditor has been approached by a debtor in financial difficulty that wants to make an out-of-court settlement on a claim of $100,000 that is now owing and past due. The regular series of collection efforts has been exhausted, and it does not appear likely that the debtor can pay all of the outstanding debt at this time. However, the creditor is satisfied that the customer proposing the settlement is an honest debtor. The analysis then seeks the choice which yields the greatest financial recovery to the creditor.

One-Time Partial Payment

The simplest offer would be for the debtor to pay a percentage of the outstanding debt and have the creditor agree to forgive the rest. For example, the agreement may be for 20 percent payment and the balance to be written off. The creditor would

Figure 18-2 The Impact of Income Taxes on a Bad Debt Expense

Original Sale:	$100,000	
Settlement:		$ 20,000
Bad Debt	$ 80,000	
tax reduction @ 50%	(40,000)	40,000
Total Funds Recovered		$ 60,000

receive 20 percent of the total receivable, or $20,000. At the same time, the creditor charges $80,000 as a bad debt expense, assuming that the creditor keeps financial records on an accrual basis and originally recorded $100,000 in sales and accounts receivable.

Tax Consequences

The bad debt expense reduces the amount of income taxes the creditor must pay. Assuming that the creditor pays combined (federal, state and city) income taxes at a 50 percent rate, the creditor's income taxes will be reduced by $40,000. Thus, the effect of the settlement for the creditor is a net financial benefit of more than the $20,000 payment. Although the tax write off of $40,000 is not income, it does flow through to the bottom line and cancel out the taxes due on the $80,000 of accounts receivable that were written off. (Figure 18-2)

Present Value of Serial Payments

In the previous example, all of the actions take place in the present. Consequently, there is no need to consider the time value or the present value (PV) of funds when deciding whether to accept or decline the debtor's offer. However, when a schedule of serial payments is offered, a new set of variables must be considered. Since a dollar collected today is worth more than a dollar collected some time in the future, the creditor should consider more than the face amount of any extended offer. Instead, the offer should be regarded as a stream of future payments to be discounted back to the present. The full offer is equal to the sum of the present values of all the payments.

Methodology

Most financial textbooks and references contain tables for calculating the present value of cash flows. The time periods are usually given in years. However, the examples here are given in half-years to conform to a typical payment schedule. The mid-year discount factors have been obtained by adding the values for the two years bracketing the mid-year and dividing by two.

In the examples that follow, the factor used for discounting future payments is equivalent to an annual rate of 15 percent. This is the assumed cost of capital of the creditor firm.

Thus, for 6 months, at 15 percent per annum, the factor would be (1.000+.870)/2=.935; for 18 months it would be (.870 +.756)/2 =.813; and so on.

Figure 18-3 Discounting Half-Year Future Payments (at 15 percent)

Payment	Periods Elapsed	Discount Factor
1	0	1.000
2	1	.935
3	2	.870
4	3	.813
5	4	.756
6	5	.707
7	6	.658
8	7	.615
9	8	.572
10	9	.535

With these calculations it is possible to construct the table shown in Figure 18-3. The left column shows the number of the payment; the second column, the number of 6-month periods elapsed since the first payment; and the right column, the discount factor, calculated for 6-month periods at the equivalent of 15 percent per annum.

Two-Year Payout

When the debtor offers five equal semiannual payments of $20,000 each, the first to be made immediately, the creditor can determine the potential total recovery at each time period by setting up a table similar to that shown in Figure 18-4.

On the left are shown the individual payments made under this schedule. Next, the dollar amount of each payment is shown: first at face amount, then after calculating the present value (PV). Total collected is tabulated at face value and at present value; the PV amount for each period is a simple sum of previous PV amounts ($20,000+$18,700+ . . . +$15,120). These figures allow the creditor to estimate the present value of the total collected after any particular payment has been made. After all five payments, the total collected will have a present value of $87,480, or 87.5 percent of the face amount. The difference between that figure and the present value of the original debt will have been eaten up by the passage of time.

With each payment the present value of the total collected increases. With the fifth payment the face amount of the debt is discharged, and the potential write-off becomes zero. The present value of the total funds recovered is $87,480. This is the highest possible amount under this plan taking into account the time value of funds.

Figure 18-4 Recovery under Two-Year Payout

Number of Payments	Payment			Total Collected	
	Face Amount	PV Factor	PV Amount	Face Amount	PV Amount
1	20,000	1.000	20,000	20,000	20,000
2	20,000	.935	18,700	40,000	38,700
3	20,000	.870	17,400	60,000	56,100
4	20,000	.813	16,260	80,000	72,360
5	20,000	.756	15,120	100,000	87,480

Figure 18-5 Recovery under Ten Equal Semiannual Payments

Number of Payments	Payment			Total Collected	
	Face Amount	PV Factor	PV Amount	Face Amount	PV Amount
1	10,000	1.000	10,000	10,000	10,000
2	10,000	.935	9,350	20,000	19,350
3	10,000	.870	8,700	30,000	28,050
4	10,000	.813	8,130	40,000	36,180
5	10,000	.756	7,560	50,000	43,740
6	10,000	.707	7,070	60,000	50,810
7	10,000	.658	6,580	70,000	57,390
8	10,000	.615	6,150	80,000	63,540
9	10,000	.572	5,720	90,000	69,260
10	10,000	.535	5,350	100,000	74,610

Figure 18-6 Recovery under Increasing Payments

Number of Payments	Payment			Total Collected	
	Face Amount	PV Factor	PV Amount	Face Amount	PV Amount
1	5,000	1.000	5,000	5,000	5,000
2	5,000	.935	4,675	10,000	9,675
3	7,500	.870	5,525	17,500	16,200
4	7,500	.813	6,098	25,000	22,298
5	10,000	.756	7,560	35,000	29,858
6	10,000	.707	7,070	45,000	36,928
7	12,500	.658	8,225	57,500	45,153
8	12,500	.615	7,688	70,000	52,841
9	15,000	.572	8,580	85,000	61,421
10	15,000	.535	8,025	100,000	69,446

If the debtor defaults before all the payments are made, the creditor still receives the tax benefit of classifying the sum of the defaulted payments as a bad debt expense and reducing its taxes by 50 percent of that amount.

Ten Equal Payments

The longer the payment schedule, the less money the creditor recovers in terms of present value. There is also no guaranty that the debtor will survive in the future. Figure 18-5, for example, shows a plan for ten equal semiannual payments, to begin at once. In this case, the maximum present value recovery is 74.6 percent. Furthermore, with more payments, the risk to the creditors is greater at the beginning of the payment schedule because each payment is a smaller proportion of the settlement than it is with a shorter payment schedule.

Increasing Payments

For this final illustration, it is assumed that the debtor's plan offers smaller payments in the beginning, then increases the amount of later payments so that 100 per cent is paid at the end of the four and one-half years. The creditor's table would look like Figure 18-6. This type of 100 percent repayment plan provides the greatest relief to the debtor. It is the most expensive plan for the creditor, as maximum present value recovery is only 69.4 per cent. The total funds recovered at any stage are less than they would be under a plan that calls for an equivalent number of equal payments.

Summary

These analyses are based purely on an application of present value concepts to repayment schedules offered to a creditor. They seek to identify the financial implications of alternative plans. They do not take into account nonfinancial factors, such as the desire to rehabilitate a particular customer or the need to make a vital penetration into a desirable market area. The consideration of nonfinancial factors may outweigh the potential financial recovery in any given instance. Even then, however, the creditor should develop the tables shown here so as to clarify the tradeoffs being considered.

Settlements that Benefit Creditors

The illustrations point to a general finding that creditors benefit most—or lose least—when a settlement plan calls for large payments made early in a repayment plan.

Settlements that Benefit Debtors

Stretched out repayment schedules cause large losses in the present value of total recovery for the creditor, even if the debtor adheres to the schedule. Schedules that provide for small early payments and large payments made later in the plan also erode the creditor's present value of total funds recovered. The worst possible plan from the creditor's point of view is one that provides for a long period of repayment and also proposes installments that are small in the beginning and increase as time goes on.

Impact of the Cost of Capital

Potential losses in the present value of total funds recovered are directly related to the cost of capital of the creditor firm: they are lowest when cost of capital is low, and increase directly as the cost of capital increases. Furthermore, if the cost of capital tends to rise while a plan is in effect, the creditor will realize a lower maximum present value recovery than was projected by the earlier calculations.

Comprehension Check

1. List seven changes in a customer's business that may signal financial distress.
2. What is a voluntary settlement?
3. What are the advantages of a voluntary settlement?
4. What is mediation?
5. What is arbitration?
6. What is the difference between mediation and arbitration?
7. List four advantages of using arbitration to settle a dispute?
8. Voluntary settlements usually take one of three forms. What are they?
9. Describe the essential elements of an extension agreement.
10. Describe the essential elements of a composition agreement.
11. Describe an assignment for the benefit of creditors.
12. What is a common law assignment?
13. What is a statutory agreement?

19 Bankruptcy Code Proceedings

Overview

The term bankruptcy comes from Latin and means "broken bench". Hundreds of years ago, when a merchant failed to repay suppliers in a timely manner, the suppliers would break the benches which displayed the goods of the merchant. With a broken bench, that merchant was unable to conduct business. Today, bankruptcy is far more complex and is governed by federal law. This chapter presents the general basics of bankruptcy. As with all legal issues, credit executives are urged to seek legal counsel.

Learning Objectives

After reading this chapter, the reader should understand:

- The automatic stay provision of the Code
- Chapters 7, 11, 12, and 13 of the Code
- How to establish a response to bankruptcy filings
- How to pursue claims
- How the U.S. Trustees work
- The basic recovery procedure

Chapter Outline

I. The History of the Bankruptcy Code

II. Federal Rules of Bankruptcy Procedure
   - A. The Automatic Stay

III. Chapter 7
   - A. Trustee's Compensation
   - B. Distribution of Assets
   - C. Discharge Litigation
   - D. Filing a Proof of Claim

IV. The Chapter 11 Reorganization Process
   - A. The Creditors' Committee
   - B. Assumption or Rejection of Executory Contracts
   - C. Plan of Reorganization
   - D. Secured Creditors
   - E. Unsecured Creditors
   - F. Interest Classification and Treatment
   - G. Provision for Execution of Plan
   - H. Voting Process
   - I. The Confirmation Process
   - J. The Absolute Priority Rule
   - K. Postconfirmation Problems

V. Basics of Chapter 12
   - A. Confirmation
   - B. Trade Creditors' Primary Concerns

VI. Basics of Chapter 13
   - A. Summary of a Typical Case
   - B. The Chapter 20 Maneuver

VII. Establishing a Systematic Response to Bankruptcy Filings
   - A. Filing a Proof of Claim
   - B. The Official Proof of Claim Form

VIII. Objections to Proofs of Claims

IX. Discharge And Dischargeability
   - A. Reasons for Denial of Discharge in Chapter 7 Cases

X. Pursuing Claims for False Financial Statements and Fraud

XI. The Trustee's Strong Arm and Avoiding Powers

XII. Basic Recovery Procedure
   - A. Settlement Considerations
   - B. The Trustee's Strong Arm Powers

XIII. Preferences
   - A. Exceptions to the Preference Rules

XIV. Fraudulent Transfers

XV. Involuntary Bankruptcy

XVI. Tactics

XVII. Master Checklist

The History of the Bankruptcy Code

The **Bankruptcy Act** *is federal law that provides an organized procedure under the supervision of a federal court for dealing with insolvent debtors.* It is found in Title 11 of the United States Code. The Bankruptcy Code was adopted in 1978 and became effective on October 1, 1979. The 1978 Code was the first substantial revision of the bankruptcy laws in effect in the United States. Prior to 1979, the **Bankruptcy Act of 1898** (or the Bankruptcy Act) was in force. *Although the 1898 Act allowed individual bankruptcy filings, it was primarily a business law for the winding up of failed businesses.* In 1994, Congress made provisions for small business and single asset reorganizations. Since 1978, Congress also added Chapter 12 to deal with the farm crisis. Also in 1994, Congress increased the debt limits in Chapter 13.

The Code consists of eight chapters. The first three chapters, **Chapters 1, 3, and 5**, *contain administrative provisions that apply in all cases under the Code.* The remaining five chapters, **Chapters 7, 9, 11, 12, and 13**, *are the operative chapters for filing different types of bankruptcies.* **Chapter 7** *is a liquidation bankruptcy*, sometimes called a straight bankruptcy, in which a trustee is appointed by the United States Trustee in every case to liquidate nonexempt assets. **Chapter 9** *pertains to municipalities and governmental units.* A Chapter 9 bankruptcy can only be filed on a voluntary basis. **Chapter 11** *is the business reorganization chapter.* Most Chapter 11s involve a debtor in possession of assets who is attempting to rehabilitate a business. A small business may reorganize under an expedited Chapter 11 proceeding. A small business is defined as a business with total debts of less than $2,000,000.

Chapter 12 *is the used only with a voluntary petition by family farmers who have debt up to $1.5 million.* The purpose of this chapter was to provide family farmers with a chance to reorganize debt and retain their land.

Chapter 13 *is sometimes called the wage earner's plan. Individuals with wages or income are eligible to file under Chapter 13 as are certain professional or business owners.* The current law establishes a threshold limit for a debtor to be eligible to file. This threshold is set at a level of secured debt of less than $750,000 and unsecured debt of less than $250,000.

One of the most important things to know about the Bankruptcy Code is that adherence to deadlines is critical; noncompliance can affect one's rights under the law.

Federal Rules of Bankruptcy Procedure

At the behest of Congress, the *Supreme Court adopted rules of procedures for bankruptcy cases, which are called the* **Federal Rules of Bankruptcy Procedure**. There are 10 chapters of rules containing deadlines and other regulations that govern pleadings in the bankruptcy court. They also provide for the bankruptcy courts and the United States district courts to adopt local rules. If there is a conflict between the provisions of the Bankruptcy Code itself and the various applicable rules, the Bankruptcy Code has priority. Current federal and local bankruptcy legislation can usually be found at a local library or on the Internet.

The Automatic Stay

The filing of a bankruptcy petition imposes an automatic stay of (holds in abeyance) various forms of creditor action against a debtor or his property. These actions include:

- actions to begin or continue judicial proceedings against the debtor
- actions to obtain possession of the debtor's property
- actions to create, perfect or enforce a lien against the debtor's property
- and actions to setoff indebtedness owed to the debtor that arose prior to the bankruptcy proceeding.

The purpose of an automatic stay is to insure a fair distribution of the debtor's nonexempt, unencumbered assets among creditors. It prohibits any action to collect the debt from the debtor or the debtor's property. Governmental agencies, such as the IRS, cannot seize the assets of or file liens against the assets of the debtor. Creditors cannot offset credits or returns against the debtor's debt. Any violation of the stay is contempt of court and punishable by fines and fees.

In order to lift the automatic stay, a creditor with a security interest in property of the estate must file a motion for relief from the automatic stay. Usually a filing fee of $60.00 or so is required. In routine Chapter 7 consumer cases, motions rarely have hearings; complicated Chapter 11 cases almost always do. An unsecured creditor should consult with counsel upon receipt of a notice for a hearing.

Chapter 7

Chapter 7 is the most common type of bankruptcy filing in the United States. *It is also called straight bankruptcy or liquidation.* Most Chapter 7 filings are consumer cases. In all Chapter 7 cases, a trustee is appointed to take possession of nonexempt assets and sell them for the benefit of creditors. There are usually few, if any, nonexempt assets to sell.

After the debtor files the bankruptcy petition and pays the current $160.00 filing fee, the bankruptcy court appoints a United States Trustee or an interim trustee. This usually is an attorney or an accountant with experience in bankruptcy. The interim trustee has two main duties. The first duty is to review the file and take possession of any unencumbered assets subject to immediate depreciation. The second duty is to preside at the §341 meeting. Creditors may elect a different trustee at this meeting if they are dissatisfied with the performance of the interim trustee. There are legal qualifications and steps that must be followed. If no trustee is elected at the §314 meeting, the interim trustee's position becomes permanent. After the §314 meeting, the creditors cannot elect a new trustee, although the court may replace the trustee.

The trustee has several legal responsibilities. The trustee must sell any assets of the estate that are not encumbered or exempt for the benefit of the creditors. The trustee also investigates the financial affairs of the debtor, investigates and examines proofs for all claims of the creditors, and in the rare instances when there are unencumbered assets, the trustee takes possession and prepares to liquidate them. The trustee also arranges to liquidate the assets and notifies all the creditors of the details in advance. Creditors may file an objection, but it must be before the sale date. Objections are usually to ensure that the creditor's security interest in the sold asset will be recognized by receiving the proceeds. Assets sold by the trustee normally come with clear title to the property and free of any liens.

Trustee's Compensation

Chapter 7 trustees are paid $60.00 per case handled plus a percentage of the assets distributed to creditors. The Bankruptcy Act of 1994 established minimum amounts. Compensation is so low that courts usually award the maximum compensation possible. Trustees may be reimbursed by the estate for their expenses except for office overhead. Creditors are notified of intended payments to trustees and others and may file objections within the stated deadline in the notice.

Distribution of Assets

To close a case, the trustee files a final report with the court and with the approval of the United States Trustee when all the issues of a case have been settled and the trustee is prepared to distribute the funds. It is common practice for the trustee to notify the creditors of the recommended distribution of funds and their fees. If there are no objections, the final hearing is waived and the distribution is approved as stated in the notice. If a hearing is scheduled, the trustee is usually required to appear before the court and will award fees. Written objections to the recommended distribution or to the tentative fees must be filed before the deadline given in the notice.

The trustees are required to satisfy claims in a particular order. The priorities are clearly established. Proceeds from assets are distributed in a sequence of priorities:

1. Secured Creditors: Secured Creditors are first in order of claims on assets. A secured creditor is entitled to have a first claim on proceeds from collateral assets. Any excess amount received from security is returned to the courts. Any deficiency in funds resulting from the sale of collateral makes the secured creditor an unsecured creditor for the amount of the deficiency.
2. Administrative Expenses: These expenses represent certain expenses related to the bankruptcy proceeding, such as professionals used during the bankruptcy.
3. Unsecured Claims for Sales to a Debtor in Possession: The purpose of this priority is to encourage creditors to extend new credit to a bankrupt business during a Chapter 11 proceeding. The theory is that the bankrupt company needs inventory to generate new sales and to continue ongoing operations. Only credit extended after the bankruptcy receives this priority. Credit executives need to determine whether there is a sufficient asset base to cover this priority claim before extending unsecured credit to a bankrupt firm during a Chapter 11.
4. Wages and Compensation Claims: Wages earned within three months plus employee benefits earned within six months prior to a bankruptcy filing receive a priority claim limited to $4,000 per wage earner.

5. Customer Deposits: A maximum of $1,800 per claimant is next in the order for priority claims. This priority is available to individuals who place a deposit on property or services for personal, family or household use.
6. Taxes: Federal, state, country or any other type of government agency receives a priority.
7. Unfunded Pension Liabilities: Unfunded pension claims are determined by professional actuaries. These claims represent estimated deficiencies in pension assets needed to make expected future retirement payments to employees. The amount of the unfunded liability, which is equal to no more than 30 percent of the common and preferred equity of the company, receives a priority about that of the unsecured creditors. The remaining unfunded claim receives the same priority as an unsecured creditor.
8. Unsecured Creditors: These claims are often referred to as general creditors' claims. They include trade creditors, deficiency claims of secured creditors and debenture holders. A subordinated debenture also holds this type of claim but must turn over proceeds to the party to whom they have subordinated until the party is paid in full.
9. Preferred Stockholders: Preferred stockholders are paid after all creditors are paid in full.
10. Common Stockholders: Last in line is the common shareholder who bears the residual risk. Any remaining funds are paid to common stockholders after all claimants are paid in full.

Trustees cannot give creditors legal advice about the case. They are fiduciaries and hold the estate in trust for all the creditors. A creditor that has concerns about how a case is being handled has two options:

1. Retain counsel to object the trustee's final report.
2. Contact the United States Trustee for the district in which the case is pending.

Monitoring the notices of sale and the notice of distribution is usually sufficient. A creditor with information about the estate or the conduct of the debtor's business may be helpful to the trustee.

The Bankruptcy Code permits individual debtors to claim either state or federal exemptions in an effort to give the debtor a fresh start after bankruptcy. Creditors that wish to file an objection to such exemptions must do so within 30 days of the §341 meeting. This requires familiarity with the exemption laws of the state where the debtor resides and some knowledge of the debtor's assets. Creditors must review notices as early as possible in order to meet the deadline.

Discharge Litigation

Only honest debtors are granted a discharge through the Bankruptcy Code. Creditors may file an objection to a discharge within 60 days of the §341 meeting.

Filing a Proof of Claim

In a Chapter 7 bankruptcy, a creditor must file a proof of claim to participate in the distribution of estate assets. By filing a proof of claim, a creditor may be waiving its right to a jury trial on certain preference and fraudulent transfer actions and submitting to the jurisdiction of the bankruptcy court for other purposes. It is prudent to discuss the filing of a claim with counsel unless there is no doubt that the debtor has no potential claim for fraudulent or preferential transfer or otherwise against the creditor.

The Chapter 11 Reorganization Process

Chapter 11 is one of the most important provisions of the Bankruptcy Code. It was designed to be a single, unified way of dealing with reorganization of most businesses. One objective of Chapter 11 is to reorganize a troubled debtor while maximizing the return to creditors. Another objective is to retain employment and other economic benefits which the community derives from the business.

The key players in a Chapter 11 case include the judge, who decides the relavent legal issues; the United States Trustee, who appoints the Creditors' Committee and has general oversight responsibility; secured creditors; equity security holders; the debtor and, of course, the Committee. In an appropriate case, the court may order the appointment of a trustee to operate the debtor's business or an examiner to investigate its affairs.

A case starts with the filing of a voluntary or involuntary bankruptcy petition. The petition may be filed by either a debtor or by creditors. In general, a petition is filed in the location where the principal assets of a debtor are located. Jurisdiction can be important to the case.

Most bankruptcy petitions are initiated by the debtor. The filing of a petition by a debtor automacically creates an automatic stay, which prevents creditors from enforcing prepetition claims or from seeking recourse against the debtor's assets, without permission from the court.

An involuntary petition may be filed by creditors under either Chapter 7 or Chapter 11. To do so, three creditors must have nondisputed claims. The three creditors' claims must aggregate $10,000 in order to force an involuntary bankruptcy. Normally, a debtor has 20 days to contest an involuntary petition.

Under Chapter 11, the United States Trustee is required to attempt to appoint a creditors' committee. The Code specifically authorizes the United States Trustee to approve and appoint a prepetition committee if it is appropriately representative. On the East Coast, and particularly New York, there is an active creditors' network that often results in the formation of a creditors' committee even before a bankruptcy is filed. In the Midwest and South, creditors' committees are appointed in fewer cases simply because creditors are less willing to serve.

Initially, the United States Trustee will contact the 20 largest unsecured creditors from the list filed with the petition for relief by the debtor and solicit their input on the appointment of a committee. Unless and until a trustee is appointed, a debtor remains in possession of its assets and will manage its own affairs, protected by the automatic stay. The debtor in possesion, or DIP, has a fiduciary obligation to the creditors, much the same as a court-appointed trustee. The United States Trustee will normally file a formal pleading with the court stating the names and addresses of the particular creditors appointed to serve on the committee.

The debtor in possession is required to make periodic, standardized financial reports to the United States Trustee and the bankruptcy court. The reports are usually made available to creditors and the creditors' committee. Creditors can review the reports to check officers' salaries and other data. The reports will show if the debtor continues to lose money. The debtor in possession has the broad authority to conduct the business under the general supervision of the United States Trustee and the creditors' committee, if there is one. The debtor usually has the exclusive right to file a reorganization plan for the first 120 days after filing the bankruptcy petition.

All creditors should always file a proof of claim. Creditors who have filed a claim but are not listed as a potential distributee must file an objection to determine why their claim is not in the distribution. It may have been a simple oversight by the trustee. A creditor that does not object may lose its claim for good when the court approves the distribution.

A superpriority claim can be authorized by a court during a Chapter 11 proceeding. The superpriority claim has a priority over other administrative claims. The court would authorize a superpriority claim when a debtor in a Chapter 11 is unable to obtain new credit during the Chapter 11. If the Chapter 11 is converted into a Chapter 7 liquidation, the superpriority claimant has the first claim on all unencumbered assets. Technically, a bank that lends to a debtor in possession during a Chapter 11 is an unsecured creditor; yet, if granted superpriority status, the bank is in a relatively safe position.

The Creditors' Committee

The Bankruptcy code requires the United States Trustee to attempt to form a Creditors' Committee of creditors willing to serve. The Committee plays a critical role. It has the responsibility to protect unsecured creditors' interests, and it oversees the debtor's operations until, and sometimes after, confirmation of the Plan. It will investigate the debtor's affairs, monitor its business and negotiate a Plan of Reorganization for the benefit of unsecured creditors. It has the right to investigate questionable transactions in which the debtor or its principals might have engaged.

Congress intended that the Committee be a key player in a Chapter 11 case. The Committee consists of unsecured creditors selected by the United States Trustee, often the holders of large claims who have the most at stake, although small, but important creditors representing a significant constituency might well be members as well. The United States Trustee can approve and name a prepetition committee if it fairly represents the creditors. The Committee has a fiduciary duty to represent all creditors rather than the specific interest of the individual creditor appointed to the committee.

The financial stake of Committee members, along with their expertise in the industry, gives them tremendous influence in a case. The Committee may participate in all aspects of a case. Courts often rely on the Committee and its positions in deciding how to act on various issues. The Committee's recommendation is often the decisive factor on the question of whether a Plan can be confirmed.

The law does not stipulate how Committees must operate. Most Committees meet at the members' convenience and are bound by a majority vote. Official Creditors' Committees are allowed to retain counsel, accountants, and other professionals at the expense of the estate, with these professional fees to be paid before any distribution is made to creditors.

The Committee cannot tell the debtor or the debtor's officers how to run the business, but if its suggestions are not considered, it may bring the issue before the court for ruling. The Committee may have to deal with fraudulent or preferential transfer actions, sometimes against committee members. The Committee may also ask the court for the authority to pursue an avoidance action against a secured creditor with an improperly perfected claim. The Committee's strength is its ability to recommend or oppose confirmation of a proposed plan of reorganization.

The Bankruptcy Code gives creditors the right to be notified about many actions that affect the operation of the business and the assets of the bankruptcy estate. The debtor is limited in its ability to use cash collateral, such as cash from the sale inventory or the collection of receivables that is subject to a prepetition lien. If the cash collateral is subject to valid prepetition security interests, the debtor needs either the express permission of the creditor holding the security interest or a court order allowing the use. Before the debtor and the bank can arrange for the use of cash collateral, the debtor must notify all parties in interest of the proposed agreement and its terms.

Any postpetition unsecured credit obtained by the debtor needs court approval before it can become effective. Some types of unsecured postpetition credit need neither notice nor court approval. Unsecured creditors should examine, and may wish to object to, notices of postpetition credit requests that may affect their claim on remaining unencumbered assets.

Assumption or Rejection of Executory Contracts

With court approval, the debtor has 60 days after filing to assume or reject executory contracts and unexpired leases. The decision in these cases is whether it will be financially more advantageous to reject the contracts or leases or to assume them and sublease or sell them.

The Committee, or another interested party, may seek the appointment of a Trustee or an examiner. While some courts direct the appointment of an examiner "with expanded powers," an examiner is not a trustee, does not operate the debtor's business, and may not review claims or file adversary proceedings. The examiner is limited to conducting an investigation of the debtor's business and assets and making a report to the court and parties in interest. The examiner will submit a written report to the court and may continue to monitor operations pending further order from the court. A Trustee, if requested and approved by the court, will manage the business.

Plan of Reorganization

Only between 25 and 30 percent of all Chapter 11 cases result in a reorganization plan. Most filings are either converted to Chapter 7 or dismissed. Congress amended the Bankruptcy Act of 1994 for small businesses and single asset real estate debtors to encourage a fast resolution to the reorganization process. A **small business** *is defined as "a person engaged in commercial or business activities, excluding real estate, whose aggregate noncontingent liquidated and unsecured debts as of the date of the petition do not exceed $2,000,000."* A **single asset real estate debtor** *is defined as "real property constituting a single property or project with less than four residential units, which generates substantially all of the gross income of a debtor and on which no substantial business is being conducted by a debtor other than the business of operating the real property and activities incidental thereto having aggregate noncontingent, liquidated, secured debts in an amount no more than $4,000,000."* A creditor's focus in a reorganization plan will be on the proposed terms and conditions.

The debtor in possession has the exclusive right to file a plan of reorganization for the first 120 days following the petition for relief. This is reduced to 100 days for small businesses. This period may be extended or terminated by the court. When a trustee is appointed, the exclusive right is automatically terminated. When the debtor's exclusive period is ended, any interested party, including the debtor, can file a reorganization plan. If the debtor is a corporation, the corporate officers or the board of directors may propose a plan. Shareholders also can propose a plan, but not on behalf of the debtor. Partners may propose a plan for a partnership. The creditors' committee or even a single creditor can propose a plan. Outsiders may attempt to acquire the debtor's assets or the debtor itself as a form of corporate takeover.

The classification and treatment of claims is the heart of any reorganization plan. *In the Bankruptcy Code,* **a claim** *is a right to payment or a right to some equitable remedy such as injunctive relief in the event of a breach of contract.* A claim may be contingent or disputed and may not have matured at the time of filing. **Secured creditors** *are creditors holding liens on assets of the estate.* **Undersecured claims** *are those where the value of the collateral is less than the amount of the claim held by the creditor; they are partially secured and partially unsecured.* All other claims are unsecured. Priority unsecured claims are entitled to be satisfied from unencumbered assets of the estate ahead of general unsecured claims.

Underlying any plan of reorganization is the method for classifying claims and the proposed treatment for each class. The Bankruptcy Code requires that at least one class must accept the plan before the court will consider it.

Secured Creditors

Usually the courts require each secured creditor to be placed in a separate class. If two or more secured creditors have equal claims against the same collateral, they all may be placed in one class. The potential treatments of secured creditors often depends on the value of their collateral. If the value is the same as or more than the amount of the claim, the proponent of the plan may surrender the collateral in full satisfaction of the claim. In other cases, the debtor may propose retaining the collateral and reamortizing the debt, selling the collateral and giving the secured creditor an equivalent lien on other assets, or selling the collateral and using the proceeds to pay administrative expenses and the secured creditor. The creditors' committee or an individual creditor should review the validity of secured creditors' security interests to see if they have cause to object if one or more of them adversely affects the payment to unsecured creditors.

Unsecured Creditors

The Bankruptcy Code requires that all claims of a similar nature in a single class be treated the same. Courts will generally approve a plan that puts all unsecured creditors in a single class, but this may cause problems when the unsecured creditors have to vote on a plan if there is great disparity among the claims. Plans must be approved by a minimum of one-half the number and two-thirds the amount of the claims in any one class. In such cases, one large claim or many small claims could prevent acceptance of the plan. Courts may also approve a plan where unsecured creditors are divided into several classes based on their relationship to the creditor or another factual basis relating to the case. This allows for more homogeneous classes. Creditors should examine plans to see how the classification process affects their interests. Specific things to watch for are:

- multiple classes of unsecured creditors where one or more classes receive more favorable treatment than their class.
- a single class of unsecured creditors that logically should be split into more than one class.
- an administrative ease class where the minimum size of the claim is set at a relatively high figure to include all trade creditors (and thus win acceptance by this class) and exclude creditors with unsecured deficiency claims.

Creditors may file objections to the classification(s) of a plan before the confirmation hearing, or earlier. Plans vary from providing unsecured creditors full payment over time (extension plans) to partial payment (compromise plans) to no payment at all. The creditors' main concern in the reorganization plan is the kind of payment the plan proposes for the creditors' class. The only reason an unsecured creditor might consider a plan that provides no payment at all for its class is if there are no assets to be salvaged by liquidation, operation, or by sale. Partial payments usually are for a percentage of unsecured claims either when the plan is confirmed or over time. The timing of payments will affect the willingness of creditors to approve the plan. Unsecured creditors evaluating a proposed reorganization plan should compare the payment being offered against the liquidation value of the debtor's assets. "Pot plans" set aside some of the debtor's assets for liquidation and distribution to the unsecured creditors. This is usually done to gain the approval of the unsecured creditors although the value of the assets in the pot to be divided is hard to estimate. Extension plans are uncommon, but sometimes the debtor will offer a debt for equity swap. A plan can include a variety of payment plans and can offer payment choices to the classes of creditors. The danger in liquidation for unsecured creditors is that priority and administrative claims may absorb all of the liquidation proceeds, leaving nothing for them.

Interest Classification and Treatment

Whether the business is a sole proprietorship, a partnership, or a corporation, the plan must classify the ownership interest and propose treatment. Equity holders are normally the last to receive any payment, and a plan must be accepted by creditors or pay them in full before equity holders may receive any payment.

Provision for Execution of Plan

A reorganization plan should spell out how the assets, the claims, and the interests will be treated, as well as give specifics and a time schedule for any sale, liquidation, or restructuring of the business, including deadlines for the distribution of any payments. A plan may also contain additional optional provisions. A plan may not discharge the guaranty claim of a creditor against a principal of the business if the guaranty holder objects.

The Bankruptcy Code requires that a proponent of a plan disclose certain information in conjunction with the solicitation of the votes on the plan and that the court must approve the disclosure statement. In general, protracted litigation over the amount of the information disclosed by the proponent of the plan is counterproductive. Such litigation wastes estate assets and can delay a plan whose success depends speedy action and distribution to the creditors. The disclosure statement is sent pro forma to the creditors' committee and the major secured creditors only and a hearing date is set. Other creditors must request a copy in writing from the debtor's lawyer. Objections must be received before a deadline set by the court and can be argued at the hearing. Under 1111(b), certain undersecured creditors may elect to have their claim treated as though it were fully secured for confirmation purposes. Creditors with this option should consult counsel. No one may solicit rejections or acceptances of a plan until the court has approved the disclosure statement.

Voting Process

For a plan to be accepted, a majority in each class must vote to accept it. A majority is defined as those holding at least two-thirds in amount and one-half in number of the allowed claims. The bankruptcy court may disallow votes procured in bad faith (e.g., in return for a payment) or not in accordance with the Bankruptcy Code. The law requires that a formal ballot either accepting or rejecting the proposed plan be returned to the court or to counsel in order to be counted.

Ballots are sent to the creditors with the proposed plan. Ballots must be returned before the deadline in order to be counted. After the deadline, counsel for the plan's proponent files a certificate of voting that lists all ballots, including those that are disputed or were returned late, and gives the result of the voting. The plan proponent or the debtor will sometimes object to a particular claim and request the court to disallow it for voting purposes. This is usually done to effect the results of the vote on the plan. Creditors that receive such an objection to their claim must respond by a given deadline and request a hearing or risk having the claim disallowed. Sometimes competing plans are sent to creditors simultaneously. It is permissable to have only one ballot that allows creditors to express their preference for one plan over the other.

The Confirmation Process

The procedure for confirming a plan follows a protocol that has been partly described. The first step is to file the reorganization plan and the disclosure statement. After the disclosure statement is approved as presenting the necessary information, all creditors entitled to vote receive a notice of the confirmation hearing as well as a copy of the reorganization plan and the disclosure statement. The court may choose to combine the hearings on the plan and the disclosure statement to save time. The notice also includes the identity of the proponent of the reorganization plan, a ballot for voting on the plan, deadlines for filing objections and for returning ballots, and giving directions on where to send completed ballots. Objections should be explained as specifically as possible and filed promptly—usually a week or so before the date set for the confirmation hearing. The ballots are tallied and reported to the court. Plan proponents are allowed to submit modifications to the reorganization plan up until the confirmation hearing. If the modification does not affect all classes or improves the treatment for one class, it does not have to be resubmitted to the creditors for another general vote. There is no set procedure for a confirmation hearing. The procedure is determined, to a large extent, by the objections filed and the complexity of the case. The court is likely to confirm the plan if all classes of creditors and interest holders have accepted it by the necessary majorities, and the unsecured creditors will get a distribution that equals or exceeds what they would receive in a liquidation. *The bankruptcy court is allowed to confirm a plan that has been rejected by one or more classes. This is known as a* **cramdown**, and is more often a threat than a reality. Cramdown procedures differ depending on the creditor class involved.

The Absolute Priority Rule

The absolute priority rule prevents confirmation of a reorganization plan without the consent of the necessary classes of creditors if the plan provides that the shareholders in the corporation or the individual debtor in an individual case will retain an interest in assets after confirmation. The rule comes into play if the debtor proposes to pay less than 100% of all allowed claims and the holders of those claims do not accept the plan by the necessary majority. The absolute priority rule bars confirmation of the reorganization plan unless the creditors accept by the necessary majorities, or the plan provides for full payment to the creditors or wipes out all junior classes.

Postconfirmation Problems

The Bankruptcy Code permits the proponent of the plan to make postconfirmation modifications only if a substantial transfer of assets as outlined in the plan has not already taken place. Only the plan proponent(s) can request such a modification. On the whole, postconfirmation modifications tend to be for the purpose of correcting technical errors and are not significant changes in the plan. If the modification will change the rights of the creditors as confirmed in the original plan, then the creditors must vote on the modifications. The court may consider dismissing a plan after it has been confirmed if, again, it has not been substantially consummated. This is rare because of the difficulties in reversing the effects of the confirmation. Postconfirmation conversion of a case to Chapter 7 is possible if the debtor fails to substantially consummate the confirmed plan or materially defaults on the plan. If this happens, the creditors are notified in advance about the court motion required for the conversion. If the confirmation was obtained by fraud, the court may revoke it, but only within the first 180 days after the confirmation order was entered. The authority for enforcing the plan is split between the bankruptcy court and the state court. The bankruptcy court usually has jurisdiction until the plan is substantially consummated. Creditors may use the state courts to sue a debtor who has defaulted on an extension payment.

Basics of Chapter 12

Chapter 12 of the Bankruptcy Code was adopted by Congress in 1986. It can be used only by farmers and ranchers. It has some of the provisions found in Chapters 11 and 13 of the Bankruptcy Code.

Only debtors who qualify as family farmers with regular income can file under Chapter 12. This includes individuals and spouses, corporations and partnerships. Total liabilities of the debtor must be $1,500,000 or less, 80 percent of which must be from farming operations. The debtor initiates Chapter 12 by filing a petition for relief with the bankruptcy court. A standing trustee is appointed in each Chapter 12 case to serve as the disbursing agent for payments under the reorganization plan.

A Chapter 12 reorganization plan must be filed only by the debtor within 90 days after the filing of the petition for relief. As in Chapter 11, plans must classify creditors and propose treatment for each class.

Confirmation

Chapter 12 eliminates the absolute priority rule, which means the farmer may retain the family farm and make minimal payments to unsecured creditors. Creditors do not vote on the plan, and the debtor is not required to make a disclosure statement. Plans must satisfy two conditions:

1. Creditors are to receive what they would receive under liquidation (the liquidation test).
2. All the debtor's disposable income for at least three years must be paid to creditors (the best efforts test).

Basically, Chapter 12 lets a debtor keep the farm, revalue secured creditors over time on the current market value of the land, treat the balance of the debt as an unsecured claim, and discharge all unsecured claims with nominal payments.

Trade Creditors' Primary Concerns

A creditors' concern in a Chapter 12 case is to protect its secured position. Unsecured creditors may assert their right to the debtor's disposable income and any liquidation dividend. The trustee usually checks the debtor's income and expenses and claims the difference for distribution to creditors.

Basics of Chapter 13

Chapter 13 is a way for people with regular incomes to reorganize their debts. In the 1978 code it was only for wage earners, now the source of income is not relevant. There are three criteria for filing under Chapter 13. The debtor must be an individual. The individual must have regular income. The debt's limits are $250,000 in unsecured debt and $750,000 in secured debt.

Summary of a Typical Case

The debtor files a petition and a plan for handling the debts with the bankruptcy court in the district where the debtor resides. A plan must be filed within 15 days of filing the petition if it is not filed with the petition. The standing trustee will move to dismiss the case if the debtor fails to file a plan.

The case is then referred to the standing trustee who handles all Chapter 13 cases in a designated locality. The standing trustee handles the administration of the case and presides at the §341 meeting and makes recommendations to the court regarding confirmation of the plan. The standing trustee is also responsible for collecting money from the debtor and distributing it to the creditors, as outlined in the confirmed plan. The standing trustee is the person to contact about questions pertaining to the status of the case or about distributed payments.

The plan must classify creditors and propose treatment for their claims. Total payments to unsecured creditors must meet the liquidation test under Chapter 7, but like most Chapter 7 cases, which make no payments to unsecured creditors, Chapter 13 cases often make no payments to them, either. The plan may provide for payments to make up a monetary default for a homestead mortgage or other secured debt to prevent these assets being foreclosed and sold by the creditors.

Creditors must file claims in order to receive any distributions under the plan. Plans tend to be either extension plans or composition plans. **Extension plans** *pay all creditors in full over the duration of the plan. There are two types of* **composition plans**. *Both make only partial repayments of the total debt to creditors, and both must continue for at least 36 months.* In one kind, the debtor pays a fixed dollar amount monthly that is the surplus of net income after deducting expenses and payments to secured creditors. This amount is distributed pro rata among the unsecured creditors. In the second kind, the plan pays a fixed percent of the allowed claims to each unsecured creditor in monthly payments that continue until the percentage of each allowed claim has been paid. The court may stipulate that payments be for more than 36 months, even if it means that creditors receive more than the plan calls for.

The confirmation hearing may be brief unless the trustee or a creditor objects. The standing trustee's main concern is meeting the confirmation tests. One test is the liquidation test: Will the total amount of plan payments equal the amount distributed to unsecured creditors via a Chapter 7 liquidation? The second test is the best efforts test: Will the debtor be paying creditors all his or her disposable income for at least 36 months? The court usually will not confirm the plan unless objections of the standing trustee are amended. Under Chapter 13, the discharge comes only after the debtor has made all payments required under the plan.

The discharge is only for the claims dealt with under the plan. The discharge under Chapter 13 does not bar the debtor from filing a Chapter 7 or another Chapter 13 petition if the debtor has paid a minimum of 70 percent of the allowed claims in the prior Chapter 13 case.

The Chapter 20 Maneuver

This refers to serial bankruptcy filings where, because of the size of the debt, a debtor files a Chapter 7 petition to discharge the unsecured claims and, as soon as the discharge is granted, files a Chapter 13 petition to deal with the secured claims. The name Chapter 20 refers to the combination of 7 plus 13. This is expected to occur less frequently as Congress raised the debt limits in 1994.

Establishing a Systematic Response to Bankruptcy Filings

Creditors must establish an efficient internal system of routing bankruptcy notices so that information gets to the proper individuals. The credit executive (or whoever is in charge of bankruptcy cases) needs to know about deadlines for meetings of creditors, filings of proofs of claim or objections to the sale of assets, etc. Copies should be routed to the sales department with instructions on the effect of the bankruptcy filing on existing credit limits and any need for consultation on postpetition sales. Many of the deadlines are relatively short, so a creditor may need to file a change of address form with the bankruptcy court if the debtors are mailing notices to a lockbox or other office where rerouting may involve unnecessary delay. It is imperative to establish procedures for the staff who deal with receipts at the lock box address for handling bankruptcy notices.

A separate system should be established to deal with adversary proceedings in which the company is sued by the debtor or some other party in the bankruptcy case. A company's bankruptcy system should include a periodic review with the sales and other staff members who have direct contact with a customer. These staff should be educated about the importance of being alert to bankruptcy danger signs and what actions to take upon learning of the bankruptcy filing.

Filing a Proof of Claim

In cases under Chapters 7, 12, and 13, the filing of a proof of claim is required to participate in any distribution of the bankruptcy estate assets to unsecured creditors. In a Chapter 11 case, a claim is deemed to be filed for any claim or interest which the debtor correctly lists in the schedules without indicating that the claim is disputed, contingent, or unliquidated. The creditor should review its claim as listed by the debtor. The creditor must file a proof of claim if the claim listed is incorrect or listed as disputed, contingent, or unliquidated. Technically any document filed with the bankruptcy court in order to set forth your rights to payment of a debt may be considered proof of claim. A proof of claim must be received by the appropriate bankruptcy court on or before the last day for filing claims.

In a Chapter 7, all proofs of claim must be filed within 90 days after the first date set for the §341 meeting. When dealing with a Chapter 11, the Federal Rule of Bankruptcy Procedure Rule 3003(c) allows the bankruptcy court to establish a deadline. Chapter 12 follows Rule 3002(c) which provides that all claims must be filed within 90 days of the first date set for the §341 meeting. Lastly, in a Chapter 13 all proofs of claim must be filed within 90 days after the first date set for the §341 meeting. If the §341 meeting is rescheduled, the filing date does not change. It is never rescheduled. If the 90th day falls on a holiday or a weekend day, the next workday is the deadline.

The Official Proof of Claim Form

Not all claims need to be on official forms. Virtually any writing that sets out an enforceable claim against the debtor that is served on the trustee or filed with the court may be deemed an informal claim. The official claim form is Form 10. It is available from the clerk of the bankruptcy court, from any office supply company, or may be completed using a computer. Claims should be prepared in duplicate and signed by an officer or an attorney of the company. It is prudent to provide extra copies of the proof to the bankruptcy clerk's office with a self-addressed, stamped envelope and request that at least one filed stamped copy be returned to the company. This protects the company against the possible accidental loss of the claim in the clerk's office. The creditor must complete the following sections of the form:

- identity of the Bankruptcy Court
- name of the debtor
- bankruptcy case number
- creditor information
- claim information
  - Section 1—basis of the claim: goods sold; services performed; money loaned; personal injury or wrongful death; taxes; retired benefits; wage, salary, and compensation; or other.
  - Section 2—date the debt was incurred.
  - Section 3—date of a judgment against the filer if that is the basis of the claim
  - Section 4—classification of claim as secured, unsecured priority, or unsecured nonpriority. Claims are secured only to the value of the collateral pledged. Partially or totally unsecured claims are nonpriority claims. Unsecured priority claims are those only for wages, salary, commissions, contributions to employee benefit plans, and taxes.
  - Section 5—statement of the unsecured, secured, and priority portions of the claim and the total of these numbers as the full amount of the claim.
- Certification of the information given
- Copies of supporting documentation
- Required number of copies plus one to be returned

Objections to Proofs of Claims

The trustee in bankruptcy in Chapters 7, 11, and 13, and the debtor in possession under Chapter 11 are statutorily responsible for reviewing claims filed, or listed in a Chapter 11 schedule, to determine whether the claims are proper claims against the estate. Objections to claims can range from inadequate documentation to lender liability lawsuits to the inclusion of precomputed interest. Routine objections often result from communication problems and can usually be resolved without much difficulty. The trustee will charge the estate for all legal expenses relating to claim objections. As this reduces the amount available for distribution to the unsecured creditors, those creditors have an incentive to present claims that are as objection-free as possible. Procedures for objecting to claims and resolving those objections vary from court to court. It is wise to use legal counsel in dealing with objections.

Discharge And Dischargeability

The goal of virtually any bankruptcy proceeding is the discharge of some or all of the debtor's debts and obligations. The Bankruptcy Code allows for a debtor to be denied a discharge completely in Chapter 7 for reasons of fraud, perjury, concealment of assets, or destruction of relevant records.

Reasons for Denial of Discharge in Chapter 7 Cases

- corporations are not normally discharged, although they may be under Chapter 11
- concealing assets
- failure to keep records
- perjury in connection with the bankruptcy case
- failure to explain disposition of assets
- failure to obey court orders to testify
- prior bankruptcy proceedings within six year limit
- waiver of discharge by the individual debtor

Certain debts are excepted from the discharge, but only upon action by the bankruptcy court. The following is a checklist of excepted debts:

- taxes due less than three months before filing bankruptcy
- credit obtained by false financial statement of fraud
- unlisted creditors
- breach of fiduciary duty claims
- intentional torts/conversion of collateral
- fines and penalties/taxes
- student loans
- Driving Under the Influence (DUI) liabilities
- debts excepted from discharge in prior bankruptcy proceedings
- FDIC claims

In order to have a debt excepted from a discharge under 11 USC 523 or to deny the discharge generally under 11 USC 727, a creditor, the trustee, or the United States Trustee must file a timely complaint under one of those sections. A complaint to deny discharge under 11 USC 727 on the other hand, may be filed up to the conclusion of the hearing on confirmation of the Chapter 11 plan.

Pursuing Claims for False Financial Statements and Fraud

Trade credit managers should be familiar with the provisions of 11 USC 523(a)(2)(A) and 523(a)(2)(B) relating to fraudulent misconduct and the use of false financial statements.

Debts arising from the extension, renewal, or refinancing of credit obtained through false pretenses, false representation, or actual fraud are excepted from the discharge under 11 USC 523(a)(2)(A). Creditors must show that the debtor made a false representation or committed fraud, that the debtor was aware of the false representation or fraud at the time it occurred, that the debtor intended to deceive the creditor, and that the creditor relied upon the misrepresentation with the resultant loss.

Under 11 USC 523(a)(2)(B), the Bankruptcy Code excepts from discharge claims arising out of the use of a materially false financial statement in writing. The creditor must show that the debt arises from the use of a false written financial statement that is materially false regarding the debtor's financial condition which the debtor caused to be published with intent to deceive. Conversions of collateral require showing a willful conversion of the proceeds, which is not easy to prove.

The Trustee's Strong Arm and Avoiding Powers

To further the equitable distribution of assets to creditors, *bankruptcy trustees have the power to recover certain fraudulent transfers, recover preferential payments to creditors, and avoid certain improperly perfected security interests and mortgages. Collectively, these rights or powers are referred to as the trustee's* **strong arm and avoiding powers**. Trade creditors want to make sure that any payments they will receive are not subject to recovery as a preference, fraudulent transfer, or otherwise. On the other hand, members of the creditors' committee want to make sure that the debtor presses all possible claims for recovery, including preferences or fraudulent transfers that benefit insiders.

Basic Recovery Procedure

For both Chapter 7 and Chapter 11 filings, the procedure for recovering preferential and fraudulent transfers and setting aside improperly perfected security interests requires the filing of an adversary proceeding under Rule 7001 of the Federal Rules of Bankruptcy Procedure. Once the adversary proceeding is filed, the trustee or debtor in possession can obtain nationwide service of the summons and complaint pursuant to the Federal Rules of Bankruptcy Procedure. If the defendant does not answer the complaint within the time specified by the bankruptcy court, a default judgment will be entered. Once the defendant files an answer, an adversary proceeding is handled as any other lawsuit. If no jury has been demanded, the proceeding is tried by the bankruptcy court.

Settlement Considerations

As in any litigation, you should always keep your eye on the bottom line: What will the action by the debtor or the committee bring into the bankruptcy estate for distribution to unsecured creditors?

The Trustee's Strong Arm Powers

11 USC §544, the **"strong arm clause"**, *empowers a trustee or a debtor-in-possession to avoid any lien or security interest in personal property or any lien or mortgage on real estate which is not properly perfected as of the date of the bankruptcy petition.* 11 USC §544 grants to the trustee the rights of three different hypothetical types of creditors or purchasers.

Hypothetical Judicial Lien Holder

This allows the trustee or debtor in possession to set aside any security interest or mortgage of creditors for the benefit of all creditors. Trade creditors that advance credit through the sale of goods should understand the purchase money security interests and their special protection under both the UCC and the Bankruptcy Code.

Any security interest or lien not properly perfected as of the date of the petition is subject to attack under 11 USC §544(a)(1). Unsecured creditor status is most frequently utilized where there has been a bulk transfer of the debtor's assets without a notice to creditors.

Bona Fide Purchaser for Value of Any Property Owned by the Debtor as of the Date of the Petition

This gives the trustee priority over the holder of an inaccurate or unrecorded deed or mortgage. When a debtor has a large business involvement in real estate and files for bankruptcy before all business is recorded, there may be a substantial recovery of assets for the general unsecured creditors.

Legal Audit

Persons dealing with security interests and mortgages in personal and real property will want to be sufficiently familiar with the law governing the creation and perfection of security interests and mortgages to perform a legal audit or review of either their own documentation or documentation of lending creditors in a case. **A legal audit** *is a review of all documentation to determine whether all security interests were properly perfected and all mortgages were correct and properly recorded, paying special attention to legal descriptions of the covered real estate.*

Preferences

A preferential payment to an unsecured creditor can be recovered by the trustee under 11 USC §547. To prove a preference, the trustee or the debtor in possession must prove:

- that a transfer of the debtor's assets were made
- to or for the benefit of a creditor
- for or on account of an antecedent debt
- while the debtor was insolvent
- within 90 days of the petition for relief, or within one year if the transfer is to an insider
- the effect of the transfer was to give the creditor more than the creditor would otherwise receive in a Chapter 7 liquidation

Exceptions to the Preference Rules

- A transfer to a creditor that is contemporaneous with the extension of credit or the delivery of goods by the creditor.
- Ordinary course of business payments.

Fraudulent Transfers

Two types of fraudulent transfers made within one year of filing for bankruptcy can be set aside under 11 U.S.C. 548 (a) and (b). The transfer of the debtor's property made with the actual intent to hinder, delay, or defraud creditors is one type. The debtor's intent is usually inferred from the circumstances of the transfer. If the court concludes the debtor had the necessary fraudulent intent, it will usually set aside the transfer unless the debtor can prove it received an equivalent value in money or money's worth for the asset transferred. The second type is the transfer of property for less than market value at a time when the debtor was insolvent. However, under the Bankruptcy Code, a transferee that takes for value and in good faith is entitled to a lien on the property transferred or may retain any interest transferred to the extent that such transferee gave value.

Involuntary Bankruptcy

The filing of an involuntary bankruptcy is used by creditors to force recovery of fraudulent and preferential transfers. As the common law does not prevent a debtor from preferring one creditor over others and gives creditors only a limited ability to recover fraudulent transfers, the filing of an involuntary bankruptcy may be the only way of stopping and recovering these types of transfers.

Tactics

Creditors that are offered payment by a debtor in financial difficulty should accept the payment. The worst that can happen is the creditor may have to return the money if it is later deemed to be preferential. The creditors' committee should carefully review all the debtor's security agreements and transfers for the year before the bankruptcy filing to rule out possible fraudulent transfers that might be set aside. It is important to evaluate the bankruptcy case at the beginning so as not to use up the assets of the estate in legal and other fees to the detriment of the unsecured creditors.

Master Checklist

This checklist will help nonlawyers make an initial evaluation of a bankruptcy case.

- *Routing System.* Bankruptcy notices must be rerouted directly to whoever is responsible for making decisions and taking action in bankruptcy cases. A single file should be established for all bankruptcy notices. It should also have sufficient information for the credit executive to determine the amount of the prepetition claim and any postpetition credit extended to a debtor in possession under Chapter 11.
- *Bankruptcy Checklist.* Review the initial bankruptcy notice and determine the size of any claim against the debtor. If the claim is small and does not justify the assistance of counsel in the reorganization process, file a claim and close the file. Gather all documentation relating to the claim for possible transmittal to counsel with instructions for action in the case. Notify the sales depart-

ment for any restrictions on postpetition credit sales to the debtor in possession.

- *Goods in Transit.* Determine whether any goods are in transmit or delivered immediately prior to the petition are subject to reclamation under the UCC. Stop all goods in transit through notice to the common carrier delivering the goods. Serve reclamation demand upon the debtor for goods received immediately prior to bankruptcy. Reclamation or stoppage of goods in transit will probably require reference to counsel for further action.
- *Deadline for Filing Claims.* Chapter 7's deadline is 90 days from the date first set for the 341 meeting. When determining the deadline for a Chapter 11, the deadline for the filing of claims from the initial notice must be determined. If the court has established a deadline for the filing of claims in the initial notice, the debtor's file should be reviewed and a decision made about filing a claim. A creditor may wish to file a claim immediately, even if the court does not establish a deadline in the initial notice. Both Chapter 12 and Chapter 13 have a deadline of 90 days from the date first set for the 341 meeting.
- *Deadlines for Objections To Discharge and Complaints To Determine Dischargeability.* Review the initial notice for the deadlines established for any objections to discharge and complaints to determine dischargeability. If deadlines are established, consult with counsel about the possibility of filing a complaint.
- *Motions for Trustee or Examiner in Chapter 11.* Creditors that intend to participate actively in the case may want to review the facts to determine whether the appointment of a trustee or an examiner is warranted.
- *Consult Counsel To File a Motion.* Subsequent notices should be reviewed in case further action is needed:
  - notice of hearing on an application for use of cash collateral
  - motion for relief of stay
  - notice of intended sale of estate assets
  - notice of Hearing on disclosure statement
  - notice of Confirmation hearing: Chapter 11, 12, or 13
  - fee applications
  - postconfirmation motions

Comprehension Check

1. Provide a brief definition of the following chapters of the bankruptcy code:
   a. Chapter 7
   b. Chapter 9
   c. Chapter 11
   d. Chapter 12
   e. Chapter 13
2. What is the purpose of an automatic stay in bankruptcy?
3. What are the basic duties of a Trustee?
4. In a Chapter 7, trustees must satisfy claims in a particular order. List the priority of claims in order.

5. What is the purpose of Chapter 11?
6. Who are the key players in a Chapter 11 proceeding?
7. What is the role of a Creditors' Committee in a Chapter 11 proceeding?
8. How long does a debtor have to assume or reject executory contracts, with court approval, under a Chapter 11 proceeding?
9. How is a small business defined under Chapter 11 of the Bankruptcy Code?
10. Define the term claim, under the Bankruptcy Code.
11. How are claims classified under the Bankruptcy Code?
12. What information is contained in a plan of reorganization?
13. In order for a plan of reorganization to be accepted, what is necessary?
14. What is the absolute priority rule?
15. What two conditions must a plan satisfy under a Chapter 12?
16. List the three criteria for filings under a Chapter 13.
17. Why is it important to establish a systematic response system for bankruptcy cases?
18. Under what Chapters of the Code must a proof of claim be filed?
19. Before a preferential payment to an unsecured creditor can be recovered, what must the trustee prove?
20. What are the exceptions to the preference rules?
21. What is a fraudulent transfer?

20 Financial Statements

Overview

An important skill that an effective credit manager should have is the ability to understand and analyze financial statements. The standard financial statements, as well as related supporting records, can provide valuable information for making informed credit decisions. In understanding and analyzing financial statements, it is also important to be familiar with standard accounting terms and conventions and the role of external financial auditors. This chapter provides the foundation for financial analysis by describing financial statements and accounting approaches.

Learning Objectives

After reading this chapter, the reader should know:

- The types of financial statements produced regularly by customers
- The major components of the balance sheet
- The major components of the statement of income
- The major components of the statement of retained earnings
- The major components of the statement of cash flows
- Key aspects of other financial reports
- The role of auditors and the financial audits
- Differences in audit reports

Chapter Outline

I. Types of Financial Statements
  A. Reporting Periods
  B. Role of Financial Statements
  C. Annual Reports
  D. Basic Financial Statements

II. Accounting Issues
  A. Generally Accepted Accounting Principles (GAAP)
  B. Accounting Assumptions
  C. Financial Accounting Standards Board (FASB)
  D. Notes to Financial Statements

III. The Balance Sheet
  A. Overview
  B. Assets
  C. Liabilities
  D. Stockholders' Equity or Owners' Equity

IV. Statement of Income
  A. Overview
  B. Components

V. Statement of Retained Earnings
  A. Overview
  B. Components

VI. Statement of Cash Flows
  A. Overview
  B. Cash Flows from Operating Activities
  C. Cash Flows from Investing Activities
  D. Cash Flows from Financing Activities

VII. Other Financial Reports
  A. Trial Balance
  B. Consolidated Financial Statements
  C. Combined Financial Statements
  D. Pro Forma Financial Statements

VIII. Audit Issues
  A. The Role of the Auditor
  B. Types of Audits
  C. Responsibility for Financial Reporting
  D. Change in Auditor
  E. Auditor-Client Relationships

IX. Audit Reports
  A. Overview
  B. Customary Schedules in Audit Reports
  C. Unqualified Opinions
  D. Qualified Opinions
  E. Reliability

X. False Financial Statements
  A. General Considerations
  B. Continuing and Acceleration Clauses
  C. Fraud
  D. Points to be Observed

Types of Financial Statements

Reporting Periods

Reporting periods are usually monthly, quarterly, or yearly, which presupposes that a company's business can be divided into regular, consistent time periods. The company is responsible for deciding in which periods to report the revenues and expenses of the business.

Two types of accounting methods may be used: cash or accrual. Using cash accounting, revenues and expenses are reported in the income statement for the time period in which the revenues and expenses occur. *The* **net income** *or (net loss) is the difference between cash revenues received and cash payments made.* Most individuals and small businesses use the cash basis of accounting. Using accrual accounting, revenues are reported when they are earned, rather than actually received, and the costs incurred in generating these revenues are recognized as expenses in the same time period as the revenues.

Recognizing revenues and their associated costs in the same reporting period is referred to as **"matching" expenses and revenues.** Most large companies use the accrual basis of accounting for measuring earnings and financial position.

Financial statements and schedules may cover an annual period, an interim period, or an operating cycle. They may be prepared by company accountants or by outside accounting services. They may be based on audited figures or on estimates. They are used to determine the financial success of a company, although, the only accurate—albeit unrealistic—way to do so is to keep track of all transactions from the beginning of the business until it ends.

Annual statements may be prepared for a calendar year, a natural year, the fiscal year peculiar to the company, or an operating cyclewhichever is longer. The **calendar year** *extends from January 1 to December 31 in a given year.* The **natural year** *is the 12-month period that ends when the activities of a business have reached the lowest point in its annual cycle.* The **fiscal year** *is a 12-month period that closes at the end of any month other than December, after which the books of a firm are closed and an annual statement is issued.* For purposes of credit analysis, the date of the annual financial statement is important in order to relate the figures to the stage or level of seasonal operations, to the condition of the industry, and to the state of the overall economy. The date of the statement is important when more than one statement is being compared, to determine the trend of operations.

Despite the fact that the natural year represents a point in time when business operations are at a low point—that is, its financial position is the most liquid—most businesses have adopted calendar year closings. Because this may be in the midst of the busy season, the customer's financial statement is likely to reflect larger inventories and short-term debt than would be expected at any other closing. A statement prepared at the end of a natural year discloses the customer's ability to liquidate short-term indebtedness.

Role of Financial Statements

Although the financial status of a business changes from day to day, the financial statements present pictures of the firm at two different time intervals. The balance sheet gives a snapshot of the firm's finances at one point in time, the last day of the reporting period. The profit and loss statement and the statement of cash flows show the firm's finances over the course of the reporting period. As such, they are key documents for the credit executive to review and understand.

Financial statements are usually produced on a regular schedule at the end of each accounting period and certainly at the end of each public disclosure period (i.e., quarterly and annually). The fiscal year is the company's tax year. There are ten related elements in financial statements that relate to measuring the performance and the financial status of a business.

1. Assets—economic benefits that are owned or controlled by the business
2. Liabilities—obligations to transfer assets or give up some economic benefits in the future
3. Equity—what remains of assets after liabilities are deducted
4. Investment by owners—increases in the equity of business when something of value is transferred to the business to obtain or increase ownership interest in it
5. Distribution to owners—a decrease in the equity of business after assets of some kind are transferred to the owners
6. Comprehensive income—all the changes in equity during a stated period except changes from either investments by or distributions to owners
7. Revenues—inflows to a business or other increases of its assets or settling of its liabilities resulting from the activities that are part of its business operations
8. Expenses—outflows or other uses of assets of a business or incurring of liabilities resulting from the activities that are part of its business operations
9. Gains—increases in a company's equity from non-core business transactions and other occurrences during a time period except those that stem from revenues or investments by owners
10. Losses—decreases in a company's equity from non-core business transactions and other occurrences during a time period except those that stem from expenses or distributions to owners

A credit manager should assume that the financial statements being reviewed represent the most liquid financial condition possible as of that date, and should then determine if the condition becomes more or less liquid at any point during the remainder of the year.

Interim Statements

The main purpose of interim statements is to give creditors a more up-to-date view of a firm's finances than can be obtained from the fiscal figures. In some seasonal lines, statements are prepared after the primary selling season, when inventories are at their lowest. Many small concerns are asked by their suppliers to work up midyear balance sheets and trial balances covering operations for one month or longer periods.

Trial balance figures differ from interim figures in that the latter contain an ending inventory while trial balance figures only have a beginning inventory. Thus, the interim figures will reflect the profit for the period. Other interim statements are issued by many firms for the benefit of investors and potential purchasers of their securities.

Estimated Statements

Unaudited statements or estimates can be erroneous and misleading, usually by accident but sometimes by deliberate intent of the preparers. Where credit exposure is substantial or the risk is sufficiently large, audited statements provide the best information and should be sought at all costs. Small concerns tend to resist the use of an auditor, frequently citing the high cost of such services, but it can be argued that an audit will provide assurance of fair and complete reports to all partners or principals and creditors. It will also make certain that tax returns are accurate, thus avoiding costly and time consuming audits by tax collectors, disputes over taxes due, and possible penalties. Despite these strong arguments, many credit decisions are based on financial estimates. If an audited statement cannot be obtained, efforts should be made to verify the assets and liabilities shown in the estimates.

Previous statements should be reconciled with current estimates, via application of the profit and loss information submitted. Cash estimates can be compared with the average balance quoted by the bank. If there is great variation, the bank can be asked to verify the figures shown in the statement. Notes payable to banks can also be verified.

Sales or service personnel calling at the customer's place of business can observe the inventory on hand and the degree of activity in the business. Accounts payable can be checked against a credit interchange or agency report. Ownership of land and buildings, as well as mortgages, can be verified through public records or a real estate search.

Annual Reports

Publicly owned corporations issue annual reports to their shareholders. These reports contain a great deal of information about the corporation, its executives, its product lines, and its performance for the past year and previous years. Public companies are companies whose stock is traded in open markets and exchanges. Private companies are companies with a relatively few number of stockholders, and whose stock is not traded in open markets or exchanges.

Publicly held corporations are required by Securities and Exchange Commission (SEC) regulations to file form 10-K, which presents detailed information regarding the business and its operations. The SEC also requires that companies use a common body of information for the 10-K report and the annual report that is sent to shareholders, including:

- audited financial statements
- notes to the financial statements
- auditor's report
- financial summary for the last five years, including: sales/revenues, net operating income/loss, income/loss per common share, total assets, long-term debt, preferred stock that can be redeemed, and cash dividends per share
- the high and low sales prices of common stock for each quarter during the past two years
- management discussion and analysis of the firm's financial condition and operating results at the time the financial statements were issued.

Publicly held companies are also required to file a 10-Q report with the SEC. This quarterly report contains a balance sheet, profit and loss statement, source and application of funds statement, and a narrative analysis that points out any exceptional changes over the previous quarter. Reports filed with the SEC are obtainable from the SEC's EDGAR (electronic data gathering, analysis, and retrieval) system that can be accessed through the SEC Internet site on the World Wide Web. Its Uniform Resource Locator (URL) is: http://www.sec.gov/index.html

Basic Financial Statements

There are four basic financial statements:

- the balance sheet
- the statement of income
- the statement of retained earnings
- the statement of cash flows

These four basic financial statements are linked. The cash account balance from the balance sheet at the end of the previous accounting period should be equal to the beginning cash figure on the statement of cash flows. The cash account balance from the current balance sheet (i.e., the one ending with the end of the period for statement reports) should be equal to the ending cash figure on the statement of cash flows. The retained earnings figure from the previous balance sheet should be equal to the beginning retained earnings figure on the statement of retained earnings. The retained earnings figure from the current balance sheet should be equal to the ending retained earnings figure on the statement of retained earnings. The figures for dividends and net income from the statement of income should be equal to the those figures on the statement of retained earnings.

Financial statements show several things about a firm, including:

- Liquidity—the firm's ability to pay its obligations as and when they become due
- Solvency—the firm's ability to pay its obligations and make a profit on its businesses—in other words, its ability to stay in business
- Management Efficiency—the ability of the firm's management to manage the overall business procedures

Accounting Issues

Generally Accepted Accounting Principles (GAAP)

Accounting principles must have public and professional support. Generally Accepted Accounting Principles (GAAP), as established by the Financial Accounting Standards Board (FASB) and the Security and Exchange Commission (SEC), represents the body of knowledge of accounting. As such, they provide a common format for preparing financial statements. Accountants and auditors must be able to reference a situation to an accounting standard to treat it properly. Accounting standards are reviewed, revised, and clarified by the FASB.

Accounting Assumptions

Basic assumptions include:

- Business Entity—the business is a separate entity from its owners.
- Going Concern—the business is assumed to continue in business indefinitely.
- Time Period—because any accounting period does not encompass the life of the business entity, it is permissible to accept some inaccuracies during the business's lifetime. Also, the typical accounting time period is assumed to be one month.
- Monetary Unit—all financial records will reflect foreign exchange translation into the business's home currency and will show the effects of inflation.
- Historical Cost and Conservatism Concept—it is assumed that the business uses measurement methods that will have the least favorable effect on net income.
- Realization—the business will decide when to recognize receipts and apply this method consistently.
- Matching—cost will be matched with receipts appropriately. For instance, one cannot be on a cash basis and the other on an accrual basis.
- Consistency—financial statements reflect the same accounting treatment from period to period unless explained in footnotes.
- Full Disclosure—the financial statements present all facts, using standard schedules, reports, footnotes, etc.
- Materiality—only transactions that are of relative size and importance to the company will be included in preparing the financial statements and footnotes, and in conducting the financial audit.
- Industry Practices—accounting practice associated with specific industries will be assumed.
- Transaction Approach—only those events that have an effect on the firm's financial position will be considered.
- Present Value Consideration—transactions will fairly represent the time value of money.
- Cash versus Accrual Basis—the company will decide on one or the other and apply it consistently. The cash basis recognizes revenue when cash is collected and expenses when cash is paid out. The accrual basis recognizes revenues when they are realized (not necessarily when cash is actually collected) and expenses when they are incurred (again, not necessarily when they are actually paid out). Accruals are adjusted at the time financial statements are prepared to reflect the delay between recording and actual cash movement.

Financial Accounting Standards Board (FASB)

FASB was formed to oversee financial accounting standards and to research new standards. It issues four types of communications:

- Statements of Financial Accounting Standards (SFAS). These establish GAAP concerning specific financial accounting issues.
- Interpretations. These provide clarifications to previously issued standards.
- Technical Bulletins. These provide guidance for accounting professionals about specific issues or events.
- Statements of Financial Accounting Concepts (SFAC). These are descriptions of financial accounting theory but are not considered parts of GAAP.

FASB has defined recognition criteria for financial statements:

- Definition. Transactions must be one of the elements of financial statements, such as assets, liabilities, etc.
- Measurability. Transactions and related issues can be measured reliably.
- Relevance. The information presented is relevant to the firm's business.
- Reliability. The information presented is reliable.
- Materiality. All information is subject to the materiality threshold for this company. This threshold need not be disclosed.

FASB has also defined several measurement attributes that can be used to determine value:

- Historical costs
- Current costs or replacement costs
- Current market value
- Net realizable value (undiscounted equivalent cash value)
- Present value of future cash flows

Notes to Financial Statements

The notes are an important part of the financial statements and must be read to understand thoroughly the presentation of specific items in the actual statements. Examples are notes for contingencies such as leases, merchandise in transit, pending purchase contracts, commitments for plant expansion, liability for dividends in arrears, events occurring subsequent to the balance sheet date, and pending litigation. The auditor may also deem it appropriate to comment upon pending tax examinations and the last tax year examined by the various authorities.

With regard to any notes referring to a firm's pension plan, it is particularly important to determine whether the actuarially computed value of vested benefits exceeds the plan assets. If so, the Pension Benefit Guarantee Corporation would have a preferred claim of up to 30 percent of the net worth if the company were to liquidate.

As a first step in analyzing the figures, the credit executive should adjust all balance sheet and income accounts for the transactions reflected in the footnotes.

The Balance Sheet

Overview

A **balance sheet** *is a statement of a company's financial position and contains specific details concerning the major financial items of a company at a specific point in time.* It is also called the statement of condition or statement of financial position. Balance sheets are static; they reflect conditions as of the date stated. It is important to note the date of the balance sheet. That is the only time the balance sheet is guaranteed to be accurate. There is no way of knowing how much accounts on the balance sheet may change after it is prepared.

The balance sheet shows, as of a particular date, what a business or person owns (expressed as assets), owes (expressed as liabilities), and its capitalization (expressed as stockholders equity), which is also the difference between assets and liabilities. The amount of detail depends on the auditor and possibly restrictions imposed by the client.

By definition, the account balances on a balance sheet must balance. The total of all assets must equal the sum of all liabilities and stockholders' equity. (Figure 20-1) The balancing equation is:

Assets = Liabilities + Stockholders' Equity

Assets

Assets *are all the resources owned by a company or a person.* They may take several forms, such as cash, accounts receivable, or physical property. They may be fully paid, in which case they are held free and clear, or they might be owned subject to outstanding debt. In any case, title to the assets is in the company's name. When ownership is acquired by lease, the lease rights are shown as an asset and the lease obligations as a liability. Assets are subdivided and listed on the balance sheet in order of liquidity (the ability to be converted into cash):

- current assets
- property, plant, and equipment
- other

Current assets *include cash and other assets expected to be converted into cash within one year or one operating cycle, beginning with the balance sheet date, whichever is longer.* The five categories of assets usually found in current assets are, listed in order of liquidity: cash, marketable securities, accounts receivable, inventories, and prepayments. With the exception of inventory, all current assets may also be called quick or liquid assets, because it is easy to convert them to cash. The relationship of these liquid assets to current liabilities (liquid or quick ratio) is an important consideration

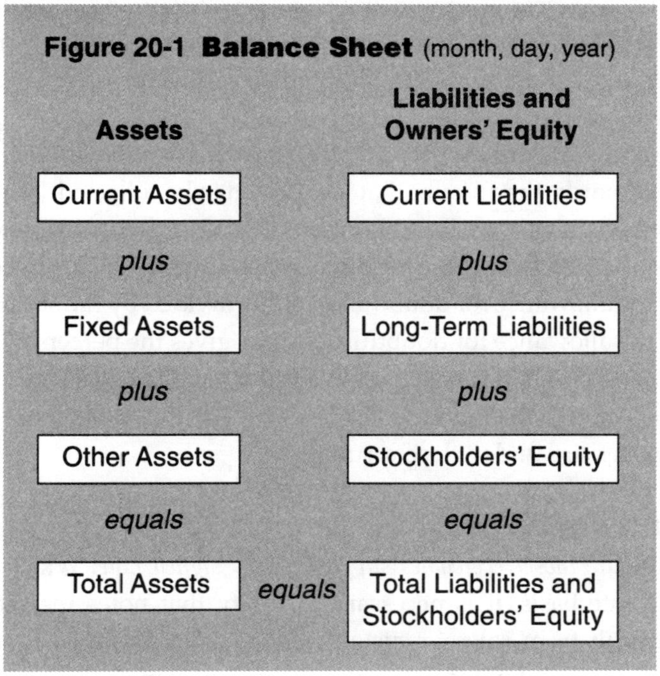

Figure 20-1 Balance Sheet (month, day, year)

for the credit executive when examining the current ratio (current assets to current liabilities) and other balance sheet ratios, because it shows the extent of liquid resources available to meet current obligations.

The term **net working capital** *is the difference between current assets and current liabilities* and, if positive, represents the amount of working capital the company expects to generate in the short-term, and have available to pay operating expenses. As such, it is an excellent predictor of future cash flows. It is also referred to as working capital.

Cash is the most liquid asset. Unrestricted balances in checking and savings accounts, checks, and money orders are considered cash, in addition to cash on hand. The cash figure shown on the balance sheet is assumed to be available for general business purposes, unless otherwise identified by the auditor. Adjustment of this amount is necessary when funds are restricted for specific projects, such as a legal reserve. Deposits under restrictions in foreign countries or funds set aside to retire funded debt, capital stock, etc., are classified as miscellaneous assets.

Marketable Securities

These are investments in short-term instruments (maturities under one year) with little risk. They are meant to be readily convertible into cash. Marketable securities are usually considered temporary or short-term investments. They are shown on the balance sheet at their fair value. Unrealized gains and losses are reported as a part of stockholders' equity.

Accounts Receivable

This represents amounts owed to the company for goods or services sold on credit. Amounts owed to a company for goods or services sold on credit should be segregated from those arising from other transactions, and the open accounts should be listed separately from those evidenced by notes. Receivables pledged as collateral for secured borrowing should be identified in the balance sheet and explained in a footnote. Receivables due from affiliated concerns should be listed separately and included among the current accounts only when representing merchandise sold on regular terms. Advances to affiliates or amounts due from officers, directors, and employees should not be listed with current assets.

Accounts receivable *are stated net of allowances to show the value they are expected to realize.* In other words, the amount that is expected to be collected. The most common allowance is for bad debts (uncollectible accounts). Other deductions applicable under special circumstances include those for discounts, returns and allowances, and freight. The amount of the allowance for doubtful accounts divided by the sum of net accounts receivable and the allowance for doubtful accounts gives the percent of total customer accounts receivable that is doubtful. Some auditors age balance sheet receivables by listing them according to the month billed. This breakdown should be required whenever the receivables are under close scrutiny.

Notes Receivables

Notes receivable *are those receivables supported by a signed note.* When normal selling terms are on a note basis, it is necessary to verify that notes receivable shown as current assets result from sales to customers. When sales are customarily on open account, the appearance of notes in the current section signals the need for additional investigation. They may represent past-due accounts for which the company has accepted notes, or may indicate activities not related to the normal course of business. It will help to know if the notes are payable in monthly amounts or by a single payment.

Merchandise Inventory

Inventory *represents goods that have been manufactured by a company for sale to customers or the components of the manufacturing process, which will be used to make finished goods for sale. It also can represent goods that have been purchased by the company in finished or unfinished (components) form for resale to customers, such as inventory maintained by a wholesaler.* Supplies used by a company are not included in the inventory figure. It is essential to know whether the inventory figure represents an actual physical stock-taking, is derived from perpetual inventory records, or is only an estimated figure.

In manufacturing, the merchandise inventory is usually in three stages: raw material, goods in process, and finished goods. This breakdown is usually shown on the balance sheet or can be obtained from the auditor.

Raw material has flexibility and can be used by others in a similar line of manufacturing. Consequently, its wholesale value is usually well established and the resale market for it is relatively broad. Under these circumstances, losses through emergency liquidation of raw material will be proportionately lower than for the other classes of the inventory and its value as collateral higher.

Finished goods, as completed products, are in an immediately salable state. The extent of loss in an emergency sale depends on the urgency of the situation, the type and quality of the product, and the demand for the goods being sold. Both raw materials and finished goods have relatively high values as loan collateral because they are relatively easy to segregate, warehouse, and sell.

Goods in process, however, have been committed but are not ready for sale. They need additional work before they can be sold and therefore represent a poorer salvage value. The proportion of goods in each stage has significance that goes beyond forced liquidation. Finished goods on hand at the beginning of a selling season can support a heavy debt position because their sale is imminent. If a disproportionate part of the inventory were in raw materials, it would mean added costs and, more important, poor timing and inability to deliver on time.

Inventory Valuation

While knowing the stages of the inventory is important to analysis, it is also essential to determine the bases and methods used in its evaluation. Inventory may be valued at cost, at market, at the lower of cost or market, or by any other recognized basis generally accepted in a given industry.

No two methods or bases give identical values for the same amount of physical goods. Because inventory is such an important component of financial statements, the value finally assigned to it will influence the financial position of the firm. The basis most commonly used is the lower of cost or market value. Conservatively, it assigns the lowest reasonable value to inventory on hand. It devalues raw material that had been purchased at a price higher than is now in effect but does not permit it to be revalued upward if its price rises after purchase. This basis always tends to understate earnings. In determining cost, any one of a number of methods may be used:

- average cost
- standard cost
- book cost as reflected in the perpetual inventory records
- estimated costs as applied to long-term contracts in process

Two commonly used methods are last-in, first-out (LIFO) and first-in, first-out (FIFO). The accounting in these two methods refers only to the costing of materials and does not necessarily relate directly to the utilization of the physical units.

The **LIFO method** *assumes that the last material acquired will be the first used.* Consequently, the inventory valuation on the balance sheet is based on earlier prices paid for material. The use of LIFO, in a period of rising prices, reports lower earnings, reduced taxes, and thereby increases cash availability. The combination of reduced taxes and increased cash availability takes on added significance during inflationary times, when it is difficult to obtain fresh money and the cost of obtaining it is high.

The **FIFO method** *works opposite to LIFO: the earliest prices of goods are charged against production and remaining inventory is valued at the more recent prices paid.* In a period of rising prices, the FIFO method will report greater profits, result in higher taxes, and yield less cash available than the LIFO method.

During inflationary times, when product cost is increasing, LIFO produces the highest cost of goods sold, which increases expenses, decreases earnings, and thus reduces tax liability. On the other hand, when inflation is not an issue, many companies want to show strong earnings. Some companies may choose FIFO despite the tax liability because it lowers their expenses and increases their earnings.

Whatever the basis or method of valuation, it should be applied consistently year after year and throughout the entire period under review. Failure to do this distorts any trend analysis. Any major changes in the basis or method of evaluation should be fully explained and its impact on profits determined. It has been noted that some companies will change from LIFO to FIFO, and back again to optimize their tax payments, depending on the rate of inflation.

Average Cost Method

This is the simplest of all the methods. *All the costs of inventory are added together and divided by the number of units to get an average price that is applied to all units of inventory, regardless of when they were purchased.* Although simple to administer, this method eliminates the tax benefits of the LIFO and FIFO methods.

Retail Method or Specific Identification

On financial statements of retail stores, the retail method of valuing inventories is in general use. Under this method, *the retailer enters the cost of each purchase item in a merchandise record, and against the entry posts a predetermined selling price. The difference between the totals of these two values at the end of the accounting period represents the anticipated markup or gross profit.*

The ratio of cost to retail is then calculated and this percentage is applied against the aggregate selling price of the unsold inventory to arrive at a computed cost of the merchandise stock.

The balance sheet inventory is often taken from the merchandise ledger or stock record but should be verified periodically by actual stock taking. The credit grantor should ask when such physical inventory was last taken.

Prepaid Expenses

These are payments that have already been made for services or benefits not yet received, such as rent and insurance. While these payments do not represent assets that can be converted into cash, they do depict funds expended during the period that will be charged to future operations. Most auditors list these items with current assets, as do such agencies as Dun & Bradstreet and Robert Morris Associates in the preparation of their industry averages.

Fixed Assets, *sometimes called tangible assets, are permanent or semi-permanent investments in tangible properties required for the conduct of the business and not subject to periodic purchase and sale.* They include land, buildings, machinery, tools and equipment, furniture and fixtures, trucks and automobiles, and leasehold improvements when the facility is not owned. In many instances, firms own properties not used in their regular business operations. These items are investments, even though they may appear as fixed assets on the balance sheet. They should be listed separately under miscellaneous assets.

Encumbrances on fixed assets should be listed among the liabilities and never shown as an offset on the asset side of the balance sheet. When only the net values are shown, the credit executive should insist on a full description of the properties, their value, mortgages or liens, and depreciation schedules. Fixed assets are subject to **depreciation**, *which is an amount regularly charged against operations to recover the cost of those assets but is not an actual cash outlay.* Fixed assets are usually shown at cost in the balance sheet, the amount of depreciation accumulated over the years listed as a deduction, and the net figure posted into the main assets column.

There are several ways to calculate depreciation: straight-line, declining balance, sum-of-the-years'-digit, and units of production. (Figure 20-2) The majority of firms use the straight-line method. Although the annual amount of depreciation varies according to the method used, the total amount of depreciation for any item is the same, regardless of method. It is customary to depreciate assets to their salvage, or residual, value.

Occasionally a company may engage a firm of appraisers to place a current value on property which has been held for a long time. This is done to obtain a more realistic valuation of the asset, particularly if it had been purchased during a period when building prices were low. The new value is assigned to the assets side of the balance

Figure 20-2 Methods of Depreciation

To illustrate the four methods of depreciating assets, the following case is used:

A company purchases a new piece of equipment that costs $28,000. It estimates the useful life of the equipment as six years, with a salvage, or residual, value of $4,000. It estimates that the equipment will be used five days a week for eight hours a day, producing four units an hour, for a total of 8160 (51 weeks) units a year and 48,960 units over the six years.

Straight-line Method of Depreciation
The rate and the amount of depreciation are constant over the estimated life of the equipment. The yearly depreciation is calculated as follows:

Cost-salvage value/estimated life = annual depreciation

In the example above, the computation of annual depreciation is:

$28,000 – $4,000/6 = $24,000/6 = $4,000

Each year, $4,000 of depreciation will be recorded for this asset.

Year	Beginning Value	Depreciation	Ending Value
1	$28,000	$4,000	$24,000
2	24,000	4,000	20,000
3	20,000	4,000	16,000
4	16,000	4,000	12,000
5	12,000	4,000	8,000
6	8,000	4,000	4,000

Declining Balance Method of Depreciation
This is a method of accelerated depreciation where the amount depreciated is enhanced when the asset is first put into service and diminishes significantly as the asset nears the end of its estimated useful life.

It is calculated as follows:

1/Estimated life of asset × 2 × Book value at year's beginning = Annual depreciation

In our example, the calculation for year one is:

1/6 × 2 × $28,000 = $56,000/6 = $9,330

The calculation for year two is:

1/6 × 2 × $28,000 – $9,330 = 1/6 × 2 × $18,670 = 1/6 × $37,330 = $6,220

The rate of depreciation over the six years is given in the table below.

Year	Accum. Dep. Beg. of Year	Book Value Beg. of Year	Depreciation for Year	Book Value End of year
1	——	$28,000	$9,330	$18,670
2	$ 9,330	18,670	6,220	12,450
3	15,550	12,450	4,150	8,300
4	19,700	8,300	2,770	5,530
5	22,470	5,530	1,530	4,000
6	24,000	4,000	——	4,000

Note that using the formula would give a year 5 depreciation amount greater than $1,530. However, then the book value would be reduced to less than the salvage value. As the salvage value is $4,000, the depreciation for year 5 is reduced to the amount that leaves exactly the $4,000 residual value, and no depreciation is allocated in year 6.

(continued)

Figure 20-2 Methods of Depreciation

Sum-of-the-Years'-Digits Method

This is another accelerated method of depreciation where the amount of depreciation is greater at the beginning and decreases over time. It is computed as follows:

Remaining number of years of useful life of asset × (Cost – salvage value) = Annual depreciation

Sum of the digits of the total number of years of use

Using our example, the depreciation for the first year is calculated as:

6/(6+5+4+3+2+1) × \$28,000 – \$4,000 = 6/21 × \$24,000 = \$6,857.14

Depreciation for the second year is calculated as:

5/21 × \$24,000 = \$5,714.29

Depreciation for the six years appears in the following table:

Year	Cost less salvage value	Fract.	Deprec. for year	Accum dep. at year end	Book value at year end
1	$24,000	6/21	$6,857.14	$ 6,857.14	$21,142.86
2	$24,000	5/21	5,714.29	12,571.43	15,428.57
3	$24,000	4/21	4,571.43	17,142.86	10,857.14
4	$24,000	3/21	3,428.57	20,571.43	7,428.57
5	$24,000	2/21	2,285.71	22,857.14	5,142.86
6	$24,000	1/21	1,142.86	24,000.00	4,000.00

Unit of Production Method

This method is not accelerated. Depreciation is tied to the use of the asset at a constant cost per output unit. The variable is the number of units. Units in our example are manufactured items. Units could also be hours the asset is used.

To calculate depreciation, the following equations are used:

Cost-salvage value = Depreciation per unit

Estimated output

Depreciation per unit × output for year = Annual depreciation

In our example, the calculations are:

\$28,000 – \$4,000 = \$0.490196, or \$0.49 per unit

\$0.49 × 8160 = \$3,998.40 annual depreciation.

If the asset should be used more than 40 hours a week in production, the amount of annual depreciation will increase. If it is used less than expected, the annual depreciation will decrease. Thus, the amount of depreciation for six years cannot be predicted in advance, as it can with the other methods illustrated. However, as with the other methods, the total amount of depreciation taken over the life of the asset cannot be more than $24,000, regardless of how much asset is used.

sheet and is offset by an equity item, unrealized capital increment per appraisal or appraisal surplus, equal to the difference between the old and new valuations.

Leases are classified as operating leases or as capital leases. If a lease is noncancelable and meets at least one of the following four criteria, it must be treated as a capital lease on the balance sheet: (1) Ownership of the property is transferred to the lessee by the end of the lease. (2) The lease includes a bargain purchase option. (3) The term of the lease is at least 75 percent of the expected economic life of the leased property. (4) At the start of the lease, the present value of all the payments equals or exceeds

90 percent of the fair market value of the leased property. If it meets none of these, it is treated as an operating lease.

This balance sheet treatment tends to show larger investment in property and greater liabilities for capital leases. Many companies prefer to keep leases off the balance sheet altogether, which is possible with operating leases. In addition to excluding the four criteria above from the lease agreement, there are other ways of circumventing the capitalization of leases, such as sale of receivables with recourse to a third party or to a captive finance company. The end result is that many corporations can avoid the capitalizing of leases on the balance sheet.

Investment in and Advances to Subsidiaries

When this item appears on a statement, it is important to know several things:

- whether the investment is carried at cost or at net asset
- the extent of intercompany relations between the parent and subsidiaries
- the financial condition of the separate subsidiaries

Individual financial statements of the subsidiaries are helpful in evaluating these points.

Miscellaneous Assets

Miscellaneous assets include all tangible assets not identified as current or fixed. They include investments, advances to or stock interests in subsidiaries and affiliates, amounts due from officers, directors, and employees, cash surrender value of life insurance policies on officers, and sometimes prepaid expenses.

Intangibles

These are nonphysical assets that are not available for payment of debts of a going concern. There is a long list of such items, including good will, patents, trademarks, brands, designs, contracts, formulas, mailing lists, franchises, and the legal costs of organizing a business. Expenditures for these assets may be incurred in a short period of time or over a number of years. On the balance sheet, they are reported at their historical cost and amortized over the shorter of their legal or useful lives.

Tangible Net Assets and Tangible Net Worth

Tangible net assets are total assets less intangibles (e.g., good will). Tangible net worth is net worth less intangibles. Tangible net assets minus tangible net worth equals total liabilities.

Contra Accounts

These are accounts used to offset or reduce an asset to its net realizable value or book value. Rather than show some financial items as one amount, proper accounting treatment provides for two amounts to be shown in order to furnish additional useful information. The allowance for doubtful accounts is a contra account that offsets accounts receivable (the primary account); accumulated depreciation is a contra account that offsets fixed assets, the primary account.

Contra accounts are sometimes shown as reserves. For example, in the above illustrations they would appear as a reserve for doubtful accounts and a reserve for depreciation. This would be incorrect, since the term reserve tends to connote something set aside for a particular purpose.

Liabilities

Liabilities *are claims against the assets of a company.* They are usually classified as current liabilities or long-term liabilities. **Current liabilities**, *by long-accepted definition, are obligations maturing within the longer of one year or one operating cycle from the date of the statement.* Examples of current liabilities are salaries, wages, taxes other than Federal income tax, insurance, interest, dividends payable, customer advances and deposits, and payables. Payables can also include short-term obligations, notes payable and promissory notes.

Deferred or long-term liabilities *are those that are due in a term longer than an operating cycle or one year, whichever is longer.* They usually fall into two types: those incurred in financing assets and those incurred in operating the business. Examples of long-term liabilities are mortgages, bonds, debentures, serial notes, purchase money obligations, credit agreements, and long-term notes which mature more than one year from statement date. Included in this category are demand notes that have been formally subordinated to all other creditors for a period of at least one year from the date of the statement.

Stockholders' Equity or Owners' Equity

The **stockholders' equity** *of unincorporated business firms may be called net worth, proprietary interest, partners' capital, or capital.* Drawings and withdrawals of capital during the auditing period are reflected in the operating statement and the balance sheet, but some auditors do not specifically cover the contingency of later withdrawals to pay income taxes on each principal's share. On the other hand, some auditors, by statement footnote or general comment, do give an estimate of probable future withdrawals that will be made to pay personal income taxes based on the partners' distributive shares in the profits. Corporate net worth or stockholders' equity is divided into various classes of preferred and common outstanding stock and retained earnings. The credit executive is interested in any asset or dividend preferences involved in the classes of stocks as well as in the relationship between owned and borrowed funds. Thus, the showing of various classes of stock by order of preference, by dividend requirements, or by indication of preemptive rights, if any, is helpful.

The credit executive should pay particular attention to preferred stock and be aware of its rights or covenants. Preferred stock, for example, may have been issued as part of an agreement to defer existing debt. In this instance, it may be preferable to remove such stock from the equity portion of the balance sheet and treat it as long-term debt. It is important to be aware of the cumulative nature of preferred stock dividends and the preemptive rights associated with preferred stock. Owners of common stock share all the rights of ownership, including voting and liquidation. If a company is liquidated, owners of common stock have a claim to the assets of the company only after all other claims have been satisfied. The order of preference for claims when a business is liquidated is:

1. secured creditors
2. administrative expenses (professionals)

3. unsecured claims for sales to a debtor-in-possession (DIP)
4. wage and compensation claims
5. customer deposits
6. taxes
7. unfunded pension liabilities
8. unsecured creditors
9. preferred stockholders
10. common stockholders

Treasury stock, representing some of its own capital stock that has been bought back or reacquired by a corporation, is shown either as an asset item or as a deduction from outstanding stock. Credit executives prefer the latter treatment. When treasury stock appears as an asset, they place this item among the intangibles, which are deducted to determine tangible net worth. The term surplus is sometimes used in this portion of the balance sheet:

- Earned surplus results from retained earnings.
- Additional paid-in capital that is contributed in excess of par, or stated value, may be called paid-in surplus.
- An increased net worth resulting from an upward appraisal of fixed assets may be termed appraisal surplus or unrealized capital increment per appraisal.

Statement of Income

Overview

It is also called the **Income Statement, the Statement of Earnings, and the Statement of Operations**. The income statement is considered to be perhaps the most important financial statement. *It provides a summary of income and expenses, and gains and losses for a specific period of time.* The relationship of the income statement to the balance sheet is important: A balance sheet provides a picture of financial condition at a given date, while a statement of income and retained earnings traces the results of corporate activity over a period of time. An income statement should contain information on sales, cost of goods sold, expenses, net operating profit, information on other income and expenses, and profit before and after taxes.

Income statements are presented in one of two ways. The single-step method totals all revenues and all expenses, and then subtracts the latter from the former to get net income. The multiple-step method matches revenues and expenses from the earliest calculation of gross profit until it derives net income. (Figure 20-3)

Components

Sales or Revenues

This refers to the dollar volume of transactions involving company products and services. It is valued at selling price rather than at cost of merchandise. Gross sales should be

Figure 20-3 Two Ways of Constructing Income Statements

Single Step	Multiple Step
Revenue	Net sales
Net sales	(Cost of goods sold)
Other income	Gross profit
Total revenue	(Operating expenses)
Expenses	Operating income
Cost of goods sold	+/– Other income/expense
Operating expenses	Income before taxes
Other expenses	(Income taxes)
Income tax expense	Net income
(Total expenses)	Earnings per share
Net income	
Earnings per share	

separated into cash sales and credit sales whenever a substantial amount of cash business is done. The net sales figure is used in credit analysis. It is obtained by deducting returns, allowances, and any applicable discounts from the gross sales figure.

Gross sales - (returns+allowances+discounts) = Net sales

Other information can be determined from this part of the income statement. Returns and allowances are clues to the quality of output and customer satisfaction with the product. It is important to determine if sales returns are put back into inventory and counted again. The figure shown as sales or revenues should represent actual transactions during which title changes hands. Goods placed on consignment, for example, are not sold, though a credit executive will see unaudited statements in which no distinction is made between the two. Further, customers' commitments are sometimes incorrectly shown as sales. Or, sales may occasionally be held off beyond the closing date of a period in order to reduce the reported income.

Intercompany sales between affiliates can also be manipulated to show a higher or lower sales volume. These practices are all misleading and can be overcome by careful reading of the financial statement figures and footnotes.

Cost of Goods Sold (Cost of Goods Manufactured)

This item represents the cost of materials, labor, and factory overhead needed to bring to a marketable state the goods that have been sold. The figure can be affected by the way purchases are listed in this part of the operating statement. Purchases can be shown net of discounts to represent the cost after trade and cash discounts. Discounts can be shown as other income, and gross purchases can be used to compute the cost of goods sold. This allows a credit executive to determine how much profit was earned by taking discounts and how much by operations. Cost of goods sold should also include freight in and technicians' wages.

Because cost of goods sold is calculated by taking the difference between beginning and ending inventory balances and adding purchases, the inventory figures are major items in determining the cost of goods sold, and gross and net profits. If inventory is incorrectly stated, profits can be materially distorted. Claims of hidden cushions in inventory (the undervaluing of inventory to reduce tax obligations) should be carefully investigated, as this practice can be used equally well to cover up losses in an unprofitable period.

Gross Profit

This is the first step in the multi-step method of developing the income statement. It is an important measure in evaluating a company's financial operations. *Cost of goods sold is deducted from net sales to arrive at the* **gross profit**.

Net sales - Cost of goods sold = Gross profit

Gross margin, *which is the percentage of sales represented by gross profit*, is a valuable analytical tool for internal analysis and for comparing the financial affairs of a concern with others in the same line.

Gross profit/Net sales = Gross margin

This percentage is stable within an industry because competitive factors tend to keep the price of purchases and selling prices in fairly close alignment. Consequently, gross profit is a major determinant of a firm's ability to stay in business. A return considerably below that of the industry may be due to insufficient volume, poor purchasing habits, or high labor costs. An explanation of any major deviation is essential for understanding the account. Year-to-year variations in a company's gross profit would be caused by changes in selling prices or cost of goods sold, variations in product mix between high- and low-priced items, or a combination of these factors.

Expenses

Operating expenses *are daily expenses associated with operating the business but are not attributable to any specific sales category*. Sometimes operating expenses are referred to as overhead or general and administrative expenses. A breakdown of operating expenses and their separate relationships to net sales are extremely helpful when appraising operations and comparing them with those of other companies. These include administrative and general expenses, distribution costs (sales, shipping, and sales advertising expenses), and changes in the allowance for uncollectibles. Certain expenses, like rent and administrative costs, tend to remain constant while others vary considerably, most often in relation to sharp increases or declines in sales. For instance, it would be normal for advertising and sales commissions to increase with expanding volume. Depreciation is a noncash expense but it is included in operating expenses to represent an allowance for wear and tear, replacement, and obsolescence of machinery, equipment, and buildings. Each expense item should be considered and its contribution to results weighed wherever possible. Depreciation, taxes, telephone costs, and rent may be apportioned among the various departments.

Selling expenses are directly attributable to the sales effort and would include such items as sales department salaries, freight out, and advertising. Administrative and general expenses are often combined and include clerical salaries, directors' fees, legal and auditing expenses, etc.

Net Operating Income

After the cost of goods sold and expenses are deducted from net sales, a firm has either an operating profit or loss. This is a good measure of ability to operate successfully because it represents income derived from normal business operations but does not take into account cash discounts given or received, interest on borrowed funds, and all extraordinary charges and income that are not separate adjustments of retained earnings.

Other Income and Expenses

Income from incidental ventures, such as rentals or interest, would be classed as other than operating income, while items such as loss on foreign exchange transactions would be classed as a nonoperating expense. Such items have a definite bearing on overall company results but should be examined separately because of their special nature. The key analysis should be directed to the customer's day-by-day operations, its line of business.

Extraordinary Items

Nonrecurring events such as fire damage, storm losses, or gains or losses on sales of plant and property would distort the income statement if credited to income or charged as an expense on a direct basis. It is preferable to set up a separate section for them on the income statement. After adjusting net operating income for other expenses and extraordinary items, the result is pretax profit.

Federal Income Taxes

The tax requirements shown in the statement of income represent those estimated by management for the period covered. The firm has made scheduled payments during the year, so this figure is not the same as that shown on the balance sheet.

Net Income

After the provision for federal income taxes has been made, the final net income remains. This is often referred to as the bottom line. This may be retained or partially paid out to stockholders and owners. Rapid growth companies normally retain earnings in order to increase their working assets, while slow growth companies distribute earnings. For closely held corporations, dividend payout constitutes additional compensation to the principals. When dividends are paid and loaned back by the principals, the creditor must be aware that the loans may be payable on demand.

Statement of Retained Earnings

Overview

The **statement of retained earnings** *reconciles the increases and decreases in retained earnings for the period stated.* The statement often appears as an addition to the income statement. It may be shown as follows:

Beginning balance, retained earnings	(First day of time period)
Add net income	(Last day of time period)
Total	
(Less dividends declared and paid)	
Ending balance, retained earnings	

Components

Retained Earnings

The current amount represents profits retained by the firm (i.e., undistributed profits) after paying taxes and dividends to shareholders. The beginning balance represents retained earnings at the end of the prior period.

Net Income

This amount, from the income statement, is added to beginning retained earnings.

Dividends

The amount of dividends is subtracted from net income to give final retained earnings.

A part of retained earnings may be restricted by legal agreement, management decision, or loan covenants. The restriction will usually be shown and explained in further detail in a footnote to the financial statements.

Statement of Cash Flows

Overview

The **statement of cash flows (SCF)** *details cash inflows and cash outflows during the same period as the income statement and the statement of retained earnings.* It is important for understanding the true cash flows of the business. The statement of cash flows separates the cash flows into three activities, listed in the following order: operating activities, investing activities, and financing activities. The sum of these three activities equals the change in the cash figure for the period.

Cash Flows from Operating Activities

Operating activities include manufacturing, or delivering goods for sale or resale, or providing services, that is, the core business of the firm. All other transactions that are not financing or investment activities are classified as operating activities. **Cash inflows** *are the receipts from the sale of goods or services, the receipt of interest on loans, or dividends received from equity ownership.* **Cash outflows** *are payments for inventory items, salaries and wages, taxes, interest expense, and other expense payments to suppliers.*

Cash Flows from Investing Activities

Investing activities include buying and selling investments and productive long-term assets and lending money and collecting interest on the loans. Cash inflows come from the sale of property, plant and equipment; from the sale of debt or equity securities of other firms held as investments; and from interest or other payments received from loans to others. **Cash outflows** *come from buying property, plant, and equipment; buying debt or equity securities of other firms as investments; or making loans to other entities.*

Cash Flows from Financing Activities

Financing activities are those related to liability and owners' equity. Cash inflows come from selling equity securities of the firm and from selling bonds, mortgages, notes, and any other short- or long-term debt instruments. **Cash outflows** *are dividend payments, repayments of debt, and repurchasing the company's own stock.*

Other Financial Reports

Trial Balance

The **trial balance** *is a list of the debit and credit balances of the general ledger accounts.* It is prepared monthly in a well-managed business as a test of the posting to these accounts and is a preliminary step when an annual or interim balance sheet and operating statement are to be prepared.

Limitations

Because of the way it is prepared, the trial balance has certain inherent limitations, including:

- While the sum total of debits balances with total credits, there is no assurance that the records are correct, as they are not audited.
- Even when monthly trial balances are prepared by an independent auditor, they usually carry notification that they were prepared from the books without audit or verification, and that the auditor assumes no responsibility for their correctness.
- The trial balance does not show a closing inventory position and thus prevents an accurate calculation of profit for the period.
- Accounts receivable represents the general ledger controlling account and may be greater than the receivables shown in the customers' ledger. It may include ledger balances of bankrupt accounts not written off and accounts long overdue, as well as advances to principals, sales representatives' overdrafts, and loans to affiliate interests or relatives. Anticipation or discounts earned by customers also would not be reflected in the account.
- Accounts payable may be understated by showing less than the total amounts that appear on creditors' ledgers. Some concerns forward purchase entries to a following month when the bills have future dating, when the bills have not been approved before the purchase book was closed, or when goods are in transit.
- Accrued liabilities are not reflected in the trial balance. Omission of the sum of accrued wages, salaries, commissions, rent, and taxes can understate expenses and current liabilities.
- Loans payable to principals, when entered as credits to their salary or drawing accounts, can understate liabilities and expenses.
- Production labor may incorrectly include indirect costs such as factory supervision because factory prime cost and expense have not been separated.

Advantages

Despite these limitations, and because many firms do not prepare quarterly or semi-annual financial statements, the trial balance is often viewed as the means to obtain the latest interim financial information.

Consolidated Financial Statements

The parent company of interrelated companies will occasionally issue only consolidated financial figures of the parent and one or more subsidiary concerns, and eliminates all intercompany accounts regarding investment, advances, revenues, expenses, and distribution of income. Only statements of subsidiary concerns may properly be consolidated with that of the parent company. A concern is designated as a subsidiary when over 50 percent of its controlling capital stock is owned by the parent concern. *When 50 percent or less of its stock is held by the parent company, the related concern is called an* **affiliate**. The interest in the affiliate is shown as an investment item in the noncurrent assets, and amounts owed between the two concerns are indicated as receivable or payable items.

The **consolidated statement** *is recognized as synthetic or amalgamated. It relates to no one corporate entity, but pools the accounts of two or more legal entities for the purpose of presenting a composite picture.* It should be kept in mind that each underlying unit still retains a separate legal corporate status, controls its own assets and distributes its own dividends, and has no general liability for the debts of the other units or the parent. A consolidated statement inadequately discloses the immediate position of the parent because it mixes corporate assets and liabilities of several individual companies. By itself, it gives no indication of the status of assets and liabilities of each subsidiary, nor does it indicate which ones are operating at a profit and which at a loss.

Varying degrees of control are exercised in consolidations. In some cases, purchasing, borrowing, and lending functions of the combine are centralized in the parent company or a designated subsidiary. In others, the separate corporations have more or less autonomy in this respect. The following points should be checked when reviewing consolidated statements:

- The consolidated units are over 50 percent owned and controlled.
- Each of the individual statements included in the consolidated statement is for or as of the same date.
- The method of consolidating has been followed consistently; departures have been noted.
- Changes in the subsidiaries making up the consolidated companies have been noted.
- The accounting methods of the companies consolidated are uniform and their business policies are substantially the same.
- The valuation bases of the assets are the same.

These assurances are usually given or implied in the opinion of a responsible auditor. Where the consolidated statement does not include all subsidiaries, the creditor should know which have been included and which have been excluded, since the choice is a prerogative of the parent concern. A complete analysis of a consolidated financial statement requires working papers showing the individual statements of the consolidated companies along with the intercompany items that are eliminated in the consolidation. Sometimes credit is checked on the consolidated statement of a parent company when analysis discloses no reason to go behind the overall figures.

Combined Financial Statements

There are instances where *the shares of two or more companies are owned by the same stockholders, who may submit a statement showing the added assets and liabilities of all the companies so affiliated, even though a parent-subsidiary relationship does not exist. This statement is properly called a* **combined balance sheet** rather than a consolidated one. The statement has no legal standing and should not be used for credit analysis.

The statement does not represent the financial picture of a legal entity but only an amalgamation of financial resources owned by the same shareholders. Therefore, it is essential to obtain separate statements on each company.

Pro Forma Financial Statements

A **pro forma financial statement** *shows what the financial condition and operating results of a company would have been if certain events had taken place in the past or will take place in the future.* For instance, if a corporation spins off an operating unit to shareholders, pro forma statements could be constructed from historical data that would show what the separate financial conditions and operations of the spun-off unit and its parent would have been at a time before they were actually separated.

A pro forma financial statement may be prepared to show the effects on the firm's financial statements from a significant future event, such as a new stock issue, major acquisition or divestiture, increase in market share, or unexpected financial crisis.

Audit Issues

The Role of the Auditor

The terms of an auditor's engagement determine the extent of the audit, the number and detail of the schedules produced, and the amount of verification work done. The adequacy of the audit and the experience and reputation of the auditor are weighed by the credit executive against the size and financial condition of the customer. This should be the initial step in financial analysis.

Types of Audits

An independent auditor is engaged to prepare or verify the financial report of a company. The audit may range from a detailed audit with verification of all items and transactions, to a simple book audit concerned only with arithmetic accuracy in transferring ledger figures into the balance sheet and statement of income and retained earnings. Between these extremes, limited audits exclude some items because of restrictive circumstances or because management insists that certain figures be accepted without complete checking. The auditor notes these limitations in order to avoid misleading others as to the extent of the verification.

Unaudited Statements

When a report indicates that the auditor has reviewed the financial data, this means that the statement has not been audited. The auditor makes inquiries concerning the internal procedures of the client, but does not make any external inquiries, observe physical inventories, review internal control, or perform other mandatory auditing procedures. Moreover, the auditor's statement attached to the review should represent a disclaimer of opinion.

A Compilation Is Even Less Assuring

Its financial information is the representation of management without any attempt by the auditor to verify figures or to provide any assurance on the statements. Interim statements are seldom audited. In large concerns, these figures are usually prepared and released by the controller. At most, they are subjected to a limited audit, even when issued on the stationery of the auditor.

Responsibility for Financial Reporting

While the auditing firm is liable for its opinion of the financial statement, company management is responsible for the statement's integrity and objectivity. A lot of information must be presented in a logical manner in order to accurately show how the company is performing. Management is responsible for writing the "Management Discussion and Analysis" section.

In a note to shareholders and directors, the management of a large company will acknowledge its responsibility for maintaining internal accounting control systems that provide reasonable assurance as to the reliability of the financial records.

An audit committee of the board of directors, consisting solely of members who are not employees of the company, oversee the financial reporting. This committee usually meets jointly and separately with the independent auditors and management to review their activities.

Change in Auditor

When the regular auditor quits an engagement, it is important to determine the underlying reason. A desire to lower auditing costs is often given as the motive, but the move may also have credit implications. A substantial cut in auditing fees may foreshadow looser auditing work and less verification effort.

The change in auditors may have been occasioned by a difference of opinion between auditor and management regarding the treatment and certification of material items in the statement. Some auditors announce they are no longer "on the books" of a former client but do not give the reason why. Credit executives should carefully compare the opinion of the new auditor with that of the former one. When a firm changes auditors, it is required to file a form 8-K with the SEC.

Auditor-Client Relationships

Auditors prepare financial statements and supporting schedules for clients and not to meet the special needs of creditors. Their work is governed by their intensive training, strict regulation of auditing procedures and conventions, and their accountability to professional societies. They do, however, have a responsibility to clarify items in their audits when questions are raised, and usually give such explanations readily.

Auditors differ as to the degree of their cooperation with small- or medium-sized clients. Some believe their audit report meets the terms of their engagement, while others give additional information that may benefit their clients. In some lines of business, notably segments of the textile industry, auditors may accompany their clients on credit interviews and supply additional information to creditors. Many credit executives and bank lending officers welcome an opportunity to become acquainted with an auditor on whom they expect to rely.

Audit Reports

Overview

The Auditor's Report: *The letter of transmittal in which the auditor reports the results of the audit to the client is termed the* **certificate**. It is a formal, written statement of the auditor's opinion concerning the financial statements after a financial audit has been completed. Statements that omit the auditor's full certificate may be withholding vital information, and should be questioned. The letter may be in a short form or in the more comprehensive long form.

Customary Schedules in Audit Reports

Primary exhibits or schedules *are the balance sheet, statement of income, statement of retained earnings, and statement of cash flows.* The report may also include various supporting and analytical schedules. Their scope and character depend on the size of the concern, the complexity of organization and operations, and the client's instructions. It is customary for comprehensive audit reports to present these exhibits and schedules for at least two successive years. Comparisons may be stated in dollars and on a percentage basis to facilitate analysis by management and creditors. Special purpose schedules are occasionally included for managerial use or because of special interest by suppliers and bankers. The first appearance of unusual schedules should suggest that special study is needed.

Unqualified Opinions

An **unqualified opinion** *is one that states that the schedules are prepared accurately, fairly present the results of operations for the period reported, and show the actual financial condition of the concern on the date of the statement, prepared in a manner consistent with that used last year, and with GAAP.* An unqualified opinion usually assures the client and the creditors that:

- The client's accounting records were actually audited for the period indicated.
- Such tests of the accounting records and other auditing procedures were made as deemed necessary under the circumstances.

- The major assets and liabilities were confirmed or checked, with exceptions noted.

Qualified Opinions

A **qualified opinion** *is one that explains the qualifications detailed in the footnotes, usually referenced by the footnote number, which may have a material effect on a company's operating results and financial condition.* With the exception of the qualification, the financial statements have been prepared in accordance with GAAP. When an opinion is qualified, a credit executive should compare successive statements to uncover material changes in phrasing or omissions that could prove significant on further inquiry. Adverse opinion: An opinion of this type means that the auditor believes the financial statements do not conform to GAAP.

Disclaimer of opinion

In this case, the auditor has not conducted a complete financial audit and, therefore, does not have sufficient data to comment on the financial statements one way or the other. Often, the auditor will have done a compilation, which means that the auditor has helped prepare the financial records to produce the financial statements or has helped in preparing the financial statements. However, the auditor has not audited the statements. A sample compilation letter and several sample opinion letters are shown in this chapter.

Reliability

The audit and certification is generally accepted as adequate endorsement of the correctness of a financial statement. Seasoned credit executives take three additional factors into consideration:

- the experience of the auditor with the type of business
- how often the client's books are examined
- keeping a close working relationship with the auditor and client, and becoming wary when the auditor is changed

Specialization by Auditors

Practically every trade and industry has a group of auditors who concentrate their practice in that field. Often this specialization is along functional lines. By cooperating with the credit executives of suppliers and with their close knowledge of specific products, processes, and market conditions, these auditors become authorities in particular lines. Consequently, their audits are preferred by some credit executives over those of less specialized auditors.

Frequency of Audit

Continuity of engagement and continuous audit are not the same type of service. In continuity of engagement, an independent auditor is regularly employed to prepare annual and other statements, and does so for successive years. Under continuous audit, the auditor makes periodic inspections of the books and records between annual statement periods, but not necessarily an audit, and may supervise or prepare monthly trial balances and quarterly or semiannual statements. Continuous audit enables the

Figure 20-4 Sample Unqualified Opinion

WOODEN & BENSON
CHARTERED
CERTIFIED PUBLIC ACCOUNTANTS

INDEPENDENT AUDITOR'S REPORT

To the Board of Directors
Model Corporation
Clientown, State

We have audited the accompanying balance sheets of Model Corporation as of December 31, 19X2 and 19X1, and the related statements of income, retained earnings, and cash flows for the years then ended. These financial statements are the responsibility of the Company's management. Our responsibility is to express an opinion on these financial statements based on our audits.

We conducted our audits in accordance with generally accepted auditing standards. Those standards require that we plan and perform the audit to obtain reasonable assurance about whether the financial statements are free of material misstatement. An audit includes examining, on a test basis, evidence supporting the amounts and disclosures in the financial statements. An audit also includes assessing the accounting principles used and significant estimates made by management, as well as evaluating the overall financial statement presentation. We believe that our audits provide a reasonable basis for our opinion.

In our opinion, the financial statements referred to above present fairly, in all material respects, the financial position of Model Corporation as of December 31, 19X2 and 19X1, and the results of its operations and its cash flows for the years then ended in conformity with generally accepted accounting principles.

WOODEN & BENSON

Baltimore, Maryland
________, 19_

100 W. PENNSYLVANIA AVENUE BALTIMORE, MARYLAND 21204 TELEPHONE (410) 825-4860 FAX (410) 828-1419

Figure 20-5 Sample Qualified Opinion - Scope Restriction - Did Not Audit Entire Entity

WOODEN & BENSON
CHARTERED
CERTIFIED PUBLIC ACCOUNTANTS

INDEPENDENT AUDITOR'S REPORT

To the Board of Directors
Model Corporation
Clientown, State

We have audited the accompanying balance sheets of Model Corporation, a wholly-owned subsidiary of ABC Corporation, as of December 31, 19X2 and 19X1, and the related statements of income, retained earnings, and cash flows for the years then ended. These financial statements are the responsibility of the Company's management. Our responsibility is to express an opinion on these financial statements based on our audits.

Except as discussed in the following paragraph, we conducted our audits in accordance with generally accepted auditing standards. Those standards require that we plan and perform the audit to obtain reasonable assurance about whether the financial statements are free of material misstatement. An audit includes examining, on a test basis, evidence supporting the amounts and disclosures in the financial statements. An audit also includes assessing the accounting principles used and significant estimates made by management, as well as evaluating the overall financial statement presentation. We believe that our audits provide a reasonable basis for our opinion.

As explained in Note X to the financial statements, ABC Corporation and its other subsidiaries conduct certain transactions on behalf of Model Corporation. Because the engagement was limited to the records of Model Corporation, we were unable to satisfy ourselves as to the full nature and volume of transactions conducted by ABC Corporation and its other subsidiaries on behalf of Model Corporation.

In our opinion, except for the effects of such adjustments, if any, as might have been determined to be necessary had we been able to audit the records of ABC Corporation and its other subsidiaries, the financial statements referred to above present fairly, in all material respects, the financial position of Model Corporation as of December 31, 19X2 and 19X1, and the results of its operations and its cash flows for the years then ended in conformity with generally accepted accounting principles.

WOODEN & BENSON

Baltimore, Maryland
______, 19_

100 W. PENNSYLVANIA AVENUE BALTIMORE, MARYLAND 21204 TELEPHONE (410) 825-4860 FAX (410) 828-1419

Figure 20-6 Sample Qualified Report - Change In Depreciation Method

WOODEN & BENSON
CHARTERED
CERTIFIED PUBLIC ACCOUNTANTS

INDEPENDENT AUDITOR'S REPORT

To the Board of Directors
Model Corporation
Clientown, State

We have audited the accompanying balance sheets of Model Corporation as of December 31, 19X2 and 19X1, and the related statements of income, retained earnings, and cash flows for the years then ended. These financial statements are the responsibility of the Company's management. Our responsibility is to express an opinion on these financial statements based on our audits.

We conducted our audits in accordance with generally accepted auditing standards. Those standards require that we plan and perform the audit to obtain reasonable assurance about whether the financial statements are free of material misstatement. An audit includes examining, on a test basis, evidence supporting the amounts and disclosures in the financial statements. An audit also includes assessing the accounting principles used and significant estimates made by management, as well as evaluating the overall financial statement presentation. We believe that our audits provide a reasonable basis for our opinion.

As described in Note X to the financial statements, the Company adopted a new method of computing depreciation for previously recorded equipment as of January 1, 19X2. Generally accepted accounting principles require that the change be reflected through current income by a cumulative effect adjustment, whereas the Company has elected to account for the change through prospective adjustment of the current and future years' depreciation expense. As a result, at December 31, 19X2 accumulated depreciation is understated by $_____ and retained earnings is overstated by $_____ and net income for the year ended December 31, 19X2 is overstated by $_____.

In our opinion, except for the effects on the 19X2 financial statements of recording the change in accounting principles as described in the preceding paragraph, the financial statements referred to above present fairly, in all material respects, the financial position of Model Corporation as of December 31, 19X2 and 19X1, and the results of its operations and its cash flows for the years then ended in conformity with generally accepted accounting principles.

WOODEN & BENSON

Baltimore, Maryland
______ _, 19_

100 W. PENNSYLVANIA AVENUE BALTIMORE, MARYLAND 21204 TELEPHONE (410) 825-4860 FAX (410) 828-1419

Figure 20-7 Sample Review Report

WOODEN & BENSON
CHARTERED
CERTIFIED PUBLIC ACCOUNTANTS

ACCOUNTANT'S REVIEW REPORT

To the Board of Directors
Model Corporation
Clientown, State

We have reviewed the accompanying balance sheets of Model Corporation as of May 31, 19X2 and 19X1, and the related statements of income, retained earnings, and cash flows for the years then ended, in accordance with Statements on Standards for Accounting and Review Services issued by the American Institute of Certified Public Accountants. All of the information included in these financial statements is the representation of the management of Model Corporation.

A review consists principally of inquiries of Company personnel and analytical procedures applied to financial data. It is substantially less in scope than an audit in accordance with generally accepted auditing standards, the objective of which is the expression of an opinion regarding the financial statements taken as a whole. Accordingly, we do not express such an opinion.

Based on our reviews, we are not aware of any material modifications that should be made to the accompanying financial statements in order for them to be in conformity with generally accepted accounting principles.

WOODEN & BENSON

Baltimore, Maryland
_____ _, 19_

100 W. PENNSYLVANIA AVENUE BALTIMORE, MARYLAND 21204 TELEPHONE (410) 825-4860 FAX (410) 828-1419

Figure 20-8 Sample Compilation Report

WOODEN & BENSON
CHARTERED
CERTIFIED PUBLIC ACCOUNTANTS

ACCOUNTANT'S COMPILATION REPORT

To the Board of Directors
Model Corporation
Clientown, State

We have compiled the accompanying balance sheets of Model Corporation as of May 31, 19X2 and 19X1, and the related statements of income, retained earnings, and cash flows for the years then ended (and supplementary information), in accordance with Statements on Standards for Accounting and Review Services issued by the American Institute of Certified Public Accountants.

A compilation is limited to presenting information that is the representation of management in the form of financial statements (and supplementary information). We have not audited or reviewed the accompanying financial statements (and supplementary information) and, accordingly, do not express an opinion or any other form of assurance on them.

WOODEN & BENSON

Baltimore, Maryland
______, 19_

100 W. PENNSYLVANIA AVENUE BALTIMORE, MARYLAND 21204 TELEPHONE (410) 825-4860 FAX (410) 828-1419

Figure 20-9 Sample Disclaimer of Opinion

WOODEN & BENSON
CHARTERED
CERTIFIED PUBLIC ACCOUNTANTS

INDEPENDENT AUDITOR'S REPORT

To the Board of Directors
Model Corporation
Clientown, State

We were engaged to audit the accompanying balance sheet of Model Corporation as of December 31, 19X2, and the related statements of income, retained earnings, and cash flows for the year then ended. These financial statements are the responsibility of the Company's management.

Management has refused to provide written representations as to its responsibility for the fair presentation of the financial statements and other matters which could materially affect the amounts and classification of items included in the financial statements. Such representations are required under generally accepted auditing standards.

Since the management of the Company has refused to provide written representations as noted in the preceding paragraph, the scope of our work was not sufficient to enable us to express, and we do not express, an opinion on the financial statements referred to above.

WOODEN & BENSON

Baltimore, Maryland
_________ ___, 19__

100 W. PENNSYLVANIA AVENUE BALTIMORE, MARYLAND 21204 TELEPHONE (410) 825-4860 FAX (410) 828-1419

Figure 20-10 Sample Adverse Opinion

WOODEN & BENSON
CHARTERED
CERTIFIED PUBLIC ACCOUNTANTS

INDEPENDENT AUDITOR'S REPORT

To the Board of Directors
Model Corporation
Clientown, State

We have audited the accompanying balance sheet of Model Corporation as of December 31, 19X2, and the related statements of income, retained earnings, and cash flows for the year then ended. These financial statements are the responsibility of the Company's management. Our responsibility is to express an opinion on these financial statements based on our audit.

We conducted our audit in accordance with generally accepted auditing standards. Those standards require that we plan and perform the audit to obtain reasonable assurance about whether the financial statements are free of material misstatement. An audit includes examining, on a test basis, evidence supporting the amounts and disclosures in the financial statements. An audit also includes assessing the accounting principles used and significant estimates made by management, as well as evaluating the overall financial statement presentation. We believe that our audit provides a reasonable basis for our opinion.

As discussed in Note X to the financial statements, the Company carries its property and equipment accounts at appraisal values and provides depreciation on the basis of such values. Further, the Company does not provide for deferred taxes with respect to temporary differences arising because of the use, for income tax purposes, of the installment method of reporting gross profit from certain types of sales. Generally accepted accounting principles require that property and equipment be stated at an amount not in excess of cost, reduced by depreciation based on such amount, and that deferred taxes be provided.

Because of the departures from generally accepted accounting principles identified above, as of December 31, 19X2 inventories have been increased $____ by inclusion in manufacturing overhead of depreciation in excess of that based on cost; property and equipment, less accumulated depreciation, is carried at $____ in excess of an amount based on the cost to the Company; and deferred taxes of $____ have not been recorded; resulting in an increase of $____ in retained earnings and in appraisal surplus of $____. For the year ended December 31, 19X2, cost of goods sold has been increased $____ because of the effects of the depreciation accounting referred to above and deferred taxes of $____ have not been provided, resulting in an increase in net income of $____.

In our opinion, because of the effects of the matters discussed in the preceding paragraphs, the financial statements referred to above do not present fairly, in conformity with generally accepted accounting principles, the financial position of Model Corporation as of December 31, 19X2, and the results of its operations and its cash flows for the year then ended.

WOODEN & BENSON

Baltimore, Maryland
________ __, 19___

100 W. PENNSYLVANIA AVENUE BALTIMORE, MARYLAND 21204 TELEPHONE (410) 825-4860 FAX (410) 828-1419

auditor to follow the client's affairs more closely than is possible during a single annual visit. As a consequence, credit executives can place greater credence on financial figures prepared under this type of arrangement.

False Financial Statements

General Considerations

Though normal credit analysis is based on the assumption that the facts submitted by the customer are true, there is always the possibility that a false and misleading financial statement may be intentionally submitted. Statements should be signed by a principal of the business. Besides the psychological effect on the business executive, the principal's signature to a financial report has legal implications.

The title of the principal should also be included, as well as the date of the signing. When unsigned balance sheets or operating statements are received, some credit executives will send them back for signature. Although this may seem time-consuming, it protects the creditor's interest in case of litigation.

Continuing and Acceleration Clauses

Most statements contain a **continuing clause**, *which is a declaration, signed by the principals, attesting that there has been no unfavorable change in the financial condition of the business from the date of the statement to the date of the signing. Further, it is declared that the firm receiving the statement will be notified of any such change.* Until notice is given, the statement may be regarded as continuing to reflect the firm's financial condition. The **acceleration clause** is ordinarily used in connection with bank loans. *It gives the bank the option to call a loan ahead of time if the financial condition of the borrower changes so much that it increases the bank's risk.*

Fraud

The essential characteristic of **fraud** *is the intent to deceive.* A principal may be incompetent or negligent in managing the business or may even be willfully wasteful of the firm's assets, by gambling, for instance. But unless creditors were at some point intentionally deceived on a material fact, the principal cannot properly be charged with fraud.

Certain essential elements, aside from use of the mail, must be proved before there can be a conviction for mail fraud by a false financial statement. The statement must be false, it must be known to the maker to be false, and it must be made with the intent that it be relied upon by the prospective creditor. Also, for all practical purposes, the creditor must sustain a loss through reliance upon it for granting credit. The falsity of the statement is proved either by an audit of the debtor's books and records following bankruptcy or an assignment for the benefit of creditors, or by a reconstruction of the debtor's records if the books are unavailable. This is a job for an auditor, retained either by the trustee or assignee under court order or by creditors acting independently.

Points To Be Observed

Certain precautions will reduce the likelihood of loss because of fraudulent statements:

- Avoid estimated statements.
- Make sure of the date, and do not accept undated or obviously incorrectly dated statements.
- Be certain of the signature, and make sure that all documents are signed and witnessed, if possible.
- Do not assist the customer in preparing a statement.
- Insist on mailed statements whenever possible.
- Retain proof of mailing, and date stamp all mail received from customers.
- Look for omissions and unanswered questions.

Comprehension Check

1. List the two types of accounting methods used for financial statement reporting.
2. What are the four basic types of financial statements?
3. What type of company is required to file a 10-Q?
4. What is the purpose of notes to financial statements? Why should the reader of a corporation's annual report always read these notes?
5. What is the purpose of a balance sheet?
6. Define the accounting term assets.
7. Define the accounting term current assets.
8. What is net working capital?
9. What is the most liquid asset on a balance sheet?
10. What four methods are used to value inventory?
11. Explain the terms LIFO and FIFO.
12. Define the accounting term liability.
13. What is the purpose of an income statement?
14. Name the two methods used to present an income statement.
15. How are net sales calculated?
16. How is the cost of goods sold calculated?
17. How is gross profit calculated?
18. How is gross margin calculated?
19. What is the purpose of the Statement of Retained Earnings?
20. What is the purpose of the Statement of Cash Flows?
21. Name the three activities into which cash flows are grouped on the Statement of Cash Flows.
22. What is a pro forma financial statement?
23. What is an unqualified audit opinion?
24. What is a qualified audit opinion?

21 Financial Analysis Fundamentals

Overview

Financial analysis is generally undertaken to determine the liquidity and debt-paying ability of a customer. It differs from the analysis that an investor or an owner would perform, but it is similar to that of a banker considering a short-term loan. The extent of the analysis is generally determined by the size of the credit availability, the potential sales to the account, the availability of guarantees or security agreements, and the ongoing relationship with the customer. In practice, there are wide extremes in the scope and intensity of financial analysis.

Financial analysis includes internal analysis, which uses financial statements and financial ratios derived from those statements to gain an understanding of the company. In addition, a comparative analysis is usually used to determine trends when two or more successive sets of figures are available. Further, a brief analysis of liquidity can highlight short-term problems or strengths. Finally, additional analysis using trial balance information or sales data can provide further insights into the customer's financial position.

Learning Objectives

After reading this chapter, the reader should know:

- How to analyze a firm within the current year and over time
- How to interpret the statement of cash flows
- The basics of using financial ratio analysis
- The differences among various types of financial ratios
- How to construct the DuPont formula
- The major sources of comparative industry financial data

Chapter Outline

I. Common-Size Analysis
   A. Overview
   B. Vertical Analysis
   C. Horizontal Analysis
II. Statement of Cash Flows
   A. General Considerations
   B. The Indirect Method
   C. The Direct Method
III. Ratio Analysis
   A. Liquidity/Solvency Ratios
   B. Efficiency/Activity Ratios
   C. Leverage/Coverage Ratios
   D. Profitability Ratios
   E. Using the Dupont Model
   F. The Cash Conversion Cycle
IV. Using Industry Comparative Information
   A. Sources of Industry Information
   B. Making Industry Comparisons

Common-Size Analysis

Overview

Common-size analysis *can be defined as accounting statements expressed as a percentage of net sales or total assets to aid comparison*. It is a technique that enables a credit analyst to determine the makeup and patterns of a firm's balance sheet and income statement. The analysis can be either horizontal (across years) or vertical (within a year). Common-size analysis expresses comparisons in percentages rather than absolute dollar amounts, revealing possible trends and changes in the internal structure of financial statements. Common-size statements are also useful when comparing different firms to one another because the information is restated in a common format, making the comparison more meaningful.

Vertical Analysis

Common-size vertical analysis *compares each amount with a base amount selected from the same year*. Accounts in the income statement are stated as a percentage of net sales. A common-size vertical analysis of an income statement is prepared by assigning net sales a value of 100 percent and then expressing each statement item as a percent of net sales. If the 100 percent net sales amount is assumed to represent one sales dollar, then the remaining accounts show how each sales dollar was distributed to costs, expenses and income.

In a common-size vertical analysis of a balance sheet, total assets are assigned a value of 100 percent. Because total assets equal liabilities and owners' equity, the amount for total liabilities and owners' equity is also assigned a value of 100 percent. Then, each asset is shown as a percentage of total assets and each liability and owners' equity account is shown as a percentage of total liabilities and owners' equity. An example of a vertical analysis of an income statement is shown in Figure 21-1 and an example of a vertical analysis of a balance sheet is shown in Figure 21-2.

Horizontal Analysis

Common-size horizontal analysis *compares several annual balance sheets or income statements*. The change in an account on a statement is compared to a base amount for a selected base year. This allows a comparison of annual changes in like accounts. It also allows annual financial statements to become statements of trends rather than a look at numbers at a point in time or on a certain date.

To construct a common-size horizontal analysis for a three-year period, select the earliest financial statement as the base year statement. Then, calculate the change in each account against the base year account and express the change as a percentage. For example, compare the following balance sheet account over a three year period.

	1998	1997	1996
Accounts Receivable	$303	$294	$210

In 1996, the accounts receivable account showed a balance of $210. This account increased in 1997 to $294 and increased in 1998 to $303. Because 1996 is the earliest

Figure 21-1 Vertical Analysis of Income Statements for a Three-Year Period

($000)	Year 3	%	Year 2	%	Year 1	%
Gross Sales	$1,585.0	113.1	$1,970.0	107.7	$1,546.0	105.9
Less returns	184.0	13.1	140.0	7.7	86.0	5.9
Net sales	$1,401.0	100.0	$1,830.0	100.0	$1,460.0	100.0
Cost of sales:						
Beginning inventory	$ 272.6	19.4	$ 116.1	6.3	101.3	6.9
Purchases	997.6	71.2	1,571.5	85.9	1,119.8	76.7
	$1,270.2	90.6	$1,687.6	92.2	$1,221.1	83.6
Ending inventory	262.2	18.7	272.6	14.9	116.1	7.9
Total	$1,008.0	71.9	$1,415.0	77.3	$1,105.0	75.7
Gross profit	$ 393.0	28.1	$ 415.0	22.7	$ 355.0	24.3
Operating expenses	263.9	18.8	263.4	14.4	208.4	14.3
Depreciation	31.3	2.3	21.8	1.2	13.5	0.9
Interest	26.8	1.9	24.8	1.4	12.1	0.8
Income before taxes	$ 71.0	5.1	$ 105.0	5.7	$ 121.0	8.3
Income taxes	31.0	2.2	49.0	2.6	57.0	3.9
Net income	$ 40.0	2.9	$ 56.0	3.1	$ 64.0	4.4

Profitability, as measured by the percentage net income of sales, is steadily declining.

year, it is the base year. Receivables increased $84 in 1997 to $294 from 1996 ($294 – $210 = $84). The percent change is 40% ($84 ÷ $210 = .4 or 40%). Receivables increased by $93 in 1998 from 1996 ($303 – $210 = $93). The percent change is 44% ($94 ÷ $210 = .44 or 44%). A horizontal analysis of a balance sheet is shown in Figure 21-3 and a horizontal analysis of an income statement is shown in Figure 21-4.

Percent changes over a base year show how the financial statement items have increased or decreased, and whether the rate of growth or decline is erratic or consistent.

Statement of Cash Flows

General Considerations

The statement of cash flows (SCF) required by Statement of Financial Accounting Standards No. 95, provides information about a firm's cash inflows and outflows during an accounting period. *The SCF reports a firm's major cash inflows and outflows for a period.* It provides useful information about a firm's ability to generate cash from operations, maintain and expand its operating capacity, meet its financial obligations and pay dividends.

The SCF restates the firm's flow of funds from an accrual accounting basis to a cash accounting basis by eliminating all noncash revenues and expenses recorded by accrual accounting. It takes the accountant's accrual-based income statement and converts it to a cash-based income statement. The restatement of financial statements to a cash basis does not suggest that accrual accounting is wrong. In fact, the purpose

Figure 21-2 Vertical Analysis of Balance Sheets for a Three-Year Period

($000)	Year 3	%	Year 2	%	Year 1	%
Current assets						
Cash	$ 0.3	0.0	$ 13.7	1.8	$ 11.4	2.5
Receivables	303.0	36.6	293.5	39.5	210.0	46.8
Inventories	262.2	31.6	272.6	36.7	116.1	25.9
Prepaid expenses	15.6	1.9	19.4	2.6	25.1	5.6
Total	$ 581.1	70.1	$ 599.2	80.7	$ 362.6	80.8
Property and equipment	$ 323.8	39.1	$ 181.7	24.5	$ 113.0	25.2
Accumulated depreciation	81.1	9.8	49.8	6.7	28.0	6.2
Net property and equipment	$ 242.7	29.3	$ 131.9	17.8	$ 85.0	18.9
Other assets	5.2	0.6	11.5	1.5	1.4	0.3
Total assets	$ 829.0	100.0	$ 742.6	100.0	$ 449.0	100.0
Current liabilities						
Accounts payable	$ 224.0	27	$ 185.5	25.0	$ 53.7	12.0
Notes payable	200.1	24.1	197.3	26.6	106.0	23.6
Taxes payable	31.0	3.7	49.0	6.6	57.0	12.7
Accrued expenses	43.9	5.3	59.6	8.0	14.7	3.3
Portion of LT debt	8.0	1.0	6.0	0.8	4.6	1.0
Bank overdraft	15.0	1.8	0.0	0.0	0.0	0.0
Total	$ 522.0	63.0	$ 497.4	67.0	$ 236.0	52.6
Long-term liabilities	$ 45.6	5.5	$ 22.8	3.1	$ 12.6	2.8
Shareholders' equity						
Common stock	$ 60.0	7.2	$ 60.0	8.1	$ 60.0	13.4
Retained earnings	201.4	24.3	162.4	21.8	140.4	31.3
Total	$ 261.4	31.5	$ 22.4	29.9	$ 200.4	44.6
Total debt and equity	$ 829.0	100.0	$ 742.6	100.0	$ 449.0	100.0

Receivables and inventories represent over two-thirds of the total assets, although the proportion for property, plant, and equipment is growing each year. About two-thirds of all financing is short-term.

of accrual accounting is to show revenues and expenses incurred by the firm, whether paid for or not. The statement of cash flows shows the true cash inflows and outflows of the firm.

The following rules should be used to construct the statement of cash flows:

- Revenue accounts are sources of cash.
- Expense accounts are uses of cash.
- Increases in asset accounts are uses of cash.
- Decreases in asset accounts are sources of cash.
- Increases in liability and equity accounts are sources of cash.
- Decreases in liability and equity accounts are uses of cash.

It is helpful to think of the statement of cash flows as a statement of sources and uses of resources. Consider cash, which is an asset, as a resource. Because an increase in cash represents an investment decision, it is a use of resources. Following the rules stated above, an increase in cash is a use of cash.

Figure 21-3 Horizontal Analysis of Balance Sheets over a Three-Year Period

($000)	Year 3	Δ%	Year 2	Δ%	Base Year Year 1
Current assets					
Cash	$ 0.3	(97)	$ 13.7	20	$ 11.4
Receivables	303.0	44	293.5	40	210.0
Inventories	262.2	126	272.6	135	116.1
Prepaid expenses	15.6	(38)	19.4	(23)	25.1
Total	$ 581.1	60	$ 599.2	65	$ 362.6
Property and equipment	$ 323.8	187	$ 181.7	61	$ 113.0
Accumulated depreciation	81.1	190	49.8	78	28.0
Net property and equipment	$ 242.7	186	$ 131.9	55	$ 85.0
Other assets	5.2	271	11.5	721	1.4
Total assets	$ 829.0	85	$ 742.6	65	$ 449.0
Current liabilities					
Accounts payable	$ 224.0	317	$ 185.5	245	$ 53.7
Notes payable	200.1	89	197.3	186	106.0
Taxes payable	31.0	(46)	49.0	(14)	57.0
Accrued expenses	43.9	199	59.6	305	14.7
Portion of LT debt	8.0	74	6.0	30	4.6
Bank overdraft	15.0	∞	0.0	0	0.0
Total	$ 522.0	121	$ 497.4	111	$ 236.0
Long-term liabilities	$ 45.6	262	$ 22.8	81	$ 12.6
Shareholders' equity					
Common stock	$ 60.0	0	$ 60.0	0	$ 60.0
Retained earnings	201.4	43	162.4	16	140.4
Total	$ 261.4	30	$ 222.4	11	$ 200.4
Total debt and equity	$ 829.0	85	$ 742.6	65	$ 449.0

Total assets have shown significant growth over the past two years. Financing has relied heavily on accounts payable.

The statement of cash flows reports cash flows by three types of activities:

1. Cash flows from operating activities
2. Cash flows from investing activities
3. Cash flows from financing activities.

Stated another way:

	Cash flows from operating activities
plus	Cash flows from investing activities
plus	Cash flows from financing activities
equal	Change in cash

The first section, cash flows from operating activities, shows cash flows from operating activities and cash generated or consumed by the productive activities of a firm over a period of time. Operating activities are the earning-related activities of a firm.

Figure 21-4 Horizontal Analysis of Income Statements for a Three-Year Period

($000)	Year 3	Δ%	Year 2	Δ%	Base Year Year 1
Gross Sales	$1,585.0	3	$1,970.0	27	$1,546.0
Less returns	184.0	114	140.0	63	86.0
Net sales	$1,401.0	(4)	$1,830.0	25	$1,460.0
Cost of sales:					
Beginning inventory	$ 272.6	169	$ 116.1	15	101.3
Purchases	997.6	(11)	1,571.5	40	1,119.8
	$1,270.2	4	$1,687.6	38	$1,221.1
Ending inventory	262.2	126	272.6	135	116.1
Total	$1,008.0	(9)	$1,415.0	28	$1,105.0
Gross profit	$ 393.0	11	$ 415.0	17	$ 355.0
Operating expenses	263.9	27	263.4	26	208.4
Depreciation	31.3	132	21.8	61	13.5
Interest	26.8	121	24.8	105	12.1
Income before taxes	$ 71.0	(41)	$ 105.0	(13)	$ 121.0
Income taxes	31.0	(46)	49.0	(14)	57.0
Net income	$ 40.0	(37)	$ 56.0	(12)	$ 64.0
Dividends	$ 1.0	(97)	$ 34.0	0	$ 34.0

Sales are up slightly from the level of two years ago. However, profits and dividends are lower by a considerable amount.

Typical inflows/sources are:

- the sales of goods or revenue from services
- returns on interest earning assets (interest)
- returns on equity securities (dividends)

Typical outflows/uses are:

- payments for purchases of inventories
- payments for operating expenses
- payments for purchases from suppliers other than inventory
- payments to lenders (interest)
- payment for taxes

The second section of the statement is cash flow from investing activities. This section summarizes the purchases and sales of investments in the firm to maintain or enhance its productive activities. It shows cash flows relating to lending money and to acquiring and selling investments and productive, long-term assets.

Typical inflows/sources are:

- sales of long-term assets such as property, plant and equipment
- sales of debt or equity securities of other entities

- returns from loans (principal) to others

Typical outflows/uses are:

- acquisition of long-term assets
- purchases of debt or equity securities of other entities
- loans (principal) to others

The final section of the statement is cash flow from financing activities. This section shows cash flows relating to liability and owners' equity accounts such as borrowing, liquidating investments or dividend payouts.

Typical inflows/sources are:

- proceeds from borrowing
- proceeds from issuing the firm's own equity securities

Typical outflows/uses are:

- repayment of debt principal
- repurchase of a firm's own shares of stock
- payment of dividends

Two methods are used for calculating and presenting the cash flow from operating activities in the statement of cash flows: the direct method and the indirect method. When the direct method is used, the indirect method must also be used to prepare a supplemental reconciliation of net income with cash flows from operations. Most companies use the indirect method when they publish this required statement.

The Indirect Method

The **indirect method** *reports the operating cash flows by beginning with net income and adjusting it for revenues and expenses that do not involve the receipt or payment of cash.* An advantage of the indirect method is that it focuses on the differences between net income and cash flows from operations. An example of an indirect presentation of a statement of cash flows is shown in Figure 21-5.

The Direct Method

The **direct method** *reports the sources of operating cash and the uses of operating cash.* The major source of operating cash is cash received from customers. The major uses of cash include cash paid to suppliers for merchandise and services and cash paid to employees for wages. The difference between these operating cash receipts and cash payments is the net cash flow from operating activities. The primary advantage of the direct method is that it reports the sources and uses of cash in the statement of cash flows. Its primary disadvantage is that the necessary data may not be readily available. An example of a direct presentation of a statement of cash flows is shown in Figure 21-6.

Figure 21-5 Indirect Presentation of Statement of Cash Flows for a Three-Year Period ($000)

		Year 3	Year 2	Year 1
	Net income	$ 40.0	$ 56.0	$ 64.0
+	Depreciation	31.3	21.8	13.5
		$ 71.3	$ 77.8	$ 77.5
–	Increase in receivables	–9.5	–83.5	–12.2
–	Increase in inventory		–156.5	–5.4
+	Decrease in inventory	10.4		
+	Increase in accounts payable	38.5	131.8	17.0
–	Decrease in accrued expenses	–15.7		–7.8
+	Increase in accrued expenses		44.9	
+	Decrease in prepaid expenses	3.8	5.7	4.8
–	Decrease in taxes payable	–18.0	–8.0	–8.4
=	Net cash flow from operations	$ 80.8	$ 12.2	$ 65.5
–	Increase in fixed assets	–$ 142.1	–$ 68.7	–$ 32.0
+	Decrease in other assets	6.3		3.1
–	Increase in other assets		10.1	
=	Net cash flow from investing	–$ 135.8	–$ 78.8	–$ 28.9
+	Increase in long-term debt	$ 24.8	$ 11.6	$ 13.2
+	Increase in bank debt	15.0		
–	Decrease in notes payable			–9.0
+	Increase in notes payable	2.8	91.3	
–	Dividends paid	–1.0	–34.0	–34.0
=	Net cash flow from financing	$ 41.6	$ 68.9	–$ 29.8
	Net cash flow from operations	$ 80.8	$ 12.2	$ 65.5
	Net cash flow from investing	–135.8	–78.8	–28.9
	Net cash flow from financing	41.6	68.9	–29.8
	Decrease in cash account	–$ 13.4		
	Increase in cash account		$ 2.3	$ 6.8

Note: + represents a source of cash: – represents a use of cash.

Ratio Analysis

Liquidity/Solvency Ratios

Liquidity or solvency ratios *attempt to measure a company's ability to satisfy its expenses and other cash requirements that come due during the current accounting period or year.* The most common of this type are current ratio, quick ratio, defensive interval, and net working capital.

Current Ratio

Obtained by dividing current assets by current liabilities. **Current assets** *is the sum of cash, short-term marketable securities, notes and accounts receivable, and merchandise inventories.* **Current debt** *is the total of all liabilities due within one year.* The higher the ratio, the greater the protection to the short-term creditor. However, it is generally

Figure 21-6 Direct Presentation of Statement of Cash Flows for a Three-Year Period ($000)

		Year 3	%	Year 2	%	Year 1	%
	Sales	$1,401.0		$1,380.0		$1,460.0	
–	Increase in receivables	–9.5		–83.5		–12.2	
=	Cash sales	$1,391.5	100.0	$1,746.5	100.0	$1,447.8	100.0
–	Cost of sales	–$1,008.0		–$1,415.0		–$1,105.0	
–	Increase in inventory			–156.5		–5.4	
+	Decrease in inventory	+10.4					
+	Increase in accounts payable	+38.5		+131.8		+17.0	
=	Cash cost of sales	–$ 959.1	68.9	–$1,439.7	82.4	–$1,093.4	75.5
	Cash gross profit	$ 432.4	31.1	$ 306.8	17.6	$ 354.4	24.5
–	Operating expenses	–$ 263.9		–$ 263.4		–$ 208.4	
–	Decrease in accrued expenses	–15.7				–7.8	
+	Increase in accrued expenses			+44.9			
+	Decrease in prepaid expenses	+3.8		+5.7		+4.8	
=	Cash operating expenses	–$ 275.8	19.8	–$ 212.8	12.1	–$ 211.4	14.6
	Cash earnings before interest and taxes	$ 156.6	11.3	$ 94.0	5.4	$ 143.0	9.9
–	Interest expense	–26.8		–24.8		–12.1	
=	Cash income before taxes	$ 129.8	9.3	$ 69.2	4.0	$ 130.9	9.0
–	Income tax expense	–31.0		–49.0		–57.0	
–	Decrease in taxes payable	–18.0		–8.0		–8.4	
=	Net cash flow from operations	$ 80.8	5.8	$ 12.2	0.7	$ 65.5	4.5
–	Increase in fixed assets	–$ 142.1		–$ 68.7		–$ 32.0	
+	Decrease in other assets	6.3				3.1	
–	Increase in other assets			10.1			
=	Net cash flow from investing	–$ 135.8		–$ 78.8		–$ 28.9	
+	Increase in long-term debt	$ 24.8		$ 11.6		$ 13.2	
+	Increase in bank debt	15.0					
–	Decrease in notes payable					–9.0	
+	Increase in notes payable	2.8		91.3			
–	Dividends paid	–1.0		–34.0		–34.0	
=	Net cash flow from financing	$ 41.6		$ 68.9		–$ 29.8	
	Net cash flow from operations	$ 80.8		$ 12.2		$ 65.5	
	Net cash flow from investing	–135.8		–78.8		–28.9	
	Net cash flow from financing	41.6		68.9		–29.8	
	Decrease in cash account	–$ 13.4					
	Increase in cash account			$ 2.3		$ 6.8	

conceded that cash and receivables have higher liquidating values than merchandise inventory. Consequently, if cash and receivables are high in relation to inventory, a lower current ratio could be satisfactory from a credit standpoint. As a general rule, analysts look for a minimum ratio of 2.0 for the current ratio. However, some caution must be used in evaluating the current ratio by itself.

$$\text{Current ratio} = \frac{\text{Current assets}}{\text{Current liabilities}} = \frac{\$581{,}000}{\$522{,}000} = 1.1 \text{ times}$$

Quick Ratio

Also called the liquid ratio and acid test, this is the sum of cash, marketable securities, and receivables divided by current liabilities. It should provide at least a small margin over current debts, and a high liquid ratio can often support a low current ratio. If the ratio is too low, the firm must rely on quick marketing of merchandise for funds to meet maturing debts. A slow turnover of receivables worsens the quality of the liquid ratio. As a general rule, analysts look for a minimum ratio of 1.0 for the quick ratio. This means that the firm should be able to meet its current liabilities with ready, or quick assets, assuming that all the receivables shown can actually be collected in a reasonable period of time.

$$\text{Quick ratio} = \frac{\text{Cash + marketable securities + receivables}}{\text{Current liabilities}}$$

$$= \frac{\$300 + \$303{,}000}{\$522{,}000}$$

$$= 0.6 \text{ times}$$

Defensive Interval

To provide additional insight into a firm's liquidity, some analysts have suggested computing this ratio. Briefly stated, *it shows how long a company can operate using its current quick (liquid) assets if it had no revenue in the next period.* It is calculated by dividing the numerator of the quick ratio (cash, plus marketable securities, plus receivables) by daily cash expenses. **Daily cash expenses** *is defined as the difference between cash collected from sales (cash sales on the direct version of the statement of cash flows, Figure 21-3), and net cash flow from operations (see Figure 21-3 for an example), divided by 360.*

$$\text{Defensive Interval} = \frac{\text{Quick assets}}{\text{Daily cash expenses}}$$

$$= \frac{\$303{,}000}{\$3640.8}$$

$$= 83.3 \text{ days}$$

Net Working Capital

This is calculated as the difference between current assets and current liabilities. Note that this is the same as the accounting definition for working capital. Even if positive, the calculated net working capital value does not necessarily mean that the company is truly liquid or solvent. High levels of receivables and inventory can create positive net working capital, but this doesn't mean the firm can easily turn these assets into cash if needed. It may be more useful to compute this value by focusing on the noncurrent items on the balance sheet. In this alternate way of computing net working capital, the total for fixed and other long-term assets is subtracted from the total of noncurrent liabilities (defined as everything except current liabilities) and equity. The alternate form, if positive, will indicate whether net working capital represents noncurrent, or permanent capital that is being invested in current assets. If negative, this means that current liabilities are being used to finance long-term assets.

Net working capital	=	Noncurrent debt + equity – noncurrent assets
	=	\$45,600 + \$261,400 – (\$242,700 + \$5,200)
	=	\$59,100

Efficiency/Activity Ratios

Efficiency or activity ratios *attempt to measure how efficiently the company's resources have been managed in financing its key assets.* The usual measures of efficiency include two ratios for current assets—average collection period and inventory turnover—and one more general ratio—investment turnover.

Average Collection Period

This represents the number of days sales represented by the level of account receivable for the period. It is computed by dividing daily sales (defined as net credit sales, divided by the days in the accounting period) into receivables. Note that this ratio is similar to a turnover ratio and can be converted to a turnover figure by dividing it into 360. A high number for average collection period usually indicates slowness in collecting from customers.

$$\text{Average Collection Period} = \frac{\text{Receivables}}{\text{Average sales per day}} = \frac{\$303{,}000}{\$3891.66} = 77.9 \text{ days}$$

Inventory Turnover

This indicates the speed with which inventory is being sold and provides a picture of how much a company has invested in inventory. It is calculated by dividing the cost of goods sold by the average inventory. Average inventory can be estimated by adding the beginning and ending inventory values and dividing by two. The higher the turnover ratio, the faster the inventory is moving, and this means that the company is effectively investing less in inventory to support its operations. High turnovers alone do not indicate efficient inventory management. For example, if the company keeps its inventory levels too low, it may be losing sales orders that it cannot fill in time.

$$\text{Inventory Turnover} = \frac{\text{Cost of goods sold}}{\text{Average inventory}} = \frac{\$1{,}008{,}000}{(\$272{,}600 + \$262{,}200)/2} = 3.8 \text{ times}$$

Investment Turnover

This provides insight into the relative efficiency of the company as a whole. It is calculated by dividing net sales by total assets. The basic interpretation of this turnover ratio is that it shows how much in sales (dollars) the firm is creating per dollar in assets. In other words, it represents the turnover of total assets. Accounting influences aside, the higher the number for this turnover, the better the firm is doing in operating its business.

$$\text{Investment Turnover} = \frac{\text{Net sales}}{\text{Total assets}} = \frac{\$1{,}401{,}000}{\$829{,}000} = 1.7 \text{ times}$$

Leverage/Coverage Ratios

Leverage or coverage ratios *attempt to measure the degree of financial and operating leverage in the company and its long-term solvency.* It attempts to do this by measuring debt capacity and the extent to which the company has used debt as a financing source to support its operations. Key financial leverage ratios include long-term debt to equity, total debt to assets, total debt to equity, interest coverage, and fixed charge coverage. The chief operating leverage ratio is the break-even sales level ratio.

Long-Term Debt to Equity

This shows the comparative value for long-term debt (debt maturing in greater than one year) versus the firm's equity. It is calculated by dividing long-term debt by shareholders' equity. If this ratio equals 1.0, then long-term debt holders have an equivalent investment in the company. If a company has significant amounts of off-balance sheet financing, this ratio will not reflect the true nature of the firm's financial leverage.

$$\text{Long-term debt to equity} = \frac{\text{Long-term debt}}{\text{Shareholders' equity}} = \frac{\$45{,}600}{\$261{,}400} = 0.174 \text{ or } 17.4 \text{ percent}$$

Total Debt to Assets

This is computed by dividing total debt (current liabilities plus long-term debt) by total assets. This gives an indication of the relative size of the company's total financial leverage by including all debt. It also shows how much assets are financed by debt, with a high number showing substantial dependence on debt sources.

$$\text{Total debt to assets} = \frac{\text{Current liabilities + long-term debt}}{\text{Total assets}} = \frac{\$522{,}000 + \$45{,}600}{\$829{,}000} = 0.685 \text{ or } 68.5 \text{ percent}$$

Total Debt to Equity

Similar to the preceding ratio, *this is computed by dividing all debt by shareholders' equity.* This also gives a relative picture of financial leverage. It differs from the first ratio by including all debt in the calculation.

$$\text{Total debt to equity} = \frac{\text{Current liabilities + long-term debt}}{\text{Shareholder's equity}}$$

$$= \frac{\$522{,}000 + \$45{,}600}{\$261{,}400}$$

$$= 2.171 \text{ or } 217.1 \text{ percent}$$

Interest Coverage

Also referred to as "times interest earned", **interest coverage** *shows the relative size of interest expense versus earnings.* It is calculated by dividing earnings before interest and taxes by interest expense. A high number is usually considered as a positive measure. This ratio does not mean that the firm will pay or be able to pay interest from its earnings. It can do this with funds from operations, so even if this ratio is negative (i.e., the firm is showing a net loss from operations), the company may still be able to meet its interest obligations.

$$\text{Interest coverage} = \frac{\text{Earnings before interest and taxes}}{\text{Interest expense}}$$

$$= \frac{\$71{,}000 + \$26{,}800}{\$26{,}800}$$

$$= 3.6 \text{ times}$$

Fixed Charge Coverage

This is computed by dividing earnings before interest, taxes, and leases by the sum of interest, leases, long-term loan principal repayments, and any dividends from preferred stock. The latter two items are adjusted for tax effects, and to put them on the same basis as expense items by dividing them by one, minus the tax rate. This ratio also shows the effects of using leases. A higher number is usually considered positive.

$$\text{Fixed charge coverage} = \frac{\text{Earnings before interest, leases, and taxes}}{\text{Interest + leases + } \frac{\text{principal repayment + preferred dividend}}{1 - \text{tax rate}}}$$

$$= \frac{\$71{,}000 + \$26{,}800 + \$0}{\$26{,}800 + \$0 + \frac{\$0}{1 - 0.437}}$$

$$= 3.6 \text{ times}$$

Break-Even Sales Level

This indicates operating leverage by computing the amount of sales at which revenues from operations exactly equal expenses from operations. It is calculated by dividing fixed operating costs by the contribution margin proportion, which is defined as the relative portion of sales that remains after variable costs are paid, or the portion of each sales dollar available to pay for fixed expenses. The contribution margin proportion can be calculated by subtracting the percentage of variable costs to net sales from one. It may be desirable to include interest expense as a fixed costs and recalculate this ratio. This will show how substantial interest expense is in comparison with operating expenses. A lower sales figure is generally considered positive.

Profitability Ratios

Profitability ratios attempt to measure how well a company has performed in terms of its profit making performance. Key ratios include return on sales, return on equity, return on assets, and sustainable growth.

Return on Sales

This shows what proportion of sales (dollars) the company retained. Also called the net profit margin, it is calculated by dividing net income by sales. Return on sales is affected by price changes and the level of operating expenses, so a declining return must be investigated further. Like many other ratios, this ratio is more meaningful when compared with other firms in the same industry or with the same profile of multiple business lines. It is also useful to calculate this ratio for each line of business when there are different business lines.

$$\text{Return on sales} = \frac{\text{Net income}}{\text{Sales}} = \frac{\$40{,}000}{\$1{,}401{,}000} = 0.029 \text{ or } 2.9 \text{ percent}$$

Return on Equity

Return on Equity (ROE) *shows how profitable the firm has been with respect to the equity invested in it.* It is calculated by dividing net income by equity. This ratio is best evaluated by comparing results over time, and with similar firms. It is also useful to analyze return on equity with other return ratios, such as return on assets. If a company has issued preferred stock and the analyst decides to regard it as debt, then the ratio as defined above should be changed. The level of preferred stock is subtracted from the numerator and the denominator.

$$\text{Return on equity (ROE)} = \frac{\text{Net income}}{\text{Equity}} = \frac{\$40{,}000}{\$261{,}400} = 0.153 \text{ or } 15.3 \text{ percent}$$

Return on Assets

This shows how profitable the assets are in terms of earning power. It is calculated by dividing the sum of net income and taxes (adjusted for any debt financing costs by multiplying it by one minus the firm's tax rate) divided by total assets. It may be appropriate to deduct intangible or soft assets from total assets when doing this calculation. By restricting the total assets to those that are tangible, any misleading effects from such intangible assets as goodwill, are ignored. If earnings before interest and taxes are used instead of after-tax net income and adjusted interest, it is possible to determine the operating return on assets. This may provide further insight into the firm's performance.

$$\text{Return on assets} = \frac{\text{Net income} + \text{interest}\,(1 - \text{tax rate})}{\text{Total assets}}$$

$$= \frac{\$71{,}000 + \$26{,}800}{\$829{,}000}$$

$$= 0.118 \text{ or } 11.8 \text{ percent}$$

Sustainable Growth

This attempts to measure what growth rate a company can maintain with its current level of equity financing. It is calculated by multiplying the return on equity times one minus the dividend pay-out percentage (retention rate), and then dividing one minus the numerator. Note that the dividend pay-out percentage is calculated by dividing the dividends paid by net income, and subtracting the answer from one. If the company wishes to exceed this rate of growth for any extended period of time, it must provide additional resources to fuel the desired growth. Although technically not a profitability ratio, the sustainable growth ratio does provide insight into the potential growth of the firm.

$$\text{Sustainable growth} = \frac{1 - \frac{\text{Dividends paid}}{\text{Profits}} \times \text{return on equity}}{1 - \left(1 - \frac{\text{Dividends paid}}{\text{Profits}}\right) \times \text{return on equity}}$$

$$= \frac{(1 - \$1{,}000/\$40{,}000) \times 0.153}{1 - (1 - \$1{,}000/\$40{,}000) \times 0.153}$$

$$= 0.175 \text{ or } 17.5 \text{ percent}$$

Using the DuPont Model

The DuPont model or formula (equation) was developed by financial analysts at that company, and provides another way of looking at performance by restating the return on equity ratio computation. It is calculated by multiplying the profit margin (net income divided by sales), times the total assets turnover (sales divided by total assets), times the equity multiplier (total assets divided by equity). It demonstrates the common links among the various ratios. It is also useful to prepare a chart of the Du Pont model or equation to better understand the company's return on equity. (Figure 21-7)

Dupont Formula = Return on sales x efficiency in managing assets x financial leverage

$$= \frac{\text{Net income}}{\text{Sales}} \times \frac{\text{sales}}{\text{assets}} \times \frac{\text{assets}}{\text{equity}}$$

$$= \frac{\$40{,}000}{\$1{,}401{,}000} \times \frac{\$1{,}401{,}000}{\$829{,}000} \times \frac{\$829{,}000}{\$261{,}400}$$

$$= 0.0286 \times 1.69 \times 3.17$$

$$= 0.153 \text{ or } 15.3 \text{ percent}$$

Figure 21-7 Example of the DuPont Model

Profit Margin (Profits ÷ Sales) **X** Turnover (Sales ÷ Assets) **X** Leverage (Assets ÷ Equity) **=** **ROE** (Return on Equity)

The Cash Conversion Cycle

This calculation shows the number of days of financing needed to support the current level of the firm's operation. It is calculated by adding the average collection period and average days inventory outstanding, and subtracting the number of days in purchases outstanding. Average collection period is calculated by dividing receivables by average daily sales. Similarly, average days inventory outstanding is calculated by dividing inventory by average daily sales. Average days purchases outstanding is calculated by dividing payables and accruals by daily operating expenses (excluding notes payable). Manufacturing firms typically have longer cycles than firms less involved with manufacturing, such as wholesalers. As with other ratios, comparing calculations with other firms in the same industry helps the analysts better understand how much financing the company requires, and whether this is reasonable for the industry.

Using Industry Comparative Information

Sources of Industry Information

To compare ratios and other financial data effectively, it is important to find detailed financial information for the firm's industry. There are a number of standard data service firms, as well as the general trade press. Primary sources include:

- Dun and Bradstreet
- Robert Morris Associates
- Moody's Investment Services
- Standard and Poor's Investment Services
- Value Line
- U.S. government sources, including EDGAR, accessible through the Securities and Exchange Commission web site
- Trade periodicals, such as the *Wall Street Journal, Fortune, Forbes, Business Week*

Making Industry Comparisons

It is important to be sure that the figures used are for the same time period. Similar fiscal years are usually required, or there may be problems in drawing meaningful comparisons. Dissimilar accounting treatment of items such as inventory can create differences among firms that are not easily understood. Company size is also a key determinant. Comparing firms that are substantially different in terms of sales size may not produce meaningful comparisons. If there are not many companies in an industry, the ratios may not be appropriate to use. Other factors that may influence financial figures include geographic differences, economic differences, and type of ownership or extent of public trading of the firm's stock.

Comprehension Check

1. What is common size analysis?
2. What is the difference between vertical and horizontal common size analysis?
3. XYZ Corporation's most recent financial statement summaries follow:

Balance Sheet

	This Year	Last Year
Cash	$ 50,000	$40,000
Accounts Receivable	80,000	60,000
Inventories	180,000	110,000
Plant & Equipment	300,000	260,000
Accumulated Depreciation	(40,000)	(20,000)
Total	$570,000	$450,000
Accounts payable	$100,000	$150,000
Accrued Liabilities	70,000	50,000
Mortgage Payable	80,000	
Common Stock	130,000	90,000
Retained Earnings	190,000	160,000
Total	$570,000	$450,000

Income Statement

Net sales	$680,000
Cost of goods sold	410,000
Gross profit	$270,000
Operating expenses	190,000
Operating income	$ 80,000
Interest expense	7,000
Profit before taxes	$ 73,000
Taxes	22,000
Net income	$ 51,000

Other data:

—Cash dividends paid this year were $21,000

—Depreciation is included in cost of goods sold.

—The change in accumulated depreciation account is the depreciation expense for the year.

A. Prepare a vertical and horizontal analyses of the balance sheets in good form. Round to one decimal place.

B. Prepare a vertical analysis of XYZ's income statement.

C. Prepare the statement of cash flows for XYZ using the indirect method. The mortgage balance this year is after XYZ made a $10,000 payment.

D. Based on the financial statements prepared in parts A and B, calculate the efficiency ratios, liquidity ratios, leverage ratios and profitability ratios for XYZ Corporation this year. Use a 360-day year. All sales are on credit to business customers. Assume an income tax rate of 30 percent.

4. List six rules that can be used to construct a Statement of Cash Flows.
5. List the typical inflows/sources and outflows/uses in the operating activity section on a Statement of Cash Flows.
6. List the typical inflows/sources and outflows/uses in the investing activity section on a Statement of Cash Flows.
7. List the typical inflows/sources and outflows/uses in the financing activity section on a Statement of Cash Flows.
8. How can ratio analysis be useful to the credit manager?

22 Analysis and Forecasting of Credit and Receivables Information

Overview

One important activity for credit managers is analyzing accounts receivable information routinely. This is important to ensure that problem accounts are identified and contacted in order to obtain payment. The longer a customer is allowed to extend payments, the less likely it is that the customer will pay at all.

Effective monitoring of accounts receivables information enhances the credit function. It should be done on individual and aggregate bases. Many of the yardsticks used as measuring tools have been used and refined over many years.

Learning Objectives

After reading this chapter, the reader should know:

- Methods used to analyze accounts receivable information effectively
- Ways to interpret days sales outstanding calculations
- Steps to take to establish and monitor sales forecasting systems
- How to identify and understand the costs associated with accounts receivable

Chapter Outline

I. Analysis of Accounts Receivable Information
   A. Aging Receivables Information
   B. Days Sales Outstanding
   C. Ways to Calculate DSO
   D. Other Collection Measures

II. Forecasting Receipts
   A. General Forecasting Considerations
   B. Developing a Forecasting System
   C. A Simple Receipts Model
   D. Variance Analysis

III. Allowances, Write-Offs, and Costs
   A. Allowances for Bad Debts
   B. Write-Offs
   C. Costs of Accounts Receivable

Analysis of Accounts Receivable Information

The basic building blocks for measuring credit performance are outstanding accounts receivable balances and sales figures. These can be tracked on an ongoing basis or at regular intervals, such as in conjunction with the monthly accounting and reporting cycles. Summary reports of these measures provide management with information about how well the credit function is performing and help identify problem areas that require more attention.

Care must be taken when evaluating many of these measures because they are often related to or derived from sales data and can be affected by shifts in sales figures. For example, as sales increase, the measures may increase even though underlying payment patterns have not changed. Some measures have been devised to eliminate such sales biases and are often used in conjunction with the more traditional measures.

Aging Receivables Information

Many accounts receivable measures start with a simple tool, the aging schedule. Developing an aging schedule is a relatively easy task. It entails classifying outstanding accounts receivable items by how long they have been outstanding. Accounts are classified as current, i.e., still within the credit period, or past due, i.e., beyond the credit period. Past due accounts are broken down further into segments, usually of 30 days, to show their relative ages.

Aging schedules can be completed in many forms. For instance, if a customer has many outstanding invoices, its entire account can be aged to show the distribution of its invoices and thus help the credit manager focus on older invoices first. This may be feasible for large customers and is helpful in managing such accounts.

In addition, it is common to prepare aging schedules in aggregate forms. By doing it over all accounts receivable, it is possible to determine how successful the credit management function has been as a whole.

A sample aging schedule is shown in Figure 22-1. In the first portion, a schedule is shown by customer. This type of information is helpful in following up with large customers that can have several invoices outstanding at any one point in time. It also helps identify possible disputed claims, as these are likely to show up as older invoices. The next two sections show aggregate agings first in dollar terms, then as percentages. By scanning the dollar amounts, it is easy to see how much is outstanding by time period. Looking at dollar amounts is important, but focusing on the relative shifts in aging can be just as important to the effective management of accounts receivable. Calculating percentages for each month for each aging bracket allows a credit manager to identify potential problems quickly. In addition, calculating an overall average (or possibly, if data are available, a rolling 12-month average) provides an internal measure of how current outstanding accounts receivable compare with past levels. This is useful in identifying trends in customer payments and can be used to initiate new or different collection efforts aimed at reducing current outstanding accounts receivable.

Days Sales Outstanding

A popular measure of accounts receivable performance and the level of "investment" in accounts receivable is given by calculating the average days sales outstanding

Figure 22-1 Accounts Receivable Aging Schedule by Customer

Customer	Total A/R	Current	Past Due 1–30	31–60	61–90	Over 90
Abel	$50,000	$30,000	$20,000			
Baker	30,000	15,000	10,000	$5,000	$2,500	
Carter	20,000	15,000				$5,000
TOTAL	$100,000	$60,000	$30,000	$5,000	$2,500	$5,000
% of total	100%	60%	30%	5%	2.5%	5%

In aggregate ($000):

Month	Total A/R	Current	Past Due 1–30	31–60	61–90	Over 90
Jan	$10,000	$ 8,000	$1,000	$ 500	$ 300	$ 200
Feb	$15,000	10,500	2,500	900	$ 800	$ 300
Mar	$20,000	13,500	3,500	1,500	950	$ 550
Total	$45,000	$32,000	$7,000	$2,900	$2,050	$1,050

In aggregate ($):

Month	Total A/R	Current	Past Due 1–30	31–60	61–90	Over 90
Jan	$10,000	0.80	0.10	0.05	0.03	0.02
Feb	$15,000	0.70	0.17	0.06	0.05	0.02
Mar	$20,000	0.68	0.17	0.07	0.05	0.03
Total	$45,000	0.73	0.15	0.06	0.04	0.02

(DSO) at any point in time. These calculations are typically done at regular intervals, coinciding with accounting periods and statement reporting. The number of days sales outstanding represent the time period it takes, on average, for accounts receivable to be collected. There are a number of ways to calculate DSO, and the method used will often depend on the firm's line of business or the historical way in which DSO has been calculated. The primary methods are briefly discussed below. Note that DSO is shown as a number in days and, because it is an average over all accounts receivable, does not distinguish between customers who are past due and others who may have paid early. Consequently, DSO should not be used as the sole means of evaluating accounts receivable collection performance or in monitoring customer payment patterns.

Ways To Calculate DSO

One of the most common ways of calculating DSO is given by the following general equation:

DSO = [Accounts receivable balance ÷ sales] × days in the period

Note that in this formula, the term sales refers to credit sales and the number of days is the period over which the sales figure is measured, which is usually equal to an exact number of accounting periods. For example, the sales could be shown monthly, in which case the number of days would be 30. Often, however, DSO is calculated for

Figure 22-2 LIFO Method

DSO = 575 - 400 = 175—unaccounted for by current sales so DSO is at least 30 days = 1 month)

Since 175 is less than the full sales amount for last month (300), compute proportion of the month it takes to equal the balance: 175/300 = 0.583

Multiply by 30 to get the number of days: 0.583 × 30 = 17.5

Adding the two figures together gives a DSO of 47.5 (30 + 17.5)

longer periods, such as 90 days or even one year (in which case 360 is often used). Obviously, individual companies may differ in how they measure the periods.

The advantages of this form of calculation are that it is simple to complete, can be done for other companies by using data available in their financial statements, and by spreading out the time period, can soften the impact or bias that sales figures may have on DSO. In general, changes in sales level will change the DSO figure and may lead to misleading conclusions about credit performance. By monitoring DSO over time and comparing similar months from year to year, it is possible to discern trends or changes in performance. Even so, most effective credit managers use more than just DSO to monitor and measure performance.

Other methods of calculation use different decision rules. For instance, the last-in, first-out (LIFO) method calculates DSO by comparing current and historical sales with current receivables. To calculate the DSO under this method, current receivables are reduced by current sales, then the previous month's sales, and backward until the amount of current receivables has been reached. For example, for current sales of 400 and past sales of 300 and 350 and current receivables of 575, DSO would be calculated as shown in Figure 22-2.

This method is preferred by credit managers who believe that most receivables are created by current or the most recent sales. It too is subject to a sales bias, but again, if used consistently over time, it can provide useful insights into credit and receivables performance.

One method to take out the sales effect on the DSO calculation is to compute a sales-weighted DSO. This is computed by dividing each month's aged receivables by the comparable sales figures for each of the aging brackets times 30. For example, if current receivables aging for current, 30 days past due, 60 days past due, and 90 days past due are 400, 200, 100, and 50 respectively, and sales figures for the current month and last three months prior are 500, 480, 450, and 500 respectively, then the sales-weighted DSO would be computed as follows:

$$\text{DSO} = [(400/500) + (200/480) + (100/450) + (50/500)] \times 30 = 46.2$$

Other Collection Measures

In addition to DSO, credit managers often calculate other measures to measure credit and receivables performance. Some of these measures may retain a sales bias while others have been developed to eliminate sales effects and give a clearer picture of performance and more objectively represent customer payment patterns. The major types include:

- True DSO: True DSO is calculated for each invoice. *It is the number of days that an invoice has been outstanding (i.e., the number of days from its issuance to the date of the report/calculation) times the invoice amount divided by the sales for the period when the sales originally occurred.* Summing the true DSO computed for all invoices gives the true DSO for all accounts receivable. True DSO does not have a sales bias, but it can be cumbersome to calculate and sum for all accounts receivable. It is useful in monitoring individual customers if there is sophisticated systems support for this type of computation. If a credit manager wishes to or has to work (because of systems or other constraints) with aggregate numbers, he or she will be better off with one of the other measures.
- Best Possible DSO: *This measure computes the DSO figure for current receivables.* For instance, if current receivables are 200 and sales for the month are 250, then best possible DSO is calculated as follows: (200/250) X 30 = 24 days. This calculation is really only valid if done on a monthly basis. If more than one month's sales are included in the calculation (as current), then there is a sales bias, which will increase best possible DSO as sales increase, or decrease it as sales decrease.
- Average Days Delinquent (Delinquent DSO): This is really a combination of "regular" DSO and one of the other measures discussed above, the best possible DSO. *It is equal to the calculated DSO minus the calculated best possible DSO.* A lower number is considered desirable. This measure retains a sales bias and may not give a true picture of performance.
- Bad Debt to Sales: *This measure is the percentage of sales written off (as bad debts) for the period being examined.* Obviously, a high percentage is undesirable. Many credit managers use bad debt to sales (percentage) as the ultimate measure of accounts receivable performance and compare it with other firms or with a budgeted target. Major sales shifts can affect the calculation, however, by lowering the percentage when sales are high and inflating it when they are lower. To be truly effective and representative, the bad debts should be associated with the sales period in which they were generated. However, this could be very difficult to calculate and could make it difficult to compare results accurately from period to period since percentages in prior periods could change when bad debt write-offs are taken.
- Days Average Collection Rate: *This measure is calculated by dividing total funds applied into the total flow of funds for the period being measured.* To compute the flow of funds, the days an invoice was outstanding (until it was paid) is multiplied by the amount of funds applied. When this is done for all paid invoices, totals are calculated for funds applied and flow of funds. Dividing them gives the Days Average Collection Rate. This ratio should be free from any sales bias and is similar to the True DSO measure. It may be misleading, however, if there is a large number of outstanding unpaid invoices since only the paid invoices are included in the computation. Regardless of how it is calculated, the measure can be indirectly affected by sales changes in that

larger amounts of unpaid receivables may be generated with large sales increases. The same effect holds for sales declines, but in reverse, of course. The measure can also be calculated by multiplying the number of days an invoice was outstanding times the proportion of total receivables accounted for by the invoice (the invoice dollar amount divided by total dollars of receivables outstanding).

- Collection Effectiveness Index (CEI): *This measure shows the effectiveness of collections over a given time period.* It is calculated by the following formula:

  CEI = {1 – [Total past due receivables ÷ (Outstanding receivables from the prior month + current month's sales)] × 100}

  The answer is expressed as a percent, and the closer to 100% the CEI is, the better the performance is rated. However, the CEI, like the DSO, is affected by sales levels and rises or falls with rises and falls in sales. It does not distinguish among different types of credit terms, so it can be used in such cases, keeping in mind the sales bias.

- Prior Month's Past Due Collected: This measure is similar to the CEI measure. *It shows the percentage of the previous month's past due accounts receivable that has been collected in the current month.* It is calculated by the following formula:

  1 – [(Current month past due, all aging brackets) ÷ (Beginning receivables last month)]

  This percentage may be too limited if it is not used in conjunction with other measures because it focuses heavily on past due amounts and not current amounts. In addition, it may give deceptive results when there are major sales changes, especially when sales decline. In such cases, it may appear that collections are better than they actually are because of the decreasing sales base.

- Payment Pattern Analysis: This measure is essentially an analysis of variance. More than a simple measure or percentage, *it is a more complex method of analyzing customer payment performance.* Current levels of outstanding accounts receivable are compared with a standard, such as past averages, budgeted amount same time periods in the previous year. Variances are recorded and evaluated. This offers a more managerial approach and is fairly complex to establish and maintain, but it does give a full picture of how customers are paying and how reliably that can be predicted. Some form of variance analysis should be included in any accounts receivable performance evaluation system as well as any receipts forecasting system that is based on estimating customer payments.

Forecasting Receipts

Forecasting receipts (customer payments) is an important aspect of credit and accounts receivable management. The credit manager may not be the direct source of the receipts forecast, but he or she is often considered as the most knowledgeable person about this information. Therefore, the credit manager should be prepared to provide or help complete regular estimates of customer payments. For forecasts to be accurate and reliable, they must be set up in a logical framework or system. A forecasting system can be a manual one, or it can be supported by computer software and communications hardware (for data collection). The technical sophistication will depend on the company.

Providing estimated receipts does not necessarily mean that a credit manager has to predict when each customer will pay because it is often possible to estimate for larger aggregates of payments. On the other hand, if there are only a few very large customers and many smaller ones, predicting when the larger customers will pay will provide most of the forecast. A standard "factor" can be used for the bulk of the smaller ones to complete the forecast in such cases.

Forecasts should be regarded as estimates, not facts. This means that they can be wrong without any repercussions to the provider of the data or the preparer of the forecast without too much difficulty. Preparers of the forecasts should learn from the forecasting process and become better at it as they gain experience. Users of the forecast owe it to the preparers to provide constructive feedback and to discuss regularly problems with the forecast as well as the importance of the forecast itself. If the sources of data know why they are being asked for the information, they are likely to provide it more willingly.

General Forecasting Considerations

In establishing a forecasting system, there are a number of key decisions that must be made. These include the reasons or the purpose for the forecast, the time horizon for the forecast, the format of the forecast, and how sophisticated the forecast will be, including whether it will require special advanced techniques, such as statistical methods.

Purpose

There should be general acceptance as to why the forecast is being prepared. Who are the users of the forecast? In other words, who is asking for the information? What will the forecast be used for? Can the forecast be produced regularly and reliably?

Timing

The time horizon and the regular reporting periods are key decision items. For instance, if the forecast is to be prepared monthly, it is important that it be coordinated with regular accounts receivable reporting so it does not create extra work for everyone and so it takes the most updated information. It should tie in to reported figures. This means that there will probably be some time delay necessary after normal accounting closing to provide the data. The time horizon is an important factor, but it is usually set when the forecasting system is first designed. For instance, the forecast may be for daily receipts for the next week, weekly receipts for the next month, monthly receipts for the next year, or quarterly receipts for the next two to three years. Obviously, the length of the time horizon will have an influence on the desired accuracy of the forecast and the amount of work required to prepare the forecast regularly. For shorter forecasts, such as daily to monthly, the credit manager will be an integral part, providing estimates. For longer forecasts, however, the credit manager may not be the main provider of forecast data. In such cases, statistical models may be more useful, thereby relieving the credit manager from long-term predictions. Shorter-term forecasts differ from longer ones in that they will usually require higher degrees of accuracy. This is because their time periods are smaller, which means that there is little time to recover from or accommodate widely inaccurate estimates that could have severely negative effects on the tactical decisions being made on the basis of the forecast. Longer-term estimates, on the other hand, may not need such accuracy as they are used to make more strategic decisions.

Format

The format of the forecast is the way in which the estimates are presented. For example, shorter-term forecasts, including those up to one year, are often more meaningful if they are presented in a receipts and disbursements format, which shows the cash flows in common terms. The opposite of this type of format is a financial statements format, which may look like a statement of cash flows or extracted items from a balance sheet and/or income statement. This type of format is fine for longer-term forecasts, such as those for longer than a year, but it is very confusing and difficult to work with for shorter forecasts. Some senior managers may be accustomed to this format and may suggest using it for shorter forecasts, but it can provide estimates that are not understandable or that cannot be reconciled easily with actual data.

Developing a Forecasting System

Developing a forecasting system often means adapting a current system. Follow these steps when evaluating and developing a forecasting system:

- Establish the scope: Define the forecasting process for your company (if you already haven't). What is the purpose of each forecast? Establish a focal point for your forecasts: i.e., is it corporate treasury, or are you going to try to forecast for each major operating area? Determine the frequency, level of detail, and accuracy desired (review your current system first). Review major problems, shortcomings, and strengths of the current system, planning to keep the good and throw out the bad.
- Structure the problem: What are you trying to predict? Try to describe each forecast. Take a step back and see if it makes sense. How should you separate the pieces of the forecast? Can you learn from the past? What makes sense for your company? How well have you predicted in the past? Review how well you did. Who are the best forecasters? Identify the best ones by type of forecast. What is the time horizon and frequency for each forecast? Can the sources of data provide information in time to meet the horizons? Who are the primary users of the forecasts inside and outside treasury?
- Assess the data flows in several ways: By type of flow, predictability of flow (certain, predictable, and unpredictable), and ease of data collection (easy, somewhat complex, hard-to-find). Determine what each breakdown (above) tells you. Essentially: How easy or hard will the data be to collect and/or predict? Will you need to spend time in improving the data collection before moving on?

- Investigate and select methods for each forecast or component: Research methods internally and externally (look for help if you need it). Try to get comfortable with each method before selecting. Estimate the resource requirements for each method, in terms of costs, time, and accuracy.
- Identify reliable (ongoing) sources: By type of data element and source (for example, staff vs. operating unit).
- Design the new system: Incorporate current system strengths. Add in new techniques or approaches as needed. Select a method. Relate the data to the observable cash flows. Try out the method to get a feel for it (use test data here). Gather data to use each method to be considered. Start with test data to keep things under control. Use several versions of test data, not just the same set. Apply the method, using test data that are typical of regular flows. Build a model, if necessary, remembering that you may have to "transform" the data. Evaluate by measuring accuracy versus historical data or versus a sample of current data. Revise the method and repeat the process as required.
- Link forecasting with existing resources: These may include credit management activities that can provide actual data on cash flows, predictive factors, etc. Look for other data bases or information flows that can be used in forecasting, such as sales estimates. Look for standard statistical packages available in other financial areas, and look for experienced users there as well. Ask other users for help or input on how easy or hard the methods are to use effectively.
- Don't forget the feedback mechanism: Make sure there is a way to get feedback and give feedback to the source(s) of the data.

A Simple Receipts Model

It may be fairly easy to construct a simple model to use in preparing a receipts forecast if there are a relatively small group of larger customers that, for instance, account for 70% to 80% of the receipts dollar volume. If this is the case, study each customer's payment history to compute the average time it has taken from the invoice date to receipt (payment) date. Usually, this will be a fairly constant number, especially if the average is computed over six months to one year in time. Use a rough estimate of timing, such as the average number of days for all the "big" customers for the aggregate of all the smaller customers (the remaining 20% to 30% of the receipts). Then, these factors can be multiplied by the issued invoices file to produce an expected collection volume over time. A computer spreadsheet model can be used, or this can even be done by hand for small numbers of invoices and customers.

Variance Analysis

An important aspect of any forecasting system is variance analysis. It is important because *it provides a regular assessment of how well the forecast is working as an estimate of the actual cash flow being predicted, such as receipts.* Variance analysis is also a means to providing two-way communications between users and providers of forecasts.

Variances should be tracked regularly over time by comparing actual data with comparable estimated figures. Usually, estimates can be updated, so the variance will possibly vary as forecasts are more recent or not.

When variances are monitored regularly, they help increase the effectiveness of the forecasting system because they can pinpoint possible errors. Major variances (e.g., those more than 5% or 10% higher or lower than the estimate) should require written explanation from the source of the data. The threshold will vary by company and by degree of accuracy desired. But the analysis will create dialog between sources and users, which can be beneficial.

Variances also should be resolved somehow. One method is to roll the variances over into the next update to the forecast. This can be a simple roll-over to the next period, or it can follow a proration of the variance over more than one period, based on past experience. The procedures to be followed should be agreed upon when the system is established and should be checked regularly to be sure that it is still appropriate. Variances are to be expected, they just have to be handled effectively.

Allowances, Write-offs, and Costs

At some point in time, nonpaying customers have to be accounted for. This usually means deleting them from the company's books and from regular accounts receivable records by writing off the outstanding receivable as a bad debt. To handle this process, credit managers use a combination of allowances and write-off guidelines. The basic guidance for these should be in the company's general credit policy.

Bad debt write-offs are not pleasant events. They have clear impact on the firm's cash flow and profit margins. They also provide tangible feedback on how effective the company's credit and receivables management has been.

Allowances are established to recognize that write-offs are inevitable and to provide management's estimate of how large the write-offs can be. The allowance is not a fact per se, but it does give some structure to this process and keeps write-offs from becoming total surprises when they do occur.

Allowances for Bad Debts

Allowances for bad debts or uncollectible accounts are established to charge off bad-debt expenses in the accounting period matching the creation of the accounts receivable record. They are contra-assets, reducing current assets (accounts receivable) accordingly on the company's balance sheet. This gives a more accurate picture of the outstanding receivables. In addition, an allowance can be related to bad debt expenses, which impact the company's income statement when bad debts are written off. This reduction from profit also provides a clearer picture of the firm's performance.

Allowances can be established annually, based on past experience as well as management's willingness to accept a certain level of bad debts or recognition that an estimated level of bad debts is inevitable. In some cases, the allowance is regarded as a kind of budgeted item, with periodic comparisons providing another form of performance measurement.

Allowances can be based on qualitative evaluation of individual accounts, by relating past levels of bad debts to current market and economic conditions, or by using more sophisticated methods such as newer forms of credit scoring. In these newer techniques, a credit score is computed for each customer in the company's credit "portfolio." The score is then analyzed to determine how likely each customer is to fail to pay. The technique is also used to develop more effective and finely tuned collection actions, but it can provide useful estimates of potential bad debt amounts.

Write-offs

Most write-offs consist of basic data—the amount and customer identification information, such as customer account number. *An account is written off when there is no probability that it will be collected.* Some companies make the write-off when an account is turned over to an outside collection agency or lawyer, while others wait until the amount of loss can be determined. Other firms may take the write-off when there is factual evidence of inability to pay, such as final bankruptcy liquidation or insolvency. It is possible that an account does not have to be written off fully. The fact that an account is in insolvency proceedings may not be sufficient to make an account completely worthless. But it may not be worthwhile to pursue a claim where the recovery expense is greater than the amount to be recovered.

Accounts are put in the suspense category when there is substantial doubt that they will be collected in full. Reasons for this include legal action, bankruptcy protection, assignment, credit extension agreement (beyond a reasonable period), compromised settlement, the death of the debtor, or the disappearance of the debtor. Often, accounts in the suspense category will carry a full allowance of 100%. However, if regular payments are being received or if an agreement or compromise settlement has been reached on an account, the allowance should be less than the total amount due.

Costs of Accounts Receivable

Accounts receivable costs fall into the following main categories:

- External processing costs: These include major expenses such as bank service charges for processing customer payments through a lockbox (for checks), related check processing and funds concentration charges, or other charges for collecting electronically. Also included in this category are materials and equipment necessary to manage receivables, such as the costs of forms for invoices, statements, and dunning letters, postage, and fax machines.
- External credit information costs: These include charges from third-party credit agencies as well as fees paid to consultants and systems providers for credit information systems and analytical tools, such as credit scoring models.
- Internal processing costs: These include direct expenses or allocated expenses associated with managing receivables, such as computer hardware and software, systems maintenance expenses, and telecommunications charges and equipment.
- Personnel and related costs: These include labor expenses, personnel benefits, office space expenses, and other types of charges associated with maintaining a credit and receivables staff.

- Miscellaneous financial costs: These include bad debts and perhaps some cost associated with the firm's "investment" in accounts receivable, possibly derived from an overall cost of short-term capital or longer-term weighted average cost of capital if accounts receivable (or some portion) is considered long-term.

These costs should be monitored over time. Some of them, such as the personnel and labor costs, will be managed and controlled through the firm's regular budgetary procedures. Others may not be so easily monitored because they are lumped in with other expenses. Bank service charges are a good example of this. Many companies pay bank fees centrally through the treasury function and may not allocate these charges directly to the accounts receivable function, although it is becoming more common to do so. Many larger firms have sophisticated, computerized systems that are used to monitor and evaluate costs for all functions, including accounts receivable.

Comprehension Check

1. How is DSO calculated?

Index